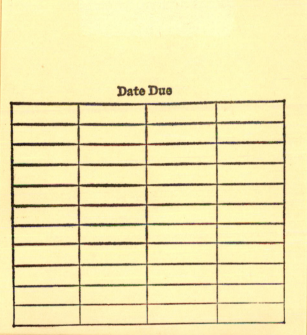

ORDER AND HISTORY

VOLUMES IN THE SERIES

Volume One - Israel and Revelation

ERIC VOEGELIN

ORDER AND HISTORY

VOLUME ONE

Israel and Revelation

LOUISIANA STATE UNIVERSITY PRESS

Coniugi Dilectissimae

In consideratione creaturarum non est vana
et peritura curiositas exercenda; sed gradus
ad immortalia et semper manentia faciendus.

(In the study of creature one
should not exercise a vain and per-
ishing curiosity, but ascend toward
what is immortal and everlasting.)

Sᴛ. Aᴜɢᴜsᴛɪɴᴇ, *De Vera Religione*

Preface

The order of history emerges from the history of order.

Every society is burdened with the task, under its concrete conditions, of creating an order that will endow the fact of its existence with meaning in terms of ends divine and human. And the attempts to find the symbolic forms that will adequately express the meaning, while imperfect, do not form a senseless series of failures. For the great societies, beginning with the civilizations of the Ancient Near East, have created a sequence of orders, intelligibly connected with one another as advances toward, or recessions from, an adequate symbolization of truth concerning the order of being of which the order of society is a part. That is not to say that every succeeding order is unequivocally marked as progressive or recessive in relation to the preceding ones. For new insights into the truth of order may be achieved in some respects, while the very enthusiasm and passion of the advance will cast a shroud of oblivion over discoveries of the past. Amnesia with regard to past achievement is one of the most important social phenomena. Still, while there is no simple pattern of progress or cycles running through history, its process is intelligible as a struggle for true order. This intelligible structure of history, however, is not to be found within the order of any one of the concrete societies participating in the process. It is not a project for human or social action, but a reality to be discerned retrospectively in a flow of events that extends, through the present of the observer, indefinitely into the future. Philosophers of history have spoken of this reality as providence, when they still lived within the orbit of Christianity, or as *List der Vernunft*, when they were affected by the trauma of enlightenment. In either case they referred to a reality beyond the plans of concrete human beings—a reality of which the origin and end is unknown and which for that reason cannot be brought within the grasp of finite action. What is knowable is only that part of the process that has unfolded in the past; and that part to the extent only to which it is accessible to the instruments of cognition that have emerged from the process itself.

The study on *Order and History*, of which the first volume is here presented to the public, is an inquiry into the order of man, society, and history to the extent to which it has become accessible to science. The principal types of order, together with their self-expression in symbols, will be studied as they succeed one another in history. These types of order and symbolic form are the following:

(1) The imperial organizations of the Ancient Near East, and their existence in the form of the cosmological myth;

(2) the Chosen People, and its existence in historical form;

(3) the polis and its myth, and the development of philosophy as the symbolic form of order;

(4) the multicivilizational empires since Alexander, and the development of Christianity;

(5) the modern national states, and the development of Gnosis as the symbolic form of order.

The subject matter will be distributed over six volumes. One volume will deal with the orders of myth and history; two further volumes will be devoted to the polis and the form of philosophy; a fourth volume will deal with the multicivilizational empires and Christianity; and the remaining two volumes will deal with the national states and the symbolic form of Gnosis. The six volumes will bear the titles:

I. Israel and Revelation

II. The World of the Polis

III. Plato and Aristotle

IV. Empire and Christianity

V. The Protestant Centuries

VI. The Crisis of Western Civilization

The inquiry into the types of order and their symbolic forms will be, at the same time, an inquiry into the order of history that emerges from their succession. The first volume, the present one on "Israel and Revelation," will explore not only the forms of cosmological and historical order, but also the emergence of the Chosen People from the ambiance of cosmological empires. A truth about the order of being, seen only dimly through the compact symbols of Mesopotamian, Canaanite, and Egyptian societies, becomes articulate, in the formation of Israel, to the point of clarity where the world-transcendent God reveals himself as the original and ultimate source of order in world and man, society and history, that is, in all world-immanent being. Under this aspect of the dynamics of history, the otherwise autonomous study of cosmological order acquires the character of a background for the emergence of history, as the form of existence in response to Revelation, gained by Israel's exodus from civilization in cosmological form. The volumes on polis and philosophy, then, will not only deal with the philosophical form of order as developed by Plato and Aristotle, but also explore the process in which this form disengages itself from the matrix of the Hellenic variant of the myth, and farther back from the Minoan and Mycenaean background of cosmological order.

The older symbolic forms are furthermore not simply superseded by a new truth about order, but retain their validity with regard to the areas not covered by the more recently achieved insights—even though their symbols have to suffer changes of meaning when they move into the orbit of the more recent and now dominant form. The historical order of Israel, for instance, approaches a crisis, both spiritual and pragmatic, when it becomes obvious that the exigencies of existence in the world are neglected in an order dominated by the Sinaitic Revelation. The cosmological symbolism pours back into the order of Israel with the establishment of a permanent government under kings, not provided by the word of God from Sinai; and the conflicts between the two experiences of order and their symbolisms occupy the major part of Israel's history. The inquiry must, therefore, extend to a sizable class of further phenomena, *i.e.*, to the interactions between symbolic forms. This part of the study will assume considerable proportions, beginning with the fourth volume, when the multicivilizational empires provide the arena for the struggle between Babylonian and Egyptian cosmological forms, the Roman myth of the polis, the Hellenic form of philosophy, the earlier Israelite historical and the later Jewish apocalyptic symbols; when all of the enumerated types of order enter into the great struggle with the new order of Christianity; and when from this welter of mutual invalidations and limitations emerges the compound of Western medieval order. And the whole of two volumes, finally, will be necessary to describe the dissolution of the medieval compound through a Gnosis that had been reduced to a thin trickle of sectarian movements during the early Middle Ages, as well as the consequences of the dissolution.

The reader who is faced with the prospect of six volumes will justly expect a prefatory word about the intellectual situation which, in the author's opinion, makes an enterprise of this nature both possible and necessary. This expectation can be fulfilled only within certain limits —for the size of the work is caused by the complexity of the situation, and the answers to the questions that impose themselves can be given only through the unfolding of the study itself. Still, a few orienting remarks are possible in brief form.

The work could be undertaken in our time, in the first place, because the advance of the historical disciplines in the first half of this century has provided the basis of materials. The enormous enlargement of our historical horizon through archaeological discoveries, critical editions of texts, and a flood of monographic interpretation is so well known a fact that elaboration is superfluous. The sources are ready at hand; and the convergent interpretations by orientalists and semitologists, by classical philologists and historians of antiquity, by theologians and medievalists, facilitate and invite the attempt to use the primary sources as the basis for a philosophical study of order. The state of science in the various disciplines, as well as my own position with regard to fundamental questions, will be set forth in the course of the study. As far as the present volume on "Israel and Revelation" is concerned, I should like to refer the reader to the digressions on the state of Bible criticism (Chap. 6, § 1) and of the interpretation of the Psalms (Chap. 9, § 5).

The second reason why the study could be undertaken in our time is less tangible than the first one, inasmuch as it can be described only negatively as the disappearance of the ideological mortgages on the work of science. I am speaking of the pervasive climate of opinion in which a critical study of society and history was practically impossible because the varieties of nationalism, of progressivist and positivist, of liberal and socialist, of Marxian and Freudian ideologies, the neo-Kantian methodologies in imitation of the natural sciences, scientistic ideologies such as biologism and psychologism, the Victorian fashion of agnosticism and the more recent fashions of existentialism and theologism prevented with social effectiveness not only the use of critical standards but even the acquisition of the knowledge necessary for their formation. The assertion that this incubus on the life of the spirit and intellect has disappeared, must be qualified, however, by the awareness that the forces of the

Gnostic age are still social and political powers on the world scene, and will remain formidable powers for a long time to come. The "disappearance" must be understood as the fact that in the course of the wars and revolutions of our time their authority has seeped out of them. Their conceptions of man, society, and history are too obviously incongruent with the reality that is within the range of our empirical knowledge. Hence, while they still are powers, they wield power only over those who do not turn their back to them and look for greener pastures. We have gained a new freedom in science, and it is a joy to use it.

The reflections on the ideological incubus have led us from the possibility to the necessity of the study on *Order and History*. It is man's obligation to understand his condition; part of this condition is the social order in which he lives; and this order has today become worldwide. This world-wide order is furthermore neither recent nor simple, but contains as socially effective forces the sediments of the millennial struggle for the truth of order. This is a question, not of theory but of empirical fact. One could draw for proof on such obvious facts as the relevance for our own affairs of a China or India that is struggling with the necessary adjustments of a basically cosmological order to political and technological conditions that are of Western making. I prefer, however, to draw the reader's attention to the analysis of the metastatic problem in the present volume on "Israel and Revelation" (Chap. 13, § 2.2), and he will see immediately that the prophetic conception of a change in the constitution of being lies at the root of our contemporary beliefs in the perfection of society, either through progress or through a communist revolution. Not only are the apparent antagonists revealed as brothers under the skin, as the late Gnostic descendants of the prophetic faith in a transfiguration of the world; it obviously is also of importance to understand the nature of the experience that will express itself in beliefs of this type, as well as the circumstances under which it has arisen in the past and from which it derives its strength in the present. Metastatic faith is one of the great sources of disorder, if not the principal one, in the contemporary world; and it is a matter of life and death for all of us to understand the phenomenon and to find remedies against it before it destroys us. If today the state of science permits the critical analysis of such phenomena, it is clearly a scholar's duty to undertake it for his own sake as a man and to make the results accessible to his fellow men. *Order and History* should be read, not as an attempt to explore curiosities of a dead past, but as an inquiry into the structure of the order in which we live presently.

I have spoken of remedies against the disorder of the time. One of these remedies is philosophical inquiry itself.

Ideology is existence in rebellion against God and man. It is the violation of the First and Tenth Commandments, if we want to use the language of Israelite order; it is the *nosos*, the disease of the spirit, if we want to use the language of Aeschylus and Plato. Philosophy is the love of being through love of divine Being as the source of its order. The Logos of being is the object proper of philosophical inquiry; and the search for truth concerning the order of being cannot be conducted without diagnosing the modes of existence in untruth. The truth of order has to be gained and regained in the perpetual struggle against the fall from it; and the movement toward truth starts from a man's awareness of his existence in untruth. The diagnostic and therapeutic functions are inseparable in philosophy as a form of existence. And ever since Plato, in the disorder of his time, discovered the connection, philosophical inquiry has been one of the means of establishing islands of order in the disorder of the age. *Order and History* is a philosophical inquiry concerning the order of human existence in society and history. Perhaps it will have its remedial effect—in the modest measure that, in the passionate course of events, is allowed to Philosophy.

1956   Eric Voegelin

Acknowledgments

An enterprise of this magnitude could not be conducted over the years without material aid from various institutions. I am indebted for such aid to the John Simon Guggenheim Memorial Foundation, the Rockefeller Foundation, the Social Science Research Council, and the Research Council of Louisiana State University. My special thanks, for aid at a critical juncture of the work, are due to an institution that wishes to remain unnamed.

The present volume on "Israel and Revelation" required a knowledge of Scandinavian literature, and especially of the more recent work of Scandinavian scholars, that could not be obtained in this country. I want to thank my colleagues in Uppsala for their generous help, and the University of Uppsala for the permission to use its excellent and efficient library.

A special pleasure is it to say my thanks to my friend and colleague Professor Robert B. Heilman (University of Washington) for his help in improving my English. His thorough analysis of sections of the manuscript, his reasoned advice with regard to grammar and style, his congenial understanding of the relations between philosophical subject matter and means of linguistic expression, have had a pervasive effect. I can only hope that the disciple will not disappoint the master too deeply.

E. V.

Table of Contents

Analytical Table of Contents

INTRODUCTION

The Symbolization of Order

God and man, world and society form a primordial community of being. The community with its quaternarian structure is, and is not, a datum of human experience. It is a datum of experience in so far as it is known to man by virtue of his participation in the mystery of its being. It is not a datum of experience in so far as it is not given in the manner of an object of the external world but is knowable only from the perspective of participation in it.

The perspective of participation must be understood in the fullness of its disturbing quality. It does not mean that man, more or less comfortably located in the landscape of being, can look around and take stock of what he sees as far as he can see it. Such a metaphor, or comparable variations on the theme of the limitations of human knowledge, would destroy the paradoxical character of the situation. It would suggest a self-contained spectator, in possession of and with knowledge of his faculties, at the center of a horizon of being, even though the horizon were restricted. But man is not a self-contained spectator. He is an actor, playing a part in the drama of being and, through the brute fact of his existence, committed to play it without knowing what it is. It is disconcerting even when accidentally a man finds himself in the situation of feeling not quite sure what the game is and how he should conduct himself in order not to spoil it; but with luck and skill he will extricate himself from the embarrassment and return to the less bewildering routine of his life. Participation in being, however, is not a partial involvement of man; he is engaged with the whole of his existence, for participation is existence itself. There is no vantage point outside existence from which its meaning can be viewed and a course of action charted according to a plan, nor is there a blessed island to which man can withdraw in order to recapture his self. The role of existence must be played in uncertainty of its meaning, as an adventure of decision on the edge of freedom and necessity.

Both the play and the role are unknown. But even worse, the actor does not know with certainty who he is himself. At this point the metaphor of the play may lead astray unless it is used with caution. To be sure, the metaphor is justified, and perhaps even necessary, for it conveys the insight that man's participation in being is not blind but is illuminated by consciousness. There is an experience of participation, a reflective tension in existence, radiating sense over the proposition: Man, in his existence, participates in being. This sense, however, will turn into nonsense if one forgets that subject and predicate in the proposition are terms which explicate a tension of existence, and are not concepts denoting objects. There is no such thing as a "man" who participates in "being" as if it were an enterprise that he could as well leave alone; there is, rather, a "something," a part of being, capable of experiencing itself as such, and furthermore capable of using language and calling this experiencing consciousness by the name of "man." The calling by a name certainly is a fundamental act of evocation, of calling forth, of constituting that part of being as a distinguishable partner in the community of being. Nevertheless, fundamental as the act of evocation is—for it forms the basis for all that man will learn about himself in the course of history—it is not itself an act of cognition. The Socratic irony of ignorance has become the paradigmatic instance of awareness for this blind spot at the center of all human knowledge about man. At the center of his existence man is unknown to himself and must remain so, for the part of being that calls itself man could be known fully only if the community of being and its drama in time were known as a whole. Man's partnership in being is the essence of his existence, and this essence depends on the whole, of which existence is a part. Knowledge of the whole, however, is precluded by the identity of the knower with the partner, and ignorance of the whole precludes essential knowledge of the part. This situation of ignorance with regard to the decisive core of existence is more than disconcerting: it is profoundly disturbing, for from the depth of this ultimate ignorance wells up the anxiety of existence.

The ultimate, essential ignorance is not complete ignorance. Man can achieve considerable knowledge about the order of being, and not the least part of that knowledge is the distinction between the knowable and the unknowable. Such achievement, however, comes late in the long-

drawn-out process of experience and symbolization that forms the subject matter of the present study. The concern of man about the meaning
of his existence in the field of being does not remain pent up in the
tortures of anxiety, but can vent itself in the creation of symbols purporting to render intelligible the relations and tensions between the
distinguishable terms of the field. In the early phases of the creative process the acts of symbolization are still badly handicapped by the bewildering multitude of unexplored facts and unsolved problems. Not much is
really clear beyond the experience of participation and the quaternarian
structure of the field of being, and such partial clearness tends to generate
confusion rather than order, as is bound to happen when variegated
materials are classified under too few heads. Nevertheless, even in the
confusion of these early stages there is enough method to allow the
distinction of typical features in the process of symbolization.

The first of these typical features is the predominance of the
experience of participation. Whatever man may be, he knows himself a
part of being. The great stream of being, in which he flows while it flows
through him, is the same stream to which belongs everything else that
drifts into his perspective. The community of being is experienced with
such intimacy that the consubstantiality of the partners will override
the separateness of substances. We move in a charmed community where
everything that meets us has force and will and feelings, where animals
and plants can be men and gods, where men can be divine and gods are
kings, where the feathery morning sky is the falcon Horus and the Sun
and Moon are his eyes, where the underground sameness of being is a
conductor for magic currents of good or evil force that will subterra-
neously reach the superficially unreachable partner, where things are the
same and not the same, and can change into each other.

The second typical feature is the preoccupation with the lasting and
passing (*i.e.*, the durability and transiency) of the partners in the community of being. Consubstantiality notwithstanding, there is the experience of separate existence in the stream of being, and the various
existences are distinguished by their degrees of durability. One man lasts
while others pass away, and he passes away while others last on. All
human beings are outlasted by the society of which they are members,
and societies pass while the world lasts. And the world not only is outlasted by the gods, but is perhaps even created by them. Under this
aspect, being exhibits the lineaments of a hierarchy of existence, from

the ephemeral lowliness of man to the everlastingness of the gods. The experience of hierarchy furnishes an important piece of knowledge about order in being, and this knowledge in its turn can, and does, become a force in ordering the existence of man. For the more lasting existences, being the more comprehensive ones, provide by their structure the frame into which the lesser existence must fit, unless it is willing to pay the price of extinction. A first ray of meaning falls on the role of man in the drama of being in so far as the success of the actor depends upon his attunement to the more lasting and comprehensive orders of society, the world, and God. This attunement, however, is more than an external adjustment to the exigencies of existence, more than a planned fitting into an order "about" which we know. "Attunement" suggests the penetration of the adjustment to the level of participation in being. What lasts and passes, to be sure, is existence, but since existence is partnership in being, lasting and passing reveal something of being. Human existence is of short duration, but the being of which it partakes does not cease with existence. In existing we experience mortality; in being we experience what can be symbolized only by the negative metaphor of immortality. In our distinguishable separateness as existents we experience death; in our partnership in being we experience life. But here again we reach the limits that are set by the perspective of participation, for lasting and passing are properties of being and existence as they appear to us in the perspective of our existence; as soon as we try to objectify them we lose even what we have. If we try to explore the mystery of passing as if death were a thing, we shall not find anything but the nothing that makes us shudder with anxiety from the bottom of existence. If we try to explore the mystery of lasting as if life were a thing, we shall not find life eternal but lose ourselves in the imagery of immortal gods, of paradisiacal or Olympian existence. From the attempts at exploration we are thrown back into the consciousness of essential ignorance. Still, we "know" something. We experience our own lasting in existence, passing as it is, as well as the hierarchy of lasting; and in these experiences existence becomes transparent, revealing something of the mystery of being, of the mystery in which it participates though it does not know what it is. Attunement, therefore, will be the state of existence when it hearkens to that which is lasting in being, when it maintains a tension of awareness for its partial revelations in the order of society and the world, when it listens attentively to the silent voices of conscience and grace in human existence itself. We are thrown into and out of existence without knowing the Why or the How, but while in it we know that we are of the being to which we return. From this knowledge flows the experience of obligation, for though this being, entrusted to our partial management in existence while it lasts and passes, may be gained by attunement, it may also be lost by default. Hence the anxiety of existence is more than a fear of death in the sense of biological extinction; it is the profounder horror of losing, with the passing of existence, the slender foothold in the partnership of being that we experience as ours while existence lasts. In existence we act our role in the greater play of the divine being that enters passing existence in order to redeem precarious being for eternity.

The third typical feature in the process of symbolization is the attempt at making the essentially unknowable order of being intelligible as far as possible through the creation of symbols which interpret the unknown by analogy with the really, or supposedly, known. These attempts have a history in so far as reflective analysis, responding to the pressure of experience, will render symbols increasingly more adequate to their task. Compact blocks of the knowable will be differentiated into their component parts and the knowable itself will gradually come to be distinguished from the essentially unknowable. Thus, the history of symbolization is a progression from compact to differentiated experiences and symbols. Since this process is the subject matter of the whole subsequent study we shall at present mention only two basic forms of symbolization which characterize great periods of history. The one is the symbolization of society and its order as an analogue of the cosmos and its order; the other is the symbolization of social order by analogy with the order of a human existence that is well attuned to being. Under the first form society will be symbolized as a microcosmos; under the second form as a macroanthropos.

The first-mentioned form is also chronologically the first one. Why this should be hardly requires elaborate explanations, for earth and heaven are so impressively the embracing order into which human existence must fit itself, if it wants to survive, that the overwhelmingly powerful and visible partner in the community of being inevitably suggests its order as the model of all order, including that of man and society. At any rate, the civilizations of the ancient Near East that will be treated in Part I of this study symbolized politically organized society as a cosmic analogue, as a cosmion, by letting vegetative rhythms and celestial revolutions function as models for the structural and procedural order of society.

The second symbol or form—society as macroanthropos—tends to appear when cosmologically symbolized empires break down and in their disaster engulf the trust in cosmic order. Society, in spite of its ritual integration into cosmic order, has broken down; if the cosmos is not the source of lasting order in human existence, where is the source of order to be found? At this juncture symbolization tends to shift toward what is more lasting than the visibly existing world—that is, toward the invisibly existing being beyond all being in tangible existence. This invisible divine being, transcending all being in the world and of the world itself, can be experienced only as a movement in the soul of man; and hence the soul, when ordered by attunement to the unseen god, becomes the model of order that will furnish symbols for ordering society analogically in its image. The shift toward macroanthropic symbolization becomes manifest in the differentiation of philosophy and religion out of the preceding, more compact forms of symbolization, and it can be empirically observed, indeed, as an occurrence in the phase of history which Toynbee has classified as the Time of Troubles. In Egypt the social breakdown between the Old and the Middle Kingdom witnessed the rise of the Osiris religiousness. In the feudal disintegration of China appeared the philosophical schools, especially those of Lao-tse and Confucius. The war period before the foundation of the Maurya Empire was marked by the appearance of the Buddha and of Jainism. When the world of the Hellenic polis disintegrated, the philosophers appeared, and the further troubles of the Hellenistic world were marked by the rise of Christianity. It would be unwise, however, to generalize this typical occurrence into a historical "law," for there are complications in detail. The absence of such a shift in the breakdown of Babylonian society (as far as the scantiness of sources allows the negative judgment) suggests that the "law" would have "exceptions," while Israel seems to have arrived at the second form without any noticeable connection with a specific institutional breakdown and subsequent period of trouble.

A further typical feature in the early stages of the process of symbolization is man's awareness of the analogical character of his symbols. The awareness manifests itself in various ways, corresponding to the various problems of cognition through symbols. The order of being, while remaining in the area of essential ignorance, can be symbolized analogically by using more than one experience of partial order in existence. The rhythms of plant and animal life, the sequence of the seasons, the revolutions of sun, moon, and constellations may serve as models for analogical symbolization of social order. The order of society may serve as a model for symbolizing celestial order. All these orders may serve as models for symbolizing the order in the realm of divine forces. And the symbolizations of divine order in their turn may be used for analogical interpretation of existential orders within the world.

In this network of mutual elucidation inevitably concurrent and conflicting symbols will occur. Such concurrences and conflicts are borne, over long periods, with equanimity by the men who produce them; contradictions do not engender distrust in the truth of the symbols. If anything is characteristic of the early history of symbolization, it is the pluralism in expressing truth, the generous recognition and tolerance extended to rival symbolizations of the same truth. The self-interpretation of an early empire as the one and only true representative of cosmic order on earth is not in the least shaken by the existence of neighboring empires who indulge in the same type of interpretation. The representation of a supreme divinity under a special form and name in one Mesopotamian city-state is not shaken by a different representation in the neighboring city-state. And the merger of various representations when an empire unifies several formerly independent city-states, the change from one representation to another when the dynasties change, the transfer of cosmogonic myths from one god to another, and so forth, show that the variety of symbolizations is accompanied by a vivid consciousness of the sameness of truth at which man aims by means of his various symbols. This early tolerance reaches far into the Greco-Roman period and has found its great expression in the attack of Celsus on Christianity as the disturber of the peace among the gods.

The early tolerance reflects the awareness that the order of being can be represented analogically in more than one way. Every concrete symbol is true in so far as it envisages the truth, but none is completely true in so far as the truth about being is essentially beyond human reach. In this twilight of truth grows the rich flora—luxuriant, bewildering, frightening, and charming—of the tales about gods and demons and their ordering and disordering influences on the life of man and society. There is a magnificent freedom of variation on, and elaboration of, fundamental themes, each new growth and supergrowth adding a facet to the great work of analogy surrounding the unseen truth; it is the freedom of which, on the level of artistic creation, still can partake the epics of Homer, the tragedy of the fifth century, and the mythopoeia of Plato. This tolerance, however, will reach its limit when the awareness of the analogical character of symbolization is attracted by the problem of the greater or lesser adequacy of symbols to their purpose of making the true order of being transparent. The symbols are many, while being is one. The very multiplicity of symbols can, therefore, be experienced as an inadequacy, and attempts may be undertaken to bring a manifold of symbols into a rational, hierarchical order. In the cosmological empires these attempts typically assume the form of interpreting a manifold of highest local divinities as aspects of the one highest empire god. But political summodeism is not the only method of rationalization. The attempts can also assume the more technical form of theogonic speculation, letting the other gods originate through creation by the one truly highest god, as we find it for instance in the Memphite Theology, to be dated in the early third millennium B.C. Such early speculative outbreaks in the direction of monotheism will appear anachronistic to historians who want to find a clear progress from polytheism to monotheism, and since the facts cannot be denied, the early instances must at least be considered "forerunners" of the later, more legitimate appearance of monotheism, unless, as a still further effort at rationalization, a search is undertaken to prove a historical continuity between Israelitic monotheism and Ikhnaton, or the philosophy of the Logos and the Memphite Theology. The early outbreaks, however, will appear less surprising, and a search for continuities will become less pressing, if we realize that the rigid difference between polytheism and monotheism, suggested by the logical mutual exclusion of the one and the many, does in fact not exist. For the free, imaginative play with a plurality of symbols is possible only because the choice of analogies is understood as more or less irrelevant compared with the reality of being at which they aim. In all polytheism there is latent a monotheism which can be activated at any time, with or without "forerunners," if the pressure of a historical situation meets with a sensitive and active mind.

In political summodeism and theogonic speculation we reach the limit of tolerance of rival symbolizations. Nevertheless, no serious break need yet occur. The theogonic speculation of a Hesiod was not the beginning of a new religious movement in opposition to the polytheistic culture of Hellas, and the Roman summodeism, through Constantine, could even draw Christianity into its system of symbolization. The break with early tolerance results not from rational reflection on the inadequacy of pluralistic symbolization (though such reflection may experientially be a first step toward more radical ventures), but from the profounder insight that no symbolization through analogues of existential order in the world can even faintly be adequate to the divine partner on whom the community of being and its order depend. Only when the gulf in the hierarchy of being that separates divine from mundane existence is sensed, only when the originating, ordering, and preserving source of being is experienced in its absolute transcendence beyond being in tangible existence, will all symbolization by analogy be understood in its essential inadequacy and even impropriety. The seemliness of symbols— if we may borrow the term from Xenophanes—then will become a pressing concern, and a hitherto tolerable freedom of symbolization will become intolerable because it is an unseemly indulgence betraying a confusion about the order of being and, more deeply, a betrayal of being itself through lack of proper attunement. The horror of a fall from being into nothingness motivates an intolerance which no longer is willing to distinguish between stronger and weaker gods, but opposes the true god to the false gods. This horror induced Plato to create the term theology, to distinguish between true and false types of theology, and to make the true order of society dependent on the rule of men whose proper attunement to divine being manifests itself in their true theology.

When the unseemliness of symbols moves into the focus of attention, it seems at first glance that there has not been much change in human understanding of the order of being and existence. To be sure, something is gained by the differentiating emphasis on the area of essential ignorance as well as by the consequent distinction between knowable immanent and unknowable transcendent reality, between mundane and divine existence, and a certain zeal in guarding the new insight against backsliding into renewed acceptance of symbols that in retrospect appear as an illusion of truth may seem pardonable. Nevertheless, man cannot escape essential ignorance through intolerance of unseemly symbolization; nor can he overcome the perspectivism of participation by understanding its nature. The profound insight into the unseemliness of symbols seems to dissolve into an emphasis, perhaps exaggerated, on something that was known all the time and did not receive more attention precisely because nothing would be changed by becoming emphatic about it.

And yet, something has changed, not only in the methods of symbolization, but in the order of being and existence itself. Existence is partnership in the community of being; and the discovery of imperfect participation, of a mismanagement of existence through lack of proper attunement to the order of being, of the danger of a fall from being, is a horror indeed, compelling a radical reorientation of existence. Not only will the symbols lose the magic of their transparency for the unseen order and become opaque, but a pallor will fall over the partial orders of mundane existence that hitherto furnished the analogies for the comprehensive order of being. Not only will the unseemly symbols be rejected, but man will turn away from world and society as the sources of misleading analogy. He will experience a turning around, the Platonic *periagogé,* an inversion or conversion toward the true source of order. And this turning around, this conversion, results in more than an increase of knowledge concerning the order of being; it is a change in the order itself. For the participation in being changes its structure when it becomes emphatically a partnership with God, while the participation in mundane being recedes to second rank. The more perfect attunement to being through conversion is not an increase on the same scale but a qualitative leap. And when this conversion befalls a society, the converted community will experience itself as qualitatively different from all other societies that have not taken the leap. Moreover, the conversion is experienced, not as the result of human action, but as a passion, as a response to a revelation of divine being, to an act of grace, to a selection for emphatic partnership with God. The community, as in the case of Israel, will be a chosen people, a peculiar people, a people of God. The new community thus creates a special symbolism to express its peculiarity, and this symbolism can from then on be used for distinguishing the new structural element in the field of societies in historical existence. When the distinctions are more fully developed, as they were by St. Augustine, the history of Israel will then become a phase in the *historia sacra,* in church history, as distinguished from the profane history in which empires rise and fall. Hence, the emphatic partnership with God removes a society from the rank of profane existence and constitutes it as the representative of the *civitas Dei* in historical existence.

Thus, a change in being actually has occurred, with consequences for the order of existence. Nevertheless, the leap upward in being is not a leap out of existence. The emphatic partnership with God does not abolish partnership in the community of being at large, which includes being in mundane existence. Man and society, if they want to retain their foothold in being that makes the leap into emphatic partnership possible, must remain adjusted to the order of mundane existence. Hence, there is no age of the church that would succeed an age of society on the level of more compact attunement to being. Instead there develop the tensions, frictions, and balances between the two levels of attunement, a dualistic structure of existence which expresses itself in pairs of symbols, of *theologia civilis* and *theologia supranaturalis,* of temporal and spiritual powers, of secular state and church.

.   Intolerance of unseemly symbolization does not resolve this new problem, and the love of being which inspires intolerance must compromise with the conditions of existence. This attitude of compromise can be discerned in the work of the old Plato, when his intolerance of unseemly symbolization, strong in his early and middle years, undergoes a remarkable transformation. To be sure, the insight of conversion, the principle that God is the measure of man, far from being compromised, is asserted even more forcefully, but its communication has become more cautious, withdrawing deeper behind the veils of the myth. There is an awareness that the new truth about being is not a substitute for, but an addition to the old truth. The *Laws* envisage a polis that is constructed as a cosmic analogue, perhaps betraying influences of Oriental political culture; and of the new truth there will be infiltrated only as much as the existential vessel can hold without breaking. Moreover, there is a new awareness that an attack on the unseemly symbolization of order may destroy order itself with the faith in its analogies, that it is better to see the truth obscurely than not at all, that imperfect attunement to the order of being is preferable to disorder. The intolerance inspired by the love of being is balanced by a new tolerance, inspired by the love of existence and a respect for the tortuous ways on which man moves historically closer to the true order of being. In the *Epinomis* Plato speaks the last word of his wisdom—that every myth has its truth.

PART ONE

The Cosmological Order of the Ancient Near East

The societies of the ancient Near East were ordered in the form of the cosmological myth. By the time of Alexander, however, mankind had moved, through Israel, to existence in the present under God and, through Hellas, to existence in love of the unseen measure of all being. And this movement beyond existence in an embracing cosmic order entailed a progress from the compact form of the myth to the differentiated forms of history and philosophy. From the beginning, therefore, a study of order and its symbolization is burdened with the problem of a mankind which unfolds an order of its own in time, though it is not itself a concrete society.

The order of mankind beyond the order of society furthermore unfolds in space insofar as the same type of symbolic form occurs simultaneously in several societies. The very title of this first part of the study, "The Cosmological Order of the Ancient Near East," raises the question: Whose order is supposed to be the subject of inquiry? For the ancient Near East is not a single organized society with a continuous history, but comprises a number of civilizations with parallel histories. Moreover, while in the civilization of the Nile Valley one can legitimately speak of a continuity of "Egypt" in spite of the interruptions of imperial order through domestic troubles and foreign invasions, in Mesopotamia the mere names of the Sumerian, Babylonian, and Assyrian empires indicate a plurality of political organizations by different peoples. And yet we have spoken, not only of the "Ancient Near East" as the subject of cosmological order, but even of a "mankind" that expressed its mode of existence by means of the cosmological myth. Such language implies that a group of societies with separate histories can be treated for our purposes as if they were a single unit in history, and even that the symbols developed to express a concrete order can be abstracted from the society of their origin and attributed to mankind at large.

The problem of mankind has not been raised in order to be resolved on this occasion of its first appearance. It will be with us throughout the course of the study. For the present, the awareness of its existence is sufficient as a basis for the following empirical observation which has a direct bearing on the organization of materials in Part I.

It is a matter of empirical knowledge that the cosmological myth arises in a certain number of civilizations without apparent mutual influences. The question, to be sure, has been raised whether the Mesopotamian and Egyptian civilizations, neighbors in time and space, did not influence one another, or have a common origin that would explain the parallel features in their political culture. Whatever the outcome of a hitherto inconclusive debate will be, the question itself will appear less pressing, if one considers that the same type of symbols occurs in the China of the Chou dynasty, as well as in the Andean civilizations, where Babylonian or Egyptian influences are improbable. The state of empirical knowledge makes it advisable, therefore, to treat the cosmological myth as a typical phenomenon in the history of mankind rather than as a symbolic form peculiar to the order of Babylon, or Egypt, or China. Still less is it advisable to indulge in speculations about "cultural diffusion" of the cosmological myth from a hypothetical center of its first creation.

The cosmological myth, as far as we know, is generally the first symbolic form created by societies when they rise above the level of tribal organization. Nevertheless, the several instances of its appearance are sufficiently variegated to allow the distinction of unmistakably Mesopotamian, Egyptian, and Chinese styles of the myth. Moreover, it is highly probable, though not conclusively demonstrable, that the differences of style have something to do with the potentiality of the various civilizations for the unfolding of experiences which ultimately result in the leap in being. In the area of the ancient Near East, the Mesopotamian empires proved most barren in this respect, while the sequence of Egyptian empires showed a remarkable but abortive development. The break-through was achieved only among the peoples of the Syriac civilization, through Israel. Hence, the varieties within the general type of cosmological myth must not be neglected.

In order to do justice to the various aspects of the problem, the historical materials will be organized in Part I in the following manner: Chapter 1 will deal with the Mesopotamian empires, because the rigidity of Mesopotamian symbols, with their negligible traces of differentiating experiences, is most suitable to the elaboration of the typical elements in the cosmological myth. Chapter 2, on the Achaemenian Empire, will deal with the modifications of the type under the impact of Zoroastrianism. Egypt will be treated in Chapter 3, because its indigenous development of experiences and symbols tended to break the form of the cosmological myth. This arrangement will provide for the type as well as for the varieties, and it will illuminate the progress of man through the sequence of civilizations.[1]

[1] The literature on specific problems will be given on the occasion of their appearance. For the political history of the empires treated in Part I, the following works, in general, were used: Eduard Meyer, *Geschichte des Altertums*, I/2 (5th ed., Stuttgart-Berlin, 1926); II/1 (2d ed., 1928); II/2 (2d ed., 1931); III (2d ed., 1937). Eugene Cavaignac, *Histoire de L'Antiquité*, I/1, *Javan* (Paris, 1917); I/2, *L'Orient et les Grecs* (Paris, 1919). M. Rostovtzeff, *A History of the Ancient World*, I, *The Orient and Greece* (Oxford, 1926). Arnold J. Toynbee, *A Study of History*, 6 vols. (Oxford, 1934-39). The pertinent chapters from the *Cambridge Ancient History*, I (Cambridge, 1924): Stephen H. Landon, "Early Babylonia and Its Cities," Chap. 10, and the same author's "The Dynasties of Akkad and Lagash," Chap. 11; R. Campbell Thompson, "Isin, Larsa, and Babylon," Chap. 13, and the same author's "The Golden Age of Hammurabi," Chap. 14. The pertinent essays from *Historia Mundi*, II, *Grundlagen und Entfaltung der aeltesten Hochkulturen* (Bern, 1953): Anton Moortgat, "Grundlagen und Entfaltung der sumerisch-akkadischen Kultur"; Guiseppe Furlani, "Babylonien und Assyrien"; William F. Albright, "Syrien, Phoenizien und Palaestina." For the background of the history of ideas these works were used: Alfred Jeremias, *Handbuch der Altorientalischen Geisteskultur* (2d ed., Berlin-Leipzig, 1929). Bruno Meissner, *Babylonien und Assyrien* (Heidelberg, 1920-25). H. and H. A. Frankfort, John A. Wilson, Thorkild Jacobsen, and William A. Irwin, *The Intellectual Adventure of Ancient Man* (Chicago, 1946). Henri Frankfort, *Kingship and the Gods* (Chicago, 1948).

CHAPTER 1

Mesopotamia

§ 1. The Creation of God and the Dominion of Man

To establish a government is an essay in world creation. When man creates the cosmion of political order, he analogically repeats the divine creation of the cosmos. The analogical repetition is not an act of futile imitation, for in repeating the cosmos man participates, in the measure allowed to his existential limitations, in the creation of cosmic order itself. Moreover, when participating in the creation of order, man experiences his consubstantiality with the being of which he is a creaturely part. Hence, in his creative endeavor man is a partner in the double sense of a creature and a rival of God.

The complex of experiences just outlined can be discerned as the motivating force of the cosmic myth in the scanty fragments of Mesopotamian origin. Its elements are preserved in the several accounts which Genesis gives of the crisis in the relations between God and man.

A first account is embedded in the story of the creation. On the sixth day the Elohim created man in their image, to resemble them, and gave him dominion over the rest of creation (Gen. 1:26). But the likeness was not complete, for the Elohim had withheld the knowledge of good and evil, and enjoined man, by the threat of death on the same day, not to eat from the tree of knowledge (2:17). But the tempter knows better: man will not die when he eats from the tree of knowledge, but will become more like the gods, knowing good and evil (3:4–5). The motif of rivalry appears, and the forbidden fruit is eaten. Man, indeed, does not die as he has been threatened; instead, a threat has arisen for the Elohim. "Man has become like one of us, he knows good and evil. He might reach his hand now to the tree of life also, and by eating of it live forever" (3:22). Man, therefore, was expelled from the dangerous neighborhood, and guards were set to bar the approaches to the tree of life (3:23–24).

A second account of the crisis is embedded in the prehistory of the great flood. The account is obscure because the Biblical narrator had to force a recalcitrant polytheistic source into his monotheistic story. Still, one can discern the origin of the crisis in some licentiousness in the "camp of the Elohim" (32:2 f.). The daughters of man were viewed with pleasure by some of the Elohim (discreetly toned down to "angels" in the Biblical narrative), and from the intermarriage of gods and men arose a race of semidivine, arrogant giants, more bent on evil than good (6:1–4). The new approach to divinity again had to be curbed, first by a divine decree denying immortality to the dangerous offspring (6:3) and, when their evil conduct did not abate, by their extinction through the great flood, from which only Noah and his household were excepted (6:5–8).

A third account is given in the story of the Tower of Babel. The descendants of Noah were one mankind, speaking one language (11:1). They settled in the plain of Shinar (Babylon) and conceived the plan of building a city and a tower that would reach to heaven in order to make a name for themselves and not be scattered all over the wide earth (11:4). Yahweh came down and watched their work, and he decided: "The people is one, and they have all one language; if this is what they start with, nothing will be restrained from them, which they have imagined to do"; and he confounded their language and scattered them over the wide earth (11:5–9).

From the three accounts man emerges as a creature in the likeness of God, specifically heightened above all other creatures through his knowledge of, and freedom for, good and evil. He has difficulties in finding the right balance of his existence, and is overbearingly inclined to reach out toward the divinity of which he is only an image. He is thrown back to an understanding of his condition by the consciousness of death, of his human passing compared with divine lasting; he is made aware of the precariousness and weakness of his existence by overpowering natural catastrophes; and the diversification of mankind into peoples teaches him that there is no "One World" of humanity which rivals heaven, but only a humble adjustment of every society in its allotted space and time to the majesty of cosmic order. With a splendid dramatic grip on his sources the author of Genesis welds the three accounts into a spiritual history of man. After the three great revolts and falls a chastened man, Abram, is called forth by the Lord to leave Babylon to settle in a new country and found the nation in whom all nations of the earth shall be blessed (12:1–3). The turbulent relations have found their balance, and the dominion of man can now sincerely be, without ambitious overreaching, an analogue of the creation of God, as it is praised in Psalm 8. In the Psalm God dwells in his majesty over all the world; his splendor is set high in the heavens to check the enemies and crush the rebels. And what is man in comparison with God?

> When I look up to the heaven, the work of thy fingers,
> The moon and the stars that thou hast made:
> What is man that thou should'st think of him?
> What is the son of man that thou should'st heed him?

And yet:

> Thou hast made him little less than the elohim,
> Thou hast crowned him with glory and honor,
> Thou hast given him dominion over the works of thy hands,
> Thou hast put all things under his feet.

The original Babylonian stories suffered mutilations and changes when they were fitted into Hebrew Genesis. Nevertheless, even in their distorted form the accounts will aid in understanding the much more archaic myth of Adapa, preserved only in fragments, that belongs in the same class.[1] The myth of Adapa has been an object of debate because some scholars wanted to recognize in it the Babylonian original of the story of Adam and his fall, while others defended the honor of the Bible by detailing the points of difference. A certain thematic relationship between the two stories, the gain of wisdom and the loss of eternal life, cannot be denied; nevertheless, we suspect that the debate was conducted in vain, because the myth of Adapa probably does not belong to the type of the Adam story at all but rather to the type represented by the second account, in Genesis 6, which tells of "the mighty men who were of renown in the days of old," of the race that sprang from the Elohim and the beautiful daughters of man. Genesis is terse on the more lusty activities of the Elohim and does not tell anything about the feats to which their offspring owes its renown. It is possible that in the Baby-

---

[1] The fragments of the Babylonian Adapa myth are available in an English translation in Alexander Heidel, *The Babylonian Genesis* (2d ed., Chicago, 1951), 147–53; analyses of the myth are to be found *ibid.*, 122 ff., and Meissner, *Babylonien und Assyrien*, II (Heidelberg, 1925), 188–89.

lonian myth we possess at least one such story of the age of semidivine heroes.

The Adapa of the myth is not the first man, as it had been assumed. He is characterized as the "seed of mankind," but philological comparison with related phrases has made it convincing that "seed" does not mean "father" but "offspring" of man. While thus being a son of man he also is the son of Ea, the god of wisdom, and hence a semidivine being, endowed by his father with wisdom but not with eternal life. Ea created him as a leader among mankind; he had perfected him to expound the decrees of the land. And Adapa functioned as a temple provisioner, the observer of rites at Eridu, the city of Ea, baking with the bakers, providing food and water, setting and clearing the table (probably in the temple), and doing the fishing for Eridu. The aggregate of the functions shows Adapa to have been a priest and ruler over the city of the god Ea.

One day, when he was fishing in the gulf, a squall of the south wind submerged him. The enfuriated Adapa, endowed with magic powers, cursed the south wind and by the curse broke his wing, thus causing a disturbance in the cosmos. After seven days Anu, the lord of heaven, noticed that the south wind was not blowing and, informed of the reason, summoned Adapa. Ea equipped his son with counsel, telling him how to conduct himself in order to win friends in heaven, and especially warning him not to taste of any food or drink offered him, for it would be the food and water of death. Thanks to the shrewd counsel Adapa could calm the wrath of Anu, and the lord of heaven began to reflect on what to do with the culprit. The original damage was done when Ea revealed to a man the secrets of heaven and earth (endowing him with magic power); Adapa now is strong and has a name; the best course will be to make him a complete god. Hence, Anu orders the food and water of life to be brought for him. But Adapa refuses to eat or drink, mindful of his father's counsel, and Anu releases him to go back to his earth. The rest (fragment iv) is too badly damaged to render a coherent story. It only appears that Anu laughed at the misdeed of Adapa, admiring the power of his curse and wondering how to increase his command. At any rate, he decreed freedom from compulsory service for Adapa's city of Eridu and granted the glory of its high priesthood (held by Adapa) unto faraway days.

The interpretation of the myth will properly start from its pragmatic setting. The story of Adapa is preserved in the form of a long preamble

to an incantation of Ninkarrak, the goddess of healing (fragment iv).
Ninkarrak will heal the illnesses and diseases which Adapa has brought
upon men when he refused to eat the food of life. From this setting we
learn, first, that the myth does not mean to tell the adventure of one
hero among others, but that Adapa is the representative of mankind;
and second, that death is not considered essential to human existence,
but a misfortune that could have been averted. The myth is clearly
concerned with human existence and being.

In dealing with its meaning, then, we must distinguish between the
content of the mythical story and the experience symbolized by it. For
if we select parts of the myth without critical caution and treat them as
if they were propositions in a discourse, carrying their own meaning, we
should arrive at dubious conclusions (which in fact have been drawn),
as for instance that the Babylonians believed death to be the consequence
of a deliberately misleading counsel of Ea or of a miscalculation on the
part of Ea and Adapa. Interpretations of this kind treat the myth as if it
were an empirical study of human behavior, which a myth of gods and
demigods obviously is not.

The symbols of the myth must be related to the experience expressed.
Human existence is deprived of the everlastingness which is the gods'.
While this nucleus is clearly indicated, it is less easy to catch the overtones of deprivation. There certainly is a feeling of "it might have been,"
and the sense of consubstantiality predominates strongly, overriding the
separateness of existences. Man can be half a god, he can have magic
powers that inflict damage through curses, and his semidivine substance
can be perfected through the physical consumption of the substance of
life; there seems to be no reason why he should not be a god. In spite of
this sense of consubstantiality, however, the motive of rivalry with the
gods, of an overbearing reaching out toward eternal life (of which Adam
is suspected in Genesis), is curiously subdued. Eternal life is not within
the reach of Adapa; his father Ea withholds it from him, and when he
has a chance to gain it, it is freely offered by Anu.[2]

The conduct of the two gods is puzzling. Ea is the god of the wisdom
which he imparts to his son. There is something Promethean in his
readiness to equip him as a leader among mankind. Why does he with-

___

[2] This restraint, however, is not characteristic of Babylonian myths in general. In the Gilgamesh Epic the hero is ardently in search of the herb that will give life. This difference would
allow the Gilgamesh Epic to be classified as the more archaic (and therefore perhaps earlier?) of
the two myths.

hold the eternal life which apparently he also could have bestowed on him? Does the myth perhaps suggest a true wisdom that will not yearn for a prolongation of existence beyond the allotted span? The possibility cannot be dismissed that there is a Homeric twilight about these gods. There is perhaps a glimmer of acceptance in the myth, of a will to be man and not to be a god. To be sure, it would be going too far to suggest that no mistake occurred when Adapa rejected the food of life, that Ea wanted him to reject it as the food that would bring death to his manhood. Still, there is something odd about this warning against the food and water of death, for the mythical substances are not poisons administered at a Renaissance banquet. And since their consequence is not a heart attack but mortality, what damage could they do to the mortal Adapa? Perhaps this mystery can be solved through recourse to a similar oddity in the myth of Genesis. When man is expelled from Eden he is thereby prevented from tasting of the tree of life. But why is the expulsion so important? What difference does it make whether the approach to the tree of life is cut off by a physical barrier or by an injunction not to touch its fruit? Does it make only the difference between a hedonistic, vegetative life and hard work? In Genesis there is an answer: The "death" that was set as punishment on the transgression is not mortality, the passing of existence, but the spiritual fall from being. The Adapa myth, now, does not raise the problem of a fall from being, but this curious warning against the food of death which ends in a rejection of the food of life perhaps hides under its compact, opaque symbolism the problem that becomes articulate in Genesis.

From such obscurity we emerge into light again with the consequences of Adapa's rejection of the food and water of life. Anu dismisses him graciously to the long-lasting, glorious dominion of Eridu. The hero who rejects eternal life is the ruler who creates and maintains order among men. Was Anu's offer perhaps a temptation? Again, this would be going too far, for this facet of the experience is not differentiated, as it is in the serpent of Genesis. But the result is the same: the dominion of man is the analogical compensation for eternal order.

§ 2. THE SYMBOLIZATION OF POLITICAL ORDER

The symbolization of political order through analogy with cosmic order in the Mesopotamian civilization did not flow from a speculative system created at a definite time, but was the result of a process in which political reality and symbolization grew toward one another until a well-defined nucleus of symbols was achieved under the First Babylonian Dynasty.[3] The political organization grew from independent city-states to empires dominating the whole territory of Sumero-Akkadian civilization, and parallel with its growth evolved the conception of empire as an analogue of the cosmos and its order.

The earliest known political form, far from primitive, was the city-state, an agglomeration of temples with large land holdings, each owned by a god and administered by the god's tenant farmer. The population of such cities ranged up to 20,000 inhabitants. The several temple units forming a city were organized into the larger unit through the rule or governorship, both priestly and civic, of the tenant farmer of the highest god in the city.[4] This personage was the *ensi* (Sumerian) or *ishakku* (Akkadian). The organization presupposed the existence of a developed pantheon with a hierarchy of gods. And this pantheon, in fact, extended

[3] Hammurabi was the sixth king of the First Babylonian Dynasty. His reign lasted forty-three years. The dates for the dynasty, and for Hammurabi's reign, have been moved down substantially during the last thirty years, in particular under the influence of the excavations from Mari. Eduard Meyer (1926) accepted for the Dynasty *ca.* 2225–1926, and for Hammurabi *ca.* 2123–2081. For the development of the debate since Meyer, cf. Sidney Smith, *Early History of Assyria* (1928); the same author's *Alalakh and Chronology* (1940); and P. van der Meer, *The Ancient Chronology of Western Asia and Egypt* (1947). The opinions for the date of Hammurabi range at present from 1848–1806 (Sidersky, Thureau-Dangin) to 1704–1662 (Weidner, Boehl). The years 1728–1686 are favored by Albright and de Vaux. Sidney Smith's date of 1792–1750 finds the approval of Parrot (*Archéologie mésopotamienne*, [Paris, 1953]). This survey of opinions is taken from the Louvre exhibition *Les Archives Royales de Mari (1800–1750 av. J.-C.)*. A similar survey is given in James B. Pritchard, *The Ancient Near East in Pictures* (Princeton, 1954), xii. Giuseppe Furlani prefers the date 1704–1662 (*Historia Mundi*, II, 262). While the reduction of dates in this particular case or the general scaling down of the dates of ancient history does not affect the details of our analysis, it is still of importance for our problems in so far as the reduction creates a denser, more probable medium for the evolution of experiences, replacing the awe-inspiring but empty stretches of time.

[4] On the internal organization of such city-states an interesting light has recently fallen through the brief Sumerian epic of "Gilgamesh and Agga," partially translated by Thorkild Jacobsen in *Journal of Near Eastern Studies*, II (1943), completely by S. N. Kramer in James B. Pritchard (ed.), *Ancient Near Eastern Texts Relating to the Old Testament* (Princeton, 1950). Gilgamesh, the king of Erech, before embarking on the war with Agga of Kish, consults the assemblies of the elders and the warriors. Thus the existence of the oldest political assemblies yet known, as Jacobsen has pointed out, is attested at least for the Sumerian city-states. I do not enter further into the question, because the materials are too scanty to base any conclusions on them. Considerable attention is given to the question, somewhat exaggerated in view of the paucity of sources, by E. A. Speiser, "Ancient Mesopotamia," in *The Idea of History in the Ancient Near East* (New Haven, 1955). No traces of such assemblies are to be found on the imperial level of organization in Mesopotamia.

beyond the confines of a single city-state to embrace the gods of the
manifold of Mesopotamian city-states. The several cities thus belonged
to one civilization in the sense that they were united by a common
religious culture. Border frictions between cities, therefore, need not
result in wars but could be settled by arbitration, the tenant farmer of a
third city functioning as the umpire whose decisions were backed by the
authority of the god he represented. The god Enlil of Nippur held highest
rank among the city gods, and his city consequently enjoyed a special
religious authority comparable to that of Delphi in Hellas.

Political organization by peaceful means beyond the level of the city-
state seems to have met with even more insuperable difficulties than in
Hellas, for we do not find federations of cities comparable to the Hellenic,
and the formation of larger territorial realms was due exclusively to war
and conquest. The victorious conquerors and unifiers assumed the title
of *lugal* (literally, "the great man"), a royal title that had been already
in use in city-states, for it signified the local rulers of Kish and Opis,
though it is not quite certain to what pre-eminence over other cities it
was due. The title was used in addition to that of a city governor, of an
ensi, and even as late as the Assyrian Empire the kings retained the title
of an *ensi* of Ashur in their style. Thus, the city-state organization was
preserved on the level of local administration even in the imperial periods.
Nevertheless, the position of an *ensi* was inevitably affected by the creation of a central administration; when the imperial government was
strong the *ensi* was hardly more than a civil servant who could be transferred from one city to another.

The growth of territorial dominion was accomplished by the development of a corresponding symbolism. From the time of Lugalzaggisi
(middle of the third millennium B.C.) is preserved an inscription which
reveals the new problem:

> When Enlil, king of all countries [*kurkur*],
> had given the kingship of the land [*kalama*] to Lugalzaggisi;
> When Enlil had directed the eyes of the land [*kalama*] towards
>   him,
> and had laid all countries [*kurkur*] at his feet;
> Enlil had conquered for him from the rising of the sun to its setting,
> and opened the roads for him from the Lower Sea at the Tigris and
>   Euphrates to the Upper Sea.

The inscription seems to be strictly constructed. The first two lines
describe the decision in the cosmic sphere, the second two lines the events

in the earthly political sphere, and the remainder of the text the resulting dominion. The god Enlil, who is the lord of all countries (*kurkur*), has decreed the kingship of the land of Sumer (*kalama*) to Lugalzaggisi. In execution of the decree the eyes of the land of Sumer (*kalama*) were directed towards Lugalzaggisi as the king, and with the dominion over Sumer as a basis he could subjugate all countries (*kurkur*) that were under Enlil. The result was a dominion which in the east-west direction extended from the rising of the sun to its setting, while in the north-south direction it extended from the Mediterranean to the Persian Gulf.[5] The dominion of the ruler reached beyond the land of Sumer proper and became co-extensive with the cosmic lordship of the god. The style of symbolization was continued under the Sargonid dynasty of Akkad, where among the royal titles are to be found "he who rules the four quarters [of the world]" and "King of the Four Quarters."

The new symbols were fully developed under the First Babylonian Dynasty. The principal document is the preamble to the Code of Hammurabi:

> When lofty Anu, king of the Anunnaki, and Enlil, lord of heaven
> and earth, who determines the destinies of the land,
> Committed the Enlil function [lordship] over all the people to
> Marduk, the firstborn son of Enki, made him great among the
> Igigi,
> When they called Babylon by its exalted name, made it surpassing
> in the world,
> When in its midst they established for him an everlasting kingdom
> whose foundations are firm as heaven and earth,—
>
> At that time Anu and Enlil called me, Hammurabi, the obedient
> prince, worshipper of the gods, by my name,
> To cause justice to prevail in the land, to destroy the evil and the
> wicked, to prevent the strong from oppressing the weak,
> That I rise like the sun over the blackheaded people, to enlighten
> the land.

The construction is the same as in the inscription of Lugalzaggisi, but it has become more elaborate.[6] There is the clear parallelism between the

---

[5] Text of the inscription in François Thureau-Dangin, *Les Inscriptions de Sumer et d'Akkad* (Paris, 1905), 219. For interpretations see Meyer, *Geschichte des Altertums* I/2, §§ 390–91, and Frankfort, *Kingship and the Gods*, 227–28. The translation follows the text given in Frankfort, with slight alterations to stress the construction.

[6] Robert Francis Harper, *The Code of Hammurabi, King of Babylon* (London and Chicago,

creation of order, the foundation of Babylon under the lordship of
Marduk in the heavens, and the creation of the earthly realm of Babylon
under the lordship of Hammurabi.[7] Moreover, there begins to emerge
something like a "system" of symbols which coherently express the
existence of an empire with regard to time, space, and substance.

A political organization exists in time, and as a recognizable unit
originates in time. In the cosmological style of symbolization, however,
there is no flow of historical time articulated by an originating event.
The foundation of a government is rather conceived as an event in the
cosmic order of the gods, of which the earthly event is the analogous
expression. What today we would call the category of historical time is
symbolized by origination in a cosmic decree.[8] There are cosmogonic
poems preserved from the period of the First Babylonian Dynasty which
describe the creation of the "heavenly earth" as preceding the creation
of the "earthly earth." The politico-religious centers of Nippur, Uruk,
Eridu, and Babylon are first created on the heavenly earth, and then the
corresponding earthly centers are built. Thus the origin of the dominant
political units is referred back to the beginning of the world.

While in time the political process is a reflection of the cosmogonic
process, the spatial organization of the empire reflects the spatial organization of the cosmos. The spatial order of the universe is determined by the
revolutions of the main celestial bodies from east to west, creating the
system of the four cardinal points, of the four corners of the world, and
of the four corresponding regions. The earthly empire corresponds to
the heavenly order in so far as the whole of the earth is divided, in the
Babylonian conception, into the four domains of Akkad (south), Elam
(east), Subartu and Gurtium (north), and Amurru (west). Conversely,
an elaborate heavenly geography finds in the sky the originals of earthly
configuration. The heavenly Tigris and Euphrates are identified with
definite constellations, and so are the great cities. Even the sun and moon
are divided into regions corresponding to the earthly quarters, "the right

---

1904); Hugo Winkler, *Die Gesetze Hammurabis in Umschrift und Uebersetzung* (Leipzig, 1904);
Chilperic Edwards, *The Hammurabi Code and the Sinaitic Legislation* (3d ed., London, 1921);
Jacobsen in *The Intellectual Adventure of Ancient Man*, 193; Theophile J. Meek in Pritchard
(ed.), *Ancient Near Eastern Texts*, 164. All of these translations were used.

[7] The echo of this parallelism is still to be found in the conception of a "heavenly Jerusalem"
that descends on the earth in Galatians 4:26 and Revelation 21.

[8] Cf. the Preamble of the "Sumerian King List": "When kingship was lowered from heaven,
kingship was first in Eridu" (translation by A. Leo Oppenheim in Pritchard [ed.], *Ancient Near
Eastern Texts*, 265). Cf. also the "Etana Legend" (translation by A. E. Speiser, *ibid.*, 114 ff.)

side of the Moon being Akkad, its left side Elam, its upper side Amurru, and its lower side Subartu." [9]

With regard to substance, once again political order reflects cosmic order. The sun-god Marduk is appointed as the ruler over all the peoples, and his earthly analogue, Hammurabi, rises like the sun over the people and lightens up the land, dispensing the essentials of just order. The empire is thus a microcosmos which by principle can exist only in the singular. And this conception remains undisturbed by its logical incompatibility with the existence of rival powers outside the cosmic analogue.

The symbolism of the microcosm was retained throughout the history of the Babylonian and Assyrian empires down to the Persian conquest. Nevertheless, there is a notable difference between Assyrian and Babylonian inscriptions which may be due to the peculiar temper of the two peoples. In the Code of Hammurabi the gods have committed the rule to the king, but the rather bloody means by which the rule must have been acquired are not mentioned. The king simply causes justice to prevail, he destroys the wicked and the evil, and he renders social service. The Assyrian inscriptions, however, give ample accounts of the royal wars. An inscription of Tiglath-Pileser III, for instance, praises the king as "the brave hero, who, with the help of Assur, his lord, smashed all who did not obey him, like pots, and laid them low, like a hurricane, scattering them to the winds; the king, who, advancing in the name of Assur, Shamash and Marduk, the great gods, brought under his sway the lands from the Bitter Sea of Bît-Iakin to Mount Bikni, of the rising sun, and to the sea of the setting sun, as far as Egypt,—from the horizon to the zenith, and exercised kingship over them." [10] For the rest, the conception of the sun-ruler remained substantially unchanged; an inscription of Tukulti-Urta I, for instance, runs: "Tukulti-Urta, king of the universe, king of Assyria, king of the four quarters of the world, the Sun of all peoples, the mighty king, king of Karduniash (Babylonia), king of Sumer and Akkad, king of the upper and lower sea, king of the mountains and the wide desert plains, king of the Shubarî and Kutî, and king of all the Nairi lands, etc." [11] Only on occasion does there appear an interesting nuance, as when the divine creation of order extends beyond the appointment of the king to his very bodily formation, as we find it

[9] Meissner, *Babylonien und Assyrien,* II, 110.
[10] D. D. Luckenbill, *Ancient Records of Assyria and Babylonia,* I (Chicago, 1926), sec. 787.
[11] *Ibid.,* sec. 142.

in an inscription of Ashurbanipal: "I am Assurbanipal, offspring (creature) of Assur and Bêlit, the oldest prince of the royal harem, whose
name Assur and Sin, the lord of the tiara, have named for the kingship
from distant days, whom they formed in his mother's womb, for the
rulership of Assyria; whom Shamash, Adad and Ishtar, by their unalter-
able decree, have ordered to exercise sovereignty." [12]

Cosmological symbolization is neither a theory nor an allegory. It is
the mythical expression of the participation, experienced as real, of the
order of society in the divine being that also orders the cosmos. To be
sure, the cosmos and the political cosmion remain separate existences, but
one stream of creative and ordering being flows through them so massively that, as we have seen, the god is the owner of a temple, while its
priest and ruler is only its tenant farmer; the earth-wide rule of Marduk
is established in heaven, while the rise to power of the earthly king is
only the implementation of the divine appointment; and the geographical
order on the earth is the image of the original in the heavens. The participation is so intimate, indeed, that in spite of the separateness of
existences, empire and cosmos are parts of one embracing order. It is with
justification, then, that one can speak of the Babylonian idea of a cosmos
ordered as a state, and that cosmos and empire are in substance one entity.
Such unity, comprehending the separate existences as parts, neces-
sitates the creation of a symbol that will express the point of physical
connection between the two separate parts, the point at which the stream
of being flows from the cosmos into the empire. A style of symbolization,
once a nucleus is formed and accepted, by its inner logic requires the
creation of further symbols. The symbol just indicated as a requirement
wherever political order is symbolized cosmologically may be called by
the Greek name *omphalos*, meaning the navel of the world, at which
transcendent forces of being flow into social order. In Hellas this omphalos was the stone at Delphi that marked the center of the universe. In
Babylonian civilization the symbol occurred, as we have seen, in the
preamble to the Code of Hammurabi. There Babylon became surpassing
in the world when it was established "in the midst of the world" as an
everlasting kingdom; and the name Bab-ilani meant indeed Gate of the
Gods. The idea could be observed in formation in the inscription of
Lugalzaggisi with its distinction of the *kalama*, the land of Sumer, and

---

[12] *Ibid.*, II, sec. 765.

kurkur, the other countries, the *kalama* forming the center of the earthly dominion, the *kurkur* its peripheral expansion. In Israelite history the symbol was elaborated, with more detail, in Genesis 28:11–22. Jacob lay down in a "certain place" to sleep on a stone as his pillow. In his dream he saw a ladder reaching from earth to heaven and the angels of God descending and ascending. At the top of the ladder appeared God himself, giving to Jacob and his descendants the land on which he was lying. "Your descendants shall be as numerous as the dust on the ground, you shall extend west and east and north and south, and all nations of the world shall seek bliss such as yours and your descendants." When Jacob awoke he recognized the place as the house of God and the gate of heaven, and he put up the stone on which he had slept as a pillar and called the place Beth-el, house of God.[13] The faint echo of the dream of Jacob is the Baitylion, the stone lying under the coronation throne of England in Westminster Abbey and believed to be the stone on which Jacob slept at Bethel.

The symbol of the omphalos proved adaptable to every empirical situation. The omphalos at Delphi has been mentioned, and the Roman milestone on the forum, in the shape of an omphalos, was the symbol of the world empire. In Mesopotamian civilization Babylon was the omphalos in the Babylonian period, while Nippur was the omphalos in the earlier Sumerian time. In Israel, besides Bethel as the older omphalos in Canaan, there are at least traces of Jerusalem as the omphalos of the world in later times. In Ezekiel 5 the prophet was entrusted with the following message to the community of Israel: "This Jerusalem! I placed her in the center of the nations, with the lands of the world around her, and she has rebelled against my laws and orders, sinning worse than the nations and the lands around her" (5:5–6). The people of the omphalos were under a special obligation to abide by the order of the Lord. What was pardonable in the outlying parts of the world was an unpardonable offense if committed by the people of the center. If the people of the omphalos imitated the ways of the outlying neighbors, they would be visited with severe punishment (5:7–17).

The stream of divine being that flows from the divine source through the omphalos into social order thus will not penetrate the world evenly into the farthest corner. The omphalos is a civilizational center from which the substance of order radiates, with diminishing strength, toward

---

[13] Compare the account in Genesis 35.

the periphery. The conception of diminishing degrees of quality with greater distance from the center is attributed by Herodotus to the Persians: "They honor most of all those who dwell nearest them, next those who are next farthest removed, and so going ever onwards they assign honor by this rule; those who dwell farthest off they hold least honorable of all; for they deem themselves to be in all regards by far the best of all men, the rest to have but a proportionate claim to merit, till those who dwell farthest away have least merit of all." Herodotus further tells that the Medes had organized their empire in such a way that they themselves had the overlordship over all the peoples in their dominion but governed directly only the immediately bordering groups, while the bordering groups in their turn governed the outer ranks of ethnic groups. The organization of the empire thus reflected the degree of excellence determined by the distance from the center.[14]

Finally, in order to stress the typical appearance of the omphalos in cosmological civilizations, there should be recalled the Chinese symbol of a *chung kuo,* of a central domain and seat of the king. The *chung kuo* was surrounded by the feudal states of lesser dignity, which in their turn were surrounded by the barbarian tribes. In the early Chou period the *chung kuo* denoted the royal domain proper, while under the Ch'in and Han dynasties its meaning was transferred to the unified empire which now was surrounded by the rest of mankind as a barbarian outer zone.

The mythical expressions of time, space, and substance of dominion, together with the omphalos, form a central set of symbols. This nucleus is surrounded by a wealth of auxiliary symbols, held together among themselves and united with the principal four by their common origin in the Sumero-Babylonian astronomic system. Only one or two of them can be treated here, and they will be selected under the aspect of their importance in later history.

Of such general importance are the symbols of the zodiac and the number twelve. They are best treated together because they merge in the symbol of the *dodekaoros* so that, especially after the fifth century B.C., it is difficult to say whether the *dodekaoros* has exerted its influence in the formation of certain ideas of order or whether it was the number twelve independently. The zodiac is the broad band in the heavens through which sun, moon, and planets take their course, bounded by two circles

[14] Herodotus I, 134; translation by A. D. Godley in *Loeb Classical Library.*

each about nine degrees distant from the ecliptic. The stars in this band were distinguished and named by the imagination of the Babylonian astronomers as a series of constellations. The history of the zodiac in this sense is obscure in many respects because of the scantiness of sources, but it seems certain that as early as the time of Hammurabi the "way of the moon" was leading through sixteen such constellations in the zodiac. The reduction of the constellations to twelve, rendering the familiar series from Aries to Pisces, is not attested before the fifth century B.C., though it may be very much older. This reduction of the zodiac to the *dodekaoros* is a feat of astronomical rationalization under the influence of the number twelve. The number itself, and its importance, results from the occurrence of twelve full moons within the solar year, so that the division of the year into twelve lunar months inevitably suggests itself. Moreover, in the Babylonian astronomic system the months were associated symbolically with the constellations which the sun touched at every twelfth of its course, so that the eights, for instance, would be known as "the month of the star of the Scorpion," and so on. The division of the zodiac into twelve sections of thirty degrees each, named after the constellation which occupies it, integrates it, in the form of the *dodekaoros,* into the solar-lunar system.

The use to which the symbolism can be put is illustrated, within Babylonian civilization itself, by the Gilgamesh epic, consisting of myths and legends of various origins. The main sources of the composition can still be discerned as the stories of the semidivine Gilgamesh, the ruler of Erech; the legends of his associate Enkidu, a primitive man; and the story of Utnapishtim, a Babylonian Noah, who witnessed and survived the great flood. The sources are of old Sumerian origin, and the time of original composition must precede Hammurabi, for Marduk, the divine ruler of the Babylonian period, has no function in the epic. The composition, however, must have undergone revisions, for the concluding episode (the present Tablet XII) looks like an appendix after Tablet XI has brought a formal ending. In the preserved form the epic consists of twelve episodes on twelve clay tablets from the time of Ashurbanipal in the seventh century B.C. This organization into twelve episodes on twelve tablets is the point of present interest for us, because it probably reflects the influence of the zodiacal symbolism. The state of preservation does not permit us to trace the full meaning of the zodiacal cycle, but at least the following points can be discerned: the episode of the divine bull killed by Gilgamesh and Enkidu (Taurus); the episode of Ishtar and Gilgamesh (Virgo); the killing of the giant Huwawa in the dark cedar forest with the aid of the sun-god Shamash, symbolizing the victory of light over darkness, which in plastic art is represented by a lion killing a bull (Leo); the encounter with the scorpion people (Scorpio); and the story of the great flood (Aquarius).

The influence of zodiacal symbolism thus makes itself felt in the more or less artificial organization of pre-existing materials under the number twelve, as well as in their association with zodiacal constellations. In Genesis 25:12–15, for instance, the sons of Ishmael are named, twelve in number; and Genesis 25:16 summarizes the enumeration as that of "the twelve princes according to their nations." In Genesis 49 Jacob blesses his sons, calling them forth and characterizing them, again twelve in number. On this occasion some of the characterizations reveal the zodiacal meaning of the twelve, as for instance Aquarius (Gen. 49:4 or 49:13?), Leo (49:9), an Ass (49:14), a Serpent (49:17), Sagittarius (49:23–24), a Wolf (49:27). And, still in the Jewish tradition, one should not forget the twelve apostles of Christ. In Hellas there is to be found a similar penchant for the number twelve in ordering the tribes. Herodotus knows of twelve Ionian, Achaean, and Aeolian cities.[15] The number twelve, finally, dominates the construction of the second best polis in Plato's *Laws*.

The zodiac gained its full possibilities for the interpretation of political phenomena in the Hellenistic period, after the development of the *dodekaoros*, when the heavenly order of the twelve constellations was related to an earthly order of twelve sections or climates. To every region important at the time was assigned one of the figures of the zodiac. The earliest preserved table, to be dated probably in the second century B.C., enumerated twelve countries together with the twelve constellations. It showed Egyptian influences in several of the zodiacal names (Cat, Scarabaeus, Ibis, Crocodile). These were the beginnings of an astrological geography which reached its full development in the *Tetrabiblos* of Ptolemy in the second century A.D. In Ptolemy's work astrological causality was extended from the regions to their inhabitants. The *dodekaoros* and the planets were supposed to influence the corresponding

---

[15] Herodotus I, 142, 145, and 149.

earthly regions, and the earthly climates in their turn to determine the characters of the nations. Astrological geography had expanded into an astrological psychology and ethnography.

The work of Ptolemy remained the standard system of ethnography through the Middle Ages and even gained in importance, measured by the numerous reprints, when the breakdown of rational culture in the late Middle Ages was followed by the astrological outburst of the sixteenth and seventeenth centuries. In the sixteenth century, however, the accumulation of geographical and ethnographic knowledge in the wake of the discoveries compelled a reconsideration of Ptolemy's division of climates and characterization of national types. Moreover, the increasing influence of Greek political theory suggested the abandoning of the Babylonian zodiacal apparatus. Bodin, in his *Methodus*, undertook the revision in the light of the new knowledge. The division of climates, as well as the characterization of types, while betraying their origin in Ptolemy, were reorganized under the marked influence of Plato and Aristotle. The world was divided into four quarters, to which national and constitutional types corresponded, with France holding a superior position in the center as the omphalos of the new order. And the astrological link in the chain of causality was dropped, so that only the climatic zones were left as the causes which showed their effects in the national characters—a system which closely resembled the meteorological ethnography to be found in the Hippocratic treatise on *Airs, Waters and Places*. In this revised form, as a theory of climatic influences on national characters, and of national characters on political institutions, the system of astrological geography and ethnography has survived through famous intermediaries, as for instance Montesquieu, into the present.[16]

The various symbols hitherto discussed reveal the importance of the sun in the Babylonian system. The zodiac is determined by the ecliptic of the sun, and the number twelve is the number of the full moons in

---

[16] The literature on the symbol of the zodiac is rather voluminous. As an access to it is suggested Jeremias, *Handbuch*, 113 ff., as well as the sections on "Tierkreis," 201, and "Dodekaoros," 242 ff., in his work; furthermore Meissner, *Babylonien und Assyrien*, especially II, *s.v.* "Tierkreisbild"; and the bibliographic references in these works. The Gilgamesh epic is available in English translation in Alexander Heidel, *The Gilgamesh Epic and Old Testament Parallels* (Chicago, 1946).

the solar year. A few remarks must be added on the political ramifications of the sun symbol.

The preamble of the Code of Hammurabi, as well as the Assyrian inscriptions, have shown the function of the sun-god as the heavenly original of earthly rule. The king was understood as the earthly analogue of the sun-god and, consequently, was styled the sun of Babylon or the sun of all peoples. The character of rulership as the analogue of heavenly order was emphasized in the decoration of the royal insignia with celestial emblems. In particular, the imperial robe was conceived as the analogue of the starry heavens and ornamented accordingly, while the heavens, in turn, were conceived as the imperial robe of the sun-god. The symbolism of the imperial robe, embroidered with the sun, the moon, the planets, and the zodiacal constellations, was continued from antiquity into the Middle Ages, since the emperor retained the character of a cosmocrator.[17] The sun as the symbol of political order spread from Mesopotamia and Egypt into the West. In the fourth century it appeared in the work of Plato in the *Republic* and the *Laws*. After the conquest of Alexander the sun that shines equally over all men became the symbol of just social order in Heliopolitan projects of the best society, as well as in the slave revolts. After the capture of Palmyra Aurelian introduced the Helios and Bel of the city as the *Sol Invictus* to Rome.[18] The solar summodeism was continued by Constantine and, though he eliminated the image of Helios from the coin of the realm, the porphyry column with the representation of the sun-god received sacrifices at Constantinople. In the fourth century, adjusting itself to the trend, the Church shifted the birthday of Christ, the "Sun of Justice," to December 25, since in pagan belief this was the birthday of the sun, the day when it began to rise again. Moreover, the day of the Lord (*dies dominicus*) has retained the name of Sunday since the constitutions of Constantine.[19]

The conception of royal rule as the analogue of the rule of Marduk, the sun-god, motivates a complicated set of symbols to which the present study can refer only briefly. The sun, the moon, and the planets are revolving celestial bodies, and the revolution of the sun in particular

[17] Robert Eisler, *Weltenmantel und Himmelszelt; Religionsgeschichtliche Untersuchungen zur Urgeschichte des antiken Weltbildes*, 2 vols. (Munich, 1910).

[18] Franz Cumont, *Les Religions Orientales dans le Paganisme Romain* (4th ed., Paris, 1929), 106.

[19] For the sources of this paragraph in general see Jeremias, *Handbuch, s.v.* "Sonne."

determines the cycle of seasonal fertility and death. The periodicity of the celestial movements lends itself to analogical representations in the political sphere through annual festivals of death and revival, of renovation of status and a new beginning. Moreover, the regularity of annual decline and revival suggests a periodicity in the order of the cosmos on the larger scale, of a periodic victory of order over chaos and relapse into chaos, that is, the idea of cosmic aeons.

In Mesopotamian state practice the cosmic revolutions found their expression in the New Year ceremonies, when the sun-king had to go through important rites as the symbol of the sun setting out for a new period. These festivals, however, were not New Year celebrations in the modern sense, but were loaded with the representation of periodicity on the three levels of a renewal of the fertility of the soil, of the renewal of the sun period on which the fertility depended, and of the aeonic victory of order over chaos of which the solar revolution itself was the symbol. In all three respects the New Year's festival was the expression of a new beginning, of a righting of all wrongs, of a cosmic redemption from chaotic evils. And in all of these respects the sun-king assumed the character of a Soter, of a savior, of the herald of a new age, of a representative sufferer for the community who carried the burden of its sins and redeemed them, and incidentally redeemed himself in order to resume his unsullied kingship. The experience of perfection and salvation was still deeply embedded in the experience of a cosmic rhythm of society; on the level of cosmological culture, one may say, the cycle of redemption corresponded functionally to the eschatology of transcendent perfection on the level of soteriological culture.[20]

Experiences and symbols are exposed to the pressure of reflective analysis, so that even in polytheistic and cosmological cultures the lines of rationalization become visible that will lead, by way of political summodeism and theogonic speculation, toward an understanding of the radical transcendence of divine being, and concomitantly to an understanding of the nature of mundane reality.

Such a line had just become visible when the experience of celestial revolutions and fertility cycles suggested aeonic cycles of chaos and

---

[20] On the soteriological function of kingship see *ibid.*, Chap. 13, on "Die Erloesererwartung als Ziel der Weltzeitalterlehre." An elaborate reconstruction and interpretation of the Babylonian New Year Festival is to be found in Frankfort, *Kingship and the Gods,* Chap. 22.

order in the cosmos. Under the conditions of polytheistic symbolization the recognition of these ranks of order, of movements within movements, of periods within periods, had to express itself in the creation of hierarchies of gods. Behind the rank of celestial gods that met the eye there were divine forces at work who decreed the rulership of Marduk, the sun-god; and behind the gods who appointed the ruler of the present aeon there were other gods who had created them. Behind the power of Marduk and the other celestial gods lay the power of Anu, the lord of heaven, and his generation of gods; and they in their turn originated from a primordial Magna Mater, Tiamat, and Apsu, the begetter of gods. While the polytheistic symbolization is preserved, it becomes clear nevertheless that theogonic constructions of this type may lead to the recognition of divine power in world-transcendent reality and result in monotheistic speculation. No such ultimate break occurred in Mesopotamian civilization, and political symbolization consequently remained on the level of complexity that we find in the Babylonian New Year's festival. The higher degrees of rationalization appeared, in continuity with Mesopotamian and Persian history, only in the Hellenistic period, under the influence of Greek speculation, and in the Roman imperial theology. However, other cosmological civilizations (China, for instance) developed within their own orbit and with their own means the conception of a world monarchy as the earthly analogue of the one god who rules the cosmos; and the state documents of the Mongol Empire, in the thirteenth century A.D., formulated with full rational clarity the principle of "One god in heaven, one emperor on earth."

Better than in the Babylonian sources themselves can stages in the struggle for rationalization be discerned in the traditions of Israel. The level of celestial symbolization has survived in the previously mentioned zodiacal symbolism of the twelve tribes of Israel, as well as in the dream of Joseph (Gen. 37:9–10) in which sun, moon, and the eleven stars bow to Joseph as their political head. And as late as Revelation 12:1 St. John sees the "great wonder in heaven: a woman clothed with the sun, and the moon under her feet, and upon her head a crown of twelve stars"—the woman that is bringing forth the child who slays the dragon and redeems the world. Genesis 6, as we have seen, retains the idea of a cosmic aeon of semidivine giants who must perish in the flood before the world of man can arise. And the Magna Mater has survived in Proverbs 8 in the figure of Sophia, the companion of the Lord before the creation of the world. Moreover, the Book of Job has preserved traces of transition from polytheism to the recognition of the one, invisible creator. The celestial temptation is still strong, but better knowledge is willing to resist it (31:26–28):

> If I looked on the shining sun,
> or on the moon that moved in splendor,
> And let my heart go out to them,
> wafting a kiss to them,
> That would be a crime for punishment,
> for I should have denied the God on high.

It is hard to abandon the gods who so convincingly reign in the sky with their splendid presence, and there is something elusive about the new God (9:11):

> He passes me—I cannot see him;
> He sweeps on—I behold him not.

It is difficult to find this God, to lay one's grievance before him and to argue with him (23:2–4 and 8–9):

> But my complaint is bitter still;
> under his heavy hand I lie and moan.
> Oh that I knew where to find him,
> how to reach his very throne,
> and there lay my case before him,
> arguing it out in the full!
>
> But I go forward, and he is not there;
> backward and yet I cannot behold him;
> I seek him on my left, in vain;
> when I turn to the right I cannot see him.

In search of his God, as the last verses show, Job moves to the four quarters like a Babylonian king or Chinese emperor, but the search in space no longer reveals a divine presence because the earth is no longer the analogue of the divine sky. A world that is empty of gods begins to cast its shadow over the mood of man (23:15–17):

> I am cowed before him;
> the thought of him dismays me.
> For God makes my heart faint,
> the Almighty cows me;
> I am appalled at his dark mystery,
> and its black shadow has bewildered me.

The dismay caused by the invisible divinity was still a problem in early Christianity, and the temptation to return to the visible splendor of the gods must have been great. In Galatians 4:8–11 St. Paul has to admonish a relapsing community:

> In those days when you were ignorant of God, you were in servitude to gods who really are no gods at all; but now that you know God—or rather, are known by God—how is it you are turning back again to the weakness and poverty of the elemental spirits? Why do you want to be enslaved all over again by them? You observe days and months and festal seasons and years! Why, you make me afraid I may have spent my labor on you for nothing!

It is sometimes not sufficiently realized to what extent Israel and Christianity were engaged in the same struggle, not against each other, but against Babylonian religious culture. The obstacle in the path of rationalization seems to have been the difficulty of experiencing in the fullness of its meaning the gulf between creative, world-transcendent divine being and being in created, mundane existence; again and again we find the attempts of softening the immediacy of relation between man and the transcendent God by the introduction or reintroduction of mediating existences. Against these tendencies was directed the assurance of St. Paul in Romans 8:38–39:

> For I am certain that neither death nor life, neither angels nor principalities, neither the present nor the future, no powers of the Height or of the Depth, nor anything else in all creation, will be able to part us from God's love in Christ Jesus our Lord.

In the practice of politics the rationalization of the forces of being, as yet undifferentiated into "religious" and "political" forces, is the condition of empire-building. The world of politics is essentially polytheistic in the sense that every center of power, however small and insignificant it may be, has a tendency to posit itself as an absolute entity in the world, regardless of the simultaneous existence of other centers which deem themselves equally absolute. Hence, an empire-builder faces the ineluctable task of inventing a hierarchy of forces which permits the welding of formerly independent units into one political cosmion. On the principal instrument of such rationalization, political summodeism, we have touched already. The Mesopotamian city-states had their local deities constituting the politico-religious unit; and with the succession of empires the respective victorious gods—Enlil of Nippur, Marduk of Babylon, Ashur of Assyria—succeeded each other as the *summus deus* of the empire. The other deities, however, were not abolished, but only assigned a lower status. The internal coherence and fighting strength of an empire, furthermore, depended on the degree to which the rationalization of symbols could be translated into techniques of governmental centralization. A decisive difference between the Babylonian and Assyrian administrations, for instance, lay in the fact that in the Babylonian Empire the New Year's festival was celebrated by the local governors at the local religious capitals, while the more centralized Assyrian organization required the local governors to perform the ceremony in the capital of the empire in the years after it had been performed by the king. The commander-in-chief and governor of the important province of Harran, for instance, had to perform the ceremony in the year after the king and could not hold office unless he was the eponymous official, the *limmu,* of the year following the king. The rise of hereditary governorships, as it had occurred in Babylonia, was made impossible by the Assyrian practice; and the superior military strength of Assyria was probably due to the centralization thus achieved. While the Babylonian Empire was rather a congeries of city-states, the Assyrian Empire came nearer to the type of an organized national state.

§ 3. The Symbolization of Cosmic Order

Cosmological symbolization in a strict sense may be defined as the symbolization of political order by means of cosmic analogies. The life of man and society is experienced as ordered by the same forces of being which order the cosmos, and cosmic analogies both express this knowledge and integrate social into cosmic order. The rhythms of the seasons and of fertility in plant and animal life, as well as the celestial revolutions on which these rhythms depend, must be understood as the order that furnishes the analogies. The knowledge of cosmic order in this sense, especially as regards astronomy, was highly developed in Sumero-Babylonian civilization.

The preceding sections, however, have revealed a much more complex structure of the problem. Mesopotamian political culture went far beyond cosmological symbolization in the strict sense and even reversed the direction of symbolization. To be sure, political order was understood cosmologically, but cosmic order was also understood politically. Not only was the empire an analogue of the cosmos, but political events took place in the celestial sphere. The establishment or change of imperial rule was preceded by political upheavals among the gods who would depose an Enlil of Nippur and transfer his jurisdiction to a Marduk of Babylon. Moreover, the relations between heaven and earth were so intimate that the separateness of their existences was all but blurred. The empire was part of the cosmos, but the cosmos was an empire of which the dominion of man was a subdivision. There was *one* order embracing the world and society that could be understood either cosmologically or politically.

The mutuality of analogical illumination, and especially the conception of the world as a political order, is peculiar to Mesopotamia; it is not characteristic of all cosmological civilizations. In Chinese civilization, for instance, the rule of a dynasty depends on its possession of a specific virtue, the *teh*. Like all things under the heavens, the *teh* is exhaustible; and when it has weakened to the point of causing suffering to the people and revolutionary unrest, a new possessor of the *teh* with his family will succeed in overthrowing the declining dynasty. This rise and fall of dynasties, then, is integrated into the order of the cosmos in so far as a heavenly decree, the *ming*, ordains the rule of a family that possesses the *teh* and also ordains its overthrow when it has lost the *teh*. The attunement of society to the cosmos depends on the son of heaven and his dynastic *teh*, while the power of heaven, the *t'ien*, will provide for the rise and fall of dynasties. Hence political events, though partaking of the nature of cosmic forces, remain strictly in the sphere of a human struggle for power; heaven preserves its majesty of undisturbed order, while society is engaged in its struggle for attunement. In Chinese civilization political order is symbolized as due to the operation of impersonal cosmic forces.

Further light will be shed on the peculiarity of the Mesopotamian symbolic form by a brief glance at the late Mycenaean civilization as reflected in the Homeric epics. In Homer, as in Mesopotamia, the society of men is duplicated by a society of gods; to the order of aristocratic warriors under a king corresponds the aristocratic order of Olympian gods under a powerful but limited monarch. The relation between the two orders is even more intimate than in Mesopotamia, for the gods direct the destinies of men not only from afar by their decrees, but descend

into the human arena invisibly or in various disguises and even participate in battle. Moreover, they find pleasure not only in the daughters of
men, as did the Elohim, but also in the sons, and the armies before Troy,
on both sides, contain a liberal sprinkling of semidivine offspring. Gods
and men form one great society, and the battle lines between mortals also
divide the immortals. Nevertheless, important as these parallels between
Mycenaean and Mesopotamian symbolic forms are, they must be considered secondary to a decisive difference. The Homeric gods have all but
lost their character as cosmic forces and celestial powers; they are hu-
manized as far as it is possible to conceive gods anthropomorphically
without destroying their divinity. In Homer, to be sure, there is present
the experience of participation in the community of being, but this
participation is not symbolized by analogy with cosmic order; the symbolization rather brings into its grasp, without mediation, the divine
forces of being themselves. The order of society depends not on the
attunement to the cosmos, but directly to the anthropomorphically conceived gods and especially, in the Hellenic period, to the Dike of Zeus.
In the transition from Mycenaean to Hellenic civilization we meet with
an early flowering of anthropological symbolization.

In comparing the three cases—the Mesopotamian, the Chinese, and
the Mycenaean—we can perhaps touch (though certainly not solve)
one of the obscurest problems in the intellectual history of mankind;
that is, the aptitude of various civilizations for development in the direction of the "leap in being." In the Mesopotamian case we find the
early interpenetration of symbolisms, the cosmological symbolization of
political order together with the political symbolization of cosmic order.
It seems possible that the mutual reinforcement of the two orders made
the symbolism particularly inflexible and resistant to dissolution by differentiating experiences. The simpler cosmological symbolism in China
left sufficient freedom in the human sphere to allow, in the breakdown
of the Chou dynasty, for a conception of social order as dependent, not
on the son of heaven alone, but on councillors and an administration
formed by the spirit of Confucius. This was a step in the anthropological
direction, but not a complete breakthrough. The intermediate position
of Confucianism is reflected in the debate on the question whether Confucianism was a "religion." It was not a "religion" because it did not go
beyond the conception of the Confucian sage as a man who was so well
attuned to the *tao* of the cosmos that he could be an ordering force in

society, supporting, if not supplanting, the dynastic *teh*. But since Confucianism was a discovery of the order of the soul, in its autonomy and immediacy under divine order it was a revolutionary break with cosmological collectivism and contained the seeds of a "religion" that might have flowered under more favorable circumstances. In the Homeric case the cosmological symbolism did break down, probably because the Doric invasion and the geographical dislocation of populations caused a much deeper disturbance than the ordinary Times of Trouble in other civilizations. The gods were no longer bound to the structure of the cosmos, and when the discovery of the soul occurred in Hellenic civilization, man found himself in his immediacy under a transcendent God. The preconditions were given for the blending of Greek philosophy with the religious insights achieved on the historical paths of Israel and Christianity.

While the political symbolization of the cosmos is presupposed in the Mesopotamian sources even in the third millennium B.C., a coherent exposition of the symbolism is preserved only in the form of a cosmogonic epic of the first half of the second millennium named the *Enuma elish* after its opening words "When Above." The hero of the epic is Marduk of Babylon, who establishes the present world order. His characteristics in the story, however, belong to Enlil of Nippur; hence the epic, in its original form, must have been a much earlier Sumerian creation. Moreover, there is preserved a later version, from the Assyrian period, in which Marduk has been replaced by Ashur. The epic is thus representative of Mesopotamian symbolism from the Sumerians to the Assyrians.[21]

The nature of the *Enuma elish* cannot easily be described because our differentiated vocabulary is not adequate to its compactness. It is a cosmogony in as much as it tells the story of the creation of the world. But a comparison with the Biblical Genesis would create an entirely false impression because in the *Enuma elish* it is not God who creates the world. The gods *are* the world and the progressive structural differentiation of the universe is, therefore, a story of the creation of the gods. The cosmogony is at the same time a theogony. The struggle of the gods for a proper organization of the universe, furthermore, requires new forms of social organization among the younger gods, culminating in

[21] The *Enuma elish* is available in the English translation of Heidel, *The Babylonian Genesis*. A careful analysis of the epic, by Jacobsen, is to be found in *The Intellectual Adventure of Ancient Man*, 168–83. The account in the text will stress only the points of special interest for our problems; for further details the reader should refer to Jacobsen.

the kingship of Marduk. Since the creation of the cosmos is at the same time a political enterprise, the *Enuma elish* is also a political epic. The three factors of cosmogony, theogony, and politics are inseparably blended into one. Hence, the nature of the epic can be determined in a first approach only by weighing these factors quantitatively. The whole poem consists of seven tablets: the first contains the cosmogony and theogony proper, Tablet V describes the creative work of Marduk, and the other five deal with the emergence of Marduk as the savior of the gods, his great battle against Tiamat, and his glorification. Thus the epic as a whole is preponderantly political; it symbolizes cosmic order as political order.

The interpretation of the poem is complicated by the same fusion of component factors that causes the difficulty in determining its nature. However, it is possible to distinguish three stages in the cosmogony. In the first stage only the watery elements are present: Tiamat (the sea), Apsu (the sweet water), and Mummu (probably cloud banks and mist). In the second stage silt is deposited at the border of sea and sweet water, represented by the pair Lahmu and Lahamu, and land is banking up; with the land begin to form the horizons of heaven and earth, represented by the pair Anshar and Kishar; with the rings of the double horizon grow into existence heaven and earth, represented by Anu and Ea (Mummud); and from Ea, finally, is born the god who in the Babylonian version bears the name of Marduk, but in the Sumerian original must have been Enlil, the god of the storm who by its blowing holds heaven and earth apart. The third stage brings the reorganization of power relations between the gods, the elevation of Marduk to kingship, and his completion of the cosmic structure. From the cosmogonic account emerges the cosmos with the structure experienced by man. The cosmogony, however, is not a "creation" but a growth of the cosmos through procreation of gods and struggles between their generations. The gods themselves are bodily the structural parts of the cosmos. And this peculiarity leads to the further problem of aeons of cosmic order.

The cosmos of the *Enuma elish* is a completed order at the end of the story. If the cosmos is understood as the finished product resulting from the growth, there are no aeons of cosmic order because there is no order before its completion. And historians have, indeed, interpreted the first stage of the watery elements as the chaos that brings forth the cosmos. This interpretation, however, puts too much emphasis on the cosmogonic factor in the epic, to the detriment of its political and even historical components. The stage of the watery elements is not a chaos but a self-contained order of the primordial trinity, and the pairs of gods who go forth from it belong to a new, incompatible psychological type that soon arouses the wrath of the powers that be. The new gods are a lively lot:

> The divine brothers gathered together.
> They disturbed Tiamat and assaulted their keeper;
> They disturbed the inner parts of Tiamat,
> Moving and running about in the divine abode.
> Apsu could not diminish their clamor,
> And Tiamat was silent in regard to their behavior.
> Yet their doing was painful to her.
> Their way was not good. . . .

The older generation at last takes action. They meet in council and Apsu declares:

> Their way has become painful to me,
> By day I cannot rest, by night I cannot sleep;
> I will destroy them and put an end to their way,
> That silence be established, and then let us sleep!

In the resulting clash the younger vanquish the older gods, and with their victory they have become a permanent part of the new cosmic order which they dominate. This is more than a cosmogonic myth, and certainly it is not the story of a victory of order over chaos. The order is already in existence, cherished by a conservative older type, and the conflict arises from the liveliness of a younger generation that disturbs the order by its activities. Certain details of the story even suggest the nature of the conflict. The leader of the younger gods is Ea, the earth, "the one of supreme understanding, the skillful and wise," the Promethean figure that we have already met in the context of the Adapa myth. By his magic he defeats Apsu, the sweet waters, and on his defeated body he erects his abode—which, if anything at all, can only mean the securing of land against the dangers from the waters. In this conflict can be recognized faint memories of a civilizational crisis from which emerged communities under the authority of wise chieftains, as well as their efforts to secure settlements and lands by dike-building and irrigation.

The main part of the epic is concerned with the transition from the

second to the third stage of order. The new order is threatened by a
revolt of the older gods who are thirsting for revenge. The revolt is well
prepared and this time the magic of Ea is of no avail. In their despair
the gods turn to the brilliant young Marduk. He is willing to undertake
the defense, but only on the condition that he will be recognized as the
supreme god in place of Anu. The gods meet in assembly and the kingship of the universe is conferred on Marduk, who then defeats Tiamat
in battle and reorders the universe:

> He created stations for the great gods;
> The stars their likenesses, the signs of the zodiac, he set up.
> He determined the year, defined the divisions;
> For each of the twelve months he set up three constellations.
>
> In the very center thereof he fixed the zenith,
> The moon he caused to shine forth; the night he entrusted to her.
> He appointed her, the ornament of the night, to make known the
>   days.

The cosmos then is completed by the creation of man out of one of the
dismembered enemies. On mankind is incumbent the service of the gods
so that they will be free from work. Grateful for this last feat of creation
the gods then assemble and resolve to build a sanctuary for Marduk, their
last labor before men take over the work:

> So shall Babylon be, whose construction you have desired;
> Let its brickwork be fashioned, and call it a sanctuary.

The epic concludes with the enumeration of the fifty names of Marduk.
About the meaning of the Marduk story there can hardly be a doubt:
it is the establishment of a Mesopotamian kingship with its center in
Babylon. If the first crisis could be understood as the transition from
primitive communities to the organized villages which grew into the
city-states, the second crisis is the establishment of a Mesopotamian empire.

From the analysis it should have become clear that the three component strands are, indeed, inextricably interwoven. Any attempt to
pull out one of them and to interpret the epic either as a cosmogony, or
a theogony, or a myth of Mesopotamian history would destroy the meaning of the epic, which rests in its compactness. This compactness is the
Mesopotamian peculiarity that we discussed in the opening pages of the
present section. The world is not created by the gods, but the gods are
massively the world itself. And even mankind participates in this mas-

sivity, for it is the dismembered body of one of the gods who in this form goes on to exist. The cosmos is, furthermore, the result of a historical struggle that now has settled down into a fixed and final order, an organized state of the world in the political sense of which mankind is a part. And, finally, the omphalos of this world-state is Babylon itself, where the *Enuma elish* was annually recited at the New Year's festival. Considering such compactness the durability of the symbolism should perhaps not be surprising. It outlasted Babylon through its survival in the Hellenistic idea of the cosmos as a polis.

CHAPTER 2

The Achaemenian Empire

The inscriptions of the short-lived Achaemenian Empire (*ca.* 550–330 B.C.) will require not much more than a postscript to Mesopotamian ideas, for the type of symbolization is substantially the same: the empire is co-extensive with the world; the king is instituted by the grace of the supreme god; and the god permits lands and peoples to fall under the rule of the king in order to transform the world into one well-ordered realm of peace. An inscription from the reign of Darius I (521–485) will reveal the typical features:

> A great god is Ahuramazda,
>> who created this earth, who created yonder heaven,
>> who created man, who created peace for man,
>> who made Darius king, the one king of many, the one ruler of many.
>
> I am Darius, the Great King,
>> the king of kings, king of the countries which have many peoples,
>> king of the great earth even to afar,
>> the son of Hystaspes, the Achaemenian.

The pathos of the construction in parallels is the same as in Mesopotamia; Darius, the ruler of the microcosmos, enacts analogically the rule of Ahuramazda over the cosmos. The first section enumerates the parts of creation in their order: earth, heaven, man, peace for man, and its guarantor, the king. The second section resumes the last term of the divine creation, the king, and elaborates its meaning: the king is not any king, but the Great King, the one ruler of the earth, participating in God's creation through his analogical terrestrial rule.[1]

---

[1] For the political history of Persia see Meyer's *Geschichte des Altertums*, and the same author's article "Persia," in *Encyclopedia Britannica*, 11th ed.; also the article "Ormazd," by A. J. Carnoy in *Encyclopedia of Religion and Ethics*; G. B. Gray, "The Foundation and Extension of the Persian Empire," *Cambridge Ancient History* (1926), IV, i, and G. B. Gray and M. Cary, "The Reign of Darius," *ibid.*, vii.

While the Achaemenian inscriptions add little to our knowledge of the cosmological type of symbolization, they are historically relevant for other reasons. The Persian symbolism results from an interpenetration of Babylonian civilizational elements and the specifically Syriac Zoroastrian religiousness (Syriac used in the sense of Toynbee); hence it is an instance of the transformation which a type may undergo when it is refracted in a new civilizational medium. Furthermore, it represents a higher stage of rationalization than was achieved within the Mesopotamian type proper. Both transformation and rationalization, finally, are related to each other in so far as the influence of Zoroastrianism must be considered the principal cause of the higher degree of rationalism that distinguishes the Achaemenian imperial theology. This complex of problems requires brief consideration.

As the previously quoted inscription from Darius I has shown, rationalization in the Achaemenian Empire assumed the form of political summodeism, as it had done in the Mesopotamian empires. Since, however, the Persian imperial theology had passed through the religiousness of Zoroastrianism, the rational pattern of speculation that overlaid the polytheistic symbolism was not developing in the direction of monotheism, as it did in Mesopotamia and Egypt. For in Zoroastrianism the plurality of divine forces had contracted into polar powers of good and evil. Ahuramazda, the lord of wisdom, was the good god of light, truth, and peace; while in his struggle he was opposed by the evil powers of darkness, lie, and discord, concentrated in Ahriman. And the Achaemenian kings transposed the cosmic struggle of good and evil divinities into the conception of a political struggle between an empire that would transform the earth into a realm of peace in accordance with the wishes of Ahuramazda and the hostile princes and nations who belong to the dark realm of Ahriman. The king is the divine tool, assisting the god in his struggle against the realm of darkness, and whosoever resists the king stands thereby revealed as a representative of the opposing evil power.

In the Behistun Inscription Darius I says: "As to the provinces which revolted, lies made them revolt, so that they deceived the people. Then Ahuramazda delivered them into my hands." [2] The dualistic theology expands into a dualistic interpretation of political order and even of

---

[2] L. W. King and R. C. Thompson, *The Sculptures and Inscriptions of Darius the Great on the Rock of Behistun in Persia* (London, 1907), § 54, p. 65.

human conduct. Not only are the king and his enemies representatives of Truth and Lie in the cosmological sense, but their personal conduct is characterized by the same terms in a pragmatic sense. A revolt is a manifestation of the power of Ahriman, but pragmatically it is a political event caused by the propagandic lies of the false pretenders. The king is living in the Truth of Ahuramazda, but his truth is also pragmatically understood as the truthfulness of the king in reporting his actions. The Behistun Inscription informs the reader: "By the grace of Ahuramazda there is also much else that hath been done by me which is not graven in this inscription; on this account it hath not been inscribed lest he who should read this inscription hereafter should then hold that which hath been done by me to be too much and should not believe it, but should take it to be lies." [3] The representative of the Truth must avoid even the appearance of untruthfulness.

Such caution was especially necessary in this case, because the Inscription was a solemn act of spreading the truth of Ahuramazda. The military expansion of the Achaemenian Empire was understood as a service of the god, and the earthly expansion of his realm required publication of the good tidings. The further spreading of the information conveyed by the Inscription was, moreover, considered religiously praiseworthy and even a duty, while the suppression of its content was equivalent to assisting the powers of darkness. This, at least, seems to be the sense of the following passage: "Now may that appear true unto thee which hath been done by me; so . . . conceal thou not. If thou shalt not conceal this edict, but shalt publish it to the world, then may Ahuramazda be thy friend, may thy house be numerous, and mayest thou thyself be long-lived. . . . If thou shalt conceal this edict and shalt not publish it to the world, may Ahuramazda slay thee and may thy house cease." [4] The immediately following lines set forth the reason why conquest is a truth that should be spread: Ahuramazda has aided the king because he "was not wicked, nor a liar"; because the king was not a servant of Ahriman, the Lie; because neither he nor his family were wrongdoers in the religious sense, but ruled "according to Righteousness." [5] The conquest was possible, according to this construction, because the king and his family belonged to the divine realm of Truth. Political power, since it participates in divine being, was a manifestation

[3] *Ibid.*, § 58, p. 68.
[4] *Ibid.*, §§ 60, 61, pp. 69 ff.
[5] *Ibid.*, § 63, p. 72.

of the power of the Good and the Truth. Spreading the news of its expansion, consequently, was more than a reporting of political events, it was a participation in the ordering work of truth. And the account published was not true merely because of its factual correctness, but as a revelation of God and his work.

The Zoroastrian cosmic dualism, by its immanent logic, superseded the culture of polytheism; and in so far as the dualistic speculation was effective, the Achaemenian symbolism displayed the rational structure just described. The Persian imperial theology, however, was not a logically coherent system but had retained older symbolic elements. The Behistun Inscription, which makes the expansion of the realm an issue between Truth and Lie, says in a later section: "Ahuramazda, and the other gods that be, bring aid unto me." An inscription of Xerxes says: "A great god is Ahuramazda, the greatest of gods"; and inscriptions of Artaxerxes I and II name Mithras and Anahita as the more important among these other gods. As will be seen from these dates, the polytheistic element, while noticeable by the time of Darius, was even gaining in strength in the later reigns. The Persian triad of Ahuramazda, Mithras, and Anahita corresponded to the Babylonian triad of Sin, Marduk, and Ishtar (Moon, Sun, Venus), and probably was formed under Mesopotamian influence in the Indo-Iranian period preceding the separation of Hindu and Persian civilization.[6]

The co-existence of polytheistic and Mazdaist elements made it possible to attempt a pluralistic construction of the empire when the Babylonian and Egyptian civilizations had been incorporated through conquest. The Mazdaist rationalism of their own imperial theology did not prevent the Achaemenians from organizing the empire polytheistically with regard to Babylon and Egypt. The kings from Cyrus to Xerxes used "king of Babylon" as part of their style and Cyrus submitted to the Babylonian ceremony of being called to the throne by Marduk. Cambyses and Darius I, when they ascended the throne of the Pharaohs, took Egyptian hieratic names, stressing their relationship to Amon. This mixture of symbols facilitated the integration of foreign civilizations into the empire. Only when the frequent revolts in Babylon and Egypt, as well as in the Ionian cities, proved the system to be a failure did the

[6] See on the question O. Schrader's article, "Aryan Religion," *Encyclopedia of Religion and Ethics,* II, 36.

Great Kings abandon the attempt and rule the conquered regions as parts of the Achaemenian Empire without regard for their politico-religious traditions.

Finally, the strong component of dynastic consciousness and racial pride should be noted. The inscription of the tomb of Darius I describes him as "a Persian, the son of a Persian, an Aryan of Aryan stock." In the Behistun Inscription Darius identifies himself as "the son of Hystaspes, the grandson of Arsames, the Achaemenian. . . . My father is Hystaspes; the father of Hystaspes was Arsames; the father of Arsames was Ariyaramnes; the father of Ariyaramnes was Teispes; the father of Teispes was Achaemenes. . . . On that account are we called Achaemenians; from antiquity are we descended; from antiquity hath our race been kings. . . . Eight of my race were kings before me; I am the ninth. In two lines have we been kings." And the tomb of Cyrus bears the inscription: "I am, Cyrus, the king, the Achaemenian."

We have spoken of the higher degree of rationalism that characterizes the Achaemenian speculation in so far as it is influenced by Zoroastrian religiousness. The precise degree of this rationalism requires some clarification, especially since the religious experiences that manifest themselves in the dualistic theology have shaped the intellectual history of mankind far beyond their Syriac area of origin. The experience of the cosmos as a struggle between forces of good and evil reappears not only in the varieties of ancient Gnosis, but also in Western political movements since the high Middle Ages. And in contemporary politics the symbolism of Truth and Lie has become generally predominant, with the result that the major political-creed movements interpret themselves as the representatives of Truth and one another as the representatives of Lie. The adumbrated type of experience is today one of the great spiritual world forces in rivalry with Christianity and the classic tradition.

The various manifestations of the experiential type will be treated in their proper contexts, but for the present it will be sufficient to dispel an unclearness that originates in the conventional designation of Zoroastrianism as a dualistic religion. Religions can be classified as dualistic or monistic only at the risk of destroying by the numerical nomenclature the experiential differences which require either a dualistic or a monotheistic symbolism for their expression. The conversion, on the one hand, which results in the previously discussed "leap in being," requires a monistic symbolism for expressing the differentiating experience of a world-transcendent divine being. Within the logic of conversion it is inadmissible to symbolize the mystery of iniquity by a second divinity. The experience, on the other hand, that can be adequately expressed by a dualism of good and evil forces must be sufficiently compact to comprehend in an undifferentiated state the experience of the world-immanent tension between good and evil. A dualistic theology, while it may carry monotheistic overtones, is by principle a speculative extrapolation of a world-immanent conflict of substantially the same type that in China has produced the yin-yang symbolism. Because of this world-immanent component the experience that expresses itself adequately in a dualism of divinities or principles can, in variegated historical circumstances, absorb the conflicts of the age and become the originating experience of political theologies which identify their own cause with cosmic truth and the enemy with cosmic evil.

CHAPTER 3

Egypt

The history of Egyptian order is at present in a state of reassessment. Sources have been made more accessible through improved translations and editions, and recent publications by members of the Chicago Oriental Institute have substantially advanced our understanding of Egyptian spiritual and intellectual development. Moreover, the methods of interpreting ancient civilizations in general, and the Egyptian in particular, have come into flux through Toynbee's *Study of History*. Toynbee's theory concerning the phases of a civilizational course was not accepted by Egyptologists, and the recent criticisms by Henri Frankfort have opened the debate on the principles of interpretation. The issues as they affect the understanding of Egyptian political order will be discussed in the following preliminary section of the present chapter so that the analysis proper will not be burdened down with parenthetical explanations and footnotes.[1]

§ 1. The Structure of Civilizational Courses

Ancient Egyptian civilization has a time span of more than three thousand years. Since the debate on the methods of interpretation presupposes some familiarity with the traditional classification of the phases in Egyptian history, a skeleton of dates will be of help to the reader. Fortunately, for our purpose, it is not necessary to enter into the vexed

---

[1] In addition to the literature given p. 15, n. 1 the following general works were used in the chapter on Egypt: James A. Breasted, *A History of Egypt* (New York, 1905). Adolph Erman, *Die Literatur der Aegypter* (Leipzig, 1923). James A. Breasted, *The Dawn of Conscience* (New York, 1933). Hermann Kees, *Aegypten* (Munich, 1933). Adolph Erman, *Die Religion der Aegypter* (Berlin, 1934). Herman Kees, *Der Goetterglaube im alten Aegypten* (Leipzig, 1941). Henri Frankfort, *Ancient Egyptian Religion* (New York, 1948). John A. Wilson, *The Burden of Egypt. An Interpretation of Ancient Egyptian Culture* (Chicago, 1951). Rudolf Anthes, "Aegypten," *Historia Mundi*, II.

Joachim Spiegel, *Das Werden der Altaegyptischen Hochkultur. Aegyptische Geistesgeschichte im 3. Jahrt. v. Chr.* (Heidelberg, 1953), was not available to me at the time this chapter was written.

questions of early Egyptian chronology—all that is needed is agreement on the relative order of dates. It will, therefore, be sufficient to accept the table of the subdivisions of Egyptian history given by John A. Wilson: [2]

Protodynastic Period (Dynasties I and II)	3100–2700 B.C.
Old Kingdom (Dynasties III–VI)	2700–2200
First Intermediate Period (Dynasties VII–XI)	2200–2050
Middle Kingdom (Dynasty XII)	2050–1800
Second Intermediate Period (Dynasties XIII–XVII)	1800–1550
New Kingdom, or Empire (Dynasties XVIII–XX)	1570–1165
Post-Empire Period (Dynasties XX–XXVI)	1150– 525
Persian Conquest	525
Conquest by Alexander the Great	332

The dates furnish the basic information on the phases of Egyptian political history. The unification of the land under a god-king, the Pharaoh, was achieved by the end of the Protodynastic Period, and the institutional form which characterized the Old Kingdom was renewed, after the interruptions of the Intermediate Periods, in the Middle and New Kingdoms.

Thus far there is agreement. The difficulties begin with the interpretation of the successive phases, and especially of the First Intermediate Period. Toynbee, in his *Study of History,* construes the Old Kingdom as the formative period of Egyptian civilization; the Intermediate Period, following the breakdown of the Old Kingdom at the end of the Sixth Dynasty, as the Time of Troubles in the civilizational course; and the reconstruction in the Middle Kingdom as the Egyptian imperial period, the time of the Universal State. The Second Intermediate Period, the time of the Hyksos invasion, is then the Interregnum following the Universal State; the New Kingdom, finally, is a last recovery, restoring the Empire for as long as it lasts.[3] This construction has provoked the energetic criticism of Henri Frankfort. While his argument falls short of a complete penetration of the theoretical issue, his empirical grievance becomes clear enough. In Frankfort's opinion, Toynbee's construction of the phases in a civilizational course is a generalization from insufficient materials. The pattern is developed in the light of Toynbee's thorough knowledge of Greco-Roman and Western history, and, while it may be

---

[2] Wilson, *The Burden of Egypt,* vii ff.

[3] For Toynbee's construction of Egyptian history see his *Study of History,* the sections *s.v.* "Egypt," in the registers of Vols. III and VI.

valid in these instances, it does not apply to all cases, and in particular not to Egyptian civilization. Western history, ancient and modern, has a dynamics peculiarly its own, and when type concepts based on this body of materials are transferred to the early Near Eastern civilizations, a progressivist bias will be injected into the interpretation of Egyptian history.

Concretely there arise the following problems: The Greco-Roman Time of Troubles witnessed the formation of the Mediterranean internal proletariat, and this social stratum became the originator and carrier of new religious movements, above all of Christianity. If this picture of a Time of Troubles is transferred to the Egyptian First Intermediate Period one would have to interpret the Egyptian lower classes of the time, as Toynbee does, as an internal proletariat, which, according to Frankfort, they were not. Moreover, one must look for a phenomenon that could be considered an equivalent to the rise of Christianity in the Roman Empire. Toynbee finds it in the spreading of Osirian religiousness in the lower classes: "When the Egyptiac Society was *in articulo mortis* it looked as though an Osirian Church were destined to assume, for this moribund civilization, that role of executor and residuary legatee which has actually been played by the Christian Church for the Hellenic Civilization and by the Mahayana for the Sinic." [4] The development of the Osirian Church, however, took a different turn from the Christian, because the Hyksos invasion produced a *union sacrée* between the dominant minority of Egyptiac society and its internal proletariat against the national enemy: "It was this reconciliation at the eleventh hour that prolonged the existence of the Egyptiac Society—in a petrified state of life-in-death—for two thousand years beyond the date when the process of disintegration would otherwise have reached its natural term in dissolution. . . . This artificial act of syncretism killed the religion of the internal proletariat without availing to bring the religion of the dominant minority back to life." [5] Against this interpretation Frankfort argues that, in the first place, an Osirian "church" never existed, if by church is meant an organized body of believers. The cult of Osiris, furthermore, did not originate in the lower classes, but widely spread among them from its original source in the cult of the ruling group. The picture of a religious movement comparable to

[4] *Ibid.*, V, 152.　　　　　[5] *Ibid.*, 28 ff.

Christianity, therefore, is wrong, and the hypothetical judgments based on the assumption are irrelevant. There is no empirical sense in surmising that a "normal" Egyptian development would have produced a victory of the "Osirian Church" and a dissolution of a "moribund civilization." The Egyptian Middle and New Kingdoms were not in "a petrified state of life-in-death," but were flourishing epochs, especially the brilliant Empire of the New Kingdom. The Greco-Roman pattern of growth, disintegration, and dissolution does not apply. An entirely different picture suggests itself: If one considers that the essential traits of Egyptian culture were developed in the Old Kingdom by the end of the Third Dynasty, the birth of Egypt will appear as an illuminating flash, a revelation followed by a lifelong struggle for its realization. The history of Egypt has a peculiarly static character because a form created at the beginning is ramified, endangered, regained, and varied, without loss of essential identity and vitality for more than two thousand years.[6]

The disagreement of Frankfort and Toynbee is a serious one, affecting the interpretation of Egyptian political history, as well as ideas, as a whole. Moreover, it is more than a difference of opinion between two scholars, for on both sides the position is supported by a respectable array of authorities. Toynbee's conception of an Egyptiac internal proletariat that produces the Osirian Church certainly is his own, but it draws for its empirical support on the work of Eduard Meyer and of Breasted. Frankfort's criticism, in its pointed sharpness, again is his own, but he finds support from others. John A. Wilson, for instance, agrees with Frankfort that Toynbee's theory of the phases of a civilizational course are inapplicable to Egypt; and with regard to the "Osirian Church" he specifically insists: "The Osirian religion was mortuary and could not be the genesis of a 'new society,' and it was originally created by and for Toynbee's 'dominant minority.'" Wilson finds it necessary, though, to warn: "These criticisms do scant justice to Toynbee's enormously refreshing influence in assailing formerly fixed ideas."[7] For his idea of a flashlike, sudden birth of Egyptian civilization, Frankfort, furthermore, can refer to the concurrent opinions of other Egyptologists, in particular those of Flinders Petrie.[8] And his assumption is borne out in

[6] Henri Frankfort, *The Birth of Civilization in the Near East* (London, 1951); the criticism of Toynbee and Spengler is to be found in Chap. 1, "The Study of Ancient Civilizations."
[7] Wilson, *The Burden of Egypt*, 32.
[8] Frankfort, *The Birth of Civilization*, 25.

detail for the history of political ideas by the recent study on the Old Kingdom by Hermann Junker.[9]

A disagreement of this kind cannot be resolved by adding to the empirical argument on either side. Since it is caused by the use of insufficiently analyzed concepts, it must be overcome by penetrating to the theoretical issue that lies at its root. If several variables of reality are included in one concept, the blend will not fit concrete situations when one or the other variable goes its own historical way. As such variables, not sufficiently distinguished by either Toynbee or Frankfort, the following three must be considered:

(1) The political institutions, their creation, consolidation, and disintegration.

(2) The socially predominant experience of order and its symbolization (cosmological, anthropological, soteriological).

(3) The welding together of institutions and experiences of order, from which results what Frankfort calls the "style" or "form" of a civilization.

In the light of the preceding distinctions Toynbee is right when he diagnoses a Time of Troubles in the institutional sense in the First Intermediate Period. The breakdown of the Old Kingdom at the end of Dynasty VI is a typical endogenous disintegration of a political institution, caused by an inefficient central administration which permits local power centers to grow, lets offices become hereditary, is too generous with financial endowments of regional notables, and unduly increases the central expenditure with consequent overburdening of the people.[10] It is a process of overstraining an institution, of letting disruptive tendencies get out of hand, which also can be observed in other instances, as in Chinese or Western civilizations, though the causes may vary in detail. If Toynbee's concept of the Time of Troubles were restricted to the phenomenon of the first great institutional disintegration of an established political culture, it would apply to the First Intermediate Period. It becomes, however, inapplicable because it includes the creation of a

[9] Hermann Junker, *Pyramidenzeit* (Einsiedeln-Zurich-Koeln, 1949).

[10] As far as the formation and revolutionary action of an internal proletariat are concerned, Toynbee's conception of an Egyptian Time of Troubles has found weighty support from Joachim Spiegel, *Soziale und Weltanschauliche Reformbewegungen im Alten Aegypten* (Heidelberg, 1950)—provided that Spiegel's interpretation of the so-called "Admonitions of Ipu-wer" proves to be substantially correct.

church by the lower classes, a creation which occurs in the Hellenic Time of Troubles but not in the Egyptian. Hence, Frankfort is right when he rejects the speculation on the "Osirian Church" and its miscarriage. The cosmological culture of Egypt never was broken effectively by anthropological or soteriological developments.

These clarifications, however, do not exhaust the problem. While Toynbee's speculation on an "Osirian Church" must be rejected, his admirable flair for historical climates lets him discern that the First Intermediate Period was more than an institutional breakdown, in so far as the breakdown affected the experiences of order, adumbrating a break with cosmological symbols. Osirian religiousness indeed expanded through the lower classes and the validity of the Pharaonic cosmological symbols was seriously drawn into doubt. An experiential climate was spreading in which a soteriological religion conceivably could have found fertile ground, if such a religion had existed. But no prophet or savior arose, and the mortuary religion of Osiris, as Wilson has pointed out, could hardly have become a community-forming church. Though Egyptian culture acquired during this period a new dimension of skepticism, the Pharaonic institution emerged from the ordeal with unbroken vitality. Hence, Toynbee is right when he senses an experiential climate, pregnant with new religious possibilities, but is wrong when he speculates on the actual presence of such a religion; Frankfort is right when he insists that no religious revolution occurred, but he stretches his point when he treats the changes of experiential structure as insignificant in comparison with the millennial lasting of Egyptian "form."

The abstract analysis will gain concreteness if we consider a source that will illustrate the nature and degree of the tension in Egyptian history. The purpose will be served by the "Song of the Harper," originally a tomb inscription, probably for a king shortly before the establishment of the Middle Kingdom: [11]

How weary is this righteous prince;
the goodly fortune has come to pass!
Generations pass away since the time of the god,

[11] For the question of the date see James H. Breasted, *Development of Religion and Thought in Ancient Egypt* (New York, 1912), 182, or the same author's *The Dawn of Conscience*, 163; and the introductory note by John A. Wilson in Pritchard (ed.), *Ancient Near Eastern Texts*, 467. The text is taken from *Ancient Near Eastern Texts*, with the variants indicated in the footnotes p. 467.

but young people come in their place.
The gods who lived formerly rest in their pyramids,
the beatified dead also, buried in their pyramids.

And they who built houses—their places are not.
See what has been made of them!
I have heard the words of Ii-em-hotep and Hor-dedef,
with whose discourses men speak so much.
What are their places now?
Their walls are broken apart, and their places are not—
as though they had never been!

There is none who comes back from over there,
That he may tell their state,
That he may tell their needs,
That he may still our hearts,—
Until we too may travel to the place where they have gone.

Let thy desire flourish, in order to let thy heart forget the beatifica-
tions for thee.
Follow thy desire, as long as thou shalt live.
Put myrrh upon thy head and clothing of fine linen upon thee,
Being anointed with genuine marvels of the god's property.

Set an increase to thy good things;
Let not thy heart flag.
Follow thy desire and thy good.
Fulfill thy needs upon earth, after the command of thy heart,
Until there come forth for thee that day of mourning.

The Weary of Heart hears not their mourning,
And wailing saves not the heart of a man from the underworld.
Make holiday, and weary not therein!
Behold, it is not given to any man to take his property with him.
Behold, there is no one who departs who comes back again!

The "Song of the Harper" shows that the Osirian religiousness, debated with so much heat, is by far not the most glaring symptom of
experiential changes in the Egyptian Time of Troubles. For the corrosion
has gone so deep that the faith in Osiris, the Weary of Heart, is itself
drawn into doubt. It is better not to think even of the "beatifying"
rituals which purport to make the deceased "effective personalities" in
the beyond. The thought is distasteful; and besides one does not know
whether the personalities in the beyond are really "effective," since no
one has ever come back from there to inform us about his state. The

result of such doubts is a hedonistic skepticism which counsels to satisfy the pleasures of life as long as it lasts. It is a hedonism without joy, reflecting surfeit with a life that has become senseless. And death has become a "goodly fortune" that releases the prince from the weariness of his existence.

The experience of lasting and passing without sense strongly predominates. The author of the song sees himself, in his present, at the end of a wearisome chain of existences. Generations have lasted and passed since the "time of the god" (presumably the founder of the unified Egypt), and all that has been achieved is that he, and the gods who succeeded him, as well as their beatified notables, lie now in their pyramids. That is the key word for the attack on the pyramids, those symbols of everlastingness, themselves. The names of the sages of the past, of Ii-em-hotep and Hor-dedef, are chosen with deliberation. For Ii-em-hotep, the architect of Djoser (Dynasty III, *ca.* 2700 B.C.), was the creator of stone masonry on a large scale and builder of the terraced pyramid of Sakkarah, the oldest still surviving, while Hor-dedef was the son of Cheops (*ca.* 2600 B.C.), the builder of the greatest of the pyramids. The wisdom of these sages was still known at the time of the song (*ca.* 2000 B.C.), but their tombs were broken. The neglect of the pyramids, which stood there worn with age for everybody to see, as well as the plundering and destruction of minor tombs, must have made a deep impression. When the symbols of eternity were themselves passing away, the attempt to build eternity materially into this world must have appeared convincingly futile. In brief, Egyptian culture had an inner past—sometimes forgotten by the modern historian who looks back on "ancient" Egypt. The Pyramid Age was rather "ancient" even for an Egyptian of the Middle Kingdom, and the man who wrote the "Song of the Harper" looked at the pyramid of Cheops over approximately the same distance in time that lies between us and the cathedral of Chartres. There certainly was enough of an object lesson to awaken a sense of the gulf that separates the achievement of man from the eternity of being. Moreover, the lesson once learned was not lost, for the song was still copied under the imperial dynasties of the New Kingdom. Thus, the experiential stratum of skepticism with regard to the meaning of the Pharaonic foundation was permanently incorporated into the Egyptian form.[12]

12 For the continuity between the skepticism of the Time of Troubles and the Enlightenment of the New Kingdom, in particular of the movement of Akhenaton, cf. Joachim Spiegel, *Soziale und Weltanschauliche Reformbewegungen im Alten Aegypten* (Heidelberg, 1950).

The "Song of the Harper" does not flower into an opening of the soul toward transcendent divinity, but flattens into hedonism and skepticism. This peculiar phenomenon, the corrosion of the Pharonic symbolism to a breaking point never quite reached, will illuminate the problem of civilizational form raised by Frankfort.

"Form," as previously suggested, results from the interpenetration of institutions and experiences of order. The institutions, to be sure, may break down under economic stresses, or through changes in the distribution of power, but when the afflicted society recaptures its strength for self-organization, the new institutions will belong to the same formal type as the old ones, unless there has also occurred a revolutionary change in the experience of order. As long as the experiences of order retain their compact structure, in spite of corrosion pointing toward new differentiation, the form will be preserved. A civilization can be profoundly shaken by institutional upheavals and still present an appearance of millennial formal stability. The problem of form need not be left at the stage of acknowledgment that some civilizations, such as the Greco-Roman, conform to the "progressive" type developed by Toynbee, while others, such as the Egyptian, have a "static" form which remains constant from beginning to end. The problem of "form" can be clarified theoretically, and its phenomena be made intelligible, through the use of the principles which govern the compactness and differentiation of the experiences of order. The three principles, as they have emerged in the course of this study, can be formulated in the following manner:

(1) The nature of man is constant.
(2) The range of human experience is always present in the fullness of its dimensions.
(3) The structure of the range varies from compactness to differentiation.

Moreover, the differentiation of the experiences of order does not run its course within a concrete society, or within the societies of only one civilization, but extends through a plurality of societies in time and space, in a world-historic process in which the various civilizations participate to their allotted measure. Hence, the "form" of a society is at the same time the mode of its participation in the adumbrated world-historic process that extends indefinitely into the future. Beyond the primitive level, the earliest civilizations known, like the Egyptian, are indeed exposed to the same institutional vicissitudes as the later ones, but since the compact experience of order does not break under the stress of institutional disasters, the actual changes of institutional order occur, with a peculiar quality of subduedness, within a cosmological form that remains stable. Hence, while the formal differences between civilizations are correctly observed by Frankfort, the language of "static" and "dynamic" types must be replaced by descriptions that will determine its form for each case of a concrete society by relating it to the supracivilizational process in which the compact experiences of order differentiate.

The method suggested has empirical advantages that become obvious as soon as a further civilizational course is introduced for purposes of comparison. A few reflections on Chinese civilization will prove helpful, as they have proved already in the analysis of Mesopotamian symbols.

In the Chinese case, the Chou kingdom disintegrated in the period of the Contending States, and this Time of Troubles in its turn gave way to the imperial unification of China under the Ch'in and Han dynasties. The institutional course thus closely resembles the Egyptian sequence of Old Kingdom, First Intermediate Period, and the following imperial reorganizations. Throughout this course, and further through Chinese history down to A.D. 1912, the cosmological symbolism remains unbroken. In both the Chinese and Egyptian cases, therefore, a "static" cosmological form prevails in a history of approximately three thousand years, with the Chinese Son of Heaven corresponding to the Pharaoh as the mediator between cosmic-divine order and society. The parallel goes even so far that in the Chinese Time of Troubles, in certain variants of Taoism, experiences and attitudes appear which resemble those of the "Song of the Harper."

However, in Chinese civilization there also occurred, in Confucianism, an experiential break with the cosmological order. And though the break did not go so deep as the contemporary one in Greek philosophy, it had institutional consequences of a magnitude without parallel in Egypt. For the disillusionment with the cosmic order of society, as well as with its preservation through the Son of Heaven, led to the discovery of the autonomous personality as a source of order. The order of society, which hitherto had depended on the Son of Heaven alone, now depended, in rivalry with him, on the sage who participated in the order of the cosmos.

In the realm of symbols the new experience of the autonomous person and his will to order became manifest in the transfer of imperial qualifications to the sage. The *tao* and the *teh,* whose possession entailed the ordering efficacy of the prince, the *ch'un,* now became efficacious forces in the soul of the princely man, the *ch'un-tse.* Confucius thus approached the sage and the prince to the point of blending them in a symbol closely related to Plato's philosopher-king. Moreover, the social effectiveness of the princely man was governed by the same cosmic fatality as that of the ruler. For the king had the *teh* (force) to mediate the cosmic *tao* (order) to society through the *ming,* the decree of heaven; and in the same manner it depended on the heavenly *ming* whether the wisdom of the sage was heard and accepted, so that he would become an effective ordering force in the community.[13] Thus the sage was no longer the member of a society which only as a whole received its order through mediation of the ruler. He himself had access to the *tao* that ordered world and society, and thereby he became a potential ruler and a rival to the Son of Heaven in mediating the *tao*—an idea which, as far as we know, never occurred to an Egyptian.

This transfer of royal symbols to the sage, however, illuminates the limitations of Confucianism as a new ordering force in society. To be sure, the autonomy of the personality, independent of the authority of society, had been gained through the immediate relation between man and cosmic *tao.* Nevertheless, the authority of the sage was of the same cosmological type as the authority of the Son of Heaven. The differentiation of experience did not advance, as with Plato, to the development of a new theology in opposition to the beliefs prevalent in the community; it did not become radically transcendental. Confucianism did not lead to a break in the cosmological form of the empire because it was not a philosophy in the sense established by Plato. And since there was no radical incompatibility in the experiences of order, the empire could even utilize Confucian scholarship as a bureaucratic support for its cosmological form.

In conclusion, it can be said that the debate about types of civilizational courses will remain inconclusive as long as it is conducted on the level of construction of empirical types. The intelligible order of history cannot be found through classification of phenomena; it must be sought

---

[13] Marcel Granet, *La Pensée Chinoise* (Paris, 1934), 481 ff. Fung Yu-lan, *A Short History of Chinese Philosophy* (New York, 1948), 44 ff.

through a theoretical analysis of institutions and experiences of order, as well as of the form that results from their interpenetration. The ultimate constants of history cannot be determined by forming type concepts of phenomenal regularities, for historical regularities are no more than manifestations of the constants of human nature in their range of compactness and differentiation. Moreover, the erection into historical constants of the phenomenal regularities, which indeed can be observed in the civilizational courses, is especially reprehensible because the civilizations are not self-contained units repeating a pattern of growth and decline. A civilization is the form in which a society participates, in its historically unique way, in the supracivilizational, universal drama of approximation to the right order of existence through increasingly differentiated attunement with the order of being. A civilizational form has historical singularity, never to be absorbed by phenomenal regularities, because the form is an act in the drama of mankind that unknowably is enacted into the future.

The preceding theoretical reflections should, however, in no way deprecate the search for the phenomenally typical in the course of civilizations. For inevitably we must start from the phenomenal regularities in order to arrive at the constants of human nature, as well as at the structural differentiation of the constant range of experiences; that is, at the dynamics of human nature that we call history.

§ 2. The Cosmological Form

The Egyptians experienced the order of their society as part of cosmic order. The expression of the experience in symbols belongs, therefore, to the same general type as the Mesopotamian. Nevertheless, from the interpenetration of experiences and institutions there resulted a civilizational form, unique in all of its principal aspects. The form is peculiar because of its sudden birth, which must be considered a flashlike outburst of creativity even if we generously accord a century or more to this "flash" for bringing the form into definitely recognizable existence. Furthermore, the form is peculiar because of several elements of structure which distinguish it from the Mesopotamian, and for that matter from the form of any other cosmological civilization. And, finally, it is peculiar because within it occurs a rich differentiation of experiences which point beyond the limits of cosmology and are interpreted, therefore, by progressivist historians as anticipations of Hebrew and Greek achievements. The last characteristic is especially noteworthy because, with regard to major literary expressions of the cosmological experience itself, Egyptian civilization proved singularly barren. Egypt has produced neither epics like the Mesopotamian *Gilgamesh* or *Enuma elish,* nor a codification of its law comparable to Hammurabi's.

In the present section we shall deal with the origin and structural characteristics of the cosmological form, concentrating the analysis on those features which distinguish Egyptian from other civilizations of the same type. In the subsequent section we shall deal with the dynamics of experience within the shelter of the form.

The birth of the Pharaonic empire is sudden in the sense that apparently it had no prehistory comparable to the genesis of the Mesopotamian empires. In Mesopotamia one can trace a political evolution from primitive village communities, through the city-states, to the empire. The imperial unifiers conquered the pre-existent city-states, but the latter preserved their institutional identity so well that the empires, ruled and administered by the one among them that happened to be the strongest at the time, even took their names from the hegemonic city. The prehistory thus left its institutional mark on the later organization.

In Egypt we are confronted with a somewhat puzzling situation. The Pharaonic empire, it is true, also shows an institutional structure that points toward a unification of pre-existent political entities through conquest in the past. The Pharaoh wears the double crown as "The Lord of the Two Lands" of Upper and Lower Egypt, and in every political crisis the empire is liable to fall apart into the two lands as separate kingdoms. Nevertheless, there are doubts about the correct interpretation of these symptoms. A generation ago historians were still willing to assume the existence of two kingdoms, as well as the conquest of Lower Egypt by the southerners. Today the hypothesis is on the point of being abandoned since the sources reveal for the Delta the existence only of small principalities which never formed a political unit prior to the conquest. It seems more reasonable to assume that the Nile Valley consisted of a string of culturally homogeneous village communities, with modest market towns dominating the surrounding district, under their chieftains, and that the resistance was not too tenacious when the conquerors from the south, about whose original source of power and enterprise we know little, imposed a common political rule on a population of common culture. A process of this kind is also suggested by the fact that the inevitable enmities of the conquest must have melted away rapidly after the establishment of the empire. There are no traces of prolonged political discrimination against the Delta population; the "Two Lands" are on an equal footing. The symbol, it seems, is irreducible to events in the sphere of institutional articulation; and we agree, therefore, with the conclusion that its meaning will have to be sought in the motivation by an experience of cosmic order.[14]

The sudden transition from primitive agricultural communities to a great imperial civilization must be admitted as historical fact, but one can do no more than form a reasonable guess concerning the circumstances which favored such an extraordinary development. Egypt is a narrow trough of fertile land along the banks of the Nile, closed in by the desert cliffs east and west. In that habitable tube the density of population is today more than 1,200 per square mile, considerably higher than in Belgium, the most densely populated industrial sector of Europe, which has about 700 persons per square mile. The density in antiquity was substantially lower, but still must have been very much higher than in any of the other civilizational areas of the time. The assumption is reasonable because the system of basin irrigation, on which the Egyptian economy and its population capacity rests, goes back to antiquity and was probably in existence even in the Protodynastic Period. Only in the nineteenth century A.D., under the Khedive Mohammed Ali, was the older system gradually supplemented by canal irrigation, which greatly increased the acreage of arable land, made it suitable for cotton and sugar crops, and resulted in a proportionately larger increase of population. The crowding of a rural population in semiurban density can therefore be assumed as the factor that appreciably contributed to the sudden outburst of civilizational energy. The life in a closely packed neighborhood, with the river running the whole length of the settlement as its highway, must have caused among these people the intense social and intellectual intercourse, the homogeneousness underlying a sophisticated local rivalry, and the mutual tolerance without dogmatic self-assertion, which indeed characterize the imperial civilization once it comes

[14] On the politically formative force of the geographical situation and on the question of the two kingdoms, the possibilities of hegemonic confederacies preceding the unification, the unification itself, and the continuation of the tension into the dynastic period cf. Rudolf Anthes, "Aegypten," *Historia Mundi*, II, 134–41.

into historical view. The assumption of such circumstances prior to the conquest will make its success more understandable.[15]

The character of the Nile Valley as a continuous, homogeneous settlement without articulation by major, undubitably dominant cities continued deep into the Pharaonic period. Politically it manifested itself in the curiosity that for more than a thousand years Egypt had no permanent capital. There was no counterpart in Egypt to a Nippur, Babylon, or Ashur from which the conqueror ruled the land. A new city, the Memphis of Menes, was founded as the symbol of the unified realm. And the actual residence moved on principle with the Pharaoh to the site where his pyramid was to be built, while the neighboring town became the seat of administration. Not until the middle of the second millennium, when Thebes acquired metropolitan character, can one justly speak of an Egyptian capital city.[16]

If, however, the symbol "Two Lands" is supposed to have cosmological character, a serious difficulty arises in so far as all other cosmological civilizations symbolize the spatial order of the land by analogy with the four quarters of the world. Why should Egypt have a dualistic symbol? And which feature of the cosmos is symbolized analogically by the dualism? Some guessing has been done, none quite convincing. Frankfort finds the source of the division in a "deeply rooted Egyptian tendency to understand the world in dualistic terms as a series of pairs of contrasts balanced in unchanging equilibrium." The universe as a whole is conceived as "heaven and earth," the earth as "North and South," and the same penchant can be observed at work in pairs of gods, and so forth. This explanation must be rejected as circular, for it is precisely the question what the "deep root" of the penchant is.[17] Wilson, after an earlier attempt rejected by himself,[18] ultimately reverses the idea of Frankfort and assumes: "Perhaps the duality of 'the Two Lands' was a stronger factor in producing the dualism of Egyptian psychology." [19]

[15] For the suddenness of the civilizational outburst cf. Frankfort, *Kingship and the Gods* Chap. 1, and the same author's *The Birth of Civilization in the Near East.* On the semiurban character of the population in the Nile Valley cf. Wilson in *The Intellectual Adventure of Ancient Man,* 31 ff. For the question of irrigation see the article "Irrigation: Egypt," in *Encyclopaedia Britannica,* 11th ed.

[16] Frankfort, *The Birth of Civilization,* 83 ff.

[17] Frankfort, *Kingship and the Gods,* 19.

[18] Wilson in *The Intellectual Adventure of Ancient Man,* 41 ff.

[19] Wilson, *The Burden of Egypt,* 17.

We agree with Wilson's assumption and support it with the reflection that it is the property of rivers to flow downhill, so that in a closed river valley the "world" will naturally have the dimensions of "upstream" and "downstream." Under the peculiar topographic conditions of Egypt the river was so impressive a feature of the experienced world that the Nile could be preferred as the source of spatial order to the horizon and the sun, with the consequence that a two-dimensional cosmos was mirrored analogically in the political institution of the "Two Lands." Other topographic dualisms may have strengthened the experience and given it the force to pervade thought at large with dualistic categories, but as far as the "Two Lands" are concerned the Nile seems to be sufficient.

The expression of political order by analogy with cosmic order is further complicated by the fact that the sun symbol has in Egyptian thought at least as dominant a place as the Nile symbol, if not a higher one. The co-existence of the two symbols reflects perhaps different historical strata in the genesis of imperial order. The two-dimensional conception of cosmic space is certainly the older one as far as its political use is concerned, for the conquest was understood from its beginning as the unification of the "Two Lands." The sun symbolism, weak in the beginning, gained in strength during the Old Kingdom, apparently under influences from Heliopolis and the Delta region in general. Under Dynasty V it became so strong that the Pharaoh assumed the title "Son of Re." Now, where the sun symbol appears there also appear on numerous occasions the four quarters of the horizon over which the sun rules, and the fusion of the horizon with the dualistic conception of imperial order in various literary documents results in clashes between the logically incompatible symbols. Moreover, on such occasions the two symbolisms have different functions in illuminating the meaning of order. It will be advisable, therefore, to examine a few sun-hymns in order to clarify the distinct functions and their relation to one another.

The first hymn that attracts our attention is a hymn to Horus. By its reversal of the normal order of "Upper and Lower Egypt" into "Lower and Upper Egypt" it can be dated as belonging in the time of Heliopolitan ascendancy under Dynasties IV–V. The following passage from the hymn is of interest because it shows the plain topographical clash between the two symbols:

> Greetings to thee, sole one, of whom it is said, he will live always!
> Horus comes, he with the long stride comes;
> he comes, he who wins power over the horizon, who wins power
>   over the gods.
>
> Greetings to thee, soul, which is in his red blood,
> sole one as his father named him, wise one, as the gods called him,
> who took his place, as the sky was separated [from the earth], at
>   the place where thy heart was satisfied,
> that thou mayest stride over the sky according to thy stride,
> that thou mayest traverse Lower and Upper Egypt in the midst of
>   that which thou stridest! [20]

Horus clearly is the power over the horizon; he is the divine soul rising in the red clothes of the sun disk and striding over the sky. The last line, viewing this course not from the sky but the earth, however, breaks the image by reminding us of the north-south axis of Lower and Upper Egypt, and lets the sun move "in the midst of," or more literally "within," the Egypt which it traverses at a right angle, to the exclusion of the rest of the world contained in the horizon. The long trough of the Nile Valley and the circular horizon are geometrically incongruent.

The same tension is still present centuries later in a hymn to Amon-Re, from the New Kingdom, but antedating the Amarna revolution. In the hymn Amon-Re appears in the double role of the ruler over the Two Lands and of the highest god, who has created all that is within the horizon, including the expressly mentioned foreign countries. The tension has become more marked because the world of the horizon and the world of the Two Lands are consciously distinguished.

The following passage from the hymn stresses the rulership of Amon-Re over Egypt:

> The goodly beloved youth to whom the gods give praise,
> Who made what is below and what is above,
> Who illuminates the Two Lands
> And crosses the heavens in peace:

---

[20] Pyramid Texts, 853a–54e. All translations of the Pyramid Texts are taken from Samuel A. B. Mercer, *The Pyramid Texts in Translation and Commentary*, 4 vols. (New York, 1952). Volume I contains the texts; the other three volumes the commentaries, glossary, and indices. The Pyramid Texts were edited in Kurt Sethe, *Die Altaegyptischen Pyramidentexte*, I (Sprueche 1–468), II (Sprueche 469–714), Leipzig 1908–10. Sethe's German translation and commentary in *Uebersetzung und Kommentar zu den altaegyptischen Pyramidentexten* comprises Sprueche 213–582.

The King of Upper and Lower Egypt: Re, the triumphant,
Chief of the Two Lands,
Great of strength, lord of reverence,
The chief one who made the entire earth.

And a further passage even singles out the north-south axis as the
dimension of this rulership:

The love of thee is in the southern sky;
The sweetness of thee is in the northern sky.

An entirely different divine personality appears in the following
passage from the same hymn:

Solitary sole one, with many hands,
Who spends the night wakeful, while all men are asleep,
Seeking benefit for his creatures,
Amon, enduring in all things, Atum and Har-akhti.

Praises are thine, when they all say:
"Jubilation to thee, because thou weariest thyself with us!
Salaams to thee, because thou didst create us!"
Hail to thee for all beasts!
Jubilation to thee for every foreign country!

To the height of heaven, to the width of the earth,
To the depth of the Great Green Sea,
The gods are bowing down to thy majesty
And exalting the might of him who created them,
Rejoicing at the approach of him who begot them.[21]

Here Amon-Re has become the great creator-god whom the gods, the
cosmos, and the human societies praise in gratitude for their existence
and his wakeful care. He is the god

Who raised the heavens and laid down the ground,
Who made what is and created what exists.[22]

In the all-embracing creation of Amon-Re Egypt is but a part along
with foreign countries. It does not seem to be the microcosmos, the human
society that in its order mirrors the cosmos. For the god himself approaches a transcendent invisibility of which no immanent visible order
can be a proper analogue. And the hymn in fact repeatedly plays with
the meaning of Amon as the *amen*, the hidden, the great one:

[21] Pritchard (ed.), *Ancient Near Eastern Texts*, 365 ff.
[22] *Ibid.*, 366.

The Sovereign. . . .
Whose name is hidden [*amen*] from his children,
In this his name of Amon.[23]

When the supremely visible God of the horizon withdraws into a divinity "whose shrine is hidden," apparently he can no longer be the source of analogical imperial order.

And yet, because of this potential transformation of the visible sun-god into the invisible transcendent creator-god, by virtue of this suspense between cosmic visibility and transcendent invisibility, has he become the Egyptian political god par excellence, deeply affecting the structure and durability of the imperial order. The experience which has this effect is expressed in the earliest extant sun-hymn, a hymn to Atum, preserved in the Pyramid Texts, but of much older though uncertain date. The hymn consists of two parts in which the same litanies are addressed first to the sun-god and then to the deceased Pharaoh who is identified with him. In the first section of the litanies is enumerated what Atum has done for "the eye of Horus," that is, for Egypt:

> Greetings to thee, eye of Horus, which he [Atum] adorned with
>   his two hands completely.
> He does not make thee hearken to the West;
> he does not make thee hearken to the East;
> he does not make thee hearken to the South;
> he does not make thee hearken to the North;
> he does not make thee hearken to those who are in the middle of the
>   land;
> but thou hearkenest to Horus.[24]

In gratitude for such divine gifts, in the second litany, Egypt offers to Atum the gifts of the land in return:

> It is he who adorned thee; it is he who built thee; it is he who
>   settled thee;
> thou doest for him everything which he says unto thee, in every
>   place whither he goes.
> Thou carriest for him the fowl-bearing waters which are in thee;
> thou carriest to him the gifts which are in thee;
> thou carriest to him the food which is in thee;
> thou carriest to him everything which is in thee;
> thou carriest it to him to every place wherein his heart desires to be.[25]

23 *Ibid.*, 366.   24 Pyramid Texts, 1588a–89a.
25 *Ibid.*, 1589b–92e, abbr.

This is an odd sun-hymn, without parallel in other cosmological civilizations. While the sun is the ruler of the visible world, indeed, in all four directions of the horizon, Egypt is *not* the earthly analogue of the embracing cosmos. For the sun-god uses his power not to ensure to the realm analogous dominion over the earth, but apparently to protect it against entanglements with earthly dominion. The point is made even more forcefully by the third litany:

> The doors stand fast upon thee like Immutef;
> they open not to the West; they open not to the East;
> they open not to the North; they open not to the South;
> they open not to those who are in the middle of the land;
> but they are open to Horus.[26]

By the grace of Atum the doors of Egypt are firmly shut upon the world; the horizon is closed out.

The oddity, without losing its historical uniqueness, will become intelligible if we consider that the hymn plays over a wide range of experiences, using for this purpose the plurality of sun-gods. Both Atum and Horus are manifest in the visible sun-disk without being identical with it; but the creator-god Atum, we may say, is remoter from this visibility than Horus, the god of the horizon. Egypt, the eye of Horus, to be sure, is within the horizon of Horus, but it needs protection against the evil forces, which also are part of the horizon, and it can receive this protection only from Atum. The forces of good and evil, represented by Horus and Set, thus become an issue in worldly existence, and in this struggle help must come from a higher source of divine being—that is, from Atum:

> It was he who rescued thee from every evil which Set did to thee.[27]

The leap in being toward more perfect attunement with transcendent divinity is not actually taken, but it is vibrating as a possibility in the hymn. Egypt, by grace of Atum, is in the world but not of it; it is closed against the evil of Set, it is open and hearkens to the force of good in Horus. Within the compactness of cosmological experience, and under the veils of polytheistic language, Egypt is the chosen people of god.

The second part of the hymn transfers the litanies of the first part to the Horus and Atum manifestations in the Pharaoh. The grace and choice of the sun-god is actualized in the order of society through the

---

[26] *Ibid.,* 1593a–94a.   [27] *Ibid.,* 1595c.

rule of a king who mediates the divine forces of cosmic order to the people. Through the god-king Egyptian society is hearkening in openness to the right order of Atum and Horus; the possession of the Pharaoh secures existence within the world without falling a prey to the evils of the world; without a Pharaoh not only the country will fall into political disorder, but the people will fall from the justice of divine being. Understood in this sense the hymn to Atum reveals the structure of the experiences which lived in the Pharaonic order. It must be considered one of the most important documents for the study of Egyptian civilizational form and the secret of its millennial stability.

When the god chooses Egypt, he does not reveal himself directly to the people, or enter into a covenant with them, but is present with the people through his manifestation in their ruler. We must now approach the most puzzling aspect of Pharaonic symbolism, the divinity of the king. Divine kingship is a rare phenomenon. It occurs in Egypt, but, except in scattered instances, occurs neither in Mesopotamia nor in any of the major cosmological civilizations. Before an interpretation can be attempted, the phenomenon itself must be clearly understood. A divine king is not a god who has assumed human form, but a man in whom a god manifests himself. The god remains distinctly in his own sphere of existence and only extends his substance into the ruler, as it were. An intelligent contemporary, Herodotus, who could ask questions from Egyptian priests, and probably had more practice in dealing with gods than we have today, confirms the strictly human status of the Pharaoh. The Greek historian received the information that Menes had been the first human king of Egypt; before him the country had been ruled by gods, in particular by Horus; but since Menes the country had had "no king who was a god in human form." [28] That point must be kept firmly in mind, especially since the Egyptian sources refer to the Pharaohs as gods, identify a Pharaoh with this or that god, or address a god as the ruler of Egypt. When reading such phraseology we must consider that Egyptian sources are not treatises on philosophical anthropology or theology. The abbreviating identifications do not mean that the Egyptians could not distinguish between gods and men. They were fully aware that their Pharaohs died like all other human beings, while the undying manifestation of Horus or Re continued in their successors for their

[28] Herodotus II, 142.

respective human life-spans. The Pharaoh thus is not a god but the manifestation of one; by virtue of the divine presence in him, the king is the mediator of divine ordering help to man, though not for all men but for the Egyptian people only.

The analysis of the symbol is not complete, nor does it explain the extraordinary occurrence of god-kings in Egypt. A complete and adequate explanation would have to penetrate to the experience which expressed itself in the symbol, as well as to the circumstances which favored its development. Such an explanation—as distinguished from the usual description of the phenomenal surface of the Pharaonic institution—is perhaps not possible at the present state of science. Nevertheless, I shall venture a suggestion.

The experience can perhaps be approached through analysis of another Egyptian curiosity—that is, of the manifestation of gods in animals. Some excellent pages on this subject of animal manifestations were written by Frankfort. In the first place, the nature of manifestation becomes clearer in the case of divine animals than in that of divine kings. The god Horus, for instance, who is manifest in the sun and the king, is also manifest in the falcon; the god Thoth is manifest in the moon, the baboon, and the ibis; the goddess Hathor in the cow; the god Anubis in the jackal. In none of these cases does the animal manifestation limit or define the god's powers; the god remains distinct from his manifestation. Secondly, some light will fall on the meaning of the symbol through the observation that in animal manifestations of the gods the individual and the species tend to blur. It is not certain whether the god is manifest in the species, or in an individual animal, or in the individual animal as a representative of the species. Frankfort concludes that animals as such inspired religious awe because "with animals the continual succession of generations brought no change. . . . The animals never change, and in this respect especially they would appear to share—in a degree unknown to man—the fundamental nature of creation." [29] In animal nature the species outweighs the individual. Hence—as we should formulate it—in the animal species, with its unchanging constancy through the generations, man senses a higher degree of participation in being than his own; the animal species, outlasting the existence of individual man, approaches the lasting of the world and the gods.

The idea that the divine should be manifest in the species is suggestive.

[29] Henri Frankfort, *Ancient Egyptian Religion* (New York, 1948), 8–14.

Could it be that divine kingship is a phenomenon of the same class, only exhibiting such differences of surface appearance as are necessitated by the difference between human and animal natures? For man, while knowing himself as more than an animal of a species, still knows himself as member of a group of his kind—that is, of a society endowed with durability far superior to that of individual man. Hence, in a civilization in which gods are experienced as manifest in the animal species because of their lastingness, one might expect this "style" of experience and symbolization to extend also to the lastingness of society. The structure of a society, however, differs from that of an animal species in so far as a society gains existence through institutional articulation among a multitude of men and the creation of a representative. The god, therefore, can manifest himself not in any random man as representative of the species but only in the ruler as the representative of society. In the Pharaoh, one might say, not "a man" but "the king" was a god—though one must beware of oversharpening the issue into a charisma of office, for in the institution of the "dynasty," in the birth of every Pharaoh as a son of god, there was also present the idea of the god-man who by virtue of his qualification was destined to succeed in the Pharaonic office. Still, through manifestation in the king the god was manifest in society as a whole; and conversely, by being an Egyptian the humblest peasant on his lands, or worker on his pyramid, participated in the divinity of the order that emanated from the Pharaoh; the divinity of the Pharaoh radiated over society and transformed it into a people of the god. If we realize the compactness of the experience of order that is implied in such symbols— the firm integration of man in society, the dependence of a sense of order in his own life on the unbroken stability of social order—we can better understand why the Egyptian "form" proved so tenaciously resistant to differentiating experiences and a reorientation of human existence toward transcendent divinity. And we also get an inkling of the scandal which Christianity must have been for men emerging from cosmological civilizations, if we consider that not a king was the god incarnate but an ordinary man of low social status who represented nobody but nevertheless was claimed by his followers to be the representative mediator and sufferer for mankind.

That leaves open the question why the manifestation of gods in animals and kings should be an important feature in Egyptian civilization and should play an insignificant role, or none at all, elsewhere. Again no more than a suggestion can be ventured. It seems possible that the Egyptian peculiarity has something to do with the previously discussed suddenness of transition from primitive village communities to an imperial civilization. As a consequence of such suddenness, perhaps elements of an older, more primitive culture were preserved—as indicated by an occasional expression of cannibalistic intentions on the part of a king—which have disappeared where political evolution passed through the phase of city-states before it issued in the imperial foundations. The suggestion would have to find support through a study of East African societies and their culture traits as the social and cultural matrix from which Egypt has grown. But that will have to remain outside the scope of the present inquiry.

Through mediation of the king the order of the cosmos radiates over society. A selection of sources will illustrate the Egyptian concept of the process. We shall begin with a few passages from the Pyramid Texts of the Old Kingdom which concern the divine status of the Pharaoh in its purity—that is, after his earthly death. The gods greet the dead king in the beyond:

> This is my son, my first born . . .
> This is my beloved with whom I have been satisfied.[30]

> This is my beloved, my son;
> I have given the horizons to him, that he may be powerful over
>   them like Harachte.[31]

> He lives, king of Upper and Lower Egypt, beloved of Re, living
>   for ever.[32]

> Thou art king with thy father Atum, thou art high with thy
>   father Atum;
> Thou appearest with thy father Atum, distress disappears.[33]

> Thou hast come into being, thou hast become high, thou hast be-
>   come content;
> thou hast become well in the embrace of thy father, in the embrace
>   of Atum.
> Atum, let N. ascend to thee, enfold him in thy embrace, for he
>   is thy bodily son forever.[34]

[30] Pyramid Texts, 1a–b.   [31] Ibid., 4a–b.
[32] Ibid., 6.   [33] Ibid., 207c–d.
[34] Ibid., 212a–13b. For this and the preceding passage see also the following paragraphs.

The new "being" of the Pharaoh, his rebirth into eternal life, is due to a second birth from a procreative act of Atum and the goddess of the lower sky; at the same time, however, the rebirth after death [35] is a birth from eternity, preceding even the creation of the world:

> The mother of N., dweller in the lower sky, became pregnant with
>   him;
> N. was given birth by his father Atum,
> before the sky came into being, before the earth came into being,
> before men came into being, before the gods were born, before death
>   came into being.[36]

This personage, the son of god, begotten from his father in eternity and returning after death into his embrace to be king with him—this being "whose spirit belongs to heaven, whose body belongs to earth" [37]—is during his human life-span the ruler of Egypt. His rule, which channels the divine-cosmic forces of order into society, begins with his coronation. The meaning of the act, that is, the birth of the god who will bring order out of chaos, is expressed in the coronation rituals of the Old Kingdom in formulas which closely resemble those of the mortuary texts. The resemblance, however, is not a mere parallelism, for, as we shall see presently, the acts of royal and cosmic ordering, of the second birth and the assumption of kingship, are experienced as consubstantial "from eternity." The interpretation of the texts is, therefore, not easy, for the flavor of such compactness will get lost by transposing the various strands of meaning into differentiating concepts. We shall begin with a passage from a coronation ritual of Buto in Lower Egypt.

When the king approaches the "Crown, Great-in-Magic," the priest pronounces:

> He is pure for thee; he is in awe for thee.
> Mayest thou be satisfied with him; mayest thou be satisfied with
>   his purity;
> mayest thou be satisfied with his word, which he speaks to thee:
> "How beautiful is thy face, when it is peaceful, new, young,
> for a god, father of the gods, has begotten thee." [38]

As in a dream-play the figures of the drama blend and change into each other. The words in quotation marks are addressed by the king to the crown. The crown which the king is going to wear is now the son of god,

---

[35] Compare Revelation 20:6, 14.
[36] Pyramid Texts, 1466a–d.
[37] Ibid., 474a.
[38] Ibid., 194d–95e.

and the king greets it as the gods would greet the reborn king. Would then the king be the god who greets the crown as his son?

The play with symbolic identifications seems, indeed, to have been possible. There is extant a curious Heliopolitan text about whose meaning the authorities are in disagreement.[39] Mercer, the translator and editor of the Pyramid Texts, considers it a coronation ritual, worked over as a mortuary text.[40] Frankfort accepts the whole piece as a coronation ritual.[41] We do not intend to take sides. Far more interesting than the question whether the document is a coronation ritual or a mortuary text is the fact that the question is difficult, if not impossible, to answer because the symbolisms are practically identical.[42]

The text opens with an admonition to the king to assume the role of the creator-god, standing on the Primeval Hill that has just emerged from the waters of chaos:

> Stand thou upon it, this earth, which comes forth from Atum . . .
> be thou above it; be thou high above it,
> that thou mayest see thy father; that thou mayest see Re.
> He has come to thee, his father; he has come to thee, Re.[43]

The ascension of the king to the throne repeats the ascension of the god to the hill of cosmic order, to the hill that all over Egypt is symbolized in the pyramids and the temples on a rising terrain. Furthermore, in ascending to the throne the king acquires the characteristics which in the former coronation ritual were attributed to the crown, the "Great One," the "Great-in-Magic": [44]

> Thou hast equipped thyself as the Great-in-Magic . . . .
> nothing is lacking in thee; nothing ceases with thee.[45]

The wearer of the crown possesses the substance of its magic, so that now it becomes understandable that the magic of the crown could be addressed as the young god, begotten from his father. And, finally, the ascension to the throne can blend intelligibly into the ascension of the dead and reborn king into the embrace of his father Atum.[46] The order-

[39] The text is Utterance 222 in Mercer's edition, *Pyramid Texts*, I, 199a–213b.

[40] Mercer assumes the part that has been worked over to be an ascension text, to begin with 207a. *Ibid.*, II, 94 ff.

[41] Frankfort, *Kingship and the Gods*, 108.

[42] For this reason we have not hesitated to include two passages from the text in our preceding documentation of royal apotheosis.

[43] Pyramid Texts, 199a–200a.

[44] *Ibid.*, 194c.

[45] *Ibid.*, 204a–b.

[46] *Ibid.*, 212b.

ing creator and the ordering king, the divine father and his son begotten from eternity, the crown and its wearer, the royal ruler and the reborn young god thus merge and are all co-present in the Pharaoh. The order of society emanating from the Pharaoh is consubstantial with the order of the world created by the god, because in the Pharaoh is present the creative divinity itself. The Pharaonic order is the continuous renewal and re-enactment of the cosmic order from eternity.

The order was seriously interrupted by the First and Second Intermediate periods, and it was also exposed to minor upheavals within the established regimes. The sources of the Middle and New Kingdoms have no longer the self-assured tone of the Pyramid Texts, but reveal in their discursive assertiveness and their exhortatory character the struggle that lies behind them. The following admonition, assuming the form of a father's instruction to his children for right living, is an inscription of the chief treasurer of Amenemhet III (Nimaatre, *ca.* 1840–1790 B.C.) of Dynasty XII:

> Worship King Ni-maat-Re, living forever, within your bodies
>> And associate with his majesty in your hearts.
> He is Perception which is in men's hearts,
>> And his eyes search out every body.
> He is Re, by whose beams one sees,
>> He is one who illumines the Two Lands more than the sun disc.
> He is one who makes the land greener than does a high Nile,
>> For he has filled the Two Lands with strength and life.[47]

Even more succinctly speaks an inscription from the tomb of Rekhmire, the vizier of Thutmose III (*ca.* 1490–1436 B.C.):

> What is the king of Upper and Lower Egypt?
> He is a god by whose dealings one lives,
> the father and mother of all men,
> alone by himself without an equal.[48]

The Pharaoh is the father of all men, as Atum or Re is his father; and men are, through his mediation, sons of the god at a second remove, participating in his life-spending force. The images of physical begetting and physical absorption into body and heart vividly express the oneness of divine order in world and society. Most striking is an inscription from Queen Hatshepsut (*ca.* 1520–1480), who, considering her difficult

---

[47] Translated by Wilson in Pritchard (ed.), *Ancient Near Eastern Texts*, 431. For the historical situation of the admonition see Wilson, *The Burden of Egypt*, 142 ff.
[48] Frankfort, *Ancient Egyptian Religion*, 43.

position as a female Pharaoh, had perhaps to be more emphatic about her consubstantiality with the god:

> I have made bright the truth [*maat*] which he [Re] loved;
> I know that he liveth by it [the *maat*];
> It is my bread, I eat of its brightness;
> I am a likeness from his limbs, one with him.
> He has begotten me, to make strong his might in this land.[49]

The brightness by which Re lives, and of which the Queen eats, is the brightness of Maat, the daughter of Re, his brilliance which expels the dawn and shines forth in the day. The substance that lives in gods and the world, kings and societies, is not a brute force, but a creative life, dispelling the darkness of disorder and radiating the light of Maat. The symbol is too compact to be translated by a single word in a modern language. As the Maat of the cosmos it would have to be rendered as order; as the Maat of society, as good government and justice; as the Maat of true understanding of ordered reality, as truth.[50]

The cosmic meaning is predominant in the following Pyramid Text:

> N. comes out of the Isle of Flame,
> after he had set truth therein in the place of error.[51]

The Pharaoh, in the role of the creator-god, emerges from the Isle of Flame, which in the theology of Hermopolis corresponds to the Primeval Hill of Heliopolis. "Truth" and "error" would here more clearly be rendered as order and disorder (or chaos). In another Pyramid Text the deceased Pharaoh expects to seat himself "upon the throne of 'Truth which makes alive.' " [52] In this passage, the meaning of Maat as a resultant order blends with the ordering force itself. And the political meaning dominates in the following passage:

> N. destroys battle; he punishes revolt;
> N. goes forth as the protector of truth; he brings her, for she is
> with him.[53]

Here Maat is the political force which establishes peace, puts down the disorder of revolts, and protects the right or just order. These functions,

---

[49] James H. Breasted, *Ancient Records of Egypt* (Chicago, 1906), II, § 299.
[50] On the multiple meaning of Maat see Wilson, *The Burden of Egypt*, 47 ff., as well as generally *s.v.* "Maat" in the Index; Frankfort, *Kingship and the Gods*, 51 ff.; Frankfort, *Ancient Egyptian Religion*, 53 ff.
[51] Pyramid Texts, 265b–c.   [52] *Ibid.*, 1079c.
[53] *Ibid.*, 319a–b.

however, are inseparable from the defense of truth in the religious sense, as revealed by an inscription of Tutankhamen referring to the abolition of the Amarna heresy:

> His Majesty drove out disorder [or falsehood] from the Two Lands,
> so that order [or truth, *maat*] was again established in its place;
> He made disorder [falsehood] an abomination of the land
> as at "the first time" [creation].[54]

The symbolic re-creation of the pristine order of creation that is the function of every Pharaoh acquires a special poignancy, because on this occasion it is a political restoration after the Aton interlude. With the last two passages we are close to the Persian world-immanent dualism of Truth and Lie; one can see the point at which a dualistic conception of the cosmos and society would branch off unless the experience were balanced by faith in the one greatest god.

The Maat of the god that is present in the Pharaoh, finally, must be transformed into an effective order of society by means of royal administration. While a description of Egyptian administration and its development lies outside the scope of the present study, a few characteristics must be enumerated nevertheless.[55] The beginnings were of patriarchal simplicity, with relatives of the Pharaoh, as well as relatives of former kings, serving in various offices as far down in the scale of importance as the available personnel would admit, in order to spread the royal substance bodily through society. The administration was rationalized and centralized under Dynasty IV with the establishment of the vizierate, a chief magistracy, at the head of the bureaucracy. The transmission of the royal Maat through princes of the blood, who at first served as viziers, was later abandoned. Even under the rationalized administration there remained, however, a fluidity of jurisdictions, with inevitable conflicts, because the Maat as a whole was conceived to be present in every official who derived his charge from the king. Egypt never achieved a rational organization of offices comparable to that of Rome. Beyond these general remarks we shall confine our analysis to the transmission of the Maat from the Pharaoh to the vizier, as the further transmission to the lower ranks of the hierarchy followed the same principles.

The meaning of transmission can be studied in the autobiography

---

[54] I am quoting the translation of Frankfort in *Ancient Egyptian Religion*, 54; Wilson's translation is to be found in Pritchard (ed.), *Ancient Near Eastern Texts*, 251.

[55] A brief survey is to be found in Frankfort, *The Birth of Civilization*, 84 ff.

of Rekhmire, the vizier of Thutmose III. The dignitary gives a proud and detailed account of his investiture:

> I was a noble, the second to the king . . . . It was the first occasion of my being summoned. All my brothers were in the outer office. I went forth . . . clad in fine linen . . . . I reached the doorway of the palace gate. The courtiers bent their backs, and I found the masters of ceremonies clearing a way before me.

After the setting of the scene, he describes the first effect of Maat on his person:

> My abilities were not as they had been: my yesterday's nature had altered itself, since I had come forth in the accoutrements [of the vizier] to be the Prophet of Maat.

The Pharaoh expresses his pleasure at seeing a person with whom his heart feels in sympathy, and lays down the rule of transmission:

> Would that thou mightest act in conformance with what I may say! Then Maat will rest in her place.

The account concludes with the consequences of conformance, as manifest in the official conduct of the vizier:

> I acted in conformance with that which he had ordained . . . . I raised *maat* [justice] to the height of heaven; I made its beauty circulate to the width of the earth . . . . When I judged the petitioner, I was not partial. I did not turn my brow for the sake of reward. I was not angry at a petitioner, nor did I rebuff him, but I tolerated him in his moment of outburst. I rescued the timid from the violent. . . .[56]

The *maat* of the cosmos thus circulates from the god, through the Pharaoh and his administrators, into the existence of the humblest, most timid petitioner in court.

§ 3. THE DYNAMICS OF EXPERIENCE

The preceding section dealt with the form of Egyptian political culture; the present section will deal with its corrosion by differentiating experiences.

Form and corrosion can be clearly distinguished as problems, but they are difficult, if not impossible, to separate in the process of history.

[56] Translated by Wilson in Pritchard (ed.), *Ancient Near Eastern Texts*, 213.

Creation and corrosion can not be assigned to successive periods, and it is even doubtful whether at any time there existed a form unmoved by the leaven of differentiating experiences, for corrosive tendencies can be discerned in the very acts of Egyptian unification, as for instance in the Memphite Theology. Moreover, these tendencies never really broke the form so that one could speak of a genuine revolution, for even in the depth of political crisis, when disillusionment was as profound as that revealed in the Song of the Harper, the contemporaries attributed the evils of the age to the fall from Pharaonic order and expected relief from its restoration. The sources analyzed in the present section, therefore, concern the form itself as much as its corrosion. They will contribute to its understanding as a form that is both alive with evolutionary forces and magnificently resistant to a new birth that would spell its death.

1. The Egyptian Type of Differentiation

A living form of this kind must be treated with circumspection. From the vantage point of the present we can discern in Egyptian sources the seeds that might have grown into the achievements of Israel and Hellas. Since, however, the promise did not mature, no purpose of science would be served by reading the flowering into the germs—as on occasion it has happened on the part of enthusiastic Egyptologists with a progressivist bias. In order to be certain about the limits of the permissible, it is necessary, therefore, to clarify the structure of Egyptian symbolization; we must penetrate the secret of an intellectual form that holds its exuberant life so sternly within its bounds. The task will best be approached by first stating what type and degree of differentiation is *not* to be found in Egyptian civilization.

A suitable illustration for the limits of Egyptian differentiation is furnished by the cosmogonies in comparison with Ionian speculation. In the various Egyptian cult centers a considerable number of different creator-gods were worshipped. In Heliopolis the creator-god was Re or Atum, the power of the sun in its noon and evening phases; in Memphis it was Ptah, the power of the earth; in Elephantine it was Khnum, an enigmatic god who made all creatures on a potter's wheel; in Thebes it was Amon, the hidden power of the wind. When we survey this list of elemental creative powers—the earth, the wind, the sun—we are reminded of the Ionian philosophers' attempt to find the origin of being in water, air, or fire. Obviously, Egyptians and Ionians engaged in the same kind of intellectual endeavor. In both instances man was in quest of the origin of the world that surrounded him in time and space, and he found the answer in an element whose constant creative presence suggested its primordial creativeness.

Beyond this point, however, the two endeavors are neither similar nor parallel. They are not similar, for the answers, in spite of their common substance, differ widely by their intellectual form. In Egypt the answer is a cosmogonic myth, a story of the creation, or rather of the ordering of the world, by a god; in Hellas it is a speculation on the principle, the arche, of being. Moreover, the differences of form do not run parallel, for in the background of Ionian speculation there still can be sensed the cosmogonic thought from which it derives. Ionian speculation and cosmogonic myth are related historically in so far as the one derives from the other through differentiation of experience and symbols. The cosmogonic myth is an older, more comprehensive form of expressing the order of being, and out of this myth Ionian speculation differentiates the idea of a being and becoming that is closed to the gods, and because of this closure demands interpretation in terms of its immanent forces. This act of differentiation, in which a world with an immanent order of being is created by the philosopher, is distinctly a Hellenic achievement; nothing of the kind occurs in Egypt.

The limitation of the Egyptian myth thus is clear. Nevertheless, today it is no longer permissible to regard the myth as having no other purpose in the history of mankind than to provide a stepping stone for more rational forms of symbolization; and by the same token, it no longer makes sense to search for the meaning of the myth in its partial anticipation of future accomplishments. We must recognize that the myth has a life and a virtue of its own. While Egyptian thought does not advance from myth to speculation, it is devoid neither of truth nor of intellectual movement. And the very comparison that reveals the limitations of the myth also points toward the source of its strength. For the fact that the speculation on being has differentiated out of the larger complex of cosmogonies suggests that the myth is much richer in content than any of the partial symbolizations derived from it. This richer content may conveniently be subdivided in two classes: The myth, first, contains the various experiential blocs which separate in the course of differentiation; and it, second, contains an experience that welds the

blocs into a living whole. That binding factor in the Egyptian cosmogonies is the experience of consubstantiality.[57]

From the interaction of these various parts of the myth results its
peculiar flavor of compactness. The previously mentioned "elements,"
for instance, are not yet distinguished as substances, as the stuff of which
the world in the immanent sense is made, but are seen as the creative
forces in their most impressive cosmic manifestations—in the sun, the
earth, the wind. Moreover, the gods are recognized as manifest in the
same cosmic phenomena. And the manner in which the gods are present
again defies distinction by a Greek or modern vocabulary. One can
hardly speak of their immanence in the world, for "immanence" presupposes an understanding of "transcendence" that is not yet achieved,
though certainly from an experience of divine manifestation can develop
an ultimate understanding of divine transcendence. The myth in its
compact form thus contains both the experiential bloc that was developed by the Ionians and their successors into a metaphysics of world-
immanent being and the other bloc, disregarded in such speculation, that
developed into the faith in a world-transcendent being.

In a compactness that can not be translated but only dissected by our
modern vocabulary, the myth holds together the blocs which in later
history not only will be distinguished, but also are liable to fall apart. If
we follow the two lines of differentiation as they emerge from the myth,
if we consider that they will be pursued to the extremes of a radically
other-worldly faith and of an agnostic metaphysics, and if we contemplate the inevitably resultant disorder in the soul of man and society, the
relative merits of compactness and differentiation will appear in a new
light. Differentiation, one would have to say, is not an unqualified good;
it is fraught with the dangers of radically dissociating the experiential
blocs held together by the myth, as well as of losing the experience of
consubstantiality in the process. The virtue of the cosmogonic myth, on
the contrary, lies in its compactness: It originates in an integral understanding of the order of being, provides the symbols which adequately
express a balanced manifold of experiences, and is a living force, preserving the balanced order in the soul of the believers.

The burden of these virtues is carried by the experience of consub-

---

[57] On the problem of consubstantiality, especially in connection with the "monotheistic"
trends to be discussed presently in the text, see Wilson in *The Intellectual Adventure of Ancient
Man,* 65 ff.

stantiality. It is, within the economy of the myth, not a mechanical clasp for the various experiential blocs but a principle that establishes the order among the realms of being. The community of being, to be sure, is experienced as a community of substance; but it is divine substance that becomes manifest in the world, not cosmic substance that becomes manifest in the gods. The partners in the community of being are linked in a dynamic order in so far as divine substance pervades the world, society, and man, and not human or social substance the world and the gods. The order of consubstantiality thus is hierarchical; the flow of substance goes from the divine into the mundane, social, and human existences.

In the light of this analysis it will now be possible to characterize nature and direction of the differentiations which actually occur within the Egyptian mythical form. The differentiation goes neither in the direction of Ionian speculation nor in the direction of a genuine opening of the soul toward transcendent being; it is rather a speculative exploration within the range of consubstantiality. The nature of the divine substance that is manifest in the existentially lower ranks of being becomes the object of inquiry, and the exploration leads—we are inclined to say inevitably—to a determination of the substance as "one" and as "spiritual." Considering that result, it is legitimate to speak of an Egyptian evolution toward monotheism as long as one remains aware that the pluralism of divine manifestations in the world is not really broken by an experience of transcendence.

A few passages from the Amon Hymns of Dynasty XIX will illustrate the nature and limitations of the development.[58] In the first place, the one god is unknown because he came into being at the beginning, alone, without witnesses:

> The first to come into being in the earliest times,
> Amon, who came into being at the beginning,
> so that his mysterious nature is unknown . .
> Building his own egg, a daemon mysterious of birth,
> who created his own beauty,
> the divine god who came into being by himself.
> All other gods came into being after he began himself.

[58] The Amon Hymns are ascribed to the reign of Ramses II (*ca.* 1301–1234 B.C.). The passages are quoted in Wilson's translation in Pritchard (ed.), *Ancient Near Eastern Texts,* 368 ff.

The god, furthermore, remains a hidden, invisible god, whose name is unknown:

> One is Amon hiding himself from them,
> concealing himself from the other gods . . . .
> He is far from heaven, he is absent from the underworld,
> so that no gods know his true form.
> His image is not displayed in writings.
> No one bears witness to him . . . .
> He is too mysterious that his majesty might be disclosed,
> he is too great that men should ask about him,
> too powerful that he might be known.
> At the utterance of his mysterious name, wittingly or unwittingly,
> instantly one falls in a death of violence.

The god mysterious of form nevertheless is a god of many forms:

> Mysterious of form, glistening of appearance,
> the marvelous god of many forms.
> All other gods boast of him,
> to magnify themselves through his beauty,
> according as he is divine.

The participation of all other gods in the substance of the one god, however, is hierarchically restricted through a peculiar trinitarian conception of the highest divinity:

> All gods are three: Amon, Re, and Ptah,
> and there is no second to them.
> "Hidden" [amen] is his name as Amon, he is Re in face, and his
>   body is Ptah.
> Their cities are on earth, abiding forever:
> Thebes, Heliopolis, and Memphis unto eternity.

In their aggregate the texts render a fairly clear picture of the intellectual situation. The movement toward monotheism is unmistakably marked by the elevation of one god as the highest above all others. Moreover, the attempt to define his nature as that of a being before the time and beyond the space of the world, as well as his further characterization as invisible, formless, and nameless, reveal the typical technique of the *theologia negativa* in circumscribing the nature of the transcendent god. Nevertheless, the differentiating movement does not break with polytheism; it preserves the experience of consubstantiality intact when it interprets the gods who are manifest in the world as participants in the one highest divine substance.

Of particular interest is the trinitarian symbol of the last passage. It is one of the texts on which an Egyptologist is now and then tempted to cast a speculative eye as a possible anticipation of Christian trinitarianism. Any suggestion of this kind seems to us inadmissible. The symbol is a plain piece of political construction with the purpose of letting the three powerful rival cities participate on an equal footing in the exalted divinity of the Amon of Thebes. There is no hidden meaning in the number three; it might as well have been four or five gods, if the political situation had required them. Still, the symbol is of considerable interest under other, less obvious aspects. In the first place, it provides decisive support to our thesis that the Egyptian monotheistic development is not motivated by a genuine experience of transcendence. The bland disregard for the conflict between the trinitarian, political speculation and the exaltation of the one, invisible god would hardly be possible, if a conflict were experienced at all. Such tolerance presupposes that both types of speculation are understood as moving within the range of mythical compactness. And the passage is, furthermore, of interest because it shows that within the range of the myth various techniques of speculation are possible. The trinitarian symbol, on the one hand, draws the other two gods into the exaltation of the hidden, invisible Amon; on the other hand, it preserves the manifest, cosmic qualities of the three gods in their unity. In so far as the triune god is hidden, he is Amon, the Wind; in so far as he has a face, an appearance, he is Re, the Sun; in so far as he has a body, he is Ptah, the Earth. In this construction of a supreme deity, by the side of which there is no second, the one god has three cosmic aspects; but precisely as the carrier of all three of them, he is not identical with any one of them taken singly. If the mythical were translated into theological language, one would have to say that the nature of the one god can be defined analogically by predicates of immanent being. The god is, and is not, the Wind, the Sun, the Earth. In the exaltation of Amon alone the hymns employed the technique of the *theologia negativa;* in the trinitarian speculation they employ the technique of the *analogia entis.*

The results of the analysis, valid for the problem of differentiation within the Egyptian cosmological form in general, can now be applied to the Memphite Theology.

2. *The Memphite Theology*

The Memphite Theology is preserved as an inscription from the reign of Shabaka, the Ethiopian king who founded Dynasty XXV in 712 B.C. The date of its composition, however, is much earlier, probably as early as the unification of Egypt under Dynasty I, *ca.* 3100 B.C. The title under which the inscription goes today is a matter of convention; the characterization as a theology certainly is not adequate. With regard to its content, we encounter the same complexity as in the Babylonian *Enuma elish,* in so far as it is at the same time a cosmogony, a theogony, and a political myth, with the political events providing the motive of the composition, as well as the key to its understanding. With regard to its form, various literary devices are used. We find mythical histories, mystery plays, pieces of speculative construction, and interspersed with them even an odd epistemological account of the formation of symbols on the basis of sensual experience. If the aggregate of these pieces had a literary form at all, it no longer can be discerned clearly, because too much, particularly in the middle part, is damaged. Still, the recognizable subdivisions are definitely parts of a composition purporting to justify the establishment of Memphis as the new center of a unified Egypt.[59]

For the purpose of our analysis we shall distinguish three strands of argument in the Memphite Theology. They are concerned with (1) the unification of Egypt; (2) the establishment of Memphis as the center of the new political world; and (3) the theological speculation that confers on Memphis superiority over all other Egyptian cult centers, especially over Heliopolis. In the text itself, however, the three strands are closely interwoven. Even where one of the arguments clearly predominates, as for instance in the section containing the theological speculation, the other themes run through in a subdued mood, so that the wider political context will not be forgotten. Moreover, the distinction

---

[59] The oldest interpretation of the Memphite Theology is Breasted's, in its latest form in *The Dawn of Conscience,* 29–42. See furthermore Adolf Erman, *Ein Denkmal memphitischer Theologie* (Sitzungsberichte der Preussischen Akademie der Wissenschaften, Berlin, 1911); Kurt Sethe, *Dramatische Texte zu altaegyptischen Mysterienspielen* (Untersuchungen zur Geschichte und Altertumskunde Aegyptens, X, Leipzig, 1928); Hermann Junker, *Die Goetterlehre von Memphis* (Abhandlungen der Preussischen Akademie der Wissenschaften, Phil.-Hist. Klasse, No. 23, Berlin, 1940); the same author's *Die politische Lehre von Memphis* (*ibid.,* No. 6, 1941); Junker, *Pyramidenzeit* (1949), 18–25. For recent American interpretations see Wilson in *The Intellectual Adventure of Ancient Man,* 55–60; Frankfort, *Kingship and the Gods,* 24–35; Wilson, *The Burden of Egypt,* 58–60. Practically all of the text relevant to our purpose is to be found in Wilson's translation in Pritchard (ed.), *Ancient Near Eastern Texts,* 4–6.

cannot render the compactness of thought that is due to the experience of consubstantiality. For in the imagery of the text the political events are at the same time a divine-cosmic drama; and this substantial oneness of events on the various levels of existence cannot be communicated by an analysis at all; we must let the text speak for itself:

> . . . Ptah, that is, this land named with the Great Name of Ta Tjenen . . .
> He who unified this land has appeared as King of Upper Egypt and as King of Lower Egypt.[60]

The fragments suggest the meaning of the great event. Ptah's name is Ta-Tjenen, that is, the "Risen Land." The name alludes to the cosmogonic belief that the creation started with the emergence of a mound of earth, the Primeval Hill, from the waters of chaos. The land of the original creation is Egypt itself; and by further mythical identification this Egypt is the god Ptah. The land is, furthermore, made one by the appearance of the conquering king, who by virtue of that act slips into the role of the Ptah, the Risen Land of Egypt. In fact, throughout Egyptian history the hieroglyph which designates the primeval "hillock of appearance" means also the "appearance in glory," especially of the Pharaoh when he ascends the throne. The references to the "land," finally, are probably loaded with allusions to the land reclaimed from the marshes by Menes in order to build Memphis and the temple of Ptah, as well as to the "Great Land," that is, the province of This from which the conquerors came. Creation and unification, the world and Egypt, the god and the king, the god and the land, the king and the land thus merge in a mythical drama of order rising out of chaos, in a drama that reaches through all the realms of being. The play with tightly packed meanings must always be remembered in the background of the following analysis.

With regard to the unification and the establishment of Memphis as the new center we can be brief, because no problems of differentiation arise.

The history and justification of the conquest is clad in a mythical story, interspersed with dramatic passages (Section II). The earth-god Geb adjudicates the strife between Seth, his younger son, and Horus, the son of his older son Osiris, concerning the rule over Egypt. Seth receives

---

[60] Translation by Frankfort in *Kingship and the Gods*, 25. This is all that is left of Section I of the inscription. In numbering the sections we also follow the convenient subdivisions made by Frankfort.

Upper Egypt, Horus Lower Egypt. On second thought Geb rescinds his judgment and awards the rulership of the whole of Egypt to Horus, the son of his first-born, as his rightful heir. The political intention of the myth is obvious: Egypt is originally one land under divine rule; a dynastic dissension among the gods separates the two parts of the country; a divine resolve restores unity under the legitimate heir. Hence, the conqueror is the Horus, who enters into his rightful heritage in accordance with a divine decree. With his victory, the strife of Seth and Horus has come to its end. As the sign of the new harmony the two symbolic plants of the Two Lands are planted at the gates of the temple of Ptah in Memphis. And the name of this temple is: "The Balance of the Two Lands in which Upper Egypt and Lower Egypt have been weighed."

The foundation of Memphis as the new center is justified by a mystery play in which the body of Osiris is transferred to the new capital (Section VI). The meaning of the transfer is summarized in the passage:

> Thus Osiris became earth in the Royal Castle on the north side of this land which he had reached. His son Horus appeared as king of Upper Egypt and as king of Lower Egypt in the arms of his father Osiris, in the presence of the gods that were before him and that were behind him.[61]

Although the sections of the Memphite Theology just discussed do not display any noteworthy differentiations, they have a bearing on the theological speculation of Section V in several respects. First, they establish the context in which the speculation belongs and reveal the political motive beyond a doubt. Second, by their rich polytheistic myth, they put a damper on any attempt to exaggerate the "monotheistic" differentiation of Section V. And, third, by their free adaptation of the myth to political purposes they reveal the general range of freedom in which mythical creation at the time moves. If that general range be taken into account, the speculation of Section V will lose much of the extraordinary character which it has if considered independently.

The theological speculation, to which now we shall turn, is a free manipulation of pre-existent cosmogonies and theogonies for the purpose of elevating the Ptah of Memphis to highest rank among the Egyp-

---

[61] Frankfort's translation in *Kingship and the Gods,* 32. For the significance of this passage for the Egyptian theory of royal succession (the living king is Horus, the dead king Osiris) see *ibid.,* Chaps. 10 and 11.

tian gods. The elements used are (1) a myth of the sun-god who rises out of chaos as the creator, and (2) a myth of the gods created by the sun-god. The first myth is best preserved in a version which ascribes the rise of Atum out of chaos to Hermopolis. The chaos consists of eight gods: the primeval waters and the sky over them, the boundless and the formless, darkness and obscurity, the hidden and the concealed one. From this primeval Ogdoad emerges Atum. According to the second myth it is Atum who in his turn creates the eight gods of heavenly and earthly order; together with Atum the eight form the Ennead. With the two myths of the Ogdoad and the Ennead as their materials, the authors of the Memphite Theology had to construe Ptah as superior to the creator-god Atum. Within the style of the myth the problem had to be resolved by placing Ptah prior to Atum in the process of creation, that is, by identifying him with the gods of the Ogdoad. He is:

> Ptah-Nun, the father who begot Atum;
> Ptah-Naunet, the mother who begot Atum;
> Ptah . . . who gave birth to the gods.

Through the identification with Ptah the original gods of the Ogdoad, however, become virtually meaningless. Instead of the chaos, there is now at the beginning a god who creates the world out of nothing.

The authors apparently were aware of the problem of a creation *ex nihilo*, for they struggled visibly, against the handicap of sensual imagery, toward an understanding of the process as spiritual. The work of creation had to begin with Atum, the head of the Ennead. The creation of the former creator-god by the new one is couched in the following terms:

> [Something] in-the-form-of-Atum became, in the heart, and became, on the tongue [of Ptah].

The crude "something in-the-form-of" would best be translated by the Greek *eidos*, or our modern *idea*. The world originates as an idea in the mind (the heart) and through the command (the tongue) of the god. But the world that comes into being in that manner is not that of Genesis 1 with its sober, systematic ontology: the inorganic universe (1–11), vegetative life (12), animal life (20–25), man (26–27); it is the Egyptian world that is "full of gods," and its creation begins with the traditional divine-cosmic forces, with Atum and his Ennead. Ptah is not yet the transcendent god, but a speculative extrapolation within the range of the myth. The meaning of the process as "spiritual" must, furthermore, be hedged in by reflections, on the "heart" and the "tongue" of the god. The two organs which the god uses in producing the idea are organic seats of divine and royal qualities known to us from other sources. The "command" or "authoritative utterance" (Hu), and "knowledge" or "perception" (Sia), are attributes of the sun-god Re, as well as of the Pharaoh. A Pyramid Text says:

> The Great [Re] stands up in the interior of his chapel,
> and lays down to the ground his dignity for N.,
> after N. had taken command [Hu] and had laid hold of knowledge
>   [Sia].[62]

Thus, the "spiritualization" of the god is inseparable from that of the king. One must not forget for a moment that by virtue of the experience of consubstantiality, the "theology" of this section is at the same time a "politics." The creation of the world as a divine "idea" is consubstantial with the creation of Egypt as the royal "idea" of the conqueror. And we may even say that the creation of Egypt out of nothing, as an idea in the heart and on the tongue of the royal conqueror, is the experience that loosens up the mythical materials and engenders the conscious freedom of the theological speculation proper.

The assumption of a new freedom, of a conscious adventure in theologizing, is not arbitrary but finds support in the text itself. For the account of the first creative act is followed by an epistemological "teaching" or "doctrine" that reads as if it were a footnote of the author who wishes to justify his extraordinary construction. Other gods, like Atum, may have created physically; Ptah created by heart and tongue, and that is what gave him his superiority:

> It so happens that heart and tongue prevailed over all other members
>   of the body, considering,
> that the heart is in every body, and the tongue is in every mouth,
> of all gods, all men, all cattle, all creeping things, and whatever
>   else lives;
> [Ptah prevails] by thinking [as heart] and commanding [as
>   tongue] everything that he wishes.

[62] Pyramid Texts, 300a–c. See also Mercer's commentaries in Volume II of *Pyramid Texts*, to 300a-c and 251b. In the later political theology Maat is added to Hu and Sia as the third attribute of the Pharaoh; a passage from the Kubban Stela says: "Thou art the living likeness of thy father Atum of Heliopolis, for Authoritative Utterance is in thy mouth, Understanding is in thy heart, thy speech is the shrine of Truth [*maat*]"; see Frankfort, *Kingship and the Gods*, 149.

The sight of the eyes, the hearing of the ears, the air-breathing of
    the nose
they report to the heart. It [the heart] causes every thought to
    come forth,
and the tongue announces what the heart thinks.
Thus are done all works and all crafts, the action of the arms, the
    movement of the legs, and the action of all other members, ac-
    cording to the command which the heart thought, which came
    forth from the tongue, and which makes the dignity [or essence,
    worth] of everything.[63]

The text contains in condensed form a philosophical anthropology.
The thought and will of man are formed as to their content by observing
the situation. The will is then translated into planned action and the
meaning of artifacts. And since, by virtue of consubstantiality, the
theory applies also to the god, the essences of all things (their dignity, or
worth) are incarnations of divine thought at the god's will. The passages
are of an importance that can hardly be exaggerated, because they show
how far the differentiation in the direction of anthropology and metaphysics can go without breaking the cosmological form. The men who
could intersperse their myth of the creation with "footnotes," relating
the principles which they used in constructing it, must have had a rather
detached attitude toward their own product. The Memphite Theology
is a rare, if not unique, document in so far as it authentically attests the
degree of rational consciousness that can accompany the creation of a
myth in 3000 B.C.

The climax of the speculation is the elevation of Ptah over Atum.
The name Atum means "everything" and it means "nothing"; he is the
"all" in its fullness before its unfolding into the order of the world.[64]
In view of his rank among the gods he bears the title of the "Great One."
Ptah is now erected into the creator of Atum and the Ennead, and in
view of his higher rank he receives the title of the "Mighty Great One."
From this "Mighty Great" creator-god, then, emanates the order of the
world, evoked on all its ranks by the "word" that flows from heart and
tongue of the god. He first creates the gods, after them the male and
female spirits who provide "nourishment," and finally the order of man:

---

[63] Contracted on the basis of the translations by Wilson (Pritchard [ed.], *Ancient Near
Eastern Texts*, 5), Frankfort (*Kingship and the Gods*, 29), and Junker (*Pyramidenzeit*, 22 ff.).
[64] Wilson in *Intellectual Adventure of Ancient Man*, 53.

> Justice was given to him who does what is liked,
> injustice to him who does what is disliked.
> Life was given to him who is peaceful,
> and death to the criminal.

Having completed his work the god can rest:

> And so Ptah was satisfied, after he had made every
> thing and every word of the god.

In surveying his creation he finds that he has made the gods, the cities, and the districts of Egypt. In particular, he has put the gods in their shrines, established their offerings, and given to every god a body of wood, or of stone, or of clay, so that their hearts would be satisfied. The success of the creation becomes manifest when all the gods and their spirits gather around Ptah, "content, because associated with the Lord of the Two Lands." This concluding line of the speculation leads the myth of the creation back again to its political motive, that is, to the unification of Egypt.

The creation of the world by the word of Ptah reminded Breasted of the divine word that created the world in Genesis, and of the Logos speculation of St. John. Ever since, the Memphite Theology has remained the pride of Egyptologists.[65] Egyptian thought, they maintained, showed itself from the very beginning on the spiritual and moral level of the Hebrews and of St. John; and by its search for a first principle of order, as well as by the discovery of the principle in a creative, divine intelligence, it gained the intellectual level of the Greeks. While undeniably there is a core of truth in such reflections, they require some critical qualification in order to become tenable; for as they stand they are all too obviously on the defensive against progressivist notions of history in so far as they argue in substance: Anybody who still believes that the beginnings of human civilization are "primitive," and that only with Israel and Hellas do we rise to a level of serious interest for Western man, should consider the achievement that speaks from the oldest extant document in human history. Against that argument must be held that it makes sense only if the idea of a progress with regard to "doctrines" be accepted at all. If, however, we replace the principle of progress in the history of ideas by the principle of compactness and differentiation

---

[65] Breasted, *Development of Religion and Thought in Ancient Egypt*, 47; *The Dawn of Conscience*, 37. Breasted's suggestion is accepted by Wilson in *Intellectual Adventure of Ancient Man*, 56, and in his *Burden of Egypt*, 59; by Frankfort in his *Kingship and the Gods*, 29.

with regard to experiences, there is nothing extraordinary about the appearance of particular ideas and techniques of thought in an ancient
civilization. The Egyptian Logos speculation should cause no surprise,
since differentiations of this kind are possible within every civilizational
form. It would be surprising only if "a man had appeared, sent by God,
whose name was John: who came for the purpose of witnessing, to bear
testimony to the Light, so that all men might believe by means of him"
(John 1:6–7). For that would not have been a matter of speculation
within the form of the myth, but an experiential break with the cosmological form and an opening of the soul toward transcendence. The
Logos of the Memphite Theology created a world that was consubstantial
with Egypt; but the Logos of John created a world with a mankind
immediate under God. The Johannine Logos would have broken the
Pharaonic mediation; it could not have unified and founded Egypt,
but would have destroyed its order. Breasted, we may say, has rightly
seen the parallel speculations on the level of "doctrine"; but since life is
not a matter of doctrine, they do not touch the form, or essence, of a
civilization. As far as the experiences of order are concerned, the parallel
cannot be maintained.

3. The Response to Disorder

The impressive construction of the Memphite Theology—One God,
One World, One Egypt—reveals the creation of Pharaonic order as the
attunement of a society with divine being. When the empire disintegrated
institutionally at the end of Dynasty VI, the horrors of the ensuing social
upheaval might well have furnished reasons for reconsidering the merits
of the fallen order, as well as of the god who had been its guarantor. It
was a time for forming new social ties, for organizing a new community,
and for propitiating the gods to endow it with sacral meaning. From
the depths of despair there might have arisen a soul purged of illusions
about the world and willing to face its iniquity with the strength that
flows from faith in a world-transcendent god. A new man, guided by the
god who was manifest nowhere except in the loving movement of his soul,
might have set himself to the task of creating a government that would
rely less on the cosmic divinity of institutions and more on the order in
the souls of the men who live under them.

The potentials of the situation, however, did not become actual under
the stresses of the Egyptian upheaval. The Pharaonic order had come

down thunderingly, but the faith in it, as the truth of human existence, was never abandoned, in spite of the acute misery of the age. While the responses of men in their loneliness were rather various, they had in common their orientation toward the paradise lost and to be regained. The extant literary documents of the period contain descriptions of the disorder, lamentations, agnostic and hedonistic reactions, expressions of skepticism and of despair to the point of suicide, and hopes for a Pharaoh who will restore the empire to its pristine glory. It is a literature always fascinating, frequently profound, and sometimes grandiose, but it never reveals a religious personality that could have become the center of a new community life beyond the range of cosmological civilization.[66]

From the considerable body of surviving literature there stands out one brief text as deserving closer attention, because it shows that revolutionary possibilities, though not realized, at least could be envisaged by the thinkers of the age. It is a Coffin Text from the Middle Kingdom, to be dated *ca.* 2000 B.C.; no copies of it are known from other periods.[67]

In the opening passage of the text, the sun-god receives the souls of the deceased; they are released from the turmoil of the world, and they will be receptive to the message which the god has to convey. He bids them peace. It is the peace that he found for himself when through creation he disengaged himself from the coils of the serpent of iniquity. While in the coils of the serpent, his heart did four good deeds for him in order to still evil; and he now repeats them so that the souls of the dead may participate in his peace. These are the four good deeds:

[66] A person of the type whose absence we have just maintained is found by Joachim Spiegel, *Soziale und Weltanschauliche Reformbewegungen im Alten Aegypten* (Heidelberg, 1950), as the leader of a revolutionary movement, attacked in the "Admonitions of Ipu-wer." Spiegel, furthermore, considers the "Dispute of a Man, who Considers Suicide, with His Soul" an autobiographical document of the revolutionary leader, setting forth the reasons for his suicide after the breakdown of the movement. I must confine myself to referring the reader to Spiegel's work, for two reasons. In the first place, the interpretation of Spiegel involves textual reconstructions and philological arguments of which the validity can be judged only by an Egyptologist. And second, the interpretations are so badly vitiated by looseness of hermeneutical technique that it is difficult to ascertain what will remain as the solid core of the work, once the anachronisms and extravagances are eliminated. At the time it seems to me at least possible that the "Admonitions of Ipu-wer" indeed refer to a popular leader. Whether to that leader can be attributed ideas that go beyond what is to be found in the documents, presently to be studied in the text, seems doubtful. The attribution of the "Dispute" to the hypothetical leader of the revolution is an interesting possibility, but no more than that.

[67] Breasted, *The Dawn of Conscience*, 221 ff.; Wilson in *The Intellectual Adventure of Ancient Man*, 106 ff. See also Wilson's translation in Pritchard (ed.), *Ancient Near Eastern Texts*, with the introductory note, 7 ff.

I made the four winds that every man might breathe thereof like
his fellow in his time. That is the first of the deeds.

I made the great inundation that the poor man might have rights
therein like the great man. That is the second deed.

I made every man like his fellow. I did not command that they
might do evil, it was their hearts that violated what I had said.
That is the third of the deeds.

I made that their hearts should cease from forgetting the west, in
order that divine offerings might be made to the gods of the provinces. That is the fourth of the deeds.

The text is a little tract on the nature and source of evil. Its author
understands creation as the overcoming of evil through an order of
"good deeds." The good order of world and society is wrested from the
iniquity of chaos by the creator-god, and in its goodness released into
existence. If there is evil in the world, it stems from the heart of man—
a heart that violates the commands of the god. These compact sentences
imply both a myth of the Golden Age and a theodicy; and they furthermore imply the hope for restoration of the good order when man sup-
presses the chaos that is in his heart and finds his peace in obedience to
the creative commands of the god. The tract is truly extraordinary,
however, because of the content of the commands: the god has created
all men equal; he has created the refreshing winds of Egypt and the
inundation of the Nile for the equal benefit of the poor and the rich;
and he has implanted equally in the hearts of all men the concern about
the "west," that is, about their death, so that by their offerings they will
have equal access to the life to come. By divine order society becomes a
community of equals; the inequality of rank and wealth is the evil that
stems from the heart of man.

The idea of a community of equals is a far cry from the Memphite
Theology. Unfortunately, it is practically impossible to determine the
meaning of the text more closely. The extant literary documents, though
numerous, are not sufficient to furnish a coherent picture of Egyptian
intellectual history. Hence, we cannot place the text in context. Do such
ideas have antecedents? Are they the work of an isolated individual? Are
they representative for a social group, or a region? There are no answers
to such questions. One can only point out the obvious: that the *conditio
humana* is here the organizing center of thought, not the Pharaoh and
his unified Egypt. The man who breathes the air and tills the soil, who
lives and dies, whose heart yearns for peace and yet trespasses in strife,

who is man before God like his brother—all this betrays a new religious-ness from which a community of men immediate under their God might have grown. But as far as we know there was no such growth.

It is possible, though not certain, that some light will fall on the brief Coffin Text from a more elaborate poem of the same period which relates the "Dispute of a Man, Who Contemplates Suicide, with His Soul." [68]

The man is dejected by the misery of the time and wants to cast off a life that has become senseless. But he hesitates before the irrevocable act; his soul is not in agreement with his resolve. In the dispute between the man and his soul the arguments for and against suicide are presented, until the decision is reached and the soul agrees to go with the man wherever he goes.

The soul disagrees with the man, because the act of self-destruction is impious and immoral. The command of the gods and the wisdom of the sages prohibit man to shorten the allotted span of his life. Against the argument of the soul, the man pleads exceptional circumstances that will justify a violation of the rule before the gods. Moreover, in order to comply with other accepted beliefs, he will make proper provisions for burial and sacrifices so that his soul will be satisfied in the beyond. The soul is not pleased by such prospects, and in order to weaken Man's will, it voices skepticism with regard to the efficacy of such provisions, using arguments that we already know from the Song of the Harper. But Man approaches the crisis, and the soul resorts to the desperate means of tempting him with the suggestion of moral as an alternative to physical suicide. Man is in deadly anguish, because he takes life seriously, because he cannot bear existence without meaning. Why not cast such worries aside? Why not simply not despair? Man should enjoy the pleasures of the day as they come: "Pursue the happy day and forget care!" That ends the dispute with the soul. Man is aroused by the baseness of the counsel; he is now at one with himself and presents his case for decision. In four great series of exclamations, in the form of tristichs, he reaches the climax of his decision for death.

The first series expresses his horror about the counsel of his soul. Merely entertaining such an idea is a disgrace, and if he followed the advice his name would become a stench:

---

[68] Translation by Wilson in Pritchard (ed.), *Ancient Near Eastern Texts*, 405–407. A careful interpretation is to be found in Junker, *Pyramidenzeit*, 162–74.

> Behold my name will reek through thee
>   More than the stench of bird-droppings
>   On summer days, when the sky is hot.

The resources of his soul are exhausted; no help is to be had from her; now he is all alone with himself in the horrors of the age. The second group of exclamations expresses his sense of being lost in the impasse of solitude:

> To whom can I speak today?
>   One's fellows are evil;
>   The friends of today do not love.
> To whom can I speak today?
>   Faces have disappeared:
>   Every man has a downcast face toward his fellow.
> To whom can I speak today?
>   A man should arouse wrath by his evil character,
>   But he stirs everyone to laughter, in spite of the
>   wickedness of his sin.
> To whom can I speak today?
>   There are no righteous;
>   The land is left to those who do wrong.
> To whom can I speak today?
>   The sin that afflicts the land,
>   It has no end.

In such utter loneliness, in the third group of exclamations, man turns toward death as a salvation from evil:

> Death faces me today
>   Like the recovery of a sick man,
>   Like going out into the open after a confinement.
> Death faces me today
>   Like an unclouding of the sky,
>   Like an illumination that leads to what one did not know.
> Death faces me today
>   Like the longing of a man to see his home again,
>   After many years that he was held in captivity.

The final group of tristichs reveals what man has to hope from the beyond:

> Why surely, he who is yonder
>   Will be a living god,
>   Punishing the sin of him who commits it.
> Why surely, he who is yonder
>   Will stand in the barque of the sun,
>   Causing the choicest therein to be given to the temples.

> Why surely, he who is yonder
> Will be a sage, not hindered
> From appealing to Re when he speaks.

The text speaks for itself. Only a few touches of interpretation need be added. The first part, the dispute between man and soul, is in the nature of an introduction. It looks like a literary device for surveying the arguments used at the time in the debate on the meaning of life. The individual arguments are known from other sources. Once they are disposed of, the author presents his own position, without further debate, in the tristichs of the main part. He rejects with horror the nihilism of moral self-destruction. The impasse which precedes a suicide is caused by the impossibility of spiritual and moral life in community with others.[69] That is not a matter of discomforts and dangers as they are inevitable in a time of social upheaval; it is rather a question of the moral disintegration of the people with whom one is compelled to live. The essence of the misery is formulated in the line "Every man has a downcast face toward his fellow." The community of the spirit (or, for Egypt, we should say, of the *maat*) is destroyed. The fellow man casts down his eyes so that you will not read in them the deal he has made with evil and know that he has become a conniver. The isolation of the spiritual man among contemporaries who have committed moral suicide lets death appear as the friend who opens the gate from the prison of life. One should observe the metaphors of life as a disease and a prison— they are the metaphors that we shall find again in the dialogues of Plato. The last group of tristichs gives the reasons for suicide as the moral solution. It is not a mere escape from an unbearable situation but the way to redeeming action. In the beyond, the man will be a living god who can help in repairing the evils of society by punishing criminals, restoring worship and offerings in the temples, and effectively appealing to the god.

The poem will gain in meaning if we remember the experience of consubstantiality. The age is in turmoil because the mediation of divine substance through the Pharaoh has broken down. In this situation man can strengthen divine substance by committing suicide and joining the living gods who can let their substance pervade society more effectively

---

[69] In the text we must concentrate on the causes of the impasse in this particular case. We cannot dwell on the brilliant psychology of impasse and suicide in general that is contained in the poem. The subtleties of Egyptian psychology have not yet received the attention which they deserve.

than a mere man. That may sound odd, but it is in keeping with the Egyptian "form" of the myth. The poet is bound experientially to the mediation of right existence through the order of society; he cannot dream of communities outside the political order immediate under God; and salvation through an effective Pharaoh is apparently not in sight. The proposed suicide is the extreme, but apparently the only effective, way for an Egyptian individual to let his substance participate in the restoration of order. If we compare the solution with the Confucian transfer of the princely *tao* and *teh* to the sage, it certainly is an extraordinary substitute for the Pharaonic ordering function.

It is possible, as we said, that this poem on suicide will cast some light on the meaning of the Coffin Text. The idea that the text contains the program of an egalitarian revolution is too improbable to be considered. It rather seems that the analysis of the impasse situation was driven in the Coffin Text one step further, to the insight that no man is without guilt, not even the author. Everybody is involved, through the passions of his heart, in the evil that preferentially he sees only in his surroundings. The Coffin Text understands men as equal, not only in their god-created capacity for good, but also in their own capacity for evil. Only in the beyond will their souls open to the peace of the god. Whether the position implies a hope, as does the poem on suicide, that the perfect community of the dead will influence the society of the living, or whether it is an expression of radical pessimism with regard to earthly affairs is a matter for conjecture. The text contains no clues.

4. Akhenaton

The tenacity of the Egyptian political form under the pressure of new experiences was put to its most spectacular test in the period of the New Kingdom, through the so-called Amarna Revolution. The events of the time are more immediately associated with the name of the royal reformer Akhenaton (Amenhotep IV, 1375–1358 B.C.); and no doubt, the revolution received its signature from the personality of the Pharaoh, from his reform of the cult, and in particular from the expression of his spiritualism in the hymns to Aton. He was the first religious reformer clearly distinguishable as an individual, not in the history of Egypt only but of mankind. Nevertheless, his politico-religious reform had its antecedents and causes; and an appraisal of its precise nature requires an understanding of the circumstances that would, for a few years, open the historical clearing in which he could move, only to close in again and cut his work short with abrupt failure.

The vicissitudes of the Pharaonic order—the disintegration of the Old Kingdom, the subsequent Time of Troubles, the restoration of the Middle Kingdom, the second breakdown and the Hyksos invasion, the expulsion of the invaders, perhaps with foreign aid, and the renewed unification under the rulers from Thebes—had left their marks on both the organization of the empire and the position of the Pharaoh. A ruler of the New Kingdom was no longer a Menes, who, in the flush of his creative victory, could shuffle the gods to suit his conquest. He was more humbly an instrument of the gods, by their grace chosen to restore and preserve a millennial order not of his making, an order that had more than once been mismanaged by his predecessors. The eclipses of the political regime had diminished the prestige of the Pharaoh in relation to the lasting regime of the gods; and correspondingly the prestige of the priesthoods of the lasting gods had noticeably increased. In particular the priesthood of the Amon of Thebes had become a political power balancing the Pharaoh's. It was a solid power, deriving its strength from long historical accumulation. Three times Egypt had been founded and restored by rulers from the South; twice the political center had moved northward, strengthening the influence of the Re of Heliopolis. This time, the third time, the southern god kept his instrument under control; Thebes became the capital of the New Kingdom, and the Amon-Re of Thebes the empire god.

Nevertheless, the Pharaoh was still the ruler of Egypt. And his position had acquired even a new poignancy, precisely because he, as an individual, was the instrument of the gods. If he no longer shone in the primordial luster of the conqueror and creator, he radiated the milder light of the savior and benefactor. This messianic quality of the individual ruler becomes tangible in the sources as early as the twenty-second century B.C.

The "Instructions" of a ruler of the Faiyum of that period for his son Merikare reveals the Pharaoh's faith in an invisible god "who knows men's characters." The son is admonished,

> More acceptable is the character of one upright of
>   heart, than the ox of the evildoer.
> Act for the god, that he may act similarly for thee. . .
> The god is aware of him who acts for him.

The god is the creator and benefactor of mankind, and in his scheme the ruler has a definite function:

> Well directed are men, the cattle of the god.
> He made heaven and earth according to their desire. . . .
> He made the breath of life for their nostrils.
> They who have issued from his body are his images.
> He arises in heaven according to their desire.
> He made for them plants, animals, fowl, and fish to feed them. . . .
> He makes the light of day according to their desire,
>   and he sails by in order to see them.
> He has erected a shrine around about them,
>   and when they weep he hears.
> He made for them rulers even in the egg,
>   a supporter to support the back of the disabled.
> Give the love of thee to the whole world.[70]

The designation of mankind as the "cattle of the god" is not an occasional metaphor; the phrase cuts to the heart of the Pharaonic ethos. The "Admonitions of Ipu-wer," of the same period, elaborate the idea in holding up the image of the perfect Pharaoh:

> Men shall say:
> He is the herdsman of all men.
> Evil is not in his heart.
> Though his herds may be small, still he has spent the day caring for
>   them.

Such a herdsman

> Would smite down evil; he would stretch forth the arm against it;
> He would destroy the seed thereof and their inheritance.

When, however, evil is rampant, man will look for the herdsman and not find him:

> Where is he today? Is he then sleeping?
> Behold, the glory thereof cannot be seen. . . .

From the contrast between function and failure of the Pharaoh will arise bitter questions and skepticism:

> Authority, Perception, and Justice are with thee,[71]
> but it is confusion which thou wouldst set throughout the land,
> together with the noise of contention.

[70] Pritchard (ed.), *Ancient Near Eastern Texts*, 417 ff.
[71] Cf. § 2, n. 6, *supra*.

Men conform to that which thou hast commanded. . . .
Does then the herdsman love death? [72]

The pointed question makes the Pharaoh responsible for the disorder; when men misbehave, they still execute the will of the ruler. The character of the individual Pharaoh, thus, becomes the condition of domestic peace. From the depth of the misery will then arise the hope for a messianic ruler who by his personal qualities will bring happier days, as we find it expressed in the "Prophecies of Neferrohu," from the beginning of the reign of Amenemhet I (2000–1970 B.C.):

> Then it is that a king will come,
> belonging to the south, Ameni, the triumphant, his name.
> He is the son of a woman of the land of Nubia;
> he is one born in Upper Egypt. . . .
> Rejoice, ye people of his time!
> The son of a man will make his name forever and ever.
> They who are inclined toward evil and who plot rebellion have subdued their speech for fear of him.
> The Asiatics will fall to his sword, and the Libyans will fall to his flame.
> The rebels belong to his wrath, and the treacherous of heart to the awe of him. [73]

In the New Kingdom the savior-king had to come to terms with the conditions of an expansive world-empire and its military, civil, and sacerdotal bureaucracies. The latent tension is noticeable in the account given by Thutmose III of his own rulership (*ca.* 1450 B.C.). On the one hand, he is the son of Amon-Re, the great conqueror who has expanded the frontiers of Egypt:

> The god is my father, and I am his son.
> He commanded to me that I should be upon his throne,
> while I was still a nestling. . . .
> He made all foreign countries come bowing down to the
> fame of my majesty. . . .
> He has given victory through the work of my hands, to
> extend the frontiers of Egypt. . . .
> He is rejoicing in me more than in any other king who
> has been in the land since it was first set apart.
> I am his son, the beloved of his majesty.

[72] Pritchard (ed.), *Ancient Near Eastern Texts,* 443.
[73] *Ibid.,* 445 ff.

On the other hand, he is a former Amon priest, advanced to rulership by the sacerdotal college for obscure reasons, and very much indebted to his god:

> I repay his good with good greater than it, by making him greater
>   than the other gods.
> The recompense for him who carries out benefactions is a repayment
>   to him of even greater benefactions.
> I have built his house with the work of eternity. . . .
> I have extended the places of him who made me.
> I have provisioned his altars upon earth. . . .
> I know for a fact that Thebes is eternity,
>   that Amon is everlastingness. . . .[74]

When reading this double account of brilliant victory and payment of debts, one begins to wonder how long the harmony could last. Sooner or later this son of the god, with his competent army, would find that he had paid his debt to the god, and that he could dispense with the priestly kingmakers of Thebes. That is what in fact happened two generations after Thutmose the Great, when the empire, thanks to his victories, had experienced a period of stability.[75]

The revolt of Akhenaton against the Amon of Thebes has a complex structure. It is both institutional and spiritual, both revolutionary and reactionary. The institutional aspects are easy to grasp. The Pharaoh, still by his Amon name Amenhotep IV, founded the cult of the new god Aton, equipped it lavishly with land grants, changed his residence from Thebes to a newly founded city farther north, on the site of the present Tell el-Amarna, and resorted to radical measures when he encountered resistance from the established sacerdotal colleges. They were dispossessed and the worship of their gods discontinued. The special wrath of the king was directed against Amon. The name of the god was erased by gangs of hatchet men from inscriptions wherever it was to be found; and the zealous employees even erased the name of the god in the name of the king's father Amenhotep. The king himself changed his own name to Akhenaton, probably meaning the Spirit of Aton. For Egyptian so-

---

[74] *Ibid.*, 446 ff.

[75] For the political history of the period see the respective sections in Eduard Meyer, *Geschichte des Altertums*, II/1; for the antecedents of the Amarna Revolution and the history of Akhenaton itself, Wilson, *The Burden of Egypt*; for the intellectual history of the period in general, Breasted, *The Dawn of Conscience*

ciety that was a major upheaval, in so far as a new ruling group of the followers of the king was established in power while the old ruling class associated with the priesthood of Thebes fell into disgrace and suffered severe losses of property. The people at large also must have been materially affected by the changes, because hordes of retainers, of craftsmen and merchants, connected with the Amon cult lost their sustenance. The institutional overthrow could be successful only because the king had the army, with its able commander Haremhab, on his side.

The other aspects of the revolt are more elusive because of the paucity of sources. In particular, the prehistory of the god Aton is obscure. He certainly was not created by Akhenaton, though his existence cannot be traced farther back than the reign of the king's father Amenhotep III, or at the utmost the reign of Thutmose IV. The word *aton* was of old usage; it designated the sun disk in its physical appearance, without reference to a god. The Aton as a sun-god appeared for the first time in inscriptions of the immediately preceding reigns; and under Amenhotep III he seems to have received a temple in Thebes, apparently not in conflict with Amon. The implications of the new divine appearance can perhaps be surmised in a sun-hymn from the reign of Amenhotep III (*ca.* 1413–1377 B.C.). It is a hymn to Amon-Re. But the term sun-disk, *aton*, is used in addressing the god:

> Hail to thee, sun disc of the daytime, creator of all and maker of their living!

Moreover, this sun-god is addressed in the previously discussed messianic phraseology:

> Valiant herdsman, driving his cattle,
> Their refuge and the maker of their living.

And, finally, he is a world-god, shining over all lands, not only over Egypt:

> The sole lord, who reaches the ends of all lands every day,
> Being thus one who sees them treading thereon.[76]

The hymn suggests that a resistance to the Amon of Thebes and his priesthood was building up under the preceding reign. Since by the rule of consubstantiality the character of the sun-god also applies to the

[76] "A Universalist Hymn to the Sun," in Pritchard (ed.), *Ancient Near Eastern Texts,* 367 ff. Breasted, in *Dawn of Conscience,* 275–77, had drawn attention to the importance of the hymn as an antecedent to the Aton cult of Amenhotep IV.

Pharaoh, the messianic terms would indicate a sharpened consciousness of the Pharaoh as the savior-king. And the insinuation of the *aton* into the appellation of the god would indicate a search for a divinity distinct from Amon-Re. The search for the nature of divine being was advancing to the point where a new name had to be found, in order to characterize its oneness and supremacy as lying beyond the Egyptian pantheon. Moreover, the accent (for the first time in the extant sources) on the sun-god's shining over all lands and all mankind suggests the expansion of the Egyptian frontiers and the creation of a world-empire through Dynasty XVIII as the experience that set into motion the new politico-theological speculation. Only such surmises are possible; but they are sufficient to assume at least a generation of experiential and symbolic preparation for the revolt of Akhenaton.

The hymns of Akhenaton are preserved through inscriptions in the tombs of his nobles. For the complete text and an elaborate interpretation the reader should refer to the work of Breasted.[77] We shall touch only on the few points that have a bearing on the development of Egyptian political form.

In the revolt, as well as in the form which it assumed, the personality of the Pharaoh was a decisive factor. The following passages will suggest the character of his spiritualism that set him apart and motivated his revolt:

> Thou dawnest beautifully on the horizon of the sky,
> Thou living Aton, the beginning of life!
> Thou art gracious, great, glistening, and high over every land,
> Thy rays encompass the lands to the limit of all that thou hast made.
>
> All cattle rest upon their pasturage,
> The trees and the plants are flourishing,
> The birds flutter from their nests,
> Their wings uplifted in adoration to thee,
> All beasts spring up on their feet,
> All creatures that fly or alight,
> They live when thou hast risen for them.
> The ships sail up-stream and down-stream alike,
> Every high-way is open at thy appearance.
> The fish in the river dart before thy face;
> Thy rays are in the midst of the great green sea.

---

[77] Breasted, *The Dawn of Conscience*, Chap. 15, "Universal Dominion and Earliest Monotheism." The quotations from the hymns following in the text are frequently adjusted in the light of Wilson's translation in Pritchard (ed.), *Ancient Near Eastern Texts*, 369–71.

This is a new voice in history, the voice of a man intimately sympathetic with nature, sensitive to the splendor of light and its life-spending force, praising the god and his creature. And the joyful response to the appearance of the god, described in the hymn, is carried on by the hymn itself as the response of the royal soul to the splendor of Aton.

> The Aton is the creator-god:
> O sole god, like whom there is no other!
> Thou didst create the world according to thy desire,
> While thou wert alone.

But he has now become expressly the creator of all mankind, including the foreign peoples:

> The countries of Syria and Nubia, the land of Egypt,
> Thou settest every man in his place,
> Thou suppliest their necessities:
> Everyone has his food and the time of his life is reckoned.
> Their tongues are divers in speech,
> And their forms as well;
> Their skins are distinguished,
> As thou distinguishest the foreign peoples.

The imperial expansion has broken the infoldedness that we could observe in the hymns of the Old Kingdom. The world has opened, and foreign peoples are within the confines of the empire. Their common humanity becomes apparent in spite of their racial, linguistic, and cultural differences. The god is now understood as a god for all men.

In spite of its universalist and egalitarian aspects, however, the hymn is neither monotheistic, nor does it proclaim a redeemer god for all men. The creation of the Aton is more radical than any of the preceding attempts to arrive at an understanding of the nature of divinity, but it still lies within the range of the polytheistic myth. Akhenaton proceeded by excluding other gods, in particular, the hated Amon. But his very zeal in eradicating the name of Amon from the inscriptions, thereby to destroy his effectiveness magically, shows that the Amon was a reality for him that had to be taken into account. Moreover, he did not prosecute the other gods with the same zeal. The Re of Heliopolis was at least tolerated; and in the hymn itself Aton was identified with the three old solar deities Re, Harakhte, and Shu. It would rather seem that there was a streak of reaction in Akhenaton's revolution in so far as he hearkened back to the divinities which had endowed with glory the Pharaohs of the Old Kingdom. The reassertion of the royal position against the sacerdotal incubus of Thebes fortified itself by remembering the older gods.

The reactionary streak, perhaps not sufficiently observed, makes itself felt also in the personal relation between the king and his god. The Aton is a god for everybody's nature, but only for the king's soul:

> Thou art in my heart,
> And there is no other that knows thee,
> Save thy son [Akhenaton].
> For thou hast made him well-versed
> In thy plans and in thy might.

The position of the Pharaoh as the exclusive mediator between god and man was re-established with a vengeance. The personal religiousness of the people, which had been growing ever since the First Intermediate Period, was to be diverted to the Pharaoh as the god on earth. At least that is what Akhenaton attempted. The Osiris cult was severely repressed. The inscriptions from the tombs of the officials reveal the new emphasis on the monopoly of divine radiation that was held by the administration under the king. In the tomb of Tutu, a high court official under the regime, the king is described as the son of Aton, living in truth, coming forth from the rays of the sun-god, and established by him as the ruler over the circuit of Aton. The god endows the king with his own eternity and makes him to his likeness; the king is the emanation of the god. Aton is in heaven, but his rays are on earth; and the king, being the son of the rays, is the god's instrument in working his designs on earth. The god hears for the king what is in his heart, and he utters for the king what comes forth from his mouth. As the god begets himself every day without ceasing, so the king is formed out of his rays to live forth the life of Aton. The king is "living in the truth" of the god as the god's truth lives in him; and the official executes this truth, and is able to do so, in so far as the king's *ka* lives in him. The substance of the god, his *maat*, thus percolates through the realm and ultimately reaches the subjects.[78] But the subject has no access to the Aton directly. When the Aton rises in the world he embraces his beloved son Akhenaton; and the royal son, through his rule and administration, returns the world to the god as his offering. The subject can participate in the circulation of divine substance only through obedience to the Pharaoh.[79]

[78] "Tomb of Tutu," in Breasted, *Ancient Records of Egypt*, II, §§ 1009–1013.
[79] "Tomb of Mai," *ibid.*, 1000.

The beauty of the hymns to Aton, the "modern" atmosphere of individualism, of intellectual excitement, of realism in art, of humanization of the court ceremonial, and of a general civilizational nervousness, have been a temptation to find in the reforms of Akhenaton more than they contain. To be sure, the king was an extraordinary individual. Nevertheless, when all is taken into account, his work reveals the impasse of the Pharaonic symbolism rather than a new beginning. He was a mystical aesthete of high rank and could animate the form, for the last time, with his spiritual fervor. But that was all, as far the political order of Egypt was concerned. He neglected the administrative and military needs of the empire, and he had nothing to give to the people. Toward the end of his regime, as far as the sources indicate the state of affairs, he was compelled to compromise. And his successor Tutankhaton became again Tutankhamon and capitulated to Thebes. The form remained unshaken to the end by foreign conquest.

PART TWO

The Historical Order of Israel

The compact experience of cosmological order proved to be tenacious. Neither the rise and fall of Mesopotamian empires nor the repeated crises of imperial Egypt could break the faith in a divine-cosmic order of which society was a part. To be sure, the contrast between the lasting of cosmic and the passing of social order did not remain unobserved, but the observation did not penetrate the soul decisively and, consequently, did not lead to new insights concerning the true order of being and existence. Political catastrophes continued to be understood as cosmic events decreed by the gods. In the Sumerian Lamentations over the destruction of Ur by the Elamites, for instance, the Elamitic attack was experienced as the storm of Enlil:

> Enlil called the storm—the people groan.
> The storm that annihilates the land he called—the people groan.
> The great storm of heaven he called—the people groan.
> The great storm howls above—the people groan.
> The storm ordered by Enlil in hate, the storm which wears away the
>   land,
> Covered Ur like a garment, enveloped it like a linen sheet.

A cosmic shroud, as it were, was thrown by the god over the city and its streets filled with corpses.[1] In Egypt, it is true, institutional breakdowns caused the variety of responses studied in the preceding chapter. The experience of order, more deeply shaken than in Mesopotamia, moved toward the limits that became visible in the Amon Hymns in the wake of the Amarna Revolution.[2] Man, in his desire for a new freedom, seemed on the verge of opening his soul toward a transcendent God; and the new religiousness, indeed, achieved a surprising feat of monotheistic speculation. Nevertheless, even in the Amon Hymns, the attraction of the divine

---

[1] From the "Lamentations over the Destruction of Ur," translated by S. N. Kramer, in Pritchard (ed.), *Ancient Near Eastern Texts*, 455–63.

[2] Chapter 3.3.1.

magnet was not strong enough to orient the soul toward transcendent being. The Egyptian poets could not break the bond of Pharaonic order and become the founders of a new community under God.

And yet, it was their age in which the bond was broken. The Amon Hymns were created under Dynasty XIX, *ca.* 1320–1205 B.C. And this was the dynasty under which, according to recent trends of conjecture, occurred the Exodus of Israel from Egypt. Ramses II is supposed to be the Pharaoh of the oppression, his successor Merneptah (1225–1215) the Pharaoh of the Exodus. While such precise suppositions may be doubtful, the thirteenth century B.C. in general was probably the age of Moses. At the time when the Egyptians themselves strained their cosmological symbolism to the limits without being able to break the bonds of its compactness, Moses led his people from bondage under Pharaoh to freedom under God.

In pragmatic history the event was too unimportant to be registered in the Egyptian records. The people who followed Moses consisted of a number of Hebrew clans which had been employed by the Egyptian government on public works, probably in the region east of the Delta. They fled eastward into the desert and settled, for at least a generation, in the neighborhood of Kadesh before advancing to Canaan. In the centralized welfare state from which they fled they had probably not been treated worse than the native population of the same social status. Nevertheless, Egypt had been a house of bondage to a people whose nomadic soul thirsted for the freedom of the desert. When the freedom was gained, however, it proved of dubious value to men who had become accustomed to a different way of life. On the material level, perhaps there was not much to choose between nomadic existence and public works in a welfare state. The frugality of desert life aroused nostalgic memories of the Egyptian cuisine; and for all we know, the house of bondage might have become a home to which the tribes ruefully returned. Even without such an anticlimax the Exodus still would hardly have been worth remembering. If nothing had happened but a lucky escape from the range of Egyptian power, there only would have been a few more nomadic tribes roaming the border zone between the Fertile Crescent and the desert proper, eking out a meager living with the aid of part-time agriculture. But the desert was only a station on the way, not the goal; for in the desert the tribes found their God. They entered into a covenant with him, and thereby became his people. As a new type of people, formed by God, Israel conquered the promised land. The memory of Israel preserved the otherwise unimportant story, because the irruption of the spirit transfigured the pragmatic event into a drama of the soul and the acts of the drama into symbols of divine liberation.

The events of the Exodus, the sojourn at Kadesh, and the conquest of Canaan became symbols because they were animated by a new spirit. Through the illumination by the spirit the house of institutional bondage became a house of spiritual death. Egypt was the realm of the dead, the Sheol, in more than one sense. From death and its cult man had to wrest the life of the spirit. And this adventure was hazardous, for the Exodus from Sheol at first led nowhere but into the desert of indecision, between the equally unpalatable forms of nomad existence and life in a high-civilization. Hence, to Sheol and Exodus must be added the Desert as the symbol of the historical impasse. It was not a specific but the eternal impasse of historical existence in the "world," that is, in the cosmos in which empires rise and fall with no more meaning than a tree growing and dying, as waves in the stream of eternal recurrence. By attunement with cosmic order the fugitives from the house of bondage could not find the life that they sought. When the spirit bloweth, society in cosmological form becomes Sheol, the realm of death; but when we undertake the Exodus and wander into the world, in order to found a new society elsewhere, we discover the world as the Desert. The flight leads nowhere, until we stop in order to find our bearings beyond the world. When the world has become Desert, man is at last in the solitude in which he can hear thunderingly the voice of the spirit that with its urgent whispering has already driven and rescued him from Sheol. In the Desert God spoke to the leader and his tribes; in the Desert, by listening to the voice, by accepting its offer, and by submitting to its command, they at last reached life and became the people chosen by God.

What emerged from the alembic of the Desert was not a people like the Egyptians or Babylonians, the Canaanites or Philistines, the Hittites or Arameans, but a new genus of society, set off from the civilizations of the age by the divine choice. It was a people that moved on the historical scene while living toward a goal beyond history. This mode of existence was ambiguous and fraught with dangers of derailment, for all too easily the goal beyond history could merge with goals to be attained within history. The derailment, indeed, did occur, right in the beginning. It found its expression in the symbol of Canaan, the land of promise. The symbol was ambiguous because, in the spiritual sense, Israel had reached the promised land when it had wandered from the cosmological Sheol to the *mamlakah*, the royal domain, the Kingdom of God. Pragmatically, however, the Exodus from bondage was continued into the conquest of Canaan by rather worldly means; further, to a Solomonic kingdom with the very institutional forms of Egypt or Babylon; and, finally, to political disaster and destruction that befell Israel like any other people in history. On its pragmatic wandering through the centuries Israel did not escape the realm of the dead. In a symbolic countermovement to the Exodus under the leadership of Moses, the last defenders of Jerusalem, carrying Jeremiah with them against his will, returned to the Sheol of Egypt to die. The promised land can be reached only by moving through history, but it cannot be conquered within history. The Kingdom of God lives in men who live in the world, but it is not of this world. The ambiguity of Canaan has ever since affected the structure not of Israelite history only but of the course of history in general.

The brief sketch of the issues raised by the appearance of Israel in history suggests a considerable amount of complications in the detail. There are difficulties of chronology; there is the relation between Hebrews, Israel, Judah, and the Jews; the relation between Israel and the surrounding Syriac society, whose importance has been revealed to us by recent archaeological discoveries; the relation between the Biblical narrative and the history that can be reconstructed from external evidence; and, finally, the relation between pragmatic and spiritual history that issued into the Christian problem of profane and sacred history. These questions should be hurdles enough for a study of the peculiar order of Israel. But they are further complicated by the state and history of our literary sources. There must be taken into account the transformations which the early traditions of Israel have undergone through the postexilic redaction; the deformations of meaning caused by rabbinical and Christian canonization and interpretations; the further subtle changes of meaning imposed on the Hebrew text of the Bible by the English translations since the sixteenth century A.D., changes which have hardened into conventions to such a degree that even contemporary translations of the Bible do not dare to deviate from them; and, finally, the cloud of debate thrown up by a century of lower and higher criticism that settles in thick layers of controversy on every problem. We have today reached a state in which competent scholars write volumes on the "Theology of the Old Testament" or the "Religion of Israel," while other, equally competent scholars raise the questions whether a theology can be found in the Old Testament at all or whether Israel had a religion.

It is dangerously easy to be swallowed up by the Sheol of history and philology. In order to avoid such a fate, we shall skirt the controversy and cut straight to the great issue that lies at its root, that is, to the creation of history by Israel. Once the great, embracing issue of history is clarified, the method that must be used in treating the secondary problems will also be clear.[3]

[3] For the state of controversy concerning Old Testament problems cf. H. H. Rowley (ed.), *The Old Testament and Modern Study. A Generation of Discovery and Research* (Oxford, 1951).
The following works were used throughout the study of Israelite problems:
GENERAL—William F. Albright, *From the Stone Age to Christianity* (1940; 2d ed., Baltimore, 1946). *Id.*, "Syrien, Phoenizien und Palaestina," *Historia Mundi*, II. S. A. Cook, the articles in *Cambridge Ancient History*, I (1924), Chap. 5; II (1924), Chap. 14; III (1925), Chaps. 17–20; VI (1927); Chap. 7. Walter Eichrodt, "Religionsgeschichte Israels," *Historia Mundi*, II. Adolphe Lods, *Histoire de la Littérature Hébraique et Juive. Des Origines à la Ruine de l'Etat Juif (135 après J.-C.)* (Paris, 1950). Meyer, *Geschichte des Altertums*, II/1, II/2. W. O. E. Oesterley and Theodore H. Robinson, *Hebrew Religion. Its Origins and Development* (2d ed., 1937; London, 1952). Johannes Pedersen, *Israel. Its Life and Culture*, 4 vols. (London-Copenhagen), I–II (1926); III–IV (1940). Max Weber, *Das Antike Judentum* (Gesammelte Aufsaetze zur Religionssoziologie, III, Tuebingen, 1921).
HISTORIES OF ISRAEL—Albrecht Alt, *Kleine Schriften zur Geschichte des Volkes Israel*, 2 vols. (Munich, 1953). Rudolf Kittel, *Geschichte des Volkes Israel* (Stuttgart-Gotha), I (5th–6th eds., 1923); II (5th ed., 1922); III (1927). Adolphe Lods, *Israel from its Beginnings to the Middle of the Eighth Century* (Engl. ed., 1932; London, 1948). *Id.*, *The Prophets and the Rise of Judaism* (Engl. ed., 1937; London, 1950). Martin Noth, *Geschichte Israels* (1950; 2d ed., Goettingen, 1954). W. O. E. Oesterley and Theodore H. Robinson, *A History of Israel*, 2 vols. (1923; Oxford, 1951). Julius Wellhausen, *Prolegomena zur Geschichte Israels* (1878; 6th ed., Berlin, 1950). *Id.*, *Israelitisch-Juedische Geschichte* (1894; 7th ed., Berlin, 1914).
INTRODUCTION TO THE OLD TESTAMENT—Aage Bentzen, *Introduction to the Old Testament*, 2 vols. (Copenhagen, 1948). Otto Eissfeldt, *Einleitung in das Alte Testament* (Tuebingen, 1934). Ivan Engnell, *Gamla Testamentet. En Traditionshistorisk Inledning*, I (Stockholm, 1945). Robert H. Pfeiffer, *Introduction to the Old Testament* (New York, 1941).
SOURCES, TRANSLATIONS, AND COMMENTARIES—*Biblia Hebraica*, ed. Rudolf Kittel (8th ed., New York-Stuttgart, 1952). *Holy Bible. Hebrew and English*, trans. Isaac Leeser (New York, n.d.). *The Old Testament in Greek According to the Septuagint*, ed. H. B. Swete, 3 vols. (Cambridge, 1930–34). *The Holy Scriptures According to the Masoretic Text. A New Translation* (1937; Jewish Publication Society of America, Philadelphia, 1945). *The Old Testament. An American Translation*, ed. J. M. Powis Smith (1927; Chicago, 1944). *Die Fuenf Buecher der Weisung*, trans. Martin Buber-Franz Rosenzweig (Berlin, 1930). *The Holy Bible. Revised Standard Version* (New York, 1953). *Goettinger Handkommentar zum Alten Testament*, ed. W. Nowack. *Kommentar zum Alten Testament*, ed. E. Sellin. *Handbuch zum Alten Testament*, ed. Otto Eissfeldt.

CHAPTER 4

Israel and History

The major theoretical issues arising in a study of Israelite order have their common origin in the status of Israel as a peculiar people. Through the divine choice Israel was enabled to take the leap toward more perfect attunement with transcendent being. The historical consequence was a break in the pattern of civilizational courses. With Israel there appears a new agent of history that is neither a civilization nor a people within a civilization like others. Hence, we can speak of an Egyptian or a Mesopotamian but not of an Israelite civilization. In the Egyptian case, people and civilization roughly coincide. In the Mesopotamian case, we can distinguish major ethnic units, such as the Sumerian, Babylonian, Elamitic, and Assyrian, within the civilization. In the Israelite case, we encounter difficulties. Following Toynbee one can speak of a Syriac civilization to which belonged such peoples as the Israelites, the Phoenicians, the Philistines, and the Arameans of Damascus. But the mere enumeration of the ethnic subdivisions makes it unnecessary to argue further that Israel's position was peculiar; for the people that produced the literature of the Old Testament without a doubt stood apart from the others. Moreover, the course of Israelite history did not coincide chronologically with the course of Syriac civilization. It began before the Syriac civilization crystallized in history, and it took an independent, rather surprising development when the Syriac area was conquered successively by Assyrians, Babylonians, Persians, Greeks, and finally Romans.

1. *Israel and the Civilizational Courses*

We shall approach the peculiar status of Israel through questions of chronology. As far as absolute dates are concerned we accept the most recent opinion without further debate.[1] What interests us rather, is the

[1] A report on the archaeological evidence for Old Testament events and dates was given by W. F. Albright in Chapters 1 and 2 of H. H. Rowley (ed.), *The Old Testament and Modern Study. A Generation of Study and Research* (Oxford, 1951). See also W. F. Albright, *The Archaeology of Palestine* (Pelican Books, 1949).

question of the persons, facts, and events to which the dates are assigned.

A first chronological table can be constructed by assigning dates to the events narrated in the literature of the Old Testament, such as the stories of the patriarchs, the sojourn in Egypt, the Exodus, and so forth, down to the postexilic history. The result, confined to the principal events, will be something like the following:

Table I

Patriarchal Age	1900–1700 (?)
Emigration of the Jacob Clans to Egypt	1700 (?)
Exodus	*ca.* 1280
Main Hebrew Conquest of Canaan	*ca.* 1250–1225
Period of the Judges	1225–1020
The Kingdom (Saul to Solomon)	1020– 926
The Split of the Kingdom	926
Israel	926– 721
Judah	926– 586
Beginning of the Babylonian Exile	586
Building of the Second Temple	520– 516
Return of Nehemiah	445
Return of Ezra	397

A second table can be constructed by assigning dates to the migration waves and political dominations in the geographical area of Syria–Palestine:

Table II

Early Semitic Waves of Settlement	*ca.* 3000–2000
The Hyksos Movement (Semitic and Hurrian)	*ca.* 1680–1580
Egyptian Conquests	*ca.* 1580–1375
Habiru Attack on Canaan	*ca.* 1480–1350
Hittite Conquests	*ca.* 1390–1300
Egyptian Reconquest of Palestine	*ca.* 1350–1200
Israelite Invasion	*ca.* 1250–1225
Philistine Invasion	*ca.* 1190–1175
Period of Philistine Ascension	*ca.* 1080–1028
Consolidation of Israelite Power	*ca.* 1020– 926
Israel–Judah to Exile	926– 586
Assyrian Conquest of Israel	721
Babylonian Conquest of Judah	586
Persian Rule	538– 332
Macedonian Rule	332– 168
Maccabaean Period	168– 63
Roman Rule	63–0–395

Finally, one can construct a table by assigning dates to the main phases of the Syriac civilization in Toynbee's sense of the term. According to Toynbee's interpretation the Israelite and Philistine invasions in the Syro-Palestinian area created the situation in which the growth of an autonomous civilization could begin. The Hittite and Egyptian domination was broken, the independent Canaanite settlements were restricted to the northern coastal strip, the Philistines had settled on the southern coast, the Israelites in the hill country south of Syria. From this initial situation emerged into permanent political organization the kingdom of Damascus, the Phoenician city-states, and the kingdom of Israel. The main shock that cleared the area for its indigenous growth came from the invasion of the Minoan sea-peoples; and to Minoan culture Toynbee would also attribute the main influences in fertilizing the newly developing civilization. He is willing, therefore, to place the Syriac by the side of the Hellenic as affiliated to the Minoan civilization. This assumption, as we shall see, is hardly tenable in its general form, but it has an appreciable core of truth. Minoan influences in the Canaanite area were strong, indeed, even before the Philistine invasion; and the discoveries of Ugaritic mythological poems since 1930 have acquainted us with a Canaanite-Phoenician theogony that was at least as closely related to Hellenic theogony, as we know it from Hesiod, as to the Babylonian myth, if not more so.[2] The Syriac civilization that can be circumscribed in such terms had a comparatively short period of growth. It began to crystallize ca. 1150 B.C. and suffered the first, decisive check to its growth as early as 926 B.C., when the Solomonic kingdom was divided into Israel and Judah. At a time when the newly rising power of Assyria would have required military co-operation for the common defence, the Syriac states were involved in suicidal conflicts among themselves. The battle of Karkar, 854 B.C., gave a momentary respite; but ultimately it did no more than show that a military alliance of the Syriac states, if it had lasted, could perhaps have stemmed the Assyrian assault. The Syriac Time of Troubles ended with the establishment of a Universal State under the Persians. From Toynbee's interpretation results the following:

[2] The Ugaritic texts are available in the English translations by Cyrus H. Gordon, *Ugaritic Literature* (Rome, 1949) and by H. L. Ginsberg in Pritchard (ed.), *Ancient Near Eastern Texts*. For an analysis see W. F. Albright, *Archaeology and the Religion of Israel* (Baltimore, 1946).

Table III

Israelite-Philistine Invasion	*ca.* 1250–1175
The Growth of Syriac Civilization	*ca.* 1150– 926
Syriac Time of Troubles (The Prophets)	926– 538
Syriac Universal State (Persian Empire)	538– 332

The method of constructing several chronological tables for various classes of events has the advantage of bringing into view the various facets of meaning attaching to the so-called historical facts. This advantage is especially clear for the cases where events appear in more than one table. There is such an area of overlapping events, in all three of the tables, for the period from the Israelite invasion of Canaan to the fall of Jerusalem. In each of the tables the conquest of Canaan, for instance, has a meaning which differs according to the context. In Table I it is the fulfillment of a divine promise; in Table II it is one of the many waves of migration that washed into the geographical area of Palestine and left their ethnic sediment; in Table III it is part of the migrations which destroyed the Hittite and Egyptian domination of the area and cleared the space for the indigenous growth of a Syriac civilization. If the three tables were pooled into one, the differences of meaning would disappear, and there would result a flat string of "facts" in the not-too-well-defined sense of positivistic historiography.

Outside the period of overlapping events, the tables show remarkable divergences. In particular, a date for Moses and the Exodus is to be found only in Table I, not in II or III.

That a date for Moses should be absent from Table II is noteworthy but not surprising, for here we are dealing with the massive events of ethnic movements and imperial dominations. On the vast scale of these movements of peoples the tribes led by Moses from Egypt were an anonymous contributory factor. One must always be aware that Israel does not owe its importance in history to numbers. By the time of Solomon, it is perhaps well to remember, the people that we call "Israel" was a population in which the tribes of the Conquest had mixed with the Canaanite remnants of the millennial Aramaic waves, with Hurrians, Hittites and Philistines; and the Kingdom was ruled by the non-Israelitic Davidic dynasty.

Rather as a shock, however, comes the omission of Moses from Toynbee's construction of the Syriac civilization in Table III. In Toynbee's con-

ception of history "religions" are the "products" of disintegrating
societies. When the Syriac civilization disintegrated it produced the
Prophets and Judaism, just as later the disintegrating Hellenic civilization produced Jesus and Christianity. There is no room for Moses in a
history of Israel that begins only after the dust of the invasions has
settled, by *ca.* 1150 B.C. Where then—unless he be eliminated altogether
as a myth—should one look for Moses in this construction of history?
Toynbee finds him by assuming a "line of spiritual enlightenment," on
which both Judaism and Christianity can be placed in succession. If the
line is traced from the Prophets back into the past, one will find on it
Moses and, still earlier, Abraham, until one reaches the primitive worship
of Yahweh, whom Toynbee describes as "the *jinn* inhabiting and animating a volcano in North-Western Arabia." The subsidiary "line of spiritual
enlightenment," while cutting across the civilizations, is related at its
decisive points with the various Times of Troubles. Moses, thus, would be
"produced" by the disintegration of the Egyptian New Kingdom, Abraham by the Babylonian disintegration after Hammurabi—always suppos-
ing, and Toynbee is not certain, that Abraham and Moses were historical
figures at all.[3]

The constructions of the distinguished historian may sound strange,
but they certainly make good sense in terms of a study of civilizations.
Their relentless consistency at the price of casting doubts on the value of
the method must even be praised. For the method, so it seems, does not
apply either to the epiphany of Moses or to the constitution of Israel
through the Covenant; a crack shows, which is insufficiently repaired by
the subsidiary construction of a "line of spiritual enlightenment." If we
follow Toynbee, we have in our hands (1) an Israel whose history begins
only after the conquest of Canaan, (2) a line of spiritual enlightenment
from *jinn* to Jesus, (3) a Babylonian Abraham, and (4) an Egyptian
Moses. And when we look at this odd assortment, we begin to wonder what
has become of the Israel whose history is preserved in the Old Testament?

The difficulties arise from the confrontation of two types of history
represented respectively by Tables I and III. The Israel whose story is told
in the Old Testament does not fit into the picture drawn by our contemporary, critical historiography. The fact must be faced, and it should
be understood that there are no easy solutions. As far as compromises are
concerned, Toynbee's "line of spiritual enlightenment" should discourage

[3] Toynbee, *A Study of History*, V, 119 n.; VI, 39.

further attempts of a similar nature. And neither is it possible to abolish the difficulty by discarding one or the other of the two tables. On the one hand, the rise and fall of ordering power certainly is the stuff of which history is made; and if we accept this principle, we must also accept the scale of relevance by which Israel has a low rank in pragmatic history and, for the period of Moses, none at all. Hence, we cannot discard Table III. On the other hand, Jews and Christians have a disconcerting habit of outlasting the rise and fall of political powers; and we cannot eliminate Judaeo-Christian spiritual history without making nonsense of history in general. Hence, we cannot discard Table I. Both tables must be accepted as legitimate; and their conflict, therefore, must be dissolved by a theoretical analysis of its source.

We shall attack the problem by taking, for the moment, the pursuit of pragmatic history, as well as Table III, for granted, and look for the source of the trouble in Table I.

In the first chronology dates are assigned to the main events narrated in the literature of the Old Testament; and this procedure will, indeed, lead to difficulties. For the story told from Genesis to the end of II Kings is not a critical history of pragmatic events—not even where the reference to pragmatic events has a solid basis in contemporary historiography and court annals, as for the period of the Kingdom—but an account of Israel's relation with God. This does not mean that the account has no pragmatic core; for we have no more reason to doubt the existence of some sort of pragmatic Moses behind the story of Exodus than of some sort of a world behind the story of its creation in Genesis. Nevertheless, the events are not experienced in a pragmatic context of means and ends, as actions leading to results in the intramundane realm of political power, but as acts of obedience to, or defection from, a revealed will of God. They are experienced by souls who struggle for their attunement with transcendent being, who find the meaning of individual and social actions in their transfusion with the plans of God for man. When experienced in this manner, the course of events becomes sacred history, while the single events become paradigms of God's way with man in this world. Now, the criteria of truth applying to paradigmatic events in this sense cannot be the same as those applying to pragmatic events. For an event, if experienced in its relation to the will of God, will be truthfully related if its essence as a paradigm is carefully elaborated. Precision with regard to the

pragmatic details of time, location, participating persons, their actions and
speeches will be much less important than precision with regard to the
will of God on the particular occasion, as well as to the points of agreement, or disagreement, of human action with the divine will. Moreover,
an original account, once it has entered the stream of oral tradition, can
be submitted to reworking for the purpose of improving the paradigmatic
essence; stories can be dramatically pointed up, if necessary through
imaginative detail; and the meaning of speeches can be made more luminous through paraenetic interpolations. A pragmatic historian, to be sure,
would regret such transformations as a falsification of sources, but the
writer of sacred history will understand them as an increase of truth.

Sometimes, however, the traditions may prove too recalcitrant for the
taste of later writers; and the reworking of detail may be deemed insufficient for arriving at the paradigmatic truth. Then it may happen
that whole bodies of the tradition are recast in a more "modern" summary. The book that by an unfortunate tradition goes under the name of
Deuteronomy, for instance, is not a "fifth" book of Moses, but a huge
paraenesis appended to the Tetrateuch. Cast in the literary form of a
speech by Moses before his death, it summarizes the paradigmatic lesson
of Exodus, Desert, and Covenant as it was understood shortly before the
end of the Kingdom of Judah. Chronicles, in its turn, recasts the traditions of Kings so as to make them a suitable introduction to the accounts
of postexilic reconstruction by Ezra and Nehemiah. Such multiple paradigmatic histories, however, are still a comparatively simple matter. The
situation becomes even more confusing when we find several accounts of
what seems to be the same event, without being able to know why there
is more than one account. Of the conquest of Canaan, for instance, the
Old Testament furnishes the two incompatible accounts of Joshua and
the opening chapter of Judges. And we are left guessing whether the
same pragmatic event could, indeed, form the core of two such widely
differing versions, or whether the so-called conquest was not rather a
gradual infiltration of Hebrew tribes of which two phases happened to be
caught in the two versions, each elaborated paradigmatically so as to give
an exhaustive account of the symbolic Conquest. And, finally, we must
remember that the multiple histories and versions were integrated by the
postexilic redactors into a body of history with a meaning of its own; and
that the work of the redactors was not done in order to be disintegrated
by modern historians into the meanings of the component parts.

Reflection on this bewildering complex of successively superimposed meanings should make it clear that paradigmatic and pragmatic histories are not rivals. Israelite history was not written in order to confuse pragmatic historians who wryly assign a date to Moses while suspending judgment with regard to his existence. It does not want to give pragmatic history at all, even though over long stretches the pragmatic core is so tangible and clear in detail that we are better informed about certain phases of Israelite history than about our Western Middle Ages. It begins to dawn on us that history is a complicated fabric of which two strands become visible in the two chronologies. Perhaps what appears as a conflict between them will disappear when the pattern in the Israelite fabric of meanings becomes somewhat clearer. Hence, we shall now change our line of attack. Table III will no longer be taken for granted, but will be set aside as suspect of causing the trouble through its relative simplicity, while Israelite history will be accepted, in the hope that its more complex structure, if properly understood, will resolve our problem.

We shall start from the observation previously made, that Israelite sacred history cannot be discarded as unimportant even in pragmatic history, since by virtue of its possession Israel became the peculiar people, a new type of political society on the pragmatic plane. The men who lived the symbolism of Sheol, Desert, and Canaan, who understood their wanderings as the fulfilment of a divine plan, were formed by this experience into the Chosen People. Through the leap in being, that is, through the discovery of transcendent being as the source of order in man and society, Israel constituted itself the carrier of a new truth in history. If this be accepted as the essence of the problem, the paradigmatic narrative, with all its complications, gains a new dimension of meaning through its role in the constitution of Israel. For the truth which Israel carried would have died with the generation of the discoverers, unless it had been expressed in communicable symbols. The constitution of Israel as a carrier of the truth, as an identifiable and enduring social body in history, could be achieved only through the creation of a paradigmatic record which narrated (1) the events surrounding the discovery of the truth, and (2) the course of Israelite history, with repeated revisions, as a confirmation of the truth. This record is the Old Testament. Precisely when its dubiousness as a pragmatic record is recognized, the narrative reveals its function in creating a people in politics and history.

Hence, there is an intimate connection between the paradigmatic narrative of the Old Testament and the very existence of Israel, though it is not the connection that exists between a narrative and the events which it relates. The nature of this elusive relationship will become clearer if one remembers that no problem of this nature did arise in the treatment of Mesopotamian or Egyptian history. No Table I worried us in dealing with the ideas of Near Eastern empires. As soon as this negative observation is made, the significance of the table, not for Israelite history only, but for the problem of history in general, becomes evident. There was, indeed, no occasion to use a table of this kind in Mesopotamian or Egyptian history—for the good reason that neither of these civilizations produced an Old Testament. Israel alone constituted itself by recording its own genesis as a people as an event with a special meaning in history, while the other Near Eastern societies constituted themselves as analogues of cosmic order. Israel alone had history as an inner form, while the other societies existed in the form of the cosmological myth. History, we therefore conclude, is a symbolic form of existence, of the same class as the cosmological form; and the paradigmatic narrative is, in the historical form, the equivalent of the myth in the cosmological form. Hence it will be necessary to distinguish between political societies according to their form of existence: the Egyptian society existed in cosmological, the Israelite in historical form.

Now that the mystery of Table I is cleared up, at least to some extent, we can return to Table III and inspect more closely the Spengler-Toynbee theory of history that underlies its construction. The theory is simple and well reasoned. Spengler conceives of a civilization (a "culture" in his terminology) as the flowering of a collective soul in its historical landscape. The souls bloom only once; and the civilizations produced each move through the same series of phases, their respective "histories," conceived by organic analogies of youth and age. When their vitality is exhausted they flatten out into *fellahim* periods of indefinite duration. Each civilization, thus, has a history; but the succession of civilizations is not an additional history. The theory has good common sense arguments on its side. For the civilizations of the past have, indeed, flowered and declined, and the mechanics of the process is well understood. One may consider it possible that the history of mankind will not always be cast in the civilizational mold, but as long as it is transacted by the societies that we call civilizations, there is no reason to assume that the present and future ones will escape the fate of their predecessors.

The excellence of the arguments, however, will not assuage our unhappiness about the consequences. For the civilizations follow each other in a meaningless sequence; and when the manifold of civilizational souls is exhausted, as for Spengler it seems to be, mankind will subside into a-historical, vegetative existence. The prospect is depressing, and it becomes even bleaker when Toynbee applies his imagination to it. With the pessimistic Spengler one could at least hope that the melancholy spectacle of flowering and dying civilizations would soon come to an end; but with the more cheerful Toynbee one must fear that this sort of thing will be going on as long as the earth holds out. For, accepting figures given by Sir James Jeans for the duration of the earth, Toynbee calculates a future of 1,743 million civilizations. "Imagine 1,743 million completed histories, each of which has been as long and lively as the history of the Hellenic Society; 1,743 million reproductions of the Roman Empire and the Catholic Church and the Teutonic Voelkerwanderung; 1,743 million repetitions of the relations between our Western Society and the other societies that are alive to-day!" [4] "Our powers of imagination fail," exclaims the great historian in view of such prospects.[5]

We shudder politely, as always when invited to contemplate the infinity of time, space, or numbers under any other aspect than its transparency for the infinity of God, but firmly refuse to play the game. In order to avoid the inevitable failure of our imaginative powers, we shall presently apply our intellect to the issue. For the moment be it stated only that the Spengler-Toynbee theory has, indeed, simplified matters—with the imaginative consequences just adumbrated. Moreover, we can now lay our finger on the defect, that is, its disregard for the problem of history as an inner form. Of the many factors which codetermine the defect, the one of most immediate interest must be sought in the historical situation in which the theory was formed. Both Spengler and Toynbee are burdened with the remnants of certain humanistic traditions, more specifically in their late liberal-bourgeois form, according to which civilizations are mystical entities producing cultural phenomena such as

---

[4] *Ibid.*, I, 463.

[5] For a further analysis of Toynbee's ideas in the "Annex" to Vol. I see the study by Friedrich Engel-Janosi, "Krise und Ueberwindung des Historismus," *Wissenschaft und Weltbild*, VI (Vienna, 1953), 13 ff.

myths and religions, arts and sciences. Neither of the two thinkers has accepted the principle that experiences of order, as well as their symbolic expressions, are not products of a civilization but its constitutive forms. They still live in the intellectual climate in which "religious founders" were busy with founding "religions," while in fact they were concerned with the ordering of human souls and, if successful, founded communities of men who lived under the order discovered as true. If, however, the Israelite discovery of history as a form of existence is disregarded, then the form is rejected in which a society exists under God. The conception of history as a sequence of civilizational cycles suffers from the Eclipse of God, as a Jewish thinker has recently called this spiritual defect.[6] Spengler and Toynbee return, indeed, to the Sheol of civilizations, from which Moses had led his people into the freedom of history.

2. The Meaning of History

The Israelite conception of history, being the more comprehensive one, must be preferred to the defective Spengler-Toynbee theory of civilizational cycles which underlies the construction of Table III. Such preference, however, does not abolish the difficulties inherent in the Israelite conception. For, if the idea of history as a form of existence be accepted, the term "history" becomes equivocal. "History," then, could mean either the dimension of objective time in which civilizations run their course or the inner form which constitutes a society. The equivocation could easily be removed, of course, by using the term in only one of the two meanings; but the result would be unsatisfactory. If the first meaning be eliminated, so that only "existence in time" could be predicated of cosmological societies, Egypt or Babylon would have no history. If the second meaning be eliminated, as is done by Spengler and Toynbee, there would be no word for what is history in the just-established pre-eminent sense of a society's moving through time, on a meaningful course, toward a divinely promised state of perfection. And it would be most inconvenient to use it in both senses, because in that case some societies would be more historical than other historical societies. If the Israelite conception be preferred, it must now be put to work to resolve the problems of its own making.

The trouble originates in the following proposition: Without Israel there would be no history, but only the eternal recurrence of societies in

[6] Martin Buber, *Gottesfinsternis* (Zurich, 1953).

cosmological form. At a first glance, to be sure, the proposition looks absurd, for it leads to the baffling equivocations, and ultimately, perhaps, to the escape, of Spengler and Toynbee. But it will lose its absurdity if it be understood in its methodical strictness as a statement about the inner form of societies. It does not mean that before a future historian there would unfold an interminable succession of Platos, Christs, Roman Empires, and so forth, as Toynbee imagines in his flight of fancy. For "eternal recurrence" is the symbol by means of which a cosmological civilization expresses (or rather, can express, if it be so minded) the experience of its own existence, its lasting and passing, in the order of the cosmos. "Eternal recurrence" is part of the cosmological form itself—it is not a category of historiography, nor will it ever have a historian. A political society which understands its order as participation in divine-cosmic order for that reason does not exist in historical form. But, if it does not have historical form, does it have history at all? Are we not back to the absurdity that Egypt and Babylon have no history? Again the absurdity will dissolve, if intellect intervenes before imagination runs away. Cosmological civilizations, though not in historical form, are not at all devoid of history. Remembering our principles of the constancy of human nature, as well as of compactness and differentiation, we may expect history to be present in them quite as much as metaphysical and theological speculation, but to be bound by the compactness of cosmological form, not yet differentiated. And this presence will be revealed as soon as, through Israel, history is differentiated as a form of existence. We began our history of order not with Israel, but with the Mesopotamian and Egyptian empires, because in retrospect the struggle for order in the medium of cosmological symbols appeared to be the first phase in the search for the true order of being that was carried one step further by Israel. In particular, the Egyptian dynamics of experience proved of absorbing interest because it revealed the movement of the soul toward an understanding, never quite achieved, of the world-transcendent God.

The equivocation of "history," thus, dissolves into the problem of compactness and differentiation. Egyptian history, or for that matter Mesopotamian or Chinese history, though transacted in cosmological form, is genuine history. Nevertheless, the knowledge is not articulated in the compact symbolism of the cosmological civilizations themselves; the presence of history is discovered only in retrospect from a position in which history as the form of existence has already been differentiated. For

the first time we encounter the problem that will occupy us repeatedly—
that is, the genesis of history through retrospective interpretation. When
the order of the soul and society is oriented toward the will of God, and
consequently the actions of the society and its members are experienced
as fulfillment or defection, a historical present is created, radiating its
form over a past that was not consciously historical in its own present.
Whether through the radiation of historical form the past receives negative accents as the Sheol from which man must escape, or positive accents
as the *praeparatio evangelica* through which man must pass in order to
emerge into the freedom of the spirit, the past has become incorporated
into a stream of events that has its center of meaning in the historical present. History as the form in which a society exists has the tendency to expand its realm of meaning so as to include all mankind—as inevitably it
must, if history is the revelation of the way of God with man. History
tends to become world-history, as it did on this first occasion in the Old
Testament, with its magnificent sweep of the historical narrative from the
creation of the world to the fall of Jerusalem.

The tendency of historical form to expand its realm of meaning
beyond the present into the past implies a number of problems that will be
elaborated in their proper places in later sections of this study. In the
present context only the three most important ones will be briefly suggested. They are (1) the ontological reality of mankind, (2) the origin
of history in a historically moving present, and (3) the loss of historical
substance.

(1) In the first place, history creates mankind as the community of
men who, through the ages, approach the true order of being that has its
origin in God; but at the same time, mankind creates this history through
its real approach to existence under God. It is an intricate dialectical process whose beginnings, as we have seen, reach deep into the cosmological
civilizations—and even deeper into a human past beyond the scope of the
present study. The expansion of empire over foreign peoples, for instance,
brought into view the humanity of the conquered subjects. In the texts
from Thutmose III to Akhenaton the god who created Egypt was transformed into the god who also created the other peoples who now had
come into the imperial fold. The course of pragmatic history itself, thus,
provided situations in which a truth about God and man was seen—

though yet so dimly that the cosmological form of the society would not break. The realm of pragmatic conquest became transparent for the truth that the society of man is larger than the nuclear society of a cosmological empire. This observation should illuminate both the causal mechanism of differentiation and the objective reality of history. The inclusion of the past in history through retrospective interpretation is not an "arbitrary" or "subjective" construction but the genuine discovery of a process which, though its goal is unknown to the generations of the past, leads in continuity into the historical present. The historical present is differentiated in a process that is itself historical in so far as the compact symbolism gradually loosens up until the historical truth contained in it emerges in articulate form. From the articulate present, then, the inarticulate process of the past can be recognized as truly historical. The process of human history is ontologically real.

Nevertheless, there remains the ambiguity of a meaning created by men who do not know what they are creating; and this ambiguity quite frequently engenders the complacency that comes with supposedly superior knowledge, and in particular the all-too-well-known phenomenon of spiritual pride, in later generations. Such complacency and pride certainly are unfounded. For the ray of light that penetrates from a historical present into its past does not produce a "meaning of history" that could be stored away as a piece of information once for all, nor does it gather in a "legacy" or "heritage" on which the present could sit contentedly. It rather reveals a mankind striving for its order of existence within the world while attuning itself with the truth of being beyond the world, and gaining in the process not a substantially better order within the world but an increased understanding of the gulf that lies between immanent existence and the transcendent truth of being. Canaan is as far away today as it has always been in the past. Anybody who has ever sensed this increase of dramatic tension in the historical present will be cured of complacency, for the light that falls over the past deepens the darkness that surrounds the future. He will shudder before the abysmal mystery of history as the instrument of divine revelation for ultimate purposes that are unknown equally to the men of all ages.

(2) The retrospective expansion of history over the past originates in a present that has historical form. There arises, second, therefore, the whole complex of problems connected with the multiplicity of historical

presents. Each present has its own past; and there are, furthermore, the relations between the various presents, as well as between the histories created by them. Israelite was a first, but not the last, history; it was followed by the Christian, which extended its own form over the Israelite past and integrated it, through St. Augustine, into the symbolism of its *historia sacra*. Moreover, parallel with the Israelite occurred the Hellenic break with cosmological form, resulting in philosophy as the new form of existence under God; and the stream of Hellenic philosophy (whose relation to historical form will occupy us at considerable length) entered, and mingled with, the Judaeo-Christian stream of history. This manifold of successive, simultaneous, and mingling presents has a suspicious color of arbitrariness. The question arises whether anything like an objective, true history can result from such subjective, fictional constructions?

The question is legitimate; and the suspicion that history is a subjective interpretation of past events cannot be overcome by any amount of "exactness" in ascertaining the events. If there is such a thing as historical objectivity at all, its source must be sought in historical form itself; and conversely, if there is a suspicion of subjectivity, it must attach again to the form. Now, historical form, understood as the experience of the present under God, will appear as subjective only, if faith is misinterpreted as a "subjective" experience. If, however, it is understood as the leap in being, as the entering of the soul into divine reality through the entering of divine reality into the soul, the historical form, far from being a subjective point of view, is an ontologically real event in history. And it must be understood as an event of this nature, as long as we base our conception of history on a critical analysis of the literary sources which report the event and do not introduce subjectivity ourselves by arbitrary, ideological surmising. If now the men to whom it happens explicate the meaning of the event through symbols, the explication will cast an ordering ray of objective truth over the field of history in which the event objectively occurred.

Moreover, since the event is not fictional but real and the symbolic explication, therefore, is bound by the nature of the event, we can expect the various symbolizations of historical order, in spite of their profound individual differences, to conform to a general type. And this expectation is, indeed, fulfilled by the manifold of historical presents and their symbolizations. Moses led Israel from the death of bondage to the life of freedom under God. Plato discovered life eternal for the erotic souls and punishment for the dead souls. Christianity discovered the faith that saves man from the death of sin and lets him enter, as a new man, into the life of the spirit. In every instance of a present in historical form, the Either-Or of life and death divides the stream of time into the Before-and-After of the great discovery.

The content of the event, furthermore, provides the principle for the classification of men and societies, past, present, and future, according to the measure in which they approach historical form, remain distant, or recede from it. This principle, while remaining the same in every instance, will inevitably render different results according to the empirical horizon in which it is applied. There will always be the division of time into the Before-and-After, as well as the classification of contemporaries into those who join the Exodus, and thereby become the Chosen People, and those who remain in Sheol. The expansion of historical order beyond this center, however, will depend on the nature of the past that is experienced as socially effective in the present. The model for treating the effective past in relation to the historical present was set by St. Paul in Romans. The historical present was understood by St. Paul as the life under the divine revelation through Christ, while the effective past surrounding the new society was furnished by Jews and Gentiles. All three of the communities—Christians, Jews, and Gentiles—belonged to one mankind as they all participated in divine order; but the order had been revealed to them in different degrees of clarity, increasing in chronological succession. To the Gentiles the law was revealed through the spectacle of the divine creation; to the Jews through the Covenant and the issuing of a divine, positive command; to the Christians through Christ and the law of the heart. History and its order, thus, were established by the measure in which various societies approached to the maximal clarity of divine revelation. This was a masterful creation of historical order, centering in the present of St. Paul and covering the high points of his empirical horizon. Obviously, the construction could not be ultimate but would have to be amended with changes and enlargements of the empirical horizon; but, at least, it remained "true" for the better part of two millenniums.

When we reflect on this long span of time, we are reminded again of the cataclysmic events which, on the pragmatic level of history, formed a horizon like the Pauline and now are changing it. The Israelite and Christian historical forms have arisen in the pragmatic situation created by the multicivilizational empires since Thutmose III, and we have noted

how the conquests, even within Egyptian civilization, induced and clarified the idea of a more-than-Egyptian mankind under one creator-god.[7]
A similar pragmatic situation, only on a much larger scale, has been
created by the earth-wide, imperial expansion of Western civilization
since the sixteenth century A.D. Civilizations which formerly were to us
only dimly known, or entirely unknown, now fill the horizon massively;
and archaeological discoveries have added to their number a past of mankind that had been lost to memory. This enormous expansion of the
spatial and temporal horizon has burdened our age with the task of relating an ever more comprehensive past of mankind to our own historical
form of maximal clarity, which is the Christian. It is a work that has
barely begun.

(3) A society in existence under God is in historical form. From its
present falls the ray of meaning over the past of mankind from which it
has emerged; and the history written in this spirit is part of the symbolism by which the society constitutes itself. If the story of mankind is
understood as a symbol in this sense, we realize that it is exposed, as is
every symbol, to loss of substance. Long after the meaning has seeped out
of it, the symbol may still be used, as for instance when the past of mankind is not related to a present under God but to the opinions of an agnostic or nationalist historian. It is not necessary, however, to dwell on instances of this type in order to see that the symbol is threatened with grave
dangers. For the mass of materials that have a bearing on the meaningful
history of mankind tends, by its sheer weight, to disintegrate the meaning
which it is supposed to serve. As an archaeologist remarked recently: "In
one's enthusiasm for archaeological research, one is sometimes tempted to
disregard the enduring reason for any special interest in Palestine—nearly
all the Hebrew Old Testament is a product of Palestinian soil and Israelite
writers." [8] The inevitable specialization will penetrate into regions of
materials and problems far distant from the center of meaning, so remote
indeed that sometimes a specialist will consider the occupation with the
center of meaning alien to the task of the historian.

These hints should be sufficient to suggest the problem. We shall now

---

[7] See Oesterley and Robinson, *A History of Israel*, I, by Robinson, *From the Exodus to
the Fall of Jerusalem*, 586 B.C., 4 (hereinafter cited as Robinson, *A History of Israel*, I):
"Modern history properly begins with the year 1479 B.C., and treats of that epoch in the story
of our race which we may call the era of territorial imperialism." Robinson's elaboration of the
idea is dubious, but the idea itself certainly deserves closer attention.

[8] Albright, *The Archaeology of Palestine*, 219.

once more consider the Spengler-Toynbee theory, under the aspect that it dissolves history into a sequence of civilizational courses. The theory will appear odd, if one considers that a historian supposedly relates the past of mankind to a meaningful present. Why should a thinker be concerned about history at all, if apparently it is his purpose to show that there are no meaningful presents but only typical, recurrent situations and responses. This apparent oddity will now become intelligible as an expression of the tension between the Judaeo-Christian historical form, in which Western civilization still exists, and the loss of substance which it has suffered. The theory of civilizational cycles should not be taken at its face value; for if its authors were serious about it, they would no longer live in historical form and consequently not worry about history. The theory is of absorbing interest not only to its authors but also to their numerous readers because it reveals to our age history on the verge of being swallowed up by the civilizational cycles. The concern about civilizational decline has its roots in the anxiety stirred up by the possibility that historical form, as it was gained, might also be lost when men and society reverse the leap in being and reject existence under God. The form, to be sure, is not lost—at least not completely—as long as the concern inspires gigantic enterprises of historiography; but it certainly is badly damaged when the mechanics of civilizations occupies the foreground with massive brutality, while the originating present of history is pushed out of sight. The shift of accents is so radical that it practically makes nonsense of history, for history is the Exodus from civilizations. And the great historical forms created by Israel, the Hellenic philosophers, and Christianity did not constitute societies of the civilizational type—even though the communities thus established, which still are the carriers of history, must wind their way through the rise and fall of civilizations.

CHAPTER 5

The Emergence of Meaning

The present chapter will deal with the meaning of history in the Israelite sense. That meaning did not appear at a definite point of time to be preserved once for all, but emerged gradually and was frequently revised under the pressure of pragmatic events. As a consequence, the historical corpus of the Old Testament, reaching from Genesis through Kings, displays the rich stratification previously indicated. All the substrata, however, are overlaid by the meaning imposed by the final redaction, as well as by the arrangement of the books so that they will deliver the continuous narrative from the creation of the world to the fall of Jerusalem.

The intention of the postexilic authors to create a world-history must be accepted as the basis for any critical understanding of Israelite history. The Biblical narrative, as previously suggested, was not written in order to be disintegrated by exploring the Babylonian origin of certain mythologemes or by studying Bedouin customs that illuminate the Age of the Patriarchs, but in order to be read according to the intentions of their authors. A first approach to these intentions is given through Psalm 136.

Organized in three distinct parts the liturgical Psalm 136 gives something like a commentary on the governing principle of Israelite history. It opens with a preamble:

> Give thanks to Yahweh, for he is good,
> Give thanks to the God of gods,
> Give thanks to the Lord of lords.

And then follow the appositions, describing the feats of Yahweh for which thanks are due. First, the creation of the world:

> To him who did great wonders alone,
> To him who made the heavens with skill,
> To him who spread out the earth upon the waters,
> To him who made the great lights,
> The sun to rule by day,
> The moon and the stars to rule by night.

Second, the rescue from Egypt:

> To him who smote the Egyptians in their first-born,
> And brought forth Israel from the midst of them,
> With a strong hand and an outstretched arm,
> To him who divided the Sea of Sedge into two parts,
> And led Israel over through the midst of it,
> And shook Pharaoh and his army into the Sea of Sedge.

Third, the conquest of Canaan:

> To him who led his people through the wilderness,
> To him who smote great kings,
> And slew mighty kings,
> Sihon, the king of the Amorites,
> And Og, the king of Bashan,
> And gave their land as a possession,
> A possession to Israel, his servant.

The Psalm concludes with a summary invocation of the god who created both world and history:

> Who remembered us in our abasement,
> And rescued us from our foes,
> Who gives food to all flesh,
> Give thanks to the God of the heavens.

The drama of divine creation moves through the three great acts: the creation of the world, the rescue from Egypt, and the conquest of Canaan. Each of the three acts wrests meaning from the meaningless: the world emerges from Nothing, Israel from the Sheol of Egypt, and the promised land from the Desert. The acts thus interpret one another as works of divine creation and as the historical stages in which a realm of meaning grows: In history God continues his work of creation, and the creation of the world is the first event in history. To this conception the term "world-history" can be applied in the pregnant sense of a process that is world-creation and history at the same time. In its sweep the Old Testament narrative surveys the process from the creative solitude of God to its completion through the establishment of the servants of Yahweh in the land of promise. As in the Amon Hymns one could discern speculative structures which in later history would be differentiated, so one can discern in the compactness of the Israelite historical symbolism the outlines of the three great blocks of Thomistic speculation: God, the creation, and the return of the creation to God. That Israelite history contains this speculative structure, though yet in undifferentiated form, is the secret of its dramatic perfection.

While Psalm 136 reveals the speculative sweep of the construction, further texts must be considered in order to understand the richness of motivations in detail. The problems of this nature have received careful attention by Gerhard von Rad in his studies on the Hexateuchal form. The following examples are chosen, therefore, from the materials assembled in his work, though they will have to be moved into a somewhat different light, in accordance with the purposes of the present study.[1]

The oldest of the several motives that have formed the Israelite meaning of history is probably to be found in the famous prayer formula of Deuteronomy 26:4b–9:

> A wandering Aramean was my father;
> and he went down into Egypt, and sojourned there, few in number;
> and he became there a nation, great, mighty, and populous.
>
> And the Egyptians dealt ill with us, and afflicted us, and laid upon
>   us hard bondage.
> And we cried unto Yahweh, the God of our fathers;
> and Yahweh heard our voice, and saw our affliction, and our toil,
>   and our oppression.
>
> And Yahweh brought us forth out of Egypt,
> with a mighty hand and with an outstretched arm,
> with great terror, and with signs, and with wonders.
>
> And he has brought us into this place,
> and has given us this land,
> a land flowing with milk and honey.

This obviously is not the great construction of Psalm 136. The prayer, concentrates, rather, on the concrete historical experience of Israel's salvation from the bondage of Egypt; and since it is a ritual prayer, to be offered with the first fruits of the land, it properly concludes on the motif of the Canaan that has produced them. Nevertheless, it has an importance of its own in so far as it shows how the meanings of history ramify from an experiential nucleus. In order to be brought out of Egypt, Israel first had to come into it. If God reveals himself as the savior in a concrete

---

[1] Gerhard von Rad, *Das Formgeschichtliche Problem des Hexateuchs* (Beitraege zur Wissenschaft vom Alten und Neuen Testament, 4:26, Stuttgart, 1938).

historical situation, the prehistory of the situation comes into view. The Exodus expands into Patriarchal history.

Once the pattern of the expanding nucleus has been set, it can be elaborated to suit further concrete situations. On the occasion of the Diet of Shechem, for instance, the tradition attributes to Joshua a speech which elaborates the prayer formula of Deuteronomy 26. The reference to the "wandering Aramaean" expands into a succinct recall of Patriarchal history, mentioning Abraham, Isaac, and Jacob (Josh. 24:2b–4). The miracles of the Exodus are then recalled with specific details (5–7). And the gap between Egypt and Canaan, finally, is filled with an enumeration of the principal events of the Transjordanian Wars, as well as of the Conquest itself, down to the present meeting at Shechem (8–13). On a similar solemn occasion, when Saul was instituted as king at Gilgal, Samuel's recall of events begins with the Exodus and brings them down through the period of the Judges to the Ammonite War, which had aroused the irresistible desire of the people for a king like Ammon (I Sam. 12:8–13). In the liturgical literature, the variations of the theme can achieve considerable length, as in Psalms 78, 105, and 135.

Not all Israelite history grows, however, through expansion from the experience of the Exodus. There are rival centers of meaning. The prayer formula of Deuteronomy 26, for instance, appears with a slight variation in a different ritual context in Deuteronomy 6:20–25. This time it is not the offering of Canaanite first fruits but the question why Yahweh's statutes and ordinances should be obeyed that occasions the recall of God's work of salvation (6:20). Exodus and Canaan together (6:21–23) now become a course of providential history which serves the ulterior purpose of establishing a Chosen People in obedience to the ordinance of God (6:24–25). While the experiential center of the Exodus is not abolished, it has become subordinate to the meaning emanating from the Sinaitic Covenant. A further complication is introduced by the speech of Joshua at the Diet of Shechem (Josh. 24:2b–13), in so far as the speech is the prelude to a ritual (24:14–27) by which the assembled tribes enter into a berith with Yahweh that presupposes, but is not identical with, the Sinaitic Berith. A third experiential center seems to exist, strong enough to have found expression in a festival and ritual of its own. Gerhard von Rad calls it the Covenant Festival of Shechem; and in the reconstruction of its ritual distinguishes:

    (a) Joshua's Paraenesis (24:14 ff.)
    (b) The Assent of the People (24:16 ff.)
    (c) The Reading of the Law (24:25)
    (d) Conclusion of the Covenant (24:27)
    (e) Blessing and Curse (Josh. 8:34) [2]

The Law that was read as part of the ritual was presumably closely related to the Sinaitic legislation, so that the Shechem festival would furnish an example of a rite that has absorbed the meaning of another rite originating in a different experiential situation. Of an independent Sinai festival traces are still to be found in Psalms 50 and 81.[3]

The rites and liturgies, thus, are the key to the process in which the meaning of Israelite history grows into its complex form. They reveal above all their own motivation through the experiences of concrete historical events; they show, furthermore, the possibilities of expanding a nucleus of historical experience into the past and the future; and the cases of interlocking rites, finally, foreshadow the method of welding traditions of different experiential motivation into a whole of meaning on the level of historiography. Before that level is reached, however, the rite gives further proof of the strength of its experiential charge in so far as it motivates the creation of cult legends as the literary form in which the historical events that have motivated the cult are presented. As such cult legends are recognizable the Passah legend, which has become the form of the Exodus traditions, and the New Year legend, which has become the form of the Sinai traditions.[4] Only beyond the traditions formed by cult legends begins the historiographic construction proper, in the ninth century B.C., when the motive for writing history is furnished by the Davidic

---

[2] *Ibid.*, 31 ff. The conclusion of a berith at Shechem implies that the constitution of Israel as a people did not occur at one time, but went through at least the phases of Sinai and Shechem. For the reconstruction of this early period of Israelite history see Martin Noth, *Das System der zwoelf Stamme Israels* (Beitraege zur Wissenschaft vom Alten und Neuen Testament, 3:10, Stuttgart, 1930), and Albrecht Alt, *Die Staatenbildung der Israeliten in Palaestina* (Reformationsprogramm der Universitaet Leipzig, 1930), now reprinted in Alt, *Kleine Schriften zur Geschichte des Volkes Israel*, II, 1–65. Cf. the chapter on "Der Bund der Israelitischen Staemme," in Noth, *Geschichte Israels*, especially pp. 89 ff. on the Diet of Shechem.

[3] That the sources betray the existence of a Sinai Festival has been recognized by Sigmund Mowinckel, *Le Décalogue* (Etudes d'Histoire et de Philosophie Religieuses, XVI, Paris, 1927) 119 ff. For the further exploration of the problem see von Rad, *Das Formgeschichtliche Problem des Hexateuchs*, 19 ff.

[4] On the cult form of the Exodus traditions (Exod. 1–15) see Johannes Pederson, "Passahfest und Passahlegende," *Zeitschrift fuer die alttestamentliche Wissenschaft*, N.F. XI (1934), 161–75; and the same author's *Israel. Its Life and Culture*, III–IV, 728–37. On the cult form of the Sinai traditions, as well as on the further application of the form to the construction of Deuteronomy, see von Rad, *Das Formgeschichtliche Problem des Hexateuchs*, 19 ff. and 24 ff.

monarchy. On that level it is, then, possible to combine the traditions of variegated origin into a coherent prehistory of the monarchy and to expand the narrative into the past, beyond the Patriarchs, into the prepatriarchal Genesis. A stream of motivations, thus, rises from the primary experiences, through the festivals, rites, and cult legends, into the speculative construction of the narrative. And since the stream rises without losing its identity of substance, the speculative form of the unfolded meaning can revert to the liturgical level, as in the great prayer of Nehemiah 9:6–37 that praises God in his works from the Creation, through the history of the Patriarchs, of Exodus, Sinai, and Canaan, of Kingdom, Exile, and Return, down to the postexilic rite of the new Covenant with Yahweh.

The construction of world-history unfolds the meaning that radiates from the motivating centers of experience. And since it is the will of God, and his way with man that is experienced in the concrete situation, world-history is meaningful in so far as it reveals the ordering will of God in every stage of the process, including the creation of the world itself. Beyond the construction of the world-history rises, therefore, a vision of the God who by his word called into existence the world and Israel. He is one God, to be sure, but he bears as many aspects as he has modes of revealing his ordering will to man—through the order of the world that embraces man and history, through the revelation of right order to the Fathers and the Chosen People, and through the aid that he brings to his people in adversity. He is the Creator, the Lord of Justice, and the Savior. These are the three fundamental aspects of divine being, as they become visible in the Israelite construction of world-history. They become something like a "theology" when they are brought into focus in the work of Deutero-Isaiah; and they remain the fundamental modes in which God is experienced in Christianity.

The experience of existence under God unfolds into the meaning of world-history; and the emergence of meaningful order from an ambiance of lesser meaning supplies the subject matter for the Biblical narrative. The term "emergence" in the present context is meant to denote the process in which any type of meaningful order is brought forth from an environment with a lesser charge of meaning. It will apply to the three main instances evoked in Psalm 136, as well to all other instances interspersed between them or following them. The Biblical narrative is built around the great cases of emergence, and gains its dramatic movement in detail as

the story of recessions from, and returns to, levels of meaning already
achieved.

Genesis establishes the dramatic pattern of emergence and recession of
meaningful order. It opens with the creation of the world, culminating in
the creation of man; and it follows the account of the original emergence
of order with the story of the great recession from the Fall to the Tower
of Babel. A second level of meaning emerges with Abraham's migration
from the Chaldaean city of Ur, with a way station in Haran, to Canaan.
That is the first Exodus by which the imperial civilizations of the Near
East in general receive their stigma as environments of lesser meaning.
Canaan, indeed, is reached in that first venture, but the foothold in the
land of promise is still precarious. Repeated famines drive first Abraham to
a temporary settlement in Egypt and later the Jacob clans to a more permanent one. Genesis closes the account of this second recession with the
return of Jacob's body to Canaan, to be buried in the field that Abraham
had bought from Ephron the Hittite, and the oath of the sons of Israel to
take the bones of Joseph with them, when they will all return to the promised land. Creation and Exodus, thus, are successive phases in the unfolding of the order of being; but the rhythm of emergence and recession was
to be beaten twice in Genesis, and the order of being is not yet completed.
Genesis is clearly the prelude to the main event whose story is told in
Exodus, Numbers, and Joshua—that is, to the second Exodus, the wandering in the Desert, and the conquest of Canaan. Only with the main event,
with the constitution of Israel as a people through the Covenant and its
settlement in the promised land, the historical present is reached from
which the ray of meaning falls over Genesis. At this point, at the complete emergence of meaning, the guidance offered by Psalm 136 properly
stops, for it is the historical present in which the postexilic redactors still
live—in spite of the course of pragmatic events which necessitated serious
revisions of the original conception. Before turning to the disturbing
events under the established present, however, a further aspect of the
emergence of meaning must be considered.

The world-history is the history of all created being, not of Israel alone.
As far as meaning emerges beyond the creation of the world in the history
of mankind proper, the Biblical narrative is therefore fraught with the
problem of understanding Israelite as the representative history of mankind. In Genesis 18:18 Yahweh asks himself:

Shall I hide what I am about to do from Abraham,
seeing that Abraham is bound to become a great and powerful nation,
and through him all the nations of the earth will invoke blessings on
  one another?

In Galatians 3:7–9, St. Paul could interpret his apostolate among the nations outside Israel as the fulfillment of Yahweh's promise to Abraham; and contemporary with St. Paul, Philo Judaeus interpreted the prayer of the Jewish High Priest as the representative prayer for mankind to God. The ability or inability of the various branches of the Jewish community to cope with the problem of its own representative character has affected the course of history to our time, as will be seen presently. For the moment it must be observed that Genesis, as a survey of the past from which emerges the Israelite historical present, fulfills two important tasks. On the one hand, it separates the sacred line of the godly carriers of meaning from the rest of mankind. That is the line of Adam, Seth, Noah, Shem, Abraham, Isaac, Jacob, and the twelve ancestors of the tribes of Israel. On the other hand, it must pay some attention to the mankind from which the sacred line has separated. That task is discharged in Genesis 10, in form of a survey of the nations that have descended from Noah after the Flood and peopled the earth. Not all of the nations mentioned can be identified with certainty. But at least the sons of Japhet are recognizable as the northern peoples, and among them the sons of Javan (the Ionians) as the peoples of Cyprus, Rhodes, and other islands. Under the sons of Ham the populations of Canaan are ranged by the side of the Egyptians, probably because the country was under Egyptian suzerainty. The sons of Shem, finally, comprise the Elamites, Assyrians, and Arameans by the side of Eber, the ancestor of the Hebrews. Certain details, such as the display of violent animosity in Genesis 9 against the Canaanites, suggest that the body of traditions incorporated in this geopolitical survey, was formed not very long after the Conquest.

The problem of emergence can now be further pursued into the course of events under the historical present created by Covenant and Conquest. As far as the course of paradigmatic history is concerned, the pattern established by Genesis simply runs on with its alternate recessions from, and recapturings of, the level of meaning achieved by the Conquest. The book of Judges is a model of this type of historiography, with its partly monotonous, partly amusing, repetition of the formula: "So the Israelites did what was evil in the sight of Yahweh in that they forgot Yahweh their God, and served the Baals and Ashtarts," followed by accounts of prompt punishment through military defeat at the hands of Midianites, Amorites, or some other neighbor, by the repentance of Israel, and by the rise of a major judge who restores independence.

The formal rhythm of the ups and downs of meaning was further formalized by using twelve judges to cover the period; and this pattern of the rhythm, with dozens of judges for punctuation, might have run on indefinitely, unless the exigencies of power politics had persuaded the confederate tribes of Israel that a more effective, centralized government under a king was needed in order to endow the conquest of Canaan with some measure of stability. It was this establishment of a kingdom which inevitably produced the conflict between the Israel that was a peculiar people under the kingship of God, and the Israel that had a king like the other nations. Whether the kingship was pragmatically successful, through assimilation to the prevalent style of governmental organization, foreign politics, and cultural relations with the neighbors, as it was under Solomon and the Omride dynasty in the Northern Kingdom; or whether it was unsuccessful, and ultimately brought disaster on Israel through hopeless resistance against stronger empires, the Prophets were always right in their opposition. For Israel had reversed the Exodus and re-entered the Sheol of civilizations. Hence, the pattern of recession and repentant return still runs through Samuel and Kings but no longer with the ease of Judges, for it is increasingly overshadowed by the awareness that the Kingdom on principle is a recession, while the carriership of meaning, running parallel with it, is being transferred to the Prophets. Moreover, the literary organization of the great historical work can no longer cope successfully with the problem of crisis. To be sure, the story is continued in a formal sense beyond Judges through Samuel and Kings; but for the period of the Kingdom the prophetic books must be read by the side of the historical if one wants to gain an adequate understanding of the spiritual struggle of Israel with the issue of the Kingdom. And with the Exile the leadership of meaning plainly passes to the Prophets.

The construction of paradigmatic history in the light of a present that had been constituted by the Covenant was obviously cracking up— even in the hands of the postexilic redactors, who apparently accepted this present still as valid. The source of the difficulties will perhaps become clearer, if we step back of the redactors and assume the more detached

view of the rabbinical canonizers. For the division of the books in the
rabbinical canon offers a valuable clue to the disturbance in the emergence
of meaning. The sacred writings were subdivided by the canon into (1)
The Law, (2) The Prophets, and (3) The Writings. The Law comprised
the Pentateuch; the Prophets comprised Joshua-Kings, Isaiah, Jeremiah,
Ezekiel, and the twelve minor Prophets; and the Writings comprised
roughly the postexilic literature, discarding, however, the Apocrypha and
Pseudepigrapha. Looking back on the great political disaster from the
vantage point of the synod of Jamnia (*ca.* A.D. 100), the emergence of
meaning seemed to have occurred in three main phases. The first phase
reached from the creation of the world to the historical constitution of
Israel under the Covenant, and the Law made in pursuance thereof, as
might be expected. The second phase, however, brought a new development, not yet envisaged by the redactors of the historical writings, in so
far as the conquest of Canaan, as well as the whole confederate and royal
history of Israel, were subordinated with regard to their meaning to the
emergent Yahwism of the Prophets. The third group, finally, under the
nondescript title of "Writings," had no more than a firm core of meaning in the books connected with the foundation of the Second Temple
(Chronicles, Ezra, Nehemiah), as well as in the hymnbook of the new
community, while for the rest it was characterized rather negatively by
the elimination of the Maccabaean history, the larger part of the Hellen-
izing wisdom-literature, and the almost complete elimination of the
apocalyptic literature, the one exception being Daniel. The canonization,
thus, formalized a situation that had been sensed to exist in fact already
by the author of the Prologue to Ecclesiasticus (*ca.* 130 B.C.), when he
wrote: "Many and great things have been delivered unto us by the law
and the prophets, and by others that have followed their steps, for the
which things Israel ought to be commended for learning [*paideia*] and
wisdom [*sophia*]." Israel with its *paideia* and *sophia* belonged to the past.
The Law and the Prophets were closed chapters of history. What finally
emerged from the double spurt of meaning was no Canaan, but the community of Jews who would preserve their past as an eternal present for all
future.

The retrospective interpretation from the rabbinical position makes
it clear that the disturbing factor in the Israelite historical form had been
the ambiguity of Canaan, that is, the translation of a transcendent aim

into a historical *fait accompli*. With the conquest of Canaan, Israelite history, according to its own original conception, had come to its end; and the aftermath could only be the repetitious, indefinite ripple of defection and repentance that filled the pages of Judges. From this rippling rhythm the historical form was regained, not by the Kingdom, but through the elaboration of the universalist potentialities of Yahwism by the Prophets. The separation of the sacred line from the rest of mankind—an enterprise that had run into the impasse of a nation among others—would have ended ignominiously with the political catastrophy, unless the Yahwism of the Prophets had made possible the genesis of a community under God that no longer had to reside in Canaan at all cost. Still, the new Jewish community, which succeeded to the Hebrews of the Patriarchal Age and the Israel of the Confederacy and the Kingdom, had to travel a hard way until it could rejoin the mankind from which it had separated, so that the divine promise to Abraham would be fulfilled. And not the whole of the community was successful in ascending to this further level of meaning. For, from the postexilic community there emerged, surviving historically to this day, the branch of Talmudic Judaism—at the terrific price of cutting itself off, not only from the abortive Maccabaean nationalism, but also from its own rich potentialities that had become visible in Hellenization, the proselytizing expansion, and the apocalyptic movements. The representative separation of the sacred line through divine choice petered out into a communal separatism, which induced the intellectuals of the Roman Empire to attribute to the community an *odium generis humani*. What had begun as the carriership of truth for mankind, ended with a charge of hatred of mankind. As the other and, indeed, successful branch, emerged the Jewish movement that could divest itself not only of the territorial aspirations for a Canaan, but also of the ethnic heritage of Judaism. It became able, as a consequence, to absorb Hellenistic culture, as well as the proselytizing movement and the apocalyptic fervor, and to merge it with the Law and the Prophets. With the emergence of the Jewish movement that is called Christianity, Jews and Greeks, Syrians and Egyptians, Romans and Africans could fuse in one mankind under God. In Christianity the separation bore its fruit when the sacred line rejoined mankind.

CHAPTER 6

The Historiographic Work

The Israelite conception of true order in the human soul, in society, and in history cannot be ascertained through consultation of treatises which explicitly deal with such subject matters. The historical narrative from the creation of the world to the fall of Jerusalem is neither a book, nor a collection of books, but a unique symbolism that has grown into its ultimate form through more than six centuries of historiographic work from the time of Solomon to *ca.* 300 B.C. Moreover, this written literary work has absorbed oral traditions which probably reach back as far as the first half of the second millennium B.C. Hence, it is possible to find a tradition from the seventeenth century, side by side with an editorial interpolation of the fifth century, in a story that has received its literary form in the ninth century B.C. One may, furthermore, find that the odd composition is not a piece of clumsy patchwork but a well-knit story that conveys a fine point of nomad ethics, or spiritual response to revelation, or diplomatic compromise with foreign divinities. And we may, finally, find that the story has an important function in a wider historical and speculative context which in its turn reveals an equally complex composition. That is a disconcerting situation, as it appears impossible to identify the object of inquiry. Do we deal with the component ideas of the seventeenth, ninth, or fifth centuries; or with the idea conveyed by the composition, which does not seem to have a date at all; or with the meaning which the piece has by virtue of its position in the larger context? Certainly no simple answer will be possible, and in many instances no satisfactory one at all. We must recognize the difficulties presented by a symbolism that has absorbed primary traditions and records of more than a thousand years, and overlaid them with interpretations, with interpretations of interpretations, with redactions and interpolations, and subtle imposition of new meanings through integration in wider contexts.

In order to cope with the difficulty, we shall deal in the present chapter with the uppermost layer of interpretation. While this procedure will not solve all of our problems, it will at least reduce them to manageable proportions. For the separate study of the uppermost layer will enable us further on to distinguish between the construction of the context and the materials embedded in it, as well as between contextual meanings and the meanings of the materials independent of the context. In the following Parts III and IV of the study, we shall then deal with the traditions that were ultimately subjected to the historiographic construction.

That the difficulty cannot be solved satisfactorily even by this method of isolating the comprehensive context is obvious from the vocabulary just used. When we speak of an "uppermost layer of meaning" and, as a matter of convenience, characterize it as the "historiographic work" proper, it must be understood that there is no reason why the designation as historiographic work should be denied to the lower strata of the narrative, which appear in the role of historical subject matter in relation to the uppermost layer. Some of the finest accomplishments of Israelite historiography, such as the memoirs of an unknown author on the reign of David and the accession of Solomon, belong in the lower stratum. History and historiography can be distinguished only by the relative position of a document in the stratification of the narrative. A document will be historiography with regard to its specific subject matter; but it will move into the position of historical subject matter with regard to a later historiographic effort that has absorbed the specific subject matter in the literary form given to it by the earlier historiographic effort. The situation is even further complicated insofar as the term "historical subject matter" is also fraught with thorny problems. In the present context, the reader should be warned, it is used only as a provisional instrument of analysis that will have to undergo serious qualifications in the further course of this chapter.

The main body of the present chapter will deal with the symbols (§ 2) and the motivations (§ 3) of the historiographic work. These two main sections will be preceded by a note on the state of Old Testament science with regard to the sources and construction of the narrative (§ 1).

§ 1. The Sources of the Narrative

At the beginning of the present part on "The Historical Order of Israel" we have skirted the controversies of Old Testament science and approached directly the issues of Israelite order, that is, (1) the historical form of existence in the present under God, and (2) history as the symbolism of that form. The procedure was permissible because Old Testament science, though involved in the issues through its materials, rarely is concerned with their philosophical penetration, and consequently has little to contribute to their direct formulation. In the measure in which our study, in its turn, is becoming involved more deeply in the concrete materials, the situation changes. When dealing with concrete problems, we have to rely on the results of Old Testament science; and even when the interpretation, in the light of our principles, has to go ways of its own, the way moves through a field that is pre-empted by competent and astute scholarship. That is true in particular with regard to authorship, composition, and sources of the Biblical narrative, and in general with regard to the complex of historiographic problems that will occupy us, not only in the present chapter, but throughout the remainder of this volume.

The adumbrated situation creates certain problems of presentation. Our study is based on the results of Old Testament science, and we cannot conduct the analysis without reference to its basis. Old Testament science, however, has its definite place in the history of Western civilization as a growth of critical science, preponderantly advanced by Protestant scholars, in connection with the concerns of theological studies. As a consequence, its controversies reach extraordinary degrees of complication. On the one hand, the debates are burdened to this day with the conditions of their theological origins; on the other hand, Old Testament scholars participate almost feverishly in the quite untheological advances in the fields of archaeology, semitology, comparative religion, and general history of antiquity. The inevitable tension between origins and direction has caused, especially during the last generation, an amplitude of opinion that makes it impossible for a student of Israelite order to justify his own position on major points in relation to the literature without writing incidentally a history of Old Testament science. This task, to be sure, could be performed. Nevertheless, the performance is not advisable, because it would easily double the size of our study and obscure the problems which are its proper concern. A policy of compromises had to be devised in order to meet this difficulty.

We have given a formal exposition of the state of the problem, that is, a critical survey of the literature and a justification of our own position, only on occasion of the Imperial Psalms, in the Digression of Chapter 9, § 5. The occasion was chosen because it offered a fortunate combination of several advantages. In the first place, Old Testament science had advanced in the study of the Psalter very close to our own problems of Israelite order, so that only a minimum of issues lay beyond our immediate interests. The controversy on the Psalter was, second, of recent origin, so that the critical survey did not quantitatively disrupt our study too badly. And third, it involved, with a comparatively high degree of theoretical clarity, the various positions which divide Old Testament scholars today, so that the account rendered a picture of the state of science beyond the problems of the Psalter. The critical Digression, thus, became representative for the relation between the current controversies and our own study in general, while the size of the Digression made it clear that the study could not be burdened throughout with such excrescences. On all other occasions, we decided to confine ourselves to the argument in support of our position, accompanied by brief references to the principal literature.

The present occasion, however, requires a form intermediate between the Digression just mentioned and a bibliographical footnote. For, on the one hand, the debate on the composition of the narrative has, as does the Homeric question, a time range of living issues going back to the eighteenth century, so that a full treatment would require a sizable monograph of the kind we want to avoid. On the other hand, there is more than one reason why the two centuries of Pentateuchal criticism cannot be dismissed with a brief footnote. In the first place, it is not easy to give satisfactory references at all, because the lack of adequate philosophical foundations, which in general is the bane of Old Testament science, makes itself especially felt in the treatment of the historiographic complex. The controversial literature is turgid, and its theoretical quality leaves much to be desired. Second, the general surveys of the controversy to which we can refer the reader are handicapped in various respects. The masterly history of source criticism in Adolphe Lods's *Histoire,* for instance, suffers from the interruption of communications during the Second World War, in so far as the recent German and Scandinavian literature could not be digested; and the bibliographical supplements by A. Parrot, while valuable, are no substitute for a critical evaluation.[1] The essay by C. R. North on *Pentateuchal Criticism* includes the recent literature, it is true, and is especially valuable because of the space it accords to the work of Ivan

[1] Lods, *Histoire de la Littérature Hébraique et Juive.* Cf. the chapter on "Critique des Sources" (pp. 83–127) and the supplements by Parrot (p. 1035).

Engnell.[2] Unfortunately, however, it is limited to the period 1920–1950, and the prehistory of the problems inevitably cannot come into proper view. Moreover, it suffers somewhat from professional exclusiveness in so far as the work of Martin Buber, which has considerable importance for the understanding of the narrative and its composition, was ignored.[3] And third, the labors of Pentateuchal criticism have had certain results. Even though their validity has become doubtful today in many respects, they must be furnished as plain information, since their knowledge is presupposed in the course of our study. Hence, in order to satisfy the needs of our study without getting too deeply involved in the history of Old Testament science, we shall concentrate on the phases of the controversy represented by the literary criticism of Wellhausen and his school and by the tradition-historic method of Engnell. Moreover, in the case of the Wellhausen phase we shall not enter into the intricacies of the argument or the personal qualifications, refinements, and reservations made by various scholars, but shall present a school picture of the typical features.

According to the Wellhausen school of criticism, there are distinguishable in the Pentateuch the narratives of the Yahwist (J) and the Elohist (E), so called after the preferred designation of the divinity as Yahweh or Elohim in the respective strands of the Biblical narrative. The narratives, drawing on oral traditions, were submitted to writing and rewriting until the preserved form emerged. The Yahwist narrative originated in the Kingdom of Judah in the ninth century; the Elohist in the Kingdom of Israel in the eighth century. In both of them can be distinguished further lines of component traditions. A third source is the Deuteronomist (D), named after its principal work, the Deuteronomy, which since De Wette (1806) is presumed to be identical with Josiah's reform-code of 621. In view of the distinguishable component strands of tradition, as well as of the recensions which the narratives presumably had undergone, the sigla J, E, and D were agreed to stand not for definite authors but rather for

[2] C. R. North, "Pentateuchal Criticism," in Rowley (ed.), *The Old Testament and Modern Study*, 48–83. Cf. also the immediately following essay by N. H. Snaith, "The Historical Books," 84–114. North had at his disposition some of the articles by Engnell that were to be published in Vol. II of Ivan Egnell och Anton Fridrichsen, *Svenskt Bibliskt Uppslagsverk*, 2 vols. (Gaevle, 1948–52). The article "Moseboeckerna" was especially used; "Traditionshistorisk metod" would also have been of importance.

[3] Cf. especially Martin Buber, *Moses* (Zurich, 1948). The work of Buber is generally ignored in Rowley (ed.), *The Old Testament and Modern Study*, nor is his *Prophetic Faith* (New York, 1949) mentioned.

"schools" of historiography. The Deuteronomist school was supposed to have flourished from at least the middle of the seventh century well into the Exile. The combination of Deuteronomy with the J and E sources probably took place in the Exile, and it was accompanied by noticeable editorial work in the Deuteronomic spirit on the earlier sources. Moreover, it appeared highly probable that the J and E sources were amalgamated by a non-Deuteronomist hand into one narrative before they underwent their integration into the Deuteronomist work. A fourth source, finally, is the sacerdotal or priestly document (P), which contains the Priestly Code of *ca.* 400 B.C., but also envelops in its text the Holiness Code (H) (Lev. 17–26), which goes back to the time of Ezekiel. The integration of J-E-D into the P narrative took place in the fourth century, and the revisions in the sacerdotal spirit may still have been going on by 300 B.C.

Bible criticism, as we have indicated, is burdened with its origins in theological concerns. Pentateuchal criticism, in particular, is a traditional unit of study, because it is in search of a substitute author for the Five Books ascribed by the Biblical tradition to Moses. It is a unit, not because philological criteria draw a forceful line between the first five and the subsequent books of the Biblical narrative, but because of its opposition to the Moses tradition. When the tension of the opposition relaxed, though it never disappeared completely, philological considerations could assert themselves more freely; and only then, as a secondary development, did the source analysis expand beyond the Pentateuch. The J and E sources, reworked by a Deuteronomist hand, seemed to extend so clearly into Joshua that the term Hexateuch was coined for the aggregate of books. And the same structure of sources was found, though with hesitations and qualifications, to continue in Judges, Samuel, and the first chapters of Kings. Continuous component narratives, thus, were considered to extend beyond the Pentateuch into the Former Prophets of the rabbinical canon. Under that assumption a J narrative would extend from the creation of the world to the accession of Solomon (Genesis 2—I Kings 2); an E narrative from Abraham to the death of Saul (Genesis 15—II Samuel 1); and a P narrative from the creation of the world to the death of Joshua (Genesis 1 —Joshua).

If these assumptions be accepted, there is no D narrative running parallel with J, E, and P. To be sure, Deuteronomy itself is the work of the Deuteronomists, but for the rest their function in the earlier part of the narrative is mainly editorial. Their independent work begins only with

Kings; and as a consequence the structure of Kings differs substantially from that of the preceding books. It is possibly written by a single author in the retrospect of the late Exile; and it is not an edited amalgamation of pre-existent narratives covering the same period, but draws for its materials on such contemporary annalistic works as the Acts of Solomon (I Kings 11:41), or the Acts of the Kings of Israel (I Kings 14:10) and Judah (I Kings 14:29), and on the cycles of Elijah and Elisha legends. Moreover, the composition has a recognizable principle in so far as the foundation of the Solomonic Temple, understood as the formal break with the false gods and the concentration of the cult on Yahweh, is considered an epoch in Israelite history. The arc of the story therefore rests on the two pillars of the Solomonic story at the beginning and the Reform of Josiah at the end. The construction is, furthermore, distinguished by a high degree of consciousness in so far as it clearly relies on a torah formulated in Deuteronomy 12: "You must not conduct yourself at all as we are doing here today, everyone just as he pleases," serving the gods of other nations; when the people is settled in the promised land, living in security, then "to the sanctuary which Yahweh your God chooses out of all your tribes as the seat of his presence, to his habitation you must resort." The conflict between the Canaanite cults and Yahweh, thus, furnishes the principle of relevance; and the history of the monarchy is narrated as a sequence of paradigmatic events in the light of the Deuteronomic torah.

From the labors of the Wellhausen school there emerges a definite conception of the composition of the Pentateuch and, beyond it, of the Biblical narrative in general. The Mosaic authorship of the tradition was the starting point for a work of literary criticism which distinguished the "sources" or "documents" designated by the sigla J, E, and P and assigned them to definite authors. With the advancing philological dissection of the documents into component strands, which underwent recensions, editions, amalgamations, and redactions, the number of "authors" had to be multiplied; and since the main units of literary criticism were retained on the whole, the "authors" had to be bunched into the "schools" corresponding to the sigla. Moses as the author of the Pentateuch had ultimately been replaced by the authors of the various component strands of the narrative. Whatever meaning could be found in the narrative had to be found on the level of the "sources" distinguished by literary criticism. The situation is well characterized by Martin Noth: "The genesis of the

Pentateuch as a whole, that is, the integration of the J-narrative, as enlarged by numerous E-elements, into the literary framework of P, is not of great importance from the point of view of a history of traditions. That was a purely literary labor, adding nothing by way of new materials, points of view, or interpretations; it was a mere drawing of a sum, of importance only insofar as the total was the Pentateuch as it lies before us in its final form." [4] Some unknown writer, for reasons unknown, fused the various narratives into an encyclopedic whole, without adding anything of his own. "It would have been important, if something new had resulted from the fusion of sources for the course of the Israelite pre-history told in the Pentateuch, or for its theological interpretation. But that is not the case. Because of the common background of fully developed oral traditions, and because of mutual literary dependence, the history had been narrated in all sources in so closely similar a manner, that even the combination of sources could bring no essential change." [5]

The methods and results of the Wellhausen school of criticism have aroused a mood of dissatisfaction which has difficulties in articulating itself and bringing the grievance into focus. Still, there are occasional outbursts hitting close to the mark, such as Volz's complaint about Eissfeldt's synopsis, which arranged the fragments of the presumed sources in parallel columns. "I see in this Synopsis the culmination of the hitherto prevailing method, and I find that it proves exactly the opposite of what it is meant to prove, for the miserable fragments of narrative which for the most part the columns contain prove precisely that there were not four original narratives, and that this entire Pentateuchal Synopsis is nothing but the artificial creation of modern erudition." [6] And in his gentler manner, Gerhard von Rad sets himself the new task of going "beyond the source analysis, which has been run to death" and then quietly proceeds "to unfold the problems of the Hexateuch from its final form." [7]

If now we try our own hand at formulating the cause of dissatisfaction, it seems to lend itself to articulation in three propositions:

---

[4] Martin Noth, *Ueberlieferungsgeschichte des Pentateuch* (Stuttgart, 1948), 267 ff.

[5] *Ibid.*, 271.

[6] Otto Eissfeldt, *Hexateuch-Synopse* (Leipzig, 1922). The review by Paul Volz was published in the *Theologische Literaturzeitung*, 1923; I am quoting the passage from North, "Pentateuchal Criticism," *loc. cit.*, 55. The reader should be aware that source criticism of the type which aroused the blast of Volz, though notably discredited today, has by no means been given up. A good example of a recent excess in this direction is C. A. Simpson, *The Early Traditions of Israel* (Oxford, 1948).

[7] Von Rad, *Das Formgeschichtliche Problem des Hexateuchs*, 1–3.

(1) The disappearance of Moses as the author of the Pentateuch entailed the disappearance of the meaning of the Biblical narrative in its final form.

(2) What was found in its place turned out to be not worth finding, measured by the treasure of meaning that had always been sensed in the narrative but now escaped the critics.

(3) It is doubtful whether, beyond the strictly philological results of criticism, anything was found at all.

The meaning of the propositions can be unfolded best by reflecting on the last one first. The critical work of the Wellhausen school moves methodologically in a haze, because it is insufficiently aware of the difference between empirical, philological work and the interpretations put on its results. One may well distinguish units of text by such criteria as the names used for the divinity, preferences of vocabulary, standard phrases, syntactical peculiarities, literary style (simple narrative or majestic oratory), degrees of anthropomorphism in the conception of divinity, art of characterization, preferences for subject matters and regions, accounts of events (primitive and legendary or spiritually articulate), and so forth; in all these respects the critical work may be impeccable and the results firmly established, but one still does not know what the units distinguished by such criteria signify in terms of symbolisms, conceived for the articulation of concrete experiences of concrete human beings. It is possible, on principle, that the "sources" are nothing but collections of stylistic debris broken from contexts which the literary critic did not understand. While, to be sure, this extreme possibility does not apply to the present case without qualifications, it must be realized that the nature of the collections cannot be determined by the philological criteria used in their formation, but only in the light of assumptions about symbolic forms. And the assumption that the collections in question are documents emanating from definite authors rests on nothing but a nineteenth-century conceit that bodies of literary text, if they have a certain length and show definite characters of style, are "books" which inevitably must have "authors." That the problem is not so simple is clear if the reader recalls Chapter 5, § 2, where the materials assembled by von Rad were used to trace the emergence of meaning from the primary motives in the experiences of historical situations and events, through festivals and ceremonial assemblies, rituals, and cult legends, to the historiographic level. A complicated, objective field of experiences

and symbolizations unfolded, in which numerous human beings participated on the levels of their collective consciousness as tribes and the
covenant people. And that field of experienced order and its symbolization is so firm in its structure that even on the level of historiographic
elaboration, while there is room for personal qualities of sensitiveness,
imagination, and gifts of linguistic expression on the part of individual
participants in the process, there is certainly no room for personal interpretations of "history" or "authorship" in the modern sense. Moreover,
the unanalyzed conception of authorship facilitated the belief, in the
Wellhausen school, that one knew what the presumed authors had written
if one called their product a "narrative" or "history," even though behind such vocabulary lurked the formidable questions of the symbolic
form not only of the narrative itself but of the canonical collection of
the Old Testament as a whole.[8] Questions of this nature, however, can
not be approached through dissection of a text into sources, by literary
criteria, but only through an analysis of the contents; and by contents are
meant the units of meaning that can be found in the text as it stands,
through the application of a theory of symbolic forms. This postulate
does not imply, to be sure, that the component strands discerned by
Wellhausian analysis are senseless. On the contrary, it is quite possible
that the units discerned by an analysis of symbols will fall in their entirety
within the range of one or the other "source"; and the sources discerned
by literary criticism should by all means be examined closely, for if separated from the context they may reveal units of meaning that otherwise
might have escaped attention. Such coincidences, however, are a question
of fact, not the consequence of a prestabilized harmony between the
sources and symbolic forms. Source analysis, thus, can be of assistance,
if used with circumspection, in the search for units of symbolic form;
but it can become utterly destructive if it pretends that the integral
text contains no units of meaning which cut across the sources.

The last reflections lead to the first and second propositions advanced

---

[8] Some of these questions were treated in the preceding Chap. 5, others will be examined in
the subsequent §§ 2 and 3 of the present chapter. Beyond the problems of order and symbolization which form the subject matter proper of our study lie the questions of a philosophy of language, as well as of the relation between the meanings of language symbols in general and of the
symbols of order in particular. For the relation between the Hebrew time conception and historical order cf. the chapter on "Die Israelitische Zeitauffasung" in the brilliant study by Thorleif Boman, *Das Hebraeische Denken im Vergleich mit dem Griechischen* (1952; 2d ed., Goettingen, 1954). Boman's work is characteristic of the shift of accents in Old Testament science; and
the fact that a second edition became possible within two years seems to indicate an increasing
awareness for the necessity of philosophical foundations.

above. The question whether a unit of symbolic form falls within the range of one of the sources of literary criticism, or cuts across several of them, is a question of fact. And our analysis will show on several occasions, especially in Chapter 12 in the study of Moses, that very important units of text, with a distinct form and meaning of their own, as a matter of fact, cut across the sources. But this is not the place to dwell on specific instances. For the Biblical narrative abounds, of course, with an infinity of meanings beyond the component sources, for the common-sense reason that it was composed for that very purpose, or as we should rather say, that it grew into its final form through the compositorial labors, over centuries, of a great number of men who selected and combined traditions in order to bring to paradigmatic perfection meanings which had not been articulated with the same degree of clarity in the component materials. If the compositorial labors had not added new strata of articulated meaning, the Biblical narrative in its final form would be the *Glasperlenspiel* of unemployed intellectuals who had better have left their sources alone. Faced with the alternatives that either the compositors of the Biblical narrative have ruined the meaning of their sources or that the literary critics have ruined the meaning of the compositorial work, we prefer the second one.

Still, the results of literary criticism are not negligible. While some units of meaning cut across the sources, there are other units, and very important ones, that coincide with them. The so-called Yahwist document, especially, is a body of text rich in meaning that seems to have furnished the historiographic nucleus for the expanding narrative. Following the characterization of the Yahwist work given by von Rad, we can summarize its achievement in the following manner: The Yahwist seems to have reached the historiographic level through expansion of the motives contained in the prayer formula of Deuteronomy 26:4b–9. He organized the materials of the Patriarchal age, through the tradition of the God of the Fathers and his promise of ultimate settlement in Canaan, in such a manner that the events became transparent for the providential guidance of Yahweh. The course of Patriarchal history, thus, was endowed with an entelechy in two respects: On the one hand, the promise of settlement found its fulfillment in the events surrounding the Conquest; on the other hand, the Covenant with Abraham found its fulfillment in the Covenant with Israel at Sinai. Moreover, the meaningful course of history from the "wandering Aramean" to the Conquest was expanded, still within the Yahwist document, through the pre-history from the creation of the world to Abraham.[9] This is, indeed, a great symbolic construction, falling completely within the range of one of the sources; and in so far as the J source is the oldest one, we touch here the beginnings of the symbolic work that ultimately has become the narrative in its extant form.[10]

Nevertheless, the fact that an important unit of meaning is to be found within a source delimited by literary criticism must not blind us for the other fact that we still know nothing whatsoever about the "Yahwist." Assumptions about the manner in which this unit came into being cannot be based on the literary characteristics, as we have stressed, but only on its contents; and the meaning of the contents does not re-quire as its creator a single author. For the entelechy of the historio-graphic symbol does no more than articulate the experienced entelechy of Israel's existence under God. The *telos* of the people's existence was ontologically real, and whoever participated sensitively and imagina-tively in Israel's order was a potential participant in the creation of the historiographic symbol. The literary characteristics indicate no more than the common language of a group of persons, perhaps numerous over a period of time, who were occupied with the traditions concerning Israel's existence under God. We have arrived at last at the basic philo-sophical weaknesses of literary criticism, that is, at the attempt to treat the Biblical narrative as if it were "literature" in the modern sense and the disregard for its nature as a symbolism which articulates the experi-ence of a people's order—of the ontologically real order of Israel's exist-ence in historical form.

The work of the Wellhausen school had resulted in a theoretical vacuum. The traditional meaning which radiated over the Biblical nar-rative from such symbols as the Old Testament of Christianity, the word of God, or the Five Books written by Moses under divine inspiration had evaporated under an empirical investigation of the narrative as a literary document with one or more authors. Furthermore, the dissection of the text into ever-smaller literary units had, while delivering results of questionable validity with regard to the early pragmatic history of Israel,

[9] Von Rad, *Das Formgeschichtliche Problem des Hexateuchs*, 58–62.

[10] Von Rad, *Das erste Buch Mose, Genesis Kapitel 1–12:9* (Goettingen, 1949), 16, assumes for the J source a date of *ca.* 950 B.C., for the E source *ca.* 850–750, for the P source *ca.* 538–450.

led far away from the meaning intended by the narrative itself. And a philosophy of symbolic forms, finally, that would have linked the symbolic narrative with the problems of human existence in response to the divine revelation in history, had failed to develop. The dissatisfaction with this state of things has caused the energetic reaction against the Wellhausen school in the work of Ivan Engnell.[11]

Engnell distinguishes four principal methods for the study of the Old Testament. They are, in the sequence of their development, (1) the source-critical method of the Wellhausen school; (2) the form-literary method of Gunkel; (3) the methods of comparative history of religion; and (4) the tradition-historical method represented by himself.[12] A description of Engnell's method must begin with the clarification of certain complexities in his position. In the first place, while the tradition-historical method invalidates and replaces the earlier ones in some respects, it only supplements them in other ones. The earlier methods, thus, will still have to be used as far as they render valid results.[13] And the tradition-historical method has, furthermore, a double concern with (1) the formation of the narrative through tradition rather than through the literary activity of definite authors, and (2) the peculiar character of a tradition-history as distinguished from pragmatic history. We shall concentrate for the present on the results of the method in so far as it is concerned with the formation of the narrative, and in so far as it replaces the conception of the Wellhausen school.

In the Old Testament, Engnell finds three great collections of traditions: The first one comprises Genesis—Numbers; the second one, Deuteronomy—II Kings; and the third one, I Chronicles—Nehemiah.[14] Our present concern is only with the first two of them. The first collection, to which Engnell briefly refers as the Tetrateuch, originates in a traditionist circle which, as a convenience of language, may be called the

---

[11] The works taken into consideration in the following summary are Engnell, *Gamla Testamentet*, I, as well as Engnell's articles "Litteraerkritik," "Moseboeckerna," and "Traditionshistorisk metod," in Engnell-Fridrichsen, *Svenskt Bibliskt Uppslagsverk*. The most recent formulations of Engnell's position are to be found in his "'Knowledge' and 'Life' in the Creation Story," *Vetus Testamentum*, III, suppl. (Leiden, 1955), 103–19. I owe this reprint to the courtesy of Professor Engnell.

[12] Engnell, *Gamla Testamentet*, I, 9 ff.

[13] Cf. the use of the other methods, for instance, in Engnell, "'Knowledge' and 'Life,'" *loc. cit.*, 104 ff., as well as the enumeration of methods to be used, running into six, not counting subdivisions, in "Planted by the Streams of Water" (reprint from *Studia Orientalia Joanni Pedersen Dicata*, 1953, pp. 85–96), 91, n. 21.

[14] Engnell, *Gamla Testamentet*, I, 209–59.

P-circle. The conventional siglum, however, does not retain its original meaning in Engnell's use. For the P-circle must be understood as a group of persons who preserved certain traditions, identical on the whole with the P-materials of the Wellhausen school, and combined them with materials preserved in other traditionist circles into the Tetrateuch. And the great P-collection, in Engnell's sense of Genesis-Numbers, is therefore an integral work in which the P-circle has imposed its own views on the whole body of traditions received into the Tetrateuch. Hence, no narratives covering the same period ever existed side by side, to be combined into an encyclopedic story by an unknown redactor who did not contribute anything of his own. There co-existed, instead, various traditionist circles, each preserving its own body of traditions and interweaving it with traditions of other circles, if that should appear desirable for one reason or another, until the P-circle combined what presumably was its own material, with the traditions of other circles, into the Tetrateuchal narrative with a meaning of its own. As the nucleus of tradition which radiated its meaning over the construction of the Tetrateuch, Engnell assumes the Passah Legend of Exodus 1–15, in this point following Pedersen.[15] The same assumptions as to the Tetrateuch will, then, apply also to the Deuteronomic work. A D-circle of traditionists must be assumed behind the Deuteronomist collection, though the probabilities of a smaller number of hands in the final redaction, something like a school of authors, are somewhat higher than in the P case. The two circles existed side by side and concluded their work in the postexilic period, perhaps both as late as the time of Ezra and Nehemiah. By whom, finally, the two collections were combined into one narrative, presumably by placing the P-story of the death of Moses at the end of the Deuteronomic speeches (Deuteronomy 34), can no longer be determined.

A comparative evaluation of the new tradition-historical and the older source-critical results must start from the understanding that two sets of assumptions must be weighed against one another. Neither the new nor the old method can draw on independent sources for information about genesis and authorship of the narrative; both have to base their argument on the contents of the narrative itself. If, therefore, the conception of Engnell be considered a distinct advance over the Wellhausen school, as we believe it must, the reason is that the tradition-

---

[15] For Engnell's own view of the Passah problem cf. his "Paesah-Massot and the Problem of Patternism," *Orientalia Suecana*, I (Uppsala, 1952), 39–50.

historical view is based on a much more thorough understanding of the contents of the narrative than the source-critical conception. What characterizes the work of Engnell, and of the Uppsala school in general, is a remarkable respect for the Masoretic Text as it stands, a reluctance to operate with conjectures and emendations (especially a disinclination to use the Septuagint as an easy way out when the Hebrew text is difficult), an excellent philological equipment for dealing with the text, and a vast knowledge of comparative materials for the elucidation of symbols and cult patterns. These technical virtues are the outer bulwark of a will, not always clearly articulated, to return to the meanings intended by the narrative and its subunits, which the Wellhausen school had replaced by the meanings of the J, E, P, and D narratives. And the tradition-historical assumption obviously fits the intended meaning of the narrative very much better than the source-critical assumption. If, for instance, the Tetrateuch is conceived as a work that has received its meaning, together with its final form, through a traditionist circle, the body of text has regained the meaning which it had lost under the assumption of a mechanical combination of sources; and, at the same time, the embarrassing redactor, who combined sources which he had better have left alone, has disappeared. Moreover, the assumption of traditionist circles is sufficiently elastic to accommodate the various genera of traditions clearly to be discerned not only in the narrative but in the Old Testament in general. There may be assumed circles of scribes and learned men for the wisdom literature, of singer groups in the temple for the psalm literature, of colleges of priests for the law collections, of groups of disciples around a master for the prophetic literature, of bards or poets (the *moshlim* of Numbers 21:27) for proverbs, and finally of storytellers or traditionists in the narrower sense for the various types of patriarchal, heroic, and prophetic legends.[16] A splendid vista opens on the culture of Israel, as well as on the variegated circles of men who preserved and enlarged it. Particularly felicitous is Engnell's deliberate anachronism when he speaks of the P-circle as an "Israelite Academy of Literature, History and Antiquities, though, of course, with its root and keen interest in the cult."[17] One wonders whether the analogy is really so very anachronistic; for the concern with the past as the paradigmatic record of God's way with man, extending over a period of more than a thousand years, could

[16] Engnell, *Gamla Testamentet*, I, 41, 105.
[17] Engnell, " 'Knowledge' and 'Life' in the Creation Story," *loc. cit.*, 105.

hardly translate itself into practice without a considerable apparatus of both personnel and material installations, for preserving this enormous body of traditions not only mechanically but with the necessary intelligence and erudition.

Into his tradition-historical method Engnell has thoroughly absorbed the knowledge that tradition-history is not pragmatic history. Since this component of the method derives primarily from Pedersen's earlier rebellion against the Wellhausen school, a few excerpts from Pedersen's study on the Paschal Legend will help in understanding the issue: [18]

> The story of the crossing of the reed sea. . . , as well as the whole emigration legend, though inserted as part of an historical account, is quite obviously of a cultic character, for the whole narrative aims at glorifying the god of the people at the paschal feast through an exposition of the historical event that created the people. The object cannot have been to give a correct exposition of ordinary events but, on the contrary, to describe history on a higher plane. . . . The legend purposes to describe the mythical fight between Yahweh and his enemies and this purpose dominates the narrative to such a degree that it is impossible to show what were the events that have been transformed into this grand drama. . . . The usual separation of the sources of that part of the festival legend which relates to the departure and the crossing of the reed sea is due to a misunderstanding of the whole character of this story. The narrative is no report but a cultic glorification.

In these remarks, on occasion of a concrete subunit of the narrative, Pedersen touches on the decisive points at stake: In the first place, the Paschal Legend cuts across the sources; its unit of meaning is ruined when the text is dissected according to the principles of literary criticism. That unit of meaning, furthermore, though embedded in what purports to be a historical account, has nothing to do with pragmatic history. The attempt at a "realistic" reconstruction of events will be futile, since the order of events within the narrative is governed by the drama of Yahweh's victory over his enemies. The meaning of the narrative, finally, is described as the "cultic glorification" of the God who created his people. At this point we can link the position of Pedersen and Engnell with our own, in so far as "cultic glorification" is a special case of what

[18] For his formal criticism of the Wellhausen school cf. Johannes Pedersen, "Die Auffassung vom Alten Testament," *Zeitschrift fuer die alttestamentliche Wissenschaft*, XLIX (1931), 161–81, and his study on the Paschal Legend in *Israel. Its Life and Culture*, III–IV, 728–37. The following excerpts are from pp. 728–31.

we have called "paradigmatic history." Moreover, we again encounter the "emergence of meaning," in so far as the paradigmatic meaning is not directly imposed by a historian on the events but grows through the stages of the events as experienced by the participants, the crystallization of the experience in a cult, the elaboration of the cult's meaning in a cult legend, and the further historiographic elaboration of the cult legend, probably before, during, and after its integration into what Engnell calls the P-collection of the Tetrateuch. And in this complicated growth of the paradigmatic meaning, finally, various traditionist circles have participated, if we assume the source criteria of the Wellhausen school to be indexes of such circles, even though the original contexts of the elements, discernible by source criteria in the final text, can no longer be reconstructed and the elements themselves, in isolation, render no worthwhile sense.

We have presented the issues by opposing a summary of Engnell's position to a summarizing picture of source-criticism. The reader must now be cautioned not to generalize the means of presentation into a formula for the state of Old Testament study with regard to historiographic problems. For Engnell, in his pointed formulations, is in rebellion against a state of science that prevailed about thirty years ago. During the last generation scholars have gradually moved away from a situation that was typical for *ca.* 1920; and Engnell himself is most eager to enlist the support, coming from various quarters, for his tradition-historical method.[19] The complexity of the Old Testament does not yield to a brief theoretical formula, and the lines of development in science do not run as clearly as our contrasting summaries might suggest. Engnell, for instance, following Pedersen, considers the Paschal Legend the nucleus of meaning in the Tetrateuch. And nobody will deny that the experi-

[19] Cf. Engnell, *Gamla Testamentet*, I, in the chapters on "Litteraerkritiken efter Wellhausen" (pp. 175–85) and "Opposition. Kritisk uppgoerelse" (pp. 186–209). In particular Martin Noth, *Ueberlieferungsgeschichtliche Studien I. Die Sammelnden und Bearbeitenden Geschichtswerke im Alten Testament* (Halle, 1943), is frequently adduced by Engnell in support of his own views concerning the collections of traditions. Of the literature after 1945, furthermore, must be mentioned Artur Weiser, *Einleitung in das Alte Testament* (2d ed., Goettingen, 1949). Weiser, who at the time of his writing had not yet access to the recent work of the Uppsala school, uses the term *Traditionsgeschichte* and recognizes the origin of numerous traditions in the cult. He is, furthermore, aware that the "sources" are no literary documents and that, in view of the changes which they have undergone in the process of oral and written tradition, they can no longer be reconstructed in an "original" form. He is willing, however, to recognize the marks of personal authorship in the sources, thus approaching the position of Gerhard von Rad in his treatment of the Yahwist. And he is, finally, aware, like Pedersen, that *Heilsgeschichte,* because of its origin in the cult, is something entirely different from pragmatic history.

ence of the Exodus is one of the great motivating centers which cannot have failed to make its strength felt in the organization of traditions. Von Rad, on the contrary, has stressed the Sinai experience as a motivating center radiating order over the narrative. And again nobody will deny the strength of the Sinai experience and its crystallizing influence on traditions—even though the result is a Hexateuch rather than Engnell's Tetrateuch. Moreover, the historiographic construction, as distinguished from the traditions submitted to its work, has an independent motivating center in the experience of the Davidic monarchy. The point of literary crystallization of the narrative probably was neither the Paschal Legend nor the Sinai Pericope but the David Memoirs—and with that observation we are beyond Tetrateuch and Hexateuch in organizational contexts in which the hand of the "Yahwist," in the sense in which von Rad has clarified his work, can hardly be denied.[20] The source criticism of the old type, we may say, is indeed dead. What has come into view through the labors of Old Testament students is the rich stratification of the narrative and the plurality of motivating centers. And that new freedom of critical exploration is about to repair much of the damage inflicted upon the meaning of the narrative by the literary conceits of the nineteenth century.

§ 2. THE SYMBOLS OF HISTORIOGRAPHY

Throughout this part we have spoken of history as the Israelite form of existence, of a historical present created by the Covenant, and of an Israelite historiography, while ignoring the fact that the Hebrew language has no word that could be translated as "history." This is a serious matter, for apparently we have violated the first principle of hermeneutics—that the meaning of a text must be established through interpretation of the linguistic corpus. It is impermissible to "put an interpretation on" a literary work through anachronistic use of modern vocab-

---

[20] On the role of the David Memoirs as the motivating center of historiography cf. Gerhard von Rad, "Der Anfang der Geschichtsschreibung im Alten Israel," *Archiv fuer Kulturgeschichte,* XXXII (1944), 1–42. Von Rad is aware that the problem of historiography cannot be attacked from the literary phenomenon of the written work but that the writing of history in the Israel-ite manner presupposes what we call "existence in historical form." "The ability to recognize a succession of events as history at all, is owed in the old Israel to the peculiarity of its faith" (p. 6). On the basis of this insight, von Rad can then distinguish between the Israelite type of historiography, the annalistic of the cosmological empires, and the immanentist Hellenic histori-ography. Our own views in these matters are closest to those of von Rad.

ulary without equivalents in the text itself. Hence, two questions will demand an answer: (1) How can the use of the term "history" be justified in an analysis of Israelite symbols? and (2) what did the Israelite authors do, expressed in their own language, when they wrote what we call "history"?

The justification demanded by the first question will rely on the principle of compactness and differentiation. The Israelite thinkers did not indeed differentiate the idea of history to the point of developing a theoretical vocabulary. Nevertheless, with due precautions, the modern vocabulary may be used without destroying the meaning of Israelite symbols, because the idea of history has its origin in the Covenant. The compact Mosaic symbolism of communal existence under the will of God as revealed through his instructions has in continuity, through the course of Israelite, Jewish, and Christian history, undergone a process of articulation from which resulted, among others, the idea of history. After three millenniums of defections and returns, of reforms, renaissances, and revisions, of Christian gains and modern losses of substance, we are still living in the historical present of the Covenant. Moreover, the work of the Israelite historiographers is still going on, although, due to theoretical differentiation, the techniques have changed. For Israel has become mankind; and the accretion of the Instructions has become the revision of principles.

The use of such terms as "history," "historical present," and "historiography," however, is more than justified in an analysis of Israelite symbols—it is a matter of theoretical necessity. For if the differentiated vocabulary were rejected, there would be no instruments for critical analysis and interpretation. Confined to the use of the Hebrew symbols, our understanding would be locked up in the very compactness which, in Israelite history, has led into the disastrous impasses previously discussed. Nevertheless, while we cannot dispense with modern theoretical vocabulary, extreme caution is necessary in its use, for the idea of history has absorbed experiences beyond the Israelite range, and we run the risk of projecting later, e.g. Christian, meanings into the earlier symbols. Hence, the interpretation must be kept as close as possible to the Biblical text. Moreover, a brief reflection on the peculiar nature of Israelite compactness will be in place.

The nature of Israelite compactness has been touched repeatedly in the analyses of Chapters 4 and 5. The events in the social sphere were no longer experienced as part of the cosmic-divine order, but became transparent for the order of transcendent-divine reality. The impact of the new experience must have been overpowering, for the community who suffered it with its leaders was thereby set off as a peculiar people from the surrounding cosmological societies, and that meant at the time, from the rest of mankind. It was perhaps this heaviness of the divine impact on a comparatively small community, traumatically aggravated by the stresses and strains of pragmatic existence, that sealed the meaning of the event ineluctably with its concrete, circumstantial features. At any rate, the universalist implications of the experience were never successfully explicated within Israelite history. The spiritual meaning of the exodus from civilization was well understood but nevertheless remained inseparable from the concrete Exodus from Egypt; the Kingdom of God could never quite separate from Canaan; the great original revelation remained so overwhelmingly concrete that its spiritual renewals had to assume the literary form of additions to the Instructions; and the word of God to mankind through Israel became the sacred scripture of a particular ethnico-religious community. The nature of Israelite compactness can be summarized, therefore, as a perpetual mortgage of the world-immanent, concrete event on the transcendent truth that on its occasion was revealed.

The compactness of the nature just described is peculiar to the whole body of symbols in which Israelite historical thought expressed itself. From this body we must now single out for consideration the few symbols that have a direct bearing on the question: What did Israelite historians do, in their own terms, when they wrote history? Of whom or of what, we must ask, did they write history? And what did they call the thing they wrote?

The subject-matter of Israelite historiography, as we have seen, is world-history in the pregnant sense of a report on the emergence of divinely willed order in world and society through the creative and covenanting acts of God. If for the moment the brief introductory account of the Creation, as well as its bearing on the further happenings, is set aside, one can say that the vastly preponderant bulk of the report is concerned with the human drama of obedience to, and defection from, the will of God. Hence, the historiographer will be, first of all, concerned with the divine instructions (*toroth*) that furnish the measure for human conduct and its appraisal. In the realm of historiographic symbols this governing theme has achieved precedence over all others in so far as it has furnished the title for the Bible: "Law [*torah*], Prophets, and Writings." This body of literature in its aggregate is briefly referred to as the "book," *sepher,* the Bible.

The drama of man under the will of God cannot unfold without the continuous existence of the mankind that is supposed to live in accordance with the Instructions. Man, therefore, with the accent on his reproductive capacity, is the second major concern of the Israelite historians.

Mankind is conceived as a clan, deriving its community bond from a common ancestor. History, under this aspect, becomes an account of the generations (*toldoth*) of man descending from Adam, down to the time of the writer. The idea, with some of its connotations, can be discerned in the opening of Chronicles. The author of this late historical work begins with a long account of Israelite genealogies from Adam to the Exile (I Chron. 1–8), in order to link the men who returned from the Babylonian Captivity, and in particular those who now held office, with the past and thereby to guarantee their legitimate descent (9).[21] The genealogical register, thus, has its immediate function in the synoecism of Ezra. Since the "holy seed" had been polluted through marriages with foreign women, they and their offspring had now to be expelled by a solemn covenant with God. It was a serious affair with a comic touch: "All the people sat in the open space before the house of God, trembling on account of the occasion itself and also because of the pouring rain" (Ezra 10:10). Clan-heads of pure descent, uncontaminated by marriage with foreigners, were to be the ruling class of the new settlements in Jerusalem and the surrounding towns. In order to establish the pure descent, the genealogy had to be traced into the pre-exilic Kingdom.

At this point of the construction, there appears a new authenticating source. Back as far as the fall of Jerusalem the author apparently relied on the memory of the living; for the period of the monarchy, however, he referred to the "Book of the Kings of Israel" as the source of his registers. (I Chron. 9:1.) Whatever that "Book" may have been, the

---

[21] This would be an odd opening for a history of the Kingdom of Judah. But the oddity disappears if we remember that the whole work of Chronicles is a report on the political disaster, meant as a warning introduction to Ezra and Nehemiah.

reference suggests the existence of literary sources dealing with the genealogies of leading Israelite families; and these sources in their turn were probably based on Temple or other public archives. How far back the written genealogies of "all Israel" extended does not appear with certainty from Chronicles; but their arrangement according to tribes in I Chronicles 2–8 suggests they were constructed on principle so as to be attached to one of the ancestors of the Jacob clans.

Beyond the tribes of the confederacy we enter the realm of legend, myth, and speculation. The great nodal point in the symbolism is the descent from Shem, "the father of all the children of Eber" (Gen. 10:21). The Hebrew word *shem* means "name." With Shem the register of names reaches the abstraction of the Name by which "all Israel" is distinguished from a symbolically anonymous mankind. From Shem, finally, the register goes back to Adam. The Hebrew word *adam* means "man." The man with the Name ultimately descends from generic Man.

The register of Chronicles illuminates the various uses to which the genealogies can be put, as well as the tension that must develop between the clan idea and the idea of mankind. The symbol of the *toldoth* applies to the whole course of Israelite history. As the phases of application can be distinguished, in chronological order: (1) The synoecism of the returned exiles; (2) the clan-heads of the Kingdom; (3) the tribes of the Confederacy; (4) the succession of the Patriarchs; (5) the second mankind from Noah to Abraham; and (6) the first mankind from Adam to Noah. The reliability of the registers in detail is not our concern; but we must note that the form of the register is applied not only to Patriarchal but even to pre-Patriarchal history, where it no longer can serve clan history, however unreliable, but obviously is the clan symbolism expanded to cover a speculation on the origins of mankind. This speculative expansion, however, has no independent function in the context of the registers of Chronicles but is subordinate to the main purpose of guaranteeing the purity of the "holy seed." For the register is rigidly constructed on the principle of separating the main line of mankind from the side lines. A series of names on the main line is enumerated until a point is reached where the heads of side lines appear; at this point the main line is interrupted, the side lines are disposed of, and then the enumeration returns to the main line. The descendants of Adam, for instance, are enumerated down to Shem, Ham, and Japheth; then the descendants of

Japheth and Ham, as well as the side lines of Shem are disposed of; and then the register returns to the enumeration of the main line from Shem to Abraham; and so forth. The procedure of recapturing the main line again and again from the mass of lesser mankind is an impressive prelude to the recapturing that is now in the offing when the men who returned from the Exile will separate as the "remnant," as the "children of captivity" (Ezra 8:35), from the "adversaries," the "people of the land" (*am-ha-aretz*, Ezra 4:1–4), that is, from the Israelites who had remained in the country when the others were carried off into captivity.

Up to this point the analysis renders the following result. The historiographic symbol of the *toldoth* had for its basis the genealogies of the clans united in the Israelite Confederacy. The genealogy, then, became the symbol for expressing the unity of groups which by their substance were no clans at all. The dominant experience in the creation of such groups was the Covenant at Mount Sinai, which constituted something like an amphictyonic league of formerly separate clans, under the name of Israel. The community originating in the Covenant was, then, submitted to genealogical work; and as a consequence the original clans, as well as others which joined them at a later time, as for instance Judah, were constructed as tribes descending from a common ancestor Jacob-Israel. The Covenant, however, was a divine revelation of true order valid for all mankind, made to a particular group at a particular time. Hence, there could be, and historically there was, differentiated from it both the idea of a mankind under one God and the idea of a nucleus of true believers. Again both ideas were submitted to genealogical work. The idea of mankind was cast in the form of a genealogy going back to Adam; the nucleus of the true believers became a "remnant" that kept a genealogical record of the "holy seed." In both instances the genealogical work was more than an innocuous formality. The idea of mankind could never be understood in its fullness, in spite of the arduous endeavors of the prophets, because through the genealogical form it remained closely linked to the idea of a genealogically separated sacred line. And the idea of a nucleus of true believers rendered, under the genealogical influence, the grotesque result of the postexilic synoecism: That a numerically small group of exiles returned to Jerusalem and excommunicated the *am-ha-aretz*, that is, the people of Israel settled in its promised land. The people of Israel had to wait for its historical revenge until from the *am-ha-aretz* there arose Jesus and Christianity.

Nevertheless, beside the genealogical contraction into the remnant there stands the genealogical expansion into mankind. We shall now turn to the speculation, in genealogical form, on the idea of mankind that is to be found in Genesis. The speculation develops a characteristic style in the construction of great registers which bridge the intervals between the major human catastrophes and regenerations. Omitting the complications of the Abel-Cain story, the first register extends from Adam to Noah (Genesis 5). After the destruction of mankind through the Flood, a second register begins with Noah (6:9–10). It is brief, comprising no more than Noah himself and his three sons Shem, Ham, and Japheth. Whether the two verses were at some time the beginning of a longer register, we do not know. But we can see the reason why the register had to break off at this point, not to be resumed until Genesis 11:10, where it continues from Shem to Abraham. For between the two parts of the second register is placed the previously discussed geopolitical register of Genesis 10. The historians who were responsible for the ultimate organization of Genesis wanted their world-history to embrace mankind and to clarify the relation of the sacred line to the rest of mankind. The logical place for the insertion of the register was the generation after Noah, when the first mankind had been conveniently destroyed and the second one began to branch out; thanks to this location, the ancestry of Israel was now coeval with the rest of mankind—a point that must have been of some importance for a people surrounded by the old Mesopotamian and Egyptian high-civilizations. Nevertheless, the tension between mankind and the sacred line is well preserved. After the interlude of the Tower of Babel (Gen. 11:1–9), which explains the linguistic and geographical scattering of mankind presupposed in Genesis 10, the main task is resumed and the register of the sacred line continued from the Name to Abraham. With the exodus of the first Patriarch from civilization the separation begins in earnest; and God in his turn now attacks in earnest the problem of establishing human order in conformity with his will, which he had failed to solve by the somewhat violent means of expulsion from Paradise, destruction by the Flood, and the scattering of mankind and its linguistic confusion after the affair of Babel.

Compared with the fanatical determination of the Chronicler to throw the people of Israel out of the main line, we are moving in Genesis in an atmosphere of intellectual detachment. There are subtleties embedded in its construction that require closer consideration. The registers are formalized, in so far as they begin with the phrase: "These are the generations [*toldoth*] of . . ." (Gen. 6:9; 10:1; 11:10). The meaning of the formalization becomes most tangible in the Adam register which begins: "This is the book [*sepher*] of the generations [*toldoth*] of Adam" (Gen. 5:1). What the word "book" means in this context can only be surmised; but we shall probably not be far wrong if we follow Buber's translation as *Urkunde* and assume it to mean something like an authentic record. The insistence on trustworthiness deserves attention, for it cannot have escaped the redactors of the narrative that the *toldoth* of Adam in Genesis 5 do not agree with the accounts of the Adam generations that begin in 4:17 and 4:25. If anything is untrustworthy on the face of it, it is this collection of reverentially preserved but conflicting registers. Moreover, one must raise the question, who in the world would have had an interest in these registers and their authenticity? One cannot dwell, in search of an answer, on nomad customs and the remarkable ability of Bedouin sheiks to remember twelve generations of ancestors, covering about four centuries. For the registers list nobody's remembered ancestors, but are constructions which use the clan symbolism as an instrument of speculation on the genesis of mankind and the world. Hence, taking it for granted that ancient symbolists were not as naïve as modern fundamentalists, the quality of trustworthiness must have been meant to attach not to the detail of the registers but to the symbolic meaning which they intended to convey.

A clue to the meaning is furnished by Genesis 2:4: "These are the generations [*toldoth*] of heaven and earth." The passage opens an account of the creation but uses the same phraseology as the genealogical registers. That is an odd usage; for the noun *toldoth* contains the verb *yalad*, "to bear," "to bring forth," and thus unmistakably refers not to creation but to procreation. Hence, we must assume that the oddity was intended, precisely in order to reveal a deeper connection between creation and procreation. The assumption is confirmed by the sequel to the odd passage. For the account of creation (2:4–7) describes it as a sequence of generations, the earlier one procreating the later one with the creative assistance of Yahweh:

> These are the generations [*toldoth*] of the heavens and earth when
>   they were created:
>
> On the day when Yahweh-Elohim made heaven and earth,
>   there were as yet no field shrubs on the earth,

and no field plants had as yet sprung up,
for Yahweh-Elohim had not caused it to rain on the earth,
and there was no *adam* [man, Adam] to till the *adamah* [soil].

But from the earth rose an *ad* [pronounced "ed," mist] and watered
    the whole face of the *adamah*,
and Yahweh-Elohim formed *adam* from the dust of the *adamah*,
and breathed into his nostrils the breath of life,
and *adam* became a living being.

No modern translation can adequately render the innuendo of the Hebrew text that the first generation of creation, that is, the heavens and earth, become procreative and co-operate with Yahweh in the work of creation. From the fertilization of *ad* and *adamah* arises, under the forming and animating action of Yahweh, the second generation of *adam*, with the double meaning of man and Adam.

The role of the passage in the symbolic construction will become even clearer when we hold by the side of it the opening passage of the Adam register:

This is the *sepher* [book] of the *toldoth* [generations] of *adam*
    [man, Adam]:

On the day when God created *adam*,
he made him in the likeness of God,
male and female he created them,
and blessed them,
and called their name: *Adam!* on the day of their creation.

And *adam* lived a hundred and thirty years,
and begat in his likeness after his image,
and called his name: Seth!

With the linguistic structure of the text before him, the reader will not doubt that the *toldoth* of Adam continue the *toldoth* of heavens and earth. The authors intended the meanings of creation and procreation to merge in a co-operative process; the order of being is meant to arise from the creative initiative of God and the procreative response of the creation. Hence, what is trustworthy about the registers is not the genealogical ascent from the presently living to some remote ancestor but the generative descent from God—generative understood in the double meaning of creative-procreative. The *adam* that was created by God with the procreative response of *ad* and *adamah* continues to generate himself in the likeness of God. To the presently living the registers authenticate their being *adam* in the likeness of God—that is, the human medium that is supposed to co-operate in generating the order of being through procreative submission to the creative will of God.

The divine creation of order is not finished with Man. The work continues through the instructions issued to *adam* and requiring his co-operative obedience. To be sure, the co-operation would be impossible if there were no *adam;* and the basic instruction, securing his continued existence, is therefore the "Be fruitful, and multiply, and fill the earth!" issued by God to Adam (Gen. 1:28) and to Noah (Gen. 9:1). But this torah, operative on the level of the *toldoth,* would not be enough to achieve the order of being; for, as experience had shown, unholy mankind was fruitful, multiplied, and filled the earth even more effectively than Israel. Hence, the process of world-history reaches its highest level with the divine choice of individuals and groups for special instruction and the trusting response of the chosen individuals and groups. The special relationship between God and man is formalized through the covenants. The covenant, the berith, must therefore be ranked with *toroth* and *toldoth* as the third great symbol used in the expression of Israelite historical thought.

The berith as a legal institution in general, as well as the Great Berith between Yahweh and Israel, will be discussed in a later part of this study. Nevertheless, we must remain aware that when we try to determine the historiographic function of the symbol, we are dealing with a layer of meaning superimposed on the two others. The problem resembles that of the *toldoth.* In the case of the *toldoth* the basic institution was the clan with a distinguished ancestor. The genealogies of the clans were a matter of public record. The form of the genealogy then was employed for symbolizing the community bond of groups that were no clans, as in the tribal construction of the Israel that had been constituted by the Great Berith, as well as in the speculation on the origin and diversification of mankind. And on the *toldoth* of Adam, finally, was superimposed the *toldoth* of the heavens and earth, so that from its origin the history of mankind would be suffused with the creatively ordering will of God. In a similar manner we find at the institutional basis in the case of the berith, the federal agreements between nomad clans and between nomads and agricultural settled groups, and in alliances in foreign relations. The form of the berith then is employed for symbolizing the relation between Yahweh and Israel, as it was established at Mount Sinai. And on the

Great Berith that constitutes the Israelite historical present, finally, is superimposed the use of the symbol for historiographic purposes.

In order to determine the historiographic function more closely, we must furthermore eliminate the institutional use of the symbol in the wake of the Great Berith. The Covenant at Mount Sinai became for Israel the prototype of its formal relation with Yahweh. Whenever at a critical juncture the relation had to be recalled or renewed or when the content of the *toroth* had to be amended, the solemn act was cast in the form of a covenant with Yahweh, or before Yahweh. The main instances were (1) the berith of Joshua, embodying its contents in a "Book of the Instructions [*torah*] of God" (Josh. 24:25–26); (2) the berith of Hezekiah, on occasion of his Reform (II Chron. 29:10); (3) the berith of Josiah, introducing the Deuteronomy as the "Book of the Covenant" (II Kings 23:2–3); (4) the previously mentioned berith of Ezra (Ezra 10:3); and (5) the covenant of Nehemiah, which, however, is not designated as berith but as *amanah* (Neh. 10:1). In cases of this kind the berith is an institutional, rather than a historiographic, symbol.

The historiographic function proper makes itself felt, as in the case of the *toldoth,* in the pre-Mosaic part of the narrative. Here, it seems, the symbol of the berith has been deliberately used to put heavy emphasis on the great epochs of history. These epochs are (1) the first mankind of Adam; (2) the second mankind of Noah; (3) the first exodus of Abraham; and (4) the second exodus of Moses. It was apparently the Priestly redaction that accentuated the epochs by expanding the symbol beyond Moses into the prehistory, and attributed to earlier covenants certain ritual institutions. The Abraham story was heightened through the berith of God with Abraham (Gen. 17:1–8), instituting circumcision (17:9–14); and the Noah story was heightened through the berith (9:9), instituting abstention from blood (9:3–6). While the epoch of Adam was not marked by a berith, the component parts of the Noah and Abraham epochs were inserted into the story, so that the effect of emphasis was the same. For the line of ritual accentuations was continued into Genesis 2:3 through the institution of the Sabbath. And in Genesis 1:29–30 was placed a curious torah, clearly for the purpose of linking the Adam epoch with the berith element in the Noah epoch. For the Noah covenant had enjoined: "Everything that moves, that is alive, is to be food for you; as I once gave you the green plants, I now give you everything. Only you must never eat flesh with the life [*nephesh,* life, soul], that is, the blood in it." [22] The phrase "I once gave you the green plants" refers back to Genesis 1:29–30: "I have given you every plant yielding seed . . . for food; and to every beast on the earth . . . wherein there is a living *nephesh*, I have given every green plant for food." The instruction to the animated creation, a kind of "vegetarian" covenant, looks like a speculative construction of the Priestly redactor, extending the berith symbol to the Adam epoch.

In view of the superimposition of the covenant symbol on the historical narrative, with its accentuation of the epochs, it is justifiable to speak of a conscious speculation on periods of history. There are the four periods already mentioned, from Adam to Noah, from Noah to Abraham, from Abraham to Moses, and from Moses onward. Unfortunately there is no means of ascertaining how far back in Israelite history this speculation on the ages may go; we only know that the redaction in its present form stems from the fourth century. Hence, it is certainly earlier than the Danielic construction of the four monarchies, of *ca.* 165 B.C.; and it may have its origin in Babylonian influences during the Exile. But not too much importance should be attached to such guesses. All one can say is that the number four, which has its symbolic function in the spatial orientation of cosmological empires, could be transferred to temporal orientation. And that could have happened at any time in Israelite history, for there was no secret about the symbolism of the number four.

The *berith* and the *toldoth* were both used for the symbolization of the historical periods. If there should be any doubt about the speculative intention as the primary motive in the arrangement of the narrative, it will be dispelled by the use that was still made of this symbolism in early Christian historiography. For the Gospel of St. Matthew opens in best Israelite style with a "Book of the generations of Jesus Christ, son of David, son of Abraham." The Greek *biblos geneseos* is the Septuagint translation of the *sepher toldoth*, the "Book of the generations of Adam,"

---

[22] For further explanation of the injunction to abstain from blood see Leviticus 17:11: "For the life [*nephesh*] of the flesh is in the blood; and I have given it to you to be placed on the altar to expiate your souls [*nephesh*]; for blood expiates because of the life [*nephesh*] in it." The difficulties of translation are the same as in the case of the Greek *psyche* in Homeric usage. The life-soul, seated in the blood, is supposed to be ontologically of the same substance as the life-soul that was breathed into man by the animating breath of God (Gen. 2:7). Hence, the injunction to abstain from the blood of slaughtered animals is immediately followed by the warning that nobody must shed a man's blood, or his blood will be shed in return, "For God made man in his own image" (Gen. 9:6).

of Genesis 5:1. In Matthew 1:2–16, then, the generations are given from Abraham to Jesus in descending line, whereas Luke 3:23–28 traces the genealogy in the ascending line from "Jesus, the putative son of Joseph" to "Adam, the son of God." The epochs covered by the genealogies, to be sure, were Christianized. Abraham was the distinguished ancestor because through his "descendants all the nations of the earth shall invoke blessings on one another" (Gen. 22:18); and David, because he received the prophecy through Nathan: "I will establish your offspring after you, who shall be one of your sons, and I will establish his kingdom. He shall build me a house, and I will establish his throne forever" (I Chron. 17:11–12). But the number four was preserved in spite of the Christianization of the periods; there were still four periods: from Adam to Abraham, from Abraham to David, from David to the Exile, and from the Exile to Christ (Matt. 1:17). The great problem of the periodization of history in Christian and modern speculation goes back in continuity to the Israelite historiographers.

§ 3. The Motivations of Historiography

The work of the historians produced a narrative that ranged from the creation of the world to the fall of Jerusalem. The narrative was the story of something. And whatever that something may have been, it stood in the relation of subject matter to the historiographic work. At least so it would seem to the modern mind which takes it for granted that a history must be a history of something.

But unfortunately it is not so. In the opening pages of the present chapter, we have warned that the terms "historiography" and "historical subject matter" were fraught with thorny problems. Our reflection now has led us back to the center of the difficulties.

That the term "historical subject matter" is not applicable without qualifications to the content of the narrative becomes apparent as soon as we realize that the narrative contains among other things an account of the creation. Such an account is not a body of propositions concerning events witnessed by a historian or, for that matter, by anybody. The stories of the Creation, of Noah and the Flood, of the Tower of Babel, and so on, are myths; and their "subject matter" is not the content of the stories but the experiences symbolized by means of the stories. Hence, over long stretches of the narrative, the historiographic work has pro-

duced not a history of anything but a purposefully devised myth. Moreover, myth and history are not clearly separate parts of the narrative but
blend into each other. Historical subject matter proper enters in increasing quantities in the course of the Patriarchal stories and bulks heavily
in the history of the Davidic Empire and the Kingdoms, but the myth
never disappears completely. And furthermore, one cannot even say that
the component of the myth gradually thins out as the narrative moves
closer toward its end, for toward the end it contains a magnificent and
complex specimen of myth in the story of the "discovery" of the Deuteronomic Code. The historical elements, to be sure, are clearly distinguishable in the account of the discovery. We can discern the authorship
of the Code, the skillful timing of its "discovery," and the contrivance
of the myth. But these elements are firmly embedded in the myth of the
discovery itself, as well as in the mythical form which presents the Code
as a series of divine instructions communicated by speeches of Moses.
Here, for once, we have a genuine myth *about* Moses, as distinguished
from the symbols created *by* Moses. The Israelite narrator accepts the
myth of the discovery and reports its content as if it were history; and
in doing so he inevitably informs us that, as a matter of historical fact,
such a myth was contrived and really enacted by the "discoverers" of the
Deuteronomic Code. The narrator is not the dupe of the myth, since he
belonged to the circle that created it and perhaps even participated in its
creation. His attitude rather resembles that of the authors of the Memphite Theology. He can contrive a myth and at the same time believe it,
for the myth embodies the truth of an experience—that the instructions
of the Deuteronomic Code authentically renew the truth of order communicated by Moses. The truth of the Mosaic instructions was experienced as rediscovered for the age. And the myth of the discovery,
accepted as history, was a subtle and effective method to express this
truth.

The historiographic work, thus, contains genuine myths, genuine
history, and the strange intertwinings of history, myth, and enactment
of the myth that we find in the affair of the Deuteronomy. The three
types of content are blended into a new type of story that is neither myth
nor pragmatic history but the previously analysed "world-history" with
its experiential nucleus in the historical present constituted by Moses
and the Covenant, and its elaboration through speculations on the origins
of being and the periods of world-history. The "narrative" thus has

absorbed variegated types of materials and transformed them according to its own principle of construction. It is a symbolic form *sui generis*. Hence, when now again we raise the question concerning the "subject matter" of the narrative, we are forced to the conclusion that it has no "subject matter," but a meaning which can be ascertained only by recourse to the experiential motivations of the form.

An access to the motivations of the form will be gained by the observation that the great narrative came to an end. The Israelite historians lost their interest in world-historic events when the kingdoms of Israel and Judah had disappeared from the political scene. But if we consider that certainly a principal motivation of Israelite historiography was the constitution of the people by the Covenant and that the narrative elaborated paradigmatically the existence of the people under divine Instructions, it will not be so obvious that the narrative should have come to an end at all, or that if it did it should have done so at this particular point. If one takes the narrative at its face value, one would rather expect it to have been continued and brought up to date as long as there were Israelites alive and able to do such work.

In order to explain the oddity of its cessation, we must assume the primary motivation of the great narrative to have been not an interest in world-history at all but rather an interest in the foundation of the Kingdom with whose end the story ends. And this assumption is borne out by the facts of literary history, in so far as the writing of history did indeed begin in the time of Solomon and its first subject matter was the origins of the monarchy. The J and E traditions, furthermore, were formed into coherent stories and perhaps committed to writing under the Kingdom and by their historical situation were intended as the early history of the Israel that was organized as a people under a king.

If, however, the foundation of the Kingdom furnished the primary motive for historiography, at least as far as written history is concerned, a conflict seems to develop between the two major events by which the people of Israel was constituted. For the assumed primary motive of written history contradicts the contents of the historiographic work in so far as, according to the narrative itself, the focus of Israelite history was not the rise of the monarchy but the constitution of the people through the events of the Mosaic period.

In order to remove the conflict the foundation of the monarchy must be recognized as an event of far greater importance for Israel than it would appear to have been according to the narrative. The Prophetic concern with the iniquities of royal conduct, foreign policy, and social evils has cast a shadow over the monarchy and minimized its pragmatic achievement while at the same time it was enhancing the rather dismal events of the so-called conquest of Canaan to heroic proportions. If we penetrate the paradigmatic redaction to the pragmatic core of the events leading up to the call for a king, it appears that the Israelite invasion of Canaan had been only partially successful, that the foothold gained was precarious, and that the attacks of the Philistines threatened the Israelite position with a reduction bordering on extinction. The situation must indeed have been desperate, because Israel before the monarchy consisted pragmatically of nothing but an unorganized willingness of various clans, united by the bond of the Covenant, to aid each other in case of an attack. And this willingness not only was unorganized but quite un-reliable even in case of a deadly emergency. In terms of power politics one would have to say that the "conquest" of Canaan was an incon-clusive penetration of the country, and by the time of Saul it was on the point of being wiped out by the better organized Philistine forces. The conquest was completed, or rather it became an effective conquest at all, only through the acceptance of kingship and the successful conclusion of the Philistine wars.

If the history of the conquest is seen in this light, the historiographic motivations will lose their contradictory appearance. For the foundation of the Kingdom was, strictly speaking, not an event within the history of Israel but the last of a series of acts through which Israel came into historical existence. This series of acts, to be sure, began with the work of Moses, with the Exodus and the Covenant, but it did not end with them or even with the penetration of Canaan. The political organization of the people on its territory, the creation of the form under which it could act and maintain itself on the historical scene, was accomplished only by the monarchy. The creation of the community substance by Moses had to be supplemented by the organization for pragmatic existence. The successful completion of Israelite existence would be the experience that motivated the writing of history because now the organized people had emerged of which a history could be written. And the historical work would have for its first topic the reigns of Saul and David and the accession of Solomon, as it did in the memoirs of an unknown author that are preserved in II Samuel 9–20 and the first two chapters of I Kings as the nucleus of the J document. Moreover, it would intelligibly come to an end with the destruction of the Kingdom, that is, with the disappearance of the motivating political existence.

Under the aspect just discussed, the foundation of the Kingdom became the motivating center of Israelite historiography. In particular, from this point of crystallization history was written backward so as to fit the realities of the new political organization. The story of the substantive constitution of Israel through the Covenant, as well as of the conquest down to the Philistine wars, had to precede the story of the Kings. And this prehistory, in order to fit the conditions of the Davidic Kingdom, had to allot an appropriate place to the tribe of Judah, though the king's tribe had in fact never formed part of the original Israelite confederacy. Furthermore, there had to be solved the question of the Canaan that now had become unequivocally the dominion of Israel. For this Canaan had been an old sacred landscape in its own right. And the numerous holy places, accepted as common sanctuaries in the course of the symbiosis of conquerors and conquered, had now to be integrated with genuine Hebrew clan traditions so that the whole would form a coherent story of the Patriarchs and their ancient relations with the present territory of the Israelite monarchy. And the construction of Patriarchal history, finally, had to be preceded by a history of mankind from the creation of the world in order to describe and explain the ethno-political environment of the Kingdom. The Israelite prehistory, thus, was a work of purposeful construction; and the primary motivation of this component in the larger historiographic work must be sought not in the events of the Mosaic period but in the political situation created by the success of the monarchy.

The contradictions, thus, disappear, when the two focuses of Israelite historiography are recognized and their relationship is understood. Nevertheless, a few misgivings will have been aroused by this peculiar bifocal structure. We have spoken of the foundation of the Kingdom as the primary motive of historiography; and certainly it is discernible as such in the literary genesis of the narrative. In the ultimate structure, however, it is completely overlaid by the motivations of the Mosaic Covenant. We must, furthermore, consider that the narrative indeed ends, as might be expected, with the fall of Jerusalem, but that the historiographic work on it continued, quite unexpectedly from the point of view of the primary motivation, for two-and-a-half centuries after the end of the Kingdom. In general, this posthumous work comprised the Deuteronomist and Priestly Codes in the Mosaic Instructions; it furthermore contributed the speculation on the four periods of history; and, finally, it expanded and sharpened the speculation on the meaning of creation. Moreover, by the subdivision of the work into the Instructions and the Prophets, it overshadowed the primary motivation so heavily that even the character of the world-history as a continuous narrative was obscured. In the posthumous work the interest in the community substance created by Moses and the Covenant took precedence of the Kingdom so decisively that it cannot be simply treated as a "secondary" motive.

Complexities in a structure of meanings cannot be dissolved by far-fetched explanations, but only by a clearer statement of the issue. We started from the observation that the world-history had absorbed variegated materials and merged them in the medium of the narrative. The narrative, with its content, was recognized as a symbolic form *sui generis*. It did not have a "subject matter"; its meaning had to be understood in terms of the experiences that motivated its construction. The literary genesis revealed the foundation of the Kingdom as the primary motive in chronological order; but the total construction, with its long posthumous work, made the historical present created by the Covenant, as well as the speculation on creative origins and periods of history, the dominating principle of the content, though this motivation was secondary in chronological order. The order of motives in the content, thus, was the reverse of the order of motives in time. Moreover, to round out the problem, the order of motivations in time—first the Kingdom, second the Covenant—was the reverse of the order of events in time. The elements which account for the complexity of the historiographic work can, therefore, be summarized in the following three propositions: (1) In the sequence of historical events the Covenant precedes the Kingdom; (2) in the sequence of motivations of the narrative the Kingdom precedes the Covenant; (3) in the content of the narrative itself the Covenant dominates the Kingdom.

Once the structure is recognized, its meaning is apparent. The cause of the difficulties is the compact experience of order. We have referred to the two focuses of Israelite history, that is, the creation of the community substance through Moses and the Covenant, and the creation of the political organization for successful pragmatic existence through the monarchy. These were the two focuses which in the later, Christian development differentiated into sacred and profane history, into Church and State. In Israelite history the differentiation, while never quite achieved, very noticeably began; and in the course of the attempts to break the initial compactness of order occurred the curious reversals in the hierarchy of the focuses. In the situation of the "conquest," under the threat of extinction at the hands of the Philistines, the organization of the people under a monarchy was understood as the fulfillment of the task imposed by the Covenant. But as soon as the monarchy was established, and had adjusted itself to the internal and external exigencies of politics, it became obvious that the new social order did not correspond to the intentions of the Covenant at all. Hence, only with the reaction to the monarchy began the intense interest in Moses and the Instructions which ultimately caused the Kingdom to appear as a great aberration. The foundation of the monarchy, thus, became an ambivalent event in both the history and historiography of Israel. Without the monarchy, the Israel of the confederacy might have disappeared without leaving much of a trace in history; with the monarchy, it survived but betrayed the Mosaic Instructions. Without the monarchy, there never might have arisen the Prophetic opposition which clarified the meaning of Yahwism; with a successfully continued monarchy, the Yahwism of the Prophets probably could never have become a universal historic force.

The nature of Israelite compactness has previously been defined as "a perpetual mortgage of the world-immanent, concrete event on the transcendent truth that on its occasion was revealed." The mortgage had become heavier and heavier down to the foundation of the monarchy because the original promise of Canaan made every advance of the people in worldly establishment appear as a fulfillment of the order instituted by the Covenant. When the Prophets began their work, the mortgage had reached staggering proportions, as it had accumulated the civilizational orders through which the people had passed. The people had started on the level of nomad life in the desert; it then had acquired the characteristics of a settled, agricultural population in Canaan; and finally it had developed an urban and a court society under the monarchy. Since the transitions from one civilizational order to the other did not affect the whole population, Israel under the Kingdom had preserved memories and appreciable, marginal remnants of nomad society, while the new urban and the court society was a heavy-handed, wealthy class ruling over a mass of impoverished peasants. Moreover, the social and economic changes were accompanied by changes in the cultic sphere. The agricultural settlement in Canaan had familiarized the people with the necessity of treating the agricultural fertility gods with proper respect; and the new power position of the monarchy had compelled respect, as well as official cult establishments, for foreign gods as a matter of diplomatic necessity. Hence, the Prophets, when they voiced the dissatisfaction with the new order, were in a peculiar position. They certainly had plenty of targets to attack. But the attack had to be made in the name of something; and wherever they looked for a basis from which to launch the attack, they found that the basis was already encumbered with a mortgage that had to be removed in its turn.

It is always easy to attack foreigners. Relatively simple and effective, therefore, was the attack on the cult of foreign gods, though it proved suicidal because of the political consequences. Not so simple was the attack on the moral iniquity of the new upper class through appeal to a glorified peasant existence, complete with independence, freedom, abundance, and peace; for the free and independent peasants in reality were the people who indulged with gusto in the cult of the Baals and Ashtarts. The foreign cults of the upper class, thus, were easy to attack because as the basis could be chosen a nationalist resentment against everything foreign. The moral order of the upper class was more difficult to attack from the basis of a free peasant order, because the peasants themselves had to be attacked on account of their cultic order. This attack with a double front, therefore, had a tendency to fall back on the order of the nomad society under the Covenant with Yahweh. And in the prophetic revolt against the Omride dynasty in the Northern Kingdom we find, indeed, the leader of the Rechabite nomads closely associated with the prophets Elijah and Elisha. The retreat to nomad civilization, however, was difficult for more than one reason. In the first place, the people at large had no intention of returning to nomad existence. As a matter of fact, nomad life had become so distant to the settlers in Canaan that only a few traces of its memory are left in the Bible, such as the isolated Song of Lamech (Gen. 4:23 ff.) with its blood-curdling boasts of revenge. Sometimes, as in the story of Hagar, we still find two versions reflecting the nomad and agricultural viewpoints of the respective traditions.[23] But the story of Cain and Abel, for instance, is the creation of agricultural settlers who wish to explain the way of life of the nomad Kenites that has become utterly strange to them. The ethics of nomad life, thus, could not be held up with any hope of success in opposition to the mores of the Kingdom. One could not undo the history of Israel and return to the desert. Worse, however, was that the Yahwism of the desert period apparently did not provide the spiritual symbols that could be evoked authoritatively against the evils of the time. What the exact nature of the difficulty was we do not know, as the original symbols of the Mosaic period cannot be disengaged with certainty from the context created by the postprophetic redactions. But we do know that it required the efforts of a whole galaxy of Prophets to differentiate the spiritual meaning of Yahwism from a symbolism that enclosed it compactly in the ordering instructions for an association of nomad clans. And once these efforts had achieved a certain measure of success, the oppositional character of Prophetism had become doubly futile. For, pragmatically, the opposition had lost its target with the destruction of the Kingdoms; and, spiritually, it became obvious that the existence or nonexistence of a Kingdom of Israel was irrelevant for the fundamental problems of a life in righteousness before the Lord.

Further light will fall on the nature of the Israelite difficulty through a comparison with the inverse difficulty that beset the early Christians. In Christianity the *logia* of Jesus, and especially the Sermon on the Mount, had effectively disengaged the meaning of faith, as well as of the life of the spirit, from the conditions of a particular civilizational order. The separation was so effective indeed that loss of understanding for the importance of civilizational order was a serious danger to many Christians. While the Prophets had to struggle for an understanding of Yahwism in opposition to the concrete social order of Israel, a long series of

---

[23] In Genesis 16 Hagar is a fierce nomad woman who resents the chicaneries of her mistress. She wanders off into the desert and shifts there quite well for herself. And there she receives the divine announcement of the great destiny that is in store for her son Ishmael. In Genesis 17 she is a helpless servant sent packing into the desert. There she waits for her child to die from exposure to heat and lack of water, and must anticipate the same fate for herself. God saves her and the child through a miracle, and then proceeds to the announcement of the great destiny. In the first version the desert is the freedom to which man can have refuge from social oppression in a settled society; in the second version the desert is the place into which man is driven against his will, and where he dies from lack of sustenance. In both versions Abraham appears in the pathetic role of a husband who discards his mistress and exposes her to misery in order to have his peace at home.

Christian statesmen, from St. Paul to St. Augustine, had to struggle for an understanding of the exigencies of world-immanent social and political order. The Prophets had to make it clear that the political success of Israel was no substitute for a life in obedience to divine instructions; the Christian statesmen had to make it clear that faith in Christ was no substitute for organized government. The Prophets had to stress that status in the social order of Israel did not confer spiritual status on a man before God; the Christian thinkers had to stress that sacramental acceptance into the Mystical Body did not touch the social status of a man— that masters still were masters, and slaves were slaves, that thieves still were thieves, and magistrates were magistrates. The Prophets had to explain that social success was not a proof of righteousness before God; the Christian thinkers had to explain that the Gospel was no social gospel, redemption no social remedy, and Christianity in general no insurance for individual or collective prosperity.

The relationship between the life of the spirit and life in the world is the problem that lies unresolved at the bottom of the Israelite difficulties. Let us hasten to say that the problem by its nature is not capable of a solution valid for all times. Balances that work for a while can be found and have been found. But habituation, institutionalization, and ritualization inevitably, by their finiteness, degenerate sooner or later into a captivity of the spirit that is infinite; and then the time has come for the spirit to break a balance that has become demonic imprisonment. Hence, no criticism is implied when the problem is characterized as unresolved. But precisely because the problem is unsolvable on principle, an inestimable importance attaches to its historically specific states of irresolution. In the Israelite case, the problem is unresolved in so far as it is on the point of emergence from the compactness of the Mosaic period into the Prophetic differentiation. And the foundation of the Kingdom was, furthermore, the specific crisis that revealed the demonic derailment of the Mosaic foundation. Here we witness the interplay of experiences in the struggle of the spirit for its freedom from encasement in a particular social organization. That struggle of truly world-historic importance has, by its experiential phases, determined the unique structure of the Biblical narrative as a literary work.

PART THREE

History and the Trail of Symbols

The historiographic work was originally dominated by the foundation of the monarchy. Under the impact of the Prophetic movement, then, the focus of interest shifted from successful pragmatic existence to the substantive order under the Covenant. The exilic and postexilic historians, finally, weighted the Pentateuch heavily with additional Codes, constructed the history of the Kingdom around the Temple of Solomon and the purity of the cult of Yahweh, and superimposed the speculation on periods of world-history.

The radical shift of interest, however, did not induce the historians to abandon the work of earlier generations. The complete work, as a consequence, assumed the symbolic form *sui generis* analysed in the preceding chapter. On the one hand, the form of the narrative absorbed into its medium the variegated contents of myth and history and transformed it into the paradigmatic world-history. On the other hand, the resulting world-history was not the work of a single historian who digested primary sources and imposed his personal literary style on them. The late historians achieved the desired changes of meaning rather through selection, repression, mutilation, interpolation, and the silent influence of context. In such fragmentized form, therefore, the narrative contains a considerable amount of source materials which, isolated from their context, still reveal their original meaning.

The peculiarity of the literary form is intimately determined by the problems of an order that oscillated between the righteousness of a life in obedience to divine instructions and the organization of a people for existence in history. The compactness of the cosmological symbolism, to be sure, was broken by the Yahwist experience, but the elaboration of the experience through new symbols never completely penetrated the consequences of the leap in being for either the life of the spirit or the life in the world. Israelite symbols have, therefore, a baffling structure.

And that is perhaps the reason why their nature rarely comes into clear view in the literature on the subject. The Yahwism of the Prophets still appears to be the best recognizable "contribution" of Israel to the civilization of mankind, whereas the symbols concerning organized existence seem so closely related to the cosmological myth of the time that the specific Israelite difference is difficult to determine.

That complexity of order must be faced just as the corresponding complexity of the historiographic work. There is neither a "religious" Israel of the Covenant and the Prophets, to which the love of theologians and Old Testament scholars reaches out, nor a "political" Israel which receives preferential treatment from pragmatic historians. There is only the one Israel, which tries to exist in the historical form centered in the Covenant, though at the same time the cosmological myth creeps back wherever the exigencies of pragmatic existence assert themselves. While the form elements can be well distinguished in the sources, one must resist the temptation to isolate them against each other and to speak, as is frequently done, of a genuine Israelite order under the Covenant and its vitiation through "oriental influences." For the people who had an incomplete understanding of their God, who deserted him for Canaanite, Assyrian, and Babylonian divinities, who even degraded him to a god of the same rank as the others, and perhaps not the most reliable one, were as much Israel as the Prophets and had as good reasons for their defection as the Prophets for their opposition. When reflecting on the tensions between the form elements, it will perhaps be better not to distinguish between the forms at all, but rather to descend to the level of experience and to speak of the two experiential forces which respectively pushed toward the full realization of a life in obedience to Yahweh, and pulled the people back toward existence in cosmological form. For if the tension is expressed in the language of experiential forces, it will become clearer that Israelite symbols, even when they approach closely to the cosmological symbolism of the neighboring civilizations, are still loaded with the opposition to, or regression from, Yahwism; while Prophetic symbols, even when they come closest to a universalist understanding of divine transcendence, are still loaded with the problems of Israel's pragmatic existence.

The two counteracting experiential forces met in the creation of the historiographic work. The fragments of traditions, oral and written, were incorporated in the great narrative because the history of Israel's struggle for survival in pragmatic history was tinged, at every turn of events, by its relation to the order of the Covenant. The pragmatic events themselves had acquired symbolic meaning as fulfillments of, or defections from, the Covenant order, or as variegated compromises between the will of God and the conditions of worldly existence. And the events had left their trail of symbols in the traditions. The later historians could follow the trail and heighten the events paradigmatically in the light of the Covenant order, but they certainly did not want to destroy a history which itself had become a symbol of revelation.

The preceding reflections will guide the presentation of the Israelite symbols of order. In the present Part Three of the study we shall take our position at the level of the pragmatic events and follow the trail of their symbols from the Abraham traditions to the end of the Northern Kingdom. When the history of Israel had ended in worldly disaster, the weight of interest shifted, in the Judah of the eighth century, distinctly toward the clarification of right order in the light of the Sinaitic revelation. The concluding Part Four of the study will, therefore, deal with the symbolism of Moses and the Prophets.

CHAPTER 7

From Clan Society to Kingship

§ 1. THE ABRAM STORY

The infiltration of Hebrew clans into Canaan, as it can be discerned in the stories of the Patriarchs, began in the first half of the second millennium B.C. For the Hebrew form of order in this early period no sources are extant that can be reliably dated as contemporary with the events. Nevertheless, an access to the political situation, as well as to the Hebrew ideas of the time, offers itself through the story of Abram as related in Genesis 14.

1. Yahweh's Berith with Abram

The Abram story opens with the brief information that a coalition of four Mesopotamian kings met in battle with a coalition of five Canaanite kings in the valley of the Dead Sea (Gen. 14:1–3). For twelve years the group of Canaanite kings had paid tribute to Chedorlaomer of Elam; in the thirteenth year they rebelled; in the fourteenth year Chedorlaomer and his allies made war on the Canaanites (4–5). The war assumed the form of a raid on the southern tribes of Canaan, and the razzia approached the rebellious center (5–7). Battle was joined in the valley of Siddim. The Canaanite kings were defeated; Sodom and Gomorrah were plundered; and the victors departed, carrying with them Lot, Abram's nephew, who had dwelt in Sodom (8–12). The abduction of Lot caused Abram's intervention. A survivor of the battle reported the abduction, and Abram, with his confederates and retainers, went in pursuit of the Mesopotamian kings. He defeated them, recaptured the whole of the loot, including his nephew Lot, and returned (13–16). On his return he was met by the King of Sodom, as well as by Melchizedek, the king and priest of Jerusalem (17–18). To the blessing of Melchizedek Abram responded with the gift of a tithe (19–20). The King of Sodom requested return only of his people, saying that Abram could keep the other loot (21). Abram, however, restored everything, with the exception of the sustenance for his own men and the portion of his confederates (22–24).

As a literary piece the story of Genesis 14 is an erratic block in so far as it cannot be assigned to any of the major sources of the Pentateuch. Up to Genesis 13 the narrative draws on the J and P sources; beginning with Genesis 15 the E source makes its first appearance. Genesis 14 is apparently an independent Jerusalemite tradition; and the assumption that it owes its present form to the recasting of an older Abram tradition for the purposes of Davidic propaganda is almost certainly the correct one. The role of the story in the context of Genesis envisages, through its present form, the original tradition of a patriarchal adventure.[1] By that original content the story dates itself "in the days of Amraphel king of Shinar." The identification of Amraphel as Hammurabi is probable; and tentative identifications for the names of the other three Mesopotamian kings have been proposed. Nevertheless, from the side of the Babylonian sources, it is impossible to find a time when any four kings of these names were contemporaries and could have engaged in an expedition of this nature. Hence, the anti-Canaanite kings must not be considered historical personages but representatives of the four main peoples at the time of Hammurabi—that is, of the Elamites, the Babylonians, the Mitanni, and the Hittites.[2] One can retain of this part of the story no more than the intention to date the events before the Egyptian conquest of Palestine. The Melchizedek episode (14:18–20), furthermore, has long been suspected as a late interpolation, because the assumption of a high priest in Jerusalem in the first half of the second millennium was considered anachronistic. The suspicion can no longer be entertained, since we know now that Canaanite cities did have high priests.[3] There is no reason why Jerusalem should not have had one, too, at the time. Hence, we shall assume that the story, however garbled with regard to

[1] For the role of the story in Davidic politics see below Chap. 9, § 4. For the older conceptions of Genesis 14 cf. Hermann Gunkel, *Genesis* (Goettingen, 1910) and Otto Procksch, *Die Genesis* (Leipzig, 1913). Gunkel assumes that the fabulous victory of a Jewish hero is typical for the legends of late Jewish history, as in Chronicles and Judith. It is a compensation of political impotence, as in Esther (p. 289 ff.). Procksch places the story in the Hellenistic period and attributes it to the desire to assign to Abraham a place in world-history. In Melchizedek he sees an authorizing projection into the past of the high-priest of the Second Temple (p. 514 ff.).

[2] H. S. Nyberg, "Studien zum Religionskampf im Alten Testament," *Archiv fuer Religionswissenschaft*, XXXV (1938), 358.

[3] Albright, *Archaeology and the Religion of Israel*, 108.

names and pragmatic details, contains a core of genuine tradition with regard to the typical features of the situation. And the meaning of the story, as conveyed by the context of patriarchal history in Genesis, must be accepted as authentic, since it contains nothing inherently improbable.

The story reveals a richly diversified political scene. There are, first, the kings of the Canaanite city-states of Sodom, Gomorrah, Admah, and Bela; and later enters a priest-king of Jerusalem. East of the Jordan and to the south live the aboriginal, primitive peoples who become the first victims of the Mesopotamian raid. They bear such names as Rephaim (giants), Emim (horrors), Horim (cave dwellers), and Zuzim (possibly the same as the Zamzummim of Deuteronomy 2:20, the howlers).[4] The kings of the city-states must be considered originally independent rulers. But at the time of the story they have been collectively the "servants" of a foreign power for twelve years, and when they break their servitude they appear as allies, *chaberim*, on the field of battle. The reason for the raid against the aboriginal tribes to the east and south is not clear, unless the city-states exerted some kind of sovereignty over them, so that a plundering raid against the tribes would be an economic blow to the kings.

Besides the city-states there is presumed a countryside beyond their control. There the Amorites settle who appear as the confederates of Abram. And on the land leased or bought from the Amorites, finally, there lives a Hebrew chieftain like Abram who for a fight can muster more than three hundred trained retainers born in the household. The Amorites stand to Abram in the relation of berith-masters, that is, of lords of the land to their vassal. And, as the course of events reveals, the berith must have stipulated assistance in case of war; for, at the end of the story, the three Amorites appear as participants in Abram's expedition and as such entitled to a share of the loot. The berith relation between Abram and the Amorites, however, is not the only one possible for a Hebrew in Canaan. The nephew Lot is settled in the city of Sodom, though his status, probably that of a ger, a protected resident, is not

---

[4] Not much is known about the Canaanite aborigines, except that they appeared as men of unusually high stature to the Hebrews. Rephaim was used as a generic term for the various subdivisions of the primitives (Deut. 2). The existence of such a Canaanite giant race is now attested outside the Biblical traditions, through Ugaritic texts which refer to "Daniel the Raphaman." ("The Tale of Aqhat," translated by H. L. Ginsberg, in Pritchard [ed.], *Ancient Near Eastern Texts*, 149 ff.). Some of the "descendants of the giants" survived into the Israelite period, appearing as warriors on the side of the Philistines (II Sam. 21:16–22). The most famous of the giants was Goliath.

specified. The status of Lot in Sodom seems not to be connected with the status of Abram. Between Lot and Abram, however, there prevails the clan law which obliges Abram to come to the rescue of his abducted nephew; and as a consequence, the fighting force of the Amorite berith-masters, who otherwise would not seem to be concerned with the affairs of the Canaanite kings, comes into play. But such unconcern is not certain, for the raid of the Mesopotamians against the aboriginal tribes also extends to the Amorites of Hazazon-tamar. Hence, the berith-masters of Abram are perhaps after all involved in Abram's expedition through their Amorite connections.

The story thus partly indicates explicitly, partly implies, an intricate system of relations between the various political groups of Canaan which can hardly function properly without divine sanctions accepted in common by the groups of the region. The assumption of a common divinity as the guardian of political compacts, a *baal berith* in Hebrew, will perhaps explain the appearance of the priest-king of Jerusalem, after the battle. He is introduced as bringing forth bread and wine in his capacity as "priest of El Elyon." And he extends his blessing to Abram in the following verses:

> Blessed be Abram by El Elyon,
> The maker of the heavens and the earth!
> And blessed be El Elyon,
> Who delivered your enemies into your hands!

The god invoked by Melchizedek is distinguished by his name from the Israelite Yahweh or Elohim; but otherwise we receive no information about his nature. The English translations as "the highest God," while correct, are equally uninformative.[5] But here again the Ugaritic discoveries come to our aid. The Canaanites had indeed a highest god, the storm-god Hadad, briefly referred to as the Baal, the king or lord of the gods; and one of the standard epithets of this Baal was *Al'iyan*, "the One who Prevails." The supremacy of the Baal as the highest divinity in the Canaanite pantheon was established very early, at the latest in the fifteenth century B.C.[6] This Baal must be the El Elyon of the temple-state of Jerusalem who, through his priest-king Melchizedek, extends blessings

[5] The Authorized Version has "the most high God." The Chicago translation, Moffat, and the translation of the Jewish Publication Society of America have "God Most High."

[6] Albright, *Archaeology and the Religion of Israel*, 73, 195. For texts in which the epithet occurs see the "Poems about Baal and Anath," translated by H. L. Ginsberg, in Pritchard (ed.), *Ancient Near Eastern Texts*, especially the section V AB C, p. 136, or Gordon, *Ugaritic Literature*, 32 ff.

and, for his service of delivering enemies into the hands of the people who recognize him, receives tithes after a successful war.

Among those who recognize the Canaanite Baal is Abram. Nevertheless, while ready to let the Baal have his share of the war loot, Abram reserves his allegiance beyond this point. Subsequent to the Melchizedek episode (Gen. 14:18–20) the King of Sodom offers to share the loot with Abram (21); but Abram rejects the offer, which must be supposed to have been generous, in violent, almost insulting language:

> I raise my hand to Yahweh, El Elyon,
> the maker of the heavens and the earth:
> If from a thread to a shoe-lace, if I take aught that is yours. . . !
> You shall not say: "I have made Abram rich."
> Not for me—
> Only what the young men have eaten,
> and the portion of the men who went with me, Aner, Eshcol, and
>   Mamre,—
> Let them take their portion.

It is a dramatic speech; an outburst, holding back on the verge of a betrayal, lapsing into silences to cover what already has been half said. It reveals more than the resentment of a proud nomad of being made rich by the generosity of a king—if this feeling plays an important role at all. For behind the overt rejection of the King's offer there lies the rejection of Melchizedek and his El Elyon. When Abram raises his hand to Yahweh, he pointedly arrogates the Baal's epithet for his own God. By Yahweh he swears his unfinished oath not to take anything of the King's possessions. His professed unwillingness to be made rich by the King, is in reality an indignant refusal to be made rich by the King's Baal. Yahweh is the god who delivers enemies into Abram's hands, not the god of Melchizedek; Yahweh blesses Abram, not the Baal of Jerusalem; and not to the El Elyon who watches over the relations between political allies in Canaan will Abram owe his prosperity, but to Yahweh alone. Hence, Abram reduces the King's offer to the payment of an ascetic expense account.

Any doubt about the intention of the story will be dispelled by a glance at its context. When Abram indignantly refuses to become rich with the blessing of the Baal, we may justly wonder how he ever will prosper in a political order under the protection of El Elyon. The concern will dissolve when we read the opening verse of Genesis 15:

> After what just has been related, the word of Yahweh came to
>   Abram in a vision:
> Fear not, Abram,
> I am your shield,
> Your reward shall be rich.

In the further course of the chapter Yahweh makes a berith with Abram
(15:18), promising the dominion of Canaan for his descendants (15:
18–21) when the guilt of the Amorites is full (15:16). The meaning of
Genesis 14 is clarified by this sequel beyond a doubt. Abram is in the
difficult situation of the Exodus. Pragmatically he has left the former
home in Chaldea, but in Canaan he has settled in an environment whose
understanding of human and social order does not substantially differ
from the Mesopotamian. He is still a foreigner, dependent for his status
on his berith-masters, the Amorites, whose principal occupation in the
spiritual order of things seems to be the accumulation of guilt, and he
must accept the system of order under the Baal after a fashion. Spiritually
he is profoundly disturbed. The Exodus from Chaldea shows that he no
longer can live contentedly in the world of cosmological experiences and
symbols, but his movements in the new world that opened to him when
his soul opened toward God lack yet in assurance. On the one hand, he
makes concessions to the Baal—and he must, if he wants to survive; on
the other hand, the new God has taken possession of him strongly enough
to strain his soul and to cause, in a critical situation, the outburst of
Genesis 14:22–24. The tension between god and God is severe indeed,
especially since the nature of the new God and the strength of his
assistance are not certain at all. The transfer of the El Elyon from the
Baal of Jerusalem to Yahweh leaves in doubt whether Yahweh is God
or only a highest god in rivalry with others. Moreover, while Abram
rejects riches that come to him under the sanction of the Baal, he is not
averse to prosperity; he does not want to be ruined for Yahweh. Hence,
he must have gone home from the dramatic scene full of sorrows. He
certainly has not made friends by his outburst. Will Yahweh now protect him against the possible consequences? And will he compensate him
for the riches renounced? In this critical hour of his life the "word of
Yahweh" comes to him with comfort for every disquieting aspect of the
situation: (1) The generally assuaging "Fear not"; (2) the "I am your
shield" in political difficulties; and (3) the promise "Your reward shall
be rich" in compensation for the economic loss.

The comforts and promises of Genesis 15 subtly dissolve the tense-
ness of Genesis 14. A masterpiece is the transformation of the berith
symbol. In Genesis 14 Abram is in bondage through his involvement in
the Canaanite system of political compacts. He lives under baals both
human and divine: the Amorites are his berith-masters (*baal berith*) in
political relations, and the Baal of Jerusalem is the guardian of the political berith. In Genesis 15 the decisive step of liberation occurs, when
Yahweh makes his berith with Abram. The worldly situation, to be sure,
remains what it is for the time being; but spiritually the bondage is
broken with the change of berith-masters. The order in which Abram
truly lives from now on has been transformed from the Canaan of the
Baal to the domain of Yahweh. The symbol of bondage has become the
symbol of freedom. On this occasion, furthermore, the peculiar nature
of a berith with Yahweh reveals itself. In the mundane situation of
Abram, as we said, nothing has changed. The new domain of Yahweh is
not yet the political order of a people in Canaan; at the moment it does
not extend beyond the soul of Abram. It is an order that originates in a
man through the inrush of divine reality into his soul and from this
point of origin expands into a social body in history.[7] At the time of
its inception it is no more than the life of a man who trusts in God; but
this new existence, founded on the leap in being, is pregnant with future.
In the case of Abram's experience this "future" is not yet understood
as the eternity under whose judgment man exists in his present. To be
sure, Yahweh's berith is already the flash of eternity into time; but the
true nature of this "future" as transcendence is still veiled by the
sensuous analogues of a glorious future in historical time. Abram receives the promises of numerous descendants and their political success
in the dominion of Canaan. In this sense the experience of Abram is
"futuristic." It is a component in the berith which lasts throughout
Israelite into Judaic history and issues into the apocalypses. Nevertheless,

[7] On the question of personal gods as distinguished from local or nature gods, cf. Albrecht
Alt, *Der Gott der Vaeter. Ein Beitrag zur Vorgeschichte der Israelitischen Religion* (Beitraege zur
Wissenschaft vom Alten und Neuen Testament, 3:12, 1929). Spiritually sensitive individuals
have revelations of a hitherto unknown numen which receives the name of "God of N.N." Such
personal gods Alt found attested by Palmyrene and Nabataean inscription of the last pre-Christian
centuries. Julius Lewy, "Les textes paléo-assyriens et l'Ancien Testament," *Revue de l'Histoire de
Religions*, CX (1934) corroborated the phenomenon discovered by Alt through the occurrence of
the phrase "God of your father" in the Kultepe Texts of *ca.* 2000 B.C. Alt observed the more
intimate relations between this type of god and man as a person, as well as the tendency of such
a numen to become a god of society and history (*Der Gott der Vaeter,* 46). Cf. Eichrodt, "Religionsgeschichte Israels," *loc. cit.,* 377–79.

the lack of differentiation must not be seen as an imperfection only. For, as has been discussed previously, compact experiences contain the bond of compactness that holds the undifferentiated elements together— the bond that all too frequently is lost in the process of differentiation. While the promises of the berith still veil the meaning of transcendence, they at least preserve the awareness that eternity reaches indeed into the process of history, even though the operation of transcendent perfection through the mundane process is a paradox that cannot be solved through Canaans or Utopias of one kind or another.

Genesis 14 and 15 together are a precious document. They de- scribe the situation in which the berith experience originates in oppo- sition to the cosmological order of Canaanite civilization, as well as the content of the experience itself. The philological and archaeological ques- tions of trustworthiness and date of the story will now appear in a dif- ferent light. For clearly we are not interested in either the date of literary fixation or the reliability of the story, but in the authenticity of the experience that is communicated by means of the story, as well as in the probable date of the situation in which the experience originated. As far as the authenticity is concerned, the problem is not too difficult, for nobody can describe an experience unless he has had it, either originally or through imaginative re-enactment. The writers to whom we owe the literary fixation certainly had the experience through re-enactment; and the masterly articulation of its meaning through the dramatic high points of the story proves that they were intimately familiar with it. The answer to the question of who had the experience originally will have to rely on the common-sense argument that religious personalities who have such experiences, and are able to submit to their authority, do not grow on trees. The spiritual sensitiveness of the man who opened his soul to the word of Yahweh, the trust and fortitude required to make this word the order of existence in opposition to the world, and the creative imag- ination used in transforming the symbol of civilizational bondage into the symbol of divine liberation—that combination is one of the great and rare events in the history of mankind. And this event bears the name of Abram. As far as the date of the event is concerned we have nothing to rely on but the Biblical tradition which places it in the pre-Egyptian period of Hebrew settlements in Canaan, that is, in the second millen- nium B.C. The date, therefore, must be accepted.

2. The Continuity of the Political Situation

Abram's berith experience did not die with the man who had it. About its expansion into the order of a community and its transmission down to the Israelite period we know nothing through reliable contemporary sources. The Biblical narrative, to be sure, traces the line from Abraham through Isaac and Jacob to the twelve ancestors of Israel, further on to the sojourn in Egypt, the recovery of Yahweh's order through Moses, and the Exodus, down to the Conquest of Canaan. This line of transmission, however, is highly stylized. It tells us nothing beyond the fact that throughout the history of Hebrew clans a trickle of the experience must have continued to run strong enough to broaden out into the constitution of Israel through the Mosaic Berith. Nevertheless, there are a few sources, partly external, partly Biblical, which indicate a constancy of the general situation of Hebrew clans settled in Canaan, as described in Genesis 14. The historical environment in which the experience could be preserved existed in continuity.

The political articulation of the Canaanite region into small city kingdoms, as presupposed by Genesis 14 for the pre-Egyptian centuries, is attested for the time of Egyptian rule, after the expulsion of the Hyksos, through the Amarna Letters.[8] The imperial administration, with a moderately effective military occupation, lies in the hands of a commissioner for Asiatic affairs in Egypt. The local princes, whose ethnic diversification probably reflects the ethnical components of the now broken Hyksos power, have a considerable freedom of movement which they use in feuds and alliances for the expansion of their respective principalities.[9] An important factor in the military and political situation are the 'Apiru tribes.[10] In some instances they are strong enough to threaten the princely territories with conquest and dismemberment; in other instances they appear as allies of the princes in their wars with one another, and are rewarded with land. Such alliances of one prince with the 'Apiru, then, could be construed as betrayal of the Egyptian sover-

[8] For an analysis of the political situation in Palestine, on the basis of the Amarna Letters, see Meyer, *Geschichte des Altertums*, II/1, pp. 362–67.

[9] On the continuity between the Amarna time and the Hyksos period cf. Albrecht Alt, *Voelker und Staaten Syriens im Fruehen Altertum* (Der Alte Orient, 34:4, Leipzig, 1936), 34 ff.

[10] The meaning of the name 'Apiru, as well as the question who the 'Apiru were, is still debated. That the name 'Apiru is philologically connected with the word Hebrew is possible, but must be doubted for archaeological reasons. But there is hardly a doubt that the 'Apiru were ethnically Hebrews.

eign; and another prince would feel justified to conduct a war against the traitor, in order to uphold the Egyptian order and, incidentally, to expand his dominion at the expense of the rival. The political situation will become clear from a letter of Shuwardata, the prince of the Hebron region, to the Pharaoh (Akhenaton):

> Let the king, my lord, learn that the chief of the 'Apiru has risen in arms against the land which the god of the king, my lord, gave me; but I have smitten him. Also let the king, my lord, know that all my brethren have abandoned me, and that it is I and 'Abdu-Heba who fight against the chief of the 'Apiru.[11]

'Abdu-Heba, mentioned as the ally of Shuwardata, is the prince of Jerusalem who otherwise appears in the Amarna Letters as Shuwardata's enemy. That the two rivals should join forces on this occasion shows that the 'Apiru danger must have been considerable. A letter from 'Abdu-Heba himself has a desperate tone:

> Let my king take thought for his land! The land of the king is lost; in its entirety it is taken from me. . . . I have become like an 'Apiru and do not see the two eyes of the king, my lord, for there is war against me. I have become like a ship in the midst of the sea! The arm of the mighty king conquers the land of Naharaim and the land of Cush, but now the 'Apiru capture the cities of the king. There is not a single governor remaining to the king, my lord—all have perished! [12]

And in the letters of Rib-Addi of Byblos, finally, the Amorites appear on the scene, in coalition with the 'Apiru. The Amorite chieftain 'Abdu-Ashirta, and later his sons, threaten to capture Byblos with connivance of the population under the leadership of Rib-Addi's brother:

> Behold our city Byblos! There is much wealth of the king in it, the property of our forefathers. If the king does not intervene for the city, all the cities of the land of Canaan will no longer be his.[13]

The Canaanite princes were too proud to mention such nomad rabble as the chieftains of the 'Apiru by name. It is, therefore, impossible to relate the events of the Amarna period to any personal or tribal names in the Biblical narrative. Moreover, the narrative has preserved no memory of Hebrew wars against Canaan in the time of Egyptian sovereignty.

---

[11] All quotations from the English translations by Albright and Mendenhall in Pritchard (ed.), *Ancient Near Eastern Texts*. The letter of Shuwardata, *ibid.*, 487.

[12] Amarna Letter 288. Pritchard (ed.), *Ancient Near Eastern Texts*, 488 ff.

[13] Amarna Letter 137. Pritchard (ed.), *Ancient Near Eastern Texts*, 483 ff. For the affair of Byblos see Meyer, *Geschichte des Altertums*, II/1, pp. 347 ff., 360 ff.

The reasons why there should be no specific references to clashes with a Canaan dominated by Egypt are a matter of conjecture. Perhaps at the time of the 'Apiru invasion the tribes who were the carriers of the Abram tradition moved on the fringe of events. Considering that the people of Israel constituted by the berith did not yet exist, the warlike exploits of one group of tribes were quite possibly of no concern to the tribes not directly involved. But it also is possible that war traditions were suppressed by later historians in their construction of the Patriarchal Age. Genesis 14 is erratic not only as a literary piece but also because it presents a Patriarch as a war lord at the head of his small but effective troop. In general, the Patriarchs are depicted as men of peace. Quite rarely is there a slip in the story, as when in Genesis 48:21–22 we find a Jacob who, somewhat surprisingly in view of his reported antecedents, bequeaths to Joseph the "Shechem, which I captured from the Amorites, with my sword, with my bow." A slip of this kind could be a reminiscence of the events which according to the Amarna Letters (see especially No. 289) led to the surrender of Shechem to the 'Apiru.[14]

Fortunately, the Biblical narrative has preserved a few fragments which reveal the political situation of Hebrew tribes in Canaan at the time of the conquest as being the same as in Genesis 14 and the Amarna Letters. Genesis 34 records a piece of tribal history in personalized form. Translated into tribal terms the source informs us that a Hebrew clan by the name of Dinah had entered into a compact, including intermarriage, with the city of Shechem, the seat of the Baal-berith (Judges 9:4). The tribes of Simeon and Levi resented the arrangement and raided the city of Shechem. But the Shechemites retaliated so effectively that the two tribes were practically extinguished. Joshua 9–10 tells the story of the city of Gibeon, which entered into a berith with Joshua after his

---

[14] I confine myself to such general conjectures in the briefest form possible. The relation between 'Apiru and Hebrews and between the events described in the Amarna Letters and the Biblical narrative, as well as the chronology of Hebrew history between Amarna and the Conquest of Canaan, are the subject of a voluminous literature. The shrewd and imaginative attempts to reconstruct the period from roughly 1500–1200 B.C. have in no case, however, produced convincing results. There simply are not enough sources. For a balanced survey of the problems cf. Adolphe Lods, *Israel*, 43–52, 181–89. Only one detail should be mentioned, as it has a bearing on the problem of continuity. The names of Jacob and perhaps also of Joseph are attested as place names in Canaan through the lists of Asiatic countries in inscriptions of Thutmose III (1490–1436 B.C.). Selections from such lists are now easily accessible in Pritchard (ed.), *Ancient Near Eastern Texts*, pp. 242 ff. The name of Jacob-el is attested as that of one of the Hyksos Kings in Egypt. Cf. Meyer, *Geschichte des Altertums*, I/2, pp. 321 ff. The best recent survey of the period from the sixteenth to the thirteenth century is Albright, "Syrien, Phoenizien und Palaestina," *loc. cit.*, 344–48. For the question of the 'Apiru see *ibid.*, 350 f.

victory over Jericho and Ai. When Gibeon ("a large city, quite like a royal city" [10:12]) came to an agreement with the invaders, the Canaanite princes were aroused to energetic countermeasures. An alliance of five "Amorite" princes under the leadership of Adonizedek, the King of Jerusalem, invested Gibeon. The subsequent victory of Joshua and its gory aftermath need not be taken too seriously, for Jerusalem was still an independent city by the time of David.

The fragments are important in so far as they prove the remarkable constancy of the pragmatic setting for the Yahwistic berith experience. Through anywhere from six to eight centuries we meet the Canaanite princes and their alliances, the Amorites, the Hebrews, a king of Jerusalem, a Baal-berith, and a system of compacts between the various political agents. The conditions under which the solitary genius of Abram had gained its spiritual freedom through the berith with Yahweh were those under which a Yahwist confederacy of Hebrew tribes now asserted its identity against the surrounding Canaanite civilization.

§ 2. The Deborah Song

1. The Transmission of Yahwism to the Time of Moses

About the originating situation, the content, and the date of the Yahwist experience we know only what can be gathered from Genesis 14–15. About the transmission of the experience down to the time of Moses, as well as about its expansion from the order of a solitary soul to the order of a community, we know nothing beyond the fact that it was transmitted and expanded. The information concerning this fact is furnished by Exodus 18.

According to Exodus 18, Moses and his people camped in the desert after the miraculous escape from the pursuing Egyptians. The father-in-law of Moses heard of the escape and advanced to meet the fugitives. In Exodus 18, this father-in-law is identified as Jethro, the priest of Midian; in Judges 1:16, as Hobab, the Kenite. Setting aside the variations of the name (there is still another one, Reuel, in Exod. 2:18), this personage apparently was the priest and chieftain of the Kenite subdivision of the Midianites. At the meeting with Moses, after the exchange of greetings and news, Jethro said:

> Blessed be Yahweh,
> who has delivered you from the hand of Egypt, the hand of Pharaoh,

who delivered the people from under the hand of Egypt.
Now I know:
Great is Yahweh above all gods—
for he prevailed over the proud foes of his folk.

Then Jethro proceeded to sacrifice for Yahweh; and Moses, Aaron, and
the elders of Israel joined with Jethro in the meal before God. The
situation reminds us of that other priest-king, Melchizedek, who came
forth to meet Abram in the name of his highest god and to extend blessings. But now it was Yahweh who had taken the place of El Elyon; and
Jethro, not Moses, was his priest. The story of the meeting, thus, indicates the existence of a cult of Yahweh among the Kenites, and quite
possibly among other tribes who came under the general description of
"Midianites," at the time of Moses.[15] Moreover, neither the god nor the
cult could have been of recent origin, for the meaning of the name
Yahweh was already forgotten and required explanation (Exod. 3:13–
14). And Yahweh was introduced, furthermore, as the "god of your
fathers," Abraham, Isaac, and Jacob, so that apparently Yahweh was a
god whose cult had fallen into desuetude among the tribes who had
descended to Egypt (Exod. 3:6, 13).

The Israel of the Biblical narrative was a Yahwist amphictyonic
league. The Confederacy consisted of tribes (*matteh, shebet*); the tribes
of clans (*mishpachah*); the clans of families (*beth-ab*). The family
heads formed a democratic community under chieftains of the clans who
owed their authority to a voluntarily accepted personal ascendancy. The
clan was the basic religious, military, and economic unit, with a fighting
force from three hundred to a thousand men—perhaps closer to the
latter figure, since the word *eleph* (a thousand) was a current equivalent
for *mishpachah*. The number of tribes in the confederacy was twelve,
though the tribes that were fitted into the symbolic number twelve were
not always the same. At the time of the settlement in Canaan, Israel had
an amphictyonic sanctuary of Yahweh at Shiloh.

When this Confederacy came into being is uncertain. Moreover, it is
at least not impossible that a tribal association by the name of Israel

---

[15] A special relationship of the Kenites with Yahweh also appears in other sources. The eponymous ancestor of the Kenites, Cain, received the "mark of Yahweh" (Gen. 4:15), a tribal tattoo
signifying the cult membership. And in the time of the Kingdom, one of the ardent supporters of
Yahwist purism was the founder of the Rechabite community who, according to I Chronicles 2,
was a Kenite.

existed before the Israel under Yahweh was constituted by Moses. The earliest external evidence for the existence of an Israel is the Victory Hymn from the time of Merneptah, celebrating an Asiatic campaign of *ca.* 1225 B.C.:

> Wasted is Tehenu; Hatti is pacified;
> Plundered is Canaan, with every evil;
> Carried off is Ashkelon; seized upon is Gezer;
> Yanoam is made as that which does not exist;
> Israel is laid waste, his seed is not;
> Hurru is become a widow for Egypt! [16]

The word Israel, in the inscription, is written with the determinative for a people rather than for a land. This would mean that Israel was in an unsettled condition in or near Canaan, just before or after the conquest. But unfortunately Egyptian scribes at this age were no longer reliable and did make mistakes, so that no definite conclusions can be drawn.[17]

2. *The Deborah Song*

The earliest source for the ideas of order in the Israelite Confederacy is the Deborah Song, in Judges 5. It is contemporary with the events, *ca.* 1125, and probably was written by an eyewitness of the battle which it commemorates. It has considerable value as a source, as it has preserved not only the "facts" of the event but the drama of experience. Together with the prose account of the war in Judges 4 it furnishes, in spite of a corrupt text, a fairly clear picture of the early Yahwist order of Israel.

At the time of the Deborah Song the infiltration of Hebrew tribes into Canaan had resulted in the occupation of three distinct regions west of the Jordan. A northern settlement extended in an arc around the Sea of Galilee, touching on the Mediterranean coast; a central group had penetrated across the Jordan into Samaria; and a penetration from the south had led to the settlement of Judah. The three Hebrew areas were separated by the territories of the Canaanite towns. Between the northern and central settlements a broad Canaanite strip wedged in from the coast, through the plain of Esdraelon, to the Jordan, while Judah in the

---

[16] Translated by Wilson, in Pritchard (ed.), *Ancient Near Eastern Texts*, 378.

[17] On the formation and history of the Confederacy cf. Martin Noth, *Geschichte Israels*, the part on "Israel als Zwoelfstaemmebund."

south was separated from the Ephraimite region in the center by a belt of towns that included the mountain-fortress Jerusalem. The southern settlement was still weak and politically insignificant; Judah was not even mentioned in the Deborah Song and apparently did not yet belong to the Israelite Confederacy. The scene of important events was the north, where a coalition of Canaanite princes, under the leadership of Sisera of Harosheth-goiim, engaged in raids against Israelite villages in order to keep the northern and central tribes apart and, if possible, to restrict their territories. The tense situation exploded in a war between the Canaanite forces, equipped with war chariots, and the primitive contingents of Israel. The main battle was fought near Megiddo, at the river Kishon. A violent thunderstorm made the ground sodden so that the war chariots could not operate; and the defeated Canaanites suffered heavy losses on their retreat across the Kishon that had changed from a dry bed to a torrent. The Canaanite leader Sisera was killed on his flight by a Kenite woman in whose tent he had sought refuge.

The song describes the suffering of the Israelite countryside under the Canaanite raids:

> In the days of Shamgar, the son of Anath,
> Traffic on the highways had ceased,
> Travellers went by the by-ways;
> The work of the peasants had ceased in Israel, had ceased,
> Until you arose, O Deborah, arose as a mother in Israel.

Deborah was a prophetess who by her songs (probably appeals for action and curses against the enemy) aroused the people to resistance. Since the Confederacy had no permanent organization for either peace or war, the lyrical activity of the prophetess had to incite a leader and to move the people to follow him:

> Awake, awake, Deborah!
> Awake, awake, utter a song!

The leader was found in Barak, who had been the captive of Sisera for a while and now had an opportunity to settle some personal accounts. But the tribes did not all participate in the common enterprise. The song accordingly distributes praises and blames:

> Ephraim surged into the valley. . . .
> The chieftains of Issachar were with Deborah and Barak. . . .
> Zebulum were a people who exposed themselves to death. . . .

But others held back:

> In the clans of Reuben great were the debates. . . .
> Gilead remained beyond the Jordan. . . .
> Asher stayed by the sea-coast. . . .

Still, it was a great uprising. The clans descended from the hills, the warriors' hair let down, according to the war ritual:

> When they let stream their hair in Israel,
> when the men volunteered, bless Yahweh,
> hear, O kings, give ear, O princes,
> I—unto Yahweh—will I sing,
> I will sing to Yahweh, the God of Israel.

And from his seat far in the south, Yahweh came to the aid of his people, driving the war chariot of his storm:

> Yahweh—when you came forth from Seir,
> when you advanced from the fields of Edom;
> The earth trembled, the heavens poured,
> the clouds poured down their waters;
> The mountains streamed down before Yahweh,
> before Yahweh, the God of Israel.

On the Canaanite side he was met by the celestial rulers, the Meleks, of the country: [18]

> The Meleks came and they fought,
> then fought the Meleks of Canaan,
> at Taanach, at the waters of Megiddo.
> They won no booty of silver.

> From the heavens down they fought,
> the stars down from their courses,
> they fought on the side of Sisera.

But their help was of no avail to Sisera and his allies, for the storm and flood of Yahweh had done its work:

> The torrent Kishon swept them away,
> The ancient torrent, the torrent Kishon.

The defeat of the Canaanites was crushing. Sisera, on his flight, took refuge with Jael, a Kenite woman. She offered him hospitality, and when he felt safe, she drove a tentpin through his head:

[18] For the following verses 5:19–20 I am using the translation suggested by H. S. Nyberg, *Studien zum Hoseabuche, Zugleich ein Beitrag zur Klaerung des Problems der Alttestamentlichen Textkritik* (Uppsala Universitets Arsskrift, 1935:6), 47: "The war between Sisera and the Israelites is depicted as a battle between the city-gods of Canaan and Yahweh."

> Blessed be among women, Jael, the woman of Heber, the Kenite,
> Among the women who live in a tent, blessed she be!

From the end of Sisera in the bedouin tent, the scene shifts to his palace, where his mother waited for him and wondered about the delay. The song dwells with gusto on the expectations of the women, soon to be shattered by the terrible news:

> Are they not finding,
> Are they not dividing the spoil,
> A girl, two girls, for each man?
>
> A spoil of dyed stuffs for Sisera,
> A spoil of dyed stuffs embroidered,
> Dyed and embroidered, from the necks of the spoiled?

The song ends with the lines, perhaps added later:

> Thus perish all your enemies, Yahweh!
> But your friends be like the sun when he rises in his might!

The Deborah Song is unencumbered by interpretations and redactions of the later historical schools; and it is so early that it has not yet suffered from Israelite-Canaanite syncretism. It is the only document extant which conveys a coherent picture of Yahwist Israel in its pristine form. Hence, in its every detail it is of immeasurable value for the historian who wants to distinguish between early Israelite ideas and later developments, between original Israelite ideas and Canaanite accretions. The main characteristics of this early order as they become visible in the song are the following:

An Israelite Confederacy existed, indeed, but without political organization. This fact alone sheds a flood of light over the genesis of the people and its order. For if there was no permanent organization, and if the improvisation in case of an emergency functioned as haphazardly as the Deborah Song reveals, "Israel" never can have "conquered" Canaan; the component tribes can only have slowly infiltrated, in a process made possible by the disintegration of Egyptian power in the area. While the infiltration was not entirely peaceable, it can have involved only minor clashes of clans and tribes with local enemies, not any major conflict with the Canaanites that could have been met only by the organized forces of the whole Confederacy. There was no political organization because no military effort on a national scale had been

necessary. As a consequence, the Yahweh of the Confederacy can hardly
have been a war god. And one can, indeed, find in the narrative traces
of pleased surprise when, in a critical situation, the "God of the fathers"
revealed himself unexpectedly as a mighty war lord, as in Miriam's out-
cry in Exodus 15:

> Yahweh is a man of war,
>   Yahweh is his name. . . .
> Sing to Yahweh,
>   For he has triumphed gloriously;
> The horse and his rider
>   He has hurled into the sea.

The same experience of surprise pervades the Deborah Song with its repeated accents on the voluntary participation of the tribes in a general
war of Israel and on Yahweh's aid. It would be rash to conclude from
this note of surprise that Israel as a whole had never fought a common
war before the Sisera battle (and thus, in a strict sense, had never existed
politically), but certainly such previous events were not impressive
enough to leave their trace in the memory of the people. The Deborah
Song can hardly be considered an accidental piece of poetry accidentally
preserved. It must be understood as celebrating the great event in which
Israel for the first time experienced itself as a people united in political
action under Yahweh.[19]

If the interpretation is correct, if the war with Sisera was indeed the
occasion for a decisive advance in the constitution of Israel under Yahweh, the details of the song gain added importance as a source of information on the genesis of a people. To be sure, the information is
spotty, for the song is a poem, not a treatise. Still, a few things become
clear.

The warriors assembled in camp for battle were called *am Yahweh*,
the people of Yahweh (Judg. 5:11, 13). The god himself was not present
with his people in Canaan, but came to their aid from his seat far in the
south (5:4). The ark as the seat of Yahweh is not mentioned in the song;
but since the ark in general was a questionable piece of war equipment,
it is difficult to draw any conclusions from its omission. In the later
Philistine wars it had an important function, but it proved so ineffective
that the enemy captured it. Once it had been captured, it became quite

---

[19] The suggestions in the text follow the study by Gerhard von Rad, *Der Heilige Krieg im
Alten Israel* (Zurich, 1951).

active in spreading pestilences wherever it was placed; and the Philistines were glad to return it. When it then continued to make a nuisance of itself among its own people, it was deposited in a barn and abandoned; and Israel concluded the Philistine wars quite well without the dangerous object. And, finally, after the conquest of Jerusalem, it was remembered by David and put in a tent in the city. Its strange absence from Deborah's war is perhaps a further indication that Yahweh had not previously been a war god and that his usefulness in this capacity was discovered on the occasion.

Yahweh himself was experienced as a god who manifested himself in natural forces. His appearance brought an upheaval of nature: the clouds poured down, the earth trembled, the mountains released floods, and even the stars joined in the fight. Yet, the presence of Yahweh in his storm differed from the storm which Enlil spread like a shroud over Ur. In the "Lamentations over the Destruction of Ur" the attack of Elam was experienced as the cosmic storm of Enlil; in the Deborah Song the real storm was experienced as the presence of Yahweh. And what revealed itself as Yahweh in the real storm was not a cosmic storm but the *zidekoth Yahweh* (Judg. 5:11), literally: the righteousnesses of Yahweh. The meaning of the term can only be conjectured as the righteous acts of the god by which he established just order among men. Yahweh was a god who revealed himself in historical action as the creator of true order. This conception, now, seems to be not too far from the Egyptian *maat* of both the god and the mediating Pharaoh. But again, the righteousness of Yahweh had a different complexion because there was no human mediator who would transform the cosmic into social order. One of the oddities not only of the Deborah Song but of the Book of Judges in general is the absence of a term for the human functionaries of political order in time of crisis. The designation of Deborah as a *shophet*, a judge, is probably anachronistic, for the term *shophet* belongs to the Deuteronomist redactions. But Deborah at least owes her public influence to her recognizable spiritual authority as a prophetess, a *nebijah* (4:4).[20] For Barak, however, the war leader, there is no term at all to designate his function. The charismatic leadership, on which the action of the Confederacy in war depended, obviously was not conceived as an analogue of cosmic order in society that would require appropriate

---

[20] It is possible that even the term *nebijah* is anachronistic. *Nebi'im* are attested with any certainty only for the time of Samuel. A personage of the type of Deborah would more probably have been a *roeh*, a seer.

expression through symbols. Hence, in spite of its brevity, the Deborah Song unmistakably reveals Israel's break with the cosmological civilizations.

The song celebrates a victory in a war. The ideas concerning warfare under the leadership of Yahweh are presupposed in the song, but their full understanding requires the use of additional sources. Military actions were numerous, but not all of them were *milhamoth Yahweh* (I Sam. 18:17; 25:28), wars of Yahweh, even though the Book of Judges sometimes gives this impression; with a rare exception, it tells only the story of the holy wars. The wars of Yahweh were engagements of the whole people, if not in fact, at least in their intention. And they were conducted according to a certain ritual. The component parts of the ritual are nowhere enumerated in their entirety but must be gathered from their fragmentary appearance on the various occasions of military action. Still, the general structure of the ritual can be discerned in the abbreviated account preserved in Judges 4:14–16:

> And Deborah said to Barak:
> "Up! For this is the day,
> on which Yahweh has given Sisera into your hand.
> Has Yahweh not gone forth before you?"
> So Barak went down from Mount Tabor, and ten thousand men
> after him.
> And Yahweh brought confusion [or panic] to Sisera, and all his
> chariots, and all his host; and Sisera alighted from his chariot, and
> fled on foot.
> But Barak pursued, after the chariots, after the host, unto Haro-
> sheth-goiim;
> and the whole host of Sisera fell by the edge of the sword;
> there was not a man left.

The beginning of the ritual is missing in the account; and some features that are known from other contexts are omitted. At the opening of the account the army stands ready to go into battle. But the moment when the *am Yahweh* stood ready for battle had to be preceded by a number of preparatory steps. There had to be a declaration, not of war against the enemy but of a state of emergency to the people, through prophetic authorities who issued a call for war. Then a charismatic leader had to be incited to action, as was Barak by Deborah; and the leader had to have sufficient authority to summon the people to action through messengers, as for instance in Judges 3:27 or 6:34. The tribes and clans deliberated and acted on the summons, with varying results, as the

Deborah Song indicates. The warrior community in camp had to be ritually pure, in particular submitting to sexual abstinence, for Yahweh was present with his people. Sacrifices were offered and oracles were obtained. Only then, when everything seemed favorable, would a leader (in the present case, Deborah to Barak) issue the verdict: "Yahweh has given the enemy in your hand"; and the army could proceed to the execution of the verdict with complete certainty of victory. For Yahweh was "going forth before them," he was conducting the war, and the army was no more than the instrument of execution. The character of the warriors as the instruments of Yahweh required their spiritual qualification. They had to have confidence in Yahweh; and they had to be conscious that not they themselves but their god was fighting and winning the war. Hence, in the war against the Midianites (Judges 7), Yahweh informed the war leader that his army was too large to give the enemy into his hand. Israel might vaunt itself to have won the war by its own human strength. The vast bulk of the army had to be dismissed, in particular those who were afraid and did not trust Yahweh sufficiently; and the victory had to be won by a few companies of hardened warriors with complete faith in their God. When the ritual and spiritual preconditions were fulfilled, the battle could begin. In the various holy wars, the external circumstances of the battles differed widely, but uniformly Yahweh came to the aid of his people by throwing a panic into the ranks of the enemy (Judges 4:15 or 7:22), a "confusion," a "terror," a bewilderment in which the enemies sometimes started fighting against one another. A numinous horror gripped the enemy, so that he was unable to offer resistance—perhaps not too surprising when a horde of seminude, fanatical dervishes came bearing down, screaming and screeching, with their hair flowing in the wind. After the defeat of the enemy in battle, the holy war came to a conclusion through the ritual of the *cherem*, the ban. Since Yahweh had won the war, the loot was his; all gold and silver went into the treasury of the god; all living beings, human and animal, were slaughtered in his honor.[21]

At the time of the Deborah Song Israel was a people when at war under Yahweh. It was a mode of existence not easy to describe, because the more obvious characterization of this period as a state of transition

[21] For further details of the war ritual, its variations, and the rich documentation see von Rad, *Der Heilige Krieg*.

from nomad tribalism to national statehood might be misleading. To be sure, there was a problem of transition. The basic units of the people still were the clans and the tribes; and the state of settlement in a foreign environment was so much in flux that one cannot speak yet of a national territory. And this tribal society was clearly developing toward more permanent and better circumscribed occupation of territory, as well as toward political organization under the pressure of wars. Moreover, certain details of the song indicate that the mores had changed substantially from those of nomads. For the feat of the Kenite woman who killed Sisera was, by nomad standards, an atrocious violation of the laws of hospitality, and the creator of the song praised the ugly murder in a fashion that smacks of jingoism at its worst; the incident is tangible proof of national progress. Nevertheless, an interpretation of this mode of existence as transitional would be rash, since it contains elements that remained constant throughout Israelite history. And these elements, far from contributing to a consolidated national statehood, proved rather the forces which disintegrated the Kingdom once it was gained. For the holy war, as described in the Deborah Song, was an institution loaded with experiential difficulties and obscurities. The wars of Yahweh were fundamentally defensive wars—at least, there is not a single instance of an aggressive holy war recorded. The people were conceived as being at peace, politically in a passive condition, and not bent on using war as an instrument of national expansion and consolidation. Israel itself did not conduct these wars at all; Yahweh conducted them for his people. They had no implication of missionary violence being used for the expansion of Yahweh's territory or the mundane success of his people, as in the holy wars of Islam. Yahweh, as we have said, was not primarily a war god but came to the assistance of his people, as in the Sisera case, only when it was endangered by oppression and aggression. In particular, Yahweh did not fight against other gods; and in fact, no gods of other peoples are even mentioned in the song. This peculiar passivity, and the relegation of all military activity to Yahweh, was, however, at the time still quite compatible with a lusty participation in war when the occasion arose. In Judges 5:23, the town of Meroz, situated close to the battlefield, was roundly cursed for nonparticipation:

> "Curse Meroz," said the angel of Yahweh,
> "Curse utterly its inhabitants;
> For they came not to the help of Yahweh,
> To the help of Yahweh, joining his warriors."

The poet was not perturbed at all by a people's coming to the help of the god while the god comes to the help of the people in an emergency. The experience of Yahweh's help could blend with the spirit of a warrior community without inducing reflections on the consistency of the conception. But obviously, there was a crack in the symbolism. The war spirit of the tribes and the experience of a god who comes to the aid of an essentially passive community could part company. The development need not go in the direction of an effectively organized people, conducting its political affairs with success under the guidance of its god. It also could go in the direction of a pacifist community that would sit back and expect the discomfiture of its enemies from divine interventions without military actions of its own.

In fact, the history of Israel has followed both of these courses. And we venture to say that the recognition of this double course is the key to the understanding of Israelite history. The improvised organization of defensive wars under charismatic leaders proved inadequate against the rising pressure of foreign powers after the Philistine invasion. The improvisations had to be replaced by the permanent kingship. But as soon as the monarchy was organized, the potential tensions that could be discerned in the Deborah Song became actual. In the situation described by the song, the prophetess and the war leader co-operated in the organization of the war. The prophetess mobilized and crystallized the sentiments of the people (today we should say, the public opinion) by her songs; and the war leader let himself be induced to assume his function. The prophetess rendered the verdict that Yahweh had given the enemy into the hand of the leader; and the leader was ready to execute the verdict. But the mere articulation of these steps in the procedure makes it obvious that an organized government with a king, his policy-making officials, and his military staff could not, in making its decision, politely request the opinion of some prophet whether a war should be undertaken or not, and whether, according to the prophet's information about the intentions of Yahweh, the time was propitious for engaging in battle or not. Serious conflicts were bound to break out when prophetic and governmental opinions about the right order and policy should differ. Moreover, the conflicts that actually did break out were shaped, with regard to the basic issue, by the inconsistencies of the Yahwist experience that could be noticed in the Deborah Song; and they were fostered by the institutional changes in the wake of the permanent political organ-

ization in monarchical form. For the monarchy, in order to become politically and militarily effective, had first of all to repair the backward-
ness of Israelite war technique. A modernized, professional army was
organized that could meet in battle the war chariots of the other military
powers; and the improvised peasant army, the *am Yahweh* of the Deborah Song, fell into desuetude, with the consequences that the native
warrior spirit of the peasantry died from atrophy. The militancy of the
people of Yahweh turned into the pacifism of subjects over whose heads
the wars were conducted by professionals. This peaceable population in
the shelter of the Kingdom provided social resonance when the prophets
accentuated the strand of passivity in the Yahwist experience. The new
climate of experience and ideas can be felt in the post-Solomonic account
of the miraculous rescue of Israel from the Egyptians in the J document.
In Exodus 14 the people were afraid of the pursuing Egyptian army and
Moses admonished them:

> Fear not, stand still, and you will see the salvation of Yahweh that he
> will work for you today. . . . Yahweh will fight for you, and you
> have only to keep still (Exod. 14:13–14).

And when the Egyptians were swallowed up by the flood, the account
concluded:

> And Israel saw the great deed, which Yahweh had done to Egypt,
> and the people feared Yahweh, and they believed in Yahweh and his
> servant Moses (Exod. 14:31).

At the time of Deborah and Gideon a warrior was qualified to fight in
the holy war when he was not afraid and trusted in Yahweh; now the people were afraid and wanted to surrender to the Egyptians. Yahweh fights
alone, and the people watch the performance; and only when Yahweh
has shown his might are they willing to believe in him. This strange
passivity that would even trust in Yahweh only after the goods of mundane success had been delivered was certainly not a civic virtue on which
a government could build; and it also gave pause to the prophets who
otherwise were inclined to mobilize such sentiments against the policies
of the royal government.[22]

---

[22] In the present context Israelite symbols are discussed under the aspect of mundane existence. The same passages, which reflect a dubious civic virtue, will appear in a quite different light
when they are considered with regard to their spiritual implications. The crude faith in Yahweh
after his show of effective military help will then become a compact expression of the insight that
faith has its origin not in human initiative but in a divine *gratia praeveniens*.

The Yahwism of the prophets will be treated in a later context. But the analysis of the Deborah Song should have made it clear that the sometimes bewildering problems of Yahwist order in the period of the Kingdom have their origin in a structure of experience that is already present in the earliest extant document.

§ 3. The Kingship of Gideon

The Book of Judges gives a highly stylized version of the events from the time of Joshua to the Philistine wars. According to the historiographic program set forth by the authors in Judges 2:6–3:6, the people were supposed to be settled in the promised land and to live happily ever after in obedience to the Yahweh who had brought them there. But the people would do evil in the sight of the Lord and serve the Baals and Ashtarts of the Canaanites. Then Yahweh castigated them by delivering them into the hands of their enemies, especially preserved by him for the purpose (2:23–3:6). When they were sufficiently in straits to repent, Yahweh would raise a leader, a judge, in order to deliver them out of the hands of the enemy; and the new harmony would last for the lifetime of the judge. After his death the cycle would begin again. The Deuteronomist redactors must have considered this an agreeable arrangement, for they concluded the book with the nostalgic phrase "In those days there was no king in Israel; every man did what was right in his own eyes" (21:25).

The events actually reported by the authors do not bear out their program in every point. Israel, it is true, succumbed to the gods of Canaan. The authors of Judges discerned correctly that the syncretism which aroused the ire of the prophets under the monarchy had its beginnings in the twelfth and eleventh centuries B.C., in the period of the Confederacy. Around this true nucleus of history they constructed, through mutilation of sources and imaginative additions, the pattern of the cycles. But fortunately their editorial work did not destroy the sources completely; and the essential features of the process which resulted in syncretism and monarchy can still be discerned. In the first place, whatever the connection between Israel's defection and the wars may have been in the sight of the Lord, on the pragmatic level syncretism was the effect of the successful wars against the Canaanites, not their cause. And second, every man did not do as he pleased, in an idyllic freedom without kings. On the contrary, nomad raids from Trans-Jordan proved so harassing to the already settled invaders that they were forced to adopt the more effective form of the monarchy. The kings at first were local princes, as in the cases of Gideon and Jephthah. But when the Trans-Jordanian pressure was aggravated by the consolidation and expansion of a Philistine power, kingship had to become national.

Syncretism, as we said, was the consequence of the Hebrews' successful penetration into Canaan. That much can be taken for granted, even if the sources do not confirm the fact. As long as there was friction between Israel and the Canaanites, the conditions for an amiable symbiosis in matters of cult were hardly given. Yahwism would be maintained at the level of relative purity that could be observed in the Deborah Song. This period of friction, however, did not last long; and it never was intense. The Book of Judges does not record any serious conflicts previous to the Sisera battle, with the possible exception of the Othniel episode (3:7–11); and that is a doubtful case since the identity of the enemy is uncertain. And subsequent to the Sisera battle, Judges records no clashes with Canaan at all. By 1100 B.C., roughly, the Hebrew penetration was an accomplished fact. Both Israelites and Canaanites were inhabitants of the same country; and their former enmity disappeared in face of the common danger from nomadic invaders who did not distinguish between the two ethnic groups when they attacked the cis-Jordanian Palestine from the east. Hebrew settlers and old residents were on their way toward becoming one people with a common culture, though the process was consummated only through the leveling effects of the Solomonic monarchy. The stylization of events on the part of the Deuteronomist redactors is apt, even today, to obscure the fact that after the Sisera battle the "judges" were the war leaders not of a confederacy of Hebrew clans against Canaan but of the inhabitants of Palestine, including the Canaanites, against external enemies. Under the name of "Israel" a new people was in the making.

The new situation becomes manifest in the story of the Midianite wars and the elevation of Gideon to hereditary kingship (Judges 6–9). The Midianite wars must be dated in the first half of the eleventh century B.C. The account in Judges is not too clear, particularly not for the early phases. Midianite nomads raided Palestine more than once, and records of several campaigns were blended by the editors into one story. Moreover, Gideon's second name, Jerubbaal, though carefully explained (6:32), suggests that the feats of two leaders were ascribed to one person. Furthermore, it is uncertain to what extent the ritual of the holy war was applied to the several campaigns. The account of Judges suggests its application to the earlier phases. But even if we accept the version, the procedure differed notably from that in the war of Sisera, in so far as no figure comparable to Deborah appeared. A nameless *nabi*, to be sure, is mentioned in Judges 6:8–10 as exhorting the people. But his connection with the subsequent wars is not clarified, and he may be an invention of the editors. Gideon himself is presented as deriving his inspirations variously from an angel of Yahweh (*malak*, 6:11), from the spirit of Yahweh (*ruach*, 6:34), or from Yahweh himself (6:23, 25). This peculiarity perhaps explains the subsequent course of events: the man who had his inspirations without prophetic assistance and took matters in his own hands must have been a more impressive figure than Barak. While the earlier history of the Midianite wars thus lies in the shadow of uncertainties, the last campaign preceding Gideon's elevation to kingship can be discerned more clearly because, through a piece of good luck, Judges 9 escaped the zeal of the editors; and the less distorted traditions of Chapter 9 cast some light on the immediately preceding events.

Gideon's last campaign almost certainly was not a holy war of the Confederacy. He is described as pursuing two Midianite chieftains who, in the course of a raid, had killed his brothers in Tabor. When he captured the Midianites and killed them in their turn, he carried out a vendetta; and more immediately, only his own clan, the clan of Abiezer in Manasseh, with its center of residence in Ophrah, was involved. Nevertheless, neighboring settlements were afflicted by the raids and, perhaps through berith relations, were obliged to participate in the campaign, for some of them were punished by Gideon for refusing support (7:14–18). At any rate, after the victory, as the story reports with some exaggeration, "the men of Israel" asked Gideon to become their hereditary king (8:22)—with some exaggeration because Gideon did not become a king over the whole of Israel, but only over Ophrah and the neighboring towns. His kingship was a political form, intermediate between the national leadership in holy wars, and the later nationwide monarchy of Saul. The Midianite danger, while not affecting the whole of Israel, was threatening enough to induce the population of a limited area to counter it with a permanent governmental organization.

As soon as Gideon was king, he claimed for himself the gold treasure of the defeated Midianites and had it made into an ephod, probably a gold-plated statue of Yahweh. The image was deposited in a sanctuary at Ophrah, the king's residence. The first act of the king, thus, was the establishment of a temple, that is, of a cult center for the monarchy in competition with the sanctuary of the Confederacy at Shiloh. While the intentions of the king are unknown, the consequences of his act are clear. Like the later Solomonic Temple, the royal chapel tended to become a popular shrine: "all Israel went awhoring after it" (8:27), as the editors peevishly remark. Whether intended or not, the Yahweh shrine at Ophrah grew into the cult center of the "kingdom" and its "people." Gideon's institution of a "temple" must, therefore, be recognized as the creation of a new symbol of political order. From the one side, Israel was developing a national consciousness in search of adequate governmental and cultic representation; from the other side, Yahweh was developing into the God of a settled and organized nation. The popular success of Gideon's temple proves that the people were experientially ready for the appearance of a particular, national divinity, of a political Yahweh who reigned over Canaan and its population. And this experiential trend showed itself even more forcefully when Solomon's royal chapel developed into the monopolistic Temple of Israel. The development was so successful, indeed, that the institution of the Temple survived the monarchy and became the rallying point of the postexilic Jewish community.

The endogenous development of Yahwism is somewhat neglected in the interpretation of Israelite history, though, in our opinion, it is important for the understanding of Israelite-Canaanite syncretism. When the Israelites accepted Canaanite gods and their cults, they were not simply disloyal to a clearly conceived "Yahweh." For apace with the political formation of the people, Yahwism was undergoing a change that brought the divinity down to the level of a particular national god. The syncretism with the gods of the land began in Yahwism itself, when the god of the fathers became a god of the country in the political sense. When Israel found its national existence through the creation of a king as its representative, it also found, in Yahweh, the transcendental representative of the nation. Political particularism, therefore, must be recognized as a movement, in Yahwism, of the same rank as the universalist movement of the prophets. And if the universalism of the prophets was never quite successful, the reason must not be sought in the people's defection to the Baals and Ashtarts, but in the political particularization of Yahweh, which the prophets themselves could never overcome radically, not even in the person of Deutero-Isaiah.

The creation of the royal cult image was followed by Gideon's attempt to consolidate his position through intermarriage with the important clans of the kingdom. It must have been a formidable effort, for the story reports a result of no less than seventy sons (9:2). With this measure, again, Gideon inaugurated a technique for stabilizing the monarchy that was further developed by Solomon and his successors in Israel and Judah. The superimposition of a monarchy over a clan society made the technique inevitable, even though it was bound to cause troubles. There were the usual harem affairs, the rivalries between the wives and their sons, the uncertainty of succession, and the wholesale slaughter of brothers in which the most energetic son had to indulge in order to secure his position as successor. This normal unpleasantness of a harem regime, however, was aggravated by the diversity of cults represented by the ladies. While Gideon did not yet encounter the difficulties of the Omrides with their international diplomatic marriages, he sowed the seed of troubles for his successors when he included Canaanite concubines in his harem. One of them was a woman of Shechem, the seat of the Canaanite Baal-berith. She bore him a son, Abimelech, but under matriarchal marriage customs continued to live with her family (8:31). What the relations between the gods of Ophrah and Shechem were during Gideon's lifetime does not become clear from the account in Judges. But it must be considered as possible that the Canaanites of Shechem were bound to the monarchy through a berith under the sanction of their own god. Anyway, as soon as Gideon died, Israel transferred its whoring activities from the Yahweh of Ophrah to the Baal-berith of Shechem (8:33). At the same time Abimelech left the brothers, to whom Gideon had bequeathed the kingship collectively, and went to his mother's clan in order to obtain their support for his sole kingship. The clan agreed and persuaded the whole citizenry of Shechem. Abimelech was equipped with funds from the treasury of the Baal-berith, hired a troop of adventurers, and killed all his brothers with the exception of Jotham who escaped (9:1–5). Here for the first time the use of hired troops by a pretender is recorded, which later played an important role in the rise of David and ultimately became the nucleus of the professional army in the national kingdom. The kingship of Abimelech did not last long. In the course of a revolt that originated in Shechem the city was razed and shortly afterwards Abimelech himself fell at Thebez (9:22–57). That was the end of the first monarchy in Israel.

In the story of Abimelech is embedded the fable of "The Trees Who Search for a King" (Judg. 9:8–15). It is the earliest piece of Hebrew didactic poetry extant, about contemporary with Gideon's monarchy, even if placed in its present context only because of its apt lesson. It has its importance as the oldest document expressing Israelite ideas on kingship:

> The trees went forth on a time
>   to anoint a king over them.
> And they said to the olive: "Reign over us."
>   But the olive said unto them:
> "Should I renounce to produce my oil,
>   which the gods and men prize in me,
>   in order to sway over the trees?"
>
> Then the trees said to the fig-tree:
>   "Come you, and reign over us!"
>   But the fig-tree said unto them:
> "Should I renounce to give my sweetness,
>   and my good fruit,
>   in order to sway over the trees?"
>
> Then the trees said to the vine:
>   "Come you, and reign over us!"
>   But the vine said unto them:
> "Should I renounce to give my wine,
>   that cheers the gods and men,
>   in order to sway over the trees?"
>
> Then said all the trees to the thorn:
>   "Come you, and reign over us!"
>   And the thorn said unto the trees:
> "If you will anoint me in good faith,
>   to be king over you,
>   come and take refuge in my shade!"
>
> But if not, fire shall proceed from the thorn,
>   and consume the cedars of Lebanon.

The lesson is clear. No man who leads a useful life by the standards of the clan society will want to be king. Only a useless individual will care to be esteemed for a function as dubious as the shadow cast by a thornbush. And besides, a king, while not of much use when you are loyal, is dangerous when you resist him. His wrath may destroy like a forest fire that starts from a dry thornbush. The fable is of great value for the history of ideas, as was the Deborah Song, because here one can touch Israelite ideas in their purity, before the Solomonic kingdom and the prophetic resistance have complicated the issues. The fable does not condemn kingship as do the later sources, because Yahweh is the king of Israel and kingship as such is a defection from the Lord; it rather reflects the resentment of chieftains who feel themselves quite capable to discharge all governmental functions at the local level and consider kingship a dangerous nuisance. It is a resentment that reached deep into the period of the national monarchy and was an important factor in the division of the kingdom after the death of Solomon.

CHAPTER 8

The Struggle for Empire

§ 1. THE AMPLITUDE OF YAHWISM

The episode of Gideon's kingship has furnished additional insight into the dynamics of Israelite order. There was apparently no factor in original Yahwism that would have imposed a particular political form on the faithful. But precisely because limiting factors of this kind were absent from his nature, Yahweh was adaptable to every social and political situation that required understanding as a manifestation of divine force. When the Confederacy was in danger and had to resort to war he could be a war god. When the nomad tribes settled and became peasants, he could become a Baal of agricultural fertility and prosperity, while at the same time he could remain for the Trans-Jordanian Hebrews a god who abhorred the agricultural perversions of his nature. When there was a question of conquering and holding a territory, he could become a god of the land like the gods of non-Yahwist peoples in other Canaanite regions. When the clan organization sufficed for political existence, he could become the god of the berith that held the tribes together by its divine life substance. When the political situation required kingship, he could become the god of royal order, in forms closely resembling the Egyptian. As a consequence, the spiritual freedom that had been wrested from captivity and desert by the inspiration and genius of Moses might have been lost again through a dispersal of divinity into particular divine forces.

The possibilities of such a relapse, in the eleventh century and after, becomes obvious in the assimilation of Yahweh's nature to that of the other Canaanite gods. A striking instance is offered by Jephthah's negotiations with the King of Moab, in Judges 11:14–28. In the debate over a contested territory the hero of the Trans-Jordanian tribes put it persuasively to the King of Moab: "Should you not occupy the territory of those whom Chemosh, your own god, drives out, while we occupy that of all those whom Yahweh, our god, has driven out of our way?" (11: 24). The relation of Yahweh to Jephthah and his Israel did not differ substantially from the relation between Chemosh and the Moabite kings, as we know it from the Mesha Stone of the ninth century B.C. On that occasion it was Mesha, the king of Moab, who could say: "As for Omri, king of Israel, he humbled Moab many years, for Chemosh was angry at his land. And his son followed him and he also said, 'I will humble Moab.' In my time he spoke thus, but I have triumphed over him and his house, while Israel has perished forever!" [1] The passages are instructive with regard to both parties. There are two peoples at war, rivaling one another in expanding their respective territories, each under his own god. But only the peoples, not their gods, are at war with one another. At least, there is no hint of one god's expanding at the expense of the other one. If a people is defeated, it is not because the enemy's god was stronger, but because its own god was angry. On the one hand, the foreign god is recognized as a force in his own right; on the other hand, there is no doubt that the own god will give victory unless the people has incurred his momentary disfavor.

This peculiar political theology is further illuminated by an equally odd casuistry. In the Moabite war of the ninth century, the alliance of Israel, Judah, and Edom was on the point of a complete victory over the rebellious Mesha. As a last resource, the King of Moab sacrificed his own son in order to secure the aid of Chemosh. That apparently was a decisive action, for "there came a great wrath upon Israel, so that they departed from him and returned to their own land" (II Kings 3:27). The "wrath" in this case, must have been the wrath of Chemosh, who, propitiated by the supreme sacrifice, would now proceed against the invaders of his territory. There is no suggestion that on this occasion Yahweh could have prevailed. On the Israelite side we find Jephthah, in the earlier war with Moab, having recourse to the same cruel sacrifice. Apparently he was not too convinced of the righteousness of his territorial claims. And in order to ensure victory, he promised sacrifice of the first member of his household that would meet him on the return from his campaign, if successful; and this person was his daughter (Judg. 11:29–40). A third case, illustrating the problem, is Ahaziah's attempt to obtain an oracle from Baal-Zebub, the god of Ekron (II Kings 1). Elijah

---

[1] The Mesha Stone is to be dated *ca.* 830 B.C. The English translation, by Albright, in Pritchard (ed.), *Ancient Near Eastern Texts*, 320 ff.

was ordered by Yahweh to intervene, with the pertinent question: "Is it because there is no god in Israel that you are sending to inquire of Baal-Zebub, the god of Ekron?" And the king must die for his violation of etiquette. Again, there was no question that the Philistine god was a divine force; but within Israelite territory Yahweh had sole competence to issue oracles for his subjects.

The various traditions, in our opinion, furnish the rare documentation for a political summodeism in statu nascendi. Civilizationally, the Syriac area was sufficiently unified to have the gods of its various peoples mutually recognized as ordering forces. The respective jurisdictions of the members of the pantheon were territorially circumscribed by the actual dominions of the peoples. But it was a question of events on the pragmatic level whether the jurisdiction of one of the gods would become coextensive with the imperial dominion of his particular people over the whole of the Syriac area. The experiential relation to the various gods of the pantheon could furnish arguments for every pragmatic contingency. Each god was ready to become the highest, if not the exclusive, god over whatever territory his people would conquer. If the people was victorious, its god had given the land to it, and it was his as much as the people's. If the people was defeated, the god was temporarily angry but remained potentially the ruler over the territory which his people might conquer in the future. But then again, the god of the enemy was recognized sufficiently as a force in his own right when in actual war conquest proved impossible; while the own god, even in defeat, could reveal himself as a formidable nuisance, if treated discourteously by the enemy, as was shown by the activities of the ark among the Philistines.

Nothing can be gained by putting a label—such as monotheism, polytheism, monolatrism, or henotheism—on this turgid experience of divine force. The experience must be taken as it is, in its unstable richness, pregnant with possibilities of development in one or the other direction. The divine force that revealed itself in such manner could become restricted political gods, like the gods of the Philistine city-states or of the shepherd kingdom of Moab; or local Baals, like the Baal-berith of Shechem or the Yahweh of Ophrah; or ultimately the god of a Syriac Empire, if one of the contestants should prevail over the others.

Thus there was a stage in the Israelite dynamics of order at which Yahweh could develop into a political god and, more specifically, into a god of the same type as Chemosh. Nevertheless, while Yahweh could descend to equality with the Moabite god on the level of experience just analysed, it does not follow that Chemosh could have ascended to the height of the Mosaic or Prophetic Yahweh. The dynamics of Yahwism in its full amplitude must be taken into consideration at every particular stage of the Yahwist experience in order not to mistake the appearance of equation with other gods as an identity of nature. For in the end it was the Yahweh of Israel who, as a political god, put the first imperial stamp on Syriac civilization, and not the gods of Moab, nor of the Phoenician or Philistine city-states, even though the Philistines came close to success before their drive was broken by the recovery of Israel under David. And while various other factors contributed to the issue of the struggle, the most important one was the latent quality of Yahweh as a nonpolitical, universal god who, because of his universality, could be the spiritual force that formed great individuals.

The dormant quality could spring to life at any time, and it actually did at critical moments, in the individual inspirations of prophetic and military figures by the *ruach* of Yahweh. The result was a spiritual formation of character which—as far as our documentary information goes—was unique in its time. The great personalities of the Israelite struggle for empire are so familiar to us through the Bible that it is difficult to imagine how their appearance, representing a new type of man on the world-political scene, must have impressed their contemporaries at large. In general, we can discern their impact only in the love and fierce loyalty which they inspired in their followers when times were hard. In their more intimate circle, we know, the formation of individual characters through the spirit, as well as the implications of the phenomenon for the conduct of politics, were fully understood. For this understanding expressed itself in the creation of history, not as an annalistic recording of external events, but as a course of actions motivated by the characters of the actors. And the historical memoirs for this period were integrated into the books of Samuel.

We have spoken of "characters" and "motives." Such language, however, should not induce the belief that the merit of the memoirs consists in the psychological shrewdness, which undoubtedly they possess, in analyzing the motives of actions. Shrewdness of this kind is a condition of survival at all times, and must be supposed to exist in a society even when it does not find literary expression, as in the much older wisdom literature of Egypt. Even in Israelite literature we find marvels of psychological observation at an earlier date, as in certain passages of the Deborah Song. What is new in the eleventh and tenth centuries of Israelite history is the application of such psychological knowledge to the understanding of personalities who, as individuals, have become the carriers of a spiritual force on the scene of pragmatic history. No such character portraits were ever drawn of Babylonian, Assyrian, or Egyptian rulers, whose personalities (with the exception of Akhenaton's, through the self-revelations in his hymns) disappear behind their function as the representatives and preservers of cosmic order in society. Their personalities are accessible, if at all, only through their recorded administrative and military actions; and even such records are frequently deceptive because the descriptions of military campaigns, for instance of the Pharaohs, were standardized to such a degree that the actual course of events can rarely be reconstructed with reliability. The nature of this outburst of brilliant historiography will perhaps best be understood if one considers that it disappeared as suddenly as it appeared. The royal personalities of Israel and Judah after Solomon have, in the Biblical narrative, no longer the clarity of the preceding period, either because no better accounts existed, or because they no longer interested the official historians; and about the greatest of the post-Solomonic kings, about Omri, we know next to nothing, since all that is preserved about his reign are the few pitiful lines in I Kings 16:21–28. The reason is that, as a consequence of the Prophetic movement, the kings had ceased to be representative of the spiritual order of Israel. The great personalities of the eighth and seventh centuries, whose characters are as vividly familiar to us as those of Saul, David, and Solomon, are the Prophets. History—that is, the existence of Israel under Yahweh—was shifting from royal to prophetic representation. Only for the short period, barely a century, when the kings saved Israel from physical extinction and built the shelter of the monarchy, was the organization of the people for worldly existence experienced as true existence under Yahweh. Take a passage like the following: "Now at the return of spring, at the time when kings go forth, David sent Joab and his servants with him, and they ravaged the Ammonites, and besieged Rabbah" (II Sam. 11:1). At no other time in Israelite history than David's could a historian have caught this vernal splendor of a king's going forth for a show of power. Once this glory had been glimpsed, however, its memory could be preserved in the conception of kingship. Still Maimonides, in his *Mishneh Torah*, speaks of the "optional wars" of a king in which he engages in order "to enhance his greatness and prestige." [2]

§ 2. THE KINGSHIP OF SAUL

1. *The Rise of Saul*

Israel had to be threatened with extinction at the hands of the Philistines in order to develop these potentialities of Yahwism. The critical struggle for imperial dominion over Palestine, in the second half of the eleventh century B.C., had its ultimate source in the situation created by the Aegean migrations about 1200 B.C. The dislocation of Aegean peoples through successive migration waves had caused, at the periphery of the movement, their attacks on the Asiatic empires of the time. The Hittite Empire was destroyed, *ca.* 1200, by the Peoples of the Sea, as they were called in the Egyptian records, so thoroughly that only small principalities, such as Aleppo and Carchemish, survived into the ninth and eighth centuries respectively. The Egyptian Empire could weather the storm, but its control over the Asiatic provinces had become, in the twelfth century, purely nominal. With the elimination of the imperial powers from the area, Syria and Palestine were a power-vacuum after 1190 B.C.

Into the vacuum the Hebrew tribes could penetrate from the east and south; but in it also could settle, on the southern seacoast, the remnants of the Peoples of the Sea, under the name of Philistines. About the first century of Philistine settlement we know nothing except what can be reasonably concluded from the state in which they appear on the scene of the Biblical narrative. They must have assimilated to the Canaanite environment rather quickly—for their language, their proper names, and their divinities were Semitic—and perhaps more thoroughly than the Hebrews, for they were organized in city-states like their neighbors. The principal cities were Ekron, Ashdod, Ascalon, Gaza, and Gath. The ruler was designated by a non-Semitic term, as *seren,* which is regularly used in the Biblical narrative when it refers to the rulers of the Philistine city-states (*e.g.* I Sam. 5:8, 11; 6:4, 12).[3] The relatively small

---

[2] *The Code of Maimonides. Book Fourteen: The Book of Judges,* trans. A. M. Hershman (New Haven, 1949), 217 ff.

[3] The term *seren* is possibly related to the Greek *tyrannos,* since the Syriac Bible renders it as *truno,* and the Targum as *turono.* Cf. Lods, *Israel,* 349.

territory of the Philistines indicates that they were much less numerous than the Hebrews. Politically, however, they were better organized; the five cities apparently were members of a federation, acting as a unit, though nothing is known about the constitutional detail. One of the city rulers, the prince of Gath, was sometimes styled "King," but the reasons for the distinction again are unknown; he certainly was only a King of Gath, not of the Philistines at large. Militarily, their equipment with armor and war chariots was superior to that of the Hebrews.

The expansion of the small but effective nucleus of city-states into a Philistine Empire is neither clearly known in detail nor datable with exactness. The events must have taken place between 1150 and 1050 B.C. Two phases of the Philistine expansion can be distinguished in the Biblical narrative. The memory of the first phase, still in the twelfth century, is preserved in the Samson stories of Judges 13–16. The friction with their Hebrew neighbors resulted in the expansion of Philistine dominion over the region of Judah (Judg. 15:11) and the migration of Dan to the north (Judg. 17). The second phase, in the first half of the eleventh century, brought the conflict with the central tribes of Benjamin and Ephraim. It resulted in the national catastrophe in which the ark was captured by the Philistines and Shiloh, the sanctuary of the Confederacy, was destroyed (I Sam. 4–6). Whether the territory of Israel was administered by Philistine officials directly or by responsible Hebrews is not clear. At a later time we find David in a position which is obviously that of a Philistine governor for the province of Judah. By the middle of the eleventh century, at the time of the first expansion, it is certain only that the Philistines resorted to such drastic measures as the disarmament of Israel through the deportation of all smiths (I Sam. 13:19–22).[4]

From its desperate situation Israel recovered, as at the time of the Sisera battle, through the combined efforts of a seer and a warrior. The narrative contains a good deal of information on details, some of it probably reliable. Nevertheless, the actual course of events cannot be reconstructed with certainty, since the genuine traditions are mixed

---

[4] For the Philistine period cf. Otto Eissfeldt, *Das Verhaeltnis der Philister und Phoenizier zu anderen Voelkern und Kulturen* (Der Alte Orient, 34:3, 1936), and Albright, "Syrien, Phoenizien, und Palaestina," *loc. cit.* The three Philistine attacks on Israel are dated by Eissfeldt *ca.* 1080 (conquest of Samaria), *ca.* 1020 (operations against Saul), and *ca.* 1000 (operations against David, after the conquest of Jerusalem). Albright assumes for the settlement of the Philistines in their five cities *ca.* 1175; for the first Philistine conquest, the middle of the eleventh century; for Saul, *ca.* 1020–1000.

with legendary elements and have undergone serious reworkings by the late editors. Particularly obscure is the point of greatest interest to us, that is, the genesis of Saul's kingship and its acceptance by the people. From the events following Saul's death, as well as from the reign of David, it is clear that hereditary kingship had indeed taken root in Israel, that the kings as persons were respected and loved by the people, that there might be quarrels about the succession, but that nobody wanted to abolish the institution.[5] Considering the jaundiced view of kingship entertained by the members of the clan society only half a century earlier—as manifest in the fable of "The Trees in Search of a King"— one would like to know what caused the reversal of sentiment. But light can be furnished only by a few reasonable assumptions. There obviously existed a national emergency. Since the clans could not cope with the Philistine power, the authority and prestige of the chieftains must have suffered, while correspondingly the war leader and king acquired the characteristics of a national savior. In the Confederacy and its cult, furthermore, all was not in good order. The story of Eli and his sons (I Sam. 2:12–36; 4) suggests a corruption of the younger generation in the priesthood that could not be controlled by the elders. And, finally, the growth of the new Israel, through amalgamation of Hebrews and Canaanites, must have advanced. The Hebrew clans, while remaining dominant, were no longer the "people" at large. The appearance of the previously unknown *nebi'im,* the prophets—that is, bands of nationalist ecstatics, spiritually respected but otherwise considered of a low social status—suggests new social strata and the formation of a "people" outside the Hebrew clans proper, with a more intense Israelite "national" consciousness.

Developments of the adumbrated type must be presupposed at the time of Saul's appearance. The circumstances of his rise to kingship are embedded in a narrative that has absorbed at least two principal versions of the events, the one royalist, the other antiroyalist.[6] The antiroyalist version betrays the prophetic influences of the eighth century and after.

---

[5] The respect for the royal institution, even when individual incumbents aroused misgivings and revolt, lasted well into the time of the prophetic movement. Kingship itself, as the institution founded by Saul, was for the first time explicitly condemned in the second half of the eighth century by the prophet Hosea.

[6] Lods distinguishes in the royalist version an older and a younger stratum of traditions. Cf. Lods, *Israel,* 352–56, the Appendix on "The Three Versions of the Founding of the Monarchy."

We shall deal first with the royalist version, as it is certainly the older one.

The royalist version tends to present the monarchy of Saul as having been instituted by Yahweh, and not created by the people or by Saul himself. This tendency is manifest in the legend of the asses lost by Kish, a man from the tribe of Benjamin. The son of Kish, Saul, was sent out by his father to recover the asses; when he could not find them, he ultimately had recourse to a "seer," a *roeh,* by the name of Samuel (I Sam. 9:1–14). Samuel, however, on the previous day had received the word from Yahweh that he should anoint the young man as the leader of Israel and its deliverer from the power of the Philistines (15–16). Samuel obeyed the command, and through him, as the divine instrument, Saul was anointed by Yahweh (10:1). In the subsequent speech Samuel ordered Saul to proceed to Gibeah, a town where a Philistine garrison or stele was placed (the reading is uncertain), and there to act as "the occasion served," for God was with him (10:7). The tradition is mutilated at this point, but the passage probably referred to the overthrow of the Philistine triumphal stele which marked the beginning of the Israelite uprising. When approaching Gibeah, Saul would meet a band of prophets (*nebi'im*) carrying a lyre, a tambourine, a flute, and a harp; they would be prophesying (10:5). The spirit (*ruach*) of Yahweh would descend upon him; he also would prophesy and be changed into "another man" (10:6). Having received these instructions from Samuel, Saul went on his way, "God gave him another heart," and the predicted signs came to pass on that day (10:9).

The story is fragmentary, but its meaning with regard to kingship is clear. The unction of a king was a general Near Eastern custom, adopted by the Israelites as the "natural" ceremony for marking a man as a king, but it acquired a specific meaning in the transfer. For the unction administered by Samuel was an objective sacrament, not a magic communication of power through the administering person. The historian was careful to point out that Yahweh, not Samuel, anointed the king. And the effect of the sacrament, "another heart," was caused by God, not by Samuel's manifest act. Kingship was instituted by Yahweh. The King was a Messiah, the Lord's Anointed.

The immediacy of the relation between the King and his God seems to have been a matter of some concern at the time, since so many of the preserved traditions stress the point. This is especially true if, following a suggestion of Lods, even the legends of the youth of Samuel must be considered to have originally been legends about Saul. In I Samuel 1, Hannah promised the Yahweh of Shiloh that if he would give her a son she would dedicate him to his service. When the son arrived, "she called his name Samuel, saying, I have asked him of Yahweh" (1:20). According to Lods it is difficult to see how the name *shemuel* could have been derived from the verb *sha'al*. "On the other hand, we should have a perfectly good etymological derivation if the original text read: 'she called his name *Saul*,' since *sha'ul* means 'asked for.' " [7] The suggestion of Lods is convincing. If we accept it, the story of the child given by Yahweh and dedicated to him is a story about Saul. And perhaps the same is true of the revelation of Yahweh to the young Samuel in I Samuel 3.

The same concern about Saul's relation with God appears in the story of his meeting with the prophets. This story requires a word of explanation—all the more so as even the Israelite historian found it necessary to add an archaeological footnote or two in order to make it intelligible to his own contemporaries. Saul "met a band of prophets" (10:10). These prophets, however, did not belong to the same type as the great prophets of the eighth century and after. The great prophets, rather, continued the type which at the time of Saul was represented by a man like Samuel. And the historian stressed the point; for in speaking of Samuel, the seer, he added that "a prophet [*nabi*] was formerly called a seer [*roeh*]" (9:9). Hence, some importance seems to have attached to the difference between the seers who only later came to be called prophets and the prophets of the band. It has proved difficult, however, to describe the two types with any precision. Attempts have been made to distinguish them as types of auditory and visual hallucinations, as interpreters of dreams or signs and ecstatics, as communicants with minor divinities and with the national Yahweh, or by their methods of inducing the ecstatic state. None of the distinctions was satisfactory, since invariably they broke down in one or the other specific instance. Nevertheless, the difference, as we have said, must have been of importance, since the Israelite historians noted it expressly. Hence, we shall fall back on the distinction made in the Samuel passages themselves: the seers and great prophets were solitary figures, while the prophets whom Saul met were a "band." That is indeed a difference of such importance that a search for further distinguishing characteristics seems superfluous. For

[7] *Ibid.*, 354.

collective prophetism, based on contagious ecstasy, was a widespread phenomenon in Asia Minor which reached into Hellenic civilization in the form of orgiastic cults of Dionysos, whereas it was not characteristic of early Israelite history. Its appearance in the time of Saul would indicate a penetration of Baalic ecstaticism into Yahwism, parallel with the blending of Canaanites and Yahwist Hebrews into the new Israel. Moreover, Saul himself was exposed to ecstatic seizures by contagion,[8] whereas in the case of Gideon the *ruach* of Yahweh still descended on the leader in a solitary experience.

Beyond this point the political significance of the new phenomenon can only be discerned in shadowy outlines. The *nabi* of the collective type was certainly considered a person of low social status. The people who had known Saul as a young man of good family, and who witnessed his prophetic fit, were astonished to see him in the company, and the psychic state, of men whose fathers were unknown (10:11–12). One senses the resentment of the Hebrew clan society against persons who either were not Hebrews at all or had sunk so low in the social scale that their clan affiliation had been lost. And the ironic question "Is Saul among the prophets?" became a proverb (10:12).

Perhaps the success of Saul and his kingship was due to his sensitiveness for a new "democratic" type of spiritual experience. The idea commends itself in the light of the story of David and his wife Michal, the daughter of Saul, which furnishes another instance of relations on the level of royal society, strained for the same reasons as in the Saul story. When the victorious King led the ark into Jerusalem he danced before it, in the procession, "with all his might" in a linen kilt (II Sam. 6:14). Michal, a fastidious lady, watched the phallic exhibition in front of the retainers and their womenfolk with disgust and later upbraided David for his lack of taste, only to receive from the King the information that he had danced before Yahweh, not before the women. Yahweh had chosen him as the ruler of his people, in the place of Saul and his house. For Yahweh he would debase himself with even more abandon than he had shown on this day. Even if she did not like the way he disported himself, the women of the retainers to whom she had referred would hold him in honor (II Sam. 6:21–22).[9] And the lady who had been so critical about the might dancing before Yahweh remained childless (23).

[8] Besides I Sam. 10:10 cf. 19:23–24.

[9] The meaning of the difficult passage cannot be determined with full certainty. The various translations differ substantially.

The exhibitionism of David points, as did the prophetism of Saul, to a cruder stratum of Yahwism, socially located in the people that won the war against the Philistines, as distinguished from the Hebrew clan society that had succumbed to their imperial expansion. And the early kings experienced themselves as representatives of this populist Yahwism and its "bands of prophets."

The Israelite traditions unfortunately have large gaps. After the encounter with Saul in the eleventh century, the collective prophets reappear in the narrative only in the ninth century, in the Kingdom of Israel. At that time numerous prophetic bands existed, running into memberships of several hundred, organized under masters, and attached to various sanctuaries. Yahweh as well as Baal inspired such associations, the "sons of the prophets" (*bene hannebi'im*). Moreover, the bands had become a political institution in that they were attached to the court and, when consulted before a military enterprise, knew how to produce the correct answers. Ahab had a band of Yahwist prophets, and his Phoenician queen Jezebel entertained a corresponding band of Baalist prophets at her table. No conflict between kingship and the collective prophets was noticeable. The only opposition to a royal plan came from the solitary figure of Micaiah, the son of Imlah (I Kings 22). Not until the conflict between Baalists and Yahwists was stirred up by the solitary prophets did Yahwist collective prophets join the opposition against the King. The co-existence, temporarily peaceful, of Yahwist and Baalist bands of prophets at the court of Samaria is perhaps the best evidence for the intimate connection between Israelite kingship and the orgiastic religiousness of the people that had grown in the area of Syriac civilization from the amalgamation of Hebrews and Canaanites. The ninth century, furthermore, furnishes literary evidence for the first time for the difference of cultural levels between collective prophets and the Hebrew tradition proper, in so far as the legends of Elisha, which originated in the prophetic bands, moved in a folkloristic atmosphere strikingly different from the intellectual climate of the David memoirs or the writings of the great prophets. And, finally, a clue to the tension is furnished by the history of the word *nabi*. Of non-Hebrew, probably Babylonian, origin, it entered the language with the bands of ecstatic tongue-speakers in the time of Saul; and it was domiciled in the language with sufficient strength to draw into the orbit of its meaning the solitary prophets of the eighth century and after who opposed the kingship and its "false" collective prophets. The history of the word reflects the politico-religious tension between the types of prophets. The opposition of the solitary prophets to the monarchy becomes more intelligible, as previously suggested, if it is seen as an attempt to recapture a purer form of Yahwism from the populist type that had become the foundation of national life with the establishment of the Kingdom. And further light also falls on the antipopulist sentiments of the postexilic prophets—on their hatred for the *am-ha-aretz,* that is, for the "people" which indeed had been the people of Israel during the Kingdom.

The decisive point in the present context, however, is that a purer Yahwism could be recaptured with remarkable success from collective prophetism because it was actually alive under the overgrowth of the royal institution. While Yahwist and Baalist ecstaticism resembled one another closely, there must have been an essential difference between them. For as far as our evidence goes, there was nothing in the apparently similar collective prophetism of the Baalists that could have been recaptured by anybody and have led to the spiritual insights of an Hosea or Isaiah. The "sons of the prophets" who supported Saul and the later kings, thus, were definitely Yahwists, not Baalists. This knowledge by itself, however, is not very illuminating because we do not know what goes on in a prophet while he is in his trance. What kind of god or demon possesses an ecstatic prophet must be tested by the communicable "word," as it results from the trance and crystallizes into message, advice, and conduct. With regard to the verbal crystallization of their trance, now, the prophets were apparently somewhat hampered. At least, we find them invariably "attached" to a high place—a sanctuary or a court, that is— to an institution which has at its disposal other means for arriving at articulate formulas of conduct, such as the word of a seer, the instruction of a priest, or the decision of a king. With regard to politics, therefore, the bands can hardly have been more than amplifiers of the national consciousness of the new Israel in search of an effective organization. They certainly were not policy- and kingmakers like the Egyptian sacerdotal colleges. Hence, the national Yahwism of the bands was inseparable from the royal institution which articulated the inarticulate contents of the trance. In so far as the bands were the voice of the people, they could supply spiritual authority from the "grass roots" for those who were willing and able to lead the nation in war and peace, but they could not supply leadership themselves. The leader had to be a man like

Saul who combined the charisma of the warrior and the statesman with that of an ecstatic. A prophet could not become king, but a king could on occasion be susceptible to ecstatic contagion. The king was the man who articulated in word and action the meaning of the ecstatic experience. This relationship between ecstaticism and articulation is not unique in the history of communal organization. We find the same problem in early Christianity when the tongue-speakers created difficulties in a community. I Corinthians 14, for instance, is a special tract by St. Paul on the method of dealing with ecstatics; and the most important point is that the tongue-speaker has to be silenced when there is nobody present who can interpret his "word." Hence, collective ecstaticism is an inrush of spiritual force whose precise nature can only be determined by the channeling to which it submits in community. Only in retrospect of a Yahwist, Christian, or tragic articulate culture of the spirit, can one speak of a Yahwist, Christian, or Dionysiac ecstaticism. Wherever collective ecstaticism occurs, there will arise the civilizational tension between a diffuse, contagious, spiritual force, on the one hand, and the articulation imposed by institutions and rational explication, on the other hand.

2. Spiritual Order of the Soul

The consequences of the tension are serious enough when the order of a community has to rely on agreement between ecstatics and articulate interpreters. And they will be even more serious when the tension occurs within the soul of one man, as it did in Saul's. A man of his ecstatic-active cast not only will feel responsible for translating the diffuse force into correct royal action but will also suffer from states of indecision and anxiety in critical moments when decisive action would be required but the spiritual force has ebbed away. In Saul's later years this strain on his soul became noticeable. He fell into periods of brooding melancholy for which he found relief in the music of David, and then again he was seized by fits of murderous distrust against the younger man—though one must take into account that his suspicion of David as a rival for the kingship was probably quite justified. Revealing for the nature of Saul's spiritual disorder is the story of his visit to the witch of Endor (I Sam. 28:3–25). It must be analyzed with some care, since the episode is of considerable importance for the spiritual and intellectual history of Israel in general.

THE STRUGGLE FOR EMPIRE

It was the eve of the battle of Gilboa, the battle against the Philistines in which Saul and his son Jonathan were to meet their death. Saul was depressed by forebodings of disaster. The spiritual force had left him, and Yahweh would not speak to him either through prophets or the oracles of priests, or through dreams. In his forsakenness he wanted to evoke the ghost of Samuel in order to receive his advice; and he called on a woman who was a "ghost-master" and could bring up the dead for questioning. This woman of Endor indeed evoked Samuel for him. The King, however, could not derive much comfort from the seer. Samuel's ghost reproached the King for having disturbed his peace wantonly. If Yahweh did not speak to Saul, the implications of the divine silence were obvious. During Samuel's lifetime, on a certain occasion well known to the King, Saul had not listened to the voice of the God as mediated through the seer; and as a consequence, Saul could no longer hear the voice. All the ghost could do now was to confirm the King's forebodings: tomorrow, Saul and his sons would die in battle, and Israel would be given into the hands of the Philistines.

At a first glance, the meaning of the story seems to be clear. The divine ordinances may be harsh, as they were on the occasion to which Samuel referred; and when man in his weakness follows the lines of expedience and compassion, the insulted God will avenge himself on the unworthy vessel of his spirit, as well as on the community which the King represents. Disobedience to the will of God is followed by personal and collective punishment.

The apparent clarity, however, vanishes as soon as Saul's action is placed in context. For previously, an ordinance of Saul had banished ghost-masters and wizards from the territory of the kingdom (I Sam. 28:3) and made their activity a capital crime (28:9). So that now, when the King had recourse to a ghost-master, he broke his own ordinance and became guilty of complicity, if not of the crime itself.

Why Saul had banished the ghost-masters is nowhere stated expressly. One of the possible motives, however, is rather obvious. The ghosts of the dead were *elohim* (I Sam. 28:13), divine beings; and their elimination as forces to be consulted would abolish rivals of Yahweh. Without questioning the plausibility or sincerity of this primary motive, there should be admitted, however, an incidental political motive which gains probability through Saul's later action when he evoked the ghost of Samuel. Since the King consulted a ghost-master himself, he clearly had not

banished this gentry because he considered them "swindlers" but, on
the contrary, because they brought up genuine *elohim*. The ghost-gods
were not false gods, or no-gods but were believed to be real gods, even
though of a minor status. The experience of divine force still was turgid,
beyond polytheism or monotheism, and in view of such turgidity, even
in a Yahwist kingdom the ghost-elohim might become rival sources of
authority in political matters. In the difficult and long-drawn struggle
with the Philistines, discontented subjects might well consult the *elohim*
in order to find out which way the war would turn; and some might
have been quite as interested as Saul himself to know whether the King
would meet his death at an early date. Hence, the banishment of ghost-
masters had been intended perhaps to prevent precisely the type of
consultation in which Saul indulged. Comparable ordinances were issued
in other political cultures for the adumbrated reasons, as for instance in
the Western Renaissance, when the Curia prohibited astrological fore-
casts concerning the death of the Pope because they were apt to cause
political speculation, unrest, and intrigue. Nevertheless, a political motive
of this kind, as we said, need not detract from the primary Yahwist
motive. The one may have no more than reinforced the other, with a
net result satisfactory to both the Yahwist and the King in Saul.[10]

The happy meeting of *raison d'état* with spiritual concern, however,
does not exhaust the complexities of the episode. The ghost-elohim must
have played an important role in the spiritual life of the Israelites, or it
would not have been necessary to sanction their consultation so severely,
and the ordinance of Saul must have been a correspondingly grave disturbance of spiritual life. Such interventions in the economy of the
psyche have consequences. What we know about the experiences and
actions of Saul is sufficient proof that his was not a well-organized soul
living in the faith in a transcendent God, but that his psyche was a field
of diversified sensitiveness for orgiastic contagion, priestly oracles, and

---

[10] The preceding analysis is based on the assumption that the ordinance of Saul against the
"ghost-masters" is historic. Excellent authorities, however, consider the respective passages an
anachronistic interpolation in the narrative. For this negative opinion see the analysis of Saul's
call on the witch of Endor in Oesterley and Robinson, *Hebrew Religion. Its Origin and Development,* 91 ff. I prefer the opinion of Lods, *Israel,* 358, who considers the tradition "entirely probable." The interpretation should be governed by the principle that a tradition must be accepted
as long as there is no conclusive evidence against it. The fact that necromancy continued in Israel
throughout its history and had to be prohibited on frequent later occasions is no valid argument
against a prohibition by Saul.

advice from seers, for divine dreams and voices, and messages from ghost-elohim. He was a man but also "another man" when in trance, and above all he was a part of the nonpersonal, diffuse humanity that went by the name of Israel and had to atone collectively for royal misconduct. In Saul's difficulties with a Yahwist order it is clear that the problems of a personal soul were involved—the same problems which, contemporaneously with Saul, became acute in the troubles of the Mycenaean civilization, in the epics of Homer. In Israelite history, however, these problems were bent in a direction widely divergent from the Greek, and in determining this bent the ordinance of Saul apparently was a causative factor of the first order. The issue, as well as the different forms which it assumed in Israel and Hellas, must be briefly characterized.

The leap in being, the experience of divine being as world-transcendent, is inseparable from the understanding of man as human. The personal soul as the sensorium of transcendence must develop parallel with the understanding of a transcendent God. Now, wherever the leap in being occurs experientially, the articulation of the experience has to grapple with the mystery of death and immortality. Men are mortal; and what is immortal is divine. This holds true for both Greeks and Israelites. Into this clean ontological division, however, does never quite fit the post-existence of man. In the Homeric epic, afterlife is the existence of the psyche, of the life-force, as an eidolon, a shadow in Hades; and in the same manner, Israelite afterlife is a shadowy, ghostlike existence in Sheol. In neither case is it an existence that would bring ultimate perfection to the order of the human personality. From this initial situation was developed, in Hellas, the understanding of the psyche as an immortal substance, capable of achieving increasingly perfect order, if necessary through repeated embodiments, until it reached permanent transmundane status. This development was due to the philosophers from Pythagoras and Heraclitus onward and achieved its climax in the dialogues of Plato. Without a doubt, the polytheistic culture of Hellas facilitated the speculative construction of the problem, since there was no deep-rooted resistance to conceiving the immortal soul as a daimon, that is, as a divine being of lower rank. In Israel a parallel development was barred by the early, even if imperfect, understanding of the true nature of a universal, transcendent God. The dead were *elohim*, and no man was supposed to be an *elohim*. Genesis 3:22–24 was uncompromising on the point: "Then Yahweh-Elohim said: 'See, the man has become like one

of us, in knowing good from evil; and now suppose he were to reach
out his hand and take the fruit of the tree of life also and, eating it, live
forever!' So Yahweh-Elohim expelled him from the garden of Eden."

The incompatibility of human and divine status seems to have been
realized fully for the first time by Saul. Since the dead were *elohim*, and
since the belief that they were continued unshaken, these gods had to be
relegated by means of a royal ordinance to a kind of public subconscious.
Ancestor worship, the myth of a *heros eponymos*, and above all the
evocation of such gods as rival authorities to Yahweh had to be suppressed. As a consequence the understanding of a personal soul, of its
internal order through divine guidance, and of its perfection through
grace in death that will heal the imperfection of mundane existence,
could not develop. The relation to Yahweh, precarious in this life, was
completely broken by death; what was not achieved in life was never
achieved. A pathetic expression of this plight was the psalm of Hezekiah
(late eighth century) by which the King thanked Yahweh for recovery
from a sickness (Isa. 38:18–19):

> For Sheol cannot praise thee,
>   Death cannot celebrate thee:
> They that go down to the Pit
>   Can not hope for thy truth.
> The living, the living, he shall praise thee,
>   As I do this day.
> The father to the children
>   Shall make known thy truth.

Throughout the history of the Kingdom the question of the soul remained in this submersion of a "public subconscious," and even the
prophets were unable to deal with it. Only in the time of Ezekiel (late
sixth century), the first step toward a solution became noticeable, from
the side of ethics, in the hesitant admission of personal responsibility and
retribution according to a man's merit (Ezek. 14, 18, and 33). But even
the break with the principle of collective responsibility did not break the
impasse of experience with regard to the order of the soul and its salvation. Only under Persian influence, in the third century, did the rigid
position weaken and could the idea of immortality enter the Jewish orbit.

The state of suspension in which the issue of the soul remained in
Israelite history had curious consequences in the realm of symbols. On

the one hand, it favored the advance of historical realism. On the other hand, it prevented the development of philosophy.

With regard to historical realism, the suppression of the ghost-elohim eliminated the ancestor myth as a constitutive form from the public sphere. This, to be sure, does not mean that ancestor-worship or even hero-worship were unknown to the Hebrew tribes. A sufficient number of traces of such cults have survived in the Bible (and been confirmed by archaeological discoveries) to prove that the Hebrew clans, before they came within the range of Yahwist religiousness, were constituted by their ancestor cults just as any Hellenic genos. In the Yahwist period we find such sanctuaries of ancestors as the Cave of Machpelah, where Sarah and Abraham were buried (Gen. 23 and 25:9); the Pillar of Rachel's Grave (Gen. 35:20); and the burial place of Joseph at Shechem (Josh. 24:32). And we find, furthermore, sanctuaries of heroes, such as the sanctuary of Deborah, Rebekah's nurse (Gen. 35:8); the grave of Miriam at Kadesh, the "holy place" (Num. 20:1); and the burial place of Samuel at Ramah (I Sam. 28:3). Nevertheless, while the ancestors and heroes were *elohim* on the popular level of Israelite religion, they never became mythological figures on the Yahwist level on which the narrative moves. On the contrary, those who had already disappeared behind the veil of the myth in pre-Mosaic times, such as the Jacob-el, or Joseph-el, of the Egyptian lists of Canaanite place names, were recovered as historical figures. Certainly Jacob, perhaps Joseph, and probably others of whom no records are preserved were transfigured from historical chieftains into mythical ancestors and then restored to their former status much in the manner in which a modern, critical historian recaptures pragmatic events from the myth. As a result, the Israelites developed a symbolic form without parallel in other civilizations, that is, the History of the Patriarchs.

The extraordinary character of the phenomenon must be realized in order to understand its extraordinary sequel. On the "public" level, the *elohim* had become the historical Patriarchs who now were definitely dead and no longer could influence mundane events. On this level the belief in an afterlife was blotted out so drastically that the late Kohelet could say: "A living dog is better than a dead lion. For the living know that they will die; but the dead know nothing at all, nor have they anything for their labor, for their memory is forgotten. Their love has vanished with their hate and jealousy, and they have no share in anything

that goes on under the sun" (Eccles. 9:4–6). The radical historization of
the *elohim* thus ran, by the logic of experience, into the impasse of
nihilism and hedonistic existentialism that we can observe in the Kohelet.

On the lower, popular level, however, the community of the living
with the dead, that is, the substance of continuous social order among
men, was maintained through the cults of clan ancestors and national
heroes, as well as by the faith in their help as advisers and avengers.
Though the historians did their best to erase all traditions of this faith,
numerous passages have escaped which manifest the belief in the
"fathers" or the "people" to whom in death a man is gathered.[11] From
this popular, living experience a prophetic spirit could break through to
the insight that the community of the *elohim* to whom man was assembled in death was the community with the divine father himself.
While dodging the issue of the ancestral *elohim* and their status, a prayer
of Trito-Isaiah transferred their function in the human community to
God in person (Isa. 63:16):

> You are our father,
> though Abraham knows us not,
>   and Israel is not mindful of us.
> You, Yahweh, are our father,
>   Our Redeemer is, from the beginning, your name.

Yahweh in this prayer takes the place of the redeemer—that is, of the
goel, the close relative and avenger under clan law—since the function no
longer is fulfilled by the *elohim* of Abraham and Jacob. And Yahweh
can help, as he did in the days of Moses, through the presence of his *ruach,*
his spirit, with the shepherds of his people. Searchingly the prophet asks
(Isa. 63:11 ff.):

> Where is he who brought them up from the sea,
>   with the shepherds of his flock?
> Where is he who put his holy spirit
>   in the midst of them;
> Who caused his glorious arm to go
>   at the right hand of Moses;
> Who divided the waters before them,
>   · to make himself an everlasting name;
> Who led them through the deep, without stumbling?
>
> As a horse through the wilderness,
> as cattle going down to the valley,

[11] For instance Gen. 25:8, 17; 35:29; 47:30; 49:29.

the spirit of Yahweh guided them safe.
So was it you guided your people,
to make yourself a glorious name.

And as in the past, the prophet hopes, the spirit of Yahweh will guide his people in the future again, and he prays (Isa. 63:17):

Return for the sake of your servants,
The tribes of your heritage!

One senses the animosity against the ancestral *elohim* of the pre-Mosaic age. The author of the prayer struggled to escape from their atmosphere and to understand the presence of the one and only Elohim through his *ruach,* in history. And, partially at least, his endeavors were successful. To be sure, Yahweh was still the God of Israel, not of mankind; and the issue of the soul was not clarified at all; but at least the questions had been sharpened in such a manner that from an apparently desperate situation emerged the vision of a solution. Opinion is divided whether the prayer was written immediately after the return to Jerusalem in 538 or during the conflict with the Persians in the fourth century B.C. At any rate, Israel was in a politically difficult time. No help was to be expected from man, either from men in this world or from men gathered to their fathers. Moreover, the feeling still prevailed that divine help had to come to society in its worldly existence; only help to the people in its historical straits was of interest, not help to the individual soul. From such negations, shutting out the conceivable alternatives, arose the idea of the God who would return as our Redeemer into history in order to rectify a condition of man beyond hope.

With regard to the form a return of God into history would assume, the prayer is silent. And one should not read more into Trito-Isaiah than can actually be found there. Nevertheless, there is enough in the prayer to suggest the experiential mood in which men were receptive for the appearance of God on earth and to become the followers of the Christ. To be sure, there was a host of other symbols approximating the god-man which would make the appearance of Christ intelligible to the civilizationally mixed humanity of the Roman Empire: there were Egyptian Pharaohs, Hellenistic god-kings, and Jewish expectations of a Davidic Messiah. Still, none of them contained the specific ingredient that made Christianity a scandal, the ingredient to be found in Trito-Isaiah: the return of the world-transcendent God into a cosmos which had become nondivine, and into a history which had become human. This gulf between God and the world, inherent in Yahwism from the Mosaic age, could be bridged through the Israelite centuries by the survivals of cosmological symbols, by the Canaanite agricultural gods, and by ancestor cults; but when the terrible implications of this separation of God from the world had been realized through the work of the prophets, and when the intramundane, political disasters had brought home the anguish of life in a god-forsaken world, the time was ripe for the return of God into a history from which the divine forces had been eliminated so drastically.

With regard to philosophy, one must say that its development in the Hellenic sense was prevented by the irresolution concerning the status of the soul. The *philia* reaching out toward the *sophon* presupposes a personalized soul: the soul must have disengaged itself sufficiently from the substance of particular human groups to experience its community with other men as established through the common participation in the divine Nous. As long as the spiritual life of the soul is so diffuse that its status under God can be experienced only compactly, through the mediation of clans and tribes, the personal love of God cannot become the ordering center of the soul. In Israel the spirit of God, the *ruach* of Yahweh, is present with the community and with individuals in their capacity as representatives of the community, but it is not present as the ordering force in the soul of every man, as the Nous of the mystic-philosophers or the Logos of Christ is present in every member of the Mystical Body, creating by its presence the *homonoia,* the likemindedness of the community. Only when man, while living with his fellow men in the community of the spirit, has a personal destiny in relation to God can the spiritual eroticism of the soul achieve the self-interpretation which Plato called philosophy. In Israelite history a comparable development was impossible for the previously discussed reasons. When the soul has no destiny, when the relation of man with God is broken through death, even a revelation of the world-transcendent divinity as personal and intense as the Mosaic (more personal and intense than ever befell a Hellenic philosopher) will be blunted by the intramundane compactness of the tribe. The God of Israel revealed himself in his wrath and his grace; he caused the joy of loyal obedience as well as the anguish of disobedience, triumph of victory as well as despair of forsakenness; he manifested himself in natural phenomena as well as in his messengers in human shape; he spoke audibly, distinctly, and at great length to the men of his choice; he was a will and he gave a law—but he was not the unseen Measure of the soul in the Platonic sense. A Prophet can hear and communicate the word of God, but he is neither a Philosopher nor a Saint.

No Platonic "practice of dying" developed in Israel. Still, the leap in being, when it created historical present as the existence of a people under the will of God, had also sharpened the sensitiveness for individual humanity. Perhaps because the soul had no destiny beyond death, triumph and defeat in life were experienced with a poignancy hitherto unknown to man. In the wake of Saul's kingship a new experiential mood made itself felt which, for lack of a better term, may be called the specifically Israelite humanism. The first great document of this mood was the grandiose *quinah*, the funeral elegy or dirge of David for Saul and Jonathan after the battle of Gilboa (II Sam. 1:19–27):

Your beauty, O Israel, on your heights lies slain!
  How have they fallen, the heroes!

Tell it not in Gath,
  Announce it not in the streets of Ashkelon,
Lest rejoice the daughters of the Philistines,
  Lest exult the daughters of the uncircumcised!

Mountains of Gilboa,
  Let there be upon you no dew nor rain,
    Nor upsurging from the deep.
For *there* was thrown aside the shield of the hero,
  The shield of Saul, no longer salved with oil.

From the blood of the slain,
  From the fat of the heroes,
The bow of Jonathan turned not back,
  The sword of Saul returned not in vain!

Saul and Jonathan, beloved and loved
  In their lives, in their death they were not divided.
They were swifter than eagles,
  They were stronger than lions.

Daughters of Israel, weep over Saul,
  Who clothed you in scarlet, and other delights,
Who put ornaments of gold upon your apparel!

How have they fallen, the heroes,
  In the midst of the battle!

Jonathan lies slain upon your heights!
I am afflicted because of you,
  My brother Jonathan!
Very dear were you to me!
Your love was more precious to me
  Than the love of women!

How are they fallen, the heroes,
  How shattered the weapons of war!

There is no touch of spiritual drama in the *quinah*, no question of
obedience or disobedience to Yahweh's will, no search for the grounds
of divine action. God might as well not exist. The disaster of Gilboa is
strictly an affair of man in his earthly habitat. A curse of sterility falls
on the mountains of Gilboa because arms and the men of Israel have
fallen on their heights. What has fallen with them is the beauty of
Israel, the splendor of its manhood, the *gibborim*, in war as well as the
enhancement of women when decked with plunder. Since it is a critical
defeat in the struggle for empire, the joy of the enemy is as much cause
for grief as the losses on the own side. And the defeat is a personal
disaster, for the community of lovers, of father and son, of friend and
friend is broken by death.

3. *Theocracy*

The second version of Saul's accession to the kingship is antiroyalist
in tendency.

In this version the story of Saul is preceded by an account of Samuel's
leadership. It is described as sufficiently successful to make kingship unnecessary (I Sam. 7). The events move in the pious rhythm of defection
and return that we know from the Book of Judges. Samuel is a judge who
persuades the people to abandon their foreign gods and to return to
Yahweh. A resounding defeat of the Philistines, with Yahweh's help,
rewards the return. Israel once more is delivered from all her enemies;
Samuel lives to a ripe old age; and he has just appointed his sons as successors (I Sam. 8:1). Israel, it appears, is safe under its judges until the
next defection disturbs the relation between Yahweh and his people.

A defection occurs, indeed, but not to the Baals and Ashtarts. At this
point of the story, when the reader is prepared for the next valley in
Israel's relations with Yahweh, the redactors place the call of the people
for a king. It is true that the "elders of Israel" who approach Samuel

with the request have a grievance, for Samuel's sons take bribes and pervert justice (8:3). Still, in the opinion of the historian, this is no reason to demand "a king to judge us like all the nations [*goyim*]" (8:5). What causes Samuel's dismay at this request (8:6) becomes clear in Yahweh's answer to the prophet's prayer (8:7–9):

> Hearken to the voice of the people in all that they say to you; for they have not rejected you, but they have rejected me from being king over them. According to all the deeds which they have done to me, from the day I brought them up out of Egypt even to this day, forsaking me and serving other gods, so they are also doing to you. Now then, hearken to their voice; only you shall earnestly warn them, and show them the ways [*mishpat*] of the king who shall reign over them.

The change from a government by judges to a government by kings is more than a change of political forms in the secular sense. It is a break with the theopolitical [12] constitution of Israel as a people under Yahweh, the King. Samuel may be displeased by Israel's rejection of his dynasty of judges, but the real issue is the defection from the kingship of Yahweh. Samuel, then, obeys Yahweh's command and earnestly warns the people of what will befall them (I Sam. 8:11–18). The king will press the young men into military service and serfdom; the young women will have to serve in the royal household; the best land will be expropriated and given to the king's officers and servants; the people will be taxed heavily for the upkeep of the royal administration and in addition will have to work part time for the king. "And in that day you will cry out because of your king, whom you have chosen for yourselves; but Yahweh will not answer you in that day" (18). But the people is insistent; they want a king "that we also may be like all the nations; and that our king may judge us, and go out before us, and fight our battles" (20).

Israel has its will. Samuel assembles the people at Mizpah, and the assembly proceeds to the election of a king (I Sam. 10:17–24). The

---

12 I am using Martin Buber's term "theopolitical" rather than the term "theocratic" in order to signify the peculiar constitution, both existential and transcendental, of Israel as a people under God. "Theocratic" will conviently be used when existential rulership, and especially kingship, is experienced as bound by the commands of God, and especially when a priesthood measures the conduct of the magistrate by divine commands and can make its criticism effective. For the formation of the concept "theocratic" in the latter sense see Hendrik Berkhof, *Kirche und Kaiser* (Zollikon-Zurich, 1947), 143 ff. As the text will presently show, the theocratic element enters the constitution of Israel precisely when the theopolitical experience is disturbed by the establishment of kingship.

election procedure is too tersely described to be quite clear. Apparently, sacred lots were cast by tribes, clans, and families in order to narrow the range of candidates; and there can be discerned the remainders of an old custom according to which the possible candidates hide themselves and the first one found is considered the choice of God. From the combination of lot with hide-and-seek Saul emerges as the royal candidate chosen by Yahweh. He stands head and shoulders above all others; and when Samuel presents him to the people he is accepted with the acclamation "Long live the King!" The following verses, however, suggest that not everybody was happy about the choice (10:26–27).

The procedure is continued in I Samuel 12. Samuel demands and receives discharge from his office with acknowledgement of his impeccable conduct (12:1–5). The new Messiah is witness to the discharge (5). And then follows a curious trial of Israel before the court of Yahweh (12:6–25). Samuel pleads before Yahweh. He recounts the "righteous acts" of the Lord toward those present and their fathers, as well as the defections of Israel from Yahweh. The final insult is the rejection of Yahweh's kingship through the choice of a king. Still, God will forgive again, but under one condition (12:14–15):

> If you will fear Yahweh and serve him and hearken to his voice,
> and not rebel against the commandment of Yahweh,
> and if both you and the king who reigns over you
> will follow Yahweh your God,
> it will be well.
> But if you will not hearken to the voice of Yahweh,
> but rebel against the commandment of Yahweh,
> then the hand of Yahweh will be against you and your king.

In confirmation of Samuel's plea and promise Yahweh grants a miracle. The people are convinced; they admit their guilt in having asked for a king and are granted a stay of divine wrath during good behavior.

As might be expected after such legal preparations the breach of good conduct is not long delayed. I Samuel 15 tells the episode of the war against Amalek. The word of Yahweh has come to Samuel that the new king should destroy the Amalekites for what they had done to Israel "when he came up out of Egypt." Samuel transmits the word of Yahweh to the King; and Saul undertakes the war with complete success. But a war against Amalek is a holy war to be concluded by the ritual of the *cherem*.[13] Both the King and the people are lax in the enforcement of the ban and keep the best parts of the loot for themselves. Samuel has to intervene and kill the King of the Amalekites with his own hands in order to fulfill the word of Yahweh. Then he announces to Saul that he is rejected because of the violation of the divine command. Saul's plea of relative innocence (that he had given in to the pressure of his warriors) is not accepted: "For, though you are insignificant in your own eyes, are you not the head of the tribes of Israel?" (15:17). Then Samuel withdraws from the rejected king and never sees him to his death. The aftermath again is the episode of the witch of Endor, on the eve of the battle of Gilboa.

The antiroyalist version of Saul's kingship has created one of the most important symbolisms of Western politics. Through the reception of the Bible into the Scripture of Christianity the relation between Samuel and Saul has become the paradigm of spiritual control over temporal rulership. From the first stirrings of theocratic consciousness in Lucifer of Cagliari and St. Ambrose, in the conflicts of the fourth century A.D., to the end of Christian imperial culture, and beyond it into the Calvinist theocracies of Geneva and the Massachusetts Bay Colony, the Samuel-Saul story was the "leading case." And even in the disintegration of imperial Christianity the warring parties still justified their positions by reference to the story, as when the Monarchomachists asserted the right of God's people to abide by the command of the Lord against an erring Saul, or when, in opposition, a James I asserted the right of the king not to fall into the guilt of Saul, but to shoulder his responsibility as the "head of the tribes of Israel" against an erring people.

A symbolism of such importance demands some circumspection of the interpreter. It cannot be dismissed simply as a late theocratic distortion of historical events. While in its present form the story has its inception certainly not earlier than in the prophetic opposition to the court of Samaria in the ninth century, and while the speeches of Samuel are delivered in the grandly flowing style of the Deuteronomist school of the seventh century, some of the historical materials as well as the issue

---

[13] In the *Mishneh Torah* Maimonides enumerates as holy wars the wars against the "seven nations" which occupied Canaan before the conquest, against Amalek, and defensive wars (XIV, 5, 1).

itself quite probably go back to the time of Saul—even though only common-sense assumptions concerning the genuine core are possible.

The center of suspicion is Samuel. Apparently, he was a seer of no more than local reputation who could be consulted when stray animals had to be recaptured. And especially if we agree with Lods that the legends of Saul's youth were transferred by later historians to Samuel, he must have been a comparatively insignificant figure, at least until the appearance of Saul himself. To be sure, that is no reason why he should not have been God's instrument in pointing out and anointing the King, but it relegates to the realm of later paradigmatic invention his position as a judge of Israel, as well as his role as the influential prophet who orders the King to conduct, for theological reasons, remote campaigns at a time when the Philistine danger is pressing. Precisely, however, when we agree with the critics that the figure of the historical Samuel must be substantially reduced, other parts of the story not only gain in probability but would have to be assumed as historical even if the tradition had not preserved them. For the lesser the role of Samuel becomes in the rise of Saul, the greater must become the role of the people in search of a war leader and the pragmatic achievement of the leader himself. Hence, the course of pragmatic events is probably best preserved in I Samuel 11 and 14. I Samuel 11 reports Saul's campaign against the Ammonites and the relief of the besieged Jabesh-Gilead; I Samuel 14, a first campaign against the Philistines. In both reports the campaign is followed by Saul's assumption of the kingship. That a successful leader in local revolts and campaigns should arouse popular hopes of delivery from the Philistines if he were elected king is a probable course of events, indeed. And the people's demand for "a king to judge us like all the nations" (8:5) fits well into this picture. But that the demand should meet with some opposition (10:27) which had to be overcome (11:12) also fits well.

In view of the pragmatic features of the situation it would be rash to say that it could not have contained, at least in an incipient form, the experiences which found their ultimate expression in the problems of the Samuel-Saul story.[14] On the contrary, it would be odd if the fateful transition from the theopolitical constitution of Israel to a national monarchy should have aroused nothing but unthinking enthusiasm.

[14] As a matter of fact, Judges projects the experiences even into the events preceding the assumption of kingship by Gideon. Cf. Judges 8:23.

There probably existed remnants of the clan opposition which, at an earlier date, had become articulate in the "Fable of the Trees." And there probably also existed a historical Samuel, or rather more than one, who pondered on the difference between a chosen people of Yahweh and an Israel under a king like all the goyim. This is the experiential area in which the theocratic symbolism is rooted. For the idea of theocratic order is not a "doctrine" invented by some thinker at a definite point of time but a symbol which articulates the experienced tension between divine and human constitution of society. As long as Israel was a confederacy, resting on the social organization of the Hebrew clans, the tension could become active only in the rare instances of charismatic leadership in an emergency, and that precisely was the situation in which the tension would dissolve before it could harden into a serious problem of order. When the emergency situation crystallized into the routine of permanent organization, even only locally, as in the case of Gideon's attempted dynasty, the outcome was disaster. Now, however, the Israelite theopolity was supplemented by a permanent kingship of national scope; and therefore, the question had to arise whether Israel, by the acquisition of a king like all the nations, had not become a nation like all the nations? whether Israel had ceased to be the chosen people of Yahweh? And if this should be the case, how could kingship be brought into accord with the exigencies of a theopolity?

In part, but only to a part, the questions were solved by the social process in which Hebrews and Canaanites merged into the new Israel that wanted a king. The amalgamated people was indeed well on its way to become a nation like all the nations until, in the eighth century, the process was stopped and partially reversed by the Prophetic Revolt. In spite of the fact, however, that the conflict was solved to a rather considerable extent through backsliding into the Sheol of cosmological civilization, the experience of the theopolity was never so completely submerged that it could not be recovered. This is the decisive fact in the Israelite experiment with kingship. And the preservation of the theopolitical consciousness is intelligible only if we assume a continuous occupation with the problem of theocratic order from the time when the theopolity was endangered by the royal institution. Under Israelite historical conditions no institutional solution could be found that would have been comparable to the Christian development of the spiritual and temporal orders. For within the history of Israel proper the idea of the theopolity did not bring forth its fruit, the idea of mankind as a universal church. Hence the theocratic problem, when it arose with the establishment of a national monarchy, moved from the early theopolity through the recession of order into cosmological form, the spasmodic interference of Yahwist charismatics with the routine of royal administration and dynastic succession, and the Prophetic Revolt, to the postexilic priestly organization of the Jewish community. The compact symbol of the Chosen People could never be completely broken by the idea of a universal God and a universal mankind. Yet the problem of the church, however imperfectly differentiated, was inherent in the situation as soon as a temporal polity was built into the Yahwist theopolity, with the national monarchy.

Hence the monarchy of Saul, indeed, marked the beginning of the theocratic problem. And the Samuel-Saul story must therefore be characterized as the paradigmatic elaboration of a problem which actually arose at the time at which the paradigmatic events were supposed to have occurred. To be sure, the events did not occur as narrated, for the highly articulate formulation of the issues, as well as the rich detail, presuppose an experience of the monarchy and its conflicts with Yahwist order which did not exist at the time of its foundation. Nevertheless, the Deuteronomist historians who created the paradigmatic story and placed it in the time of Saul had a finer sense for the essential origin of the theocratic problem than the modern critics who want to place the issue in the time of its literary articulation. One may go even one step further and assume that the late historians were in possession of traditions which lent themselves to paradigmatic elaboration in the theocratic sense, even though they can no longer be ascertained. For the theocratic problem of Saul cannot be considered a whole-cloth invention as long as we accept as authentic the spiritual disorder of his later years. The charismatic war leader who rose to permanent kingship in an emergency and then lost his charisma must have experienced, with a high degree of consciousness, the need of spiritual guidance in temporal affairs. The forsakenness of his soul which drove him to the witch of Endor and his frantic search for an authentic word from Yahweh indicate a historically real experience of the tension between spiritual and temporal order. Whatever doubts may be raised with regard to the historical Samuel and his role in the anxieties of the King, there can be no doubt about the Samuel in the conscience of Saul.

§ 3. THE RISE OF DAVID

With Gilboa the cause of Israel seemed lost. The Philistines again were in control of Palestine west of the Jordan. A few years later, however, the resistance could be resumed, and this time the war ended with a complete success through the establishment of the Davidic Empire. The causes of the surprising recovery, as well as the events in detail, are the subject matter of political history rather than our concern.[15] Nevertheless, the general characteristics of the period must be recalled since, in their aggregate, they determined a new phase in the Israelite occupation with the problem of political order.

During the reign of Saul (*ca.* 1020–*ca.* 1004) not only had the formation of the new Israel progressed further in the old area of the Hebrew confederacy but the process had expanded beyond it into the Judaite region south of Jerusalem. The drawing of Judah, which had not been a member of the Israelite Confederacy, into the formation of the national Israel was an event of momentous consequence for several reasons. In the first place, the material expansion of Israel broadened the territorial and ethnic basis for the struggle against the Philistines. The increase of power could not yet be utilized to the full by Saul, but it substantially contributed to the successful conclusion of the struggle by David, as well as to the strength of his kingdom. Second, geographically, the inclusion of Judah reduced the group of Canaanite towns to which Jerusalem belonged to an enclave in the territory of Israel. The geopolitical temptation to abolish the awkward wedge of towns between the northern and southern parts of the kingdom was irresistible. David's conquest of Jerusalem not only rounded out the territory but also was the precondition for his political master stroke of making the mountain fortress, which hitherto had preserved its unconquered independence and never formed part of either Israel or Judah, the neutral capital of the new empire. Third, Judah was more than a simple addition to the territory and population of Israel. In the struggle for empire the increase counted double, because previously Judah had been in the Philistine sphere of influence; the Philistine power was diminished by the amount of Israel's growth. Moreover, the long period of Philistine suzerainty

[15] For the history of the period cf. the chapters on "Saul" and "David" in Robinson, *A History of Israel,* I.

over Judah had resulted in a partial community of the peoples. When Judah became part of Israel, it drew with it that part of the Philistine federation which had exerted the specific control over Judah. The control had not been exerted by the Philistines at large, since they had no central government, but by the inland city of Gath. The relations with Judah cannot have been entirely hostile, for David found a refuge in Gath during his outlaw existence; and when his own wars had ended with success, Gath and its dependent towns were absorbed into the empire. The Gittite guards became an important part of the army; and their personal loyalty to David proved his principal support in the Absalom crisis. And finally, the fusion of Israel with Judah, while it brought the short-lived united kingdom under Judaite leadership into existence, proved also the cause of the division from which Judah emerged as the carrier of the Israelite Yahwist order.

The origins of Judah are obscure. It is certain only that its growth was independent of the northern and central tribes which infiltrated Palestine from the east. Genesis 38 suggests an early mixture of nomadic invaders from the south with the Canaanite population. But the ethnic situation is not clear enough to allow the conjecture that the name of Judah attached to the original Canaanites rather than to the invaders. Moreover, Kenite and Kenizzite tribes formed part of the composite population. And they were perhaps the preservers of a Yahwism less affected by Canaanite syncretism than the Yahwism of the northern and central tribes west of the Jordan. The capital of Judah was Hebron. The few traditions of the political history, preserved in Judges 1:1–21, are too unclear to permit unraveling with any certainty. The capture of Jerusalem reported in 1:8, if it is historically reliable at all, can have been only an ephemeral success. And there is reason to doubt the membership of Judah among the tribes of Israel as presupposed in Judges 1 for the time of the conquest. The absence of Judah from the praises and blames of the Deborah Song rather indicates nonmembership (Judges 5). Moreover, the Samson anecdote of Judges 15:9–13, referring to the situation in the twelfth century, clearly speaks of Philistine "rule" over the region. This early and enduring rule by a foreign people was perhaps a factor in blending the populations of the region into a people that later could pass as a "tribe." [16]

---

[16] For the history of Judah cf. *ibid.*, especially the note on "The Origin of the Tribe of Judah," 169 ff. For a more detailed study of the tribal movements in the southern regions, as well as of the tribal organization, cf. Noth, *Geschichte Israels*, 74 ff., 167 ff.

The fusion of Judah with Israel during the Philistine wars is only slightly less obscure than the origin of Judah itself. One gains the impression of a loosening of the older clan organization under the impact of continuous warfare. The normal life courses of individuals were interrupted, and at the same time new centers of social organization arose, in the armies and retinues of war leaders which could absorb such dislocated individuals. The unsettlement through military conquests, the plunder and expropriation of land holdings, and their redistribution among distinguished military and administrative personnel created a common lot for a new type of subject-population, while it produced a new ruling class of comrades-in-arms with common interest in the preservation of power over the whole area that had been drawn into the whirlpool of warfare. Moreover, new connections were formed among people who had formerly led their quiet lives in widely separate regions, when members of distant clans and tribes were thrown together and formed common loyalties through military and court careers in the king's service. A few examples from the Biblical narrative will illustrate the process.

The decisive factor in the Israelite struggle for empire, as well as in the building of the new order, was the creation of troops of professional soldiers personally attached to the war leader. We have met with this instrument of royal politics, for the first time, in the case of Abimelech's *coup d'état* against his brothers. It appeared again in Jephthah's rise to power, when "worthless fellows collected round Jephthah, and went raiding with him" (Judg. 11:3). In David's case, then, we learn more about the reservoir from which the "worthless fellows" were drawn: "And every one who was in distress, and every one who was in debt, and every one who was discontented, gathered to him. And he became captain over them. And there were with him about four hundred men" (I Sam. 22:2). And in a similar manner Saul recruited the nucleus of his permanent military retinue: "There was hard fighting against the Philistines all the days of Saul; and when Saul saw a strong man, or any valiant man, he attached him to himself" (I Sam. 14:52).

The enumerated cases, however, reveal subtle differences in spite of their apparent similarity. While Jephthah and David in their outlaw days had to be satisfied with adventurous malcontents and fugitives from justice who "gathered" to them, Saul was in a legitimate position and could "choose" his warriors, as suggested by the phrase: "Saul chose three thousand men of Israel" in order to organize them as fighting contingents for himself and his son Jonathan (I Sam. 13:2). And these men, recruited by Saul into his military establishment, were at least sometimes men of good family. David, who entered the King's service, was recommended to Saul as "the son of Jesse the Bethlehemite, skilled in playing, a landowner, a man of war, prudent in speech, a man of good presence, and Yahweh is with him" (I Sam. 16:18). The manner in which the features are assembled to form the picture of a *kalokagathos* may belong to a later age, but even under more rustic conditions we see the handsome, well-bred son of a family of substance. Further insights into the growth of the new society are furnished by the career of David. He became the berith-brother of the King's son Jonathan (I Sam. 18:3), distinguished himself against the Philistines and was promoted to a commander of the king's men (18:5), and finally became the King's son-in-law (18:20 ff.). The young commander, however, became too popular. When the women greeted the returning warriors with the song "Saul has slain his thousands, And David his ten thousands," Saul began to "eye" David and to suspect in him the rival for kingship (I Sam. 18: 7–9). In order to dispose of the rival he sent him on ever more dangerous missions (18:13 ff.), a device which later David used with more success against the husband of Bathsheba. When ultimately David had to flee from the murderous intents of Saul, the potential future king was in spite of his youth already a power in his own right. Adventurers gathered to him by the hundreds, certainly in expectation of great rewards when the promising young man should succeed. And not only adventurers, but his whole clan (22:1).

Here a further important element of the new order becomes visible, that is, the clan to which the successful war leader belongs. From the King's clan emerge the influential dignitaries of the realm. The main support of Saul, and after his death, of the dynasty, was Abner, the King's cousin and commander in chief. David's general, Joab, was his nephew. When Saul, in the conflict with David, assembled his officers, they turned out to be Benjaminites, men of the King's tribe; and Saul addressed them: "Hear now, you Benjaminites; will the son of Jesse give every one of you fields and vineyards, will he make you all commanders of thousands and commanders of hundreds?" (I Sam. 22:7). The son of Jesse indeed would not; when he rose to power he had to provide for his own people. The passage reveals the material interest which the King's men, including his tribe, had in the success of the struggle for empire, as well as the pay-as-you-go technique of financing the struggle. With every Canaanite town wrested from the Philistines rich loot flowed in. And this source of revenue was sufficient to finance the further expansion under the primitive conditions of Saul, when the King had not yet a residence or palace, but continued to live on his estate, and assembled his officers under a tamarisk tree or seated in the hall of his peasant home with his spear leaning beside him against the wall. Even under David, when the kingdom was still growing, until it extended its control over Edom, Moab, Ammon, and the Arameans of Damascus, the continuous flow of loot was an important source of revenue. Not until the reign of Solomon did a rational administration of finances become necessary, because of the luxurious increase of expenditure, parallel with the tightening of resources. And in the course of this rationalization the prerogatives of the king's tribe became most firmly entrenched. For Judah was exempt from the division of the empire into twelve administrative districts; and in all probability this meant exemption from the taxes and services imposed on the districts. The readiness of Israel to separate from the Davidic kingdom after the death of Solomon was motivated largely by the favored position of the king's tribe.

In spite of the important role which the clan played in the rise to power of a war leader, in the struggle for empire, and finally in the exploitation of the resources of the kingdom, David did not derive much comfort from the support of his clan when he had escaped from Saul to Judah. For Saul's kingship of Israel effectively controlled the south, though the Biblical narrative has preserved no tradition concerning the process in which the control was acquired. Saul could pursue David and his followers from one hiding place to another and punish his supporters until David would be forced to take refuge, together with his men, with the King of the Philistine Gath. He was given residence in Ziklag, a town dependent on Gath, and could hold his men together by the technique of plunder, derived from raids against the non-Judaite populations to the south (I Sam. 27). After Gilboa David could move in a peaceful march with his followers and their households to Hebron, take residence there, and have himself anointed King of Judah (II Sam. 2:1–4). At the same time, Saul's general and cousin Abner took Saul's son Ishbaal east of the Jordan and established him as King of Israel in Mahanaim (II Sam. 2:8–9). The arrangement apparently found favor with the Philistines, who were content with the control of west-Jordanian Palestine and could expect the two rival kings to be no danger for the future.

The peace lasted seven-and-a-half years (II Sam. 2:11). Then the social forces which had been activated by the kingship of Saul became virulent again. The kings' clans had tasted of the spoils that came with conquest and empire. And if the kings kept their peace, as apparently they did, their generals had other ideas. The struggle for empire started moving again, not through any conflict with the Philistines, but through an encounter between "Abner and the servants of Ishbaal" and "Joab and the servants of David" (II Sam. 2:12–13). The reason for the meeting between the two armed forces of the generals at the pool of Gibeon, north of Jerusalem, in a territory which belonged to neither of the two royal domains, is not explained in the Biblical narrative. In view of later events the meeting appears to have had more behind it than the officially ascribed desire for a sham-fight between twelve young warriors from each side. Anyway, the sham-fight, in which all participants actually killed each other, developed into a real fight between the troops of the opposing camps; and the real fight, in which Abner in self-defense killed a brother of Joab, developed into "a long war between the house of Saul and the house of David" (II Sam. 3:1). The fortune of the long war turned against the Benjaminites. At this juncture Abner provoked an incident with his king Ishbaal which permitted him to transfer his loyalty to the rival for kingship (3:6–11), with a show of righteous indignation; he thereupon offered David a berith with the promise of bringing all Israel over to him (3:12). David was ready to accept, under the condition that his wife Michal, the daughter of Saul, would first be returned to him—apparently in order to improve the legitimacy of his succession to the kingship of Israel. Abner fulfilled his part of the berith. He delivered Michal to David and gained the approval of the elders of Israel, and especially of the Benjaminites, for going over to David (3:13–20). He was ready to assemble the Israelite notables for the formal berith with David. At this point of the transaction, when he was about to become David's kingmaker and when substantial power in the future kingdom presumably was to pass into the hands of the Benjaminites, Joab intervened and without much ado murdered Abner, under pretext of the blood feud which had its origin in the fight at the pool of Gibeon (3:21–30). The deed had the result which Joab probably had calculated. With their strong man dead, the Benjaminites had little hope of ever again achieving power under their sole control. Two of them murdered Ishbaal, who had become useless for their purpose, and brought his head to David at Hebron (II Sam. 4). David was properly shocked at all these bloody doings. He had the murderers of Ishbaal executed, and he went to the length of composing a funeral elegy for his former comrade in arms Abner (3:33–34)—though he prudently did not touch the valuable Joab, who had committed the murder. Then he accepted the kingship (5:1–5). Yahweh was with him.

When the Philistines at last took military measures to prevent the unification, they were defeated (5:17–25).

CHAPTER 9

The Mundane Climax

§ 1. The Davidic Empire

From the position of the post-Solomonic historians the united kingdom was the climax toward which Israel had been moving ever since
Exodus and Conquest. The actual course of events, however, as far as it
can be discerned through the editorial manipulation of traditions, does
not reveal such an entelechy at all. On the contrary, Israel's destiny was
deflected toward a mundane adventure, with the character of an impasse rather than of a climax. It will, at least, appear as an impasse if the
struggle for empire be reduced to its pragmatic phases: In the first of these
phases the Philistines expanded their dominion at the expense of Israel
and provoked the Israelite war of liberation under Saul. The second phase,
after the defeat of Gilboa, was the war between the "houses of Saul
and David" for the prize of kingship over a united people. In the third
phase, finally, the double victory of David over both Israel and the Philistines led to the conquest of Jerusalem and the united monarchy under
a Judaite dynasty. If we survey the pragmatic course from the beginning
to the end, the result seems to have been a disaster for Israel rather than
a success. At the beginning, there existed an Israelite Confederacy, even
though its Yahwism was in a state of decomposition and the ethnic amalgamation of the Hebrew clans with the Canaanite population had far advanced toward the making of a new nation. At the end of the struggle,
the territory and population of the formerly independent Confederacy
had been absorbed into a kingdom which included not only Judah but
also further Canaanite areas and was ruled by a Judaite clan. Moreover,
under the Solomonic administration the position of Israel degenerated
even further through discrimination, in matters of taxation and services,
in favor of Judah. To be sure, Israel regained its independence after
the death of Solomon. But the very fact that it separated from the kingdom proved that the unification was not experienced as a climax of
Israelite history proper. Nor could the restored independence be con-

sidered a solution of Israel's problems, since after a bloody internal history of little more than two centuries the independent kingdom fell under the Assyrian onslaught and, as a consequence, Israel ceased to exist as a distinguishable political and civilizational entity.

These are the stark facts of pragmatic history. But they have been so successfully overlaid by the paradigmatic construction of the Biblical narrative that even today the lack of critical concepts makes it difficult to treat adequately the problems of continuity and identity. On the one hand, the language of "Israelite history" must arouse misgivings in view of the fact that the most important event in its course was the disappearance of Israel. On the other hand, the language is justified because certainly something continued, even if the "something" defied identification by a name. The problems of this nature, however, will be treated in their proper place in the further course of this study. For the present, we need only draw attention to their existence, in order to conduct the analysis with awareness of the pragmatic context.

The pragmatic context for the period under discussion is furnished by the united monarchy of Israel and Judah which, for lack of a better name, we shall call the Davidic Empire. It does clearly not continue the monarchy which the Israelite Confederacy had developed as an emergency organization, but must be considered a new imperial foundation imposed by the conqueror, his army, and his clan, on the territories and peoples of Israel, Judah, and the Canaanite towns. The elements of conquest and force which entered into the making of the empire, however, were balanced, at least in the early years of David's reign, by a genuine popular support engendered by the relief from Philistine dominion as well as by the appeal of imperial power and courtly splendor. Nevertheless, the empire did not outlast the reigns of its founder (*ca.* 1004–966) and his son (*ca.* 966–926). And a careful observer of the eighty years might arrive at the conclusion that the empire in a stable form did not last for any time at all, for during David's reign the empire was still in the making, gradually expanding its dominion over Edom and Damascus through military governors, and over Moab and Ammon through tributary princes. But under Solomon, though the direct administration was extended over most of Ammon and Moab, the empire as a whole was crumbling, as Edom in the south and the Aramean Damascus in the north regained their independence. If the territories and peoples assembled by conquest at the time of David's death could have been held together by his successors for a few generations, a stable Syriac Empire, comparable in type to the Egyptian and Mesopotamian empires, might have come into existence. But whether such an imperial organization of the Palestinian and Syrian territories and peoples, when stabilized, would have been an Empire of Israel, even if it should have adopted the style, may justly be doubted.

The rapid succession of rise and fall, without a breathing space for stable existence, left no time for problems of this kind to develop. The causes which determined the rapid decline and the division of the empire were rather variegated. Certainly David's weakness in dealing with his sons had something to do with it, as well as the personality of Solomon, which, through the rare openings in the veil of glorification thrown around it by the Biblical narrative, looks somewhat less than wise. But there is no profit in pursuing details difficult to ascertain at best. For even men of impeccable character and statesmanship might have floundered in the attempt to overcome the fundamental obstacle to the building of a durable empire, that is, the hopeless poverty of the Palestinian soil. Palestine was too poor to maintain a first-rate military power, not to mention a magnificent court, in the style of the rich river civilizations in Mesopotamia and Egypt. We have touched already on the financial aspects of Saul's warfare and David's conquest. Loot as a major source of revenue had to cease when the conquest had reached its limits and the dominion had to be administered rationally within its boundaries. Labor in the king's service, taxation, and income from the control of trade had to replace the unorthodox financial methods of the war period. And when that point had been reached, the scarcity of resources quickly proved to be the limiting factor.

The actual difficulties, as we have indicated, have disappeared behind the veil of glorification surrounding the reign of Solomon. Nevertheless, certain incidents allow at least a glimpse of the true situation. We find in I Kings 9:15-22 that Solomon recruited his slave-labor force from the descendants of Amorites, Hittites, Perizzites, Hivites, and Jebusites, that is, of non-Israelitic peoples whom "the people of Israel were unable to destroy utterly." Neither the wholesale destruction of people who, when alive, could have produced revenue, nor the use of their survivors as slave laborers on royal building projects, can have improved the wealth of the country. Moreover, contrary to the suggestion of I Kings 9:22, Israel was not a military aristocracy ruling over slave laborers, but the Chosen People itself was pressed into service by a "levy of forced labor out of all Israel" (I Kings 5:13–18) for the unproductive purpose of building the Temple. And the twelve "officers over all Israel," at the head of twelve administrative districts, who each provided for the King's household for one month of the year (I Kings 4:7–19) can hardly have levied the provisions from anybody but the Israelites themselves. The country suffered and the revenue for royal projects was running low. In the twentieth year of luxurious building, I Kings 9:10–14 reports, Solomon could obtain a sum of gold only by selling twenty cities in Galilee to Hiram of Tyre. But when Hiram inspected his new territory he found the cities in poor condition, and "so they are called Cabul [no good] to this day" (13). It is not surprising, therefore, that Israel broke away from the house of David when after Solomon's death the successor threatened to increase the burden, and that the superintendent of slave labor, Adoram, was stoned to death on the occasion (I Kings 12:16–18).

§ 2. THE DAVID-BATHSHEBA STORY

For the period of the Davidic Empire, and especially for the reign of David and the Solomonic succession, the Biblical narrative of II Samuel and I Kings abounds with information on pragmatic events, on the motivations and actions of the leading personalities, and even on institutional details. We know more about these two generations than about any other period of human history prior to the Hellenic fifth century as narrated by Thucydides. When from this richly flowing source we attempt, however, to extract the experience of order, as well as the symbols which governed the new monarchy, we encounter difficulties, since the narrative contains no episodes that would concentrate the issue of order in a manner comparable to the great episodes of pre-Davidic history. There is no Abraham wresting the idea of the berith from a more compact context of experiences, no "Fable of the Trees," no Deborah Song, no Saul and Samuel struggling with the idea of kingship and its relation to Yahwism. Not that sources of this kind are altogether missing—they are hidden away, as we shall see, in other sections of the Bible. In the narrative itself the problem of order is curiously subdued; and the one great occasion on which the question of just order becomes articulate, the Nathan episode of II Samuel 12:1–15a, is a paradigmatic interpolation whose lateness only accentuates the absence of such elaborate concern with the issue of justice at the time itself.

The peculiar twilight in the spiritual atmosphere will be sensed when we study the Nathan episode in its setting.

The context of the Nathan episode is provided by the story of David and Bathsheba. It is the eternal, sordid story of the man who stays home and takes advantage of a soldier's absence in war to have an affair with his wife. The old story acquires historical importance because the man who stayed home was the King of Israel, the Messiah of Yahweh, and the soldier was one of the "King's servants," Uriah the Hittite. The King tried to obscure the paternity of the expected child by ordering a furlough for Uriah. But the attempt failed because the Hittite observed the sex taboo on Israelite warriors during a holy war. Then Uriah was sent to his death by David's famous letter to Joab. The war widow performed the ritual lamentations for her husband and then joined the King's harem (II Sam. 11). Yahweh was displeased and took measures. The child died within a week of its birth. During the illness of the child David was disconsolate, he fasted and prayed and waked. When the child at last was dead, David immediately stopped his disconsolation, washed, ate, and went to the house of Yahweh to worship. To his servants, who were astonished at his conduct, he explained that while the child was still alive he could hope that Yahweh would be gracious and save him, but now that the child was dead no useful purpose was served by acts of mourning and contrition. Then he went in to Bathsheba and produced Solomon (II Sam. 12:15b–25).

The story forms part of the Memoirs on the reigns of Saul and David, probably written by a man whose youth was in part contemporary with the events and released to the public about 900 B.C.[1] Into this story was fitted the Nathan episode. The train of the narrative was interrupted after the birth of the child. At this point Yahweh sent Nathan to the King (II Sam. 12:1–15a), and the prophet approached the King with the parable of "The Poor Man's Lamb" (12:1b–4):

> There were two men in a certain city: the one rich, and the other poor. The rich man had exceeding many flocks and herds, but the poor man had nothing save one little ewe lamb, which he had

[1] For the debate about the Memoirs, their authorship, purpose, and date, see Lods, *Histoire de la Littérature Hébraïque et Juive*, 160–68.

bought. And he reared it; and it grew up with him and with his children; it used to eat of his own morsel, and drink from his own cup; and it lay in his bosom, and it was like a daughter to him. Now there came a traveler to the rich man, and he was unwilling to take of his own flock and of his own herd, to dress for the wayfaring man that had come to him; but he took the poor man's lamb, and dressed it for the man that had come to him.

David was indignant about the rich man's action (5–6), only to learn that he was in the evildoer's position and would have to suffer Yahweh's punishment (7–10). The more detailed description of the punishment anticipated later historical events (11–12) and then returned to the punishment immediately at hand, to the death of the child (13–15a), so that now the original story could continue and still make sense.

An analysis of the David-Bathsheba story, as well as of the interpolated episode, must beware of the misinterpretations so generously bestowed by later generations, down to our own, upon an anecdote which seems to have the *haut goût* of human interest. It should be clear, therefore, that we are dealing neither with a sentimental love story nor with horrors of royal treachery. There will be no occasion either to condemn the morals of the King or to come to his defense with the argument that other oriental monarchs have done similar things, and worse, without compunction. As far as the present study is concerned, the story is relevant under three aspects. In the first place, the story is told in a book of political memoirs. Whatever the anecdotal value of its subject matter or the literary art of the narrator, it has its place in the Memoirs because the mother of Solomon was an important political figure. We may assume there was more than one Bathsheba in the neighborhood of the royal residence who hopefully took a bath where she could be seen from the roof of the King's house; and quite possibly more than one succeeded in the immediate purpose; but only one of them became the woman who played a decisive role in the struggle for succession and brought Solomon to the throne. Hence, the anecdote is preserved in its original context not because of the interest attaching to the details of its subject matter but because it is part of the political, and especially of the court, history of the Empire. As a matter of fact, the author is so vague on the issues—rather grave issues—raised incidentally by the detail of his story that a later historian would find it necessary to interpolate the Nathan episode in order to clarify at least one of the strands of meaning. In the second place, therefore, the story is relevant as the occasion for the fable of "The Poor Man's Lamb." And in the third place, finally, the story together with the interpolation is relevant to us as a source for understanding the crisis of Yahwist order in the Empire, as well as for the manner in which it was sensed by a man who was close to it in time, if not a contemporary.

The story is told with the restraint that characterizes the Memoirs as a whole. This restraint, which seems to tell everything and yet leaves the decisive issues in semiobscurity, is their signature. It is a cultivated, courtly style, far from the spiritual fierceness and uncompromising clarity of earlier periods. Hence the anecdote as told is rich in implications, but short on direct formulation. Still, it is outspoken enough to make the restraint recognizable as a style that is caused by spiritual disintegration as much as it serves as an instrument for its description. The silences and omissions betray the discretion of a highly placed person who is writing on the affairs of a regime, as well as the uneasiness of a man of the world when he senses his realm of immanent action, with all its glory, charm, passion, tragedy, and *raison d'état,* threatened with disaster from such an uncomfortable quarter as the spirit. All of the problems in the anecdote are fairly obvious, but almost none becomes quite clear.

The lack of clarity in the story becomes noticeable as soon as one tries to interpret it consistently in the light that radiates from its one absolutely clear point, that is, from the sex taboo that had to be observed by warriors during a holy war. When David tried to cover the affair with Bathsheba by giving the husband an opportunity, he received a stern lesson from Uriah (II Sam. 11:11):

> The ark, and Israel, and Judah, dwell in booths;
> and my lord Joab, and the servants of my lord, are encamped in the open field;
> shall I then go into my house, to eat and drink, and to lie with my wife?
> As you live, and as your soul lives, I shall not do this thing.

The unexpected obstinacy of a Hittite warrior who took the ritual of the Wars of Yahweh seriously must have greatly embarrassed the more sophisticated Messiah. He saw to it that the man was made drunk, hoping that in a state of intoxication his principles would mellow. And only when this attempt failed did he send him off with the letter to the faithful Joab, to his death. But even with the husband dead it seemed wise to move the woman into the harem quickly; for the case of Uriah had shown that not everybody in the kingdom took the war ritual as lightly as the King and his court retinue.

If the interpretation be assumed as correct, the story reveals a serious crisis of Yahwist order in the empire. And it reveals not only the crisis but also the reluctance to talk about it, or perhaps even a lack of sensitiveness for its nature. According to the story David's affair with Bathsheba was no more than a moment of passion. The King accepted what must have looked like an invitation, and perhaps was one; he had no intention of taking the woman into the harem and of having her husband killed for this purpose. On the contrary, he wanted to hush up the matter and have it forgotten. What then forced the extraordinary course of action on the King? Was it the necessity to protect the woman, or himself, against the consequences of adultery? The story is silent on the point. Nor does it mention why Yahweh was "displeased" with the affair. And the virtual murder of Uriah does not seem to have caused anybody to raise an eyebrow. The only motive mentioned at all is the sex taboo, placed forcefully in the center of the story in the address of Uriah. If, however, the war ritual is the core of the royal difficulties, as we must assume, then the state of Israelite order appears in a somber light, indeed. There is a King of Israel, though of a Judaite clan, who takes the sex taboo during a holy war lightly enough to break it, but seriously enough to make at least an attempt to cover his violation. His court personnel is sufficiently obedient to aid him in the affair and can be relied upon not to gossip in indignation so that the King's violation would reach the husband. And the King expects the warrior on furlough also not to be squeamish about the rules. But then comes the surprise that, of all people, a Hittite would take the taboo seriously. That situation in itself indicates a deep corrosion of the Yahwist order.

Even more revealing, however, is the circumstantial content of Uriah's answer, as it raises the question how holy the holy war of the time could have been. For here we receive the information, important for Israelite military history, that the armed forces were organized in the two groups of the militia and the professional "servants of the King." The people of Yahweh, both Israel and Judah, with the ark, were employed as a reserve, and at the moment were encamped in the rear, while the professional army was engaged in the more dangerous and tactically more difficult siege operations against Rabbah. When we reflect on this new role of the Chosen People as the strategic reserve of the imperial army, and compare it with the holy war at the time of Deborah, when Israel gained its active existence under Yahweh, we must wonder not only about the holiness of the war but about the very identity of the actors. To be sure, the wars were still fought under Yahweh, and even the people's militia did not always have a secondary role. In the first phase of the great war against the Ammonites the professional army fought alone, and on this occasion Joab himself addressed his brother before the battle (II Sam. 10:12): "Be strong, and let us prove our strength for our people, and for the cities of our God; and Yahweh do what seems good to him." And in the second phase of the war (II Sam. 10:15–19) it was the militia alone who did the fighting—one suspects because the professional army had to be husbanded. But again one must wonder about the identity of Israel, when a professional army fights not only for the people but also for the "cities of our God," that is, for the cities of Canaan, and when the ritual of war under a charismatic leader has been reduced to the sedate piety of the commanding general's invocation. The holiness of the third phase, in which Uriah found his death, is even more questionable, since the account of the campaign opens with the previously quoted verse (II Sam. 11:1) which suggests an "optional war" at the return of spring, "when kings go forth to battle," not a defensive war under Yahweh at all. The Israel of the holy wars was giving way, so it seems, to the exigencies of the empire's rational administration and warfare. As far as the professional army was concerned—which definitely was not the old *am Yahweh*—it is difficult to see how it could maintain the pathos of the Chosen People's war under Yahweh. And this must have become especially difficult when Solomon introduced the weapon of the war chariots. For the garrison towns for the charioteers—Hazor, Megiddo, Beth Horon, Baalath, and Thamar—were old Canaanite towns and the military personnel was professional (I Kings 9:15–19).[2] As far as the people of Israel was concerned the process of gradual dissolution was not entirely painless. That much can be gathered from the story of the population count in II Samuel 24. Apparently, a rational administration of the army required a count of "the valiant men who drew a sword." David ordered the census, but on this occasion he

---

. [2] On this question see von Rad, *Der Heilige Krieg*, 36, as well as the further literature given there.

was opposed even by Joab and the army commanders. The knowledge that the strength of Israel depended not on the number of divisions, but on Yahweh's aid and the warriors' faith, was still deep-seated. But David prevailed and found his mechanization of the holy war promptly punished by a pestilence sent by Yahweh.[3] The story of the census therefore confirms our interpretation of the David-Bathsheba story, in so far as interferences with ritual and symbolism of the holy war—that is, with the form of Israel's existence—were indeed the occasions on which the crisis of the Yahwist order became tangible for the people at large.

Still, while the nature of the issue can be discerned under the surface of the story, the veiling obscurity of the surface remains real. And the veil does not cover only the drama of Bathsheba-Uriah-David but also the conduct of David after the birth of the child. This aftermath of the drama proper is of special interest because it shows that the obscurity is not all due to the narrator's manner of presentation but attaches to the events themselves. The conduct of David was so strange, indeed, that even his court retinue demanded an explanation and the author of the Memoirs took care to report it. The man who indulged in acts of contrition as long as he could hope to obtain a divine favor by his performance, who stopped his contrition as soon as the incentive of a tangible advantage was removed, whose conscience clearly was not burdened either by adultery, or the violation of the sex taboo, or the murder of Uriah, or the death of the child, and who merrily proceeded to enjoy the profits of his crimes certainly was an unusual personality—unusual enough to astonish even the court personnel who might have known him. The character of David as it emerges on this occasion is confirmed by his conduct in all other critical situations of his life, amply recorded in the Memoirs. It is historically authentic, and must not be passed over with irony or moralizing criticisms. For apparently this character was the secret of his success. Here was a man who could live with himself, with his virtues and vices, because when balancing the gains and losses of his existence, he found a success

---

[3] David's census must have stirred the consciousness of the people deeply and given rise to various speculations. In the later parallel account of the census in I Chronicles 21 it is Satan who incites David to his breach of the Yahwist order. The history of Satan in the Old Testament, however, is rather complicated, and it will be excluded from our study. Cf. the studies contained in the volume *Satan*, of the *Études Carmélitaines*, 1948, especially the study "Ange ou bête?" by A. Lefèvre, S.J.

that permitted only one conclusion: Yahweh was with him! We remember the scene when David, reproved by Michal for his dance before the ark, answered:

> Before Yahweh, who chose me above your father, above all his house,
> to appoint me prince over the people of Yahweh, over Israel,
> before Yahweh will I make merry.

This mixture of sincere piety and shrewd brutality, this readiness to bewail and punish crimes and then to pocket the profits, to accept the deeds of Joab during his lifetime and then to provide in his testament for his servant's execution by the successor—all this is not pleasant, but it is not immoral. It is primitive and lusty. It is Yahwism pulled down to the level of mundane success. And the mixture never becomes shabby or hypocritical because it is held together by that authentic wholeness of personality for which we use the term charisma. Yahweh was with him, indeed—one can say no more.

One can understand that later generations were baffled by the enigma of the charismatic brute as much as his contemporaries, and more so. The Nathan episode, not precisely datable but belonging to the prophetic period, was an attempt to make sense of a drama whose meaning had been lost. If this attempt failed to bring out the essential point, that is, the violation of the sex taboo, this was perhaps due not to a lack of understanding but to the obscurity of the Memoirs on the point. In a comparable case, in the violation of the ritual of the holy war by Saul, in I Samuel 15, the point was well understood by the historians who created the paradigmatic elements of the Samuel story, probably because in this case the traditions were sufficiently well preserved to make the issue clear. In the David-Bathsheba story, however, the issue was so obscure that other elements of the situation suggested themselves for elaboration. One must be aware, as Gerhard von Rad has pointed out justly, that none of the historians who welded the traditions into their final literary form had ever witnessed a holy war, a ritual which by their time belonged to a distant past.

Nevertheless, while the fable of "The Poor Man's Lamb" did not touch the issue of the sex taboo, neither does it indicate simply a misunderstanding of the David-Bathsheba story. As the theocratic interpolations in the Samuel-Saul story brought to paradigmatic clarity issues implied in the situation, so the Nathan episode brought a newly emerging problem into

focus. When the old order of Israel and its wars under Yahweh was dis-
solving under pressure of the rising forces of kingship, court, professional
army, and the rationality of imperial administration and warfare, the
problem of the order governing the new forces became acute. When the
king was elevated by the permanence and authority of his office far above
the common people, when his conduct was no longer governed by the
ritual of a charismatic war leader, when the king's interest in her must
have been a great temptation for a woman, when the king had means, not
at the disposition of a commoner, of dealing with an annoying husband,
the king's conduct was bound to emerge as a new topic of reflection and
speculation. The possible misuse of power would impose special duties of
restraint on the king, while correspondingly a sphere of personal rights of
the subject, inviolate to royal action, had to be circumscribed. Under
David's kingship questions of this nature began to become crucial. Hence,
the Nathan episode dwelt on the king's power and its range under the
aspect of its origin in the favors showered by Yahweh on David (II Sam.
12:7–8). As a consequence, the taking of Bathsheba and the murder of
Uriah appeared as an arbitrary human addition to the divine gifts, and
had to be interpreted as contempt of "the word of Yahweh" (9). The
episode tended to form the notion of an "estate of the king," comprising
the king's conquests and possessions, his office and powers, as well as the
privileges and duties of the incumbent. In all these respects the estate was
a divine trust, to be held under the conditions imposed by Yahweh. While
the old order of the Israelite Confederacy was disintegrating, a new Yahwist order for the mundane forces of the empire began to crystallize. In
the Nathan episode the degree of articulation was comparatively low; and
never in Israelite history did it reach the level of a philosophy of law in
the technical sense. Nevertheless, even in the compact form of the episode
the substance of the issues—of royal conduct, of justice, of the subject's
rights—became clear. As far as the literary form is concerned, the fable
of "The Poor Man's Lamb" must be ranked with the fable of "The
Trees in Search of a King" as one of the Israelite "Fables for Kings"—if
we may use the term which Hesiod has coined for the literary genus.

§ 3. DAVID'S KINGSHIP

To the historian as well as to the reader who desires clarity about the
ideas of a period, the preceding analysis will appear tortuous and un-

satisfactory. We should like to know with a higher degree of precision what the status of the king at the time actually was: How his position was experienced by the people, as well as by himself; how the experience was symbolized; and how the position was institutionalized under rules of law.

Regrettably such precision cannot be achieved. The vagueness of the David-Bathsheba story with regard to spiritual issues was not the author's fault, as we have indicated, but characterized the historical situation. The texts concerning the position of the king were generally vague, not because they were defective but because the royal position grew under the uneasy pressure of necessities and would not bear too close inspection in the light of Yahwist order. Hence, the following analysis of the texts concerning David's kingship will try to paint as carefully as possible the aura of spiritual uncertainty that surrounds the evolution of the royal institution.

The twilight hovers over the royal institution of the Davidic Empire from the beginning in that David was twice anointed king, first of Judah, and later of Israel.

After the death of Saul, David moved with "his men" and their households "to Hebron," and settled with them "in the towns of Hebron." "And the men of Judah came, and there they anointed David king over the house of Judah" (II Sam. 2:1–4). That is all we learn with regard to his first kingship. One is left to surmise whether Hebron was coextensive with the settlement of the "house of Judah" or whether it was larger or smaller; whether other tribes or clans lived within the territorial jurisdiction of the king; and if so, whether they were among the "men of Judah" who came to anoint David, or whether he was a Judaite tribal king who ruled over other tribes by force. Neither do we know what form the unction assumed nor who administered it. It looks as if David moved to Hebron at the behest of Yahweh (2:1), at the head of his army, supported by his clan, and as if the inhabitants of the region thought it wise to submit to a king whom circumstances had put in their midst *de facto*.

Moreover, it is odd that a region with a heterogeneous population became all of a sudden a "house" and anointed a king as if that were its immemorial practice. If we remember the difficulties surrounding the emergence of kingship in Israel, the smooth transition from political non-existence to kingship in Judah becomes suspicious. Most probably the conqueror established himself with his army as the ruler over a defenseless population. To be sure, the establishment would have met with little resistance anyway because on the one hand, the reign of Saul had familiarized the people with the institution of kingship as well as its advantages in the struggle with the Philistines, and on the other hand, the Yahwism of Judah was less articulate than that of the confederate Israel.

In the background of David's kingship in the towns of Hebron, however, there lurked from the beginning the idea of a succession to Saul's kingship over Israel. For from the point of view of Abner, who had made Ishbaal the king over "all Israel" (II Sam. 2:9), the kingship of David can have been hardly more than high treason against the King of Israel. Under the shadow cast by illegitimacy and usurpation was conducted the war between the houses of Saul and David that ended with the murder of Ishbaal. On occasion of the subsequent surrender ceremony, the "elders of Israel" somewhat belatedly discovered that they were of the same bone and flesh as David, and that even at the time of Saul Yahweh had ordained David to be shepherd and prince of Israel (II Sam. 5:2). With the stain of illegitimacy removed by the formal declaration of the "elders of Israel," David made a berith with them before Yahweh, and they in return anointed him "king over Israel" (5:3). While the source has nothing to say about the content of the berith, the sequence of events suggests that its stipulations had been the condition for the unction which ultimately conferred the kingship over Israel on David.[4]

At first sight, the berith seems to be a relatively clear element in the royal institution. The Davidic kingship rested on a contractual relationship between the ruler and the representatives of the people. As soon as the berith is examined more closely, however, its meaning becomes uncertain. Whatever the stipulations from both sides may have been, the situation of II Samuel 5:3 marked the berith as a treaty of surrender in a politically and militarily dismal, if not hopeless, situation. It sanctioned the rule of a semiforeign conqueror. Moreover, the other elements of the situation must be taken into account. In the first place, David was already king of Judah, without benefit of berith with anybody. Furthermore, on this occasion he became king not only over the Israel whose elders concluded the berith with him, but also over the Canaanite towns about whose

---

[4] For a more elaborate reconstruction of the pragmatic events, using conjectures to fill the gaps of the narrative, cf. the chapter on "Der Grosstaat Davids" in Noth, *Geschichte Israels*.

representation in the act we hear nothing. And subsequent to the berith, he established a capital for the united kingdom in a region and town which at the time had yet to be conquered from non-Israelite populations. Hence, the berith at Hebron, far from being the basis of David's kingship, can be considered no more than the form in which the clans of Israel submitted to the ruler of the growing empire. It is not surprising, therefore, that we hear nothing of a berith when the empire passed from David to Solomon. The succession was regulated by the entirely different means of (1) the murder of Amnon, David's oldest son, by Absalom (II Sam. 13); (2) the abortive revolt of Absalom and his murder by Joab (II Sam. 15–18); (3) the formation of a court party in favor of Adonijah (I Kings 1:5–10); (4) the formation of an opposition and the harem intrigue in favor of Solomon, resulting in the latter's unction as king while David was still living (I Kings 1:11–53); and (5) the murder of Adonijah after David's death (I Kings 2:12–25). To be sure, the berith was not entirely without importance, for it kept alive the Israelite identity within the empire, an identity which could break out in rebellion and separation at any time. Absalom, for instance, utilized in his revolt the unrest of Israel caused by the partiality of the King's judicial administration for Judah (II Sam. 15:2–6). And after Absalom's death the revolt continued under the leadership of Sheba, a Benjaminite, one of those "worthless fellows" (20:1) whom on previous occasions we have found in the retinue of future kings. David was probably right when he judged Sheba's revolt more dangerous than Absalom's, for Sheba was an authentic Israelite leader, not handicapped by his relation with the king's clan (20:6). After Solomon's death, furthermore, when Rehoboam went to Shechem to be made king by "all Israel" (I Kings 12:1), Israel asserted its freedom to negotiate a berith with the heir presumptive. The meeting that had been intended as a ceremonial formality ended as a revolt. With the war cry

> What portion have we in David?
> We have no inheritance in the son of Jesse.
> To your tents, O Israel
> Now see to your own house, O David!

Israel left the empire. The act of separation inevitably raised the question who had left whom; and the answer was not the same north and south of the new border. The Judaite legitimists who ultimately edited the Biblical narrative were certain that Israel had broken away from "Israel": "So Israel has been in rebellion against the house of David to this day" (I

Kings 12:19). But in Deuteronomy 33:7 there is preserved a northern prayer:

> Hear, Yahweh, the voice of Judah,
> and bring him in to his people!

The confusion suggested by the sentence that Israel broke away from "Israel" did not escape the contemporaries and it worried the later historians. The Davidic Empire was pragmatically a foundation in its own right. Israel could join it in ill grace; it could revolt against it under a native leader; it could finally break away from it; but David's foundation existed, whatever Israel felt about it. Nevertheless, the new political entity was not much of a power in pragmatic politics without Israel. And even worse, its legitimacy was doubtful when the Israel from which it had borrowed its symbolism openly rejected it. David had a shrewd politician's understanding for the precariousness, in both respects, of his foundation. He carefully propped the legitimacy of his succession to Saul's kingship over Israel by keeping Michal in his harem; he insisted on the formal acceptance of his rule by Israel, through the berith at Hebron; he even had himself anointed a second time to make sure that his already existing kingship was really a kingship over Israel; he developed, in the Michal episode, the notion of a *translatio imperii* by Yahweh from the house of Saul to himself and his successors; and he was worried more about the revolt of Sheba the Benjaminite than about the outburst of sedition and murder in his own family. But no amount of understanding could change the fact that Israel was the Chosen People. The confederate Hebrew clans were Israel in that Yahweh was their God; and Yahweh was the God of Israel. Any conflict between Israel and the Davidic foundation stirred up the crucial question: was Yahweh with Israel, or was he with David?

The problem was not resolved until, with the fall of the Northern Kingdom, Israel disappeared as a rival, so that Judah could not only claim Yahweh for itself but also inherit the history of Israel as its own. Only then was the field free for the paradigmatic elaboration of a symbolism whose initial construction can be traced back to the conflict of David's time. The Either-Or of Israel and David could be overcome only by the assumption that Yahweh's choice of Israel included the choice of the house of David as its ruler, that the Berith of Yahweh with his people was at the same time a Berith with the house of David for perpetual kingship. The beginnings of the construction can be discerned in David's notion of a *translatio imperii*, developed in the Michal episode (II Sam. 6:21–22), in so far as Yahweh was interpreted in these verses not as the god of Israel only but also of the kingship, as well as of the order of its succession, over the people of Yahweh. And the historian of I Kings 12:19 went one step further when he destroyed the idea of the theopolity that had prevailed in the time of Saul and Samuel. In the earlier reign Israel's call for a king was still a revolt against Yahweh; now, at the time of Solomon's death, the rejection of the king meant not a return to Yahweh, but a new rebellion against Yahweh in the person of his royal representative. From the Philistine wars and the Davidic victories there emerged the experience of a Chosen King who, in case of conflict, took precedence from the Chosen People. Yahweh was with Israel when Israel was with David and his house. The king became the mediator of Yahwist order in the same sense in which a Pharaoh was the mediator of divine order for his people.

The lines along which the construction would have to move, thus, were clear even by the time of David. But no source which can be reliably dated as contemporary seems to have taken the decisive step. As in the case of the David-Bathsheba story, the solution was elaborated in a Nathan episode, in II Samuel 7.[5] The nature of the episode as an elaboration is assured by its position. It follows immediately the story of David's dance before the ark and his answer to Michal, which belongs to the oldest stratum of traditions in the Second Book of Samuel. David's claim to be prince of Israel by Yahweh's appointment is the theme taken up by the word of Yahweh, as communicated by Nathan (II Sam. 7:8b–9):

> I took you from the pasture, from following the sheep,
> that you should be prince over my people, over Israel.
> And I have been with you, wherever you have gone, and
> I have destroyed all your enemies from before you.
> And I will make you a great name like the name of the
> great who are in the earth.

The promise to David, then, was linked with the promise to Israel (10):

> And I will appoint a place for my people Israel, and will plant them,
> that they may dwell in their own place, and they shall be disquieted
> no more.

And, finally, the two promises to David and Israel were blended in a formula that from now on forever should be associated with the name of Yahweh (26):

> Yahweh of the hosts is god over Israel;
> and the house of your servant David shall be established before you.

[5] Cf. the parallel account, with slight variations, in I Chronicles 17.

The word (*dabar*) of Yahweh, spoken through the mouth of the prophet, had the character of a covenant with David, though the term berith did not occur in II Samuel 7. That this, however, was the meaning intended was confirmed by II Samuel 23:5: "For he has made with me an everlasting *berith*, ordered in all things and secure." Yahweh's Berith with Israel had been expanded to comprise the house of David.

§ 4. DAVID AND JERUSALEM

David's kingship, as will have become clear, differed fundamentally from Saul's. In the case of Saul the royal institution developed out of the charismatic leadership of the Israelite Confederacy; and the transition from leadership in an emergency to permanent rule, while it seriously disturbed the symbolism of the theopolity, gave rise to no more than the theocratic problems. In the case of David kingship developed out of the leadership of a professional army which could be used for or against Israel. The Davidic kingship was the institutional form of a conquest; and this new royal form, in the process of acquiring the larger part of the Syriac civilizational area as its imperial body, followed its own laws of symbolization, on principle not different from the forms developed in the neighboring Mesopotamian and Egyptian civilizations. The language of the imperial symbolism was determined by the most important event in David's career, that is, by the conquest of the Jebusite Jerusalem and the need to come to terms, shared by every Near Eastern conqueror and empire builder, with the principal god of the newly acquired territory, in his case with the El Elyon of the new capital.

The Davidic form, however, developed unique characteristics, since it was diverted from an evolution toward pure cosmological symbols by the fusion of Jebusite forms with the noncosmological Yahwism of Israel. The meeting between the high-god of the Syriac civilization and the god of the Chosen People resulted in a syncretistic cult. El Elyon and Yahweh blended into a god who retained the characteristics of Israel's Yahweh while acquiring from El Elyon the features of the *summus deus* of a cosmological empire.[6] The exploration of this new syncretistic form has begun only recently and the debate is still in flux. A well-rounded picture of

---

[6] For the blending of the two gods and the Davidic syncretism see Ivan Engnell, *Studies in Divine Kingship in the Ancient Near East* (Uppsala, 1943), 175: ". . . David, the actual and intentional founder of Israelite sacral kingship in the real sense of the term and of the 'syncretistic' royal official religion." Cf. Engnell, *Gamla Testamentet*, I, 138 ff.

the state of the problem would require a monograph. In the present context we shall restrict ourselves to the most important sources and their implications.

In a study of the imperial symbolism David and Jerusalem are inseparable, because the symbolism of the conqueror is involved in that of the conquest.

The question who David was has been a burning issue in Old Testament science ever since it has become certain that "David" was originally not a proper name but designated a military function, a royal office, and perhaps even a divinity.[7] In the Mari Texts we find frequently the term *dawidum* with the meaning of a "general" or "troop commander."[8] While in the face of these texts alone there can hardly be a doubt that David adopted the term as his name, the opinions diverge with regard to the occasion and the time of the event. Noth conjectures that the title may go back to the time of David's command of a mercenary troop and was transformed into a name at an indeterminate later time, while Johnson is sure that "only after the capture of Jerusalem" was Saul's successor known "by what may be interpreted as a divine name."[9] We are inclined to agree with the view that the conquest of Jerusalem was the occasion for elaborating the imperial symbolism, including the king's name, and endowing it with official sanction—even if the name should have been applied to David by his entourage or by the people at large before that event—because the imperial cult, of which numerous liturgies and hymns are extent in the Psalms, must have been created at some time and the period following the capture of Jerusalem is the most likely one. Nevertheless, a consensus in this matter will hardly be achieved in the near future, for a number of reasons. Above all, the narrative is silent on the measures which must have been taken at the time; and, as a consequence, we do not even know what David's original name was.[10] And the matter is further complicated by the range of meaning which the

[7] Sigmund Mowinckel, *Han som kommer* (Copenhagen, 1951), 45.

[8] *Archives Royales de Mari.* Publiées sous la direction de André Parrot et Georges Dossin. XV. *Répertoire Analytique des Tomes I à V.* Par Jean Bottéro et André Finet. (Paris, 1954.) In the "Lexique," p. 200, *s.v. dawidum* are given more than twenty references to the term.

[9] Noth, *Geschichte Israels*, 165. Aubrey R. Johnson, "The Role of the King in the Jerusalem Cultus," in S. H. Hooke (ed.), *The Labyrinth* (London, 1935), 81.

[10] If the tradition of the single combat between David and Goliath is reliable, the alternative version, in II Samuel 21:19, in which Elchanan performs the feat, will be of interest in this connection. Against the assumption that Elchanan is the original name of David it may be argued, however, that the Elchanan of the story is one of David's *gibborim*, clearly distinguished from David himself.

words derived through vocalization from the consonantal complex *dwd* have in the Semitic languages.[11] In the Mari Texts the *dawidum* designates a military leader; in the Jebusite Jerusalem at the time of the conquest, however, the term was probably "a Canaanite priestly-royal denomination taken over by David." [12] The view is supported by the rubric *ledawid*, which precedes a considerable number of Psalms. The traditional translation of *ledawid* as "of David" or "by David," assuming David as the author, is certainly wrong. The Psalms in question are meant "for David," that is, for the use of the King when he officiates in the cultus. Moreover, they are not meant for the conqueror of Jerusalem in person but for any David, that is, for any of the kings of the Davidic dynasty, including its founder. And, finally, Engnell is quite possibly right when he assumes the *ledawid* to be "an original cultic-liturgical rubric inherited from pre-Israelite Jebusite times with the actual import of 'a psalm for the king.' " [13] All of this, of course, does not preclude that one or the other of the Psalms has David for its author.[14] In addition to the meanings of military commander and king, *dwd*, vocalized *dod*, finally has the meaning of "the beloved one," probably designating "a vegetation deity corporalized in the king." [15] Within the Old Testament the *dod* occurs as applied to Yahweh in the song of Isaiah 5:1. From these variegated materials we tentatively conclude that the name David was assumed by the conqueror of Jerusalem (whatever his original name may have been) for the purpose of symbolizing his position as ruler of the empire under all of its aspects of military commander, priest-king, representative and beloved of the god.

The conquest of Jerusalem was part of David's imperial program.

[11] The consonants *dwd* can be vocalized in several manners, the most important ones for our purpose being *dawid, dod, dodo*. It should be noted that only Chronicles vocalizes unequivocally as *dawid* by inserting a *yodh* after the *waw*. That practice reflects a late, selective intention, for Samuel, Kings, and the Psalms confine themselves to *dwd*, leaving the vocalization open. The pointing of the Masoretic Text accepts the vocalization of Chronicles also for Samuel, Kings, and Psalms. It should be further noted that in the passages on the early feats of David and his *gibborim* there appears an odd number of Dodos. The aforementioned Elchanan is, in II Samuel 23:24, the "son of Dodo of Bethlehem"; and the Eleazar of 23:9 is equally the son of a Dodo. The difficulties and uncertainties of vocalization become apparent when the meaning of the context is in doubt. The passage II Samuel 21:15–16 is translated by RSV as: "David grew weary. And Ishbi-benob, one of the descendants of the giants . . . thought to kill David"; while the Chicago translation has: "Then arose Dodo, who was one of the descendants of the giants, . . . and he thought to slay David."

[12] Engnell, *Studies in Divine Kingship*, 176.

[13] *Ibid.*

[14] On the complicated question of the *ledawid* see Sigmund Mowinckel, *Offersang og sangoffer. Salmediktingen i Bibelen* (Oslo, 1951), 87 ff., 360 ff., and the long Note 31 on pp. 601 ff.

[15] Engnell, *Divine Kingship*, 176.

About this program, as well as about its import for the creation of the Jerusalem cultus, we know today a good deal thanks to the ingenious interpretation of Genesis 14 by Umberto Cassuto, Julius Lewy, and H. S. Nyberg.[16] In Chapter 7, "From Clan Society to Kingship," Genesis 14 was our source for Abram's experience of Yahweh as his personal God and for the transformation of the berith symbol. On that occasion we confined our interpretation to the meaning which the text was intended to have in its present position in the history of the Patriarchs, but at the same time we noted that the story was a literary oddity, in that it represented an independent Jerusalemite tradition and could not be ascribed to any of the major J, E, and P sources. The question why the Abram story was preserved in the peculiar form of a tradition attached to Jerusalem is answered by the scholars just mentioned with the assumption that the text in its present form is a piece of imperial propaganda originating in the time of David.[17] The intervention of Abram on the side of the Canaanite kings against their Mesopotamian enemies had the purpose of legitimatizing the rule of Israel, especially under David, over the conquered peoples. They had formerly been under the dominion of the oriental kings and were liberated by Abram; hence, the conquerors of Canaan, from Moses to David, exercised a right that had belonged to Israel since Abraham.[18] The territorial claims of the Empire were expressed by the extension of Abram's pursuit of the enemy to "Hoba, north of Damascus."[19] The intervention in favor of Lot, the ancestor of Moab and Ammon, had the purpose of reminding Ammonites and Arameans of

---

[16] Umberto Cassuto, *La Questione della Genesi* (Florence, 1934). Lewy, "Les textes paléo-assyriens et l'Ancien Testament," *loc. cit.*, 29–65. H. S. Nyberg, "Studien zum Religionskampf im Alten Testament," *loc. cit.*, 329–87. The reader should be aware that excellent Old Testament authorities still have their misgivings about the new interpretation. Cf. Albrecht Alt, "Das Koenigtum in den Reichen Israel und Juda," *Vetus Testamentum*, I (1951), 2–22. Alt (p. 18) considers it possible that Jebusite forms were taken over by David, but finds the materials of Genesis 14 and Psalm 110 too thin to furnish a secure foundation for the interpretations put on them.

[17] I should like to stress that the assumption concerning the present form of the text, which I accept, does not affect the interpretation of the Abram story given previously. We have to distinguish in Genesis 14 between (1) an original Abram tradition which is not preserved, (2) the present form, in which the tradition has been couched by the Davidic propaganda, and (3) the return to the Abram element, contained in the present form, by the redactors of the Patriarchal history. Old Testament texts quite frequently have more than one meaning, due to the levels of oral tradition and literary elaboration. The problem of multiple meanings regrettably is not yet fully realized by Old Testament scholars. The discovery of new meanings is, therefore, all too often accompanied by the assumption that meanings previously found were errors of interpretation.

[18] Cassuto, *Genesi*, 372. Nyberg, "Studien," *loc. cit.*, 377.

[19] Cassuto, *Genesi*, 372. Nyberg, "Studien," *loc. cit.*, 360.

their former oppressors and their salvation by Abram: "an Israelite pro-
tectorate over these peoples lies in the air." [20] With regard to the relations
within the Empire, David recognized Jerusalem and its El Elyon, as had
his ancestor Abram, but rejected the recognition of other Canaanite kings,
as Abram did in the person of the King of Sodom.[21] Hence, the text can
be characterized as "the ideological document, by which David wanted to
set forth his right to Jerusalem. The ancestor Abram in Hebron is the
cover-figure for the young Jewish tribal king David in Hebron." [22]

The symbolic form which the kingship and the empire had to adopt
was intimately connected with the character of Jerusalem as a Jebusite
town and the seat of the high-god El Elyon. The Abram story is again the
reflection, and perhaps the justification, of David's compromising identification of Yahweh with the Canaanite god, which entailed the acceptance
of Jebusite cult forms into the Yahwism of the Empire. Traces of this
syncretism can be frequently found in the hymnic literature, as in the
Yahweh who is incomparable among the "sons of god" (*bene elohim*)
(Ps. 89:7), to whom the surrounding *bene elohim* ascribe glory and
strength (Ps. 29:1), and who is the greatly terrific *El* in the secret council
of his divine entourage (Ps. 89:8). This Yahweh-Elyon sits on "the
Mount of Assembly, in the farthest end of the north"; and the Babylonian
tyranny is described as the attempt to scale the Mountain of God and to
become "equal to Elyon" (Isa. 14:12–15). The "city of God" is "the
dwelling of Elyon" (Ps. 46:5); and "David" is his first-born, the "Elyon
among the kings of the earth" (Ps. 89:28).[23] Moreover, El Elyon has the
aspects, or hypostases, of Shalem and Zedek, who appear in a supporting
position.[24] The name Jeru-shalem itself means the "creation of Shalem";
and Shalim is an old, west-Semitic deity, attested through theophorous
names as early as the Kultepe Texts of *ca.* 2000 B.C.[25] That he probably
was a wine-god is suggested by Genesis 14:18, where Melchizedek, the
king of Shalem and priest of El Elyon offers wine and bread to Abram.[26]
El Elyon's aspect of Shalim (Hebrew, *shalom*: prosperity, success, har-

[20] Nyberg, "Studien," *loc. cit.*, 376.
[21] Cassuto, *Genesi*, 374: Israel owes nothing to Canaan. All that Israel possesses is exclusively the gift of Yahweh, who is identified with the El-Elyon of Jerusalem. Nyberg, "Studien,"
loc. cit., 361.
[22] Nyberg, "Studien," *loc. cit.*, 375.
[23] Johnson, "The Role of the King," *loc. cit.*, 87, 95, 77.
[24] Engnell, *Gamla Testamentet*, I, 119.
[25] Lewy, "Les textes paléo-assyriens," *loc. cit.*, 62.
[26] Nyberg, "Studien," *loc. cit.*, 355.

monious situation, peace, but also a *shalom* war, a war that will lead to the desired peace) is paralleled by Zedek (righteousness). In the Biblical narrative we meet two kings of Jerusalem who bear the theophorous names of Melchi-zedek ("Zedek is my King"; Gen. 14:18) and Adoni-zedek ("Zedek is my lord"; Josh. 10:1, 3). In the hymnic literature Yahweh will speak *shalom* to his people, his *zedek* will go before him, and "*zedek* and *shalom* kiss each other" (Ps. 85). The extraordinary importance which *zedakah* has as the cardinal virtue in the prophets, as well as the realization of Yahweh's kingdom as a realm of peace through a prince of peace, derive from the Jerusalemite El Elyon who at the same time is *shalom* and *zedek*.

The policy of establishing a dominion of Shalem finds its expression in theophorous names. Illuminating are the names of the sons born to David at Hebron (II Sam. 3:2–5; I Chron. 3:1–4) and Jerusalem (II Sam. 5:14–16; I Chron. 3:5–9). Among the Hebron sons we find, aside from names indifferent to our problem, formations with Yahweh such as Adoni-yah and Shephat-yah, while only one of the names, Ab-shalom, is formed with Shalem. Among the Jerusalem sons formations with Yahweh have disappeared entirely, while the preferred combinations are with El (Elishama, Eliyada, Eliphelet) or Shalem (Shelomo).[27] The occurrence of Ab-shalom among the Hebron sons perhaps indicates that David's imperial, syncretistic program was already in preparation before the conquest of Jerusalem itself, during the years in Hebron.[28] Moreover, the same symbolism was also used by the enemies of the Davidic Empire and its successor states. Several of the Assyrian kings combined in their name Shalmanassar the names of Ashur and Shalem, the great divinities of the eastern and western Semites. "In the names Ashur and Shulmanu is contained the whole political program of the Assyrian Empire" to establish a universal state over the eastern and western Semitic peoples.[29] And Shalmanassar V (727–722) became indeed the destroyer of the Kingdom of Israel. The symbolic claim was, finally, renewed after the Exile, when Zerubbabel named his son Meshullam and his daughter Shulamit (I Chron. 3:19).[30]

About the arrangements following the capture of Jerusalem we receive only scanty information from the narrative, and even this must be

---

[27] Lewy, "Les textes paléo-assyriens," *loc. cit.*, 62. Nyberg, "Studien," *loc. cit.*, 373 ff.
[28] Engnell, *Gamla Testamentet*, I, 139.   [29] Nyberg, "Studien," *loc. cit.*, 353.
[30] Franz M. T. Boehl, "Aelteste Keilinschriftliche Erwaehnung der Stadt Jerusalem und ihrer Goettin?" *Acta Orientalia*, I (Leiden, 1923), 80.

interpreted in the light of the symbolism that pervades other sections of the Bible. We hear neither about a destruction of, or even severe damage to, the city in the course of the conquest, nor about an extermination or decimation of the population—though its composition must have been strongly affected by the influx of the Davidic court officials and of the military and administrative personnel. The narrative thus offers no reason to assume that Jerusalem after the conquest was not substantially the same Jebusite city it had been before. Of the institutional changes the priestly appointments are of interest. David made several of his sons priests, though we do not learn of whom or of what temple; specifically named as priests are Zadok and Abiathar (II Sam 8:16–18). The latter two were obviously of the highest rank, and both officiated with the ark (II Sam. 15:24–29). Of Abiathar we know that he belonged to the family of Eli, the priest of the Yahweh sanctuary at Shiloh. In Zadok Nyberg wants to recognize the last priest-king of Jerusalem, who abdicated in favor of David and was rewarded with the priesthood. The suggestion has much to recommend itself, especially in that it would explain the role assigned to Melchizedek, the ancestor of Zadok, in the Abram story of Genesis 14.[31] In evaluating the suggestion one must also consider the respective positions taken by Zadok and Abiathar on occasion of Solomon's succession to the throne. Abiathar supported Adoniyah, while Zadok took the part of Solomon: it looks as if Yahwist and Zadokite factions had formed at the court with the result that, after the accession of Solomon, Zadok could get rid of his Yahwist rival in the priesthood (I Kings 2:26–27). With Abiathar's banishment to Anathoth the Yahwist dynasty of priests disappeared from Jerusalem.[32]

The Biblical narrative received its final form after the return from the Exile, when the high priests had usurped the former functions of the king. It is not surprising, therefore, that we learn little from the narrative about the king's position in general, and about his function as the high priest in particular, which David and his successors inherited from the Jebusite rulers of Jerusalem. Nevertheless, we have a fairly clear picture of the continuity, because a sufficient number of coronation oracles, liturgies, and hymns has survived. Psalm 110 is of special importance for

[31] Nyberg, "Studien," *loc. cit.,* 375.
[32] Geo Widengren, *Psalm 110 och det sakrala kungadoemet i Israel* (Uppsala Universitets Arsskrift, 1941:7, 1), 21.

our present context, as it establishes the continuity between Melchizedek and the Davidic institutions.[33]

Psalm 110 is preceded by the rubric *ledawid* and thus is characterized as a piece to be used in a ceremony involving the King. The text itself consists of a series of oracles which, by their contents, reveal themselves as a coronation ritual, or at least as important parts of it:

(1) The Psalm opens with an oracle, ostensibly spoken by a temple prophet to the King on a ceremonial occasion which appears to be the first act of the coronation:

> The word of Yahweh to my lord:
> "Sit at my right hand,
> till I make your enemies your footstool."

Yahweh invites the King to sit at his right hand, and the throne to which the King must be imagined to ascend is understood as Yahweh's throne. Of this first act we can speak as the enthronement.

(2) When the King has followed the invitation and is presumed to be seated, the speaker continues with a description of effective rule under the power of the god, supported again by a direct word from Yahweh:

> The sceptor of your strength will Yahweh stretch forth from Zion:
> "Rule in the midst of your enemies!"

In this second act of the ceremony the King apparently is endowed with the scepter. It is stretched forth from Zion by Yahweh himself, and its principal effect is victory over enemies.

(3) The third oracle presents great difficulties of translation. It probably is to be rendered as:

---

[33] For the Canaanite and general Near Eastern background of the Psalm cf. *ibid.*, and Widengren's *Sakrales Koenigtum im Alten Testament und im Judentum* (Stuttgart, 1955), 44 ff. See also Aage Bentzen, *Messias. Moses Redivivus. Menschensohn* (Abhandlungen zur Theologie des Alten und Neuen Testaments, Zurich, 1948), 12, 17 ff. and Mowinckel, *Offersang og sangoffer,* 75 ff. With regard to the date of Psalm 110 Mowinckel thinks that the oracles of the Psalm could hardly have applied to David himself, but possibly to Solomon (*ibid.*, 411 ff.), because David was already king at the time he conquered Jerusalem. The argument is plausible but not conclusive, because we know too little about the ceremonies involved or the occasion of their use to draw such conclusions with certainty. The text of the short Psalm is difficult and in some spots not well preserved, so that the traditional translations are practically useless. We use Widengren's translation in *Psalm 110*, p. 3 ff., as amended in *Sakrales Koenigtum,* 44 ff. We differ, however, from Widengren in the assignment of lines to the speakers, in order to make better sense of the sequence of oracles. Incidentally, our assignments fit Widengren's interpretation of the Psalm as a series of oracles for a coronation ritual better than the sense which he creates by his own inverted commas. The rich comparative material which justifies both translation and interpretation cannot be reproduced here; the reader should refer to Widengren's works, as well as to the bibliography attached to *Sakrales Koenigtum.*

Your people offer themselves freely on the day of your strength.
In holy array go forth!
    "From the womb of the Dawn, as Dew have I brought you
    forth!"

In the third act the King is endowed with the robe of the cosmocrator, after the usurpation described as the robe of the high priest, the "holy array," in which he is now to go forth to show himself to the people. The "day of your strength" is probably the coronation day, on which the people offer themselves freely to the King's rule, but possibly a day of war on which the people volunteer in the militia. In either case, the third act makes effective the King's domestic rule, as the second act makes him victorious over enemies. Again the picture of effective rule is supported by the oracle from its source in Yahweh who certifies the King as the new-born son, fathered by the god with his divine consort.

(4) The ritual reaches its climax with the declaration of the King as the priest of Yahweh:

Yahweh has sworn and will not repent it:
    "You shall be a priest forever, after the manner of Melchizedek!"

Geo Widengren's translation follows the Septuagint (*kata ten taxin Melchizedek*), as most translations do, in speaking of a priesthood in the manner, or after the order, of Melchizedek. The Hebrew text, however, would render, instead, "You shall be a priest forever, because of me a Melchizedek." [34] In that case the proper name Melchizedek would carry the overtones of "a King of Righteousness," deriving the righteousness (*zedek*) of the King from his priestly function and its source in Yahweh.

(5) Verses 5 and 6 resume the temple prophet's description of the King's dominion by the will of Yahweh:

The lord at your right hand will shatter kings on the day of his wrath. He will execute judgment among the nations, filling with corpses, shattering heads, over the wide earth.

I assume "the lord at your right hand" to be the King, in accordance with the first oracle's request that the King take his seat at the right hand of Yahweh. Hence the prophet's words would be addressed to Yahweh, as a confirmation of the newly created King's proper functioning. The English translations (RSV, Jewish Publication Society, Chicago, Moffat) capitalize the "Lord," referring it, with several manuscripts, to Yahweh.

---

[34] Insisted upon by Duhm, and followed by the Chicago translation.

(6) The concluding verse of the Psalm, "From the brook will he drink on his way; therefore will he lift up his head," seems to be a ritual direction for the king, who is supposed to drink from the brook Gihon the water of life.

Since an important phase in the creation of a king, the unction, is missing, Psalm 110 is perhaps a fragment. It will be good, however, to reserve judgment in such matters, because there are no independent sources for Israelite rituals; on the contrary the rituals must be reconstructed from sources like Psalm 110. The absence of the unction would be explained if the Psalm were a complete ritual for one day of a ceremony which extended over several days. It would also be explained if it were a ritual for the anointed David, who on this occasion entered into the cosmological symbolism of the Jerusalem priest-kings. Whatever the precise nature of the ritual in question may be, it shows conclusively how the imperial symbolism of the cosmological civilizations entered Israel by way of the Jebusite succession.

§ 5. The Imperial Psalms

The principal source for the imperial symbolism in the wake of David's foundation is the Psalter. The discovery of this source, however, is so recent, and the debate about its nature is so strongly in flux, that we cannot proceed to a presentation of the symbols themselves without first clarifying our own position in the matter. This is especially necessary in view of the fact that the very terminology of "imperial Psalms" and "imperial symbolism" is not the usage of the literature on the subject but our innovation.

1. The Nature of the Psalms

The discovery that the Psalms are not original expressions of personal or collective piety written in postexilic or perhaps even post-Maccabaean times, but derive from hymns, liturgies, prayers, and oracles to be used in the cult of the pre-exilic monarchy, is one of the important events, perhaps the most important one, in the Old Testament study of the twentieth century. While the discovery has by now been almost generally accepted,[35] the exploration of details, far from being concluded, furnishes

[35] The principal exceptions are American: M. Buttenwieser, *The Psalms. Chronologically Treated with a New Translation* (Chicago, 1938), and R. H. Pfeiffer, *Introduction to the Old*

occasion for wide disagreements. Moreover, the symbols of the Psalms and their "patterns" were found to have radiated over the forms of both the prophetic literature and the historical narrative, so that the interpretation of the Old Testament as a whole is faced with entirely new problems.[36] While some of the results of this comprehensive task of re-interpretation can be considered well established, the task itself is so enormous that consensus, even with regard to fundamentals, has not yet been achieved. The pursuit of the discovery has, finally, encountered serious questions of methodology, and even of a philosophy of order and history. With regard to this last class of problems, the present state of Old Testament study can be described only as bewilderment; and the difficulties arising from this source have even become a handicap for the further advancement of substantive problems.

Of the reasons why the nature of the Psalms has remained obscure for so long, two have been especially noted:

(1) The first one is the romantic notion of the poet as a man who, in definite circumstances of his life, expresses his experiences or sentiments in "poetical" form. Under the influence of this notion the Psalms were treated as *pièces de circonstance*, either national or individual, which could be examined by historians of literature with regard to the circumstances of their creation, or to the personal style of their authors.[37] The Psalms were, however, written for generic situations and therefore rarely contain allusions to specific historical circumstances; and they conformed to cultic patterns and therefore betray no personal style of an author. Hence, their treatment as romantic poetry was inevitably misleading.

(2) The second reason must be sought in the fact that Old Testament study in the nineteenth century was predominantly an occupation of Protestant scholars, whose "eyes were not sufficiently open for the fundamental place which cult in general has in the development of religion" because of "the low esteem for the cult," which has characterized the prevailing trends in Protestantism since the age of Pietism.[38]

Testament (New York, 1941). Rather hesitant with regard to the new issues is Lods, *Histoire de la Littérature Hébraique et Juive.*

[36] More recently the re-examination of texts has extended even to the New Testament. Cf. Harold Riesenfeld, *Jésus Transfiguré. L'Arrière-Plan du Récit Evangélique de la Transfiguration de Notre Seigneur* (Acta Seminarii Neotestamentici Upsaliensis, XVI, Lund, 1947): and Goesta Lindeskog, *Studien zum Neutestamentlichen Schoepfungsgedanken,* I (Uppsala Universitets Arsskrift, 1952:11).

[37] Lods, *Histoire,* 724.

[38] Mowinckel, *Offersang og sangoffer,* 24.

The obstacle to an adequate understanding of the Psalms was the *Zeitgeist* of the nineteenth century, with its individualism in "poetry" and "religion." Romanticism and Pietism conspired to obscure the generic and cultic nature of the Psalms.

The process in which the obstacles were overcome and the nature of the Psalms gradually brought to light has a recognizable beginning but as yet no end. The following characterization of the principal phases, as well as the exposition of the problems which they have engendered, will therefore be governed by the solutions which the present study itself offers tentatively.[39]

2. *Form-critical and Cult-functional Methods*

The foundations for the new study were laid by Hermann Gunkel. He started from the observation that the civilizations of the ancient Near East were more conservative in their symbolic language, in art, literature, and religion, than is modern Western civilization. In the light of this insight he then laid down two postulates for the study of the Psalter: In the first place, personal literary achievements, if there were any at all, could be distinguished only against the background of generic forms, of literary *Gattungen*. The first task of a critical study would therefore have to be the establishment of the principal *Gattungen* of Psalms. And second, since the types did not receive their meaning from personal authorship, they had to be made meaningful by the description of the generic situation for which they had been created. This situation Gunkel called the setting in life, the *Sitz im Leben*. The terminology developed by Gunkel is still in use; and his principles have remained the basis for the study of Israelite literature, though they are no longer considered its end and all.

Under the first of his postulates Gunkel engaged in a classification of the Psalms according to *Gattungen* or types. Of special interst for the imperial symbolism is his recognition of the Enthronement Songs (Ps. 47, 93, 97, 99) as a type which clearly has something to do with the

---

[39] A survey of the study of the Psalter, both old and new, is to be found in Lods, *Histoire*, 718–42. For the new study of the Psalter there is available in English the excellent chapter by Aubrey R. Johnson, "The Psalms," in Rowley (ed.), *Old Testament and Modern Study*, 162–209. Very illuminating are the brief surveys of the process in Hans-Joachim Kraus, *Die Koenigsherrschaft Gottes im Alten Testament. Untersuchungen zu den Liedern von Jahwes Thronbesteigung* (Beitraege zur Historischen Theologie 13, Tuebingen, 1951), 15–26; and the same author's *Gottesdienst in Israel. Studien zur Geschichte des Laubhuettenfestes* (Beitraege zur Evangelischen Theologie, 19, Munich, 1954), 9–17. The recent publication by Sigmund Mowinckel, " 'Psalm Criticism Between 1900 and 1935,' (Ugarit and Psalm Exegesis)," *Vetus Testamentum*, V (1955), 13–33, has particular weight because of the person of its author.

enthronement of Yahweh as King, and of the Royal Psalms (2, 18, 20, 21, 45, 72, 101, 110, 132) as a type which just as clearly has something to do with a king, presumably the pre-exilic monarchs of Israel and Judah. In the work with his second postulate, the search for the *Sitz im Leben,* Gunkel was less successful, because the official cult of the monarchy had not yet been properly understood as the setting of the Psalms. Thus, while he assigned the Royal Psalms to various settings in the pre-exilic period, he saw in the Enthronement Songs a type of postexilic spiritual poetry under the influence of the canonical prophets—a view which today is difficult to maintain.[40]

While the second phase of the process is richer in motivations, it can be characterized succinctly through the work of Mowinckel which focused the variegated influences and partial insights into a new picture of the Psalms.[41] Mowinckel received the problem at the stage to which it had been advanced by Gunkel, and recognized the weakness of the form-critical method. The *Gattungen* had to be constructed with the means of literary criticism. Recurrent formulas and subject matters, recognizable to the careful reader, had to be used as criteria of the types; and the sense of the type depended on the setting in life that was found for it—if one was found at all. The classification thus proceeded under the assumption that to every type constructed by the form-critical method, there corresponded unequivocally a setting which had motivated this particular literary form. In the practice of analysis, however, difficulties were encountered from both terms of the relation. On the one hand, the types did not form a simple catalogue—the system was complicated by the classification of numerous Psalms under more than one head, as well as by the construction of subtypes and mixed forms. On the other hand, Gun-

---

[40] The work of Gunkel extends over a considerable period of time and has undergone revisions, especially under the influence of Mowinckel, whose work will be discussed in the following paragraphs. The earliest systematic presentation of his principles was given in "Die Israelitische Literatur," Paul Hinneberg (ed.), *Die Kultur der Gegenwart,* I/7 (Leipzig-Berlin, 1906). His main work on the Psalms is *Die Psalmen* (Goettingen, 1926). His last work, completed by Begrich, is the *Einleitung in die Psalmen. Die Gattungen der religioesen Lyrik Israels* (Goettingen, 1933).

[41] The first broad elaboration of his ideas was given by Mowinckel in the six volumes of his *Psalmenstudien* (1921–24). The most important volume for our purposes is *Psalmenstudien, II. Das Thronbesteigungsfest Jahwaes und der Ursprung der Eschatologie* (Videnskapsselskapets Skrifter, II, 1921, No. 4, Kristiania, 1922). The last comprehensive restatement, with modifications, is *Offersang og sangoffer.* A few special points were restated in *Zum Israelitischen Neujahr und zur Deutung der Thronbesteigungspsalmen* (Avhandlungen, Norske Videnskap-Akademie, Oslo, II, 1952, No. 2, Oslo, 1952). Cf. also the previously quoted survey of Psalm criticism in *Vetus Testamentum,* V.

kel had no well-founded theory about what constituted a setting in life—
hence, the assignment of settings had no more critical weight than could
be gained from the types themselves in combination with a few general
notions about the course of Israelite religious history. A considerable degree of arbitrariness and uncertainty attached to Gunkel's work because
of its character as a botanical classification in the manner of a Linnaean
system. Since this analogy was drawn by Gunkel himself, we may be
allowed to draw it out and formulate the task that had become obvious as
the advance from Linné to the genetics of Mendel and Weismann.

It was Mowinckel who took this step deliberately and formulated it as
the advance from the "form-critical method" to "the cult-historical or
cult-functional conception of the Psalms." The cult became for Mowinckel the new genetic principle that would assist in the construction of
types. The types in the form-critical sense, to be sure, retained their
relevance as a first approach to classification, but the cult as the setting
in life would permit the grouping of several literary types into one class,
if they could be referred to the same cult. To the Jerusalem New Year
Festival Mowinckel was able to refer not only the five or six Enthronement Songs of Gunkel but several other *Gattungen,* totaling more than
forty Psalms.[42]

The impetus for Mowinckel's theoretical improvement—setting aside
for the moment the logic of the problem—was provided by the increase of
comparative materials from the Near Eastern civilizations and from
primitive peoples. The rapidly expanding knowledge of the ancient world,
in particular through archaeological discoveries, which today affects all
historical sciences in general and creates havoc among well-established conceptions, is especially noticeable as an influence at all the stages of the
process that is our present concern. It provided the impetus even in the
work of Gunkel, who had become aware of the generic, static character
of religious institutions and literary forms through his comparative studies in Mesopotamian materials.[43] At the time when Mowinckel's conception was in formation, the comparative materials from Babylon and Egypt
had increased substantially, and in addition he had experienced the influence of the Danish anthropologist Vilem Groenbech.[44] The idea of a

---

[42] The study of the New Year Festival, as well as of the Psalms connected with it, which
filled the whole of Volume II of Mowinckel's *Psalmenstudien* (1922), still occupies the longest
chapter, "Salmer til Jahves tronstigningsfest," in *Offersang og sangoffer,* 118–91.

[43] Cf. Gunkel's early work *Schoepfung und Chaos in Urzeit und Endzeit* (Goettingen, 1895).

[44] The impact of Groenbech on Israelite studies made itself felt a second time through his
influence on Pedersen, *Israel. Its Life and Culture.*

unique spiritual history of Israel began to be overshadowed by the recognition of the close resemblance between the institutions and cults of Israel and those of the neighboring civilizations. As far as the interpretation of the Psalter was concerned, Mowinckel saw that a considerable number of Psalms became intelligible if they were understood as connected with an Israelite New Year festival of the same type as the Babylonian, which had become better known recently, especially through the studies of Zimmern.[45] Since the Old Testament does not so much as mention a New Year festival at which an enthronement of Yahweh was celebrated, the assumption was an admirable feat of imagination. Not only the contents of the cult but its very existence had to be inferred from the Psalms. Nevertheless, the assumption proved so convincing that even Gunkel accepted it.[46]

3. Divine Kingship and Patternism

While Mowinckel's cult-functional conception was a definite improvement on Gunkel's form-critical method, it still suffered from the same weaknesses, though to a lesser degree. To be sure, Mowinckel had penetrated from the "botanical" surface of literary forms to the "genetic" depth of the cult that motivates the form. Nevertheless, the cult itself has a function in the order of society, and while it is a distinguishable unit, it is not an ultimate object in a critical science of order. Unless one penetrates beyond the cult into the order of which it is a function, the botanical superficialism with its theoretical weaknesses will repeat itself on the level of a cult-functional study of the Psalms. The difficulty of Mowinckel's position has become apparent in the continuing debate about his assumption of an Israelite New Year festival with a ritual enthronement of Yahweh, for the existence of the festival, which explains the Psalms, is inferred from the Psalms it is supposed to explain. This circle cannot be broken through reference to other sources that would unequivocally attest the existence of the festival, since the silence of the sources made

[45] At the time he wrote his *Psalmenstudien,* Mowinckel did not know that his idea had been anticipated by Paul Volz, *Das Neujahrsfest Jahwes* (*Laubhuettenfest*) (Tuebingen, 1912). The monographs of Heinrich Zimmern, *Zum Babylonischen Neujahrsfest,* were published in the Berichte ueber die Verhandlungen der Saechsischen Gesellschaft der Wissenschaften, LVIII (1906) and LXX (1918). More easily accessible is Heinrich Zimmern, *Das Babylonische Neujahrsfest* (Der Alte Orient, 25:3, Leipzig, 1926).

[46] Gunkel-Begrich, *Einleitung in die Psalmen,* 105, stresses the irrelevance of the argument that such a festival (procession of Yahweh to his sanctuary, glorification of the enthroned God) is not attested in the Old Testament, since a whole series of ceremonies, which can be inferred from the Psalms, are not otherwise known. A survey of such otherwise unknown festivals and ceremonies is given, *ibid.,* 61–65.

the circular assumption necessary in the first place. And since an alternative solution can be offered after all, as was recently done in the previously mentioned work of H.-J. Kraus, the debate is apt to run on indefinitely. The position can be strengthened and the circle broken only through the theoretical argument that the assumed enthronement festival belongs essentially to a complex of symbols which is characteristic for a certain type of order, and that an order of this type is present in Israel because other parts of the characteristic complex of symbols can be found in the Old Testament beyond a doubt.

While the theoretical issue has not yet been formulated in this manner either in Old Testament studies in general or in Psalter studies in particular, a long step in this direction has been empirically taken in the third phase of the process. The impetus was again provided in part by an increase of knowledge, especially through the Ugaritic materials from Ras Shamra, in part through the logic of the problem which induced a closer examination of the cults in question with regard to their meaning. The result was, on the one hand, a better understanding of the cultic "pattern" of the Near Eastern New Year festivals, and on the other hand, the recognition that the meaning of the pattern was intimately connected with the role of the King as the mediator between God and man in the ancient civilizations. As a consequence, the line from the "religious phenomenon" of the Psalm literature was at last drawn, beyond the "religious phenomenon" of the cult, to the institutional center of a cosmological empire, that is, to the King.[47]

On the basis of the Egyptian and Babylonian sources, S. H. Hooke distinguished the following main phases in the ritual pattern: (a) The dramatic representation of the death and resurrection of the god; (b) the recitation or symbolic representation of the myth of creation; (c) the ritual combat, in which the triumph of the god over his enemies was predicted; (d) the sacred marriage; (e) the triumphal procession, in which the king played the part of the god, followed by a train of lesser gods or visiting deities. This skeleton ritual Hooke found underlying New Year festivals, coronation rituals, initiation ceremonies, and even occasional rituals.[48]

---

[47] The conventional terminology of "religion" and "religious phenomena" is still a serious obstacle to an adequate understanding, not only of Israelite but of ancient Near Eastern history in general. One cannot repeat often enough that the word "religion" does not occur in the Bible.

[48] S. H. Hooke, "The Myth and Ritual Pattern of the Ancient East," in S. H. Hooke (ed.), *Myth and Ritual* (London, 1933), 8. Cf. in the same volume Hooke's essay on "Traces of the

For the Israelite Feast of Tabernacles, as a New Year festival, A. R. Johnson distinguished the following phases of the ritual: (a) Yahweh, the leader of the Forces of Light, triumphs over the Forces of Darkness as represented by the Chaos of waters or primeval monsters; (b) Yahweh's enthronement as King over the Floods and Ruler in the Assembly of the Gods; (c) Yahweh's mysterious works in Creation. The festival was understood by Johnson as the annual revival of the social unit. It formed the background for the re-creative work of the King, that is, of the representative of the people, in the ritual drama. The people's salvation, its victory over death, was assured through a ritual combat in which the representative King triumphed over the kings, or nations, of the earth who have combined, as the Forces of Darkness, to destroy the people. In the course of the combat the King, who was variously designated as the Son, the Servant, or the Anointed of Yahweh, suffered an initial humiliation. "But this proved his salvation and that of his people, for it involved an ultimate dependence upon Jahweh and so demanded the SEDEK, the loyalty or right relation, of the social unit as a whole." [49] From the empirical side, Johnson has gone as far as one can go in the clarification of the theoretical issue without laying new foundations for a philosophy of order and symbolic forms.[50]

A process of study that began as a form-critical analysis of the Psalms has ended with the establishment of divine kingship as the focus of relevance. The shift of relevance expresses itself in the remarkable increase of the number of studies which use the Psalms as source materials for the exploration of kingship, clearly taking it for granted that the setting in life for the Psalms is the cult of the pre-exilic monarchy. One may indeed say that a new genus of literature on divine kingship has developed, as instanced by the works of Engnell, Bentzen, Frankfort, and Widengren, to mention only the major treatises.[51] Of special importance in this

---

Myth and Ritual Pattern in Canaan." Hooke's interpretation of the pattern was still rather inadequate, in that he considered it the function of the ritual "to deal with the unpredictable element in human experience." Nevertheless, he recognized the pattern as adapted to a social structure of which the King was the center (p. 4).

[49] Johnson, "The Role of the King," in Hooke (ed.), The Labyrinth, 110 ff.

[50] That Johnson is methodologically conscious of the importance of his work is conclusively shown by his restatement of the issue in "The Psalms," in Rowley (ed.), The Old Testament and Modern Study, 193–95.

[51] Ivan Engnell, Studies in Divine Kingship, I (1943), Aage Bentzen, Det sakrale Kongedoemme (Copenhagen, 1945). Henri Frankfort, Kingship and the Gods (1948). Geo Widengren, Sakrales Koenigtum im Alten Testament und im Judentum (1955). The work by Aubrey R. Johnson, Sacral Kingship in Ancient Israel (Cardiff, 1956), was not yet published at the time of this writing.

series is the work of Engnell because of its thorough treatment of the Ugaritic materials and the bearing which they have on the understanding of Israelite institutions.[52] And finally, the shift of relevance makes itself felt in the late work of Mowinckel, in the treatment which he accords to divine kingship in his *Han som kommer* (1953).[53]

4. The Difficulties of the New Position

The rapid changes of method and the mountains of materials to be digested have absorbed the energies of Old Testament students and historians of religion so completely during the last half century that the task of laying new philosophical foundations has been neglected. Traditional conceptions of the place of Israel and the Bible in the spiritual history of mankind, the notion that "religious phenomena" can be treated in isolation from the order of a society, survivals of nineteenth-century evolutionism and positivism, and last but not least the makeshift terminologies developed by the scholars of the twentieth century have today accumulated to the point of obstructing the pursuit of substantive problems.

We can approach the nature of the difficulty through an occasional remark of one of the finest Old Testament scholars of our time, Gerhard von Rad, who declared himself puzzled by the universal claims of the Imperial Psalms. To be sure, he accepted the cultic interpretation of the Psalms, and he used the new methods himself in his studies on the Hexateuchal form, but he nevertheless found the cosmological symbolism of the imperial type somewhat ridiculous under the conditions of the small Kingdom of Judah.[54] The remark illuminates a situation which must be negatively characterized through the absence of a philosophy of symbolic forms. The question raised by von Rad would be justified if the imperial symbolism were a program of world dominion in pragmatic politics; it will dissolve once it is recognized that we are dealing with the ex-

---

[52] Cf. the chapters on "The Evidence of the Ras Shamra Texts" and "The Krt Text," in Engnell, *Studies in Divine Kingship*. For a brief characterization of the Canaanite cult pattern, as distinguished from the general Near Eastern, cf. Engnell, *Gamla Testamentet*, I, 116 ff. and 118 ff. For the relation between the Canaanite and Israelite cult patterns cf. the "Exkurs II: Ueber das israelitische Neujahrsfest" in Widengren, *Sakrales Koenigtum*, 62–79. On the Ugaritic background, especially of the Psalms, cf. Albright, *Archaeology and the Religion of Israel*, 14–16.

[53] Cf. the survey of the institution of divine kingship in Egypt, Babylon, and Canaan, in Mowinckel, *Han som Kommer*, 25–44, followed by the study of "Israels kongeideal," 46–68. The intimate connection between the New Year Festival and the role of the king, as stressed by Johnson, was acknowledged by Mowinckel in "Psalm Criticism," *Vetus Testamentum*, V, 17.

[54] Gerhard von Rad, *Erwaegungen zu den Koenigspsalmen* (Zeitschrift fuer die alttestamentliche Wissenschaft, N.F. XVII, Berlin, 1940–41), 216–22.

perience of cosmic order as the source of social order and with the articulation of that experience in the language of the cosmological myth. In a given instance, the language of the myth is motivated by the experience of order; it has nothing to do with the size or success of the social unit which uses the language. I want to stress that I am characterizing a situation and not perhaps criticizing my distinguished colleague von Rad. On the contrary, he was puzzled by an incongruity between literal language and reality that required further attention, while others did not even raise the question.

Not only were questions of this type not raised, but terminologies were developed which by their appearance of critical finality veiled the existence of the problem. Especially unfortunate under this aspect is the indiscriminate use of the term "ideology," prevalent among the Scandinavian scholars when they speak of the King's position in a cosmological civilization.[55] The scholars in question are, of course, not Marxists; and quite probably they are not even aware what they are doing when they apply a symbol developed by Karl Marx for his fight against the Western bourgeois culture of the Victorian Era, to a Pharaoh or a King of Judah. The oddity can only be explained by suggesting that Old Testament students, historians of religion, and orientalists, were ill prepared to suddenly encounter "divine kingship," a phenomenon which looked like "politics." In that situation "ideology" offered itself as a term much in use among sophisticates in political debate.

While the usage, thus, is not a symptom of Marxist infiltration in the study of the Psalter, the new terminological convention is not entirely harmless. In the first place, it continues the series of insufficiently analyzed concepts that we have traced from the *Gattungen* and the *Sitz im Leben*, through the cult, to divine kingship; it is one more word-fetish that blocks the construction of critical concepts. And second, it helps to cover a dubious theoretical position which can be discerned behind the equally indiscriminate use of the term "cult pattern." The term "pattern" refers to the symbolic drama in which the order of existence is periodically restored, in cosmological civilizations, to its accord with the order of being. The symbolic drama itself, as well as the motives of its periodic re-enactment in a cosmological order, are quite intelligible. It is, further-

---

[55] For the extent of the usage cf. the references *s.v. kungaideologi* in the subject matter indexes of Mowinckel's *Offersang og sangoffer* or Engnell's *Gamla Testamentet*, I; or most recently, the section entitled "Die Kroenungsorakel und die Koenigsideologie" in Widengren's *Sakrales Koenigtum*.

more, intelligible that the same type of symbolism will recur in every cosmological order and that the similarities of symbols in a manifold of such orders will increase through cultural diffusion, if the several orders are geographically neighbors. And it is, finally, intelligible that the symbolism will remain the same in time, if necessary through several millenniums, until the compactness of cosmological experience is broken through the opening of the soul to the revelation of God. Order is intelligible, and its intelligible meaning can be communicated through adequate language, as we are doing right here and now. The language of "patternism," however, is unable to touch the meaning of order. It transforms the intelligible, substantive constancy of symbols into an unintelligible phenomenal stability of cult-patterns in "early civilizations." And this effect of "patternism" is strengthened through the use of the unanalyzed, and therefore substantively unintelligible, term "ideology." In so far as the fetish-words phenomenalize the intelligible symbolizations of experiences into dead patterns, they betray their origin in survivals of an evolutionist philosophy of history.

The consequences become painfully apparent when the description of "phenomena" extends beyond primitive cultures and cosmological civilizations to the existence of the Chosen People in its truly historical form under God. A study like Pedersen's *Israel*, for instance, will impress the reader by its magnificent array of comparative materials as much as by its regrettable historical flatness. To be sure, the "cult patterns" of cosmological civilizations can be found in Israel, too, for the good reason that Israel "wanted a King like the other nations." And since a king is the symbolic mediator between cosmic and social order, and not perhaps a ruler whom one can have with or without "ideology," his appearance in Israel was accompanied by the appearance of cosmological symbols of mediation and restoration of order. Nevertheless, it was Israel that wanted a king; and its historical form of existence, though seriously affected, was not abolished by the cosmological admixture. Hence, the heavy accent in recent literature on "divine kingship," "ideology," and "cult patterns" leaves the uneasy impression of more than a temporary neglect of the truly unique Israelite problems of existence in the presence of God: The neglect seems due, at least in part, to a genuine distortion of Israelite order as a consequence of its insufficient philosophical penetration.

5. *The Resistance to Mythologization*

The uneasiness aroused by the work of the Scandinavian scholars is not so much caused by tangible misinterpretations that would provoke the criticism of historians, or by heterodoxies that would offend the theologians, or by theoretical propositions to which philosophers would take exception, as by a lack of clarity about principles. The heavy accent on the mythical elements in the Old Testament, without proper qualifications, engenders suspicions, as far as I know unjustified, that a radical mythologization of the Bible and Christianity is intended. And the suspicions are further nourished by exaggerated and theoretically loose formulations which probably would be hastily withdrawn by their author if their implications were spelled out to him.[56] In recent years this uneasiness has grown into critical resistance. German scholars, especially, have tried to determine the actual extent of the influx of mythical elements into the Old Testament, as well as to arrive at greater clarity about the change of meaning which they have undergone within the historical form of Israel. The complexion of this resistance, now, is significant for the state of science in that the work of the Germans is handicapped by the same insufficiency of philosophical foundations as the work of their Scandinavian and English *confrères*. We shall use as an example the treatment accorded a decisive point in the problem of "divine kingship" in Israel.

The German scholars resist the mythologization (*Mythisierung*) of the Old Testament and, in further course, of Christianity. While they accept the Royal Psalms as belonging to the cult of the monarchy—though a postexilic date for the Enthronement Songs remains in debate—they raise the question whether the symbolism of divine kingship retains its meaning when it enters the orbit of historical form.

In order to answer this question in the negative, it had first to be shown that an orbit of historical form existed indeed in the cult of Israel; that the cosmological symbolism was not as pervasive in the cult of the monarchy as the Scandinavian accents made it look; but that another, specifically Israelite cult dominated the order. And the existence of such a

---

[56] Kraus, *Die Koenigsherrschaft Gottes im Alten Testament*, 145, n. 1, assembles a number of passages from the late Aage Bentzen's *Messias. Moses redivivus. Menschensohn*, which are indeed surprising. But I hesitate to agree with Kraus that such propositions "mean a serious crisis of theology." This particular "crisis" looks as if it could be overcome through the application of intellectual energy to the theoretical problems involved.

cult was proven with a high degree of probability indeed by the studies of Gerhard von Rad, when he demonstrated the character of the Sinai pericope (Exod. 19–24) as a cult legend and, furthermore, showed that its form was used in the construction of Deuteronomy.[57] Moreover, Psalms 50 and 81 were found to contain elements (the Sinaitic appearance of Yahweh, the pronouncement of the Decalogue) that would be explained best by the assumption of a "Covenant Festival" at which Psalms of this type had a cultic function.[58] Mowinckel's cult-functional method was thus used by von Rad to show the existence of a cult which had its place not in the ritual re-creation of cosmic order, divine and royal, but in the context of the Sinaitic revelation.

With the demonstration that two symbolic forms actually coexist in the order of the Chosen People, the vista has opened on a whole field of problems which as yet have received scant attention. Von Rad has shown above all that a unique historical event such as the constitution of Israel at Mount Sinai through Yahweh and his servant Moses, when it becomes effective in the order of the people, does not have to remain in the sphere of remembrance through oral tradition or written narrative, but can be submitted to ritual renewal in a cult in the same manner as the cosmological order of the neighboring empires.[59] The earlier symbolism does not disappear altogether with the cosmological form of order, but at least some of its elements are found again in the historical form, though their context of meaning is now determined from the newly differentiated organizing center of divine revelation.[60] Moreover, as the present case shows, the relations between the various form elements cannot be reduced to a simple

[57] Gerhard von Rad, *Das Formgeschichtliche Problem des Hexateuchs,* and *Deuteronomium-Studien* (Forschungen zur Religion und Literatur des Alten und Neuen Testamentes, N.F. XL, Goettingen, 1947). That a cult problem of this type existed had already been noticed by Sigmund Mowinckel, *Le Décalogue,* especially p. 129.

[58] Von Rad, *Das Formgeschichtliche Problem,* 19 ff.

[59] The point was elaborated, though its implications were not fully realized, in Hans-Joachim Kraus, *Gottesdienst in Israel,* 55 ff.

[60] The point again has been seen by Kraus, *Die Koenigsherrschaft Gottes im Alten Testament,* 70, n. 1: "It is our task to interpret the Old Testament, not from the myth of the Ancient Orient, but from itself, though with proper regard for the foreign myth." That leaves the question open as to what "the Old Testament itself" really is. Kraus's reference to "the prophetic-historical events in the Covenant people of the Old Testament" points in the right direction, but the construction of concepts appropriate to the task has hardly yet begun. Kraus himself insists (p. 145 ff.): "Under all circumstances the Old Testament concept of history must now be clarified. The conservative theologoumena of *Offenbarungsgeschichte* and *Heilsgeschichte* are of no use to theology, unless it is clearly defined what these concepts mean." We agree with him that the categories of the theological seminar, which have their origin in the Augustinian concept of the *historia sacra,* today need considerable refinement to meet the demands of a theoretically much more complex situation.

formula.[61] For first, the historical symbol of the Covenant enters, without impairment of meaning, into the cosmological form of cultic renewal; while second, the tradition of the historical event is couched in the form of a cult legend which no longer permits a reconstruction of the course of events in terms of pragmatic history; and third, the form of the cult legend, which has absorbed the historical events, is applied to the organization of a literary work like Deuteronomy which poses quite difficult formal problems of its own.[62]

While the attempt to clarify the organizing center of Israelite form was successful and led to important results, the direct attack on the problem of "divine kingship" has, for the time being, not been able to overcome the difficulties just indicated.[63]

First the Israelite component in David's kingship had to be clearly circumscribed. The kingship was built, as we have seen, into the Yahwist tradition through an expansion of the berith symbol which purported to legitimate the dynasty through a special berith between Yahweh and David, briefly called the David Covenant to distinguish it from the Sinai Covenant. Moreover, the expansion was not an irrelevant intellectual construction, but assumed the form of a word, a *dabar*, of Yahweh communicated through the prophet Nathan. Here we have the genuinely Israelite core of David's kingship: its institution through a prophet under the revealed will of Yahweh. By the heavy accent on this core, the center of Israelite form was again moved into the foreground from which it had receded in the treatment accorded to "divine kingship" by the Scandinavian scholars.

With the prophetic institution of kingship secured, the attack could be undertaken. The kingship in Jerusalem as the point of irruption for the oriental symbolism, as well as the massiveness of the irruption, were acknowledged.[64] The question now was "how far these mythical elements became subordinate to the main statements of the royal cult, or how

---

[61] Mowinckel operates with the term "historical myth"; Kraus prefers "mythical history."

[62] For the purpose of characterizing the state of the problem, we have singled out one instance from the German effort to arrive at a more critical understanding of the specifically Israelite form. The effort is, in fact, rather broad in scope. In particular must be mentioned the work of Albrecht Alt, most of whose numerous studies are now more easily accessible in *Kleine Schriften zur Geschichte des Volkes Israel*. Alt, "Die Urspruenge des Israelitischen Rechts" (1934), "Die Wallfahrt von Sichem nach Bethel" (1938), and "Gedanken Ueber das Koenigtum Jahwes" (1945), have a special bearing on the present problem. Martin Noth, "Gott, Koenig, Volk im Alten Testament. Eine methodologische Auseinandersetzung mit einer gegenwaertigen Forschungsrichtung," *Zeitschrift fuer Theologie und Kirche* (1950), was not available to me.

[63] The principal monograph is Kraus, *Die Koenigsberrschaft Gottes im Alten Testament*.

[64] *Ibid.*, 67; Kraus, *Gottesdienst in Israel*, 77.

far they preserved themselves as components in their own right"—a question to be answered in favor of the first alternative.[65] Alt found it difficult to believe that "the supposedly general oriental divine kingship" should have been received into the Israelite order unless it had been transformed (*umgebildet*) so far that it had become compatible with the strict subordination, precisely of the kings of the house of David, under Yahweh.[66] Kraus spoke of the irruption of "the oriental ideology of kingship into the David traditions"; and he made it his program to show that "the David tradition as basically determined by the prophetic word of II Samuel 7, while admitting the foreign elements of the oriental ideology of kingship, nevertheless did not permit their continued existence in their own mythological essential form [*mythologische Wesensgestalt*]." [67] He considered it impossible in particular that an Enthronement Festival of the Babylonian type could have been part of the "foreign elements," since such a festival would have "fundamentally transformed the whole belief [*Glauben*] and thought of Israel." Only less noxious elements could have been received; and they, like the symbol of the king as the son of God, were "profoundly reshaped [*tiefgehend umgepraegt*]." [68] With regard to the Enthronement Songs, Kraus therefore went back to Gunkel's date and declared their setting in life to be a postexilic festival of the return of Yahweh from Babylon to Zion.[69]

We have given some of the programmatic formulations in direct quotation in order to show the source of the difficulty: The passages abound with unanalyzed concepts and a generally uncritical vocabulary which make it impossible to come to grips with the issue of the relation between the different sets of symbols in the Nathan prophecy of II Samuel 7. We recall that the kingship was instituted through a word of Yahweh, as communicated by Nathan, which declared the king to be the son of God. That event is the point of confluence of the Israelite historical with the Near Eastern cosmological form in that the prophet legitimates the Davidic dynasty through a word of Yahweh, whereas the word spoken

[65] Kraus, *Gottesdienst in Israel*, 77.
[66] Alt, "Das Koenigtum in den Reichen Israel und Juda," *loc. cit.*, 18.
[67] Kraus, *Die Koenigsherrschaft Gottes im Alten Testament*, 67.
[68] *Ibid.*
[69] This is the burden of Kraus's study on the *Koenigsherrschaft Gottes*. The attempt to find in the Enthronement Songs the influence of Deutero-Isaiah, thus justifying their postexilic date, seems to have failed for the reasons advanced by Aubrey R. Johnson, "The Psalms," in Rowley (ed.), *Old Testament and Modern Study*, 193 ff., against the similar earlier attempt of N. H. Snaith, *Studies in the Psalter* (1934) and *The Jewish New Year Festival* (1947).

by Yahweh on this occasion happens to be an Egyptian coronation formula. The juxtaposition of the two form elements (as for the moment we
shall say neutrally) is further complicated by the fact that on occasion of
the Exodus from Egypt, Yahweh had declared Israel to be his first-born
son, in opposition to the Pharaonic sonship. Hence, the declaration of the
king as the son of God not only introduced the Egyptian symbolism, but
also affected the sonship of Israel. A number of questions inevitably suggest themselves: Has Israel now ceased to be the son of God? Or has an
order of the Pharaonic type been reimposed on Israel, by a new dispensation? Or is the monarchy perhaps the alembic in which Israel will be
transformed into the remnant that is fit to enter into a new Covenant
with Yahweh? Such questions will occupy us in the further course of this
study. For the present they are raised only in order to suggest that the
history of Israel rather than the text of the Old Testament is the region in
which the issue is located.

The "transformation of the mythological elements," or at least of their
"essential form," is not an issue on the level of literature. The Nathan
prophecy, or the Psalms, give rise to the thorny problems precisely because they contain the mythical elements without any transformation. We
shall not be surprised, therefore, that the efforts of Kraus to resolve the
problem through text interpretation have meager results. With regard to
the symbols of the "son" who is "begotten" by Yahweh (Ps. 2:7) just as
the Pharaoh is by the sun-god, he can only persuasively plead that such
"concepts are hardly to be understood in a physical or mythical sense."
Once they are placed in the Israelite context, they are "adequate expressions" for the prophetic institution of the King; and, even more, they
"point toward the creative act of Yahweh's word." [70] That is all. The
text interpretation does not carry us beyond the assurance that mythical
symbols don't mean what they mean when they occur in the Old Testament.

In order to overcome the impasse, we must abandon all attempts to
harmonize the text. Both the historical and cosmological symbols must be
accepted at their face value as the expressions of the corresponding experiences of order; and it must be recognized, consequently, that the
Davidic Empire, as well as its Israelite and Judaite successor states, were
built on conflicting experiences of order. How such a composite order
can function at all is not a question of the "subordination" of one set of

[70] Kraus, *Die Koenigsherrschaft Gottes im Alten Testament*, 69 ff.

symbols to the other one through the interpretative skill of contemporary Old Testament scholars, but of the balance of the conflicting experiences in the Israelite society from the tenth to the sixth centuries B.C. The history of Israel must be examined if we want to know whether the motivations of action, originating in the conflicting experiences whose coexistence is conclusively proven by the symbols, were held in such balance that the order remained stable. Only the actions of individuals or groups can indicate the relative vigor of the experiences, as well as the corresponding strength or loss of substance of the symbols.

We do not have to engage in profound research in order to find the indexes of the conflict. In the ninth century, for instance, when the cosmological form of kingship in the Northern Kingdom threatened to take final precedence of Yahwism in the cult, the prophetic revolt against the Omrides revealed the strength of the historical form. And as far as Judah is concerned, the David Covenant and the Sinai Covenant were in permanent conflict throughout the period of the monarchy, with wave after wave of reform movement which reasserted the Sinaitic foundations of the old theopolity against the ascendancy of kingship. The tension between "divine kingship" and the Sinaitic tradition came to an end only with the kingship itself. And by that time there had already emerged from the conflict the indications of a new type of order, in the prophetic symbols of the remnant, the new Covenant, and the Messiah of Yahweh. The conflicts of this nature are difficult to overlook in the history of Israel, and they have, of course, not escaped the German scholars. On the contrary, they have contributed brilliantly to their exploration.[71] Nevertheless, it has not yet been seen that here lies the answer to the questions which defy treatment on the level of literary criticism.

6. Conclusion

Our own position with regard to the various issues has been intimated on the occasion of their emergence. We shall now bring the scattered remarks into focus by recalling an early study by Wensinck on the subject of cosmological symbolism.[72] Wensinck had seen that each New Year is

[71] Cf. Leonard Rost, "Sinaibund und Davidsbund," *Theologische Literaturzeitung,* LXXII (Leipzig, 1947). For the reform waves in Judah see Kraus, *Gottesdienst in Israel,* 70 ff., 82, 90. Of particular importance are the *Deuteronomium-Studien* of Gerhard von Rad, which reveal the non-Jerusalemite landed gentry as the social force behind the Deuteronomic reform (p. 43).

[72] A. J. Wensinck, "The Semitic New Year and the Origin of Eschatology," *Acta Orientalia,* I (Leiden, 1923), 158–99.

a memorial and repetition of Creation. Order is not an eternal status of things, but a transition from chaos to cosmos in time. Once created, order requires attention to its precarious existence, or it will relapse into chaos. In the New Year festivals are concentrated the cults which restore order under all its aspects: The order of the world under the rule of the creator god; the renewal of the cycle of vegetation; the foundation and restoration of the Temple; the coronation of the King and the periodic restoration of his ordering power. The drama of transition from chaos to cosmos, which draws its primary symbols from the vegetation cycles, is therefore a form that can be applied wherever a problem of order is at stake. As the principal examples of its application in the Old Testament Wensinck enumerates the story of Creation, the Exodus from Egypt and the passing through the Red Sea, the wandering in the Desert and the conquest of Canaan, the Babylonian captivity and the return from the Exile, the prophetic visions of a destruction of the world and its renewal through Yahweh. More subtly he finds the form applied to the prophetic writings with their sequence of prophecies of doom and blessedness, as well as to the figure of the Suffering Servant who emerges in triumph from humiliation. And the prophetic application of the form, finally, inspires Wensinck to the definition that "eschatology is in reality cosmology applied to the future."

While the formulations of Wensinck were frequently unprecise, his vision was admirable. From his study we can reap the enduring insight that the symbolic forms of the cosmological empires and of Israel are not mutually exclusive. Although each of the great forms has an organizing center of experience of its own, they are parts of a continuum in so far as they are linked by the identity of the order of being and existence which man experiences, on the scale of compactness and differentiation, in the course of history. Neither does the cosmological form become senseless when the organizing center of symbolization has shifted to the experience of God's revelation to man, nor does the history of the Chosen People become senseless with the advent of Christ. The ritual renewal of order, one of the symbolic elements developed within the cosmological civilizations, for instance, runs through the history of mankind from the Babylonian New Year festival, through Josiah's renewal of the Berith and the sacramental renewal of the sacrifice of Christ, to Machiavelli's *ritornar ai principij*, because the fall from the order of being, and the return to it, is a fundamental problem in human existence. Once the adequate expression for an experience of order has been developed within the cosmological form, it does not disappear from history when divine revelation becomes the organizing center of symbolic form. For within the historical form created we must distinguish between the area of experience which is more immediately affected by revelation and the much larger area which remains relatively unaffected. The relation between God and man requires new symbols for its adequate expression, such as the *dabar* (the word of God), the *nabi* (the revealer of the word), the *berith* (the covenant), the *da'ath* (the knowledge of God), and so forth. But the conditions of existence in the world, such as the celestial and vegetational cycles, birth and death, the rhythm of the generations, the work to sustain life, the necessity of governmental organization, remain what they were and do not require new symbolization. A large part of the cosmological symbolism will therefore be received into the historical form, though that transmission without transformation is liable to produce tensions within the new symbolic form. We have noted the conflicts of this type in the tension between Sinai Covenant and David Covenant.

In the light of these observations, the irruption of the "oriental myth" into the "order of Israel" will appear more intelligible and less disturbing than it does in the debate on the Psalms. We must realize that what we briefly call the "order of Israel" is the history of a society, held together by a core of ethnical identity and the forming power of the Sinaitic revelation. Within the course of its history, now, the order of that society has undergone remarkable changes. It was originally created by the Sinai Covenant. And the Berith was somewhat extraordinary under the aspect of order, for it provided for the right relation between God and man, as well as for the relations between the members of the Chosen People, but made no provision whatsoever for a governmental organization that would secure the existence of the people in the power field of pragmatic history. This gap was now filled by the organization of David's conquest in the wake of the Philistine wars. And since the symbolism emanating from the Covenant center had not extended beyond the range just indicated, the cosmological symbolism poured into the vacuum left by the Covenant.

This problem of the vacuum left by the Covenant must not be glossed over by the language of a genuinely Israelite order that emanated from the Sinai Covenant, and of foreign elements that entered with David's kingship. For such a distinction, perhaps motivated by theological or "religious" concerns, implies that the Covenant provided a complete order for a society. The conditions of existence in the world, which in fact were sorely disregarded in the Covenant order, would then be considered factors of reality which can be changed in such a manner that the existence of a society under the Covenant, and nothing but the Covenant, will become historically possible. If we take that position, however, we have introduced the prophetic vision of a new mankind in a realm of peace into the premises of our interpretation. And that is impermissible in a critical philosophy of order and history.

Hence, we shall deal with the Psalms under the aspect not of an intrusion of "oriental" elements into the existent order of Israel but of the completion, through governmental institutions, of an order that was about to cease to exist because the conditions of existence had as yet not found their place in the order of revelation. These institutions were provided by the Davidic Empire, and their symbolism is consequently as much a part of the complete order of "Israel" as is the Covenant. We shall speak, therefore, of the "imperial symbolism" and, in so far as that symbolism can be found in them, of the "imperial Psalms." This terminology will have to take precedence of such categories as the "Royal Psalms," which have their origin in literary criticism. All other questions, important as they are in their own right, will be considered secondary to the function which the symbols have in the imperial sector of Israelite order. The fact, for instance, that the symbolism of Empire and Kingship is cosmological in nature must be accepted as a matter of course, since a king like the other nations had was the supplement to the Covenant order which Israel not only wanted but badly needed in order to survive. The question of Egyptian, Babylonian, and Ugaritic parallels is of minor interest, because the symbolism has its origin not in literature but in the exigencies of imperial existence in the world. The much debated question whether the Enthronement Songs really have their function in a cult of the monarchy becomes less burning because a symbolic ramification more or less does not affect the principle of the matter. The presumption will be that imperial symbols have their origin in the imperial order, unless the sources clearly indicate another place. The following selection of representative examples from the Psalms can, therefore, be brief. They have only to demonstrate the appearance of the cosmological symbolism within the order of Israel, in preparation for the study of the ensuing conflicts.

The indigenous Israelite problems of the imperial symbolism begin *after* the fusion of the Sinaitic order with the Davidic kingship. On the one hand, the symbols exert the pressure of their cosmological compactness to bring Israel nearer to the point where it becomes a nation like the others. On the other hand, the center of the Sinaitic revelation exerts pressure to differentiate the compact meaning of the symbols so that they will fit into the historical form. On this differentiating power of the historical form we must reflect in conclusion, because it has strongly affected the meaning of the Psalms. The opening phrase of the Enthronement Songs, the *Yahweh malak,* will illustrate the problem.

The *Yahweh malak* (*e.g.,* Ps. 93) is translated by the King James Version summarily as "The Lord reigneth!"—and the translation is not wrong. Nevertheless, the original meaning has to be rendered as "Yahweh has become King!", right here and now in the cult of Yahweh's enthronement which the faithful in the time of the monarchy attended. Nobody can say, however, to what extent the phrase in the perfect tense was loaded, for the attendants of the cult, with the differentiated understanding that "Yahweh has become King!" in the ritual renewal of his cosmic rule, because "Yahweh is King!" in eternity. The symbols are compact indeed, and they carry the meaning of a divine force that is both eternally beyond the world and, in a rhythm of defeat and victory, within the world. Moreover, the rule in eternity cannot only differentiate from the compact meaning but separate from it entirely. The average reader of the King James Version will hardly have heard of the "cult-functional conception" of the Psalms and be blissfully unaware of the original cult meaning of the *Yahweh malak.* And, finally, nobody can say with certainty at which point in the history of Israel the *Yahweh malak* in the sense of a present rule of the God over his Chosen People has begun to taste bitter on the tongue of the singer who suffered the misfortunes of Judaite history, and out of despair arose the hope that someday Yahweh would be really the king of his people in a perfect realm of peace. That would be the point at which the ritual renewal of Yahweh's rule in the cosmological sense began to shift into the eschatological hope of a restoration of order, never in need of renewal, at the end of time.

The connection between cosmology and eschatology was seen by Wensinck and expressed in such formulas as: eschatology is "a cosmogony of the future." [73] Mowinckel made the connection the main issue of his *Psalmenstudien II,* which bears the subtitle "The Enthronement Festival of Yahweh and the Origin of Eschatology." He summarized his results

[73] *Ibid.,* 170. Cf. the previously quoted formula, *ibid.,* 198.

in the following two theses: (1) The contents of eschatology stems from the cultic Enthronement Festival; and (2) eschatology has developed by moving into an indeterminate future what originally were the immediate consequences, realized in the course of the year, of the annual enthronement of Yahweh.[74] The realm of God, originally a cultic presence to be renewed every year, has finally become the eschatological realm of God at the end of days.[75] Wensinck, while he had seen the connection, did not touch the question why anybody should "apply cosmology to the future" and thereby produce eschatology. Mowinckel went one step further and described what happened to the cosmological symbols as their "historization," but he did not explore the question why the myth was historized in Israel but not elsewhere.[76] Gerhard von Rad, finally, with his unerring sensitiveness for problems, warned against the language of "historization," because history is in Israel a primary factor.[77] We can now formulate the problem as the unfolding of meanings implied in the compact symbols when they enter the historical form of Israel. When the revelation of the transcendent God has become the experiential center of order and symbolization, the transcendental implications of the compact symbols are set free; and correspondingly the volume of meaning in the symbols shrinks until the ritual renewal of order in time becomes a prefiguration of its ultimate restoration in eternity.

§ 6. The Imperial Symbolism

The symbolism of the imperial order is an amalgamate of Yahwist with cosmological symbols drawn from the Canaanite environment, as well as from the neighboring imperial orders. With regard to the principal source of Israelite imperial institutions, liturgies, and coronation rituals, opinions are shifting, parallel with the increasing knowledge of the surrounding civilizations, from Babylonian and Egyptian to Ugaritic. More recently the understandable enthusiasm for Ugaritic sources has encountered the warning of Gray: "It has been too freely assumed that the Hebrew kingship was modelled on a Canaanite prototype."[78] For king-

[74] Mowinckel, *Psalmenstudien II*, 226.
[75] On the realm of God as cultic presence cf. *ibid.*, 213.
[76] *Ibid.*, 214.
[77] Von Rad, *Das Formgeschichtliche Problem des Hexateuchs*, 20.
[78] John Gray, "Canaanite Kingship in Theory and Practice," *Vetus Testamentum*, II (1952), 219.

ship in Canaan had long been reduced to the rule of commandants of mercenary troops, a process that is visible even in the Amarna Letters; and the royal personnel recruited itself largely from a non-Semitic class of military professionals.[79] Canaanite kingship, far from illuminating Israelite institutions, will become more understandable in its turn through the process in which Israelite kingship came into existence in the transition from Saul to David.[80] And Alt flatly asserts that Egyptian traditions seem to have been the principal source of the imperial claim of the Davidic dynasty, especially in the time of Solomon.[81]

In order to find our bearings among the changing opinions, we shall distinguish between sources in the literary and the experiential sense. As far as literary derivations are concerned, the question of sources is of minor interest in the present context, for the reasons set forth in the preceding section. The affinities with neighboring symbolisms become of importance, however, when they betray an experiential relation with the neighboring order whose symbols are adopted—be that relation one of compromise, emulation, or opposition. In § 4 of this chapter, on "David and Jerusalem," we have studied the compromise between Yahwism and the Jebusite symbolism. In the present section we shall start from the reception of Egyptian symbols, because they betray an emulation of Egyptian order. This relation is of special interest, as we have adumbrated in § 5, because it is at variance with the Mosaic opposition to Egypt.

We have spoken of the prophetic institution of kingship as the point of confluence of Yahwist and cosmological symbols. In the Nathan episode of II Samuel 7 Yahweh promised to David (7:12–16):

> When your days are finished,
> and you are laid with your father,
> I will raise up your heir after you,
> who shall be born of your body;
> and I will establish his kingdom. . . .
>
> I will be his father,
> and he shall be my son. . . .
> Your house and your kingdom shall be confirmed before me forever;
> for all time your throne shall be established.

[79] *Ibid.*, 218.   [80] *Ibid.*, 220.
[81] Albrecht Alt, "Das Koenigtum in den Reichen Israel und Juda," *Vetus Testamentum*, I, 18 ff. The same opinion is advanced in Kraus, *Gottesdienst in Israel*, 72, n. 125 and 77, n. 134, making allowance for the Jebusite elements of Jerusalem.

The formula "I will be his father, and he shall be my son," followed by the promise of everlasting rule, echoes the Pyramid Texts 1a-b and 4a-b:

> This is my son, my first born . . .
> This is my beloved with whom I have been satisfied

and:

> This is my beloved, my son;
> I have given the horizons to him, that he may be powerful over
> them like Harachte.[82]

While the kingship, according to the Nathan tradition, was instituted by a "word of Yahweh," there can be no doubt that it was conceived on the Egyptian model.

As far as the Judaite kings were concerned, the symbolism could not fail to induce a sense of imperial superiority when dealing with surrounding enemies. This imperial consciousness was well expressed in the stanzas of Psalm 2. The first stanza voices the astonishment that anybody should dare to assume a hostile attitude at all:

> Why do the nations conspire
>   and the peoples mutter in vain?
> The kings of the earth set themselves,
>   and the rulers take counsel together,
>   against Yahweh and his Messiah:
> "Let us break their bonds asunder,
> and fling away their cords from us."

Such seditious roaring and conspiring was futile. For, as the second stanza explains:

> He that sits in the heavens laughs,
>   the Lord has them in derision.
> Then he will speak to them in his wrath,
>   and affright them in his sore anger:
> "I have established my king
> upon Zion, my holy mountain."

---

[82] The Pyramid Texts quoted are of importance in the present context as well as for the relation between Mosaic and Egyptian symbolism that will be treated in Chapter 12, § 2, 1. Since Kurt Sethe's translation in *Uebersetzung und Kommentar zu den altaegyptischen Pyramidentexten* begins only with *Spruch 213*, and Mercer's English translation has met with critical misgivings, I have had the correctness of Mercer's translations in these particular instances confirmed by an Egyptologist. I am indebted for this kindness to Dr. Ursula Heckel of the Aegyptologische Seminar in Munich.

Then, in the third stanza, the King himself informs us about the source of his assurance:

> Let me tell of the decree—
> Yahweh said unto me: "You are my son,
> > This day I have begotten you.
> Ask of me, and I will make the nations your heritage,
> > and the ends of the earth your possession.
> You shall break them with a rod of iron;
> > you shall dash them in pieces like a potter's vessel."

The words in quotation marks probably have preserved the text of a coronation liturgy used by the Davidic dynasty. On the day of the accession the king was adopted by Yahweh as his son. And the divine promises made on the occasion were quite as cosmic as those of the Egyptian sun-god to his son, the Pharaoh. Moreover, the coronation ritual only executed the "decree," that is, the divine-cosmic order. Hence, the fourth stanza could well admonish the foolhardy rulers:

> Now therefore, ye kings, be wise;
> > be admonished, ye judges of the earth.
> Serve Yahweh with fear,
> > kiss his feet with trembling,
> lest he be angry and ye perish in the way,
> > for his wrath is quickly kindled.

Yahweh is no longer the god of Israel but the divine world ruler, who establishes order among mankind through his son, the King from the house of David. In this role, as the King of Glory, Yahweh appears in the antiphonic liturgy of Psalm 24:7–10, perhaps used on a New Year's festival when the ark re-entered the sanctuary to renew the rule of Yahweh over the world:

> Lift up your heads, O gates!
> > And be lifted up, O ancient doors,
> > that the King of Glory may come in!
>
> "Who is the King of Glory?"
> > "Yahweh, strong and mighty,
> > Yahweh, mighty in battle."
>
> Lift up your heads, O gates!
> > And be lifted up, O ancient doors,
> > that the King of Glory may come in!

> "Who, then, is the King of Glory?"
> "Yahweh of the hosts,
> he is the King of Glory."

Other Psalms stress the justice of the world ruler, rather than his glory, as does Psalm 97:1–2:

> Yahweh has become king! let the earth rejoice! . . .
> Righteousness and justice are the foundations of his throne.

And Psalm 99 construes the parallel between Yahweh's world rule and the earthly establishment of justice through the King: [83]

> Yahweh has become king! let the people tremble!
> He sits enthroned upon the Cherubim; let the earth quake! . . .
>
> Might of the king, lover of justice,
> you have established equity,
> you have wrought justice and righteousness in Jacob! . . . .

Yahweh had assumed a new form as the god of a cosmological empire. In this capacity he attracted to himself, from Egypt and Babylon, elements of cosmogonic symbolism. Psalm 93, for instance, presents him as the ruler of a firmly established cosmos:

> Yahweh has become king! he is clothed with majesty.
> Yahweh is clothed, he is girded with strength.
> Yes, the world is established; it shall not be moved.
> Your throne is established from old.
> You are from everlasting.

But under this world, established from old and forever, one still can hear roaring the waters of the chaos from which order had been wrested:

> The floods have lifted up, O Yahweh,
> The floods have lifted up their voice,
> The floods lift up their roaring.
> Above the voices of many waters,
> The mighty waves of the sea,
> Yahweh on high is mighty.

From the struggle with the waters of chaos Yahweh emerges victorious; and the earth that has been ritually re-created sings its new song of joy to the creator as in Psalm 96:

---

[83] In Psalm 99 the parallel of Yahweh and the King is overlaid by additional content in such a manner that the second member of the parallel, the King, can also be construed as meaning Yahweh.

> Sing to Yahweh a new song;
> sing to Yahweh, all the earth;
> sing to Yahweh, bless his name.

This is the Psalm in which Yahweh is introduced as the highest of all gods and the creator of the heavens:

> For great is Yahweh, and greatly to be praised;
> He is to be feared above all the gods;
> For all the gods of the peoples are nonentities.
> But Yahweh made the heavens;
> Honor and majesty are before him;
> Strength and beauty are in his sanctuary.

While the assignment of precise dates to the single Psalms is impossible except in rare instances, the general assumption will be justified that the time of the imperial Yahweh was a period of heightened receptiveness for the hymn literature of the neighboring imperial civilizations. The results of the foreign influences were sometimes unusual. Psalm 19, for instance, adapted a Babylonian hymn to the sun-god Shamash (19:1–6) and combined it with an authentically Israelite praise of the torah (19:7–10), so that in the aggregate the Psalm praises God as revealed in both the cosmos and the law. But in other instances a magnificent new hymn has resulted from the combination of Babylonian with Egyptian elements, as in the famous Psalm 104 with its leanings toward a sun-hymn of Akhenaton. Of particular importance for the present context, however, was the infiltration of the cosmological style into the imagery of royal rule, as it appeared in Psalm 72:

> Give the king your justice, O God,
> And your righteousness to the king's son,
> That he may judge your people with righteousness,
> And your afflicted with justice!
>
> .   .   .   .
>
> May he live while the sun endures,
> And as long as the moon, through all generations!
> May he descend like rain upon the mown grass,
> Like showers that water the earth!
> In his days may the righteous flourish,
> and peace abound till the moon be no more!
>
> .   .   .   .
>
> For he delivers the needy when he calls,
> And the poor, and him who has no helper.

He has pity on the poor and the needy,
    And the lives of the needy will he save.
From oppression and violence he redeems their life,
    And precious is their blood in his sight.

Yahweh had become the *summus deus* of a cosmological empire, while Israel had merged into an empire people under a Pharaonic mediator from the house of David. The order of the Covenant, to be sure, had not been abolished; but the beauty of the Psalms must not deceive us about the change which the order of Israel had undergone since the Confederacy of Deborah's time. A tension had been created through the introduction of a rival experience and its symbolization that troubled the history of the Kingdom to its end. And for the Davidic and Solomonic period, at least, it is justifiable to speak of a decomposition of the old Yahwist order.

Nevertheless, the Psalms have an importance far beyond that of symptoms of the new tension in the order of the Kingdom. Our selection of examples not only maps out the topics of imperial symbolism but also conveys the future development with which they abound. For the imperial Psalms were included in the hymnbook of the Second Temple, not as souvenirs of a dead past, but as the expression of Messianic hope. As the Davidic Empire had emerged from Israel and gained a life of its own, so from the Davidic Empire emerged the symbol of the Lord's Anointed, of Yahweh's Messiah, with a life of its own. The fading memories of the mundane climax could be filled with new substance from the eschatological hopes for a spiritual savior king who would deliver Israel forever from the tribulations by its enemies. To be sure, as Martin Buber has seen rightly, that was still the great fall from existence as a Chosen People in the historical present under its God, but certainly it also was one step closer to a humanity in the historical present under Christ. From the first century before the Christian Era there is extant a collection of hymns, under the title of the Psalms of Solomon. Psalm 17, written after the conquest of Jerusalem by Pompey in 54 B.C., has preserved the last phase of the Messianic hope in its Davidic, pre-Christian form: [84]

> See to it, O Lord, and raise up unto them their king, the son of
> David,

[84] R. H. Charles (ed.), *The Apocrypha and Pseudepigrapha of the Old Testament in English*, II, *Pseudepigrapha* (Oxford, 1913), 647–51. The following quotations in the text have been slightly altered in the light of the translation by Paul Riessler in *Altjuedisches Schrifttum ausserhalb der Bibel* (Augsburg, 1928).

> At the time that you choose, O God,
> That he may reign over Israel, your servant.

The actions of the Davidic redeemer are anticipated in the very phraseology of the imperial Psalms:

> He shall destroy the pride of the sinner as a potter's vessel,
> With a rod of iron he shall break in pieces all their substance.

But the result of his actions will be a sanctified people, a community of the
sons of God:

> And he shall gather together a holy people,
>   whom he shall lead in righteousness.
> And he shall judge the tribes of the people,
>   that has been sanctified by the Lord his God.
> And he shall not suffer unrighteousness to lodge anymore in their
>   midst.
>   Nor shall there dwell with them any man that knoweth
>   wickedness,
>   For he shall know them, that they are all sons of their God.

The imperial symbolism flickered for the last time in the Messianic
hopes of the Solomon Psalms. Then it was extinguished by the theology of
the Epistle to the Hebrews. The author of Hebrews returned to the
original "I will be his father, and he shall be my son" of II Samuel 7:14, as
well as to the related passage in Psalm 2:7, but he eliminated the institutional implications of the Nathan vision. The Son of God, the Messiah of
Yahweh, was no longer the head of a Judaite clan; and the cosmic god no
longer presided over a mundane empire. The house of David had been
transformed into the house of God the Father, to be built with man as the
material, by the Son.

CHAPTER 10

The End of Israel's Worldly Existence

§ 1. THE DIVIDED KINGDOMS

The revolt of Israel against Solomon's successor marked the end of the Davidic Empire. It was never to be restored. The northern part, comprising ten tribes, organized itself as the Kingdom of Israel. It lasted until 721 B.C., when it fell to the Assyrians. The southern part, comprising the tribe of Judah and the region of Jerusalem, continued as the Kingdom of Judah, under David's dynasty, to its final destruction by the Babylonians in 586 B.C.[1]

Israel maintained its independent organization for more than two centuries. The newly won independence, however, did not bear fruit in a great political form. Even if allowance is made for a considerable amount of sources suppressed and destroyed by Judaite historians, it remains unlikely, in view of the known course of events, that a major symbolic literature has been lost. The Kingdom of Israel, to be sure, had its fleeting moments of glory, but the disorder of political existence was so profound that a stable form could hardly rise above the convulsions of war, murderous changes of dynasties, and social unrest. The worldly existence of Israel was drawing to its end. In the much smaller Southern Kingdom, where no allowance for the destruction of sources need be made, the symbolic landscape was equally arid during the two centuries. The symbolism of the Davidic kingship continued; but no noteworthy developments seem to have taken place.

Nevertheless, the period was not barren at all. It teemed with literary activity. This was the age in which Israelite intellectual and literary culture began to flourish. The David Memoirs received their final form and were given to the public. The songs and antiquities of Israel were col-

[1] At the time only eleven tribes were counted: I Kings 11:29-39.

lected in the Book of Yashar and the Book of the Wars of Yahweh. The Royal Annals and Temple Records from the time of David and Solomon were continued; and they furnished the source materials for unofficial historical enterprises such as the Book of the Acts of Solomon. To a Book of the Acts of the Kings of Israel we owe the important sections in Kings on the fate of the Omride dynasty and on Jehu. The Yahwist and Elohist schools of historiography sprang into existence. The first law code, the Book of the Covenant, was collected and organized in written form. The prophetic revolt of the ninth century found its literary expression in the Elijah and Elisha stories. The first great "writing prophets," Amos (*ca.* 750) and Hosea (*ca.* 745–735), flourished toward the end of the period. And even the early years of Isaiah (from *ca.* 738 onward) still fell within its range.

As far as the distribution of the literary outburst over Israel and Judah is concerned, the Northern Kingdom seems to have had the greater share. That is hardly surprising. In spite of the passing ascendancy of Judah in the Empire, Israel was still the Chosen People of Yahweh. Israel was the ferment of history, not Judah; and the Northern Kingdom, furthermore, was much richer, more numerous in population, and more powerful than the southern late-comer to the expanding nation. That the capital of the Empire, with its court society and administrative personnel, remained with Judah did not seriously weight the balance against the spiritual and political preponderance of the North. For Jerusalem was at the time still the "city of David"; and Solomon's Temple was a royal chapel. Neither the city nor the sanctuary had yet the importance which it gained in the second half of the seventh century, through Josiah's reform and the monopoly of sacrifices. At any rate, the prophetic revolt of the ninth century occurred in the Northern Kingdom; the Book of the Covenant was a northern production; Hosea was an Israelite prophet; and even the Judaite Amos chose Beth-El in Israel as the place for his short public activity.

Behind the literary flowering there was a movement of experiences in search of expression; and the experiences pointed toward a communal order under Yahweh beyond the mundane existence of either Israel or Judah. The analysis of this class of experiences and their symbolic expression will occupy us in the present section. Before entering on it, however, we must consider certain formal aspects of the process in which Israel, while losing its existence as a power in pragmatic history, became a greater power in the order of mankind. The problem of Israel's continuity and identity that had intruded itself in the preceding section must now receive some further clarification.

The first formal aspect to be considered is the combination, in Israelite history, of intensive with lateral growth. On the scale of civilizational intensity Israel grew from a clan society on the nomad level to an imperial nation with a rational administrative and military organization, as well as a differentiated intellectual and literary culture. At the same time it expanded laterally from a nucleus of Hebrew clans to an empire people with a fairly homogeneous civilization, through absorption of both the Canaanites and Judah. This process, moving in two directions at once, endangered the proportionate growth of Israelite society. The infiltration of the Hebrew clans west of the Jordan had, through amalgamation with the Canaanites, led to the formation of a new society with enough national coherence, by the eleventh century, to conduct common wars against Midianites and Philistines, to organize itself under a king, and to develop even such expressions of national consciousness as the bands of ecstatic prophets. Whereas this first phase of growth, to be sure, had seriously impaired the pristine purity of the Yahwist order, the various manifestations of syncretism had not endangered the mundane existence of Israel. The Canaanites apparently were well digested, and they even added to the strength of Israel in pragmatic politics. In the second phase the dangers of rapid growth became unmistakable. By ways no longer traceable in detail Judah had been drawn into the national orbit of Israel during the reign of Saul. And this second increase of pragmatic power could no longer be digested organizationally—Israel, as part of the united kingdom, had to submit to a foreign dynasty. In the third phase, organizational freedom of a sort had been regained at the price of withdrawal from the Empire. But on the cultural level the growth of Israel continued with unbroken vitality, in both the Northern and Southern kingdoms. The impulses imparted by the luxurious and humanistic rule of Solomon, by the administrative and temple scribes of an imperial civilization, by the increased literacy of a well-to-do upper class, by the consequent literary activity of private persons who wrote court memoirs and survey histories of the reign, did not lose their effectiveness with the end of the Empire. On the contrary, they set moving the massive literary production that we have briefly sketched. While in the realm of organization for action the growth of the people had suffered a severe setback, a literary dimension had been acquired in which Israelites and Judaites could move in common in spite of their political separation. And in that dimension the expansion and unification of the people, including the southerners, advanced. The cultural absorption of Judah was so successful, indeed, that in the literary construction of Israel's pre-Davidic history the Yahwist school of the south preceded the northern Elohists.

By means of a common literature historians and prophets created an Israel that could survive in Judah even after the ethnic Israel had disappeared from history. This ultimate transformation brings to our attention the second formal aspect of Israel's growth. There is a pattern of death and survival running through Israelite history. That is not surprising in itself, for every growth, to be sure, is the death of the phases outgrown. The growth of the Chosen People, however, left a peculiar paradigmatic trail in history. The forms of existence superseded by further growth did not sink back into a dead past, but survived as symbolic forms. From the original Yahwist Confederacy that had occupied Canaan emerged the charismatic kingship of Saul. The old theopolity had to be replaced by a more effective organization of the people. But its symbolism, the Kingdom of God, remained a living force—so forcefully living indeed that the symbol of God's *mamlakah* motivated the further symbolism of a theocracy, that is, of a political organization adjusted to the exigencies of the original theopolitical idea. From the charismatic kingship, then, emerged under the pressure of the Philistine wars the Davidic Empire. Again the older forms of existence had been organizationally outgrown, but again the symbolisms of theopolity and theocracy survived with such strength that a further symbol, through the extension of the berith idea, had to be created so as to include the house of David in the system. And with the breakdown of David's organization that new component of the symbolism did not disappear either, but became the starting point for the Messianic idea with its long chain of metamorphoses ending in Christ the Messiah. From the Davidic Empire, finally, emerged the Kingdoms of Israel and Judah. And during the period of this further organizational adjustment, the surviving older symbols proved, in the revolt of the ninth century, strong enough to check the politics of the Omride dynasty and to prepare the growth of an Israel beyond the troubles of political organization. The sequence of symbols on occasion of organizational changes certainly falls into a pattern. It looks as if it had been the destiny of Israel, during the short five centuries of its pragmatic existence, to create an offspring of living symbols and then to die.

The word "destiny" as just used signifies the meaning which the order of an existent has in relation to its own lasting and passing, as well as in relation to the order of mankind in historical existence. No romantic connotations should be evoked by the term. Such mysteries as there really attach to the destiny of Israel are profound beyond penetration and at the same time flat on the surface of facts.

The first of the mysteries is the conspiracy of historical contingencies with the survival of meaningful order. In that respect the destiny of Israel is indeed peculiar in so far as it found in Judah, with its meteoric rise from nonexistence to political rivalry and cultural equality, the partner that could develop the inheritance with brilliance and authority after the demise of the older people. Even so the success of survival was achieved by a hair's breadth. If Jerusalem had fallen to the Assyrian power in 721 together with the Northern Kingdom, the upper class of the one southern tribe would have disappeared in the Asiatic hinterland as deeply as that of the ten northern tribes, leaving no more memory than they. The contingency of Jerusalem's escape in 721 granted the breathing space, until 586, in which the national substance of Judah grew firm enough to survive the Exile.

Even historical contingencies, however, could not have secured the survival of Israel in its symbols unless there had been something worth transmitting. That is the second of the mysteries attaching to the destiny of Israel: Here was a people that began its existence in history with a radical leap in being; and only after the people had been constituted by that initial experience did it acquire, in the course of centuries, a mundane body of organization to sustain itself in existence. This sequence, reversing the ordinary course of social evolution, is unique in history. It is so unbelievable that positivist historians, as for instance Eduard Meyer, do not believe it at all; while even more sensitive historians, as sensitive for instance as Adolphe Lods, have difficulties in adhering to their own belief when it comes to such a crucial test as admitting the possibility that the Decalogue of Exodus 20 is really Mosaic in content (though not in form), and not a late Deuteronomist creation. A society is supposed to start from primitive rites and myths, and thence to advance gradually, if at all, to the spirituality of a transcendent religion; it is not supposed to start where a respectable society has difficulties even ending. Nevertheless, the mystery of Israel's start at the wrong end of evolution must be accepted, the progressivist thesis that first things come always first notwithstanding. In this one case the sequence actually was reversed; and the reversal was the cause of Israel's extraordinary creativity in the realm of symbols. For the disorderly beginning of existence with a leap in being provided the experiential motivations for the people to respond to its gradual descent into Sheol with the creation of symbols that would preserve its attunement with transcendent being on each new level of mundane involvement. Each step of further adjustment to the pragmatic conditions of existence had to be measured by the standards of the initial existence as the Chosen People under God. The result was something in the nature of a model experiment in the creation of symbols of mundane existence under the conditions of an already enacted leap in being.

In the ninth century, the exigencies of the power game brought the experiment to an end. The diplomacy of the Omrides had to compromise with the cosmological order of the surrounding powers to such a degree that a solution to the problem could no longer be found within the range of Yahwist symbols. At the risk of destroying the conditions of Israel's mundane existence, the response had to be a revolutionary return to the origins. The archaic Israel reasserted itself in the political revolt of Elijah, Elisha, and the Rechabites. On the level of pragmatic history the movement was a ruinous reaction that broke all hopes for a recovery of Israelite power; on the spiritual level, however, it preserved Israel from sinking insignificantly into a morass of ephemeral success.

On the following pages we shall first sketch the pragmatic situation that faced Israel with the dilemma of spiritual or worldly suicide. We shall then deal with the Book of the Covenant as our principal source for the general mood of discontent with the internal development of Israelite society, and finally with the revolt against the Omride dynasty.

§ 2. The Pragmatic Situation

When Israel withdrew from the Empire, Judah was left in possession of the capital, its administration, and the Davidic dynasty, and continued to exist with a minimum of internal difficulties. The Israelites themselves, however, were faced with the task of organizing themselves as a state. It was a throwback to pre-imperial times; and the social forces that could be observed at work in the rise of David to kingship were released to find a new balance. Jeroboam, the first king, belonged to the tribe of Ephraim. The struggle of the clans for control of the kingship was renewed.[2] Jeroboam's son, Nadab, lasted only two years. He was assassinated by Baasha, from Issachar, the founder of the next dynasty, whose son Elah was also assassinated after a reign of only two years. With the end of the Baashide dynasty the role of the army became more marked. Elah was murdered by an ambitious officer, Zimri, one of the two generals of the war chariots. But the new king had apparently acted without securing the consent of his superior officers. The commander in chief, Omri, marched on the capital; and Zimri died in the flames of the palace after a reign of only seven days. Omri, who because of his position must be assumed to have been a member of the murdered king's clan, became the founder of the next dynasty, but had to fight for four years against Tibni, another pretender who had wide support. The domestic and foreign policy of the Omride dynasty (886–841), finally, brought into play the forces of the archaic Israel that had caused the difficulties and the undoing of David's Empire. The movement found its royal executor in one of the generals, Jehu, who exterminated the Omrides and founded his own dynasty (841–747). The following years of brief regimes and civil wars ended with the Assyrian Conquest in 721.[3]

The split of the Empire reduced both Israel and Judah to the same rank of minor powers as their neighbors. For the time being a reconstruction was impossible, since both kingdoms regarded each other as usurpers and were engaged in continuous warfare during the first two dynasties of Israel. The bitterness was so great that neither of the two antagonists hesitated to enter into alliances with the Arameans in order

---

[2] Alt, "Das Koenigtum in den Reichen Israel und Juda," *Vetus Testamentum*, I, stresses the factor of charismatic leadership in the beginnings of the Northern Kingdom. After the experience with the Davidic dynasty, the independent Israel wanted to return to the model of Saul's charismatic kingship (pp. 4 f.; 7–9). I hesitate to accept this interpretation without qualifications. While it is true that the memory of Saul's kingship may have furnished a contributive motive in the overthrow of the first two dynasties, the brief accounts in I Kings do not refer to a particular charisma of Jeroboam or Baasha. Moreover, the dynasties had to be formed, through succession of the son to the father, before they could be overthrown. And the sources reveal no antidynastic motive on the occasion of either the succession or the overthrow. It seems to be preferable, therefore, to put the accent on the fact that the throne of the new kingdom was free to be taken by the strongest competitor.

[3] The dates for this period are taken from the note on "The Chronology of the Regal Period," in Robinson, *A History of Israel*, I, 454–64.

to gain a passing advantage. The worst, however, was that the wars among the states of the Syriac area had already to be conducted in the shadow of the reviving great powers in Egypt and Mesopotamia. The opportunity for an indigenous organization of Syria and Palestine, as it had opened around 1200 B.C., was rapidly passing. In "the fifth year of Rehoboam" Egypt invaded the area, Jerusalem was taken and plundered, and the campaign seems to have extended into Israel and along the coast to the Phoenician cities.

While the Egyptian invasion was a military foray without lasting political consequences, there was perhaps more to it than the tantalizingly fragmentary sources permit to discern with any certainty. We must indicate its probable implications for the understanding of Israelite history—with the reservation, however, that no more than the barest surmises are possible.

Jeroboam, the founder of the first dynasty of Israel, had been an administrative official under Solomon. What exactly he did to rouse the King's suspicion we do not know. But he received word from a prophet that he was to be the future king of Israel (I Kings 11:26–39), and he had the fatal attraction for "worthless fellows" which in Israel marked the pretenders for kingship (II Chron. 13:6–7). He escaped murder at Solomon's order by seeking and receiving asylum in Egypt (I Kings 11:40). When Solomon had died he returned to Israel and became the leader of the revolt against Rehoboam. A generation earlier, a similar story had been told about Hadad, the young prince of Edom who escaped David's conquest and massacre of his people. He too found refuge in Egypt, married an Egyptian princess, and after David's death returned to Edom and established himself, apparently with success (I Kings 11:14–22). The Pharaoh, it would seem, as well as the rulers in the Delta (the personalities on the Egyptian side are uncertain), kept a hand in Asiatic politics, even though the hand moved remotely now compared with the time of the Amarna Letters. The third story of such contacts concerned Solomon himself. He "became allied to Pharaoh king of Egypt by marriage" (I Kings 3:1), and the Egyptian princess was the political gem of his harem.

At this point, however, the sources become so reticent that there can be hardly a doubt about extensive suppression of the Egyptian aspects of Solomon's reign. Royal marriages were an important instrument of domestic and foreign politics. In order to fulfill their purpose of consolidating the king's power, the foreign women had to be treated with courtesy and in particular their religious preferences had to be cultivated. I Kings 11 deplores Solomon's defection to the gods of his wives, and especially the building of sanctuaries for the Sidonian Ashtarte, the Ammonite Milcom, and the Moabite Chemosh. "And so he did for all his foreign wives, who burned incense and sacrificed to their gods" (11:8). It is curious that the Egyptian princess should not be among those expressly enumerated as receiving a chapel for her god.

In search of an explanation it will be necessary to give more weight than is usually done to the rare references to "Pharaoh's daughter." I Kings 3:1 informs us that Solomon "brought her into the city of David, until he had finished the building of his house and the house of Yahweh and the wall around Jerusalem." The passage stands by itself, without elucidating context. Possibly it contains no more than a piece of factual information about the temporary quarters of the princess in the old city —though one might justly wonder why the information should have survived the centuries and been preserved in the narrative. It seems to us suggestive, however, to extract from the passage the full meaning which the text allows: that both the house of the King *and* the house of Yahweh were prepared as the environment for the princess. In that case Solomon's temple would have been the house of a Yahweh who also could be interpreted as the divinity of Pharaoh's daughter. No special reference to a sanctuary for the Egyptian wife was necessary, because the temple of Yahweh had been built for her as much as for the King. The assumption is suggestive, because the historian of Chronicles confirms that something had been going on that later generations found embarrassing. For II Chronicles 8:11 relates that

> Solomon brought up the daughter of Pharaoh from the city of David to the house which he had built for her; for he said: "No wife of mine shall dwell in the house of David king of Israel, because the places are holy, wherever the ark of Yahweh has come."

Again the passage stands by itself; but it clearly conveys the meaning that an Egyptian princess should *not* dwell where Yahweh dwelt. And this meaning is in conflict with the action related. For the ark dwelt in the city of David, where the princess dwelt as long as the temple was not finished; and the princess was moved to the new palace, where also the ark dwelt in the adjoining temple. The passage looks like an attempt to cover up the fact that Pharaoh's daughter and the ark were inseparable.

The idea gains in probability if we consider that the Davidic Empire was indeed an empire founded by a conqueror and not a Kingdom of Israel. The marriages, as well as the cult establishments in the capital, served and enhanced the position of the ruler, not the people of Israel. We remember the imperial psalms, drawing on Egyptian and Babylonian models, which symbolized the royal mediator of a cosmic Yahweh. And what we know about Solomon's Temple, with its orientation toward the rising sun, the pylons channeling the rays of the sun into the interior, the Babylonian "brazen sea" on the twelve bulls, oriented in groups of three toward the four cardinal points, and its various other equipment and decoration, looks more like a connoisseur's collection of Near Eastern cosmological symbols than like the sanctuary of the Yahweh who led his Chosen People from the Sheol of civilization into the freedom of his realm.[4] Furthermore, there must be considered the robe of the high priest, with its symbols as described in Exodus 28 and as interpreted by Philo in his *Vita Mosis*. In its colors and ornaments the robe was "a copy and imitation" of the universe,[5] so that its wearer would be "transformed from a man into the nature of the world," that he would become an "abbreviated cosmos." [6] Dressed in this robe the high priest, when ministering to God the Father, would be assisted by the Son of God, that is, by the cosmos created through the Word of God.[7] And there must be considered, finally, the words of Solomon when dedicating the Temple. The Septuagint has the fuller text in III Kings 8:53:

> The Lord has lighted [or: revealed, *egnorisen*] the sun in the heavens,
>> But declared he himself would dwell in deep darkness.
> "Build a house for me, a house splendid for yourself,
>> To dwell therein forever."

The Masoretic Text has in I Kings 8:12–13:

> Then Solomon said:
>> Yahweh has said he would dwell in deep darkness.
>> I have surely built you a house of habitation,
>> A place for you to dwell in forever.

[4] For the symbols of the Temple see Albright, *Archaeology and the Religion of Israel*, especially Chapter 5 and the bibliographical references.

[5] Philo, *Vita Mosis II*, 117 and *De specialibus legibus I*, 95 (Loeb Classical Library, *Philo*, Volumes VI and VII).

[6] Philo, *Vita Mosis II*, 135.

[7] Philo, *De specialibus legibus I*, 96. Cf. also *The Wisdom of Solomon* 18:24.

One must not press a poorly preserved text too far. Still, the very mutilation in the Masoretic Text indicates the important point that was the source of embarrassment. For the God who manifested himself by setting the sun in the heavens, while remaining himself in darkness, could hardly be anybody but the God of the Amon Hymns of Dynasty XIX, Amon the "Hidden," who was Re in face. This identification should not be understood crudely as a "reception" of Amon by Solomon, but rather as a meeting of the Yahweh who approached a cosmic divinity with the Amon whose nature was experienced as "hidden" behind all cosmic manifestations. With due precautions one can say, therefore, that Solomon's Temple, while built for Yahweh, was built for a god approximating in nature the Amon of the New Kingdom.[8]

When all is considered, the connections between the Davidic Empire and Egypt must be assumed to have been more intimate than would appear from the sources in their present state. On the court level, though not in popular cults, a *rapprochement* between Yahweh and Amon had been achieved that could well be construed from the Egyptian side as a suzerainty over Solomon's domain. When the King died, an important realignment of forces must have taken place, now covered by an unrelieved, suspicious silence. For Solomon had seven hundred wives and three hundred concubines (I Kings 11:3). Even if we make generous allowance for exaggeration, there must have been hordes of sons, one or more of them perhaps from "Pharaoh's daughter"—and we hear nothing at all about the intrigues and murders that might be expected to surround the succession. Rehoboam, the son of an Ammonite wife, followed his father as if he were the only son living. What had become of the grandsons of Pharaoh, presuming there were any? Had a nationalist court party taken matters in hand and broken the Egyptian connection? We do not know; but whatever had happened ought to have furnished ample reason for an Egyptian intervention.

Into the context of a revolt against the Egyptian influences represented by the Temple must also be placed the cult reforms of Jeroboam

---

[8] Hubert Schrade, *Der Verborgene Gott* (Stuttgart, 1949), 46 ff. draws attention to the darkness of the Debir in the Solomonic Temple as an unusual feature in the temple architecture of the time, as well as to the debate about light or darkness of the sanctuary in the poems of the Ras Shamra tablets (the relevant passages of the "Poems about Baal and Anath" can be found in Pritchard [ed.], *Ancient Near Eastern Texts*, 134). It is possible that the Phoenician debate was stirred up by the Amarna Revolt of Akhenaton with its lighting of Egyptian sanctuaries, and that the reaction accentuated darkness. But that is a matter for archaeologists to explore.

in Israel. He set up two golden bull calves, the one in Beth-El, the other in Dan, as the true gods who brought Israel up from Egypt, in rivalry with the Temple at Jerusalem (I Kings 12:26–33). These bulls, the thrones of the invisible Yahweh who is present wherever he chooses to be, were probably not a defection from Yahwism, as the Judaite historians presented the matter, but on the contrary a protest against the defection of the Temple and a return to a purer form of Yahwism. The adamant silence with regard to the Egyptian elements in Solomon's reign would have a further weighty motive if the separation of Israel had been more than a clan rivalry and expression of economic discontent, if it had been a genuine Yahwist revolt against the foreign god in the Temple. It could have been a revolt similar in motivation and structure to the Israelite revolt against the cult policy of the Omrides, to which we now must turn.

The Egyptian invasion was a disaster for the cities and peoples in its path, but it receded and was not renewed. The real danger was brewing in the East with the spasmodic increase of Assyrian power. After the expansion of the fourteenth and thirteenth centuries Assyria had been seriously reduced in power, economic wealth, and territory through the events subsequent to the fall of the Hittite Empire. The recovery under Tiglath-pileser I (1116–1093) was followed by a century and a half of wars against Aramean nomads who threatened Assyria with extinction. In 932 began the first western expansion under able rulers, carrying the wars into the area of Syria, Palestine, and Phoenicia. This was the period in which the Syriac alliance, forged by the Omrides, fought the battle of Karkar, in 853, with a measure of success, though Jehu had to pay tribute to Shalmanezer III in 841. From 782–745 the Syriac states had some peace because the less energetic Assyrian kings of this period had difficulties in warding off the rising power of Urartu. In 745, with Tiglath-pileser III, began the second great expansion toward the west; it brought the end to Israel when Samaria was conquered by Sargon II in 721.

At the time of Omri's accession to the kingship in 886, two generations of wars among the clans of Israel, aggravated by the wars against Judah in the south and the Arameans in the north, would have convinced a lesser man that energetic measures had to be taken in order to save Israel from extinction, especially since the Assyrian power was tangibly growing even if it had not yet reached out toward the seacoast.

Unfortunately most of the sources concerning the pragmatic events of the Omride period have disappeared, and what has been preserved is badly mutilated and distorted, because the dynasty did not find favor with the Judaite historians. Nevertheless, the fragments are sufficient to let us discern an attempt on the part of Omri and his son Ahab to reconstruct a major Syriac power on the Davidic model, with its center in Israel.

Omri had first to consolidate his power internally. He built a new capital in rivalry with Jerusalem. The foundation of Samaria (I Kings 16:24) was intended to create a neutral center beyond clan rivalries in the same manner in which David's Jerusalem had moved the royal residence beyond the rivalries of Israel and Judah. Moreover, his own easy conquest of the old capital Tirzah, where Zimri had entrenched himself, must have been a lesson to Omri. The new capital was built as a strong fortress, strategically located on a hill difficult of access—again emulating Jerusalem—in order to give the regime security against domestic uprisings as well as against the Aramean enemies. The kingdom was furthermore divided into administrative districts under military commanders (I Kings 20:14-15), presumably with the same intention as Solomon's administrative districts to break up the tribal organization.[9] The internal consolidation of power was then supplemented by a diplomacy of marriage alliances with Tyre and Judah. The following table will show the connections and dates:

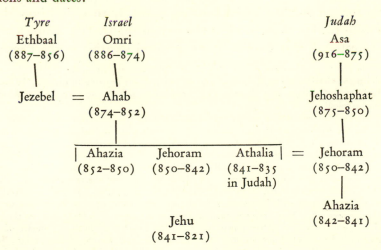

	Tyre	Israel			Judah
	Ethbaal	Omri			Asa
	(887–856)	(886–874)			(916–875)
	Jezebel =	Ahab			Jehoshaphat
		(874–852)			(875–850)
	Ahazia	Jehoram	Athalia =	Jehoram
	(852–850)	(850–842)	(841–835 in Judah)	(850–842)
					Ahazia
					(842–841)
		Jehu			
		(841–821)			

---

[9] The passage I Kings 20:14-15 suggests the coexistence of a standing army organized by administrative districts and a people's militia.

The alliance of Tyre, Israel, and Judah would have been a power of some weight indeed, strong enough to become attractive for the other peoples of the Syriac area and to form a nucleus of resistance against Assyria and Egypt. It certainly proved its value on occasion of Karkar. Whether it would have held together under the pressure of repeated Assyrian attacks, or could have been developed into a strong empire, is doubtful.[10] But the question was never put to the test because of the resistance aroused in Israel by the international form of the alliance. For the guardian of the alliance (its *baal berith*) was the Baal of Tyre on an equal footing with the Yahweh of Samaria. When the daughter of the priest-king of Ashtart came to Israel, a personal sanctuary of the Baal was not enough. The political partnership of Yahweh and Baal Melqart required an official temple of the Baal in Samaria with a public cult in which the king had to participate (I Kings 16:32–33). And the passage in II Kings 8:18 suggests that an official cult of the Baal was also organized in Jerusalem, when the alliance was extended through the marriage of the King of Judah with Ahab's daughter. On the question of whether the exchange of gods was reciprocal and Yahweh received a cult in Tyre, the sources are silent.[11] The reception of the Baal Melqart as a political god in Israel was a clear break with the idea of a theopolity of the Chosen People under Yahweh. The Solomonic sanctuaries for the foreign wives could be regretted as weaknesses of a king; and the Temple, however Egyptian it may have looked, was still a Temple of Yahweh; but now a foreign god had received public status. If Israel had been threatened with the loss of its ethnical identity in the Davidic Empire, it now was threatened with the loss of its spiritual identity in the Phoenician

[10] The power of Phoenicia, at the time very high, was rapidly waning. The great age of Phoenician colonization, from the twelfth century onward, was drawing to its end. The last great foundation was Carthage in 814. Phoenician power was actually shifting westward into the area of the colonies.

[11] Since no further sources are extant, speculations on the structure of the triple-alliance are useless. We have spoken of the "equality" of Yahweh and the Baal Melqart. Such language should mean strictly that the Baal received a public cult in Samaria by the side of the god of the country. How the relationship looked from the Phoenician side we do not know. The temples of Baal Melqart were placed in all Phoenician colonies as the politico-religious guarantee of permanent affiliation with the mother city. It must be considered as possible that the relationship with Samaria was not reciprocal. What from the Omride side was presumably considered a triple alliance with its center in Israel may well have appeared from Tyre to be the political measure of a Mediterranean thalassocracy to protect its trade routes in the Asiatic hinterland against Aramean interruptions. Ethbaal, the proud and energetic founder of a new dynasty, may have looked on Samaria as a valuable inland march of his empire. The assumption of mutuality in the relations, with a cult of Yahweh in Tyre, is reasonable in view of what we know about the Omride policy, but no more than probable.

alliance. The *raison d'état* had brought Israel to the point of losing its *raison d'être*. The revolt, both popular and prophetic, of which Jehu made himself the political and military executor broke out. Its successful conclusion entailed the extermination of the Omrides. The alliance was not only dissolved, but the former partners became bitter enemies, because the relatives of the royal houses of Tyre and Judah had been murdered.

§ 3. THE BOOK OF THE COVENANT

In the crisis of the ninth century begins the Israelite concern with the codification of the law in written form. Probably the oldest code extant is the brief collection of commands in the Yahwist (J) account of the Sinaitic legislation, in Exodus 34:17–26. Not much later but considerably more extensive is the Elohist (E) code of Exodus 20:23—23:19, commonly designated as the Book of the Covenant by modern historians.[12]

A study of the Book of the Covenant requires, first of all, a preliminary understanding of the "law" contained in it. For the code was a private undertaking. To be sure, the collection had to be organized by someone who was familiar with the law; and it is therefore reasonable to assume a priest, or a group of priests, as the codifiers. But there is no indication that the task was undertaken at the behest of the royal administration; and certainly the collection was not a statute of the realm

---

[12] The Book of the Covenant is an object of controversy with regard to (1) its literary structure and genesis, (2) the date of composition of the whole and of its parts, and (3) the origin and date of the contents of the various parts. We cannot avoid the controversial issues altogether, since several of them affect the meaning of the law book and its contents, but we shall confine the discussion in the text to the questions that have a direct bearing on our specific problems. For a fuller analysis see J. M. Powis Smith, *The Origin and History of Hebrew Law* (Chicago, 1931), as well as the literature quoted in the work. The study of Smith is not always the most penetrating, but it conveniently supports its comparisons of the Hebrew with other Oriental codes by appendixes which contain translations of the Code of Hammurabi, the Assyrian Code, and the Hittite Code. For a more judicious analysis of the relations between the Book of the Covenant and the other codes cf. Lods, *Histoire de la Littérature Hébraique et Juive*, 1950, 204–19. Lods should also be consulted for the present state of the controversy and the literature since 1931. Moreover, since the study of Smith, fragments of Babylonian codes antedating the Code of Hammurabi have been published. Their English translations, by Kramer and Goetze, can be found in Pritchard (ed.), *Ancient Near Eastern Texts*. The same collection of texts also contains new translations of the Code of Hammurabi (Meek), of the Assyrian Code (Meek), and the Hittite Code (Goetze). Of special value for the subsequent analysis in the text were Alfred Jepsen, *Untersuchungen zum Bundesbuch* (Stuttgart, 1927), and Albrecht Alt, "Die Urspruenge des Israelitischen Rechts" (1934) in *Kleine Schriften zur Geschichte des Volkes Israel*, I (Munich, 1953), 278–32.

to be enforced by the courts. There is, furthermore, no indication whether the author intended to collect the law that was in force in the Israel of the ninth century, or whether he intended to hold up a mirror of the law to an age which did not observe it. And if the latter should be the case, it would be difficult in many instances to decide whether a specific rule was old but not observed at present, or whether it was a new rule which, in the opinion of the author, should supersede a practice that had become undesirable. Hence, the problems of the book cannot be approached through a scrutiny of the single rules contained in it. We rather must start from the fact that a private person, or group of persons, suddenly displayed a burning interest in the "law" and engaged in its systematic codification.

In search of the reasons for the enterprise we find some enlightenment through Hosea, the great Israelite prophet of the eighth century. In Hosea 4:1–2 we read the following:

> Hear the word of Yahweh, O children of Israel,
>> For Yahweh has a quarrel with the inhabitants of the land.
> There is no truth, nor kindness,
>> Nor knowledge of God in the land.
> Swearing and lying, and killing and stealing, and committing adultery—
>> They break all bounds. And blood touches blood.

The offensive conduct of the people has its root in ignorance of the law of Yahweh. In 4:6 Yahweh himself complains and threatens:

> My people are destroyed for want of knowledge—
> Because you have rejected knowledge,
>> I will reject you from being my priest.
> Since you have forgotten the law of your God,
>> I likewise will forget your children.

The divine threat of destruction becomes even more intense in 8:1:

> Set the trumpet to your lips,
>> Like a watchman, against the house of Yahweh!
> For they have broken my covenant,
>> And sinned against my law.

When the covenant and the law are broken, then the people have no knowledge; and a people without knowledge of the order of God will perish, as 4:14 formulates it succinctly: "A people without insight must come to ruin." The passages in their aggregate characterize a society in spiritual and moral confusion; and in grieving over the state of confusion they develop a technical vocabulary for its description. Men are in a state of ignorance. But it is not an ordinary ignorance, in the sense of not knowing what never was learned. For the children of Israel have heard a good deal of the God whom they now do not know. The ignorance is a forgetfulness. And since God is a being not to be forgotten involuntarily, the want of knowledge is a rejection of God.

In order to appraise the meaning of Hosea's prophecies, we have to recall what appeared in the section on "The Struggle for Empire" as the difference between the Israelite and Hellenic types of symbolization. The idea of the psyche, we said, could not be fully developed in Israel because the problem of immortality remained unsolved. Life eternal was understood as a divine property; afterlife would have elevated man to the rank of the Elohim; and a plurality of elohim was excluded by the radical leap in being of the Mosaic experience. As a consequence, the eroticism of the soul that is the essence of philosophy could not unfold; and the idea of human perfection could not break the idea of a Chosen People in righteous existence under God in history. Instead of philosophy, there developed the construction of patriarchal history, a specific kind of humanism, and ultimately the apocalyptic hope for divine intervention in history.

The prophecies of Hosea reveal the limitations imposed by the initial compactness of Israelite experiences. The prophet tried to describe a society in crisis, and he found the root of the evil in the "want of knowledge" concerning matters divine. Up to this point his analysis was literally the same as Plato's in the *Republic*. Plato, as Hosea, diagnosed the evil as an ignorance of the soul, an *agnoia* concerning the nature of God. But Plato could proceed from his insight to an analysis of the right order of the soul through its attunement to the unseen measure. And he even developed the concept of "theology," in order to speak in technical language of true and false conceptions of divinity. Under the condition of the more compact experiences and symbols in Israel, Hosea could not find the answer to his problems in the attunement of the soul to the divine measure, but had to seek it in a renewed conformity of human conduct to the measure as revealed in the "word" and the "law" of God. Not the advance toward philosophy but the return to the covenant and the law was the Israelite response to the challenge of the crisis.

If the new concern about the covenant and the law is understood as the response to a crisis of mundane existence, functionally of the same type as the response through philosophy in Hellas, certain problems of Israelite history will become more intelligible. Before the ninth century we hear little of Moses and his work. To be sure, it was alive in the very existence of Israel as a theopolity under Yahweh, as well as in the oral traditions which, beginning with the ninth century, formed the raw material for historiography. Nevertheless, the events of the Mosaic period belonged to the past. The present was concerned with such pressing issues as the occupation of the promised land, the wars with Canaanites and Midianites, the growth of the new Israel in symbiosis with the inhabitants of the country, the friction between the clan society and the charismatic war leaders and kings, the wars with the Philistines, the rise of the Davidic Empire and its dissolution. Moses and the law were distinctly not topics of current interest. Only when the involvement in mundane existence had reached the impasse of the ninth century, when the *raison d'être* of Israel was at stake, did the meaning of Israel's existence become topical. Through the combined work of the historians, prophets, and code makers the meaning of Israel's existence under the revealed will of God was clarified; and the work found its center in the figure of Moses, the original prophet and lawgiver, as the instrument of God in bringing the Chosen People into existence. The prophets could reawaken the sense for the meaning of a people's existence under the will of God. The code makers could express the meaning in systematically organized rules of conduct, taking into account the conditions of the age. And the historians could ascribe the codes to Moses, until the Torah achieved the bulk of the extant Pentateuch. The three types of work— prophetic, legal, and historiographic—were inseparable in the response of Israel, and in its succession of Judah, to the crisis of mundane existence.

In the light of the foregoing reflections we shall now analyze the so-called Book of the Covenant, or rather a text whose precise limits have yet to be established. For the term "Book of the Covenant," in so far as it refers to the text of Exodus 20:23—23:19, is a concept of modern Old Testament philology, which has its good sense in the debates of higher criticism but cannot be used for our purposes. If we want to understand the concern about the "law" in the ninth and eighth centuries, we must accept the structure of the text as intended by the authors of the Biblical narrative. The Book of the Covenant in the modern philological sense does not form an independent unit of meaning, but is embedded in the Elohist account of the Berith concluded between Yahweh and his people at Mount Sinai. The account comprehends Exodus 19–24. Prophetic sensitiveness, nomoethetic skill, and historiographic imagination have joined forces to create a unit of meaning that must be treated on its own terms.

Within this body of text, in 24:8, occurs the term "Book of the Covenant" which the modern critics have used for their own purposes. As intended by the authors of the narrative it refers to the body of Sinaitic legislation in Exodus 20–23. That body consists of two classes of rules, designated in 24:3 as the "words [*debharim*] of Yahweh" and the "ordinances" (*mishpatim*) or decisions. The legislation itself distinguishes between the two classes in so far as Exodus 20 opens: "And God spoke all these words [*debharim*], saying . . ."; while Exodus 21 opens: "Now these are the ordinances [*mishpatim*], which thou shalt set before them. . . ." The *debharim* of Exodus 20:2–17 are today commonly referred to as the Ten Commandments, or the Decalogue, because in the Yahwist version of the *debharim* their number is expressly given as ten (34:28). The *mishpatim* of Exodus 21:2—22:15 form the nucleus of the law code to which modern usage refers as the Book of the Covenant. The term in the Biblical sense, thus, comprises both the *debharim* and the *mishpatim*.

The meaning of the term in Exodus 24:8, however, seems to be an enlargement of an originally narrower meaning. For in Exodus 24:3 the people take the oath of the covenant on the *debharim* alone; and in 24:4 Moses writes down only the *debharim*, not the *mishpatim*. The Yahwist account of the Sinaitic legislation, furthermore, contains only the *debharim*. And in Exodus 34:27 it refers to the covenant with Israel as made in accordance with the *debharim*; no *mishpatim* are mentioned. Deuteronomy 5:22, finally, insists that Yahweh pronounced the *debharim* "and added no more." From the passages quoted we infer an oral tradition of a Sinaitic Decalogue that was accepted by all of the historical schools. In their historiographic work it could be used to crystallize the essence of Yahwist order according to the lights of the historians and their age. In the realization of the purpose, however, the practice differed. The oldest narrative of the Sinaitic legislation, the Yahwist (J) of Exodus 34, was satisfied to use the Decalogue alone. The youngest one, the Deuteronomist, returned to the practice with a note of criticism. For in between, the Elohist account had expanded the Sinaitic legislation paradigmatically through the inclusion of the *mishpatim*. It appears that the term "Book of the Covenant" referred originally to the *debharim* alone. Moreover, the Elohist procedure furnishes a valuable hint that the code of the *mishpatim* should be understood as an expansion, through elaboration into more concrete rules, of the essence of order contained in the *debharim*.

The problems of literary structure are not yet exhausted. For the Sinaitic legislation of Exodus 20–23 is not clearly divided into the two formal parts suggested by the self-declarations as *debharim* and *mishpatim* in the openings of Chapters 20 and 21 respectively. The Elohist Decalogue comprises only Exodus 20:2–17. It is followed by the brief interlude of 18–21. And the rest of the chapter, 20:23–26, consists of a few rules which by their phrasing are "words of Yahweh" but do not belong to the *debharim* of the Decalogue. The older work of Baentsch, resumed in the fine analysis of Lods, has shown that 23–26 is part of a further decalogue of which the remnants are scattered through Exodus 21–23. The complete decalogue consists of the following passages: 20: 23–26; 22:29–30; 23:10–19.[13] For purposes of identification we shall call this further decalogue the second Elohist Decalogue.

Altogether there are four decalogues, which can be divided into two groups by their contents. The decalogue of Deuteronomy 5 is closely related to the first Elohist Decalogue in Exodus 20:2–17. The second Elohist Decalogue, with its preponderance of *debharim* concerning cult, festivals, and sacrifices, is closely related to the Yahwist Decalogue in Exodus 34. Which of the two types is the older one and comes closer to the original Mosaic contents is a matter of controversy. We are inclined to agree with Martin Buber that the first Elohist Decalogue, of Exodus 20:2–17, has the probabilities of age and originality on its side, because it concentrates on the essentials of the theopolitical order of a society under Yahweh.[14] The type of the second Elohist Decalogue would then have to be considered a secondary creation, though some of its materials may also be old enough to reach back to the time of Moses.

The first decalogue, as we said, concentrates on the essentials of the

---

[13] Bruno Baentsch, *Das Bundesbuch* (1892). Lods, *Histoire de la Littérature Hébraique et Juive,* 205 ff.

[14] The Decalogue of Exodus 20:2–17 will be treated in Chapter 12 on "Moses."

theopolitical order of a people under Yahweh and, perhaps for that reason, contains nothing that could not be Mosaic. The second decalogue contains provisions that make sense only under the conditions of the post-Mosaic agricultural society in Canaan, such as the institution of festivals of harvest and in-gathering (23:16), or of a sabbatical year for the fields, and especially for vineyards and olive groves which take a long time to grow (23:10). The existence of such widely differing versions of what purports to be the original ten "words of Yahweh" raises the issue of a decalogic form that could be filled with varying contents. We assume (for nothing can be proven in the matter) that the decalogue had been devised originally as a form that would accommodate the essentials of Yahwist order in a series of points easily countable by the fingers. And such a form, once it had been created, could be used to accommodate "words" on various levels of concretization. Rules concerning the cult or the calendar of festivals, rules concerning the Yahwist order under changing economic and social conditions, rules governing specific subject matters of civil or criminal law, and so forth— all of them were potential material to be cast in decalogic form, if the desire for systematic collection should arise. And if the form was actually used for the purpose, a series of decalogues would then form a code of legal rules in the spirit of the original, theopolitical Decalogue.

The Sinaitic legislation in the Elohist form suggests that something of the kind must have happened in the crisis of the ninth century. For Exodus 20–23 contains not only the theopolitical and cultic decalogues of *debharim*, but several more decalogues under the head of *mishpatim*. Four such *mishpatim* decalogues are still preserved intact; they are:

   (1) the decalogue concerning the status of slaves (Exod. 21:1–11)
   (2) the decalogue concerning personal injuries (Exod. 21:12–27)
   (3) the decalogue concerning injuries by animals or to animals (Exod. 21:28—22:4)
   (4) the decalogue concerning various property damages through burning over of fields, loss of deposits, theft, damage to borrowed animals, and so forth (Exod. 22:5–14)

Beyond the fourth decalogue the structure of the text can no longer be discerned clearly. It is possible that remnants of a decalogue of *mishpatim* concerning sexual offenses are preserved in 22:16, 17, and 19. And it is almost certain that a decalogue of social duties is scattered through 22:21—23:9. But we shall not venture into these areas of controversy.

For our purpose the clearly recognizable decalogues are sufficient to allow the conclusion that a corpus of *mishpatim*, organized by subject matter in decalogues, had been assembled by some priestly group in the ninth century. Four of the decalogues, and perhaps fragments of a fifth one, were incorporated by the Elohist historian into his account of the Sinaitic legislation. Several more decalogues may have existed, for a legal expert would hardly have left such obvious gaps as the law of inheritance, divorce, adultery, or procedure. Why they were omitted from the account (if they existed) is a matter of unprofitable speculation.

Besides the formal decalogues the legislation of Exodus 20–23 contains further materials which never have been, or no longer are, in such form. Nevertheless, the whole body of rules is not a haphazard agglomeration. There are lines of meaning running from the *debharim* of the theopolitical Decalogue at the beginning, through the *mishpatim* decalogues, to the counsels of social conduct at the end. We must now touch on some of these subtler elements of structure.

The ascription of the *mishpatim* to Moses, as well as their combination in one text with the theopolitical *debharim*, confers on them the character of a statutory elaboration of the principles contained in the Decalogue. The *dabar* of Yahweh says (Exod. 20:15): "Thou shalt not steal"; the *mishpat* elaborates the legal rule (22:1): "If a man steal an ox or a sheep, and kill it, or sell it; he shall pay five oxen for an ox, and four sheep for a sheep." The *dabar* says (20:13): "Thou shalt not kill"; the *mishpat* elaborates (21:12): "Who smites a man, and he dies; die he must, die." In such cases the line of meaning is relatively clear. The *dabar* is Yahweh's command to man, couched in the form "Thou shalt": [15] the *mishpat* elaborates the command into a legal rule, couched in the form of an "if"-law with a sanction attached. But the line is only relatively clear, for we do not know whether the *mishpatim* were actually enforced at the time or not. And, hence, we do not know yet whether the *debharim* are the preface to a code of positive law, illuminating the source of its authority; or whether the *mishpatim* are an appendix to the Decalogue, showing to a lawless age what the law should be in the light of the divine commands.

The motives of the authors will become clearer if we examine some rules outside the intact *mishpatim* decalogues. The *dabar*, for instance,

---

[15] I am referring to the form in its English translation. The Hebrew has the verb in the singular of the imperative.

will say (20:7): "Thou shalt not invoke the name of Yahweh your God in vain" (that is, for magic practices); and a rule will say (22:18): "Thou shalt not suffer a sorceress to live." In this case the rule concretizes the general command to the level of a *mishpat* but retains the "Thou shalt" of the *dabar*. This peculiar mixed form looks like a lawgiver's way to remind the people of the divine authority behind a *mishpat* (perhaps Saul's?) that has fallen into desuetude. Or the *dabar* says (20:3): "Thou shalt have no other gods before me"; and the *mishpat* elaborates (22:20): "Who sacrifices to gods, save to Yahweh alone, shall be destroyed under the ban [*cherem*]." This could be a genuine *mishpat* of high antiquity, but it certainly was not enforced at the time of Israel's official cult for the Baal of Tyre, to say nothing of the general cult practices of the people. Its inclusion among the rules looks like a prophetic protest against the iniquities of the age. Examples of this kind make it probable that the Elohist text of the Sinaitic legislation is not a code of positive law at all, but rather a complex attempt to weave the meaning of the terse *debharim* into concrete rules of social order. For his purpose, we assume, the Elohist historian found various means at his disposition. He could use the four *mishpatim* decalogues, because quite probably they were already collected under the aspect of their conformity with the spirit of the *debharim*, regardless of the enforcement practices of the time. And he could draw on the cultic decalogue that had been used also by the Yahwist historian.

The materials formalized in the recognizable decalogues, however, were not sufficient to execute the plan completely. The want of "kindness" about which Hosea complained required the formulation of counsels beyond the letter of the law. A few examples will reveal the final intentions of the Elohist. "A resident alien shalt thou not ill-treat, nor oppress" (22:21); "If thou lend money to any of my people, any of the poor among you, thou shalt not be toward him like a creditor" (that is, take no interest; 22:25). The rules move on the level of concreteness of the *mishpatim*, and even may have the form of the "if"-law, but they carry no sanction. And the absence of a human sanction is stressed when a divine sanction is attached: "If thou take, take in pledge the cloak of thy neighbor, before the sun goes down shalt thou restore it to him; for it is his only covering, the garment for his skin; wherein shall he sleep? and it shall come to pass, when he cries unto me, I will hear; for I am kind" (22:25–26). In this case the "if"-law with a divine

sanction is further amplified by a reasoned appeal to the moral sensitiveness of the rich man. In still other instances, the reasoning is attached to
the command without threats of divine sanction: "Thou shalt not take a
bribe [in a law suit]; for a bribe blinds the open-eyed, and perverts the
words of the righteous" (23:8). The counsels are concerned with the
misery of the poor and the uncharitable conduct of the rich in a community that has split into a wealthy upper class and an impoverished
subject population. The rift can be remedied not by enforcement of
mishpatim but only by return to the community spirit of the *debharim*.
To exist as a people under the covenant with Yahweh requires more than
obedience to the letter of the law. And the Elohist provides counsels of
equity and charity that will, if observed, transform the spirit into concrete social order.

The account of the Sinaitic legislation concludes, in Exodus 23:20–
22, with Yahweh's appointment of a Messenger who will go before the
people and guard it on its way. "Take heed of him and hearken unto
his voice . . . for my name is in him." If the people oppose the voice,
there will be no pardon for the offense; if the people heed the voice,
Yahweh will be on their side against all enemies. From the words, the
ordinances, and the counsels we return to their origin in the present
under God created at Mount Sinai. That present has not become past,
but is a living present through the Messenger whose voice is with the
people—right here and now in the work of the Elohist. The eternal voice
speaks always in the present. As it spoke through Moses, so it now speaks
through the historian who is lawgiver at the same time and prophet.
Through paradigmatic reconstruction the past is re-created as a present.
And it is the historian—not the king and his administration—who
re-creates Israel's present under Yahweh. The historian's work subtly
transfers the authority of Israel's order from the Kingdom to the new
carriers of the spirit.

§ 4. The Prophet Elijah

The Yahwist movement against the Omrides found its support in a
group of solitary prophets—a support that could be intensified to revolt
and incitement to murder. Three of them are known by their names,
Elijah, Elisha, and Micajah; two more have remained anonymous. The
great spiritual force among them was the prophet Elijah, even though the

actual extermination of the royal house falls in the time of his successor, Elisha.

The picture of the man who intervened decisively in the crisis of the ninth century is not easy to draw. For the Elijah legends cannot be used as direct historical sources because of their legendary form; and the prophet himself did not write, nor were his sayings preserved by faithful disciples as they were for the prophets of the eighth and seventh centuries. His giant stature can, therefore, only be inferred from the impression he made on his own generation, and the contours of his work from the splendid garment of symbols thrown over him by posterity. And since the symbolism connected with the epiphany of Elijah is of an eschatological nature, a study of his person and work will become, at the same time, an inquiry into the origin of eschatological experiences and their expression.

The prophet is the Messenger (*malakh*) of the Covenant (*berith*). The meaning of the function emerges from the paraenetic conclusion (Exod. 23:20–33) of the Book of the Covenant. When the Covenant is concluded and the law pronounced, Yahweh lets his people know: "Behold, I send a Messenger [*malakh*] before you, to guard you on the way, and to bring you to the place that I have prepared." The people must heed the voice of the Messenger, for Yahweh himself is manifest in it. If the people heeds the voice, then Yahweh will come to its aid, and provide for its economic prosperity and political success. But precisely in the hour of success, when Israel is victorious over other peoples and settles in their land, it must be careful not to abandon its God (Exod. 23:32–33).

> You shall not make a covenant with them, nor with their gods;
> you shall not let them dwell in your land, lest they make you sin
>   against me;
> for if you serve their gods, it would be a snare to you.

The admonition may be as old as the Canaanite temptation, but in the time of the official alliance with the Baal it must have had a special weight when the Messenger recalled it. What would happen, however, if neither the king nor the people heeded the voice of Yahweh, as they certainly did not in the Baalist crisis of the ninth century? In such an age of defection the voice would become heavy with the threat of judgment. The *malakh* would assume the role of a precursor of Yahweh's coming in his glory to administer judgment to his people.

The prophet as the Messenger of the Covenant, the Messenger as the Precursor of divine judgment, and Elijah as the prototype of Messenger and Precursor—that is the combination of elements that we find in the symbolism of Malachi. The book is probably to be dated in the fifth century B.C., and it is ascribed to "Malachi" because it announces the coming of "My Messenger" (*malakhi*). The symbolic formula is developed in 3:1:

> Behold, I will send forth My Messenger,
> and he shall prepare the way for me!
> And the Lord for whom you are longing,
> will suddenly come to his temple!

An editorial addition, immediately following the quoted passage, identifies the messenger as the "*malakh* of the *berith*"; and the concluding passage of the brief book (3:22–23) makes the prophecy more specific by saying:

> Remember the law of Moses, my servant,
> which I commanded him in Horeb for all Israel,
> the statutes and ordinances.
> Behold I will send you
> Elijah the prophet
> before the coming
> of the great and terrible day of Yahweh!

The analysis of the text will start from the assumption that the Elijah prophesied by Malachi is the speaker of the truth that had been spoken by the historical Elijah of the ninth century—though not necessarily in the form of Malachi. In the corruption of Israel the tension between divine will and human conduct broke out in the voice of the *malakh* who announced the judgment of God. The historical Elijah had become the prototype of that voice in the wilderness; and at the hands of Malachi he was transformed into the symbol of the recurrent call to restore the order from which the people was in the habit of falling away. The symbol was created consciously, and it is permissible, therefore, to draw conclusions from the symbol to the historical substance that has been absorbed into it. That the creation was conscious is confirmed by Malachi himself in so far as the transformation of historical events and persons into symbols that express the experience of judgment is in general his style. Not only does the eternal call appear in the historical costume of Elijah, but the divine order from which man falls away has to be concretely the Law of Moses. And it is worth noting that here for the first time in Israelite history, as far as sources are extant, the phrase "Law of Moses" is used to designate the Sinaitic legislation. Moses has become the lawgiver in the same symbolic sense in which Elijah has become the messenger. Moreover, the content of Elijah's prophecy, the coming Day of Yahweh, is a divine punishment in form of a political catastrophe in historical time. And the warning itself, finally, is to be understood in historical concreteness, in so far as the Day of Yahweh can be averted, if the people heeds the warning, repents, and returns to the Law of Moses. In 3:24 Malachi lets Yahweh assign to his Messenger the function of a historical savior:

> And he shall turn the hearts of the fathers to their sons,
> and the hearts of the sons to their fathers,
> lest I come and smite the land with a ban [curse—*cherem*].

The warning cry of the symbolic Elijah, thus, is richly loaded with historical contents: The voice of the Messenger announces the judgment of Yahweh on his people in the present; and for the future it holds out the alternatives of the Day of Yahweh, if the voice be not heard, or the restoration of the Law of Moses, if the call for repentance have success.

The historical substance of Malachi's symbolism does not permit us, however, to identify the symbolic with the historic Elijah. The prophet of the ninth century can be used by Malachi as a symbol because the historic Elijah was the speaker of a related experience. The historic figures are reasonable, in Hegelian phraseology, because there is reason in history; the texture of history can become the symbolic language for Malachi's experience of judgment because the judgment is present in the texture of history. We have spoken, therefore, of the historical substance that has entered into the symbolism. While this substance, the experience of divine judgment, is associated by Malachi with Elijah, the language in which Elijah expressed it cannot be inferred from Malachi. In order to find the probable form of Elijah, further sources must be considered.

The awareness of alternative symbolisms will be sharpened if we remember that the experience of judgment was not new—certainly not for Malachi, but neither for the Elijah with whom Malachi associates it. The Book of Judges, with its recurrent calls for return to the will of

Yahweh, reflects in its construction the early occupation with the problem. The rhythms of defection and return, as well as the corresponding misfortunes and restorations of Israel, must be considered an attempt to cope with it. The attempt had to remain unsatisfactory, however, because the symbolism was too deeply embedded in the historical events. If the rhythm of Judges were repeated a sufficient number of times, even a naïve historian would suspect he was dealing not with phases of pragmatic history but with a constant tension in the relation between God and man. The defection from God, he would discover, was an ever-present state of man; ever-present, therefore, was the crisis in the literal sense of the judgment; and ever-present was the voice of the Messenger, as well as the need for restoration.

The symbolism of Malachi has advanced far beyond Judges in that the historical events and figures no longer serve the narration of history but are clearly symbols for the experienced presence of defection, voice of the spirit, judgment, and restoration. Nevertheless, the contours of the symbols are still blurred so strongly by the concreteness of imagery that a discrepancy between expression and intended experience makes itself felt in so far as the presence of the judgment in the voice of the prophet is overshadowed by the future of a catastrophic judgment on the Day of Yahweh. And that discrepancy, the consequence of the concreteness of images, even affects the complexion of the experience itself. For the component of restoration is submerged with Malachi, as a hardly to be hoped for alternative, by the despair of the inevitable disaster. The restorative element achieved its full weight and distinctness only in the New Testament, when this part of Elijah's function acquired precision through the symbol *apokatastasis*.

The eschatological problems, which Malachi associated with Elijah, were advanced to further clarity through the profound scene in Matthew 17:1–13. It consists of two parts: (1) The vision on the high mountain which an early Christian tradition identified as Mount Tabor; and (2) the Logion of Jesus, which explained the drama of the vision. We shall again, first, secure the relevant text:

Jesus, so the Gospel tells, took three of his disciples and ascended with them a high mountain. There he was transfigured. Then Moses and Elijah appeared and talked to him. And, finally, a voice spoke from a bright cloud: "This is my Son, my Beloved. In him is my delight.

Listen to him" (Matt. 17:5).[16] When they descended from the mountain, Jesus cautioned his disciples not to divulge what they had seen, until the Son of Man was raised from the dead (17:9). The disciples, however, began to wonder. The Son of God was with them. Why, then, should the scribes say that first Elijah must come? (17:10). The question was answered by Jesus in the Logion 17:11–12:

> Elijah does come, and he is to restore [*apokatastasei*] all things.
>
> But I say unto you: Elijah has come already,
> And they did not recognize him, and did to him at their will.
> And in like manner the Son of Man will suffer at their hands.

The Logion is followed by the Evangelist's information that only then the disciples understood Jesus was speaking to them about John the Baptist (17:13).

The drama of the vision on Mount Tabor and the Logion form together one unit of meaning. The best, though not the most obvious, access to it is given through the structure of the Logion. For that structure, far from being a mere literary device, is a form that grows from the contents conveyed by its means. In the Logion, Jesus first restates the prophecy of Malachi—though with emphasis on the *apokatastasis* wrought by Elijah rather than on the Day of Yahweh; and then with the "But I say unto you," introduces the new meaning of the Elijah symbol. The same structure is to be found in other Logia, in particular in the Sermon on the Mount, where Jesus first states the old teaching ("You have heard that it was said to the men of old") and then (with the grandiose "But I say unto you") opposes his own message. In the context of the Sermon on the Mount, now, the meaning of the opposition is made explicit in Matthew 5:17:

> Do not imagine that I have come to destroy the Law or the Prophets.
> I have come, not to destroy them, but to bring them to their full
> meaning.[17]

---

[16] Goodspeed's translation "He is my Chosen" instead of "In him is my delight" comes perhaps closest to the intended meaning.

[17] No translation of the passage is satisfactory without an explanation. The King James Version has "I am not come to destroy, but to fulfill"—which is literal, but leaves us in the dark about the intended meaning. Goodspeed has "enforce"—which leans too much on the legal sense. Rieu has "to bring them to perfection"—which in our opinion comes closer to the sense of saturation, with a meaning already present in the Law and the Prophets, in the Greek *plerosai*. We prefer our rendering in the text.

The passage, with its discursive pronouncement on the purpose of Jesus'
coming, reads like a prologue to the drama on Mount Tabor where the
purpose was enacted. For in the vision the Law and the Prophets appeared, personified by Moses and Elijah. This was the old teaching. And
when Peter saw the appearance, when he saw the two men of old talking
to Jesus, the scene apparently pleased him. For he found it "good to be
here," and offered to build three huts, "one for you, and one for Moses,
and one for Elijah" (17:4). His friendly readiness to have the Conference
of Three comfortably settled, however, was frighteningly interrupted
by the voice from the bright cloud which declared Jesus its Beloved Son.
And when the disciples, who in fear had fallen on their faces, looked up
again, "they saw no one but Jesus alone" (17:8). Jesus was now alone.
The *malakh* of Yahweh, indeed, had come in the person of John the
Baptist. And the precursor of the Day of Yahweh had been recognized
no more than his predecessors. His voice remained unheard and he was
put to death. But John was the last Elijah. God himself, through his Son,
would now suffer the fate of his *malakh*. Not until the Son of Man had
risen from the dead as the Christ must the disciples reveal the mystery
that now God himself was present in history. The Day of Yahweh was
no longer an impending catastrophe in the history of Israel, to be announced by a Messenger. It was transformed into the presence of God's
eternal judgment in the time in which he suffered his murder through
defection from his spirit. No *malakh*, no prophetic precursor was possible
after the Incarnation.

In the symbolism of Malachi the presence of the judgment could not
assert itself against the Day that lies in the future. And the restoration of
the Law through Elijah, as we said, was submerged in the despair that the
voice would remain unheard. From its dominant position in the complex
of Elijah symbols we infer that the Day of Yahweh had a strong,
independent life of its own, rooted in a specific experience.[18] Unfortunately no sources are preserved that could with certainty be said to reveal
the origin of the symbol. The Day of Yahweh appeared for the first time
in the eighth century, in a prophecy of Amos. And on its first occur-

---

[18] Malachi 3:23 of the Masoretic Text is repeated at the end of the prophetic Book: "Behold
I will send you / Elijah the prophet / Before the coming / Of the great and terrible Day of
Yahweh." Since Malachi is the last of the Twelve, the repetition under the text (not in the King
James or the Revised versions) endows the Day of Yahweh with the character of a quintessence
of the prophetic message as a whole.

rence it obviously had a prehistory, for Amos (5:18–20) opposed a threatening catastrophe to the popular expectation of the Day as a joyous event:

> Woe to you who desire the Day of Yahweh!
> Why would you have the Day of Yahweh?
> It is darkness, not light!
>
> As though a man were fleeing from a lion,
> And a bear should meet him!
> Or went into the house and rested his hand on the wall,
> And a serpent bit him!
>
> Is not the Day of Yahweh darkness and not light,
> And blackness with no brightness in it?

Hence we have to deal not with one but with two conceptions of the Day of Yahweh.

Amos referred to the Day, in the sense of a joyous event, as if it were a well-known symbol, generally accepted by the people. With regard to its origin we can only surmise that it belonged in the complex of symbols of which remnants have survived in the Imperial Psalms. The promises of the coronation liturgy in Psalm 2, for instance, would almost inevitably provoke the creation of a popular symbol of glory, of a day of Yahweh's and Israel's rule over the nations and the earth. We are inclined, therefore, to have the joyous Day blossom from the general upsurge of cosmological symbolism in the period of the Davidic Empire. Hence, it will not be necessary to search for specific literary antecedents in Egyptian Messianic expectations. The presence of such influences can be taken for granted at a time when Israel entered on its imperial phase and consequently was receptive for foreign symbols which conveniently expressed the experience of the newly gained Empire. Even if such antecedents, more convincing than the texts from the Middle Kingdom usually adduced on the occasion, should ever be found, the root of a symbol of this nature is not literature but an indigenous experience of Israel. Moreover, we doubt that striking prefigurations of Israel's joyous Day will ever be found in the literature of the older Near Eastern empires. For after all Israel was not Babylon or Egypt. The susceptibility of the Davidic Empire for cosmological symbols never superseded the experience of the Chosen People. The new symbolism had to blend with Israel's destiny to reach its promised land in the *mamlakah* of God. If we look at the late apocalyptic treatment of the Day in Joel (hardly earlier

than the fourth century B.C.) we find the judgment terrible for the
persecutors of Israel and Judah, but joyous for all those "who call on
the name of Yahweh" (2:32). And those who escape will be set off from
those who go to destruction by an outpouring of the spirit (2:28–29):

> It shall come to pass afterward,
> That I will pour out my spirit upon all flesh;
> Your sons and your daughters shall prophesy;
> Your old men shall dream dreams;
> And your young men shall see visions.
> Even upon the manservants and the maidservants,
> In those days I will pour out my spirit.

That is the passage of Joel which Acts 2 resumed in its interpretation of
the Pentecostal outpouring of the spirit. No meaning of this nature
could be developed from cosmological symbols without the leap in being
that was Israel's claim to be the Chosen People.

Whether the threatening day of Yahweh was the creation of Amos
or not is an open question. The fact that in his prophecies it occurs for
the first time in the extant literature proves nothing either way. The
text, by the form of the question in 5:20, suggests that the people whom
he addressed were familiar with the threatening variety of the symbol
and could be reminded through the question of the less popular meaning.
In weighing this matter we must rely on the argument previously used
in dealing with the idea of theocracy and its ascription to Samuel. While
the paradigmatic ascription could not be considered proof that the historical Samuel had elaborated the idea, the later historian showed considerable insight into the connection between experience and symbol
when he discerned the situation of Samuel as a source of experiences
which, if articulated, would have to find their expression in the theocratic idea. We face a similar problem with regard to the threatening
Day of Yahweh. Malachi associated it paradigmatically with Elijah.
The historical Elijah was heightened to the prototypical figure who
announced the impending catastrophe. As in the Samuel case, the paradigmatic association is no proof that the historical Elijah created the
symbol. But again, the Malachi oracle has well discerned the situation of
the ninth century as the likely source of experiences which, if articulated,
could be expressed in the symbol of the terrible Day. And as we suggested, in the case of Samuel, that theocratic ideas must have occurred
to more than one prophet of the age, so now we assume that in the crisis

of the ninth century more than one prophet in Israel conceived the idea of a Day of a somewhat different complexion than the one expected by the people in their chauvinistic, cosmological defection from Yahweh. For in the logic of symbols the terrible Day was related with the joyous Day as a reaction to it. In so far as the joyous Day with its exuberant expectation of world-rule originated in the Empire and its symbolism, the terrible Day was a distinctly antiroyalist protest. There is no historical situation where it would fit better than in the prophetic revolt of the ninth century.

In postexilic Judaism, as well as in Christianity, Elijah was considered one of the great figures in the drama of God's revelation to man. That much is certain. In order to determine his role more clearly, we shall now list, in systematic order, the main stages in the development of eschatological symbols which in the preceding analysis had to be mentioned incidentally:

(1) The problem of eschatology was given with the ambiguity of Canaan. The Kingdom of God was understood as the establishment of a Chosen People in historical existence in a definite geographical area. In order to disengage the idea of a kingdom that was not of this world from the compact symbol, there had to be eliminated the following components: (a) that a particular people in the ethnic sense was the carrier of the kingdom in history; (b) that the kingdom could be realized through mundane organization of a people; (c) that the kingdom could be realized in history as a continuous state of perfect conduct under the will of God by any human group.

(2) Canaan was put under strain after the Conquest. Peaceful existence of the Chosen People in form of the theopolity proved impossible in the new habitat; and the amalgamation with Canaanites diluted the original Yahwism through various forms of syncretism. The two disturbances of order were connected by the symbolic rhythms of Judges as defection and divine punishment. The idea of peace and prosperity as a reward for good conduct was primitive, to be sure, and even had a touch of magic, but at least the sense of guilt and divine judgment was alive in it.

(3) With the success of kingship and Empire two further elements entered the complex of symbols. On the one hand, the role of the prophet became marked as the guardian of Yahwist order, through Samuel and

Nathan, and the outlines of the theocratic problem appeared. On the other hand, the general defection from Yahwism reached a new low in the tenth century with the transformation of Yahweh into a cosmocrator. To this period we assigned the transformation of the Canaan symbol into a glorious Day of Yahweh that would establish the rule of the Empire people over the nations and the earth.

(4) After the separation of Israel from the Empire, in the ninth century, the defection affected the public cult. That was the critical period, as we suggested, in the formation of the complex of eschatological symbols. The code makers and historians returned to the sources and tried to re-establish the standards of order by which defection could be measured. The "*malakh* of the *berith*" appeared as the permanently present voice of the spirit. And the prophets transformed Israel's Day of cosmic victory and glory into a terrible day of judgment visited by Yahweh on the Kingdom in form of a political catastrophe.

(5) The complex was formed, but in the crisis of the ninth century it was still directed against the dynasty and foreign influences. The revolt against the Omrides, although led by a general, had the support of the people and, in particular, of the Rechabites. The organization of the Kingdom in its specific form was the source of the evil. The people itself was yet guiltless and could be relied upon to realize the state of perfection unless misguided by kings and their foreign wives. In the eighth century, with Amos, began the line of the great prophets who understood that the people itself was guilty. The intoxication with the monarchy was passing and the Chosen People of the premonarchical time came into view again. The terrible Day of judgment was now threatening the people itself. At the same time, in the eighth and seventh centuries, the historians further elaborated the early Patriarchal and Mosaic history, while the code makers concentrated the standards of Yahwist order in the Deuteronomic speeches of Moses.

(6) In the postexilic Malachi, in the fifth century, the elements that had entered into the complex congealed into a pattern. Moses and Elijah became the prototypes of the lawgiver and the prophetic voice. The two Days of Yahweh became the alternatives of Israel's final restoration or destruction. And, what easily might be forgotten, the anonymous "Malachi" was the prophet who combined the symbols of past and future into a new, integral symbol in order to express his sense of defection and judgment in the present.

(7) With Malachi the symbols loaded with historical imagery of past and future had achieved something like a balance. And at their center became visible the eternal present in which the divine-human drama of history was enacted. With the appearance of Jesus, God himself entered into the eternal present of history. The Kingdom of God was now within history, though not of it. The consequences of the Incarnation for the historical order of mankind were not realized at once; and it took some time to find even moderately suitable forms of expression.[19] The symbols of the past lost their dominant position first. In the vision on Mount Tabor, Moses and Elijah talked to Jesus—and then they disappeared, even though Peter was willing to accommodate them as members of a spiritual trinity. The Law and the Prophets were now "fulfilled." The symbols of the future were more tenacious. In the very context of the vision on Mount Tabor, Jesus himself (Matt. 16:27–28) assured his disciples: "For the Son of Man is to come, in the glory of his Father, with his messengers; and then he will repay everyone according to his deeds. I tell you truly, there are some among those standing here who will not taste death till they see the Son of Man coming in his kingdom." Only gradually, in the early Christian centuries, were the futuristic, historical images transformed into the genuine eschatological symbols of the coming of the Antichrist, the Parousia, and the Last Judgment— events no longer within historical time.

The ninth was the crucial century in the history of eschatology, in so far as in that period the assembly of elements that entered into the complex of symbols was completed. The law as the standard of order, the defection of Israel, the experience of judgment, the alternatives of restoration and catastrophic punishment—all were present, though they had not yet found the balance of Malachi. The completion was associated with Elijah. Through Moses his servant Yahweh had concluded his covenant with Israel; through Elijah his messenger, in the depth of defection, he threatened the offenders with judgment and destruction. Through

[19] This sentence refers strictly to the problems of adequate symbolization. The mystery of the Incarnation itself, of the consubstantiality of God and man, is impenetrable. And its consequences for the substantive order of history are not fully realized as long as history lasts. Even in reference to adequate symbolization the sentence must be taken with proper qualification, for the meaning of history under the Christian dispensation is as far from satisfactory positive expression today as it was at the time of Jesus and his generation. The sentence, thus, means only that it took some time to overcome even the most obvious inadequacies of traditional symbols of historical order.

Moses the people had made the leap in being and gained its freedom in the present under God; through Elijah it was reminded that Yahweh's choice could be renounced and the covenant be undone. To be the Chosen People was not an insurance of success in pragmatic history, but a form of existence that could be lost as it had been gained. The leap in being was fraught with the possibility of the fall from being. Moses and Elijah, the prophets of the rise and the fall, belonged together. The dynamics of existence under God required the warner and restorer as much as the founder.

In the dynamics of existence Moses and Elijah complemented one another. In the process of history the foundation of the people through Moses was followed by the defection of Israel, as represented by the Omride dynasty. Elijah, the warner and restorer, entered history as a third force. The triangle of historical forces is essential for the understanding of the situation. If the prophetic revolt had been nothing but a political opposition to the government of Israel, it would hardly have been successful. The prophets were a force because even the dynasty did not question a spiritual authority derived from Moses. Regrettably we know very little about the interplay of the forces. And in particular, we know nothing about the origins of Elijah. The prophet was all of a sudden there, in the presence of the King, and announced to him from the blue sky: "As Yahweh, the God of Israel lives, before whom I stand, there shall be neither dew nor rain these years, except by my word" (I Kings 17:1). Having pronounced these words he was no longer there; and the sky remained blue for years on end without a drop of rain. Drought and famine followed. A man like Elijah must have been a headache for a government, even if it was concerned about the welfare of the people only after a fashion.

The abruptness of the prophet's interference with the affairs of Israel deserves attention. In part it must be explained by the nature of the sources, as well as by the use which the writer of Kings made of them. His main sources were the Acts of the Kings of Israel and the Acts of the Kings of Judah. From the Acts the historian made brief extracts for each reign, such as we find for the reign of Omri in I Kings 16:21–28, or the reign of Ahab in 16:29–34, and referred his readers for further information to the Acts themselves. When in I Kings 17 the narrative broadens out into a wealth of detail concerning the prophetic revolt, it is clear that the extracts from the Acts are now interrupted by the stories and legends about Elijah, Elisha, and the other prophets. The abrupt appearance of Elijah, who in the preceding abstract of the reign of Ahab had not been so much as mentioned, can thus be explained by the patching of sources. Nevertheless, the explanation will carry only part of the way—and it is generally advisable, when dealing with the Biblical narrative, not to attribute peculiarities of contents to the clumsiness of the historian. While the abrupt appearance can be explained by the beginning of a new source, the abrupt disappearance after Elijah's pronouncement to the King is part of the story itself. Hence, we rather imagine the author in search of literary devices to convey the inexplicable suddenness of a spiritual outbreak. The legend itself valiantly grapples with that problem by picturing Elijah as the sole survivor after massacres of all Yahwist prophets at the instigation of the royal house (18:22; 19:10, 14). The picture is flatly incompatible with the appearance of single Yahwist prophets, as well as of a whole band of four hundred, as advisers to Ahab in I Kings 20 and 22. It can only have the purpose of enhancing, by the imagery of loneliness, the figure of Elijah as the great spiritual opponent to the forces of the age.

Of the conflict of forces we catch a glimpse now and then through phrases which have an authentic ring. After three years of drought Elijah appeared again before Ahab. The meeting was a terse drama (I Kings 18:17–18):

> Now as soon as Ahab saw Elijah, he said to him:
>> "Is it you, you troubler of Israel?"
> And he answered:
>> "I have not troubled Israel. You have, and your father's house,
>> in that you have forsaken the commandments of Yahweh and
>> have gone after the Baalim."

Another meeting occurred when the royal couple had engineered the judicial murder of Naboth in order to obtain his vineyard. When the King took possession, again Elijah appeared (21:20–21):

> And Ahab said to Elijah:
>> "Have you found me, O my enemy?"
> And he answered:
>> "I have. Because you have sold yourself to no purpose, to do
>> that which is evil in the sight of Yahweh, behold I am about
>> to bring evil upon you."

On a third occasion, through his humiliation of the Baalist prophets at Mount Carmel, Elijah came into direct conflict with the Queen, the daughter of the priest-king of the Baal of Tyre. The phrase that sum-

marized the conflict of forces, the opening phrase of a message sent by
the Queen to the Prophet, is preserved in the Septuagint (19:2) but not
in the Masoretic Text:

> If you are Elijah, I am Jezebel. . . .

The message itself contained the threats which induced Elijah to leave
the neighborhood of the residence with precipitation.

The three little dramas reveal the forces whom Elijah opposed, and
at the same time they reveal how Elijah appeared to the powers of
the age. He was the troubler of Israel in opposition to the King, who
had to bear the responsibility for the political existence of the people,
both domestically and in foreign relations. He was the personal enemy
of the King with regard to the latter's misuse of his position in cases
like Naboth's. And he was the prophet of Yahweh in opposition to the
Baalism represented by the Queen. In all three relations it is clear that
the powers of the day neither could nor did take his opposition lightly.
There is a touch of intimacy in the enmity when King and Prophet
accuse one another of being the troublers of Israel. And there is the
weariness of expectation fulfilled in the King's "Have you found me, O
my enemy?" Even the Queen's self-assertion is defensive, for she must
raise herself through a formal act to equality with the Prophet. A twilight of tragedy lies over the encounters, for the truth in the voice of the
prophet is sensed even by those who fall under his judgment. The authority in Israel was indeed passing from the Kingdom to the Prophet.

The attack of Elijah was directed against the heart of Israel's defection, that is, against the cult of the Baal. The episode of I Kings 17–18,
which opened with the sudden announcement of the drought, questioned
the power of the Baal of fertility. If Israel prospered with rich harvests,
it owed the blessing to Yahweh, not to the Baal. The lesson could be
taught most convincingly by Yahweh's drought, prolonged to the point
of famine, which the Baal was powerless to break. Three years were
considered sufficient by Yahweh to carry conviction. Elijah received word
from his God that he would let it rain. The prophet presented himself,
therefore, to the King and proposed the public contest with the prophets
of Baal on Mount Carmel. But it is not among the properties of a people
to learn a lesson. When Elijah put the question, 18:21:

> "How long are you going to limp on two diverse opinions?
> If Yahweh be God, follow him;
> But if the Baal, follow him,"

the people were sullen and did not answer. A response came only at the miraculous climax of the contest. Elijah prayed (18:36–37):

> Yahweh, God of Abraham, Isaac, and Israel, let it be known today that thou art God in Israel and that I am thy servant, and that I have done all these things at thy word.
> Answer me, Yahweh, answer me, that this people may know that thou, Yahweh, art God, and that thou hast turned their heart back again.

Then the fire of Yahweh fell and consumed the sacrifices, the altar, and the water in the trenches. And when the people saw it, they fell upon their faces and said (18:39): "Yahweh, he is God! Yahweh, he is God!"

The precise nature of Elijah's Yahwism is a matter of controversy among modern historians. Did Elijah have a monotheistic conception of divinity, as suggested by the cry "Yahweh, he is God"? Or did he recognize the divinity of the Baal and want only to assert the exclusive jurisdiction of Yahweh in Israel, as suggested by the prayer? The advocates of the first opinion can point to the scorn poured by Elijah on his Baalist *confrères* in 18:27. He taunted them to cry louder, for after all Baal was a god: "Either he is meditating, or he has gone aside [*i.e.*, to satisfy a natural need], or he is on a journey, or perhaps he is asleep and needs to be awakened!" Nobody who believed the Baal to be a god, is the argument, would use such irreverent language. The defenders of the second opinion can point to the prayer, as well as to the story in II Kings 1, where Elijah recognized the divinity of the Baal-Zebub of Ekron but insisted on Yahweh's exclusive jurisdiction in Israel. We do not intend to take sides in the controversy, since we suspect it to be anachronistic. For Elijah had to deal not with theology but with the cult of Baal in Israel. If Yahweh was God in Israel, that cult had to be abolished whether Baal was a god or not. The primary purpose to be achieved was the monopoly of Yahweh's cult. In addition it is quite possible, and indeed made probable by various formulations, that Elijah's experience of God was profound and clear enough to discern Yahweh as God beside whom no other gods could be held because they were no gods.

The sorrows of the messenger of God were not of a theological nature. His danger was despair. The contest with the Baalist prophets had ended with the victory of Yahweh—though the slaughter of the enemies should be discounted just as much as the wholesale slaughter of Yahwist prophets. Nevertheless, when the miracle had happened, and rain began to fall, everything went on as usual as far as the cult of Baal was concerned. Elijah's mission had ended in a failure. Moreover, his life was in danger. He fled the country, accompanied only by a servant. In Beersheba, in Judah, he left the servant behind and went alone into the desert, a day's journey. There he sat down under a tree to die.

Elijah in the desert is one of the great scenes in the history of mankind. The theme of Exodus is running through it—but in a new spiritual key. Moses had led his people from the Sheol of civilization into the Desert; and from the Desert where it found its God into Canaan. Now Israel and Canaan had become Sheol; and Elijah went into the Desert, alone, without a people. When the existence in freedom under God had failed, the time for the last emigration had come, into death. Or rather, that is what Elijah must have felt. For in the Desert God again revealed himself. An angel came to Elijah in his sleep and ordered him to proceed to Mount Horeb. Strengthened with miraculous food and the word of Yahweh he undertook the long journey. And on Mount Horeb, Yahweh appeared to him (19:11–13):

> And behold, Yahweh was passing by.
>
> And a great and mighty wind was rending the mountain and shattering the rocks before Yahweh. But Yahweh was not in the wind.
> After the wind came an earthquake. But Yahweh was not in the earthquake.
> After the earthquake a fire. But Yahweh was not in the fire.
> And after the fire a sound of gentle stillness.
>
> Now as soon as Elijah heard it, he wrapped his face in his mantle and went out and stood at the entrance of the cave.
>
> And behold, there came a voice to him and said:
> "What are you doing here, Elijah?"

What indeed was he doing there? When the sensual machinery of divine appearance had duly run off—preparing the appearance, but not the appearance itself—there was a gentle stillness. And at that moment the sensual symbolism of Exodus, Desert, Canaan, and Death fell apart and revealed its secret as the life of the spirit right here and now in the world. As Plato's prisoner, after the vision of the Agathon, must return to the Cave and rejoin his fellow-prisoners, so Elijah is sent back, by the gentle stillness, from the Mountain of God to Israel.

The task of Elijah in the world to which he returned was the establishment of the prophetic succession. On the way back from Horeb he found Elisha and threw his mantle over him. "Then Elisha arose and went after Elijah and became his attendant" (19:19–21). When death approached—the death willed by God, not the death of despair—Elijah went down to the Jordan with his successor. There, on the bank of the river, he took his mantle, rolled it up, and struck the waters. They divided as the Red Sea had done before Moses and Israel, so that the two could cross over on dry ground. That was the crossing into the last Desert and its freedom. "As they still went on and talked, behold, a chariot of fire and horses of fire separated the two of them. And Elijah went up by a whirlwind into heaven" (II Kings 2:11). Elisha saw it and cried out: "My father, my father! the chariot of Israel and its horsemen!" Then he took up the mantle that had fallen from Elijah, used it as Elijah had done to part the waters of the Jordan, and walked back into the world.

PART FOUR

Moses and the Prophets

CHAPTER 11

The Deuteronomic Torah

1. The Prophets and the Order of Israel

History as the present under God was the inner form of Israel's existence. As it had been gained through Moses and the Berith it also could be lost through defection of the people from Yahweh and his instructions. Whenever such a crisis of defection occurred, it would be the function of the "*malakh* of the *berith*" to recall the people to its obligations, to restore its inner form. While the phenomenon of prophetism is far from exhausted by this characterization, the *malakh* function must be the guide for its interpretation in a study of Israelite order.

When the function of the prophet is defined in such terms, the precariousness of Israelite order, as well as the difficulties of the prophet's task, become clear. Above all, the prophet to whom Yahweh spoke his word might arrive at the conclusion that the situation was hopeless and return his mandate to his God. That was the conclusion at which Elijah arrived; and on the level of pragmatic history, it was a possibility that the potential prophets renounced their mission in face of its futility. Israel might, indeed, have relapsed into a nation among others, and Yahweh might have ended as one of the many Near Eastern divinities. The spirit of Yahweh, however, proved a power of its own in the person of Elijah. The prophet could not despair of his people without despairing of the spirit; he could not go into the desert in order to die in God. The spirit, while not of this world, was nevertheless experienced as the source of its order; and the solitude from which it suffered in historical existence could not be relieved by the solitude of escape. The flight to Mount Horeb was halted by the question "What are you doing here?"

The experience of Elijah precluded the reversal of the leap in being. The place of the *malakh* was with his people. Still, when the prophet, in obedience to the injunction of the divine question, retraced his steps, he met on his return with the other question, what he and his successors should do in the world. The situation in which the prophets found themselves was indeed desperate because it was fraught with the complications of Israel's pragmatic existence. For on the one hand, when the prophets were successful to a certain degree, as they were in the revolt of Jehu, they endangered the diplomatic relations on which the survival of the country depended; and when on the other hand, the existence of the people as an organized community was threatened with annihilation, the value of a covenant with Yahweh, which included the promise of a glorious future in Canaan, became doubtful.

Hence, under the impact of the prophetic movement, there developed the vacillations in the adherence to Yahwist order which accompanied the history of the people from the ninth century into the Hellenistic and Roman periods. Under the pressure of the Empires, Israel would assimilate itself to the culture of the more powerful neighbors, and then suffer a revival of Yahwist nationalism which precipitated a political disaster. The diplomatic loosening of the Yahwist order under the Omride dynasty, in the ninth century, provoked the prophetic revolt which made a policy of alliances impossible. Two centuries later the assimilation to the Assyrian pantheon, under the reign of Manasseh in Judah, provoked the Deuteronomist reform which stiffened disastrously the resistance to Babylon. And the same tension was still present, in the Maccabaean period, in the struggles between Hellenizers and nationalist zealots. The prophets themselves were more or less helplessly caught between the forces of the age. A Jeremiah, for instance, was first a propagandist for the Deuteronomist reform because it enacted prophetic demands for the purification of Yahwism; he then was its opponent, when he recognized the Deuteronomic Torah as an ossification of the prophetic spirit; and the tradition, finally, is believable that he was killed in Egypt by Jews who attributed the fall of Jerusalem to the wrath of the foreign divinities that had been insulted by the prophetic reforms. The present under God had become a suicidal impasse when it was conceived as the institution of a small people in opposition to empires.

The scriptures of Israel have become the Old Testament of Christianity, and the prophetic *dabar* of Yahweh to his people has become the word of God to mankind. It requires today an effort of imagination to realize that the prophets were concerned with the spiritual order of a concrete people, of the people with whom Yahweh had entered into the

Berith. Under the conditions of Israel's history, the concreteness of their task faced them with problems that were never quite resolved. On the one hand, the prophetic experience moved toward the clarity of understanding that Yahweh was not only the one God beside whom Israel must have no other gods, but the one God for all men beside whom no other gods existed. On the other hand, the concrete Israel was changing its identity from the Hebrew clans of the conquest and the amalgamation with Canaanites, to the people of the Davidic Empire that included Judah, further to the divided Kingdoms and then to Judah alone, and finally to the organization of the postexilic community around the restored Temple. Yahweh tended to become a universal God of mankind, while the protean Israel became smaller and smaller. Hence the prophets were torn by the conflict between spiritual universalism and patriotic parochialism that had been inherent from the beginning in the conception of a Chosen People.

The tension was to reach tragic proportions when it became fully conscious, in the exilic Deutero-Isaiah's symbol of the Suffering Servant for mankind, before it dissolved anticlimactically in the restrictive reforms of Nehemiah and Ezra. Nevertheless, even when the remnant had thus withdrawn into its shell, the consciousness of the dilemma remained alive, as in the unknown author of the Book of Jonah. At this late date, however, in the story of a prophet who received Yahweh's order to save Nineveh through his preaching but tried to evade the divine command by fleeing in the opposite direction, the consciousness had become ironic:

> The word of Yahweh came to Jonah . . . : Arise, go to Nineveh,
> that great city, and preach against it . . . . Then Jonah arose and
> fled to Tarshish, from the presence of Yahweh. . . .

One need not agree with enlightened critics who consider Jonah the profoundest book of the Old Testament, but neither should one forget that by the fourth century, within the orbit of the canonized literature, the tragic dilemma of Israel had acquired a comic touch.

While in the pre-exilic literature of Judah the dilemma certainly had nothing comic, one sometimes wonders to what degree the tragic implications became ever fully conscious. To be sure, the problems were clearly articulated, but the articulation provoked no reflection; the conflicts were submerged, as it were, by a fanatical will of collective existence. The catastrophe of the Northern Kingdom had the serious repercussions in the Judaite experience of order that expressed themselves in the creation of the Deuteronomic Torah, and one should suppose that such a radical reorganization of symbols would have aroused some critical observation, expression of grief, or reflective apology. Israel, after all, had perished; and Judah was the surviving heir of its traditions. The transfer, though, caused nothing more than the slight ripple of terminology that can be observed in Isaiah and Micah. In a phrase like "The Holy One of Israel," for instance, the term "Israel" still meant for Isaiah the community that had been constituted by Yahweh through the Berith. But it also could absorb the political contingencies and mean the people as organized in the two Kingdoms, as in the verse 5:7:

> For the vineyard of Yahweh of the hosts is the house of Israel,
> And the men of Judah are his cherished plantation.

And once the Yahweh of Israel had become the Yahweh of the Kingdoms, the politically separate Judah could slip into the symbolism of Israel, as in 8:14:

> For to both the houses of Israel shall he prove a holy place,
> A stone to strike against, and a rock to stumble upon.

From the Judah that had become one of the houses of Israel, then, it was only a small step further to the Judah which in political fact had become the only house of Israel after the disasters of 734 and 722, as in Micah 3:1:

> Hear now, you heads of Jacob,
> And rulers of the house of Israel.

The ease of the transition, the sleight of hand by which the Israel that had lost its political existence was thrown out of its symbolic existence and replaced by Judah, recalls the charismatic brutality of David in his acceptance of success and survival.

With a similar brutality the splendid rhetoric of Deuteronomy rolls over the tension between the one God of mankind and the Yahweh who is Israel's (now, Judah's) personal possession. Deuteronomy 4:35 admonishes the people: "You were made to see, that you know that Yahweh is God, none beside him"; and 4:39 continues: "Know it this day, and lay it to your heart, that Yahweh is God, in the heavens above and on earth below, none else." Since the language is unrestrained by qualifications, the verses can be understood (as by some historians indeed they are) as the first formulation of theoretical monotheism. And yet, doubts with regard to their precise meaning will arise when we read in 6:4–5 the famous invocation:

> Hear, O Israel: Yahweh—Our God, Yahweh—One!
> And you shall love Yahweh your God with all your heart, and all
>   your soul, and all your might!

For the oneness of Yahweh, as the context shows, is compatible with the existence of the gods of other peoples whom Israel is warned to follow (6:13–15). And the oneness and universality of a God of all mankind is, furthermore, difficult to reconcile with the surrender of other peoples' cities, houses, and property to Israel (6:10–12), or with the injunction to exterminate the conquered peoples in order not to be contaminated by their gods (7:1–5; 7:16–26). But then again it seems to be the universal God who, through a free act of love, has singled out Israel for the covenant (5:2) and consecrated it as his people in preference to other peoples whom he might have chosen as well (7:6–8). And Israel is assured that "Yahweh, your God, he is God; the trustworthy God, who keeps covenant and faith with those who love him and keep his commandments, to a thousand generations" (7:9). From the conflict of formulations one can only conclude that the level of doctrinal articulation, of a "theology," was reached by Deuteronomy no more than by the earlier documents we have studied. To be sure, the tendency toward a differentiated understanding of the one, universal God is marked, but still it is so deeply embedded in the compact experience of the people and its destiny, that the context deprives the monotheistic passages of the meaning they would have in isolation. The fierceness of collective existence will not yet admit dissolution into the freedom of individual souls, whether Israelite or not, under God.

2. The Speeches of Moses

The book of Deuteronomy is the symbol in which the spirit of the prophets blended with the Judaite will of collective existence. According to the most plausible conjectures it is the work of priests under prophetic influence, or in cooperation with disciples of the generation of Isaiah and Micah, who had to grapple with the problem of a Yahwist order for Judah during the reign of Manasseh (692–639). It is a code of law, couched in the form of speeches by Moses, in order to endow the demands of the *malakh* with the authority of the founder.

The conjectured time of its creation, the period of Assyria's greatest strength under Essarhaddon (681–668) and Ashurbanipal (668–625), was also the period of Judah's most intensive assimilation to the surrounding cosmological civilization. The enumeration of Josiah's acts of purification, in II Kings 23, suggests the extent of the defections from Yahwism: In the courts of the Temple, Manasseh had built altars to the divinities of the Assyrian pantheon, as well as to the hosts of heaven (II Kings 21:5), which now had to be removed (23:4–5), and there were a chariot and horses dedicated to the sun-god (23:11); the ministers and servants of some fertility cult, who had received quarters in the Temple, were thrown out (23:7); the roof-altars for astral gods had to be abolished (23:12); the reformer-king, furthermore, tried to stop the burnt-offering of children to Molech (the Baal-Melek) (23:10), a sacrifice in which Manasseh himself had indulged (21:6); and finally, the sanctuaries of foreign gods established by Solomon for his wives were defiled in the general sweep (23:13). In the shadow of Assyrian power, it is clear, the government and people of Judah had accepted the gods of the stronger battalions into their religious culture, as it was customary for the vanquished at the time. In spite of such a thoroughgoing assimilation, however, there is no reason to assume that the cult of Yahweh himself had suffered during the period. The prophets of the eighth century, after all, had done their work; and the miraculous escape of Jerusalem from conquest at the hands of Sennacherib in 701 had greatly enhanced the prestige of Yahweh as a local and territorial God. Moreover, the kings of the Davidic dynasty continued to rule as the "sons of God" under the "Yahweh who made the heavens"; and it is quite possible that some of the formulas of the Imperial Psalms achieved their popularity only under Manasseh. Yahweh may well have approached, in that reign, the position of a Lord of the Heavens similar to that of the Mesopotamian Anu, as at the time of Jephtah he had become an Israelite Chemosh, and at the time of Solomon perhaps a divinity close to the Egyptian Amon. At any rate, Yahweh moved unscathed, as the one God of Israel, through the mythological clouds of the age.

Under Manasseh the Deuteronomy could be conceived and written, but it could not reach the public. To be sure, the cult monopoly of Jerusalem provided by the new Torah had made serious concessions to popular sentiments, in so far as (1) the concentration on the cultic aspects of Yahwism abandoned the prophetic insistence on the purity of heart, and as (2) the monopoly of the cult in Jerusalem accorded to the Temple a fetishistic quality, comparable to the concession which Mohammed had to make when he left the Kaaba in Mecca to the people. In spite of such dilution, however, the King, even if he had been so inclined, could not tolerate an effective Yahwist opposition since it would have endangered the relations with the powerful neighor. And the gap between the generation of Isaiah and Micah (*ca.* 740–690) and of Zephaniah, Nahum, and Jeremiah (*ca.* 637–580) suggests that the prophets were driven underground. Hence, the manuscript of the new Torah, while preserved in the Temple, fell into oblivion, to be rediscovered only *ca.* 622/21, in the reign of Josiah. By that time the Assyrian power had passed its zenith, and Nineveh had already experienced the first siege by Cyaxares of 625. The prophetic party, with a king favorably inclined, could make the rediscovered code public and have it enacted as the law of the realm.

The story of the discovery and enactment is told in II Kings 22–23. The code, it seems, had been really forgotten and was discovered by accident, though quite possibly the priestly discoverers knew about the nature and origin of their find. A prophetess, Huldah, was approached in order to authenticate the "book of the law" by a direct word from Yahweh; and Huldah obliged by promising dire vengeance of Yahweh for the defection from his law as set forth in the book, and at the same time a stay of execution if the pious Josiah would return to the obedience together with the people. Thereupon, in a solemn ceremony (23:1–3), after the code had been read to the assembled people, the King "stood to the pillar" and made a berith before Yahweh to keep the provisions flowing from the covenant, as set forth in the book, and "all the people stood to the *berith*." The text enacted on the occasion is variously designated as "the book of the Torah" (22:8), "the words of the book of the Torah" (22:11), "the words of the Torah written in the book" (23:24), and in a probably postexilic passage, "the Torah of Moses" (23:25); it is also referred to as "the book of the Covenant" (23:2, 21). Since the text had been the object of editorial revisions before it was incorporated into the present Deuteronomy, its precise limits can only be conjectured. Chapters 31–34, which relate the death of Moses, certainly must be excluded from the text, since they belong to the J and E narrative. Within the remaining Chapters 1–30 must be distinguished the Torah proper (12–26) from the Introduction (1–11) and the Conclusion (27–30). The introductory chapters show elements of at least three introductions, the concluding chapters of at least two conclusions, while the Torah itself betrays by its repetitions the inclusion of alternative versions. Hence the original Book of the Torah must have been a briefer, more tightly constructed document.[1]

3. The Instructions of Yahweh and the Torah of Moses

An interpretation of the Deuteronomic code and its history must distinguish between the discovery of the manuscript as a physical object and its discovery as the Torah of Moses. The manuscript as a physical object may have been indeed stored away when it was completed, since it could not be put to any public use; it may indeed have been forgotten and found accidentally, though it is probable that its finding was helped by somebody's memory of its existence and the vague idea that it might be of interest under the changed political circumstances. One cannot assume, however, that the priestly circle to which the finder belonged did not know what they had found. They must have known that what they held in hand was not the "Torah of Moses," but a literary production, conceived and written by one or more members of their own group no longer than a generation ago. When they agreed to have discovered not a manuscript of comparatively recent date but the genuine Torah of Moses, they entered into the myth created by the author of the book, though the sources do not reveal the degree of deliberateness of any of the persons involved. Neither can one assume that the historians of II Kings did not know about the origin of Deuteronomy and the true circumstances of its "discovery"; they also entered into the myth when they wrote their history in apparent good faith. Hence, we have to deal with a complicated symbolic form that reaches from the narrative of II Kings, through the play of discovery and enactment as told in the narrative, to the myth created by the author of the code as acted out by the

---

[1] We assume the identity of Deuteronomy, that is, of its original nucleus, with Josiah's law book, an assumption that has remained predominant since de Wette (1805). In the 1920's the seventh century date was frequently challenged. G. Hoelscher wanted to move the date down to the sixth or fifth century (1922); A. C. Welch wanted to move it up to the Solomonic time (1924). On the literary genesis and structure of Deuteronomy, as well as on the controversy surrounding it, cf. Lods, *Histoire de la Littérature Hébraique et Juive* (1950), 345 ff.; on the variegated theories since 1920, C. R. North, "Pentateuchal Criticism," in Rowley (ed.), *The Old Testament and Modern Study* (1951), 48 ff. The extant form of Deuteronomy seems to be modeled on the Sinai Pericope (Exod. 19–24). The main divisions are (1) historical account of the Sinai events and Paraenesis (Deut. 1–11); (2) reading of the Law (Deut. 12–26); (3) the Covenant (Deut. 26:16–19); (4) Blessing and Curse (Deut. 27 ff.). On this question cf. Von Rad, *Das Formgeschichtliche Problem des Hexateuchs*, 24.

discoverers, further on to the traditions about Moses in so far as they have entered into the myth, and ultimately to Moses himself.

In an earlier context, when we had to touch upon the problem of Deuteronomy, we briefly suggested the Memphite Theology as a parallel case. The comparison extended to the element of consciousness, in both instances, in the creation of a myth of political order. Beyond this point, however, the differences between the two cases will become illuminating. The Memphite Theology is a body of tales about the gods, skillfully contrived to let the unification of Egypt and the foundation of Memphis appear as the social manifestation of events in the cosmic-divine sphere. It is a genuine myth in the sense that it casts the foundation of Egyptian order in the appropriate form of cosmological symbols. The Deuteronomy, in its turn, is a tale not about the gods but about a historical personage. The unknown author presents the people of Israel at the moment of its entrance into the promised land; Exodus and Desert lie behind it, Canaan lies before it. At this critical juncture of its history Moses assembles the people and addresses to it the speeches which contain the Deuteronomic *toroth* (1:1–5; 4:45–49).

While it is justifiable to speak of this tale as a myth, as we shall see presently, its structure must be carefully distinguished from that of the Memphite Theology, for the Deuteronomic myth is secondary in the sense that it has been grafted on the nonmythical symbolic form of Israelite history. The peculiarity of the structure becomes clear through a comparison with the Book of the Covenant, which we have studied in the preceding chapter. In the narrative of Exodus, which rests on the J and E historians, no Moses is interposed as a speaker between the author and the events narrated; the historian speaks in direct attention to his object and tells the story of the actual constitution of Israel through the Berith with Yahweh (even though the story has been paradigmatically elaborated through the insertion of new legal materials). Yahweh, Moses, and the people are the actors in the drama from which Israel emerges as the Chosen People in the present under God. In Exodus we are moving in the sphere of paradigmatic history; and in so far as that symbolic form is elaborated by the historians on the basis of traditions, in continuity with the events themselves, the history of Exodus is, by its nature of an original creation, closer to the Memphite Theology than to Deuteronomy, though the symbolic forms created in the two instances differ profoundly. In Deuteronomy the history of the Berith is no longer told in continuity with the traditions. Moses is now the fictitious historian who tells his people his and their own history of Exodus, Berith, and Desert and presents them with the alternative of the blessing or the curse (11:26–29):

> Behold,
> I set before you a blessing and a curse:
> The blessing—if you shall hearken to the commandment of Yahweh
>   your God which I command you today;
> The curse—if you shall not hearken to the commandment of Yahweh
>   your God, and swerve from the way which I command you to-
>   day, to go after other gods which you have not known.

Moses, not Yahweh, sets before the people a blessing and a curse; Moses, not Yahweh, commands the way from which the people must not swerve. The words and ordinances which in Exodus emanate from Yahweh, flow in Deuteronomy from the authority of Moses. The actual constitution of Israel in historical form through God has become in Deuteronomy a story of the past on which is grafted the legislative authority of the fictitious Moses.

The author of the people—if we may borrow the phrase from Giambattista Vico—has become the author of a book; the existence in the present under God has been perverted into existence in the present under the Torah. That perversion was not a relapse into the cosmological myth, for the memory of the Sinaitic leap was preserved as the legitimating background of the Mosaic speeches, but it nevertheless partook of the myth, in that the immediate existence under God now was broken through the mediation of the fictitious author of the Torah. The Moses of the Deuteronomic Torah must be compared, with regard to his function, to the Pharaoh as the transformer of the cosmic-divine *maat* into the statutory *maat* of social order. While the present under God did not give way to a living Pharaoh, the man to whom God had spoken face to face was now embalmed and had become a mummified Pharaoh.

When the instructions of Yahweh were transformed into the Torah of Moses, an epoch was marked in the history of Israel—if we may use the term loosely so as to include the Judaite successor—for the continuity of the tradition was now broken by the introduction of a new mythical element. The tradition, to be sure, had not disappeared but was preserved in the contents of the Deuteronomic speeches. Nevertheless, a break had occurred, when the present under God had become a past under

God. The Torah of Moses was not the living constitution of Israel in historical continuity, but an archaistic myth by which the author tried to reconstitute, in the spirit of Israel, a Judah that was on the point of disappearing in the Sheol of civilization. The original experience of the Berith was no longer alive enough to be a freely flowing source of order in the community, but it was still enough of a living force to recapture itself by the violence of an artifice.

The word of God had become the Book of the Torah, written by a Moses who had become a Pharaonic mummy. A new myth had been created, with consequences as far-reaching as they were unexpected. We shall briefly suggest the more obvious effects of the myth, for they make themselves felt even today and affect the methods of scriptural interpretation:

(1) The Speeches (words—*debharim*) of Moses, which in their present form comprise Chapters 1–30 of Deuteronomy, are the first pseudepigraphic book in Hebrew literature. When the D and P historians inserted the book in the J and E narratives, its pseudepigraphic character pervaded vast sections of the historiographic work. Since it seemed appropriate to interpolate the Speeches immediately before the traditions concerning the death of Moses, the present Deuteronomy 31–34 became part of the book of the Speeches, so that the authorship of Moses extended to the narrative of his own death. Moreover, the whole body of the narrative to the death of Moses fell under the form of the new myth: the Priestly and Holiness codes were interpolated, as the present book of Leviticus, into the narrative; the authorship of Moses was extended to cover the history from Genesis down; and even the character of "torah" was transferred to the historiographic work. The evolution toward the Five Books of Moses as the Torah must have been completed by the late fifth century, for the Israelites of Samaria, who at that time began to separate from the Jews of Jerusalem, could adopt the Pentateuch, alone, as their sacred scripture.

The Mosaic authorship of the Pentateuch remained unchallenged for the next fifteen hundred years. The first cautious questions were raised by R. Isaac of Toledo (A.D. 982–1057) and R. Abraham ibn Ezra (A.D. 1088–1167), when they recognized certain passages, which referred to later events and institutions, as irreconcilable with the authorship of Moses. They found no immediate followers, however, and another four hundred years of silence lapsed before the questioning of details became more frequent in the wake of the Reformation. From the eighteenth century onward one can speak of a continuous critical occupation with the structure of the Biblical narrative until in the nineteenth century, with the Graf-Wellhausen hypothesis, the solid basis for Pentateuchal criticism was secured. The myth of Moses, thus, had lasted for two-and-a-half millenniums before it was ultimately dissolved, and before a reliable picture of genesis and structure of the Pentateuchal books had been gained through the efforts of generations of Old Testament scholars. Only in the twentieth century has it become possible, therefore, to discern behind the mythical Moses the great contours of the man who created history as the inner form of human existence in society.

(2) The myth of Moses-the-author would not have resisted dissolution so tenaciously unless it had found shelter in the conception of the Bible as the "word of God." The origins of the conception can still be discerned in the ambiguous phraseology concerning the reception of the Book of the Torah by Josiah, in II Kings 22–23. When the King had heard "the words of the Book of the Torah" (22:11) he was shocked and frightened. Not only had the fathers not hearkened to "the words of the book," but Yahweh had now to be expected to act any day "according to all that was written therein concerning us" (22:13). The royal suspicions concerning the imminent divine sanction were confirmed by the prophetess Huldah: Yahweh was just now about to bring evil on the place and its inhabitants, "namely all the words of the book which the King of Judah has read" (22:16). In order to avert the disaster the King accepted the book as the law of the realm in the previously mentioned ceremony; and again, on the occasion were read "all the words of the Book of the Covenant which was found in the house of Yahweh" (23:2). In the several passages the term "word" refers not only to the commandments of the Decalogue, or to the provisions of ritual, constitutional, criminal, and civil law, but also to the surrounding Introduction and Conclusion, which contain the abbreviated history of Exodus, Berith, and Desert, as well as the blessing and the curse. The "word of Yahweh," thus, was expanded to embrace "all the words that are written in the book"; furthermore, the *toroth*, the instructions addressed by Yahweh to his people, were expanded into a new genus of scripture, the Torah; and the new scripture, finally, was elevated to a special rank of sacredness through a type of act which, on occasion of its later recurrence, came to be called "canonization." The consequences

of expansion and canonization made themselves immediately felt in the tension between the word of God that had been mummified in the sacred text and the word of God that continued to be spoken through the mouth of his prophets. One can imagine how horrified Jeremiah must have been when he saw conformity of action to the letter of the law supersede the obedience of the heart to the spirit of God.

The myth of the Word had an even greater success than the myth of Moses. From its origin in the Deuteronomic Torah it pervaded not only the Pentateuch but the whole body of literature eventually included in the rabbinical canon; and it imposed its form, through canonization, also on the Christian literature. While it did not destroy the life of the spirit, it inevitably proved an obstacle to its free unfolding. For when the historical circumstances under which the word of God is revealed to man are endowed with the authority of the word itself, the mortgage of the world-immanent circumstances, of which we have spoken previously, will become something like a sacred incubus. Statutory elaborations, which are meant to penetrate social order with the spirit of the "essential" Decalogue under varying economic and political conditions, tend to become canonical fossils and prevent further reforms. Mythical elaborations of the origin of the world in divine creativeness, as we find them in Genesis, are understood literally as information about the physics of the universe and give rise to formidable "conflicts between science and religion." And the myth of the Word extends even to translations, so that the philological correction of some old translator's mistake will be condemned by fundamentalists as a tampering with the "word of God." The myth of the Word, finally, had a prodigious career in the modern centuries. For the late-medieval fatigue of spiritual order led to a reform movement which, in a manner strangely resembling the Deuteronomic reform of the seventh century B.C., assigned to the New Testament the function of a Torah of true Christianity. And the vehement reassertion of the myth in the Christian sphere was followed by the expansion of its form into the various Gnostic creed movements, as for instance in the Comtean creation of a Torah for the *réligion de l'humanité*, or the formation of a Marxist Torah in the Communist movement.

4. *The Regulation of Revelation*

Because of the characteristics just adumbrated, the Deuteronomic Torah has become more than one book among others in the Bible. If it had remained the literary exercise of its unknown authors, preserved perhaps and discovered only centuries later as a forgotten scroll, it would be no more than a piece of evidence for the degree to which existence in historical form had weakened in the reign of Manasseh. Priestly and prophetic circles, we would have to say, had been capable of transforming the historical Moses into a novelistic figure. The discovery of the manuscript at the opportune moment, however, as well as its acceptance as the symbolic form for the Kingdom of Judah in the last generation of its existence, has made it the crystallizing nucleus of the Bible. One might even say there would have been no Bible, that is, no Book, unless *the* book had metamorphosed the history of Israel into the Torah and existence under God into existence under the written Law. That is a strange success for a book; and it suggests forces stronger than a mere literary whim, or the skill of a codifier, or the propitious moment of discovery.

The Torah could not have had its fateful success unless the genius of the unknown author had summarized and brought to their fulfillment century-old motivations of Israelite order, reaching back at least into the time of the prophetic revolt in the Northern Kingdom. In the preceding chapter, in the section on the Book of the Covenant, we have studied the peculiar response to the crisis of the ninth century. The "forgetfulness" of the people about the *toroth* of Yahweh provoked the construction of a paradigmatic code, organized into the *debharim* and the *mishpatim*— that is, into a decalogue of principles followed by statutory elaborations and counsels of conduct. The nature of the work was peculiar in that it was neither a code of law enacted by the royal administration nor probably even meant by its authors as a project to be enacted, nor a collection of laws actually observed; but rather an attempt to cast in the form of divine instructions (in their varieties of words, "if"-laws, and counsels) what under Hellenic conditions would have become a philosophy of right order supported by a theology.

Under the conditions of Israel in the ninth century the philosophic solution was precluded, as we have seen, because the conception of an immortal psyche as the field of right order had not differentiated, and was even prevented from being formed by, the taboo of Genesis on man's striving for immortality like the *elohim*. The prophets were not philosophers, and the hearing of the specific word was not the ordering of the soul by the unseen measure. The instructions had been the symbolic means for transforming the leap in being into the concrete order of Israel; and the revision of instructions remained the means for bending the order, under changed economic and social circumstances, again to the spirit of Yahweh. Since the Sinaitic revelation, however, had been the constitution of Israel in historical form, the revised instructions, in order to be authoritative, had to be integrated into the growing corpus of the narrative. We had to stress, therefore, the inseparability of the prophetic revision from the legislative and historiographic aspects of the Book of the Covenant.

While the conditions of the solution had not changed by the seventh century, the reflection on the conditions had entered, as a new factor, the problem to be solved. At the time of the prophetic revolt the solution was limited by the degree of differentiation which the experiences and symbols had reached, but the field was open for further changes on principle. And the history of prophetism from Amos and Hosea to Deutero-Isaiah furnishes rich evidence for the tendencies to break the parochialism of Israel through the universalism of a mankind under God and its collectivism through the personalism of a berith that is written in the heart. The mortgage of the historical circumstances of revelation could have been gradually reduced, if the men who were willing and able to do it had found followers. In the actual course of events, however, the tendency prevailed to make the mortgage permanent by including the circumstances of revelation into its contents. That, of course, could not be done by turning the wheel of history backward and recapturing the situation of Israel in the desert; it could only be done by including the organization of the Kingdom of Judah in the seventh century in the contents of revelation.

In the Deuteronomic Torah we find, therefore, two strata of contents. In the basic stratum the Torah reproduces the structure of the Book of the Covenant of the ninth century: The *toroth* are again divided into the *debharim* of Deuteronomy 5 and the *mishpatim* beginning with Deuteronomy 12; and the purpose is again the reconstruction of the concrete order in the spirit of the decalogic words. In this stratum we are still moving in the continuity of Israelite traditions; and underneath the layer of paradigmatic revision there are still present elements of high antiquity. Superimposed, however, is a second stratum in which the historical contingencies of revelation are submitted to permanent regulation. The *toroth* of this second class, in Deuteronomy 17:14—18:22, pertain to the king, the priests, the prophets, and Moses. In their aggre-

gate they freeze the historical form of existence in the present under
God, as it had been created by Moses potentially for all mankind, into
a constitutional doctrine for the people of Judah, as organized in the
Kingdom of the seventh century, and their descendants.

Deuteronomy 17:14–20 regulates the kingship of Judah. Moses anticipates the settlement in Canaan. When the people will have come to the
point where they want a king like the surrounding goyim, they must be
sure to set themselves a king chosen by Yahweh—one of their brothers,
not a foreigner. While the author accepts the institution of kingship,
as it is willed by the people, he surrounds it cautiously with a few re-
strictions. The king must not increase his horses, so that the people will
not return to Egypt—perhaps a discreet allusion to a royal (Solomonic?)
practice of acquiring horses from Egypt in exchange for slave laborers;
nor must he have too many wives, so that his heart will not turn away—
an allusion to the practice of foreign concubines and the introduction of
their cults; nor must he increase his treasure of gold and silver too much
(17:16–17). The special limitations, inspired by the memory of royal
abuse of power in the past, are followed by the general provision that the
king must abide by the new Torah like any commoner. In order to keep
him on the path of the law the king, as soon as he has ascended to the
throne, will himself have to write out in a book a copy of the Torah,
of which the original is in the custody of the Levitical priests.[2] He then
shall read therein all the days of his life so that he will fear God and
abide by the words of the Torah, that his heart will not be uplifted above
his brethren, and that his kingdom will last, for him and his children,
in the midst of Israel (17:18–20). The origin of the Davidic dynasty
from a clan of Judah makes itself strongly felt in the provisions. The
ruler is conceived as a tribal king who will be bound by the same law
as the people and whose position of power is hedged in by the injunctions
against specific abuses.

Deuteronomy 18:1–8 regulates the status of the Levitical priests who
are the custodians of the Torah. The whole tribe of Levi shall have no
personal property or heritage like the rest of Israel, but live as priests
on the sacrificial dues (18:1–5). Since the situation of the Levites in the
villages would become precarious under the new cult monopoly for

---

[2] The phrase "a copy of the Torah" is translated by the Septuagint as *deuteronomion*, the
term which has given the fifth book of the Pentateuch its name; the Hebrew title is *debharim*—
"Speeches."

Jerusalem (Deut. 12), a special provision entitles them to transfer their residence to Jerusalem and to have an equal share in the dues of the Temple (18:6–8). That provision, however, had to be abandoned in practice, for the priesthood of Jerusalem defended its position, as well as the new affluence, against the starved brethren who flocked into the capital city; and the Levites from the province had to be satisfied with an inferior position and a small stipend. From this time dates the division of priests and Levites.

Deuteronomy 18:9–22, finally, regulates the status of the prophets and of Moses himself. The provisions are of particular interest, because they allow us to discern the picture which the Deuteronomist circles had of Moses. The section starts with an attack on "the abominations of the goyim." When Israel has come into the promised land, there shall not be found one among them who makes a child pass through the fire or who uses divination, not a soothsayer, augur, sorcerer, or charmer, not one who consults ghosts, or familiar spirits, or the dead (18:9–11). Yahweh has driven the inhabitants of Canaan out, in favor of Israel, because he abhors such practices. Israel must hearken to Yahweh alone; and since the people will not hear the voice of God himself for fear they might die (18:16), he will raise up from their midst, from time to time, a revealer (*nabi*—prophet) like Moses through whose mouth Yahweh will speak his word (18:15, 18). Moses, thus, is a prophet, the first of the series of the revealers who, for Israel, take the place of the diviners, soothsayers, sorcerers, and necromancers. Their primary function is the mediation of "the word of Yahweh" so as to make the consultation of other divine forces superfluous. Under this aspect Moses is the man who has freed Israel from polytheism and superstition and brought it into the presence of the one God. The function of his prophetic successors is less clear. The question would have to be raised what they could reveal after the "word" has been so amply revealed in the speeches of the Deuteronomic Moses? Could later revelations contradict the contents of the Torah? Was it permissible for a prophet to question the importance of sacrifices and cults prescribed by the Torah, or even to consider them an obstacle to a true obedience of the heart to the spirit of Yahweh? The Deuteronomic authors, however, avoid such issues. They only reflect on the obvious question of how the people should know whether the word of a prophet is indeed the word of Yahweh; and they offer as a criterion the actual occurrence of the event predicted in the name of Yahweh

(18:21–22). This meager answer, if we take the Torah by its word, would reduce prophetism to predictions which in a reasonably short time can be verified or falsified by the observation of tangible events.

Through the second stratum of the Deuteronomic Torah the Israel that had been chosen to receive the revelation of God for mankind has contracted into the unique society that ultimately came to be called the "Jews." The future that had been open for spiritual clarification and a universal missionary reception of mankind into Israel was now closed through the limitation of the choice to a concrete and rather small people. And the meaning of revelation itself had been compromised when the royal, sacerdotal, and prophetic organization of a people had been endowed with the authority of the word. With the inclusion of the historical circumstances into the contents of revelation the history of its recipient had truly come to its end. To draw the dividing line between the history of Israel and the history of the Jews at this point will be especially justified if we follow the assumption of Old Testament scholars who attribute the intimate relationship between the part of the Torah to which we referred as its basic stratum and the traditions of the Northern Kingdom, to the strong influence of refugees from Samaria after 722.

5. Deuteronomy and the Beginnings of Judaism

The Deuteronomic Torah stands on the border line between the orders of Israel and of the Jewish community. On the one hand, a chapter of history had come to its end when the author of a people had become the author of a book. On the other hand, the book unfolded a life of its own, when it motivated the postexilic circles of traditionists to organize the memories of Israel into the Bible (sepher) with its main division into the Law (torah) and the Prophets (nebi'im)—a division which characteristically overlays and breaks the narrative as the symbol of Israel's existence in historical form. Deuteronomy, thus, is the area of symbolization in which the order of Israel blends into the entirely different order of the Jewish community; and the Torah will show correspondingly different physiognomies when viewed from the Israelite past and the Jewish future.

In the literature on the subject the futuristic view predominates, because the study of Deuteronomy is broadly determined by the concern with the Bible as the Book of the Jews that in due course has become the Old Testament of Christianity. The fundamental fact that the Bible was

never the book of Israel lies so deeply below the historians' consciousness
that today it is practically forgotten. Hence, the aspects of the Torah,
which occupied us in our study of Israelite order, in particular the problems of the mythical Moses, are hardly ever touched in the work of Old
Testament students—though one would assume that the fight against
Mosaic authorship of the Pentateuch might arouse some interest in the
genesis and meaning of the myth. The Torah as the symbolic end of
Israel's life, as the contraction of the universal potentialities of the
Sinaitic revelation into the law of an ethnic-religious community, as the
occasion on which the historical circumstances of revelation were transformed into the revealed word, and as the instrument used by the sages
to suppress prophetism—all that is understandably of less importance in
the orbit of exegesis than the spiritual treasure which after all was preserved in this magnificent sum of the Sinaitic tradition. The heritage of
Israel was saved, for the first time, when the Southern Kingdom survived the Assyrian onslaught; in the century and a half thus gained for
mundane existence, that heritage was greatly enriched through the
prophets of Judah; and in this enriched form it was saved for the second
time through the energetic repristination of traditions in Josiah's Reform, before Judah fell to the rising tide of Empire. The exegetes and
historians of religion are interested in the Torah not as the entombment
of Israel, but as the transmitter of its spirit to Judaism and Christianity.
Hence, when now we turn to the preservative aspect of the Torah, our
account can be based on the sensitive and sympathetic interpretations by
Gerhard von Rad and Walther Eichrodt.[3]

In the first of his studies, Gerhard von Rad touches the decisive point,
the "relaxed theology" of the Torah as it expresses itself in Deuteronomy
30:11–14:

> For the commandment, which I command you today,
> it is not hidden from you, nor is it far off.
> It is not in the heavens, that you should say:
> "Who will go for us to the heavens, and bring it down to us,
> and make us to hear it, that we may do it?"
> Nor is it beyond the sea, that you should say:
> "Who will go for us over the sea, and bring it here to us,
> and make us to hear it, that we may do it?"

[3] Gerhard von Rad, *Das Gottesvolk im Deuteronomium* (1927); *Das Formgeschichtliche Problem des Hexateuchs* (1938); *Deuteronomium-Studien* (1947); *Der Heilige Krieg im Alten Israel* (1951). Eichrodt, "Religionsgeschichte Israels," *loc. cit.*, 377–448, the chapter on "Die Politische Theokratie der Reformkreise," *ibid.*, 421–27.

No, very near to you is the word,
in your mouth and in your heart,
that you may do it.

The atmosphere is relaxed indeed, for these words are not spoken by Yahweh to Israel, but by the mythical Moses who reminds his people that the will of God is now spelled out to them, for everyone to hear, in unequivocal language. No longer will there be a soul in anguish like Saul's when God is silent; no longer will there be a trembling in fear that existence in truth might be missed. "The search of man for the possibility of his right relation to God has become superfluous with the promulgation of Deuteronomy. The people can now live in fulfillment of their duties; their position before God is quite uncomplicated." Life can be conducted in a *nunc aeternum*, as it were; there is no crisis in the present, and the future holds no threat.[4] Von Rad especially stresses the recurrent "today": The commands are given "today"; the people vow acceptance and obedience "today"; the blessing and curse are put before the people "today"; and the Jordan will be crossed "today." [5] The *hayom* of Deuteronomy, in fact, symbolizes a peculiar time experience of "today and always today," in which the transcendent-eternal presence of God with his people has become a world-immanent, permanent presence of his revealed word. The mediation of the divine word through Moses (Exod. 20:19) has been accomplished, the word as communicated is now within history, and the eternity of the divine will has become the everlasting presence of the Torah. The Law, thus, far from being the burden it is frequently imagined to be on the part of Christian thinkers, is on the contrary the great liberation from the tension of existence in the presence of God. The *hayom* of the Torah, while originating in Israel's historical form, is the symbolic expression of a new experience of order in which the inrush of the Holy Spirit has been toned down to the inspired exegesis of the written word. A permanent peace of mind has replaced the existential anxiety of the fall from being —though not everything is quite peaceful in this new mode of existence.

For the law book of the Bible is its war book. The word of Yahweh flattened into the law of Moses, when existence in historical form flattened into the desperate aggressiveness of survival in pragmatic existence. The

---

[4] Von Rad, *Das Gottesvolk,* 59–61.

[5] Deut. 5:2–4; 9:1; 15:15; 26:17; 27:9; 29:10; 30:15, 19. Cf. von Rad, *Das Formgeschichtliche Problem des Hexateuchs,* 25 ff.

causes of the change in the experiential climate from the eighth to the seventh century are difficult to ascertain in detail because of the paucity of sources, but the nature of the process on principle has been well established by von Rad. After their victory of 701 and the territorial restriction of Judah, it must be assumed, the Assyrians followed their usual practice and took over the Judaite professional troops, together with their equipment of horses and chariots, and integrated them into their own army. A period of military organization that had begun under David and Solomon had come to its end. During the long reign of Hezekiah's successor, Manasseh, the disarmed, impoverished, and restricted Judah, then, remained the vassal of Assyria. Under Josiah, however, when the Assyrian power declined and fell, Judah was suddenly again engaged in effective warfare, even though the military exploits ended with the disaster of Megiddo in 609 B.C. Since, in view of the economic situation, the rebuilding of a professional army had hardly been possible, the new military strength can have been due only to a revival of the people's militia.[6] And the reorganization of the people's army cannot have been a mere matter of enacting a draft law, but must have involved something like a national resurgence among the social strata who had to furnish the manpower of the militia, that is, among the *amharetz* who had politically and socially receded into the background under the Empire and the Kingdom. It is possible, to be sure, that the peasantry with its clan traditions re-entered active politics only in the wake of Josiah's Reform, but more probably the Reform was the expression of a movement that had gathered momentum ever since the catastrophe of 701.[7] At any rate, the contents of Deuteronomy requires the assumption of its origin "in circles, in which the conception of divine kingship, of an Anointed of Yahweh, had perhaps never really taken root,"[8] for it is characterized by the resurgence of warlike traditions from the period of the Yahwist Confederacy and by a corresponding recession of the role of the King. The "Law of Moses" is, in fact, distinguished from all other codes of the Bible, and especially from the Book of the Covenant, in that it contains detailed rules for the conduct of officers and men in camp, for their conduct before, during, and after

[6] On the military history of the period cf. Eberhard Junge, *Der Wiederaufbau des Heerwesens des Reiches Juda unter Josia* (Beitraege zur Wissenschaft vom Alten und Neuen Testament, 4:23, Stuttgart, 1937).

[7] Von Rad, *Der Heilige Krieg*, 79 ff.

[8] Von Rad, *Deuteronomium-Studien*, 43.

battle, as well as rules for the siege of cities. It furthermore abounds with bloodthirsty fantasies concerning the radical extermination of the goyim in Canaan at large, and of the inhabitants of cities in particular.[9] And the law to exterminate the goyim is, finally, motivated by the abomination of their adherence to other gods than Yahweh: The wars of Israel in Deuteronomy are religious wars.[10]

The conception of war as an instrument for exterminating everybody in sight who does not believe in Yahweh is an innovation of Deuteronomy. The Holy Wars of the Confederacy had been defensive wars, in which Yahweh came to the aid of his people when it was attacked by its enemies.[11] While the new fierceness fortunately could be practiced only in rewriting Israel's history of the Conquest with streams of blood that had not flowed at the time, this kind of warfare more mythical than holy is nevertheless of importance in so far as it reveals the same change in the structure of experience and symbolization as the transition from existence under God to acceptance of the Torah. We are dealing here with phenomena that have been little explored; and caution is, therefore, in place. Nevertheless, it looks as if in Deuteronomy we were touching the genesis of "religion," defined as the transformation of existence in historical form into the secondary possession of a "creed" concerning the relation between God and man. In the case of Deuteronomy, this first "religion" in the history of mankind would have to be described as the Sinaitic revelation, mediated through Moses, when broken by the belligerence and civic virtue of a little men's patriotic movement.

The last sentences must not be understood as depreciatory. The spirit lives in the world as an ordering force in the souls of human beings. And the human *anima naturalis* has an amplitude of characterological variety that breaks the ordering spirit in a broad spectrum of phenomena. Plato and Aristotle, in the construction of their paradigms of the best polis, which must accommodate the variety of characters, have made this fundamental problem of social order explicit. The prophets, philosophers, and saints, who can translate the order of the spirit into the practice of conduct without institutional support and pressure, are rare. For its sur-

---

[9] For instance Deut. 11:23 ff., 19:1, 20:16 ff. For the documentation of these aspects of Deuteronomy cf. von Rad, *Der Heilige Krieg,* 68 ff.

[10] *Ibid.,* 70. For the formal organization of Deuteronomy, following the model of the Sinai pericope, cf. von Rad, *Das Formgeschichtliche Problem des Hexateuchs,* 23–30.

[11] Cf. Chap. 7.2.2.

vival in the world, therefore, the order of the spirit has to rely on a fanatical belief in the symbols of a creed more often than on the *fides caritate formata*—though such reliance, if it becomes socially predominant, is apt to kill the order it is supposed to preserve. With all its dubious aspects admitted, Deuteronomy is still a remarkable recovery of Yahwist order, when held against the practice of Judah under Manasseh; and when held against the alternative of a complete destruction of Yahwist order through the Exile and the dispersion of the upper class, it has proved to be its salvation in the form of the Jewish postexilic community.

Under this aspect of the preservation of Yahwist order in a concrete community in pragmatic history, Deuteronomy is considered by Eichrodt. As an attempt to reform the Kingdom of Judah, Deuteronomy was "a romantic dream," followed by the rude awakening under Jehoiakim. Its greatness lies in its general "religious orientation" that was apt to induce a new attitude toward governmental order in the people. The love of Yahweh has selected the insignificant people, and the divine love permeates its order. Before God all men are equal; and the legal order of Deuteronomy stresses, therefore, brotherly aid, the protection of the weak and the poor, and the administration of impartial justice with circumstantial detail (Deut. 15:22–25; 16:18–20; 17:1–13). The king himself, not excepted from the rule of equality, is no more than the specially responsible guardian of the order and protector of the weak (17:14 ff.). In their imaginative project of the rule of law (*Rechtsstaat*) the codifiers have successfully translated the divine order of love into an institutional model, counteracting thereby the apotheosis of the state, as well as the conception of a secular order of law and government in isolation against spiritual order. This translation makes sense only if it is more than mere legalism. Hence, at the center of the conception is placed the personal obligation of every member of the community to obey the law of God; the personal appeal and personal commitment of Deuteronomy 6:5 guarantees the survival of the order, not through external security, but through the conviction of the men living under it. This model is not an Utopia, nor can it be criticized as unrealistic. "It is the vision of might overcome by right, of egoism by consecration, of material interests by the power of the spirit; it is the vanguard of implacable resistance against the externally successful powers of this world, of the camp that from now on will call the history of urges and instincts before the tribunal of moral obligation and change its victory into defeat." [12]

In the perspective of the people that had been created by Yahweh and Moses his servant at Sinai, the living order of Israel was now buried in the "religion of the book." In the perspective of exilic and postexilic Judaism, the "book" was the beginning of communal existence under the Torah. Between the Israelite past and the Jewish future, did the Deuteronomic Torah have no meaning in the present at all? As a matter of fact, it had—though this is the obscurest of all its problems, and no more than a suggestion concerning its nature is here possible.

In terms of pragmatic history, the Josianic Reform seems to have originated in the movement of a social stratum that had been shouldered aside by the political exigencies of the Davidic Empire and the successor Kingdoms. Only when Israel had been destroyed, and Judah had surrendered, in the struggle against Assyria, had the historical hour come for the political ineffectuals of the past to try their hand at the task at which the ruling class had failed. And in this task they failed in their turn so completely, that the very existence of the movement and its efforts is a matter of reconstruction on the basis of Deuteronomy and of assumptions about the military and economic situation. In terms of spiritual order, then, the great asset of the movement, the source of its vitality, seems to have been the preservation of the Sinaitic traditions, which in the public order of the Kingdom had been overlaid by the institution of kingship, as well as by the diplomatic and voluntary compromises with foreign cults. Even at this center of its strength, however, we had to note the flattening effect of the movement in the transformation of revelation into the written word and of the holy war into the bloodthirsty religious war. And nevertheless, from these negatives emerged a positive communal consciousness, a fierce adherence to the collective identity, however much damaged pragmatically and flattened spiritually; and especially there emerged from it the gigantic effort of the exilic and postexilic community in preserving its traditions and organizing them into the Bible.

This aggregate of traits is a phenomenon to which historians refer on occasion as "repristination," or "archaism," or "nationalism." All of these terms have a certain justification, but since they suggest unrelated phenomena none is quite adequate to the specific aggregate. The peculiar

[12] Eichrodt, "Religionsgeschichte Israels," *loc. cit.,* 426.

phenomenon will be understood best if one recalls that repristinations and archaisms are a general trait of the age. While the Deuteronomists of the seventh century and after were occupied with the repristination of Sinaitic traditions, Assurbanipal collected in Nineveh the enormous library to which we owe principally our knowledge of Mesopotamian literature, and the Egypt of the Saitic period went two millenniums back for an archaistic revival of the literary and artistic styles of the Old Kingdom. The parallel cases of repristination and archaic interests suggest the breakdown of the older civilizational order, under the impact of the wars among the empires, as the common cause of this frantic struggle for the preservation of historical identity. Not only the most obvious victim, Judah, but the warring empires themselves were gripped by the *malaise;* and the worst offender among them, Assyria, went to a destruction as sudden as it was complete even before Judah. The expansion of the cosmological empires beyond the boundaries of their civilizational origin, the displacements of populations, and the foreign dominations created, in the souls of the victims of such violence, a disorder which no empire of the cosmological type could repair. And from the struggle for the bare survival of order in the soul of man emerged the Jewish community victoriously, both in its own right and as the matrix of Christianity.

CHAPTER 12

Moses

§ 1. The Nature of the Sources

Of the man who has created history as the present under God no "historical image" can be drawn, as no sources in the conventional sense are extant.[1] Neither has Moses left any writings; nor have there survived, if they ever existed, any contemporary records of Israel; nor have his life and his work left any traces in Egyptian monuments. Nevertheless, we need neither doubt his existence nor grope in the dark about the nature of his work, for there is extant the work itself, a source difficult to overlook: the people of Israel that preserved the memory of its own miraculous creation through Yahweh and Moses his servant. In Deuteronomy 4:32–34 we read:

For inquire now from the early days that were before you,
from the day when God created man on the earth,
from the end of the heaven to the end of the heaven,
whether anything happened as this great thing,
or whether anything has been heard of like it:
Did ever a people [*am*] hear the voice of God, speaking mid out of
the fire, as you have heard and did live?
Or has a god ventured to come and take him a nation [*goy*] from
inside a nation [*goy*],

[1] Of the older literature on Moses, Paul Volz, *Mose und sein Werk* (1907; 2d ed., Tuebingen, 1932), and Hugo Gressmann, *Mose und seine Zeit* (Goettingen, 1913), were used. The understanding of Moses has been put on a new basis by Martin Buber, *Moses*, 1948, in so far as the paradigmatic picture of Moses, as it appears in the text of the narrative, has been taken seriously. Buber, however, has not remained faithful to his own method; all too frequently he wanted to see the paradigmatic as a "historical" Moses. Elias Auerbach, *Moses* (Amsterdam, 1953), is more conservative in his method and disagrees with Buber's interpretation frequently. A summary of his reconstruction of a historical Moses and his work is to be found therein on pp. 238–43. The best recent reconstruction of a life of Moses, on the basis of empirical evidence, with ample bibliographical references, is Henri Cazelles, "Moïse devant l'histoire," in *Moïse. L'Homme de l'Alliance* (Desclée et Cie., Paris, 1955), 11–27. A good picture of Moses, blending empirical evidence and the results of Buber, is to be found in Hans Joachim Schoeps, *Die grossen Religionsstifter und ihre Lehren* (Darmstadt-Genf, 1950), 25–42.

by tests, by signs, by wonders, by war,
by a mighty hand, by an outstretched arm, by great terrors,
as Yahweh your God did for you in Egypt, before your eyes?

And in another version of the theme, expressing more clearly the paraenetic motivation, in Deuteronomy 6:20–25, we read:

When your son will ask you in time to come, saying: What is it
about the testimonials, the statutes and ordinances, which Yahweh
your God has commanded you? speak to your son:

Bondsmen we were of Pharaoh in Egypt, and Yahweh brought us
out of Egypt, with a mighty hand,
Yahweh showed signs and wonders, great and sore, against Egypt,
against Pharaoh, and against all his house, before our eyes,
and us he brought out from there, that he might bring us here, to
give us the land he swore to our fathers.
And Yahweh commanded us to observe all these statutes, to fear
Yahweh our God, for our good all the days, to keep us alive as at
this day.
And righteousness shall it be to us, if we are careful to observe all
this commandment, before the face of Yahweh our God, as he
commanded us.

The people itself, as it is alive at this day, is the witness to its origin in the
miraculous events by which Yahweh brought the nation forth from inside
a nation. And in the continuity of Israel's memory these events are inseparable from Moses, as the human instrument of Yahweh, as the prophet
(*nabi*) from the midst of the brethren to whom the people shall hearken
(Deut. 18:15). "By a prophet [*nabi*] Yahweh brought Israel up from
Egypt" (Hos. 12:14).

   We have no sources for the understanding of the person and the work
of Moses except the memory, as preserved in the Bible, of the Israel he
founded. This fact must be accepted with its methodological consequences:

   (1) The first of these consequences concerns the questions that can
be legitimately asked. We must not indulge, for instance, in speculations
about Moses as the "founder of a religion," for nowhere in the Bible does
he appear in this role. The questioning, if it wants to remain critical, must
accept him as he was known by his people, that is, as the man who brought
Israel up from Egypt, in the sense circumscribed in a preliminary fashion
by the passages from Deuteronomy just quoted. There he appears, first of

all, as the man who could form the Hebrew clans into a people in the ethnico-political sense, into a goy, that was willing to follow where he led. That extraordinary achievement was apparently due, furthermore, to his ability to influence the people spiritually so that it would "hear the voice of God," to form it into the *am* of Yahweh. And he could exert the spiritual influence, finally, because he had heard the word of Yahweh himself and obeyed its command.

(2) The second consequence concerns the answers that are possible in view of the nature of the Biblical source. In Chapter 6 we have briefly sketched the layers of meaning in the Biblical narrative, from the late historiographic stratum to the traditions absorbed into them. In the detail, and in particular with regard to Moses, the stratification of forms absorbed by forms is even more complicated. In the preceding Chapter 11, for instance, we have studied the form of the Torah, which has come to dominate not only the history of Moses but even the structure of the Bible as a whole. From sources of this type the only answers which can be extracted are those their nature allows them to give. An analysis of the Biblical narrative will not lead us, by a circuitous route, to the "historical Moses" whose picture cannot be drawn because of the complete lack of conventional sources. The oral and written forms of saga and legend, of the paradigmatic elaboration of traditions, and of the Torah have penetrated their materials so thoroughly that the construction of a reliable biography of Moses, or of the pragmatic course of events, has become impossible.

If we want to extract the historical substance from such sources, we must first ascertain the characteristics and motivations of the form, and then reconstruct the essence of the situations and experiences which lent themselves to the literary formation. That task, while it is not simple, is not as hopeless as it may look at first sight, because it receives variegated support from the source itself. Above all, historical substance has been formed by the Biblical narrative quite frequently for the very purpose of heightening paradigmatically its essential meaning, so that we find the object of our search without difficulty because the source has anticipated our intention; in such instances the meaning of the form is an extrapolation of the meaning of the substance formed. Moreover, in important instances the form is self-reflective and eloquent on its own motivations, so that the purpose of the formation can be easily distinguished from the situations and experiences absorbed by it. Furthermore, the rich stratification of forms that is peculiar to the Biblical narrative, while it complicates the analysis, lends a higher certainty to its results, because the lines of meaning from several layers of form converge on the same historical substance. And to such variegated help as comes, sometimes surprisingly, from the source itself must, finally, be added the critical support which the closer determination of essential situations and experiences receives from the weighing of historical probabilities, as well as from the principles of this study.

The methodological situation can best be illuminated by a few examples which, at the same time, will serve as an introduction to the Mosaic problem itself.

The Deuteronomic Torah is the literary form which most strongly has molded the figure of Moses as he lives in our tradition. Since the analysis of the Mosaic problem could be undertaken with any hope of success only when the formal elements of the source had been ascertained, it had to be deferred until the nature of the Torah had been studied. For the same reason we must now begin the analysis by removing the Torah which has imposed its form so forcefully over the others. The task is comparatively easy, since in this case, as we have seen in the preceding chapter, the formal element is clearly set off against the historical substance absorbed. The Moses introduced as the speaker of the Deuteronomic discourses is, without a doubt, a product of mythical imagination. He must be eliminated —and even more so the inflated Moses who authored the Pentateuchal Torah. The operation, while drastic, should not engender any doubts, however, concerning the historicity of Moses; for the myth of Moses would neither make sense, nor could it have taken hold of the people of Judah in the seventh century B.C., unless it had been grafted on the living tradition of the historical Moses. Still, a good deal of the traditional Moses disappears with his myth. For not only the speaker has been eliminated who delivers historical discourses, blessings, and curses, but also the function of the legislator is seriously affected. Even if we assume that the *debharim* and *mishpatim* contained in the speeches have preserved materials of the Mosaic period under their heavy layer of paradigmatic incrustations, adaptations to the changing economic and social conditions, and obviously recent additions, they certainly have lost their character as a Torah issued by Moses, since in the contents of the speeches the *toroth* emanate from Yahweh directly. God himself, not Moses, is the actor in history. Even in the passages previously quoted it was Yahweh, not Moses, who brought Israel up from Egypt. That does not mean, of course, that Moses disappears altogether. He still remains the *nabi* who transmits the word of the God whom the people are afraid to face directly (Deut. 18:15–18); and, as the Hosea passage has shown, he remains the human instrument that brings Israel up from Egypt; but his role in the drama of history has become distinctly secondary.

Let us assume for the moment (what has yet to be shown more convincingly) that we have touched genuine historical ground when we have penetrated from the imposing figure of the Deuteronomic myth to the self-effacing Moses who plays no more than a mediatory role in a drama which is enacted fundamentally between Yahweh and his people. It would then become intelligible why we hear so little about Moses in the period from the Deborah Song to the end of the Davidic Empire. If Israel experienced itself as a people under the order of Yahweh, the mediatory function of Moses in bringing the people into existence under its God could indeed have only secondary importance for the symbolization of Israelite order. While traditions of Moses and his work were preserved, they entered the foreground of symbolism only through the prophetic revolt in the crisis of the ninth century. When the Yahwist order was endangered, visibly to everybody, by the Omride policy of alliances, and when the spiritual responsibility passed from the organs of government to the prophets, the appeal to Moses could provide the background of legitimacy for prophetic action. An effective *imitatio Mosis*, however, required a paradigmatic prophet and lawgiver who could be imitated. That is the situation, as we have suggested in the preceding chapter, from which ultimately grew the Deuteronomic original prophet, giver of the Torah, and historian of the history which he had made.

If we regard the Deuteronomic myth as the end of an evolution that begins in the ninth century with the prophetic *imitatio Mosis*, the body of traditions in which Moses appears with the characteristics of a *nabi* will become suspect as legendary formation of the prophetic period. A further stratum of form will have to be removed before we can find the historical substance. A few examples will illuminate the problems that arise from the prophetic legend.

(1) In Exodus 5–12 Moses and Aaron obtain repeated audiences from the Pharaoh, first to persuade him, later to intimidate him through the

threats of plagues and the actual disasters, to let their people go. Even if one considers that Moses had been brought up as an Egyptian and may well have had court connections, the picture of a Pharaoh negotiating with the leaders of workers on a building project about their release is too improbable to be accepted as historical. The story of the audiences makes good sense, however, if we ascribe it to the prophetic legend. For in the Moses facing the Pharaoh and calling on him to obey the will of Yahweh, we can recognize the paradigm of the prophet facing the king of Israel. The typical situation of Samuel and Saul, Nathan and David, Elijah and Ahab, as well as of later prophets in relation to their kings, has been extended to Moses and Pharaoh. While the repeated audiences, as well as the face-to-face negotiations, must be eliminated as formal elements of the prophetic legend, we must beware, however, not to throw out the substance together with the form. And in search of the substance we must beware of the positivistic trap to substitute more probable pragmatic events for the legendary ones. For the detail of pragmatic events is of little interest. We need no legend in order to be sure that a sizable tribe of construction workers could not emigrate from Egypt without extensive preparations which must have involved some sort of negotiations between their leaders and officials of the Egyptian administration. The legend assures us on the much more important historical point that in the Exodus there was involved an issue of spiritual order, of a conflict between Yahweh and cosmic-divine civilization, of a conflict of the type which in Israelite history led to the clashes between prophets and kings. Whatever the personal relations between Moses and the Pharaoh may have been, the legend has preserved the memory of a clash between Moses and the principle of Pharaonic order.

(2) In the story of the negotiations between Moses and the Pharaoh there are embedded numerous sub-legends which equally betray their prophetic origin. Moses and Aaron appear, for instance, as magicians; and in Exodus 7:8–13 they try to impress the Pharaoh with portents. Aaron throws down his staff and it becomes a serpent. The unimpressed Pharaoh summons a band of his own magicians, and each one of them throws down his staff and lets it become a serpent. Then, however, the Yahwist reptile tops all the others by swallowing them; it is obviously superior to the Pharaonic product. The legend reminds us strongly of Elijah's contest with the prophets of Baal, and generally of the competitive bands of prophets at the court of Samaria in the ninth century. It probably orig-

inated in circles of the type which created the rich literature of legends
surrounding Elijah and Elisha. With regard to its meaning one must again
avoid the positivistic fallacy of using the story as a piece of ethnographic
evidence that Moses was a primitive sorcerer. It only proves that the
superiority of Yahweh over other gods could also find its expression on a
primitive level.

(3) If any doubt about the proper method of interpretation should
still remain, it will be dispelled by the subsequent stories of the plagues
which Moses and Aaron bring on with their staff. Nothing could be more
inapposite than an attempt to save the historicity of the stories by surmises about natural phenomena which conceivably could have been their
raw material, for the legends of the plagues, as they follow one another,
become increasingly self-reflective and reveal the superiority of Yahweh
as the historical substance consciously submitted to their formation. On
the occasion of the last but one of the plagues, the darkness over Egypt,
even the symbolism of the plagues themselves becomes transparent for the
spiritual issue, for there was a darkness over Egypt that one could touch,
"but with the sons of Israel there was light in their abodes" (Exod.
10:23). And with the last plague, the slaying of the first-born in Egypt,
the struggle between light and darkness reaches its climax. Exodus 11:4–5
circumscribes nature and extent of the plague:

> Thus says Yahweh:
> At the mid of the night I shall go forth mid through Egypt.
> Then all the first-born in the land of Egypt will die,
> from the first-born of Pharaoh who sits on his throne,
> to the first-born of the slave-girl behind her mill,
> and all the first-born of the live stock.

Israel, however, will be exempted from the plague "so that you will know
that Yahweh makes a distinction between Egypt and Israel" (11:7). And
Exodus 12:12, finally, formulates the nature of the distinction:

> For I shall pass through the land of Egypt in that night, and smite
>   all the first-born in the land of Egypt, both man and beast,
> and execute judgments on all the gods of Egypt,
> I, Yahweh.

The darkness over Egypt is the darkness of its gods, while the light over
Israel is the light of Yahweh. And the slaying of the first-born, while it
inflicts misery on man and beast, is—in a manner yet to be clarified—a

judgment of God on the gods. Through the various layers of form we always penetrate to the same historical substance, that is, to the conflict between the Yahweh of Moses and the cosmic-divine civilization of Egypt.

The historical substance, especially in Exodus 1–15, finally, has been molded by the form of a cult legend which can be traced to the vernal New Year festivals of Passah and Mazzoth. Almost certainly these festival rites were brought by the immigrant tribes with them to Egypt, and could supply the form elements for expressing the historical experience of rescue from a great danger in terms of the victory of the divine forces of fertility and order over the dark forces of death and disorder. "There is a unity in the whole legend which is dominated by the contest between Yahweh and Pharaoh, the aim of which is the deliverance of Israel while at the same time it has the Paschal feast in view, to the contents of which there are constant allusions." [2] Pedersen, who was the first to recognize this form problem, saw that the imposition of the legend had made it impossible to discern the pragmatic events underneath: "The legend purposes to describe the mythical fight between Yahweh and his enemies and this purpose dominates the narrative to such a degree that it is impossible to show what were the events that have been transformed into this grand drama. It is through the feast that events have been condensed and exalted to the dimensions they have assumed in the sacred story. Therefore it is only conceivable that they have acquired the form we know through the practical cult. Here the events have been re-lived in the Paschal night by the whole of the festival legend being reviewed. Therefore the night that is passed in the crossing of the reed sea is for the participants identical with the Paschal night itself, the night they experienced in the holy place, and which was not of course different from its archetype in Egypt." [3]

An element of the cult that is of special importance for our purpose has been discerned by Ivan Engnell in the legend, that is, the role of the king in the fertility rite. The characteristics of the king have been transferred to the Moses who bears the old royal title of the *ebed Yahweh*, the servant of Yahweh, and who is the god's *shaliah*, his messenger. The angel of God walks in front of him (Exod. 14:19); he is upheld by the divine spirit, the ruach; he carries the miraculous staff, the royal scepter; and he is the lord of the winds which overcome the sea (*tehom*), as in the creation story and the flood story. "Moses is indeed the saviour-Messiah, leading

[2] Johannes Pedersen. *Israel. Its Life and Culture*, III–IV, 731.
[3] *Ibid.*, 730.

the 'exodus' of his people—its 'exodus' to the *Paesah* celebration!" He overcomes the god's enemies in a ritual combat, represented by the plagues of Egypt. "And that combat culminates in the victory over Pharaoh who is, in his turn, a parallel figure to *Kingu,* the Accadian personification of the 'counter-king,' the *shar puhi,* Pharaoh who, exactly like Kingu, is not killed but—according to Rabbinic tradition—kept prisoner in the Red Sea (Sheol, the Underworld) during fifty days in order to be placed, immortal as he is, at the gates of Hades for ever." [4]

The figure of Moses, thus, has been molded by more than one form. From the Paschal Legend stem the elements which place Moses in the role of the savior-king who overcomes the forces of chaos. In so far as this legend could attract variegated materials in the course of elaboration, there have entered the form elements of the prophet who opposes the King. And, finally, his figure has been overlaid by the Deuteronomic myth.

§ 2. THE SON OF GOD

Through the analysis of forms, both of the Torah and of prophetic legends, we have penetrated to the common historical substance. It proves to be the clash between the Yahwist experience of Moses and the cosmological order of the Egyptian empire. From the result falls a new light on the difficulties which beset a critical understanding of Moses. Since the clash between the two orders, as well as its issue into the actual constitution of a people under the order that had its origin in the soul of Moses, was a unique event in history, general categories do not apply to Moses, on principle, but can be used only as approximations with careful qualifications. There was something of the *nabi* in the man in whose soul occurred the leap in being when he heard the word of Yahweh; but the man who concluded the Berith with Yahweh for his people was not one of the indefinite number of "messengers of the Berith" who came after him. There was something of the legislator in the man who on innumerable occasions rendered judgment in the spirit of the *debharim,* which he perhaps had formulated himself, on cases submitted to him; but he was not himself a codemaker, though many of his decisions may have become precedents for later codifiers. There was something of the historian in the man who

---

[4] Ivan Engnell, *"Paesah-Massot and the Problem of 'Patternism,'"* Orientalia Suecana, I, 39–50. Condensed from pp. 46 ff. Cf. also Wensinck's study, "The Semitic New Year and the Origin of Eschatology," *loc. cit.,* pp. 158–99, as well as our presentation of the general problem of cults and patterns in Chapter 9.5.3 and 6.

made history and, in the course of a long life, must have had frequent occasion to correct the stories that were forming around the memorable events in which he had been an actor; but he certainly was not the historian as which he appears in Deuteronomy. There was something of the liberator in the man who led his people from servitude to political independence; but he was not an Israelite Garibaldi, for the people, in order to be freed by him from the bondage of Pharaoh, had to enter the service of Yahweh. And, finally, while he was a spiritual founder he did not found "a religion," but a people in the present under God. Hence, in order to characterize adequately the essence of the Mosaic person and work, we are forced back from the type concepts to the symbols by which the unknown authors of the respective sections of the Biblical narrative tried to express the unique essence of the issue in continuity with their traditions. That essence is contained in the formula: Yahweh brought Israel, through Moses, up from Egypt. And we must look for the symbols in which the meaning of the terse formula is made explicit.

Fortunately such symbols can be found embedded in the narrative. The decisive passage is Exodus 4:21–23:

> (21) Yahweh said to Moses:
> As you go to turn toward Egypt, see:
> All the portents, which I lay in your hand, you will do before
>   Pharaoh,
> but I shall strengthen his heart, that he will not let the people go.
>
> (22) Then you will say to Pharaoh:
> Thus Yahweh has said:
> My son, my first-born, is Israel;
>
> (23) I said to you: "Let my son go, that he may serve me";
> and you refused to let him go;
> So now I shall slay your son, your first-born.

The structure of the passage is somewhat complex. It is not part of a legend, but stands for itself as a word of Yahweh addressed to Moses; and yet it clearly refers to the legendary sources just considered. It is placed at the point in the narrative where Moses starts on his return from the Midianites to Egypt in order to free his people; and it clearly interrupts the narrative which is resumed in 4:27 with Aaron's meeting his brother on the Egyptian side of the desert. Old Testament scholars are therefore inclined to treat it as a misplaced piece of tradition. Nevertheless, we hesitate to accept the verdict because we reject, on principle, the assumption that the meaning of a passage can be exhausted by cutting it into the pieces which, by philological criteria, must be assigned to various component sources. In our opinion the passage in its present form stems from a hand which combined the various J and E strands into the story of the encounters between Moses and Pharaoh, and was deliberately placed where it stands today in order to serve as a summary of the leitmotifs which run through the legends of the audiences and the plagues.

The first motif, in 4:21, concerns the magical activities of Moses and Aaron, as well as the prolonged obstinacy of Pharaoh, which allows for the series of legends and the *crescendo* of the plagues. Since this motif belongs to the form of the prophetic legend analyzed previously, it is of no further interest to us here. Its date must be late, since it presupposes the existence of the legends; the contents of the verse may even be as late as its formulation.

Relevant for our present purpose, however, are 4:22–23, since the motifs assembled in them concern the historical substance. The conflict between the Yahwist experience and the pharaonic order is brought on a formula as simple as it is perfect. We remember the Pyramid Text in which the Pharaoh is greeted by the gods:

> This is my son, my first-born;

and we find now opposed to it in 4:22 the new formula:

> My son, my first-born, is Israel.

In adapting the Egyptian symbol to the new experience the same method is followed as in the Abram episode of Genesis 14, where the symbols of the *berith* and the *baal-berith* are transferred from the Canaanite El-Elyon to the god of Abram. The argument with regard to the date of both experience and symbol used on that occasion will also apply to the present problem. Experience and symbol fit the situation of the conflict with Egypt; there is no reason why the formula should not be dated in the Mosaic period, or why its authorship should not be ascribed to Moses himself.[5]

The formula is brief and clear, but its implications are manifold and sometimes obscure. First of all, it is not an exercise in adequate symbolization but a principle of order. It occurs in the summary of leitmotifs for the legends of the plagues and the Exodus; and the first point of order

---

[5] Nowhere in the literature have I found a reference to the relation between Exodus 4:22 and the Egyptian coronation ritual.

flowing from the principle of 4:22 is the command of 4:23 to the Pharaoh: "Let my son go, that he may serve me." The motif has to be hammered persistently through the legends, for the Pharaoh understandably is not inclined to accept the command. When Moses and Aaron inform him that in obedience to the command of Yahweh he must let the people go so that they can hold a feast for their God and offer sacrifices to him (5:1, 3), the Pharaoh roundly questions (5:2):

> Who is Yahweh, that I should heed his voice and let Israel go?
> Yahweh—I don't know him,
> and Israel—I shall not let go!

and he orders more severe treatment for the mutinous people (5:6–23). But the command is inexorably repeated (7:26; 8:16; 9:1; 9:14; 10:3); [6] the people must serve their God in the desert. In the course of the retardations it becomes, furthermore, increasingly clear that the Exodus is not an affair of Israel alone, but that the Pharaoh is fatally involved in the reordering of relations between God and Man. The emigration of Israel means more than the loss of a working force; the Egyptian ruler has been spiritually demoted and must surrender his position as Son of God to Israel. Yahweh demands Israel for his service, but he commands the Pharaoh to recognize the new order; he reminds the ruler, through Moses, that he could efface the Egyptians from the earth, but that he wants to spare them (9:16): "so that I will show you my power, and that my name be declared all on the earth." The Egypt after the Exodus will not be the same as before, for now a greater power than the Pharaonic will have been recognized. At last, when the first-born are slain, the ruler breaks down; in the middle of the night he summons Moses and Aaron and desperately orders them (12:31–32):

> Up, out from the midst of my people, you, and the sons of Israel!
> Go, serve Yahweh, as you have spoken,
> and take your sheep and your kine, as you have spoken,
> and be gone!
> and also work a blessing for me!

Still, there is a rest of resistance. When Israel has gone, the Pharaoh and his advisers reconsider. They go in pursuit with their army to bring the people back. And Yahweh has to enforce the new order with symbolic finality through the miracle of the Red Sea: The army of the former Son

---

[6] References to the Hebrew text. The first two references are 8:1 and 8:20 in the RSV.

of God is enveloped in darkness (14:19), thrown into a panic (24), and submerged in the floods (27–28), while the new Son of God, his people Israel, walks safely up to dry ground and into the desert. The scene closes with Miriam's song of triumph:

> Sing to Yahweh,
> For high he rose, high,
> The horse and its rider,
> He hurled in the sea.

When now we take a closer look at the new Son of God, as he emerges from the darkness of Egypt into the light of the new dispensation in history, we find him an odd creature. He is, first of all, not an individual human being but a social group; he has, furthermore, not the least desire to be a son of God; and finally, he expresses his disgust with, and resistance to, the new role so outspokenly that we begin to wonder what conceivable meaning the phrase "Son of God" could have when applied to an obstreperous bundle of humanity that hardly can be called even a people. When, after the first audience, the work-load for the Israelites is increased, the foremen wish the attention of Yahweh on Moses for getting them into difficulties (Exod. 5:21). And when, at the Red Sea, the Egyptian army draws near, the people turn against Moses: "Was it because there were no graves in Egypt that you have taken us away to die in the desert? What a way to treat us, bringing us out of Egypt! Isn't this what we told you in Egypt would happen, when we said: 'Leave us alone and let us serve Egypt, for it is better for us to serve in Egypt than to die in the desert'" (Exod. 14:11–12). There never would have been a first-born son of Yahweh if the God had had to rely on the people alone; there never would have been an Israel without the leadership of Moses. If there was a clash between the orders of Israel and Egypt, it had its origin in an experience of Moses.

The transformation of the indifferent and recalcitrant Hebrew clans into the Israel of Yahweh must have taken some time, as well as the efforts of a strong personality. It presupposes the existence of the man who could bring the people into the present under God because he had entered into it himself. Moreover, the formula of Israel as the Son of God could hardly have been intelligible and effective, unless the people had been penetrated with Egyptian civilization to a certain degree; and its creation, in particular, points to a man who lived so intensely as an Egyptian that he could conceive it in its full weight as the abrogation of Pharaonic order.

The traditions preserved in Exodus which suggest the Egyptization of the clans and their leaders are so well known that they require only the briefest recall. Exodus 12:40 gives the time of Israel's sojourn in Egypt as four hundred and thirty years. Whether the figure is correct or not we do not know. We know just enough about the general history of the area at that period to make more than one conjecture concerning the date of entrance and exit possible, but not enough to make one of them convincing beyond a doubt. The clans may have entered Egypt during the Hyksos period (1680–1580) and been driven out along with the foreign dynasty, or they may have left a generation later, or during the Amarna period (fourteenth century), or in the late thirteenth century. They also may have entered only during the Amarna period and left about a century later. The Biblical figure would fit best an entrance during the Hyksos period and an exit in the thirteenth century. With regard to the date of entrance we have no opinion of our own to offer; with regard to the exodus we prefer the latest date, under Dynasty XIX, for reasons that will be set forth in the present chapter. Under any assumption the sojourn of the clans was long enough for Egyptian influences to make themselves felt in the people at large. And in particular it was long enough for individuals to rise in the hierarchy of Egyptian society, as suggested by the traditions about Joseph, whose mummy the emigrants took with them (13:19). A similar rise must be assumed behind the traditions about Moses, though all concrete details have disappeared behind the veils of the legend. The story of the exposure of the infant, his preservation, and upbringing as the son of Pharaoh's daughter (2:1–10) is a typical legendary form, which has its closest parallel in the Near East in the story of Sargon of Akkad.[7] No biographical circumstances can be extracted from a form that would fit any Egyptianized Hebrew of high social rank once he has, for other reasons, become important enough to be a suitable target for legendary treatment.

In the legend of exposure and rescue there is embedded, however, a detail of nontypical, specific character, that is, the reference to the name of Moses and its meaning. When the child entered the household of the princess, "she called his name: Mosheh; and said: For out of the water I drew him" (Exod. 2:10). The passage has the more immediate purpose of

---

[7] For an English translation of Sargon's legend see Pritchard (ed.), *Ancient Near Eastern Texts*, 119.

putting a Hebrew veneer on the Egyptianized Moses, for the name is almost certainly the same element as appears in such Egyptian names as Thutmosis or Ahmosis. Since the element means "son," it is not likely to have been used alone, and the conjecture is plausible that the missing father was an Egyptian god. In that case the name would have been shortened to Moses (perhaps by himself?) because the theophorous name did not sit too well on the bearer who was in revolt against the Egyptian Son of God.[8] Apparently, however, that was still too Egyptian a name for the founder of Israel, and a Hebrew interpretation was put on it, as in Exodus 2:10, by deriving it from the verb *mashah*—to draw out, so that Moses would be "the one who was drawn out" of the water.

The more immediate purpose of the passage, thus, is clear. The interpretation of the name, however, has its difficulties, for, as Martin Buber has pointed out, the form *mosheh,* if derived from the verb *mashah,* does not mean passively "the one who was drawn out," as Exodus 2:10 wants it, but means actively "the one who draws out." [9] Buber suggests, therefore, the passage had the ulterior intention to point to Moses as the man who drew Israel from the flood. That such an interpretation of the name actually existed in the tradition of Israel Buber finds confirmed through a passage in Isaiah 63:11 which does not make sense under any other assumption. The verse begins, with Yahweh as the subject: "He remembered the days of old"; and then continues: *"Mosheh ammo,"* which means "Moses, of his people." The sequence of words does not render a satisfactory sense. It becomes meaningful, however, if *mosheh* is understood as an exegesis of the name Moses, for then the line would have to be translated:

> He remembered the days of old,
> "the one who draws out" his people.

And then also would make good sense the immediately following cry of the prophet for the Yahweh who apparently does not remember his people in the present distress:

> Where is he who brought them up out of the sea,
> with the shepherd of his flock?
> Where is he who put in their midst
> his holy spirit?

[8] Lods, *Israel* (1948), 169; Robinson, *A History of Israel,* I (1950), 81. A. S. Yahuda, *The Language of the Pentateuch in its Relation to Egyptian,* I (London, 1933), 258–60, doubts the abbreviation of a theophorus name and considers the meaning "Child of the Nile" preferable.

[9] Cf. the same observation in Ivan Engnell, "Mose," *Svenskt Bibliskt Uppslagsverk,* II, col. 311, and also the references to II Samuel 22:17, Psalms 18:17, and Isaiah 63:11.

We are inclined to accept Buber's suggestion.[10] If we accept it, how-ever, we cannot be satisfied with the assumption of a secret or ulterior in-tention of Exodus 2:10. There apparently really existed two traditions concerning the name of Moses linked by the experience of the Red Sea miracle. He was both "the one who draws out" his people and "the one who is drawn out" together with his people by Yahweh, as he appears in Isaiah 63:11. And once the suggestive connection of the name with the "drawing out" from the Red Sea was established, a little grammar more or less would probably not have been the primary concern of the men who played with the symbolism when they wanted to affix a Hebrew meaning to a name they knew to be Egyptian. The ungrammatical exegesis of Exodus 2:10 makes it probable that in the chain of symbolic motivations the link between the name and the verb *mashah* was already established when the legend of the Sargon type offered itself for adaptation to Moses. In that case, however, if the connection with the Red Sea miracle was pri-mary, something really impressive happened on the occasion which justi-fied its connection with the name—not necessarily the miracle described, or even a substitute suggested by "natural explanations," but some mir-aculous escape from a great danger to which the phrase "to be drawn from the floods" could be applied.

One cannot be restrained enough to draw naturalist conclusions from symbols—always allowing for the possibility that in a concrete instance the conclusion would be justified—for the symbols weave their own way through experiences which are not sense perceptions. There is one more place in the Bible where the verb *mashah* occurs, in Psalm 18. In II Samuel 22 the psalm is ascribed to David, and perhaps he really "spoke" it, bar-ring a few suspect passages. As the preamble informs us, it is a hymn of thanks for delivery from his enemies, in particular from Saul, as well as for ultimate victory through the intervention of Yahweh. In this context it is David who is "drawn out" from the flood (17–18):

> He reached from on high, he took me,
> he "drew me out" of many waters.
> He delivered me from my strong enemy,
> and from those who hated me;
> for they were too strong for me.

In isolation the passage only proves that the phrase "he drew me out from the waters" was freely movable and could be applied to miraculous rescues

[10] Buber, *Moses*, 51 ff.

in general. In the later course of the hymn, however, the nature of the rescue is narrowed down and approaches closely the complex of the Red Sea miracle. The hymn is one of the Imperial Psalms, if we may stretch the genus so as to include the *imperium in statu nascendi,* and David is drawn from the waters in order to emerge as the ruler over the nations (42–46):

> They cried for help, but there was none to save;
> They cried to Yahweh, but he answered them not.
> And I beat them fine, like dust before the wind;
> I cast them out, like the mire of the streets.
> You have rescued me from the strife of the people;
> You have made me the head of the nations;
> A people whom I had not known serve me.
> As soon as they hear of me, they submit to me;
> The sons of the stranger come cringing to me.
> The sons of the stranger lose heart,
> And come trembling out of their fastnesses.

At first sight that seems a strange way for the symbol of the "drawing out" to take. If we remember the sequel to the Davidic victory, that is, the coronation liturgy of Psalm 2 in which the King has become the Son of Yahweh, the meaning of the symbol appears to have been reversed. When Moses brought Israel up from Egypt, he drew the new Son of God from the waters in which the old one perished; and now Yahweh draws from the waters a ruler who resembles the Pharaonic Son of God. Has Israel now been demoted and Pharaoh resurrected? Has the symbol of the Son of God gone full circle, back to cosmological rulership?

In order to understand the issue, we must first realize that the evolution toward the Davidic Son of God was one of the possibilities inherent in the Mosaic conflict with Pharaonic order. The exodus of the Hebrew clans, as we have stressed, was more than a national liberation in the romantic sense. The Egyptian ruler did not have to set them free because of some principle of national self-determination, but in order to let them change their subjection to the service of Yahweh; he had to recognize Yahweh as the God who issued the command. The divine-cosmic order of Egypt was abrogated; and the release of Israel implied the recognition of Yahweh's historical order in which the new Son of God held first place. The god of Moses was the God not of Israel only but of mankind; when Moses led his people into the desert, the result was not two peoples in political co-existence under different gods but one historical dispensation with its center in the Chosen People. In spite of appearances, that new spiritual order established by Moses was not abolished by the Davidic kingship. The Yahwist order of history in the Mosaic sense, as well as the relations between Yahweh and his people remained intact, when Israel, under the pressure of necessities, had to acquire a king like the other nations. One can speak of no more than a deformation of the original theopolity through the intrusion of a royal Son of God into the system of symbols.

Again, however, restraint is indicated. The order of the theopolity, of the free existence of the people under Yahweh, to be sure, was deformed, when the Israel that already was the Son of God acquired a second Son of God as its ruler. The incongruity will appear in a different light, however, if we consider that the existence of a collective Son of God was in itself a deformation of the order of mankind under Yahweh, so strongly stressed in the legends of Exodus. Should "Egypt" be permanent, in order to provide the Chosen People, set off against the rest of mankind, with a pleasant sense of superiority? In the process of the spirit the Son of God had to become personal again, without becoming a Pharaoh, in order to break the collectivism of Israel and to release the universalist potentialities of the Yahwist order. And the Davidic kingship was indeed instrumental in this process. For the Imperial Psalms, as we noted in our analysis, were preserved and elaborated not because of nostalgic memories of the kingdom (though that factor may also have played its role) but because the royal symbolism became the vessel of Messianic hopes in the spirit of Yahweh, once the institution of kingship had disappeared under the blows of history. Moreover, the Psalm 18 at present under consideration lends itself to the double meaning so well that it is a matter of controversy whether certain sections, especially verse 43 ff., should be ascribed to the Davidic period, or rather be considered a late reworking with Messianic tendency. And it concludes on the ambiguous tone:

> For this I will extol you among the nations, Yahweh,
> and will sing praises to your name:
> Great triumphs he gives to his king,
> and shows kindness to his *mashiach*,
> to David and to his seed, forever.

The royal Son of God, far from destroying the order of Moses, served the unfolding of the universalism which it contained in its compactness.

The continuity of experiences and their symbolic expression, from the Mosaic foundation to the Messianic unfolding, will become clearer when

we compare the conclusion of Psalm 18 with a passage from Hebrews
13:20:

> The God of peace, who brought back from the dead the great shep-
> herd of the sheep, by the blood of the eternal covenant, our Lord
> Jesus Christ, may fit you by every blessing to do his will: working
> in you what is pleasing to him through Jesus Christ: to whom be
> glory for ever and ever.

The Anointed of Yahweh, who first was the King of Judah and then the
Messiah of the Prophets, has ultimately become the Christ in his glory for
ever and ever. And from Christ a ray of light falls back over the past to
illuminate Moses. For among the various allusions to the Old Testament
in the passage just quoted there is one, the recall of Isaiah 63:11, that links
Jesus with Moses: Jesus is the shepherd of the flock who is brought up out
of the sea with his people. He is "the one who is drawn up" from the dead
by God; and at the same time "the one who draws up" his people by working in them, as the divine instrument, what is pleasing to God. Through
the tortuous ways of the Messianic symbolism the characteristics of Moses
in the dynamics of divine order have now become the characteristics of
Jesus; and conversely the characteristics of the Son of God are those of
Moses.

The unique position of Moses has resisted classification by type concepts, as well as articulation through the symbols of the Biblical tradition.
He moves in a peculiar empty space between the old Pharaonic and the
new collective sons of God, between the Egyptian empire and the
Israelite theopolity. On the obscurities surrounding the position of Moses
now falls a flood rather than a ray of light, if we recognize in him the
man who, in the order of revelation, prefigured, but did not figurate himself, the Son of God. It is the compactness of this intermediate position
which resists articulation and makes it impossible, even in symbols of his
own time, to answer the question: Who was Moses?

Once we have become aware of the problem, however, we can search
the Biblical text for attempts to overcome the difficulty and to break
through, however imperfectly, to a symbolization of the man who stands
between the compactness of the Egyptian and the lucidity of the Christian
order. One or two passages suggest themselves, more or less clearly, as such
attempts.

One such attempt culminates in the designation of Moses as a god. When Moses is ordered by Yahweh to lead his people from Egypt and to plead with Pharaoh for their release, he resists obstinately—almost as obstinately as the Pharaoh himself. In a long dialogue Yahweh has to beat down one argument after another why the mission should be unsuccessful, until Moses refers to his personal incapacity as a negotiator (Exod. 4:10):

> O Lord,
> Not a man of words am I,
> neither in the past, nor recently, nor since you have spoken to your
>   servant,
> but heavy of mouth and heavy of tongue am I.

With that argument the dialogue approaches its climax, for the "words" which Moses has to speak as a man bodily, handicapped by his heaviness of mouth and tongue, are spiritually the words of God. And Yahweh indeed points out to Moses his twofold impertinence. For in the first place, the physical handicap is part of God's creation and therefore none of Moses' business when he is faced with the divine command (4:11); and second, Yahweh will be spiritually with his mouth and instruct him what to speak (4:12). When Moses still resists, Yahweh breaks out in anger (4:14–16): Is there not Aaron, a ready speaker, in whose mouth Moses can put his words? Aaron shall speak to the people:

> He shall be to you a mouth,
> and you shall be to him a god.

A second version of the episode, in Exodus 6:28—7:5, is pointed even more clearly toward the conflict between Moses and the Pharaonic order. Again Moses pleads his "uncircumcised lips" as the obstacle to successful negotiation (6:30), but this time Yahweh answers:

> See, I give you to Pharaoh as a god,
> And Aaron your brother shall be your revealer [*nabi*—prophet].

The language of the passage must not be mistaken for genuine symbolization which authentically expresses an experience of transcendence. Moses is not ontologically, but only metaphorically, a god. In spite of its inadequacies as a symbol, however, the language admirably expresses the feeling that Moses, while not God, is something more than man. In an undefinable manner the presence of God has become historical through Moses.

Another text, finally, cannot be omitted, though it resists conclusive interpretation, because its position in the narrative marks it especially relevant to the present complex of problems. It is the night episode of Exodus 4:24–26:

> And it happened on the way at the night-camp:
> Yahweh encountered him and tried to kill him.
> Zipporah took a flint and cut off the foreskin of her son,
> and with it touched his feet, and said:
> "In the blood so you are my bridegroom!"
> Then he let him alone.
> "In the blood bridegroom" she said with regard to circumcision.

Neither the ethnographic aspects of the episode, nor its etiological use for explaining the circumcision of infants, are our concern here. What matters is that Yahweh tried to kill Moses. Various possibilities of interpretation suggest themselves:

(1) A clue to the meaning of the strange incident, suggested by Martin Buber,[11] is perhaps that it happens on the travel from Midian to Egypt. Moses, at last, has obeyed the command and is on his way. But in the darkness of night the confidence of the day will succumb to depression. The "killer" is perhaps the daemonic negativity which Yahweh, as the exclusive Elohim, has absorbed with all other divine force. It would be the Satan in Yahweh who leads Moses into temptation.

(2) In addition to the clue suggested by Buber, we should like to draw attention to the fact that the episode immediately follows the summary of leitmotifs of Exodus 4:21–23, in which Israel is declared the son, the first-born, of Yahweh. The summary of leitmotifs and the night episode belong together, in that they interrupt the narrative as one body of text and provide the introduction to the story of the exodus proper. Hence, the possibility must not be neglected that the meaning of the episode is somehow connected with the sonship of Israel. In the spiritual situation of Moses, defection from Yahweh through simple inaction was indeed impossible. Inaction would have been active desertion to the enemy; he could not disobey the command of Yahweh without consciously reaffirming the order of Pharaoh. That the Israelite historians were aware of the problem is proven, in our opinion conclusively, by their parallel construction of the conduct of Moses and Pharaoh. The obstinate resistance of Moses in the thornbush dialogue, which precedes the interruption of the narrative by

---

[11] *Ibid.*, 82–87, the chapter on "Goettliche Daemonie."

Exodus 4:21–26, balances the resistance of Pharaoh in the legends of the plagues, which follows the interruption. And both Moses and the Pharaoh resist once more, with a last vehemence, after they have apparently bowed to the divine command. In the parallel construction the night episode, in which Moses was almost killed, would correspond to the Red Sea disaster, in which the Pharaonic order was actually engulfed. Perhaps it was the Egyptian in Moses, the old Son of God, who rose for the last time and had to be "killed" in order to establish the new Son of God. From the last temptation, in which the Pharaoh was submerged, rose Moses to victory. The action of Zipporah would then have to be understood as the assurance of the sonship of the people through the mother of the people. The collective element of the sonship needed a special guaranty.

(3) A final suggestion by Buber draws attention to a possible connection between the circumcision of the episode and the repeatedly stressed "uncircumcised lips" of Moses (Exod. 6:12, 30). The dialogue with Yahweh, as well as the repetitions, make it abundantly clear that the resistance of Moses to the divine command had something to do with the "uncircumcised lips." There was something unfree in the man whose heavy mouth spoke the word of God not willingly to the people he led though he did not quite belong to it. The anger of Yahweh that blazed forth at the climax of the dialogue had perhaps to be intensified to the threat of the night encounter, in order to make the uncircumcised lips speak the creative words and bring into existence the people whose covenant with God is confirmed through the rite of circumcision.[12]

Moses was barred from common humanity by his suffering of the solitude with God. As he had lived by the command of his God, he died by his command. The extraordinary destiny provided for him found its last symbol in the tradition of his death, on Pisgah, overlooking the promised land he was not permitted to enter:

> Thus died Moses, the servant of Yahweh,
> in the land of Moab, at the command of Yahweh,
> and he buried him,
> in the vale in the land of Moab, toward Beth-Peor,
> and no man knows his burial-place to this day.

---

[12] The night episode is painful to more conservative historians. Auerbach, *Moses*, 51, says: "It is an unsufferable thought that God, who just has uncovered his name to his favorite Moshe in a great revelation and charged him with his mission, should immediately afterwards, at night, attack him murderously." The way out of this difficulty is found by Auerbach through a generous rearrangement of the text.

The Hebrew text says literally that Moses died "at the mouth of Yahweh," a figure of speech which usually means "at the command." Perhaps the trope was used on this occasion intentionally: The man with the uncircumcised lips found his freedom at last at the lips of God.

§ 3. THE GOD

"By a prophet Yahweh brought Israel up from Egypt." The order of Israel has its origin in Moses; and the order in the soul of Moses has its origin in the leap in being, that is, in his response to a divine revelation. Two principal sources for the understanding of the Mosaic experience are extant. The first is the prologue to the revelation, in Exodus 2; the second is the account of the revelation itself, in the thornbush episode of Exodus 3:1—4:17.

The firm circumscription of the object of inquiry as well as of the sources is necessary in order to prevent derailment into the innumerable side issues which inevitably have accrued in the literature about an event of world-historic importance. We are not concerned, for instance, with pre-Mosaic Yahwism, except to the extent to which it reaches into the Mosaic experience itself. The Yahweh who revealed himself to Moses was known to him, as the Biblical narrative relates, as a tribal god of one or more Hebrew clans. Yahweh was perhaps the god of the Midianites or Kenites with whom Moses found refuge in the desert—though it should be understood that the formerly favored assumption, the so-called Kenite hypothesis, is today badly shaken; and he certainly was the god of the fathers, of Abraham, Isaac, and Jacob. He stood, furthermore, probably in a closer relationship to the family of Moses, for twice he is designated as the god of his father (in the singular: Exod. 3:6; 18:4); and the name of Moses' mother was Jochebed (Exod. 6:20), the only theophorous name composed with Yahweh before the Sinaitic Berith. The fact that Yahweh was a well-known divinity is important, however, only in so far as it attests the continuity of symbols; it has no bearing on the contents of the revelation. God, when he revealed himself to Moses, could be identified by him as a familiar divinity; and especially he could be so identified by the Hebrews whom Moses had to bring up from Egypt, or they would hardly have followed him. Nevertheless, while the continuity of the symbol could engender trust, the Yahweh of Moses was God in the mode of his revelation to Moses; no pre-Mosaic Yahweh has anything to do with the constitution of Israel as the Son of God in history. Hence, we must also exclude all speculations which try to reduce Yahweh to the primitivity that befits a god of the second millennium B.C. in the progressive order of things—whether he was, for instance, a "mountain god" (because he appeared on Mount Sinai), or a "fire god," a "*jinn*" (because the Sinai of the narrative seems to have indulged in volcanic eruptions, throwing up fiery clouds most suitable as seat for a god), or a "tree god" (because he revealed himself in a thornbush). All such speculations are impermissible in face of the Biblical information that Yahweh "descended" to the thornbush (Exod. 3:8) and Mount Sinai (19:11) from somewhere "up" where the cry of his people reached him (2:23). He was a *deus absconditus*, hidden in heavenly regions, and manifested himself in such places and forms as the occasion required. He appeared to Moses on Horeb; he accompanied him on the way and even tried to kill him; he was with him in Egypt to help his heavy mouth; and he descended on the Egyptians to slay their first-born. The mobility of Yahweh, it is true, varied in the course of Israelite history; in the seventh century B.C., for instance, when he became increasingly associated with Jerusalem, it was low; but it never completely disappeared, and the exiles gratefully discovered that Yahweh was still with them in Babylon.

Our first source, the prologue of Exodus 2, is a unit of literary work, composed from various traditions by an artist of considerable psychological and dramatic skill. Of the subsections, 2:1–10 is usually attributed to the E source, 11–22 to J, and 23–25 to P, unless one prefers an even more subtle distinction of sources. We mention the attributions, not to pursue them any further, but on the contrary because we want to stress that the meaning of the composition cannot be found through tracing the component sources. The increase of spiritual tension in Moses conveyed by Exodus 2 does not stem from the distinguishable J, E, and P sources, but has an independent origin which defies dating. The literary form, to be sure, is late, as it has absorbed the datable sources, but the contents, the growth of Moses toward his encounter with God, is an undatable description of a spiritual process. When the tradition that ultimately received the literary form of Exodus 2 started we do not know, but there is nothing in it that would not fit the time of Moses.[13]

[13] For a very minute distinction of sources in Exodus 2 cf. Simpson, *The Early Traditions of Israel*, 160–63, as well as the page references for Exodus 2 in the Index of Scriptural Passages.

The unknown author proceeds by chaining together a number of paradigmatically heightened episodes so that by their mere sequence, with a minimum of commentary, they communicate the growing tension. Moses is first the infant between the races, an exposed Hebrew child brought up as the son of Pharaoh's daughter (2:1–10). He then is the young man, Egyptianized but not ignorant of his origin, who feels himself strangely drawn toward his Hebrew brethren. Various incidents provoke interventions, which reveal his character as much as they bend it toward its destiny. On one occasion, when an Egyptian kills a Hebrew, Moses takes matters in his own hands and kills the Egyptian. On another occasion, he observes a fight between two Hebrews and points out their wrong to them. This time, however, his intervention takes an unpleasant turn, as one of the Hebrews asks him pointedly who had set him as a foreman and judge over them, and whether he would perhaps want to kill him as he did the Egyptian. Suddenly Moses awakens to his situation: He has assumed authority in rivalry with the Egyptian administration; by an unreflected sense of responsibility he has set himself as judge in affairs of his people; and his people, far from accepting his authority, threatens him with betrayal to the Egyptians. The danger is real; and Moses must flee into the desert, in order to escape execution as a rebellious Hebrew leader (2:11–15). Moses is now a fugitive in the desert into which later he will lead his people, but he is still the man of authority. When he sits at a well in Midian, a group of shepherds want to drive off the daughters of a neighboring priest who have come there to water their father's flock. Again he intervenes and helps the women; and thereupon he is invited to stay with the priest and is given a daughter in marriage. Nevertheless, he remains keenly aware of his being a stranger, a man who is not with his people. In Egypt he could not be quite Egyptian because he was a Hebrew; in Midian he is the Egyptian stranger, with status of a resident (*ger*). When a son is born to him, he calls him Gershom, "for I am a resident stranger [*ger*] in a foreign land" (2:16–22). Years have passed, the former Pharaoh has died, and the unfortunate incidents of Moses' youth are forgotten. The old man who once assumed authority as a Hebrew over Hebrews is now ripe in God's own time to assume authority over Israel as the servant of Yahweh. The last episode introduces the God to whom

---

For other subdivisions of sources cf. Auerbach, *Moses*, 13–29—very illuminating for the destruction of the meaning of the integral text. Buber, *Moses*, does not discuss Exodus 2 as an integral text.

rise the cries of Israel in bondage. Now is his time to hear, to remember the covenant with Abraham, Isaac, and Jacob:

> And God now saw the sons of Israel,
> And God knew.

The knowledge of God is his action. When God "knew," Moses was ready for the revelation (2:23–25).

The second source, the thornbush episode of Exodus 3:1—4:17, does not at first sight show the clarity of construction which distinguishes the prologue. The text as it stands today is linked through the previously discussed summary of leitmotifs with the episode of the plagues, and is intended to balance the story of the encounter between Moses and Pharaoh in the larger unit of the exodus narrative. With that layer of meaning we shall deal in the subsequent analysis of the Berith. The purpose, now, of balancing the encounters of Moses with God and with Pharaoh has been achieved through the expansion of an original account of the revelation by additions which point toward the later events. Fortunately, however, the interpolations are clearly recognizable by contents and style, and we shall follow Martin Buber in eliminating the following passages as additions: [14] (a) 3:15–22, as it is partly repetitious, partly anticipates details of the conflict with Pharaoh; (b) 4:1–9, as it anticipates the *portenta* of Moses which have no inner connection with the divine revelation; and (c) 4:13–17, as it prepares the participation of Aaron in the conflict with Pharaoh. What remains, that is, the body of text comprising 3:1–14 and 4:10–12, is again a spiritual drama of the first rank, though we do not know whether it was written by the same hand as Exodus 2. It is this remaining text that we now shall analyze. As in the case of the prologue, it should be mentioned, the attribution of component parts to the J and E sources is of no assistance for the understanding of the composition.[15]

The drama of the revelation is organized as a sequence of clearly distinguishable scenes:

(1) Exodus 3:1–3: Moses, while tending the flocks of his father-in-law, comes to the Horeb, the Mountain of God:

---

[14] Buber, *Moses,* 67–70.

[15] For another delimitation of the nucleus of the episode, taking into account the J and E sources but neglecting the meaning of the text which cuts across the sources, cf. Auerbach, *Moses,* 31–36.

> And the messenger of Yahweh let himself be seen by him, in a flame
>   of fire from the midst of a bush [*seneh*].
> And he looked: Behold, the bush [*seneh*] burned with fire,
>   and the bush [*seneh*] was not consumed.
> And Moses said: I will turn aside and see this great sight,
>   why the bush [*seneh*] is not burned up.

The repetitious insistence on the *seneh*, with its allusion to *Sinai*, draws attention to the two stages of the revelation. God reveals himself first to Moses from the *seneh*, then to the people from the *Sinai*. Seneh (Exod. 3) and *Sinai* (Exod. 19) are linked as the two acts in which the constitution of Israel is completed.[16]

(2) Exodus 3:4: The divine presence has brought itself to the attention of Moses by arousing in general the awareness of his senses. It now makes itself a presence meant for him personally:

> When Yahweh saw that he turned aside to look,
> God called to him from the bush [*seneh*],
> and said: Moses! Moses!
> And he said: Here I am!

Through the plain answer Moses puts himself in the presence of the voice, whoever the speaker may be, and is ready to hear.

(3) Exodus 3:5–6: The voice reveals itself as divine and thereby introduces the proper distance into the mutual presence. Moses is on holy ground and must not come nearer. When he has stopped accordingly and taken his sandals off, the voice then identifies itself as the god of his father, as the god of Abraham, Isaac, and Jacob. Whereupon Moses hid his face, for he was afraid to look at God.

(4) Exodus 3:7–10: To see God is to die. Moses has hidden his face from the terrifying sensual presence, and he listens, with his soul, to whatever the voice has to say. And the voice tells him of the divine knowledge that is action. The revelation opens: "Seen I have, seen the oppression of my people who are in Egypt"; and it closes: "Lead my people, the sons of Israel, out of Egypt!" Here, for the first time, appears the theme of "my people [*ammi*]," firmly framing the promise of freedom in 3:8. As the *seneh* points forward to *Sinai*, so the *ammi* points forward to the Berith through which the Hebrew clans, who as yet are ignorant of the fate in store for them, will be transformed into "my people." In the knowledge

---

[16] *Seneh* and *sinai* probably have a common root. Besides Gesenius cf. Engnell, "Mose," *loc. cit.*, col. 312; and Auerbach, *Moses*, 32 ff., 168 ff.

of God the action distended in historical time is completed. Moreover, the historical action has subtly begun with the revelation, for the knowledge of God has now become the knowledge of the Moses who, in the course of his life, has grown to the point where he can hear the divine voice articulate its command. When Moses can hear the voice appoint him the servant of Yahweh, he has grown spiritually into the servant of Yahweh. The command could be rejected only by a man who could never hear it; the man who can hear cannot reject, because he has ontologically entered the will of God, as the will of God has entered him. When the consciousness of the divine will has reached the clarity of revelation, the historical action has begun.

(5) Exodus 3:11–14 and 4:10–12: When the command strikes Moses it cannot be rejected, but it can be received with misgivings about his human ability to accomplish the apparently impossible. Who is he to persuade Pharaoh and bring Israel out of Egypt (3:11)? And how can he explain to the prospective people that the god of their fathers, who has taken his good time to hear their cries from bondage, is the God, who now will indeed help them (Exod. 3:13)? Such misgivings are overcome when the god of the fathers reveals his true nature through the self-interpretation of his name, "Yahweh." The interpretation is part of the action that has begun in Moses with the revelation, and it also determines the literary form of the scene. As in the preceding scene the promise of freedom was framed by the introductory and concluding references to "my people," so now the supreme revelation of God's nature is framed by the "I will be [*ehyeh*] with you" of Exodus 3:12 and 4:12. In the exegesis at the center, the meaning of God is then revealed as "I am who I am [*ehyeh asher ehyeh*]." To the skeptical sons of Israel Moses will have to say: "*Ehyeh* has sent me to you" (3:14). The people thus will break the bondage of Egypt and enter the present under God, once they have responded to the revelation of God's presence with them. The mutual presence of God and Moses in the thornbush dialogue will then have expanded into the mutual presence of God and his people, through the Berith, in history.[17]

---

[17] Our analysis follows on the whole Buber, *Moses*, the chapter on "Der brennende Dornbusch," 56–81. Against Buber cf. Auerbach, *Moses*, 39–44. In Auerbach's opinion Moses tries to discover the true name of God because it gives power over the divinity; and he refers to comparable episodes in Genesis 32:28, Judges 13:17, Proverbs 30:4. The interpretation is in conflict with the overt contents of the episode and can perhaps best be explained as an attempt to save the meanings of the component J and E sources. Important for the exegesis of the divine name is the recent study by E. Schild, "On Exodus III 14—'I AM THAT I AM,'" *Vetus Testamentum*, IV (1954), 296–302: "The answer to Moses' question is not an evasive circular

The thornbush dialogue could be written only by a man who had an intimate knowledge of the spiritual events of divine revelation and human response. He was a prophetic mind of the first rank; and the fact that in the composition J and E sources were used allows us to place him at the earliest in the eighth century B.C. The question will have to be raised whether a work so distinctly prophetic in form contains a historical substance that can be assumed to go back in an unbroken tradition to the time of Moses. And in particular, we must ask whether the exegesis of the divine name as I AM WHO I AM can have had Moses as its author. Since these questions are today obscured by an immense controversy which, first, is not always too clear in the statement of the issues and, second, is all too frequently biased by progressive ideology, we must briefly clarify what in our opinion the nature of the problem is.

We must realize first of all that we are dealing with a revelation presumably received by Moses, and nothing but that revelation; and second, that with regard to the contents of the revelation we have no source but the episode just analyzed. Hence, the rich etymological debate concerning the name of Yahweh, with its variegated conjectures, some more plausible than others but none conclusive, must be excluded as irrelevant to our problem. The narrative itself does not refer to any meaning attached to the name of Yahweh that could have influenced the contents of the revelation. On the contrary, it presents the name as one whose meaning is unknown, so that an exegesis is necessary in order to endow it with spiritual vitality. The exegesis, furthermore, is not intended as an etymology. As far as we know, the *ehyeh* has etymologically no more to do with *yahweh*, than *mashah* with *mosheh*, that is, nothing at all. The exegesis plays with a phonetic allusion, but its meaning is autonomous.[18]

As far as the autonomous meaning is concerned, a formidable issue is injected into the controversy through the fact that since the time of the Patres, the divine self-interpretation (*Ego sum, qui sum*) has been the

definition 'I am whatever I am,' i.e. I am I, and I am not telling you any more—but it is a positive answer in which God defines himself as the One Who Is, who exists, who is real" (p. 301). The thesis that the second *ehyeh* refers to God's reality is based on grammatical reasoning concerning the construction of clauses after *asher*. If the Old Testament specialists in 1954 still debated the grammar of the relative clause, the layman in 1955 will perhaps be permitted to read the passage in the sense suggested by the context.

[18] On the probable meaning of the tetragram cf. Auerbach, *Moses*, 44–49. Auerbach assumes the tetragram to be an enlargement, for cultic purposes, of the short form of the divine name through *He emphaticum*, and points to a similar development of *elohim* from the plural *elim*. If Auerbach's assumption of an artificial formation is correct, no etymological exegesis of "Yahweh" can even be attempted.

basis of Christian speculation on the nature of God. The primacy of the divine *esse,* in opposition to the Platonic primacy of the divine *bonum,* is so distinctively the great issue of Christian philosophy with regard to the essence of God that it has been justly called the philosophy of Exodus. The assumption now that the member of a nomad people in the thirteenth century B.C., or earlier, should have coined a formula which contains a metaphysics of being is preposterous to the enlightened, and too much even for more conservative historians. Oesterley and Robinson, for instance, say:

> We may be fairly sure that Israelite theology in Moses' day did not differ materially from that of other peoples at the same stage of development. The meaning of the name has evoked a good deal of discussion. The ancient Hebrew derivation suggested by Exod. iii, 14—"I AM THAT I AM"—has been suspected, as implying too advanced a metaphysical conception of God for an early nomad people.[19]

And even Lods, the most sensitive of the historians of Israel, says:

> The essential nature of the God of Israel is and must remain inscrutable. According to our account, the word Yahweh is merely a formal title which the God of Horeb revealed in answer to the practical needs of the cult, but it was intended to be a continual reminder of the phrase of which it was the epitome: "He is that he is," the Being whom none may know. While such an explanation is a lofty one, it seems too theological, too artificial to convey the original meaning of the name of the Midianite god.[20]

The passages are illuminating for several reasons. In the first place, the authors take it for granted that nothing extraordinary can happen in history; no unique personality, even if God so wills it, can break the "stage of development." They can make their assumption, second, because they remain unaware that the revelation creates history as the inner form of human existence in the present under God and therefore inevitably must be a break with the "stage of development," at whatever time it occurs. The "development" would be no less broken if the break occurred a few centuries later. And third, since they are not aware of the nature of revelation as a "break," as the leap in being, they both confuse the exegesis of the name, which in fact is an explication of the experience of divine presence,

---

[19] Oesterley and Robinson, *Hebrew Religion,* 153.
[20] Lods, *Israel,* 323.

with an etymology of the name "Yahweh." Obviously, the issue cannot be successfully treated on this rather low level of methodical precision.

And yet, while the arguments advanced in the two passages can hardly be called even debatable, they are motivated by a quite reasonable reluctance to read metaphysics into the thornbush revelation. Hence, we are faced with a dilemma. On the one hand, the authors just quoted (and many others) sense rightly that the exegesis of Exodus 3:14 cannot be a philosophical proposition concerning the nature of God—not because it presumably occurred in the thirteenth century B.C. among a nomad people, but because for reasons previously discussed no philosophical propositions occurred in the history of Israel at all. On the other hand, when we read in the Damascene:

> The foremost of all names applied to God is "HE WHO IS." For, as it comprehends all in itself, it includes being itself as an infinite and indeterminate ocean of substance;

we cannot deny that the Christian interpretation is well founded on the text.[21] While we cannot escape the dilemma either by doubting the text or by moving it down a few centuries, a solution suggests itself if we consider a distinction made by Gilson:

> One can, of course, not maintain that the text of Exodus bestowed a metaphysical definition of God on mankind. Still, if there is no metaphysics *in* Exodus, there is a metaphyics *of* Exodus.[22]

Gilson's distinction applies to a concrete case, in effect, our principle of evolution from compactness to differentiation. While the Exodus passage is not a metaphysical proposition, it contains in its compactness the meaning differentiated by the Christian philosophers.

Once we have recognized the exegesis of the thornbush episode as a compact symbolism in need of explication, not only will the philosophical interpretation appear well founded, but the labors of analysis bestowed by Christian thinkers on the episode in general can be accepted as an important aid for the understanding of the symbol. We shall use for this purpose the summary of the problem given by St. Thomas in the *Summa Theologiae*.[23] Thomas considers the HE WHO IS the most proper name

[21] Johannes Damascenus, *De fide orthodoxa I*, 9. (Migne (ed.), *PG*, XCIV, 836.)

[22] Etienne Gilson, *L'Esprit de la Philosophie Médiévale* (2d ed., Paris, 1948), 50, n. 1.

[23] Thomas, *Summa Theologiae*, I, q. 13, 11.

of God for three reasons: (a) because it signifies God according to his essence, that is, as being itself; (b) because it is universal and does not more closely determine the divine essence which is inaccessible to human intellect in this life; and (c) because it signifies being in the present which is appropriate to God, whose being has not past or future. Thomas, however, goes beyond the implications which the *ehyeh* has for a philosophy of being and brings the other components of meaning into play. While the name HE WHO IS is the most appropriate one with regard to the mode of signifying the divine essence, the name *God* is more appropriate with regard to the object intended to be signified by the name; and even more appropriate is the name *tetragrammaton* for the purpose of signifying the singular, incommunicable substance of God. The three names which occur in the last section of the thornbush episode—*ehyeh, elohim, YHWH*— are co-ordinated by St. Thomas with the structure of the divine being in depth, leading from the philosophically communicable essence, through the proper name of the object, into the depth of the incommunicable substance.

If now we place the issue of the "philosophical proposition" in the context of the Thomist analysis, the *ehyeh* will no longer appear as an incomprehensible philosophical outburst, but rather as an effort to articulate a compact experience of divine presence so as to express the essential omnipresence with man of a substantially hidden God. The "I will be with you," we may say, does not reveal the substance of God but the frontier of his presence with man; and precisely when the frontier of divine presence has become luminous through revelation, man will become sensitive to the abyss extending beyond into the incommunicable substance of the Tetragrammaton. As a matter of fact, the revelation of the thornbush episode, once the divine presence had become an historical experience of the people through the Berith, had no noteworthy sequel in the history of Israelite symbols and certainly no philosophical consequences. The unrevealed depth, however, that was implied in the revelation, has caused the name of God to become the unpronounceable Tetragrammaton YHWH. Philosophy can touch no more than the being of the substance whose order flows through the world.

The great issue of the "philosophical proposition" has given way to the insight that a metaphysics of being can be differentiated from Exodus 3:14, but is not the meaning of the compact symbol itself; and the summary of the problem by St. Thomas has led us back to the full meaning of the thornbush episode as the revelation to Moses of the divine presence with him and his people.

The revelation of the hidden God, through Moses, reveals his presence with his people; revelation and historical constitution of the people are inseparable. There is extant an interesting text, in the prophecies of Hosea, which proves beyond a doubt that this was indeed the sense in which the Israelites themselves understood the formulas of the thornbush episode. Hosea, as we have seen, diagnosed the "forgetfulness" of the people about their God and his instructions as the symptom of impending disaster. The God and the people who had been brought historically into their mutual presence through the revelations from *seneh* and *sinai* could separate again. The God who had disclosed himself as present could also withdraw; and then he would be no longer the "I will be with you," and the people would be no longer "My people." The prophet knew that the separation was already in process and would be consummated by disaster in pragmatic history, unless the people returned and remembered their God. As in the revelation to Moses the divine knowledge had embraced the actual constitution of Israel in historical time, so the revelation to Hosea embraced the actual dissolution of the people, accompanied by the external destruction of the Northern Kingdom. In order now to bring the divine foreknowledge to the knowledge of the people, Hosea chose the method of giving his son a symbolic name (1:9):

> And he [Yahweh] said:
> Call his name Lo-ammi [not-my-people];
> for you are not my people [*lo-ammi*];
> and I not I-am [*lo-ehyeh*] to you.

The text is important in that it proves not only the role of the symbolism in the constitution of the Israelite theopolity but also the existence of the formulas in the middle of the eighth century. Moreover, since the naming of the unfortunate child was meant to be generally understood as a revelatory action, the symbolism presumably was familiar to the people whom Hosea wanted to impress. Hence, it can hardly have been created by Hosea, but must belong to a tradition of considerable age.[24]

The structure and date of the symbol have been clarified sufficiently to prepare the crucial question whether the *ehyeh asher ehyeh* can be at-

---

[24] For the Hosea prophecy see Buber, *Moses*, 79.

tributed to Moses himself. An affirmative answer can be based on the close relation between the thornbush symbol and the Amon Hymns of Dynasty XIX (*ca.* 1320–1205 B.C.). We shall briefly establish the parallel:

(1) In the framing passages of the thornbush episode, 3:12 and 4:12, the *ehyeh* has the meaning "I will be with you"; and the Chicago translation justly paraphrases the *ehyeh* in 4:12 as "I will help you"—though the paraphrase destroys the structure of the text. The meaning that God will be present as the helper, furthermore, is confirmed by the instruction to Moses to tell the people: "*Ehyeh* has sent me to you" (3:14). The passage would have to be paraphrased: "The one who is present as your helper has sent me to you." In the light of this meaning, supported by the prophecy of Hosea, must be understood the central *ehyeh asher ehyeh,* usually translated as I AM WHO I AM. Unless we introduce extraneous "philosophical" categories, the text can only mean that God reveals himself as the one who is present as the helper. While the God himself is hidden (the first *ehyeh*) and, therefore, must reveal himself, he will be manifest whenever, and in whatever form, he chooses (the second *ehyeh*).

(2) This conception of divinity as a being hidden in his depth and, at the same time, manifest in many forms of his choice, however, is precisely the conception of divine being that we have found in the Amon Hymns of Dynasty XIX. Let us recall some of the characteristic passages:

> The first to come into being in the earliest times,
> Amon, who came into being at the beginning,
> so that his mysterious nature is unknown . . .
>
> His image is not displayed in writing;
> no one bears witness to him. . . .
> He is too mysterious that his majesty be disclosed,
> he is too great that men should ask about him,
> too powerful that he might be known.
>
> Mysterious of form, glistening of appearance,
> the marvelous god of many forms.
>
> "Hidden" [*amen*] is his name as Amon,
> he is Re in face,
> and his body is Ptah.[25]

Moreover, even within the cosmological form there become apparent the motives which tend to transform the highest empire god into the God who is present to man in his needs:

[25] Translated by Wilson, in Pritchard (ed.), *Ancient Near Eastern Texts,* 368 ff.

> Do not widows say: "Our husband art thou,"
> and little ones: "Our father and our mother"?
> The rich boast of thy beauty,
> and the poor worship thy face.
> He that is imprisoned turns about to thee,
> and he that has a sickness calls out to thee. . . .
> Everybody is turned back to thy presence,
> so that they may make prayers to thee.[26]

One must not forget, however, that approximations to an experience of divine presence of the type just quoted remain within the sphere of personal piety and prayer. They do not break with the cosmological myth of the Empire.

The parallel between the Yahwist and the Amon symbols is clear enough not to require elaboration. The tension between the hidden depth in God and his manifestations has been transposed, by the thornbush episode, from the form of cosmological myth to the form of revealed presence in history.[27] Such a transposition could well have been the decisive work of Moses, if we consider the fundamental issue of his existence as it has emerged from the previous analysis, that is, the conflict between the orders of Yahweh and the Egyptian empire. It is highly probable that the revelation of the new order was couched in symbols which clearly abrogated the order of the Egyptian gods as it was understood at the time. It would be the same type of symbolic opposition that we could observe in the Abram episode of Genesis 14. The revelation could break with the cosmological experience, but it could not be communicable unless it continued the symbols while changing their meaning. The God of Moses had to make himself intelligible to his people, not only as the God of the fathers, but also as the God of the new historical dispensation in opposition to the Amon of the empire. Hence, we are inclined to attribute the symbolism of the thornbush episode to Moses; and since the Egyptian texts which supply the continuity are later than the Amarna period, a date for Moses will have to be assumed in the thirteenth century B.C.

[26] *Ibid.*, 371.

[27] Parallels between Israelite and Egyptian symbols have been frequently drawn, in particular the parallel between the supposed "monotheisms" of Moses and Akhenaton. For a survey of such attempts, as well as for the reasons why they are not tenable, see Lods, *Israel,* 318 ff., the Appendix on "The Theory of the Egyptian Origin of the Work of Moses." Our own attempt in the text operates with a method not previously used.

§ 4. The New Dispensation

The historical action that had begun with the revelation from the thornbush was completed through the revelation from Sinai. The creation of the Israelite theopolity through the Berith is the last act of the drama in which the new dispensation of history under God was established in opposition to the Pharaonic order. In dealing with the act of foundation we shall use the same method as in the preceding sections. No more than brief reminders concerning fundamental points are necessary:

Again, there are no sources for the foundation and its meaning but the Biblical narrative itself. Hence, all extraneous speculations, especially those of an ideological nature, must be excluded. Moreover, as the question of the "philosophical" proposition had to be eliminated, in the preceding section, as anachronistic in face of compact symbols, so now the parallel question whether ideas of such lofty and pure "morality" as those contained in the Decalogue of Exodus 20, can be attributed to the famous "nomad people of the thirteenth century B.C." has to be eliminated. While the Decalogue, to be sure, has something to do with "morality," just as the thornbush episode had with "philosophy," it is not a moral catechism but the body of fundamental rules which constitute a people under God. In referring to the community as constituted under God, furthermore, we prefer the term "theopolity," coined by Martin Buber,[28] to the term "theocracy," coined by Josephus Flavius,[29] for the reasons previously discussed.[30] The Sinaitic foundation, finally, occurs no more in a historical vacuum than does the thornbush episode, but opposes its new order to the symbols of the Egyptian empire. Hence, we shall again pay careful attention to parallels with, and differences from, the cosmological form.[31]

[28] Buber, *Moses*.

[29] Josephus, *Contra Apionem*, 2, 16. The "theocracy" of Josephus—a form of government established by Moses which places supreme authority in the hands of god—has substantially the same meaning as Buber's "theopolity."

[30] Chap. 8. 2. 3.

[31] Our analysis is greatly indebted to Martin Buber's work for numerous details, as the frequent references in the footnotes have shown. It will be apposite, therefore, to characterize briefly the nature of the work, its achievements, and shortcomings, especially since we are not only indebted for details but find ourselves also in agreement with Buber's fundamental thesis: "Historisch betrachtet ist der in dem Adlerspruch und den mit ihm verknuepften Texten zum Ausdruck kommende Gedanke die Absage einer aus Aegypten in die Freiheit ziehenden Hebraeer-Schar an das ewige Pharaonentum. Die Freiheit, in die sie ziehen, wird von ihrem Fuehrer als Gottesfreiheit, und das heisst: als Gottesherrschaft verstanden. Historisch betrachtet bedeutet das: Herrschaft des Geistes durch die jeweils von ihm ergriffenen und beglaubigten Charismatiker auf Grund der im Namen des Geistes erlassenen gerechten Gesetze" (*Moses*, 158).

The action that culminates in the Berith begins when God hears the cry of his people and reveals himself to Moses. The series of events is a unit of action in so far as the begining and the end are one in the knowledge of God; in the distention of historical time, however, the unit has to be brought into being, step by step, through the human response to divine revelation. The problem of historical execution is formulated in the thornbush episode. When Moses pleads his human insignificance against the divine command, God answers (Exod. 3:12):

> But I will be with you [*ehyeh*];
> and this shall be the token for you, that I have sent you:

Buber, thus, has seen the great conflict between Mosaic and Pharaonic order, but in the execution of the idea he has frequently not applied the general insight to the specific problems. The declaration of Israel as the Son of God in opposition to the Pharaoh, for instance, is not mentioned, nor the relation between the conceptions of God in the Thornbush Episode and the Amon Hymns; nor has he seen the cosmological pattern in the conception of the Chosen People that will occupy us presently in the text.

In part, such shortcomings can be explained by the author's lack of familiarity with Egyptian and Far Eastern cosmological sources and in part, by his understandable reluctance to use Patristic and Scholastic sources as the guide to the clarification of Mosaic problems. The decisive handicap, however, seems to have been the methodological situation, which also is forcing on our analysis the frequent critical side glances. The serious study of symbolic forms and their literary expression has begun only recently. And the study of the Biblical narrative, in particular, is still heavily burdened with the disentanglement of the component sources—an indispensable task, to be sure, but no solution to the problems on the higher levels of meaning, such as the construction of the prologue to Moses' revelation, or of the Thornbush Episode.

The difficulties which have to be overcome will become clearer if we quote a few passages from the great authority of the last generation, Eduard Meyer's *Geschichte des Altertums:* "Aus dem Feuer am Dornbusch ist Jahwe selbst nach Aegypten gezogen, um sein Volk zu befreien. . . . Dadurch ist dann auch Moses selbst nach Aegypten gebracht worden. Nach dem Jahwisten ist er hier geboren; dabei ist ein allgemein verbreitetes Maerchen auf ihn uebertragen. . . . Bezeichnend fuer die Mache ist, dass die Motive, die dabei angeschlagen sind, in der Fortsetzung sofort fallen gelassen werden. . . . Auch ist Moses nichts weniger als ein Krieger und Held . . . sondern immer nur ein durch seine Verbindung mit der Gottheit mit Zauberkraeften ausgestatteter Wundertaeter . . . und ebenso zwingt er den Pharao zur Bewilligung des Abzugs nicht durch Heldentaten, sondern durch Zauberkuenste. . . . Ein Aegypter namens Moses mag in der Tat irgendwie nach Qades verschlagen worden sein und hier bei der Priesterschaft eine fuehrende Stellung gewonnen haben, so dass sein Name als der des Begruenders ihrer Kunst weiter lebte. Aber weiter laesst sich ueber ihn nichts ermitteln, von irgendwelchen aegyptischen Einfluessen in Religion und Kultus Jahwes findet sich gar nichts, diese tragen vielmehr durchweg das Gepraege eines echt semitischen Wuestenstammes" (II/2, pp. 207–209).

The attitude toward Biblical problems that manifests itself in the passages is certainly inadequate. Nevertheless, it is a powerful influence even today: The oddities in matters of religion to be found in Toynbee's *Study of History* can be explained to the larger part by the latter's incautious reliance on the authority of Eduard Meyer. Hence, even though Buber's *Moses* is unsatisfactory in many respects (the pivotal position of the summary of leitmotifs, discussed in the preceding section, for instance, was not observed by him), the work is of the greatest importance, because it breaks on principle with the spiritual oddities of the positivistic era and points the way towards a more realistic treatment of the sources. If our critical remarks can be restricted to a minimum, it is largely due to the fact that Buber, at patient length, has clarified the situation.

When you have brought up the people from Egypt,
you shall serve God at this mountain.

The divine presence assures man that he can fulfill a command he feels
beyond his human powers; and the fulfillment is the "token" of the
presence. In the concrete case: Moses can fulfill his mission because God
will be present with him; and the actual fulfillment, the service of the
people at the mountain, will be the "token" of the presence. Since in
historical time the "token" lies in the future, the end that in eternity is
joined to the beginning through the knowledge of God can be joined in
the human sphere only through the responsive trust of man in the
presence of God. There is no revelation to Moses as a historical event, unless
through the experience of revelation Moses becomes the servant of Yahweh; and no people will be brought forth from Egypt, unless in the act of
leaving Egypt it enters the service of Yahweh at the mountain. The gift
of revelation requires acceptance in order to become the form of historical
existence.

The Exodus, as it extends between the revelations from *seneh* and *sinai*,
is the historical drama *kat'exochen* in so far as it brings the order of existence into historical form through the human response to revelation. Moses
must accept the leadership of his people, as well as the mission to Pharaoh;
the Pharaoh must be made willing to let the people go; the people must be
induced to leave and to enter the service of Yahweh. At every stage of the
drama the performance can break down if the proper response is not
forthcoming; and it comes forth, indeed, only with reluctance, hesitations,
retardations, and even with resistance that must be broken. The very
substance of the drama is the molding of human action into the action
known by God; and the main stages in overcoming the resistance of man
determine, therefore, the literary construction of the Exodus story. The
great individual protagonists are Moses and the Pharaoh, the creator of
the new and the defender of the old order. Their stories are organized so
as to balance each other. In the first story, God has to overcome the resistance of Moses; in the second one, Moses, who is set as "a god to Pharaoh,"
has to overcome the resistance of the Egyptian ruler. Pre-existent treat-
ments of single episodes have been absorbed and subordinated to the
comprehensive construction of the conflict of orders. We have noted the
additions to the thornbush episode; and we have now to stress that
the interpolations, while they must be eliminated in order to clarify the
original construction of the episode, cannot be dismissed as displaying

the clumsiness of a second-rate redactor, but are carefully considered elaborations which fit the original episode into the larger context of the conflict of orders. The added retardations in the story of Moses are calculated to balance the series of Pharaonic retardations and of the plagues, which in their turn are assembled from various independent legends about the disasters inflicted on the Egyptians. Moreover, the parallel is accentuated through the climactic episodes: The declaration of Israel as the Son of God balances the destruction of the first-born of Egypt; the enigmatic night scene, in which Moses is almost killed by Yahweh, balances the Red Sea disaster in which the strength of the Egyptian Son of God is actually engulfed. Only through the overlaying construction of the whole narrative can we find the great issue—that would disappear if the component episodes were taken in isolation—that is, the transition of historical order from the Empire to the Chosen People. The elaborate presentation of the individual protagonists in their resistance to God is, furthermore, calculated to bring into proportion the resistance of the collective protagonist, of the people of Israel. The new dispensation will after all be the order neither of Moses nor of the Pharaoh but of the people under God; and the people resists, from the first treachery against Moses, through the grumbling against his liberating action and the reproaches when the Egyptian pursuers draw near, to the moods of despondency and the acts of mutiny and defection in the desert. Moses and the Pharaoh are representatives of mankind in their resistance to the order foreknown by God. And the climax of the Exodus, the actual establishment of the new dispensation through the Berith, is not at all a happy ending but the very beginning of the perpetual rhythm of defection from, and return to, the order of human existence in the present under God. Hence, while the action that began with the revelation to Moses indeed ends with the revelation to the people, the resistance to the order continues within the new historical form. History, in the sense of the perpetual task to regain the order under God from the pressure of mundane existence, has only begun.

The last act of the drama is the constitution of Israel as the people under God through the Berith. The problems of literary stratification in this part of the narrative resemble those of the thornbush episode, except that now they occur on a quantitatively larger scale. There is again a basis of materials which can be attributed to the J and E sources. With the J and E materials as his building stones, then, an unknown master has composed a paradigmatic drama which illuminates the meaning of the theo-political constitution. And the masterpiece of literary construction has, finally, been used by later historians for ulterior purposes, so that today it is badly distorted and even partly destroyed through vast interpolations and additions. The middle stratum, the spiritual drama of the Berith, is the one of primary interest to our problems. It consists of three main scenes:

(1) When the people arrived at Mount Sinai, Moses "went up to God" to receive further instructions (Exod. 19:1–3), in the form of a Message which he had to transmit to the sons of Israel. The Message (4–6) informed the people about conditions and meaning of the Berith. Moses assembled the elders and set the Message before them. It was accepted by the elders as well as by the people. Then Moses reported the acceptance back to Yahweh (7–8).

(2) When divine revelation and human response had been brought into agreement, the Berith itself could be concluded. The ceremony was prepared through ritual purifications and the delimitation of a sacred precinct (Exod. 19:9–15). Then Yahweh descended upon Sinai (16–25) and the people assembled at the foot of the mountain (Exod. 24:1–3). And when the God and the people were in their mutual presence, the Berith was concluded through a cultic act (4–11).

(3) When the Berith had been concluded, Moses was ordered to ascend to the Mountain again, there to receive the stone tablets on which Yahweh had written the fundamental rules governing the relation between the people and himself, as well as the relation among the members of the people (Exod. 24:12).

The whole action of the Covenant, thus, is clearly organized on this level of the narrative as, first, the revelation of the meaning of the Berith and its acceptance by the people; second, the cultic act of the Berith; and third, the proclamation of the rules which constitute the people as a theopolity.

The clear construction, however, is disturbed and partly destroyed through the aforementioned extensive interpolations. Between the descent of Yahweh to the Mountain (at the end of Exod. 19) and the assembly of the people at its foot (beginning of Exod. 24) has been inserted the Book of the Covenant (Exod. 20–23). Moreover, when the Berith is concluded and Moses ascends to the Mountain in order to receive the stone tablets, he is presented instead with elaborate instructions for the building of a "Tent," as well as for its equipment and ritual (Exod. 25–31). Only at the end, as an afterthought, God hands him the tablets, though we do not learn what is inscribed on them (Exod. 31:18). Then follows the episode of the golden calf (Exod. 32–33), which induces Moses to smash the tablets, their contents still unrevealed (32:19). Again he has to ascend, for a second set of tables (Exod. 34), and at last we get them down to safety and learn that they contain the cultic decalogue of Exodus 34:10–26. It is obvious that law collections of various periods were clustered around the Sinaitic Berith in order to let them partake of the dignity of the original foundation. As the thornbush episode had been inflated to make it balance the story of the plagues, so the drama of the Berith was inflated to let originate in it as many legal developments as possible.

The Berith drama has been seriously affected through the interpolations in that the rules of the theopolity, which were to be inscribed on the tablets, have disappeared from what must have been their original place, that is, the end of Exodus 24. Moreover, the rules and commandments that were supposed to be issued in pursuance of the Berith now not only follow but also precede its conclusion. As a consequence, it is today a matter of controversy whether the Berith was concluded on the basis of the Decalogue, or whether the Decalogue was issued on the basis of the Berith. The confusion has its specific origin in the interpolation of the Book of the Covenant before the conclusion of the Berith, a procedure which has forced a double meaning on certain terms of the cultic act of Exodus 24:3–8. For in 24:8 the Berith is concluded "according to all these words [*debharim*]"; and as the text stands today, the term *debharim* can refer back either to the *debharim* of the Message in Exodus 19:4–6 or to the decalogic *debharim* of Exodus 20. In the first case, the Berith would be concluded on the basis of the divine Message and its acceptance by the people; in the second case, on the basis of the Decalogue, which, according to the drama, should be inscribed on the tablets afterwards. The interpolating historians have made the second interpretation their own, for in Exodus 34 we find the meaning of the Covenant identified not with the Message but with the Decalogue itself (34:27–28). And finally, since the words inscribed on the tablets have disappeared from their proper place, we must decide which of the various decalogues, if any of them, could be the fugitive one. With regard to this question we favor the Decalogue of Exodus 20:1-17 because first, its clear theopolitical contents fit the intentions of the drama in three scenes, and second, its formal excellence and spiritual profundity match the high quality of the little drama.

With regard to historical reliability and date of the drama, one cannot go beyond probabilities. After the spiritual biography of Moses in Exodus 2, and the thornbush episode, we encounter now for the third time a brilliant author of the "middle stratum." We do not know who he was or whether the three pieces were written by one or more persons. We can only say that the authors must have been men of great spiritual sensitiveness, who were able to capture in paradigmatic dramas the essence of Moses' person and work. From the anaylsis of the component sources we know, furthermore, that they used the J and E materials, or—more cautiously—the traditions which also found their way into the work of the J and E historians. About the tradition of the meaning which the unknown authors superimposed on the materials, however, we know nothing. And with regard to historical reliability we can say only that on the one hand, the dramas of the "middle stratum" contain nothing that would be historically impossible while on the other hand, they let emerge a Moses of convincing stature.

We shall now deal with the three scenes of the Berith drama in their sequence.

When the people had at last arrived at Mount Sinai, Moses "went up to God" to receive his instructions. He was ordered by Yahweh to transmit to the sons of Israel, for their acceptance, the following Message (19:4-6):

> You have seen for yourselves: what I did to Egypt,
> and how I bore you on eagles' wings and brought you to myself.
>
> And now hear you, hear my voice and keep my covenant,
> and you will be my own possession [*segullah*] from among all peoples.
>
> For mine is all the earth
> and you shall be to me a kingdom of priests [*mamlekheth kohanim*],
> a holy nation [*goy qadosh*].

The first two lines restate the great historical issue: The people have seen what has happened to Egypt, while the sons of Israel have been brought to God. If the action of God now will be complemented by the human response, then God is ready to establish the new order, expressed in imperial symbols: The jurisdiction of God will embrace "all the earth" with its inhabitants. From among all the peoples, however, the people of Israel will be chosen as the specially treasured possession (*segullah*) of the ruler's household. They will be the royal domain (*mamlakah*); and as members of the household domain they will be *kohanim*, that is, personal aides to the king. The word *kohanim*, which in most cases has the meaning of priests, is indeed used in some instances in the sense of royal aides; [32] and perhaps a suspense of meaning was intended on the present occasion, when the royal domain was the *segullah* of God and its members, therefore, were a "holy nation."

The meaning of the imperial imagery is clarified by its elaboration in Deuteronomy 32:8–9:

> When the High One [Elyon] gave their portions to the nations,
> when he divided the sons of Adam [or, man],
> he set the boundaries of the peoples
> according to the number of the sons of Israel [or, God-El].
> For the portion of Yahweh is his people,
> Jacob the measuring-line of his property.

The text is difficult; it may also render the meaning that God, when he fixed the boundaries for the peoples, gave every one its guardian angel, while keeping Israel for his own portion. [33] Whatever translation we prefer, there remains the picture of a mankind divided into peoples according to a divine plan, with Israel as the personal share of Yahweh. Moreover, the text is clearly connected with the Message from Sinai, for the immediately following verses (10–12) resume the image of the eagle who protects his nestling and carries him on his pinions from the desert to safety.

From the Message, thus, emerges a new order, not of Israel alone, but of mankind, expressed analogically through the symbols of an empire with a royal domain at the center, surrounded by the provinces. [34] That was precisely the language required to make the new dispensation intelligible

[32] II Sam. 8:18; I Kings 4:5; I Chron. 18:17. References from Gesenius. For further discussion of the question cf. Buber, *Moses*, 155.

[33] Cf. the translation in Jewish Publication Society, RSV, Chicago, Moffat. I have followed Martin Buber's translation, because it renders the Hebrew text more literally than any other. The passage is further complicated in that the world-god El is perhaps not identical with the regional god Yahweh to whose lot Israel has fallen. On this question cf. H. S. Nyberg, *Hoseaboken* (Uppsala Universitets Arsskrift, 1941:7, 2), 34, and the same author's "Studien zum Religionskampf im Alten Testament, *loc. cit.*, 365 ff.

[34] The construction, while characteristic of all cosmological empires, is of prototypical purity. A similar purity was achieved in the later Chinese conception of the *chung kuo*, the central domain.

to a people on the point of separating from Egypt and its cosmological symbols.[35] Because of this cosmological continuity, however, it was also a language that could become opaque for spiritual universalism, if the symbols were understood in a terrestrial sense.[36] As a matter of fact, a millennium and a half had to lapse before the *segullah* of Yahweh, the *mamleketh kohanim*, had fully unfolded its meaning in the invisible *civitas Dei*.

The ceremony of the Berith, the second scene of the drama, was a sacrifical rite (Exod. 24:4–11). By its nature as a cultic act it can reveal little of the meaning attached to it by the participants.

The ceremony began with Moses' building an altar at the foot of the mountain, as well as twelve pillars, "according to the twelve tribes of Israel" (4). The erection of the pillars suggests that through the Berith the agglomeration of Hebrew clans was constituted as a people, organized for the first time in twelve tribes. A distinctly archaic detail is the next step, when "the young men of Israel" are ordered to conduct the sacrifice (5) —apparently there were no priests at the time. Then the bond between God and man was forged through Moses. He dashed half of the blood on the God's altar and half on the people, and said: "That is the blood of the Covenant which Yahweh has made with you, in accordance with all these words" (6–8). "All these words" we take to mean the words of the Message, rather than the words of the interpolated Decalogue. And, finally, Moses and the elders went up to consume the sacrificial meal in the presence of God (9–11):

> And they beheld God,
> and ate and drank.

That was all. And the paucity of information should cause no surprise, for the establishment of order in the present under God is an event not in literature but in the souls of men. "And they beheld God, and ate and

[35] From the fact that the symbolism fits the situation of the Exodus, no conclusions can be drawn with regard to the time at which the text received its present form. The date of the Berith drama is certainly very much later. The same argument applies to the fact that the theme of the passage, though not its precise language, is on numerous occasions resumed in Deuteronomy (Deut. 7:6; 10:14; 14:2; 29:2; 32:8–11). The Deuteronomic preoccupation with the theme does not necessarily indicate a Deuteronomic date for the drama. All arguments of this type unfortunately work in both directions.

[36] Within the history of Judaism, the symbolism was continued into the Diaspora, with the accent on its terrestrial implications. Cf. the special holiness of the land of Israel above all other lands, as well as the concentric regions of holiness within the land of Israel until the Holy of Holies is reached in the Temple, in the *Mishnah*, Tractate Kelim I, 6–9 (trans. Danby, Oxford, 1933).

drank" is the perfect formula for an event in which divine order becomes established in history, while externally happens nothing at all.

While nothing happens externally when man beholds God and the leap in being occurs in his soul, a good deal happens afterwards in the practice of conduct. The Hebrew clans who concluded the Covenant with God, even though under considerable persuasion on the part of Moses and the elders, became a new people in history through their response to revelation. They became Israel, in so far as their existence was now ordered as a theopolity under fundamental rules emanating from their God. These rules, supposedly to be inscribed on the tablets, are now missing from the context of the drama; and we have expressed our inclination to recognize the Decalogue of Exodus 20:1–17 as the body of the missing rules for reasons of contents, as well as of formal and spiritual quality. With regard to the textual quality of the source certain reservations have to be made. The motivations attached to the commands in 20:5b–6, 7b, 11, and 12b look like additions and should be eliminated. The specifications of commands in 9–10 and 17b could be later elaborations. The "thou shalt not carve an image . . . ," which today is counted as one command, actually contains three commands, each beginning with *lo*; perhaps the three commands, related by their subject matter, were contracted into one, in order to satisfy the desire for decalogic form; otherwise the ten commandments would be twelve.[37]

---

[37] We can accept the Decalogue of Exodus 20 as a legitimate source without difficulty because we are only interested in the question whether by substance and form it fits into the Berith drama that we are analyzing at present. Historians who raise the question whether it is the "original" Decalogue written by Moses himself confront a more complex situation. Our analysis is based on the assumption that the Berith drama has extracted a paradigmatic essence from the traditions, so that the question of originality in a pragmatic sense becomes secondary. We do not know, of course, whether the Berith drama is a reliable report or whether the Decalogue has not undergone transformations in the process of clarifying its essential contents to paradigmatic purity. Nevertheless, we should like to stress that in this particular case we know of no reason why the substance of the Decalogue should not have Moses as its author. On this point, however, the best authorities disagree widely. Lods, for instance, says: "The Decalogue of Exodus xx. and Deuteronomy v. is wholly occupied with moral and social responsibilities. We have no proof that such an attitude was ever characteristic of early Israel, whereas it is one of the distinguishing features of the prophetic movement, especially in its beginnings: Jahweh desires justice and mercy, not sacrifices (Amos v. 21–5; Hos. vi. 6; Mic. vi. 1–8). The Decalogue is, like Deuteronomy, a faint echo of the message of the prophets of the eighth and seventh centuries" (*Israel*, 316). For his view Lods can find strong support from Mowinckel, *Le décalogue*, especially p. 60. Oesterley and Robinson are more cautious: "While there is nothing in [the commandments] which prohibits a wilderness origin, the evidence is hardly strong enough to justify us in being dogmatic either for or against their Mosaic authorship.—This much, however, we can say. Whether these commandments are the work of Moses or not, they do represent very fairly the general moral standard

The meaning of the Decalogue is determined by its own contents, as well as by the context of the drama which begins with the Message of Exodus 19:4–6. The Berith has been concluded, and Israel is accepted as the royal domain of Yahweh the King. Hence, the Decalogue is not a catechism of religious and moral precepts, but a proclamation of the God-King laying down the fundamental rules for the order of the new domain. It opens with a declaration of the authority from which the commands emanate:

> I, Yahweh,
> thy God who brought thee
> out of the land of Egypt, out of the house of bondage.

Yahweh is the lord of history who has brought his people from the service of Egypt into his own service. In this capacity, as the new ruler, he issues a series of commands, organized by subject matter into three groups:

1. Thou shalt have no other gods before me (literally, to my face).
2. a. Thou shalt carve no image, or any likeness of what is in the heaven above, or on the earth beneath, or in the water under the earth.
   b. Thou shalt not bow down thyself to them.
   c. Thou shalt not serve them.
3. Thou shalt not invoke the name of Yahweh, thy God, to evil intent.

4. Remember the sabbath day, to keep it holy.
5. Honor thy father and thy mother.

---

which we may ascribe to Israel in the days preceding the Settlement" (*Hebrew Religion*, 168 ff.). The reader can take his choice: With Lods, we have no proof that the attitude of the commandments "was ever characteristic of early Israel"; with Oesterley and Robinson, the commandments "represent very fairly the general moral standard" of early Israel. He can, furthermore, assert with Mowinckel—who seems to have been impressed by Lévy-Bruhl—that the "prelogical mentality" of the primitives makes a decalogue without cultic provisions inconceivable. And he can consider it improbable with Nowack (*Der erste Dekalog*, quoted in Buber, *Moses*, 179), that Moses was a religious genius who had his parallel only in Jesus. Our own position with regard to the ideological assumption that such things cannot happen in the thirteenth century B.C. has been set forth on previous occasions. Of interest for our position is the argument of Rudolf Kittel, *Geschichte des Volkes Israel*, I, 383 ff. and 445–48. Kittel accepts the Decalogue as Mosaic in spite of what he considers its "moral" contents, because he considers the ideological conception of an evolution from cult to morality erroneous. In support of his position he refers to "moral" commandments in the Egyptian Book of the Dead, as well as among Australian primitives. The Decalogic commandments 4–8 he assumes, therefore, to be even older than Moses, since they are more primitive. Elias Auerbach, *Moses*, 198–203, pleads for a Mosaic date, because especially the tenth commandment seems to express the "ideal of the desert." Against Auerbach's argument cf. Immanuel Lewy, "Auerbachs Neuester Beweis fuer den Mosaischen Ursprung der Zehngebote Widerlegt," *Vetus Testamentum*, IV (1954), 313–16.

6. Thou shalt not kill.
7. Thou shalt not commit adultery.
8. Thou shalt not steal.
9. Thou shalt not bear false witness against thy neighbor.
10. Thou shalt not covet thy neighbor's house.

The commands are addressed both to Israel collectively and to each member of the people individually. We have retained the form of the "Thou shalt," though recent translations have abandoned it, in order to stress the character of the word that is spoken personally to the individual man, in so far as he is a member of the divine domain. The commands are not general rules of conduct but the substance of divine order to be absorbed by the souls of those who listen to the call. Only to the degree to which the divine substance of the proclamation has entered the human substance will the people indeed have been transformed into the royal domain under God.

The first group of three or, with the subdivisions of the second one, of five commandments deals with the relation between God and man. The commandments contain no "monotheistic doctrine"; they rather prohibit fallacious conduct that would obscure the nature of the God who has revealed himself as the *ehyeh asher ehyeh*. Yahweh is the hidden God who manifests himself in the form, and at the times, of his choice. He must not be made manifest through images of human device, because his nature as the hidden God would be obscured—and man cannot obscure the nature of God through symbolic action without affecting the order of his relation with God. Moreover, behind all attempts to image God in the likeness of anything within the visible cosmos, even though the attempts are apparently harmless, there lurks the desire to bring God within the reach of man. Man cannot bow to the image (2.b), or serve it (2.c), without substituting the imaged divine force for the divine reality that calls on men, at its own discretion, through the "word." And from such possessiveness, it is only a small step further to the magic misuse of a divine power that has been brought under the control of man (3). The author of the Decalogue has discerned the human desire to create a manageable God as the source of the attempts at representation, whatever form they may assume. In the first commandment he goes to the root of the issue, when he prohibits the "having of other gods," not because Yahweh is polytheistically jealous of rivals, or monotheistically denies their existence, but because man is in rebellion against God when he has other gods "in his face." The phrase "in the face," in the sense of rebellious or antagonistic existence, occurs also in other contexts, as for instance in Genesis 16:12 and 25:18, where the outcast Ishmael lives and settles "in the face" of his brethren. The recognition of other gods is an act of rebellious self-assertion which disrupts the relation between God and man.[38]

The third group of five commandments is self-explanatory. The commandments transfer the rules of internal clan solidarity to the new social body of the people of Israel. The injunctions protect the basic goods of life, marriage, property, and social honor. And the last commandment again penetrates to the source of disturbance when it prohibits the cherishing of covetous sentiments, of envy, which ultimately might break out in the specific disturbances.[39]

The two groups of injunctions are skillfully linked by the positive commandments of the middle group. The order of a people lives not only in the here and now of man's right relations with God and fellow man but in the rhythms of the people's existence in time. The articulation of order in time, through both the divine rhythm of the holy day and the human rhythm of the generations, must be honored. The command to remember the divine rhythm (4) concludes the commandments concerning the relation with God; and the commandment to honor the human rhythm (5) opens the commandments concerning the relation with fellow man.[40]

Clearly, the Decalogue is not an accidental collection of "religious" and "moral" precepts, but a magnificent construction, with a firm grip on the essentials of human existence in society under God. While the compact symbol offers an explicit "philosophy of order" no more than the thorn-bush episode offered a "philosophy of being," it certainly is animated by the insight that right order will somehow grow in a community when the attunement to the hidden divine being is not disturbed by human self-assertion. Since it does not issue positive rules, either cultic or moral, the field remains wide open, in both respects, for civilizational growth. Nevertheless, the Decalogue restrains and directs the growth by its injunctions against rebellious existence. It is framed by the firm blocks of the first and tenth commandments with their injunctions against the antitheistic rebellion of pride and the antihuman rebellion of envy. Between the two protective dams, in the middle, can move the order of the people through the rhythm of time. Through the articulation of the divine will into the commandments of the Decalogue Moses, indeed, has given Israel its constitution as the people under God in historical existence.

[38] Buber, *Moses*, 93.   [39] *Ibid.*, 195 ff.   [40] *Ibid.*, 194.

CHAPTER 13

The Prophets

§ 1. THE PROPHETIC EFFORT

Without the revelations from the Thornbush to Moses and from the Sinai to the people, there would have been no messengers of the Covenant; but without the messengers we would probably know little about Moses and the events of his time. The great question of the "historical Moses," which agitates the moderns, must be considered of secondary importance compared with the real issue, that is, the prophetic effort to regain, for the Chosen People, a presence under God that was on the point of being lost. It was in order to re-establish its meaning, as constituted by the Sinaitic events, that unknown authors elaborated such traditions as were preserved in cult legends, poems, and prose accounts into the paradigmatically heightened dramas that we have studied in the preceding Chapter. From those scenes of the "middle stratum" of the Biblical narrative emerges the Moses who lived, in historical continuity, in the medium of prophetic experience in Israel. The Moses of the prophets is not a figure of the past through whose mediation Israel was established once for all as the people under Yahweh the King, but the first of a line of prophets who in the present, under the revelatory word of Yahweh, continued to bring Israel up from Egypt into existence under God.

If we distinguish, thus, between the "historical" and the living Moses and, furthermore, define the prophetic experience as the medium of his life, the problems of the prophetic movement, from the crisis of the ninth to the exile of the sixth century, will come more clearly into focus:

(1) When prophetic authors recalled the work of Moses and heightened it paradigmatically in dramatic scenes, their work was not an end in itself. It served the purpose of awakening the consciousness of the Chosen People for the mode of its existence in historical form. The people had to be reminded, first, of its origin in the response of the fathers to Yahweh's revelation through Moses and, second, of the fact that its

continued existence depended on its continued response to Yahweh's revelation through the prophets. The recall of the past blends, therefore, into the call in the present. They both belong to the same continuum of revelation, which creates historical form when it meets with the continuum of the people's response. The historical form of the people unfolds in time; but it remains historical form only as long as the people, while lasting in time, lives in the tension of response to the timeless, eternal revelation of God.

(2) The prophetic blending of past and present in a continuum of living tension between time and eternity, however, has its dangers. For precisely when the defection of the people has reached such proportions that repeated, energetic reminders of the conditions of existence in historical form become necessary, the recall of the past may have effects as unexpected as they are undesired. We have studied such an unwanted effect in the chapter on the Deuteronomic Torah, when we traced the line that led from the recall of the origins to the Myth of Moses. Far from resulting in a new response of the people to the living word of Yahweh as pronounced by the messengers, the prophetic effort derailed into a constitution for the Kingdom of Judah which pretended to emanate from the "historical" Moses. The past that was meant to be revitalized in a continuous present now became really a dead past; and the living word to which the heart was supposed to respond became the body of the law to which the conduct could conform.

(3) This evolution toward the mythical Moses and the Torah, although caused by the persistent recall of Israel's theopolitical constitution and at times perhaps even favored by prophetic circles, was certainly not their ultimate intention. Hence, as the first symptoms of the derailment became noticeable, that is, as early as the eighth century, the recall of the origins was accompanied by warnings against the misapprehension that Yahweh would be satisfied with ritual observances and a conformity which disregarded the spirit of the law. As a consequence, the struggle of the prophets for the historical form of Israel had to cope with two evils at the same time: On the one hand, the prophets had to bring Israel back from its defections to Canaanite and Mesopotamian gods, to the obedience of Yahweh; on the other hand, when in the first respect they were successful, they had to convert Israel from its chauvinism and reliance on external performance, to a communal life in the spirit of the Covenant.

(4) The most serious problems of the prophets, however, arose from the very nature of their work, that is, from their effort to clarify the meaning of existence in historical form. When the revelations of the Mosaic period were studied and relived by men of such spiritual sensitivity as the authors of the thornbush episode and the Berith drama must have been, implications of the experience would unfold which required symbolizations of a new type. The universalist implications, for instance, which could be suppressed on the popular level by the fierceness of collective existence, had to loom large in the souls of solitary spiritualists tortured by the sorrow about the destiny of the Chosen People. When the syncretistic defections raised the question in what sense Israel could still be regarded by Yahweh as "My People," the possibility of God's choosing another people had to be considered. Moreover, when the rising danger from the neighboring empires had to be interpreted as divine castigations, the foreign peoples became instruments of Yahweh in the execution of a historical plan; and consequently the features of Yahweh as the universal God of mankind became increasingly marked. The appearance of prophetic personalities, succeeding one another through the generations in opposition to the people, furthermore, had to raise the problem of personal existence under Yahweh, in his spirit, independent of Israel's collective existence. If Israel as a people was doomed, could not a remnant, consisting perhaps of the followers of the prophets, escape and be saved for a better future? Could the people of God not contract into a group of spiritual personalities in free association under God? Should those who were willing to walk humbly with their God suffer the fate of the defectors? Was Israel really identical with the "historical" people? The implications, unfolding in such questions, would raise the ultimate issue: Had the Kingdom of God, of necessity, to assume the form of a political Israel; and if that question should be answered in the negative, had it, of necessity, to assume the form of a politically organized people at all? If Israel relegated Moses and the Covenant to a dead past by transforming them into a constitutional myth, the prophets were about to relegate Israel to a dead past by transforming the Kingdom of God into something which, at the time, was no more than the shooting lights of a new dawn on the horizon.

In the present, concluding chapter we shall deal with the transformation of the theopolitical symbols of the Mosaic period through the prophets. The first section will treat the unfolding of the problems, contained in a compact form in the older symbols, under the pressure of new experiences. For this section the prophecies of Jeremiah will be our guide. For at this late hour, in the last period of the Kingdom of Judah, the two and a half centuries of resistance to defection and chauvinism, as well as of continuous occupation with the meaning of the Sinaitic foundation, had differentiated the experiences to the point where new symbols for their adequate expression, though not always found, were clearly required. The second section will deal with the search for new means of expression. Beyond Jeremiah, with his clarity of issues and the veil yet drawn over the solutions, lead the prophecies of the unknown genius of the sixth century to whom philological convention refers as Deutero-Isaiah. His symbol of the Suffering Servant stands on the borderline between Prophetism and Christianity.

§ 2. THE UNFOLDING OF THE PROBLEM

The creation of Israel as the people under God begins with the Message of Yahweh to Moses, proceeds to the Covenant, and concludes with the constitution of the people under the Decalogue. Since the violations of the decalogic constitution are massively the occasions on which the problem of Israelite order becomes tangible, it will be convenient to reverse the sequence of the Berith drama in an analysis of Jeremiah's concern with Israel's theopolitical existence.

1. The Decalogue

We shall begin with "the word that came to Jeremiah from Yahweh" to stand at the gate of the Temple and to address the people, because the Temple Address (Jer. 7) refers directly to the text of the Decalogue. According to the information of Jeremiah 26 the Address was delivered in 609/8 B.C.

Yahweh, through Jeremiah, warns the people as they enter the Temple to mend their ways, or he will not make their home in this place (7:3). They must not trust: "The Temple of Yahweh is this!" For it will not be their home unless they practice strict justice among themselves, do not oppress the resident stranger, the fatherless, and the widow, do not shed innocent blood nor follow other gods to their hurt (7:4–8). As it is, they "steal, murder, and commit adultery, offer sacrifices to

Baal, and follow other gods," and leave to continue their abominations (7:9–10). "Has this house which bears my name become a robbers' cave in your eyes?" (7:11).

The passages from the Temple Address furnish valuable information on the sense in which admonitions of the prophets must be read. The categories so frequently used by modern historians when they speak of the ethics, or politics, or religion, or theology of the prophets may have their taxonomic uses, but they are anachronistic when applied to the prophets' intention, because the Israelite symbolism has its own logic: When the prophets raise problems of order, they refer them, through extensive interpretation, to the decalogic constitution. The Jeremiah passages have their climax in direct quotations from the Decalogue in its form of either Exodus 20 or Deuteronomy 5, and they interpret all types of offensive conduct as ultimately a violation of the Commandments. And such interpretation is possible, because the Decalogue, while a collection of substantive rules, is at the same time an exemplification of the injunctions to restrain self-assertiveness with regard to God and man. As a consequence, its meaning can ultimately be concentrated in the one command: "Listen to my voice and I will be your God, and you shall be my people; and walk consistently in the way that I command you" (Jer. 7:23); and the violations can, therefore, be correspondingly concentrated in the one offense: "Yet they neither listened, nor inclined their ear to me, but walked in their own counsels and the stubbornness of their evil hearts, and went backward instead of forward" (Jer. 7:24).

Because of this intricate structure of the Decalogue the prophets are able to classify social evils in general under the categories of theft, murder, adultery, false witness, and covetousness; and they wield this formidable instrument ruthlessly, in order to tear the web of institutions and customs, of the convenient distances which social stratification, vested interests, professional habits, and inherited positions put in a complex society between actions and their human effects, and to make visible the direct attack of man on man in situations which more laxly may be viewed as regrettable but inevitable social evils. Amos, for instance, in a magnificent short circuit of cause and effect speaks of the rich (3:10):

> For they do not know how to do right,
>   who store up robbery and violence in their palaces.

Hosea brings a series of unidentified offenses under the decalogic categories (6:8–10):

> Gilead is a city of wrong-doers,
> > it is covered with footprints of blood.
> As robbers lie in wait for a man,
> > so the priests are banded together;
> they murder on the way to Shechem,
> > yea, they commit villainy.
> In the house of Israel I have seen a horrible thing,
> > harlotry is found in Ephraim, Israel is defiled.

Micah is explicit on the acquisition of wealth as a case of decalogic covetousness (2:1-2):

> Woe to them who devise wrong,
> > and work out wickedness upon their beds.
> When the morning dawns, they execute it,
> > because it is in their power.
> They covet fields, and seize them,
> > and houses, and take them away.
> They crush a man and his house,
> > a man and his inheritance.

And he even sees the order of the people perverted into a civil war conducted by the upper class against the poor (2:8-9):

> But you rise against my people as an enemy,
> > you strip the robe from the peaceful,
> from those who pass by trustingly,
> > with no thought of war.
> The women of my people you expel
> > from their comfortable homes;
> from their young children you take away
> > my glory forever.

A century later, Jeremiah still voices the same complaints: One can range through the streets of Jerusalem and not find a man who does justly or seeks truth (5:1-2); and the judgment extends equally to the poor and the rich (5:4-6), though the rich are still singled out for specific denunciation of their misdeeds (5:26-28).

Disorder in Israel thus was measured by the comprehensive order of the Decalogue. As far as persons were concerned, the rich and the poor, the king and the priests, the sage and the false prophets were equally judged by the standard of antidivine or antihuman self-assertiveness; and as far as subject matter was concerned, civil and criminal, ritual and constitutional offenses, abuses of power, station, and wealth, hardness of heart and indifference to the misery of fellow men were all equally

classified as violations of the fundamental command to listen to the voice
of God. Since the prophetic method of interpretation was not a whim or
a novelty but the accepted principle of Israelite order; since, furthermore,
the people at large, and in particular the ruling classes and the court,
were convinced that their conduct was an impeccable fulfillment of the
laws which had been elaborated in pursuance of the Decalogue; and
since, finally, the Deuteronomic constitution, with its provisions for
kingship, priesthood, and the cult monopoly of Jerusalem, was understood as Mosaic legislation, the prophecies of the adumbrated type raised
a serious problem of public order. Jeremiah's prophecies not only insulted influential sectors of the people, but were in conflict with the
constitution of Judah. When in his Address he threatened the Temple
(7:12–15), Jerusalem, and the people (7:16–20) with destruction
through Yahweh, if Israel persisted in conduct which every Israelite of
importance, from the King down, considered legal and constitutional
under the Sinaitic Covenant and Decalogue, his action bordered on
high treason; and when he defined as offensive any conduct at variance
with the word of the prophets (7:25–26), that is, with his own word in
particular, he pitted his prophetic authority against the public authority
of Israel. Was Israel identical with the Kingdom of Judah, organized
under the Torah as interpreted by the King, his officers and priests; or
was it identical with an entirely different community that lived under
the Decalogue as interpreted by Jeremiah?

The question could not be compromised. At the time, however, the
two Israels were still held together in one community by correlative hopes
and fears. The court and the ruling class, while rejecting the word of the
prophet, did not dare to attack on principle an authority on which they
depended for their own legitimacy; and the prophets, while pronouncing
Yahweh's death sentence on the corrupt society and its rulers, hoped for
a miracle of conversion that would avert the disaster from their people.
The conflict, thus, remained a tension within the Kingdom of Judah.

Nevertheless, it was a conflict of formidable proportions. We learn
something about it from the sequel to the Temple Address, as reported
in Jeremiah 26. The Address is reduced to a summary of essentials which
reads almost like an indictment. Jeremiah is reported to have said: If the
people will not listen to Yahweh, that is, follow his law (*toroth*) and
heed the words (*debharim*) of his servants the prophets, the Temple will

be destroyed like Shiloh and the city will be made a curse to all the nations of the earth (26:4-6). The audience was incensed. They surrounded Jeremiah and held him, crying he would have to die for his prophecy, in the name of Yahweh, that Temple and city would be destroyed (26:7-9). The princes (the judicial officers) were informed; they came from the neighboring palace and sat at the Gate to hear the case (26:10). The priests and prophets were the accusers and demanded the death of Jeremiah; but the princes and the people were impressed by the prophet's assurance that he had indeed spoken at the command of Yahweh (26:11-15). The temporal prevailed over the spiritual party in the conflict. Princes and people decided that a man who truly spoke in the name of "Yahweh our God" did not deserve to die (26:16). The decision was strongly influenced by the precedent of Micah under the reign of Hezekiah. Micah had pronounced substantially the same prophecies as Jeremiah (Mic. 3:12); and he had been pardoned, with the result that Yahweh could be persuaded not to fulfill his threat. It would be more cautious to follow the same course as in the Micah case (26:17-19). That was a worldly wise decision not to kill a prophet: If he was not sent by Yahweh, nothing would happen anyway; if he was sent by Yahweh, his execution might precipitate a disaster, whereas his acquittal left the hope that things would be no more terrible in the end than after Micah. But Jeremiah's escape from a death sentence was nobody's escape from the problems his prophetism raised.

Not every prophet was as lucky as Jeremiah on this occasion. The story of his trial is followed by the information that a certain Uriah, who prophesied "against the city and the land" in the same manner as Jeremiah had done, was slain with the sword by the King in person, after he had been extradited from Egypt, where he had sought refuge (26:20-23). King Jehoiakim, on whom after all rested the responsibility for the order of the realm, was apparently not inclined to take the prophetic challenge to his authority lightly. And the conflict between the King and Jeremiah was indeed only delayed. For five years later (ca. 603 B.C.) the prophet, who did not dare to come near the Temple again, sent at the command of Yahweh his secretary Baruch with a scroll, on which were written the words of Yahweh, to have them publicly read in the Temple on a day of ritual fasting so that perhaps the people would turn from their evil ways (36:1-7). After the reading, the scroll was confiscated by the princes and examined. They had to transmit it to the

King, but again were cautious enough to advise Baruch to go into hiding with Jeremiah where nobody could find them (36:8–19). At last the scroll reached Jehoiakim. It was in the wintry season, and a fire was burning before him in a brazier as an attendant read the scroll to him. Whenever three or four columns had been read, the King, who had listened in stony silence, would cut them off with his knife—and then Jehoiakim, the King of Judah, dropped the words of Yahweh, the King of Israel, on the brazier until the whole scroll was consumed by fire (36:20–24).

The trial of the prophet and the mutual death sentences when the order of God is about to disengage itself from the order of man form an aggregate of symbols that recurs, at a distance of two centuries, in the Hellas of Socrates and Plato. Now the philosopher represents the order of the God of Delphi; the "priests and prophets" reappear as the sophistic intellectuals and politicians in the role of the accusers; there is again the strong minority of the "people" who vote against the death sentence; and there is Plato, who, in his dialogues, continues the trial and makes it clear that the gods had condemned Athens when Athens had condemned Socrates. The comparison should make us aware that we are dealing not with contingent events but with essential processes of experience and symbolization. Parallels of this kind are neither historical curiosities, nor do they suggest mysterious laws of history. They rather show that the relation between transcendent and mundane order, when it reaches the level of conscious experience in prophets or philosophers, will become articulate in closely related symbols; and when the men in whose experience the problem lives become a force in community life, the responses again will be so closely related that the pattern of action will become a symbolic play, acting out the drama of revelation.

The drama, as it was acted out at the end of the seventh century by Jeremiah and his antagonists, originated in the prophetic experience of the conflict between the historical order of society and the divinely revealed order. Fortunately there is extant, in Isaiah's account of his first revelation, an autobiographical report of the type of experience which unfolds, when it enters the stream of communal life, into the drama of Jeremiah and his trial. In Isaiah 6:1–5 we read:

> In the year that King Uzziah died, I saw the Lord sitting upon his throne, high and lifted up, the skirts of his robe filling the temple.

Above him stood the seraphim; each had six wings: with two he
covered his face, and with two he covered his feet, and with two he
hovered in flight. And they called one another, and said:
> "Holy, holy, holy, is Yahweh of the hosts;
>   the whole earth is full of his glory."

And the foundations of the threshold shook at the sound of those
who called, and the house was filled with smoke.

Then said I:
> "Woe is me! I am lost—
>   for a man of unclean lips am I,
>   and among a people of unclean lips dwell I—
>   for the King, Yahweh,
>   of the hosts have seen my eyes."

While the reference to the death of Uzziah permits us to date the revelation *ca.* 740 B.C., the information is not tendered for that purpose. It
rather suggests that a revelation is not a prophet's private affair, but the
entrance of God, at a specific time, through the prophet, into the public
order of the people. The occasion of the King's death, furthermore,
stresses the meaning of the revelation as an irruption of eternal being
into an order that is characterized by the representative mortality of the
King. When the mortal King of Judah passes away, the eternally living
King of Israel lets himself be seen by Isaiah. But to what avail can the
revelation be, when it confronts death with life? Will the dead come to
life again? Isaiah is unclean, a man of an unclean people; and the unclean
must die when they see Yahweh the King in his glory. The theme of
death is subtly varied from the demise of the King to the spiritual death
of the people he represented.

The contents of the revelation (6:6–13) is, therefore, not a piece of
information, but the beginning of a purification. The revelation will
indeed be of no avail when even the human instrument is unclean. Hence,
the seraphim touch the lips of Isaiah with a red-hot stone, so that his
guilt will be removed (6:6–7). Only when the instrument of transmission for divine being is cleansed can Isaiah hear the divine voice itself
and put himself in its presence as Moses did in the thornbush revelation
(6:8). And from the voice he receives the terrifying order to tell "this
people" (6:9):

> "Hear and hear, but do not understand;
>   see and see, but do not perceive."

And to his question "How long, O Lord, how long?" he hears the answer (6:11–13): until the cities lie waste, and the inhabitants have fled, and the land is a desolation.

> And though a tenth remain in it,
> this will be burned again,
> like a terebinth or an oak,
> whose stump remains when it is felled.

The living fire that has burned Isaiah clean will also have to burn the people. As they are, they hear and will not understand, they see and will not perceive. And whatever emerges from the ordeal, the imagery of destruction makes it clear that the Kingdom of Judah will no longer be recognizable in it. The old Israel, as it was constituted by the Covenant, is unclean to death, and a new one will arise from the fire.

If we pursue Isaiah's revelation to this point, however, the question must be asked: What has this new Israel to do with the old one? The continuity seems to be broken by an epoch as incisive as the Sinaitic revelation. Is the old Covenant not dead when the people with whom it was made has died? And is "Israel" not about to become the name of whatever human society lives in historical form, in the presence under God? We seem to have reached the limits of the Covenant symbol.

2. *The Covenant*

Since the Decalogue was accepted as Israel's fundamental law, the prophetic criticism not only could but had to judge the people's conduct by its standards. Nevertheless, while the complaints, reproaches, and admonitions of the prophets construed reprehensible conduct as violation of the Commandments, obviously more was at stake than an interpretation of legal rules. One might even say the prophets weakened their case, when they involved themselves in arguments about offenses against decalogic injunctions, for a man could well plead that he had not committed murder or theft when he used his business acumen to increase his property at the expense of an unwise peasant who had gone into debt too deeply. Once the expansion of the Decalogue into codes like the Book of the Covenant or the Deuteronomic Torah had been admitted at all as the adequate unfolding of its meaning, an alternative interpretation, even if it was not meant as legal argument, could be understood as such for the purpose of misunderstanding. While the appeal to decalogic standards lent authority to prophetic criticism, it obscured rather than clarified the real issue: that the prophets judged conduct in terms of its compatibility not with a fundamental law but with the right order of the soul.

The ambiguity of the prophetic appeal was inevitable in view of the compact form of the Decalogue, which did not allow for a distinction between existential and normative issues. While the construction as a whole made it clear that the concrete offenses were prohibited as manifestations of self-assertive existence in rebellion against God and man, the Commandments which concentrated the existential issue were couched in the same normative form as the other ones. In particular, the positive relation between God and man, man and God, was expressed negatively in the injunction not to have other gods in the face of Yahweh. We have previously studied the meaning of this peculiarity when we reflected on the difference between Israelite Revelation and Hellenic Philosophy: A positive articulation of the existential issue would have required the experience of the soul and its right order through orientation toward the invisible God; and that experience never in Israelite history clearly is differentiated from the compact collectivism of the people's existence—not even in the prophetic age, and certainly not in the age that formed the Decalogue. Hence, at a time when a theory of the psyche and a theology would have been required to unfold the meanings implied in the Sinaitic legislation, the prophets were badly handicapped by the want of a positive vocabulary. They had at their disposition neither a theory of the *aretai* in the Platonic-Aristotelian sense so that they could have opposed character to conduct in human relations, nor a theory of faith, hope, and love in the Heraclitian sense so that they could have opposed the inversion of the soul toward God to ritual observance of his commandments. In particular, the lack of a differentiated theology must have been a tremendous obstacle to a proper articulation of the prophetic intentions: When reading the story of Jeremiah's squabbles with the Judaite refugees in Egypt (Jer. 44), one wonders whether the Israelite common man, and even more so the common woman, had ever really understood why they should have no other gods besides Yahweh; and one begins to wonder whether the prophets had ever been able to make the reasons clear to them. The famous defections from Yahweh to Canaanite and Mesopotamian gods will appear in a new light if one considers that the people at large probably never had understood a Commandment whose spiritual meaning had remained inarticulate.

The insight that existence under God means love, humility, and righteousness of action rather than legality of conduct was the great achievement of the prophets in the history of Israelite order. Even though their effort to disengage the existential issue from the decalogic form did not lead to expressions of ultimate, theoretical clarity, the symbols used in their pronouncements leave no doubt about the intended meaning: The normative component of the decalogic constitution was a source of evil in as much as it endowed the institutions and conduct of the people, which derived through interpretation from the Decalogue, with the authority of divinely willed order, however much the actual institutions perverted the will of God. Moreover, the prophets recognized that any letter, as it externalized the spirit, was in danger of becoming a dead letter, and that consequently the Covenant written on tablets had to give way to the Covenant written in the heart.

A few representative examples will illustrate the prophets' struggle with the variegated phenomena of externalization, their inquiry into its motives, their search for a language that would positively express the right order of the soul in openness toward God, and their ultimate vision of a Covenant that would preclude the danger of externalization.

To the heart of the prophets' difficulties leads Jeremiah's attack on offenders against the First and Tenth Commandments. The text (10: 1–16) shows a Jeremiah at the moment less aggrieved by the violations of the Decalogue than concerned with explaining to the defectors why their conduct is senseless. He admonishes them not to be dismayed by the signs of the heavens just because the goyim are dismayed by them (10:2). The alien gods are no more than a tree cut from the forest, shaped with an ax by the hands of a craftsman, decked by men with silver and gold, and fastened with hammer and nails so they will not topple (10:3–5). There is no reason to be afraid of them, for they cannot do either harm or good (10:5). Once the people have become conscious of the senselessness of their fears and beliefs, that seems to be the assumption, they will see (10:10) that

> Yahweh is God in Truth;
> he is the living God, and the everlasting King!

The form of an argumentative exhortation, however, is deceptive. Behind the persuasive language, almost that of an Enlightenment philosopher who wants to dissolve superstition through information, lurks a problem which even a Jeremiah hesitated to articulate plainly.

The argument, to be sure, is not insincere, but it certainly is devious. Jeremiah knew, of course, that the alien gods were false gods because Yahweh had revealed himself as the true God, and not that Yahweh was the true God because of somebody's discovery that images of gods were no more than pieces of woodwork; and he knew, furthermore, quite well that the carving of a god was prohibited precisely because it was not as innocuous an action as carpentering a piece of furniture. Moreover, as early as the eighth century, Hosea had said of the Bull of Samaria (8:6):

> A workman made it;
> and it is not God.

Hence, by the time of Jeremiah the argument must have been a prophetic staple that impressed nobody, because it was too obviously wrong. More than once must he have heard the answer to his expostulations which he puts himself in the mouth of the people (2:25):

> "It is hopeless! for I love alien gods,
> and after them will I go!"

The texts of Jeremiah should therefore not be considered an argument calculated to persuade anybody, but rather as a desperate attempt to veil the true reasons, that will not give way to argument, of Israel's defection by the pretense that argument will overcome them.

The true reasons of defection did not escape Jeremiah: The people went after alien gods, there could be no doubt, because it loved them; it preferred the manifestations of divine force within the world to the world-transcendent, invisible God. With grief he noted the unheard-of spectacle of a nation abandoning its gods (2:11–12):

> Has ever a nation changed its gods,
> even though they are no gods?
> Yet my people have changed their glory,
> for that which is useless.

And it has changed so thoroughly that "as many as your cities are your gods, O Judah" (2:28). Jeremiah had made the discovery (today it would be called an insight of cultural anthropology) that peoples, as a rule, don't change their gods; hence, if they change them nevertheless, the reason would have to be as extraordinary as the event. He had, furthermore, discovered, that they don't change their gods as long as they are false gods; and that in the one, extraordinary instance of change the god was "God in Truth." Could it be that the nature of the "God in Truth" was the cause of the singular defection? It became clear, in brief, that Israel, while it did not mind being a Chosen People, did not care to be chosen at the price of ceasing to be a people like the others. If Jeremiah rejected the cosmic gods as useless, the people rejected, if not as useless, at least as defective, a world-transcendent God in Truth; the gods who were false to Jeremiah were not so false to an Israel that wanted to be both a Chosen People and a people like the others. The time was drawing critically near when the God of the prophets, in order to establish his Kingdom, would have to separate from a people that understood its chosenness as no more than an agreeable premium put on its unregenerate cosmological existence.

The deviousness of the Jeremiah texts thus veils the insight that Israel's defections had something to do with the construction of the theopolity as an embodiment of the Kingdom of God in a concrete people with its institutions, and that they would cease only with the theopolity under the Covenant itself. In the history of prophetism from the eighth century to the fall of Jerusalem we must distinguish, therefore, between (1) the prophets' complaints about Israel's misconduct and (2) the varying degree of their awareness that admonitions were not only hopeless, but perhaps even pointless. We shall first deal with the complaints.

The complaints, though variegated in form, were remarkably constant with regard to substance. Every prophet from Amos and Hosea to Jeremiah recognized the symptoms of the trouble. That substance we find most clearly expressed in Hosea's plain indictment (8:4):

> They made kings, but not from me;
> they set up princes, and I knew it not.
> With their silver and gold they made idols,
> for their own destruction.

The kings and gods of the people, thus, were the representative symptoms of Israel's fall. The frequently made suggestion that Hosea condemned only the institutions of the Northern Kingdom, but not the national kingship of Saul or the Davidic monarchy can hardly be maintained in face of 13:9–11:

That will be to your destruction, O Israel,
that it is with me you find your help.
Where is now your King, that he may deliver you in your cities,
where are your judges, to whom you said:
"Give me a King and Princes!"
I have given you a King in my anger,
and I have taken him away in my wrath!

The kingship as it existed in Israel from Saul to the present was to Hosea the great defection (10:13–15):

You have plowed iniquity, you have reaped injustice,
You have eaten the fruit of lies,
in that you trusted in your chariots,
and the multitude of your warriors.

But a revolt shall arise among your people,
and all your fortresses shall be destroyed . . .
And at that dawn shall be cut off, cut off
the King of Israel.

From the institutional nucleus of the kings, the gods, and the army the condemnation of the prophets, then, ranges widely over the phenomena of a people's civilization. In Hosea 8:14 we read:

For Israel has forgotten his Maker, and built palaces;
and Judah has multiplied fortified cities.

Jeremiah warns (9:23):

Let not the wise man boast of his wisdom,
Nor the strong man boast of his strength,
Nor the rich man boast of his riches.

Isaiah displays a remarkable circumspection in spotting phenomena of rebellious pride against Yahweh (2:12–17):

For Yahweh of the hosts has a day
Against all that is proud and high,
    and against all that is lofty and tall:
Against all the cedars of Lebanon, high and lofty,
    and against all the oaks of Bashan;
Against all the high mountains,
    and against all the lofty hills;
Against every tall tower,
    and against every fortified wall;
Against all the ships of Tarshish,
    and against all the gallant craft.

In particular, the women attract Isaiah's unfriendly attention (3:16):

> The daughters of Zion are haughty,
> and walk with outstretched necks,
> glancing wantonly with their eyes,
> mincing along as they go,
> and jingling with their feet.

Terrible things will befall such creatures (3:24):

> Instead of perfume there shall be rottenness,
> and instead of a girdle, a rope;
> instead of curls, baldness,
> and instead of a rich robe, sackcloth.

A great change had come over Israel indeed since the days when David could speak:

> Daughters of Israel, weep over Saul,
>   Who clothed you in scarlet, and other delights,
>   Who put ornaments of gold upon your apparel!

If one isolates the complaints of the prophets, as we have just done in our selection, one is inclined to wonder what the servants of Yahweh wanted. Should Israel have submitted to the Philistines instead of creating a king and an army? should the ships of Tarshish stay in port? should the cedars of Lebanon grow only half size? and should the daughters of Zion be dowdy? It is important to realize that no prophet has ever answered a question of this kind. If such were the complaints of the prophets, we may say, the people could well have answered that the prophets had no respect for the beauty of God's creation, that they did not permit man to unfold his God-given faculties of mind and body, and that they could not distinguish between pride and joy of life. And the countercharges would have been justified indeed—if the people had been able to articulate such charges at all. The people, however, no more lived in the tension of temporal and spiritual order (which had not yet differentiated) than did the prophets, but in the tension between cosmological myth and a Yahwist order that was yet badly lacking in clarity about the relations between the spirit and the world. And the prophets' attempt to clarify the meaning of the Sinaitic revelation was therefore as right in rejecting the mythical form of the people's order as it was wrong in rejecting the order of mundane existence together with the mythical form.

The atmosphere of strangeness, and even of morbidity, that hovers

over the complaints of the prophets will be alleviated when the violent
rejections are placed by the side of the positive demands. When Jeremiah
enjoins the wise, the strong, and the rich not to boast of their advantages,
he continues his admonition (9:24):

> But if he boast, let him boast of this,
> that he understands and knows me:
> How I, Yahweh, exercise mercy [*hesed*]
> justice [*mishpat*], and righteousness [*zedakah*], on earth.

The text assembles the principal positive terms which the prophets had
evolved for designating the desired traits of the soul; it furthermore
attributes them to Yahweh and assumes that man will acquire them too,
if he "understands and knows" God; by this assumption it moves the
knowledge of God into the position of a comprehensive, formative virtue
of the soul, comparable to the Platonic vision of the Agathon; and it
finally couples the positive traits with the complaints, which reject the
mundane order on principle as an externalization. Under all of these
aspects of the text Jeremiah had predecessors. The coupling of rejection
and demand is a literary type that goes as far back as Amos (5:21–25):

> I hate, I despise your feasts,
> and I take no delight in your solemn assemblies.
> Even though you bring me your burnt-offerings
> and your meal-offerings, I will not accept them,
> and the peace-offerings of your fatted beasts, I will not regard them.
>
> Take away from me the noise of your songs,
> the melodies of your harps, I will not hear:
> But let justice roll down like waters,
> and righteousness as an everflowing stream.

The Amos text is important, not only because it sets the literary type,
but especially because the prophet rejects even sacrifice to Yahweh as an
externalization of the qualities of man which in philosophical language
would have to be called virtues. Moreover, Amos makes the attempt to
legitimate his demands by deriving them from the reality of the Mosaic
period (5:25):

> Did you bring me sacrifices and offerings
> in the wilderness for forty years, O house of Israel?

As far as we know, it did; and in particular, the Berith was concluded
with a sacrifice. The passage shows how far the prophets would go in
their desperate effort to disengage the order of the soul under God from

a mundane order that was formed by the myth. To Amos' virtues of *mishpat* and *zedakah* Hosea, then, adds *hesed*, to be translated variously according to the context as mercy, piety, grace, loving-kindness, and so forth (6:6):

> For I desire *hesed*, and not sacrifice,
> the knowledge of God, rather than burnt-offerings.

And on this occasion also appears the virtue of knowledge (*daʿath*) of God as the general, formative force in the soul. From the gradual clarification of the issue and the corresponding development of a positive vocabulary there emerges, toward the end of the eighth century, the beautiful summary of the prophets' exhortation in Micah 6:6–8:

> Wherewith shall I come before Yahweh,
> and bow myself before God on high?
> Shall I come before him with burnt-offerings,
> with calves a year old?

> Will Yahweh be pleased with thousands of rams,
> with ten thousands of rivers of oil?
> Shall I give my first-born for my transgression,
> the fruit of my body for the sin of my soul [*nephesh*]?

>> "You have been told, O man, what is good,
>> and what Yahweh requires of you:
>> Only do *mishpat*, and love *hesed*,
>> and walk humbly with your God."

The juxtapositions of rejection and demand make it clear that the prophets wanted to overcome the externalization of existence; and the texts reveal the remarkable degree of success their efforts achieved: They disengaged the existential issue from the theopolitical merger of divine and human order; they recognized the formation of the soul through knowledge (Hosea) and fear (Isaiah) of God; and they developed a language to articulate their discoveries. They were handicapped, to be sure, by their inability to break through to philosophy, but the part of their work we are examining at present runs parallel, without a doubt, to the discovery of the *aretai* in Helles. Nevertheless, the rejections of the mundane order remain as an oddity. The prophets apparently were not only unable to see, but not even interested in finding, a way from the formation of the soul to institutions and customs they could consider compatible with the knowledge and fear of God. The attitude of the prophets is tantalizing in that it seems to violate common sense.[1]

We have reached the core of what may be called the prophets' ontology. Their strange conception of the order of being will become more intelligible if a case be examined where the question what to do concretely in a situation affecting public order was not evaded. For that purpose will be used certain prophecies of Isaiah concerning the conduct of war.

During the wars with Israel and Syria of 734, and with Assyria toward the end of the century, Jerusalem herself was threatened with conquest by the enemy. Here was the occasion for a prophet to say what a people should do in an emergency, whether it was an insult to Yahweh to rely on an army and even to have a king and an administration. And Isaiah indeed, at the command of Yahweh, approached the King when he was engaged in a fearful inspection of the water supply and tendered

---

[1] We interpret Prophetism as the struggle against the Law, as the attempt to disengage the existential from the normative issues. That this is indeed the essential core of the prophetic effort is confirmed by the Talmudic interpretation of prophecy, which has for its purpose the reversal of the effort and the assertion of the supremacy of the Torah. On this subject cf. Nahum N. Glatzer, "A Study of the Talmudic Interpretation of Prophecy," *The Review of Religion* (1946), 115–37. In the Talmudic conception "the task of the prophet is understood to be the same as the task of the interpreter of the Law: to teach the Torah to Israel." "Prophetic words of general and comprehensive nature are referred to a specific law or observance" (p. 128). By the words "of general and comprehensive nature" Glatzer means the passages which develop the prophetic vocabulary of the "virtues," or *aretai*, just discussed in the text: "To walk humbly with thy God" (Micah 6:8), according to R. Eleazar b. Pedat (third century), means "to escort the dead to the grave and to lead the bride to the bridal chamber" (Sukkah 49b). "To seek the Lord" is interpreted as seeking him in the houses of prayer and study, "to forsake the Lord" as disobedience to a certain commandment or usage. The prophetic "word of God" is identified with "the word of the Torah." Even the prophetic "knowledge of God" is reversed. To "I desire knowledge of God rather than burnt-offerings" (Hos. 6:6) R. Simeon b. Yohai (second century) remarks: "The words of the Torah are dearer to me than burnt-offerings and peace-offerings." The motives of the reversal are various. One of them is the desire to depreciate the prophets, because in the early Christian writers "Jesus appears as the termination and culmination of prophecy." A more immediate problem was the suppression of pneumatic irrationalism within the Jewish community. "The rabbis pointed out indefinite, vague, and more theoretical prophetic terms, which lent themselves to support pneumatic religions, and translated them into concrete demands. Terms like 'Knowledge of God,' 'Covenant,' 'Way of the Lord,' opened the way to uncontrolled religious emotional experience. The Talmud, without losing sight of the deeper issue in the relation of man to God, stresses 'study of the Torah' and 'observance of the Law' as the concrete meaning of 'Covenant' and 'Knowledge of God,' thus demonstrating the common task of prophet and rabbi" (condensed from *ibid.*, 127–29). Back of the Talmudic interpretation lies, of course, the transformation of the Sinaitic revelation into the written word of the Torah that we have studied in the chapter on the "Deuteronomic Torah."

his advice. The prophet went out to meet Ahaz and said to him (7:4):
"Take heed: Be quiet, do not fear, let your heart not be faint because of
these two tails of smoking firebrands [*i.e.* Syria and Israel]." Things
would come out well, if the King accepted the counsel, for Yahweh had
said "it shall not stand, and it shall not be" that the designs of the enemy
be crowned with success (7:6–7); but if the King did not accept the
counsel, Yahweh had said: "If you do not trust, you will not last"
(7:9).[2] That was all.

On the occasion of the Assyrian threat and the alliance with Egypt,
Isaiah again spoke the word of Yahweh. The first of the prophecies,
30:15, no more than confirms the earlier one: The "strength" of Israel
lies in "returning and resting," in "sitting still and confidence." We pass
on, therefore, to the more revealing 31:1:

> Woe to those, who go down to Egypt for help
> and rely on horses,
> who trust in chariots, because they are many,
> and in horses, because they are very numerous,
> but do not look to the Holy One of Israel
> and do not consult Yahweh.

Such conduct is foolish because (31:3)

> Egypt is man, and not God,
> and his horses are flesh, and not spirit [*ruach*].

The analysis of the passages by Gerhard von Rad has shown that
Isaiah resumed the traditions of the war ritual, long dormant in his
time, and transformed them strangely.[3] He cast himself in the role of the
nabi, of the time of Judges and the early Kingdom, who sanctioned the
Holy War. These wars of the Confederacy, we recall, were defensive.
Since they were conducted for the Chosen People, on principle, by
Yahweh himself, trust in Yahweh and his help was a condition of membership in the fighting forces. Moreover, victory was achieved by the
numinous terror cast by Yahweh into the ranks of the enemy. Now,
as long as this confidence was coupled with the people's fierce lust to
fight, everything went as well as the fortunes of war would permit.

---

[2] The RSV translates: "If you will not have faith, surely you shall not be established." No
translation can convey that the "trust" and "last" of our translation are forms of the same verb
in Hebrew. It has the meaning of being steady or reliable, of having trust, with the consequence
of being steadfast and quiet oneself. Such qualities of character, then, will help a man to per-
severe and to last through a critical situation, the "being established" of the RSV.

[3] Von Rad, *Der Heilige Krieg* (1951), 2d ed. (1952), 55–62.

When, however, as we anticipated, confidence assumed the form of a prophetic demand to remain passive, to sit still and let Yahweh do the fighting, and to rely on the numinous panic to discomfit the enemy, difficulties had to arise from the conflict between the demand and the exigencies of mundane existence. That conflict became real in the case of Isaiah. The prophet demanded the "House of David," *i.e.*, the King and his court, not to trust in the army or the Egyptian auxiliaries, but to "consult Yahweh," *i.e.*, Isaiah. And what he offered as advice was trust in the *ruach* of Yahweh that lived in him.

The Isaiah prophecies require for their full understanding the consideration of earlier and later texts concerning warfare. The advice to replace the army by the *ruach* of God living in the prophet, incredible as it may sound at first hearing, will make sense of a sort, if we remember the old appellation: "My father, my father! the chariots of Israel and its horsemen!" (II Kings 2:12). The meaning of the cry emitted by Elisha when Elijah was taken to heaven in a fiery chariot remains unclear on the basis of this text alone—one can only say that at least as early as the ninth century (the formula may be much older) "my father," *i.e.*, the prophet, was considered the true armor of Israel. The implications unfold, however, when the cry recurs on occasion of the death of Elisha in II Kings 13:14–19: The prophet was lying in his last illness, and King Jehoash (804–768 B.C.) came to see him. It was a time of war with the Syrians of Damascus. The King in his sorrow addressed the prophet with the words "My father, my father!" and so forth; and Elisha responded to what he must have understood as an appeal to his function as "the chariots and horsemen of Israel," by guiding the King's hand in acts of sympathetic magic that were to ensure the victory over Syria. The scene serves as an introduction to the actual victories reported in 13:25.

On the prophecies of Isaiah, finally, falls some light from the late historiographic work of the Chronicler (fourth, perhaps even third century), in as much as the history of the decisive battle in the war with Mesha of Moab (II Kings 3), in which Elisha took a hand, was rewritten from the position of Isaiah in II Chronicles 20: On the morning of the battle the King of Judah addressed his people in the very words of Isaiah: "Trust in Yahweh your God, and you will last; trust in his prophets and you shall prosper" (II Chron. 20:20). Then a choir was ordered to sing praise to the Lord; Yahweh dispatched supernatural powers to spread confusion among the enemies; and the enemy forces destroyed each other to the last man (20:21–23). Judah had to do nothing but trust and collect the spoils (20:24–25).

These are the texts. How to categorize their meaning is a thorny problem. We shall first consider the comments of Gerhard von Rad. In the case of Isaiah, von Rad speaks of a "spiritualization" of the ritual of the Holy War. The works of Yahweh in history have, as a whole, become the God's Holy War for Zion in the eschatological sense (Isa. 5, 12, 19), a war which requires no human synergism, especially no military action. And Prophetism has become the successor to the old institution of the war ritual so completely that the prophet and his charisma have replaced the defense by armed force.[4] That is a correct description as far as it goes—but it does not touch the crucial question how the prophetic charisma can be considered by anybody an effective substitute for weapons on the battlefield. The ontological question of the *ruach* of Yahweh, manifesting itself efficaciously in the prophet, rather points toward a development from the sympathetic magic of Elisha to the sublimated magic of Isaiah's charisma. "Trust" alone, without the material operations of Elisha, will produce the desired results. That at least seems to be the sense in which the "trust" was understood by the Chronicler. With regard to Chronicles, now, von Rad observes the "resolute correlation between piety and earthly prosperity." And while the predominant element in this correlation is "the strong faith in divine blessing," the confidence that "nobody has put his trust in Yahweh in vain," there can also a "utilitarian component" be discerned in such piety.[5] The problem of magic, it appears, cannot be dismissed altogether, for the "utilitarian component," that is, the conviction that prosperity is the reward of faith, has something to do with magic in so far as it can be understood either as a spiritualized magic or as a faith that has sunk to the magic level. Nevertheless, however interpreted, this secondary magic requires the previous differentiation of trust in a transcendent God from the compact experiences of divine presence, as well as of a human power that can influence the consubstantial divine power.

The comments of von Rad, while not conclusive, point toward the magic complexion of the Isaianic experience as the source of the difficulty. The efficacious trust of Isaiah seems to lie somewhere between

---

[4] *Ibid.*, 62, 67.

[5] Gerhard von Rad, *Das Geschichtsbild des chronistischen Werkes* (Beitraege zur Wissenschaft vom Alten und Neuen Testament, 4:3, Stuttgart, 1930), 16.

the sympathetic magic of the Elisha legend and the utilitarian flattening of faith in Chronicles. On the one hand, the severe repression of human synergism, the reduction of man's role in the drama of history to a trusting abnegation of action, is definitely not magic in the sense of human action that intends to compel favorable action of divine forces. On the other hand, the formula "If you do not trust, you will not last," carries the implication that you will last, if you trust. Isaiah's counsel does not originate in an ethics of nonviolence; it is not calculated to lose the war in order to gain something more important than earthly victory but on the contrary to win the war by means more certain than an army. In the counsel of Isaiah, we may say, the element of faith in a transcendent God (which is also contained in the compactness of magic) has differentiated so far that a practice of sympathetic magic, as in the Elisha legend, has become impossible; and the sensitiveness for the gulf between divine plan and human action has even become so acute that all pragmatic assistance in the execution of the plan is considered a display of distrust. And yet, an aura of magic undeniably surrounds the counsel: It is due to the fact that the divine plan itself has been brought within the knowledge of man, in as much as Isaiah knows that God wants the survival of Judah as an organized people in pragmatic history. With that knowledge is given the trust, not in the inscrutable will of God that must be accepted however bitter it tastes when it does not agree with the plans of man, but in the knowable will of God that conforms with the policies of Isaiah and the Chosen People. That knowledge of the divine plan casts its paralyzing spell on the necessity of action in the world; for if the concrete human action will achieve nothing but what God intends to do himself, it may be indeed considered a distrustful officiousness on the part of man. This is a subtlety of experience beyond magic in the ordinary sense. What can be observed here in the making rather reminds of the later phenomena of Gnosis. With regard to the more immediate setting of the experience one may say: The infusion of society with cosmic-divine order through the cult and myth of the cosmological empires has become, in Israel, the cultic presence of the Kingdom of God in the annual festivals; and it now becomes, in the prophetism of Isaiah, a pragmatically effective presence in the history of the Chosen People. The knowable divine plan, that requires for its embodiment in pragmatic history nothing but the unbounded trust of the "House of Judah," is the cosmic-divine order of the empires, in an ultimate transformation through the medium of Israelite historical existence.

The conflict between the compact experience of order, of the cosmological type, with the historical form of existence creates the Isaianic problem. In the Introduction to this volume we have explained that the leap in being is not a leap out of existence; the autonomous order of this world remains what it is, even when the one world-transcendent God is revealed as the ultimate source of order in the world, as well as in man, society, and history. Isaiah, we may say, has tried the impossible: to make the leap in being a leap out of existence into a divinely transfigured world beyond the laws of mundane existence. The cultic restoration of cosmic divine order becomes the transfiguration of the world in history when carried into the historical form of existence. To be sure, this peculiar transformation is not a matter of necessity, perhaps inherent in the logic of experience and symbols. The transformation is due to the element of "knowledge" concerning the divine plan. And this "knowledge" seems to link the revelation of God to man with the pragmatic victories of Judah in the same manner in which the Deuteronomic Torah linked the Sinaitic revelation with the constitution of Judah. A common style of symbolization must be noted in the Law and the Prophets. Through the intervening "knowledge," thus, the recurrent restoration of order through the cosmological cult becomes, when it enters the historical form of existence, a unique transfiguration of the world according to the divine plan. A gulf opens between the world as it is and the world as it will be when it has been transfigured.

No technical terms exist for describing the state of the psyche in which the experience of cosmic rhythms, in the medium of historical form, gives birth to the vision of a world that will change its nature without ceasing to be the world in which we live concretely. I shall introduce, therefore, the term *metastasis* to signify the change in the constitution of being envisaged by the prophets. And I shall speak of metastatic experiences, of metastatic faith, hope, will, vision, and action, and of metastatic symbols which express these experiences.[6]

[6] In a first attempt to deal with this problem I had driven the analysis only so far that the line of magic becomes visible that runs from the Elisha legends, through the Isaianic trust, to the historiography of the Chronicler. And I had spoken of a "magic component in the prophetic charisma," especially with regard to the Isaiah prophecies. In conversations with several Old Testament scholars, however, the notion of a "magic component" in Isaiah met with serious misgivings, though on the spur of the moment no alternative solutions were developed for the problems undoubtedly presented by the prophet's faith and counsel. I want to express my gratitude in

The constitution of being is what it is, and cannot be affected by human fancies. Hence, the metastatic denial of the order of mundane existence is neither a true proposition in philosophy, nor a program of action that could be executed. The will to transform reality into something which by essence it is not is the rebellion against the nature of things as ordained by God. And while the rebellion has become sublime in Isaiah's trust that God himself will change the order of the world and let Judah win its victories without battle, the danger of derailment in various directions is obvious. This metastatic faith, now, though it became articulate in the prophets, did not originate with them but was inherent, from the very beginnings of the Mosaic foundation, in the conception of the theopolity as the Kingdom of God incarnate in a concrete people and its institutions. It could rest dormant or remain comparatively innocuous, deeply embedded as it was in the compactness of early experiences and symbols, for centuries, but it had to become virulent when under the pressure of historical events it became obvious that the reality of Israel was not exactly a Kingdom of God and showed no inclination to become one. The growing realization of the conflict aroused a whole series of attempts to bring the obstreperous reality of the world, through metastatic imagination and action, to conformity with the demands of the Kingdom. These operations can best be classified by the time dimension, as symbolic actions concerning the future, the present, and the past of true order:

(1) *Pro futuro*: a. Israel will suffer punishment at the hands of Yahweh, because its misconduct is the cause of the conflict. The obstreperous reality will be destroyed altogether. That is the response represented by Amos' terrible Day of Yahweh. In this context (Amos 2:13–16) occurs significantly the numinous terror of the Holy War as the mode of punishment inflicted on Israel. b. Israel will emerge from its present and future miseries into a true Kingdom of God, in which the conditions of existence have given way to something like a Golden Age. The date of the numerous prophecies of this type (*e.g.*, Amos 9:13–15;

---

particular to Professor Nahum N. Glatzer (Boston), Professor Gerhard von Rad (Heidelberg), and Professor Rudolf Bultmann (Marburg) for a sympathetic resistance that forced me to resume the analysis. The ontological implications of the prophetic symbolism have attracted little attention. As far as I know, the problem has never been formally treated. The literature on the metastatic class of experiences in detail, however, is enormous. Especially since the discovery of the Psalms as cult hymns and rituals, the transition from the cultic to the eschatological meaning of the Psalms has become the subject of a far-flung inquiry. On these problems cf. Chapter 9.5.

Isa. 2:2–4; Mic. 4:1–5; Joel 3:18–21) is a matter of controversy. They do perhaps not always belong to the pre-exilic prophets to whom they are ascribed. Nevertheless, there is no reason to doubt that the type itself, as in the cases of Hosea 2:16–25 or Isaiah 9:1–7, goes back at least to the eighth century.

(2) *Pro praesente:* a. The Kingdom of God will be forced into the present reality through myth and constitutional enactment, as in the Deuteronomic Torah. b. The Kingdom of God will be forced into the present reality through metastatic trust, as in the Isaiah case.

(3) *Pro praeterito:* Reality will be metastically transformed in retrospect through the rewriting of history, as in the case of the Chronicler.

In the variety of symbolic forms is recognizable the common substance of the metastatic will to transform reality by means of eschatological, mythical, or historiographic phantasy, or by perverting faith into an instrument of pragmatic action. This metastatic component became so predominant in the complex phenomenon of prophetism that in late Judaism it created its specific symbolic form in the apocalyptic literature. As the decline of Israel and Judah was accompanied by the forms of prophetism, so the Judaism of the new imperial age was accompanied by the symbolism of the apocalypse. Moreover, the recognition of the metastatic experience is of importance for the understanding not only of Israelite and Jewish order but of the history of Western Civilization to this day. While in the main development of Christianity, to be sure, the metastatic symbols were transformed into the eschatological events beyond history, so that the order of the world regained its autonomy, the continuum of metastatic movements has never been broken. It massively surrounds, rivals, and penetrates Christianity in Gnosis and Marcionism, and in a host of gnostic and antinomian heresies; and it has been absorbed into the symbolism of Christianity itself through the Old Testament, as well as through the Revelation of St. John. Throughout the Middle Ages, the Church was occupied with the struggle against heresies of a metastatic complexion; and with the Reformation this underground stream has come to the surface again in a massive flood—first, in the left wing of the sectarian movements and then in the secular political creed movements which purport to exact the metastasis by revolutionary action.

The analysis of the metastatic problem will now illuminate the aspects of the prophetic position which defied common sense. The drastic rejections of the people's order, as we have seen, had a number of motives. They served analytically the purpose of opposing the order of a soul formed by the knowledge and fear of God to mere conformity of conduct; they were motivated by moral sensitiveness in as much as they denounced various forms of oppression and callousness in social relations; they came spiritually to the defense of Yahwism when they castigated the people's preference for alien gods; they were archaistic, and understandably so, when they expressed nostaligia for the early times of the theopolity; and their vehemence was necessary to counter the fierce collectivism of the people. Nevertheless, when all the motives were given due weight, they did not account for the qualitatively different rejection of the institutional order on principle. No list of grievances, however long and formidable, adds up to an ontological denial of the conditions of existence in the world. The enigmatic factor, which caused this additional effect, is now found in the metastatic experience. Precisely, however, when this experience is recognized as the missing factor in the field of variegated motivations, it becomes no more than one component in the complex effort of the prophets to clarify the existential issue under the concrete conditions of Israelite order in the eighth and seventh centuries B.C. The nature of this further problem, that is, of the relation between the metastatic experience and the existential issue, will become apparent if we consider the above-mentioned text, Hosea 2:14–23 (Engl. vers.).

Drawing out his beautiful symbolism of the faithless wife who returns to her husband, Hosea develops a typical apocalyptic vision of the future (2:16):

> And it shall be at that day, says Yahweh,
> that you will call me *ishi* [my husband],
> and you will no longer call me *baali* [my Baal-master].

And on that day it shall be (21–23) that:

> I will answer the heavens,
> and they shall answer the earth
> and the earth shall answer the corn, and the wine, and the soil,
> and they shall answer Jezreel [Sown-by-God].

> And I will sow her for me in the land,
> and I will have pity on Not-Pitied [*lo-ruchamah*];
> and I will say to Not-my-people [*lo-ammi*] You-are-my-people,
> and they shall say My-God.

The constitution of being is transfigured into a state of perfection, the world we know has given way to a new world through an act of divine grace. And Hosea not only is conscious of a new act of creation that will surpass the Creation and Covenant of the old order, but also finds the language for it (2:18):

> And I will make in that day a covenant [*berith*] for them
>   with the beasts of the field, and the fowl of the heavens, and the
>   creeping things of the ground;
> and I will break the bow, and the sword, and the war from the land,
> and I will make them lie down in safety.

The metastasis, thus, affects the whole creation, but it will specifically change the relation between man and God (2:19–20):

> And I will betroth you to me forever.
> I will betroth you to me in righteousness [*zedek*], and in justice
>   [*mishpat*],
> and in loving kindness [*hesed*], and in compassion [*rachamim*].
> And I will betroth you to me in faithfulness [*emonah*],
> and you shall know Yahweh.

The metastatic yearning of the prophet expresses itself starkly in the vision of a transfigured world. The yearning, however, does not obscure his knowledge that the change cannot be brought about by human action, not even by a will to believe; and the vision expands, therefore, to include a divine act of grace that will bestow ultimate order on the world. Surrounding it with the metastatic symbols, Hosea, finally, articulates the real issue, that is, the reordering of human existence through the knowledge (*da'ath*) of God. With a profusion of terms he describes the bethrothal of man to God in steadfastness, righteousness, lovingkindness, justice, and compassion. As far as one can judge this intricate weave of motives and symbols, the metastatic experience, while it finds odd expressions in the prophets and derails dubiously in later phenomena, is with Hosea not a disturbing but rather a maieutic factor in his effort to bring the Kingdom of God in the souls of men forth from its theopolitical matrix.

When now we return to Jeremiah, we find that the differentiation of the existential issue has remarkably advanced beyond Hosea. In Jeremiah 31:29–30 we read:

> In those days they shall say no more:
> "The fathers have eaten sour grapes,
>   and the children's teeth are set on edge."
> But every one shall die for his own guilt [*awon*]:
> every man who eats the sour grapes shall have his own teeth set on edge.

The collectivism of existence, while not completely broken, is at least seriously shaken by a conception of personal responsibility and punishment that was further developed by Ezekiel (Ezek. 18). And even when the people still appears as a body, the metaphors stress the personal state of order, as in Jeremiah 17:1:

> The sin of Judah is written
>   with a pen of iron;
> with a point of diamond it is engraved
>   on the tablet of their hearts.

The hearts have now become the Tablets on which the Commandments were written, and what is written on the hearts of the Chosen People is not the Covenant with God, but the entirely different *berith* about which Isaiah (28:15) had let the people boast:

> We have struck a *berith* with Death,
> and have formed a compact with Sheol.

From the depth to which the old Covenant had fallen, then, rises the climactic prophecy of Jeremiah (31:31–34):

> Behold, the days are coming, says Yahweh, when I will make a new covenant with the house of Israel and the house of Judah,
> not like the covenant which I made with their fathers on the day that I took them by their hand to bring them out of the land of Egypt,
> my covenant [*berith*] which they broke, though I was their master [*baal*], says Yahweh.
>
> But this is the covenant, which I will make with the house of Israel after those days, says Yahweh:
> I will put my law [*toroth*] within them, and will write it on their hearts;
> and I will be their God, and they shall be my people.

And no longer shall each man teach his neighbor and each his
   brother, saying "Know the Lord";
for all of them shall know me, from the least of them to the greatest of them, says Yahweh.
For I will pardon their guilt, and their sin will I remember no more.

3. The Message

To be Israel meant to exist in continuity with the action of the
Berith drama. In the first act of this drama, in the Message of Exodus
19:4–6, Yahweh had promised to make Israel his own possession (*segullah*) among all peoples, the royal domain of his immediate servants
(*mamlekheth kohanim*), and a holy nation (*goy qadosh*), on the condition that the people hear his voice and keep his covenant. The cosmic-
divine order of Egypt was to be superseded by a new order of history
under the world-transcendent God who had revealed himself from
Sinai. In the realm of symbols, the royal domain as the divine center of
order in the cosmological empire was accordingly transformed into the
Chosen People, the holy omphalos of world-history. Only when the
Message had been accepted, followed the second act, the ritual conclusion of the Berith between God and the people that now had become
"his people." And in pursuance of the Berith, finally, Yahweh proclaimed
the Decalogue as the fundamental law of the people's order. The meaning
of the drama, though it unfolded in a sequence of three distinct acts,
was one and indivisible; no part of it could be removed without affecting
the whole. The people that emerged as Israel from the Sinaitic events
could not disobey the commandments of the Decalogue without breaking the Covenant; it could not break the Covenant without reversing
the acceptance of its status as the Chosen People; and it could not refuse
to be the *goy qadosh* without being in revolt against the revealed will of
God. This chain of meaning running through the acts in which Israel
gained its existence in historical form had not been made explicit, however, in the traditions of the events. It had remained indeed so deeply
embedded in the accounts of the events themselves that even in the
extant form the narrative is unclear on the point whether the Berith
precedes the Decalogue, or the Decalogue the Berith. Only in the crisis
of Israel, when the continuity of its existence as the *goy qadosh* had been
made problematic by the empirical conduct of people, ruling class, and

court, as observed by the prophets, was the experiential motive given for an inquiry into the precise meaning of existence under God.

The prophets tried to save the order of Israel through clarification of its meaning. We followed this struggle, in the reverse order of the Berith drama, through Decalogue and Covenant, because the empirical observation of conduct in violation of the commandments furnished in fact the motive of inquiry. Under the impact of this inquiry, as we have seen, the symbols of the Berith drama disintegrated, because their compactness of meaning proved inadequate to express the differentiated experiences of the prophets. The normative and existential issues of the Decalogue had to be distinguished, as far as the lack of a philosophical vocabulary permitted the distinction; and a catalogue of virtues, describing the existential order, was developed. This new table of virtues, expressing the spirit contained compactly in the decalogic table of commandments, then, seemed to require a Covenant, different from the Berith on the basis of which the Decalogue had been proclaimed; and the symbol of a covenant written in the heart was formed. And the Covenant, finally, was based on the Message, its promises and their acceptance. Could the Message escape the fate of the other symbols? Was the revelation still valid in the form in which it had been cast in the time of Moses? To be sure, that the symbolism of the Message had not spent its force by the time of Jeremiah was proven by the Deuteronomic Torah, which still referred to Israel as the *segullah* and *goy qadosh* of Yahweh (Deut. 7:6; 14:2; 26:18–19). Only the *mamlekheth kohanim* had disappeared, probably because the *kohanim* had so unequivocally become priests in the sense of cult officials that the symbol would no longer evoke the sense of royal aides. Nevertheless, while the continuity of tradition made it possible, at least for the Deuteronomist circles, to apply the symbols in the archaistic reform of the seventh century B.C., the order of Israel had changed so profoundly, through the misconduct observed by the prophets, that the Torah as a whole expressed no more than one of its component factors—and that was, in the judgment of the prophets, no longer the most important one. The forceful separation from Egyptian order, the declaration of Israel as the son of God in opposition to the Pharaoh, and the creation of the *goy qadosh* had receded six centuries into the past. The springtime of the new dispensation could not be recaptured by an act of archaising violence for an Israel that was in revolt against God. Under the circumstances, this identification of the Kingdom of Judah with the *goy qadosh* through a metastatic myth was, on the contrary, for Jeremiah one symptom more of the rebellion against the word of God as spoken through the prophets' mouth. Hence, the symbolism of the Message could not be exempted from the prophetic attack, though with this target the struggle for clarification reached the originating center of historical existence in the revelation of Yahweh. The prophets were faced with the task of reformulating the problem of history in such a manner that the empirical Israel of their time could disappear from the scene without destroying by its disappearance the order of history as created by revelation.

When the prophetic critique of symbols reached the center of revelation, it was no longer possible to restrict the argument to specific issues of misconduct. The chain of meaning contained in the Berith drama burst at once in violent articulation. The constitution of being as a whole, with the origin of its order in God, was at stake. The magnitude of the conflicts can better be understood by first listing the three sets of arguments which had to be taken into account at once:

(1) When the prophets measured the empirical conduct of Israel by the symbols of the Berith drama, they could observe that the people neither heard the voice nor kept the covenant of Yahweh. They knew that the Decalogue had become a matter of legal and cultic observance in violation of the spirit, and that the Covenant had been broken. In this situation of disorder on the human side, when the people no longer fulfilled their obligations under the Covenant, the question imposed itself whether the divine partner was still bound by his promise. Was the Message still valid? Was Israel still the Chosen People in the Sinaitic dispensation of history? These were the questions suggested by the contractual symbolism of the Berith.

(2) As soon, however, as the prophets raised them, the abyss of revelation and faith proved incommensurate with the logic of contract. For the substance of the Covenant was provided not by the meeting of the minds of equal partners but by the revelation of God as the source of order in man, society, and history. The set of legal argument concerning conclusion, violation, and dissolution of an agreement had to be supplemented by a second set of argument concerned with the substance of revelation and its consequences. On the level of substantive order, the

God who had revealed himself and made the choice could not be assumed either to have deceived the people with false promises or to have deceived himself about the qualities of the human partner. Moreover, the revealed will of God to create a new order of history could not be assumed to be stultified by the opposing will of the human subject of order. The revelation of God, once it had entered the reality of history, could not be thrown out of history by a human decision to ignore it.

(3) This second train of reflections, conducted in the certainty of prophetic faith, of the knowledge of God, however, encountered the incontrovertible facts of Israel's misconduct, the empirically observed symptoms of the crisis of order which motivated the prophetic struggle: that revelation could be ignored, that faith could be abandoned, that the covenant could be broken, that the Chosen People even did not care to be chosen, and that it was on the point of being annihilated by imperial powers who were no more paragons of virtue than was Israel.

For the first time men experienced the clash between divinely willed and humanly realized order of history in its stark brutality, and the souls of the prophets were the battlefield in this war of the spirit.

The bearing of the prophets in this storm, their action and passion, their speeches and silences have created symbols of a validity as permanent as the conflict itself. This validity is due to the conspiracy of faith and reason. The intellectual penetration of the issues has forced the symbolism to the point at which, under the sensuous concreteness of prophetic language, the ontological problems become clearly visible. And this force of intellectual penetration has its source in the prophets' faith, their *da'ath* of God, which maintains in their tension the lasting of divine order and the passing of human disorder. In whatever manner the empirical Israel conduct itself, the divinely revealed order is beyond doubt the immutable order of history; what God wills cannot be undone by the doings of man. The symbolism of the thornbush episode, in which Yahweh revealed himself to Moses as the I AM WHO I AM, has been brought by the prophetic faith close to unfolding the metaphysics of being contained in it. When the prophets struggle with the meaning of the Message, the principles of a philosophy of history become at least discernible, though they do not achieve conceptual articulation.

In the first place, the prophets penetrated what in modern terminology may be called the dialectics of divine foreknowledge and human decision. On the side of divine foreknowledge they knew: God had chosen Israel as the holy nation of the new order; since God did not use the method of trial and error, the revealed order had to be realized; whatever Israel did, it had to remain the Chosen People. On the side of human decision they knew: The empirical Israel did not realize the revealed order; and a terrible disaster, amounting to extinction, was impending in pragmatic politics. In the face of this conflict between revealed and empirical order, the prophets spoke the word of Yahweh in the dual symbolism of the prophecies of punishment and salvation. The prophecies of the terrible day were intended to induce the change of heart that would avert the punishment; and the prophecies of ultimate salvation held out the future that would follow the concrete change of heart. The prophecies will become senseless if they are understood as flat predictions of future events, without any bearing on the attunement of human to divine order through the change of heart. This proposition, that the prophecies will become senseless unless they are understood as the alternatives hinging on the change of heart, is valid, however, only on the level of prophetic existence. The literal, or fundamentalist, understanding of prophecy as flat information about the future acquires a sinister and even deadly sense if it is the deliberate misunderstanding by the people of whom the change of heart is demanded. For the dialectics of divinely foreknown and humanly realized order is not merely a "theoretical problem," but the ontologically real struggle for order conducted in every man's existence. Moreover, it is the struggle for the order in society conducted among the men who take sides for or against the attunement to divine order. And in this struggle no holds are barred on the side of the resisters. Precisely because the prophetic concern is not with future events but with the existential order in the present, the prophecies will be understood by the people to whom they are addressed as literal information about the future. The stubborn of heart are clever dialecticians themselves; they know quite as well as the prophets that the will of God, expressed in his choice, cannot be stultified by the people. Hence, they will pretend not to hear the existential appeal in the prophecy of disaster; for if they do not hear it, they not only need not respond to the appeal, but can construe the prophecy as an insult to God and his choice, and gain the right to persecute and martyrize the "prophet of doom." The prophecy of salvation, in its turn, lends itself so easily to the not-hearing of the appeal, that its misuse for evading the issue of existential order had become the prosperous business of the "false prophets," against whom Jeremiah conducted his lifelong campaign. The authentic prophets were forced, as a consequence, to lay their accents in public on the prophecy of disaster, thus exposing themselves even more to the fate of the "prophet of doom" who blasphemously attacks the revealed order, as in the case of Jeremiah. And Isaiah, in his endeavor to prevent the misuse of his words, apparently went even so far as to entrust his prophecies of salvation to a circle of disciples, to be kept secret for the time being. The prophets thus forced the dialectics of order into articulation over the wide range of ontological distinctions between the world-transcendent God and the world, the tension between divinely willed and humanly realized order, the types of existence in faith and defection, the existential appeal and the stubbornness of heart, the dual symbolism of the prophecies of punishment and salvation, the fundamentalist device of literal misunderstanding, the exploitation of the device by the "false prophets," the suffering of persecution and martyrdom, and the prophetic device to protect and preserve the truth of salvation through schools of disciples who became the carriers of the secret. The range of articulation from ontological distinctions to the physical conflict between the prophets and their enemies suggests that with the entrance of revelation into history a new order has been established indeed. For even those who reject it cannot create an alternative order, but are forced to create its semblance by perverting the symbols of revelation and prophetism. Even perdition must speak the language of salvation. We recall the profound prophecy of Hosea 13:9: "That will be to your destruction, O Israel, that it is with me you find your help." With regard to the prophecies of punishment and salvation, we conclude therefore that the two must not be separated: Together they are the one symbolism by which the prophets articulated their experience of the conflict between divine order and human realization, of the mystery that God suffers human rebellion against his foreknown order in the distention of historical time. And as far as the interpretation of prophetic texts is concerned, we therefore cannot follow historians who doubt the authenticity of the prophecies of ultimate salvation in the great prophets, who will for instance assign Amos 9 to a later period on the ground that it glaringly contradicts the main body of Amos' prophecies of disaster. For such reasoning would introduce the category of the "prophet of doom" into the premises of interpretation and make nonsense of the prophetic problem.

On several occasions we have spoken of the ontological distinctions implied in the prophetic concern with the order of history. The distinctions themselves, as well as the mode of their implication, require our attention because on the one hand, these questions touch the fundamentals of a philosophy of history, whereas on the other hand, in our contemporary state of intellectual confusion their fundamental character is rarely understood. The prophets had no doubts about the ontological presuppositions of their problem of order: Without the God who "knows" his people and the prophet who "knows" God, there would be no Chosen People, no defection from the commandments, no breaking of the Covenant, no crisis of Israel, no prophetic call to return, and no suspense between destruction and salvation. Existence in historical form presupposes the existence of the world-transcendent God, as well as the historical fact of his revelation. This presupposition, embedded in the prophetic *da'ath*, did not require articulation at the time because the prophets' environment did not yet contain philosophical atheism among its variegated phenomena of defection from order. Nevertheless, although in the absence of articulate doubt the corresponding positive articulation was unnecessary, the issue was fiercely alive in the contents of prophecy. For the prophets lived concretely as members of a people called Israel, which experienced its order, in historical continuity, as constituted by the Sinaitic revelation. While they anticipated disasters for the empirical humanity surrounding them, they never doubted for a moment that the dispensation of history created by the Message would continue, whatever "remnant" of Israel or "offshoot" from the House of Jesse would be its empirical carrier in the future. History, once it has become ontologically real through revelation, carries with it the irreversible direction from compact existence in cosmological form toward the Kingdom of God. "Israel" is not the empirical human beings who may or may not keep the Covenant, but the expansion of divine creation into the order of man and society. No amount of empirical defections can touch the constitution of being as it unfolds in the light of revelation. Man can close the eye of his soul to its light; and he can engage in the futility of rebellion;

but he cannot abolish the order by which his conduct will be judged. Modern symbolic expressions of the crisis, as Hegel's dictum "God is dead" or Nietzsche's even stronger "He has been murdered," which betray the degree to which their authors were impressed by massive events of their time, would have been inconceivable to the prophets—to say nothing of the rebellious fantasy of having the order of history originate in the will of ideological planners left and right. If the prophets, in their despair over Israel, indulged in metastatic dreams, in which the tension of historical order was abolished by a divine act of grace, at least they did not indulge in metastatic nightmares, in which the *opus* was performed by human acts of revolution. The prophets could suffer with God under the defection of Israel, but they could not doubt the order of history under the revealed will of God. And since they could not doubt, they were spared the intellectual confusion about the meaning of history. They knew that history meant existence in the order of being as it had become visible through revelation. One could not go back of revelation and play existence in cosmic-divine order, after the world-transcendent God had revealed himself. One could not pretend to live in another order of being than the one illuminated by revelation. And least of all could one think of going beyond revelation replacing the constitution of being with a man-made substitute. Man exists *within* the order of being; and there is no history *outside* the historical form under revelation. In the surrounding darkness of Israel's defection and impending political destruction—darker perhaps than the contemporary earthwide revolt against God—the prophets were burdened with the mystery of how the promises of the Message could prevail in the turmoil. They were burdened with this mystery by their faith; and history continued indeed by the word of God spoken through the prophets. There are times, when the divinely willed order is humanly realized nowhere but in the faith of solitary sufferers.

Their faith in the time of crisis forced the prophets to oppose the order of society and to find the order of their existence in the word spoken by Yahweh. Suffering in solitude meant suffering, in communion with God, under the disorder of a community to which the prophet did not cease to belong.

The participation in the conflict reached its extreme when Jeremiah enacted in his life the crisis of Israel. Both disaster and salvation, the dual symbolism held together by the existential appeal, were acted out by him at the command of Yahweh:

(1) Jeremiah remained without family because the divine word had come to him, saying: "You shall not take a wife, neither shall you have sons and daughters in this place" (16:2). For children and parents would die of starvation, unlamented and unburied (16:3–5); the voice of gladness and the voice of joy, the voice of the bridegroom and the voice of the bride, would be banished from this place "before your eyes, and in your days" (16:9). The disintegration of Israel's order had reached the point where the first of the *toroth,* the "Be fruitful, and multiply," was suspended; the people was to be destroyed physically, through breaking the chain of the *toldoth.*

(2) And yet, life will continue "in this place." For the word came also to Jeremiah ordering him, as the next of kin, to buy a field at Anathoth from a relative (32:7–8). The prophet obeyed and ordered Baruch to place the deed of purchase, together with a copy, in an earthen jar, "so that they may last many days." "For thus says Yahweh of the hosts, the God of Israel: Yet again shall there be bought houses and fields and vineyards in this land" (32:15).

(3) To the intense enactment of the symbolism corresponded the intense experience of the appeal which it had become Jeremiah's fate to make to the people. In the oracle of 1:14–19 Yahweh summoned "all the kingdoms of the north." They shall set up their thrones before the gates and the walls of Jerusalem, and of every city of Judah. And Yahweh will pronounce his judgments against them for all their defections. In this situation Jeremiah would have to speak all that Yahweh commanded him; and he was assured by his God: "Do not be dismayed before them, lest I dismay you before them. For behold! I make you this moment a fortified city, and an iron pillar, and brazen walls above the whole land—against the kings of Judah, against its princes, against its priests, and against the people of the land. They shall fight against you, and shall not overcome you. For I am with you, to deliver you" (1:17–19).

The oracles reveal a new structure in the field of historical forces. The prophet had to act out the fate of Israel in his own life, because the holy omphalos of history had contracted from the Chosen People into his personal existence. In the world-historic crisis, involving the goyim together with Judah, he had become the City of God above the doomed cities of the land, not to be overcome either by the "kingdoms of the north" or by the people and government of Judah. He was the sole representative of divine order; and whatever the inscrutable will of God might hold for the future, the meaning of the present was determined by the Word that was spoken from the divine-human omphalos in Jeremiah. The Chosen People had been replaced by the chosen man.

The symbols of the Message were not suitable to express the changed structure of the historical field. New symbols had to be found; and they were found indeed by Jeremiah, through the method of transfer, in the oracles of his call (*ca.* 626 B.C.):

(1) In the first oracle (1:5) the word of Yahweh comes to Jeremiah, saying:

> Before I formed you in the womb, I knew you;
> and before you came from the womb, I consecrated you;
> a prophet to the nations I ordained you.

The prophet is the Son of God. The child is formed by God in the mother's womb. Even before his formation he is "known" by God; and before his birth he is consecrated for the God's service as the prophet to the nations. The language is borrowed from the royal symbolism of the cosmological empires—it closely resembles an inscription of Assurbanipal, the ruler of Assur and overlord of Judah in the time of Jeremiah's youth.[7] As the Assyrian ruler, the prophet is ordained for his service by the God from distant times before the time of the world; and the "distant times" of the Assyrian inscription now blend into the eternity of the divine will that had been revealed in the Message from Sinai. The will of God is not stultified after all by the recalcitrant people, but continues, with historical effectiveness, in the ordination of Jeremiah from eternity. The sonship of God, moving from the Pharaoh to Israel, and from the people to its Davidic king, has at last reached the Prophet. While this is by far not yet the Christian revelation that only God can be the Son of God—the mystery expressed in Trinitarian theology and the Christology—it is a long step toward the insight that the order from eternity is not incarnate in a people and its rulers in pragmatic history. The transfer of the royal symbolism to the institutional outcast Jeremiah is a decisive advance in the clarification of the Messianic problem that

---

[7] For the Assurbanipal inscription cf. Luckenbill, *Ancient Records of Assyria and Babylonia*, II, s. 765. The inscription has been quoted in Chapter 1.2.

will occupy us presently; and the consequences make themselves felt, only a few decades later, in the prophecies of Deutero-Isaiah.

(2) When Jeremiah receives the word of his ordination as a prophet to the nations, he protests humbly (1:6):

> Ah, Lord Yahweh! I cannot speak;
> for a youth am I.

And he is answered (1:7–8):

> Say not: A youth am I.
> For to whomever I send you, you shall go;
> and whatever I command you, you shall speak.
> Be not afraid of them;
> for I am with you to deliver you.

The second oracle transfers the symbolism of Moses to Jeremiah—it is the hesitation, overridden by Yahweh with his promise to be with the prophet, that we know from the thornbush episode. Both oracles, held together by the identity of the Jeremiah to whom they are addressed, form one body of meaning, in that the royal figure of the first one is a Moses standing before Yahweh, while the Mosaic figure of the second one is a Son of God. In their combination they illuminate the changes in the experience of authority that had occurred since the time of Moses. We remember the difficulties in answering the question "Who was Moses?", arising from the fact that, with the exception of the "servant of Yahweh" (ebed Yahweh), no symbols were available to characterize his status in the creation of Israel's order—between the Pharaonic and the new Son of God the status of Moses remained strangely inarticulate. Now, when the prophets move ever more distinctly into the position of preservers and restorers of order, their self-understanding can be increased through Mosaic symbols, while the figure of Moses becomes more intelligible through the prophetic effort at self-understanding. In particular, the vicissitudes of the Ebed-Yahweh symbol will illuminate the process in which the meaning of authority emanating from God becomes clarified. The original Ebed-Yahweh is Moses (Josh. 1:1), and in his succession the symbol applies to Joshua (Josh. 24:29; Judg. 2:8); it moves further on to David (especially II Sam. 7) and Solomon (the transfer in I Kings 3:7); it then wanders to the bands of prophets of the ninth century (II Kings 9:7) and the solitary prophets of the eighth century (Amos 3:7); and it is applied for the first time to a concrete prophet in the phrase "my servant Isaiah" (Isa. 20:3). Jeremiah does not use it for himself specifically, because with him the symbol has become the general designation of the prophets (Jer. 7:25; 25:4; 26:5; 29:19; 35:15); and he uses it even for designating such nonprophetic instruments of Yahweh's will in history as the King of Babylon (Jer. 25:9; 27:6; 43:10). The wandering of the symbol reflects the wandering of authority in Israel from Moses, over the conqueror of Canaan and the founder of the Empire, to the prophets, until the concentration of authority in himself permits Jeremiah to use the symbols of the earlier carriers of authority, as far as they seem suitable, in the expression of his own prophetic existence. The fluidity of the symbols, their meandering through the process in which the meaning of authority becomes clarified, must be realized if one wants to understand the interchangeability of symbols, as in a dream play, in Deutero-Isaiah. Moreover, its recognition will make it clear why today it has become impossible to know to what extent the prophetic existence was formed by traditions of Moses, or to what extent the traditions of Moses have been formed by the prophetic experience.

(3) In the third oracle the divine authority is actually transferred to Jeremiah. Yahweh stretches forth his hand and, touching the prophet's mouth, he says (1:10):

> Behold! I put my words in your mouth.
> See! I have put you in charge, of this day, over the nations and over
>   the kingdoms,
> to root up and to pull down,
> to destroy and to overthrow,
> to build and to plant.

This is the new message, replacing the one from Sinai to Moses. The prophet is no longer the founder and legislator of his people but something like a lord of history under God, "set over," or "put in charge of," the nations and kingdoms, for their good or their evil as they respond to the appeal. The charge is elaborated in Jeremiah 18:1–12, where the prophet is ordered to go down to the potter's house and to watch how he turns the clay in his hand into another vessel when the first one seems to be spoiled. "As the clay in the potter's hand, so are you in my hand, O House of Israel" (18:6). If God intends to destroy a nation, he will repent if it turn from evil. And if he intends to plant, he will repent if the nation does what is evil in his sight (18:7–10). On principle, this is still tne dual prophecy, hinging on the appeal to return. But in the case of Israel, there is no hope—not because Yahweh has decided against his people, but because the people answers to the appeal: "There is no hope! For we will walk after our own plans; and we will do everyone after the stubbornness of his evil heart" (18:12). This is the juncture of history in which Jeremiah becomes the sole vicar of God.

The experience of Yahweh as the universal God of history, and of the speaker of his word as a "prophet to the nations," has become fully articulate only in Jeremiah, but it was present even in Amos, the first in the line of the solitary prophets whose sayings are extant. In Amos 9:7 we read:

> Are you not as the children of the Kushites to me,
>   O children of Israel?—the oracle of Yahweh—
> Have not I brought forth Israel
>   from the land of Egypt,
> And the Philistines from Caphtor,
>   and Aram from Kir?

A more drastic ranking of the nations with Israel and of Israel with the nations is hardly conceivable than through the suggestion that the divine choice for the Exodus was not restricted to the *goy qadosh*. Such freedom from bondage as the nations achieved, they also were granted by Yahweh; and with the Exodus from bondage they accepted, as did Israel, the law of Yahweh, though in the restricted form of a commandment to recognize the fellow-humanity among themselves in their conduct. Hence, they fall under Yahweh's judgment, like Israel, when they grossly violate the rules of humane conduct in their quarrels, as Amos casuistically details in his prophecies against the nations (Amos 1:3–2:3). This constancy of the prophetic problem from Amos to Jeremiah, and even to Ezekiel, has resulted in a distinct literary form—if the term may be used for spoken words and their tradition—which is still discernible even in the secondary, postexilic organization of the prophetic books. In this form must be distinguished (1) the types of oracles which enter into larger complexes of meaning, (2) the variety of meaningful combinations of the basic types, and (3) the superimposed order of the collections. The basic types are determined, on the one hand, by the alternatives of the appeal to Israel as oracles of disaster and salvation concerning Israel and Judah; on the other hand, by the inclusion of the nations in the historical plan of Yahweh as oracles concerning the nations. Meaningful simple combinations are: (1) the sequence of oracles of disaster and salvation concerning Israel; (2) the sequence of oracles of disaster concerning Israel and the nations; (3) the reverse sequence of oracles against the nations climaxed by the oracles of disaster against Israel; (4) the sequence of Israel oracles followed by the oracles against the nations; (5) the sequence of Israel oracles interrupted by the oracles against the nations; (6) various sequences of oracles rounded out by a final sequence of disaster and salvation (this last form probably reflecting the rituals of defeat and victory in the royal cult). A simple form of organization is to be found, for instance, in the small book of Zephania, the older contemporary of Jeremiah, with its division into the prophecies of judgment against Judah and mankind in general (Zeph. 1), the prophecies against the nations (Zeph. 2), and the resumption of the prophecies against Jerusalem, followed by the prophecies of salvation, in a typical concluding chapter (Zeph. 3). Of the larger collections, the organization is clearest in Ezekiel with its chronological order of oracles of disaster preceding the fall of Jerusalem (Ezek. 1–24); oracles against the nations, mostly during the siege of Jerusalem (Ezek. 25–32); and oracles of restauration, after the fall of the city (Ezek. 33–48). The Isaiah collection proper (Isa. 1–35) follows the form of Ezekiel in its superimposed organization but is extremely complex in the subdivisions. And both Isaiah and Jeremiah are further complicated by the insertion of biographical and historical pieces. Still, one can discern in Jeremiah the three main bodies of the prophecies against Judah and Jerusalem (Jer. 1–24); the oracles against the nations (Jer. 46–51); and the little book of comfort, containing the prophecies of salvation (Jer. 30–33) — though the Septuagint lets the oracles against the nations immediately follow (inserted in Jer. 25 of the Masoretic text) the prophecies against Israel. In the book of Amos, a firmly organized body of text begins with the oracles against the nations (1:3–2:3) and is climaxed by the prophecies against Judah (2:4–5) and Israel (2:6–16), while the last chapter is organized in the same manner as Zephania 3, as a resumption of the prophecy of disaster (9:1–8) followed by the prophecies of salvation (9:9–15).

From the middle of the eighth century B.C. to the fall of Jerusalem, the historical order under a universal God is the constant concern of the prophets—that much is confirmed by the pervasiveness of the literary form just described. This general problem, though, is no more than the background for the prophets' specific concern with the fate of Israel on the suddenly enlarged world scene. For the recognition, in Amos, that Yahweh is the God of the nations as much as of the Chosen People does not abolish the peculiar status of Israel as the center from which radiates the order of history. While the concrete terms of the Message will no longer apply to the recalcitrant people, its intention is not invalidated by the defection of the empirical Israel; and that intention can be realized only if the intended historical order has an omphalos. For the order of society and history participates in the order of God only in as much as the universal, transcendent God is experienced as such in the faith of men who order their existence in the light of their faith and thereby become the representative center of society and history. If the Kingdoms of Israel and Judah are doomed, the question becomes ever more burning: Who will be the carrier of historical order in the future? If it is no longer the people and the king of Judah, who then will be "Israel"? What kind of "people" under what kind of "king" will emerge from the imminent destruction as the new Israel under the new Covenant? Since in the prophetic occupation with such questions the figure of a ruler more satisfactory than the contemporary Davidic Kings looms large, the whole complex of questions has come to be called, by a historiographic convention, the "Messianic problem."

The term "Messianic problem," which originates in Christian exegetic interests, is justified in so far as the Christian symbolism of the Messiah has indeed unfolded in continuity with the prophetic symbolism developed in the articulation of these questions. It is misleading, however, in so far as the Christian overtones of the term tend to obscure the fact that the prophets in their time were not concerned with the revelation of the Logos—for which the world still had to wait some seven hundred years—but with the characteristics of a political ruler of Israel in their lifetime, or in a near future to be measured in a few decades. Hence, in a critical study of the question the term "Messiah," loaded as it is with Christian connotations, should be avoided whenever possible. The problem, in order to be placed properly in its historical context, must be stated in terms of the prophetic sources. In the continuity of symbols, the way must be traced back from "Christ the Messiah" to the Greek *christos* of the Septuagint, which translates the *mashiach* of the Hebrew text; and *mashiach* means "the Anointed," that is, the King of Israel.

Hence, in the crisis of Israel the prophets were interested not in a Messiah but in the conduct of their kings; and when the conduct seemed to accelerate rather than to avert the disaster, they became interested in the type of ruler who would succeed the Davidic Anointed of Yahweh, as soon as some semblance of organization would rise again from the "remnant" left by the storm of history.

The terms of the prophetic problem, as well as its symbols, were set by the founder of the Empire, by David himself. In his famous "last words" he had drawn the picture of the true ruler of Israel (II Sam. 23:1–4):

> These are the last words of David:
>
> A saying of David-ben-Jesse,
> a saying of the man raised high,
> of the Anointed of the God of Jacob,
> of the favored of the songs of Israel—
> the spirit of Yahweh spoke through me,
> and his word was upon my tongue—
> said the God of Israel,
> spoke to me the Rock of Israel:
>
> "Who rules over men be righteous,
> who rules be in fear of God,
> and as light of a morning at sunrise,
> of a morning with no clouds,
> as from radiance from rain,
> as young green from the earth."

The oracle in its context breathes the spirit of imperial order in cosmological form. Here speaks the ruler who is placed as the mediator between God and the people, the man raised high to rule over man; he is a man like the others (David-ben-Jesse) and yet more than the others (the Anointed), by ontological status somewhere between God and man. The construction of the "last words" is reminiscent of nothing so much as a Babylonian proverb:

> The shadow of God is Man,
> and the shadow of Man are men,

which is accompanied in the text by the gloss: "Man, that is, the King, who is the image of God." [8] And through this image of God at the first remove, this "Man who rules over man," the *moshel* of 23:3, the *ruach*

---

[8] For the text and its implications cf. Franz M. Th. Boehl, "Der Babylonische Fuerstenspiegel," *Mitteilungen der Altorientalischen Gesellschaft*, IX/3 (Leipzig, 1937), 49, 41, 46.

of Yahweh speaks, drawing the image of the true ruler. For the status of this image the text has no term—we must describe it as something like a Platonic paradigm, an idea that will enter reality through *methexis* of a man in it. Only when the idea has become reality in a man, through existential participation, can it be pronounced, as by David, with authority as the paradigm of rulership. And David apparently was clear about this connection between existential participation and the speaking of the *ruach,* for he concludes his oracle with the questions (23:5): "For is not like that my house with God? For has he not made the everlasting *berith* with me?" The man who participates in the paradigm of rulership, "speaks" the image that has become reality in him and, as he hopes, in his house.

Once the image of the ruler has become articulate, it can be converted into a standard by which the conduct of the concrete ruler is to be measured. This possibility, which also exists in cosmological civilizations, acquires a peculiar importance in Israel because the kingship was syncretistic in the sense that a rulership in cosmological form had to find its place in the theopolity created by the Sinaitic revelation. And the combination of the two forms was achieved, as we have seen, through the prophetic institution of David and his house by a word of Yahweh which declared the king to be his son. Hence, while the monarchy developed its cosmological ritual, the restoration of order did not rely on the annual catharsis through the cult festivals alone, but was supplemented by prophetic criticisms and admonitions addressed to the King. The "Man who rules over man" had to conform to the model adumbrated in II Samuel 23:3–4 and further elaborated in Psalm 72; and the prophets, who had instituted him, could remind him of the model when his conduct fell short of it. Through the history of the monarchy runs, from its beginnings, the theocratic tension between prophet and king—from Samuel and Saul, through Nathan and David, to Elijah and Ahab, and to the revolt against the Omrides. And this theocratic tension in the royal institution forms the never-to-be-forgotten background for the concern of the great prophets, since the middle of the eighth century B.C., with the figure of the King.

In the prophetic occupation with the problem three phases can be distinguished: (1) an institutional phase, represented by Amos and Hosea; (2) a metastatic phase, represented by Isaiah; and (3) an existential phase, represented by Jeremiah.

In the first phase, when the great prophets began to express the crisis of Israel in the alternatives of disaster and salvation, the criticism of the present order was no more than supplemented by the evocation of a future perfect order. The faith in a cultic restoration of the present order was broken, to be sure, when the restored order of the future was separated from the present state of things by an abyss of destruction. But the future was conceived as an institutional order, not so very different from the present one, minus its imperfections. When Israel had to be destroyed because of the misconduct of the people and the king, the end would be a restoration of the survivors under a king after the model held up by Yahweh in the oracle of David. With regard to the people, Amos 9:8 envisages the survival of a "remnant" as the ethnic nucleus for the future:

> Behold! the eyes of the Lord Yahweh are upon the sinful kingdom—
> and I will destroy it from off the surface of the earth,
> save that I will not utterly destroy the house of Jacob.

With regard to institutions, the threats of destruction in Amos 9:9–10 are followed by the promise that "the fallen tabernacle of David" will be raised again from the ruins (9:11). With regard to the general state of things, the concluding oracles (9:13–15) envisage the fortunes of Israel restored, with the countryside flourishing and the cities rebuilt. And Hosea, finally, completes the picture with the oracle (Hos. 3:4–5):

> Many days shall remain the children of Israel
>   with no king, and no prince,
>   no sacrifice, no pillar, no ephod, no teraphim.
> After that shall return the children of Israel,
>   and seek Yahweh their God, and David their King.

The last line confirms our previous reflections on the "Man who rules over man" as the paradigm, briefly called "David," that must be humanly realized through "seeking" as God must be realized existentially through faith.

In Amos and Hosea, the cosmological form still exerted a strong influence on their conception of the process of history. Although their alternatives of disaster and salvation went beyond the restoration of order through the cult, they substantially did no more than break the cosmic rhythm down to a sequence of disorder and order in historical time. With Isaiah, the younger contemporary of Hosea, begins the insight that one cannot advance from the cycle, in which institutions are restored through the cult, to the irreversible emergence of ultimate order in history without radically recasting the symbols. When the ebb and flood of cosmic order becomes the darkness and light of successive periods in history, new expressions for the dynamics of order, not yet provided in the compactness of cosmological symbols, must be differentiated. With Isaiah the experience of metastasis, of the substantive transfiguration of order, that was inchoately present even in Amos and Hosea, enters the prophetic concern with Israel's rulership. The motivations of Isaiah's experience, as well as its evolution in the course of about four decades following the call of *ca.* 740/34, are still discernible in the sequence of prophecies which at present form the text of Isaiah 6–12.[9]

The first of the distinctive Isaianic symbols is the Lord, who sits on his throne "high and exalted," while the skirt of his robe fills the Temple. Yahweh is the thrice-holy King above the earth, while at the same time "the fullness of the whole earth is his *kabhod*," his glory or divine substance (6:1–5). The symbolism of the Trisagion passage is of cultic origin,[10] but Isaiah employs it to express the presence of the divine *kabhod* over all the earth throughout the time of history. And from this ever-present *kabhod* derives the Isaianic dynamics of history. For the *kabhod* can become the substance of order in society and history only when men let themselves be penetrated by it through faith; order depends on the human response to the *kabhod*. The historical metastasis of the world, as distinguished from the cultic restoration, into the realm of God the King requires the responsive change of heart. Moreover, this knowledge of historical dynamics comes to Isaiah (and through him), because in the vision of the call he responds to the revelation of the *kabhod* by volunteering as the messenger of Yahweh to his people (6:8). The metastasis has actually begun in his person and is to expand through the prophecies that Isaiah will address to Israel, though the message will be effectively heard only after the terrible disasters caused by the stubbornness of the people (6:9–13).

How Isaiah's understanding of his call developed through the next five to ten years, we do not know. As the text stands, the account of the call is the preface to his great political intervention, to his appeal to King

[9] The following interpretation of Isaiah relies strongly on Martin Buber, *The Prophetic Faith* (New York, 1949).

[10] Ivan Engnell, *The Call of Isaiah. An Exegetical and Comparative Study* (Uppsala Universitets Arsskrift, 1949:4), 11, 16, 35–37.

Ahaz in the hour of danger to place his trust in Yahweh rather than in military preparations for the clash with the Northern Kingdom and Syria. The Davidic institution of the Anointed of Yahweh still has so much weight with Isaiah, at least at this time, that he re-enacts the encounter Prophet-King even now, when the King is to be drawn beyond the institution into transfiguration. The metastasis that has begun in the prophet can gain its social dimension of order in Israel only through co-operation of the "Man who rules over man," of the King of Judah. The trust of the King will transfigure the order of history, so that not only will the imminent disaster be averted, but the *kabhod* will actually fill the order of Israel forever (7:1–9). But the King responds to the appeal with eloquent silence, and the prophet is forced to offer him a "sign" of his choice to confirm the truth of the oracle (7:10–11). This time the King politely declines, for the acceptance of a "sign" would commit him and perhaps interfere with his more earthy plans for the defense of Jerusalem (7:12). With the King's refusal to have anything to do with Isaiah's appeal, the attempt to operate the metastasis through the present ruler has come to its end. At this juncture, Isaiah turns from the present to the future, without abandoning the conception of order through kingship. At the command of Yahweh he gives the King the "sign," though he does not want it, but it is a "sign" concerning Ahaz' successor in the kingship. "The young woman," says the oracle, presumably the queen, is about to bear a son. She will call him *immanu-el*, With-us-God—a symbolic name that spins out the theme of Isaiah's call, of the "Fullness of the whole earth—his *kabhod*." This child, in whom the *kabhod* of God will be "with us," is the future King, who knows to refuse evil and to choose good. But by the time he will be able to make the choice, the country will have been devastated by wars so thoroughly that it has reverted from an agricultural to a pastoral economy, thanks to the present King, who refuses good and chooses evil (7:13–17).[11] The scene between the Prophet and the King closes with this threat and this promise.

About the sequel to the encounter between Prophet and King again

[11] The much-agitated question whether the Immanuel prophecy of Isaiah 7:14 speaks of a "young woman" (Masoretic Text), or a "virgin" (Septuagint), is of little importance for the understanding of the passage. Considerably more important is the fact that both the Hebrew and Greek texts have the definite article before the noun rather than the indefinite article of RV, or RSV, or even the Chicago translation. Through the switch of articles in the ecclesiastic versions "the" definite young woman, probably the King's bride who is pregnant with the successor to the throne, becomes "an" indefinite young woman who will bring forth a child in an indefinite **future.**

we know nothing. Nevertheless, since the following text 7:18—8:10 brings a series of oracles which elaborate the Immanuel prophecy, we can surmise that Isaiah's situation must have become difficult: When a prophet, perhaps accompanied by a group of disciples, proclaims in public that he is waiting for an Immanuel to replace the reigning King, his activity can be construed as incitement to rebellion. Some friction of this kind must have developed indeed, for in 8:11 Yahweh has to grasp his prophet's hand strongly so that he will not give in to the ways of the people. He must not call a conspiracy what they call a conspiracy, nor fear what they fear (8:12); Yahweh he must call holy, and him he must fear (8:13). Difficulties of this kind must be assumed as the background for Isaiah's immediately following resolve to withhold his prophecies of a metastatic ruler from the public and to entrust them as a secret to his disciples (*limmudim*) (8:16). In the meanwhile, waiting for the coming of the *kabhod*, Isaiah and his children would "remain as signs and wonders in Israel from Yahweh of the hosts" (8:17–18). The remnant of Israel, as the bearer of the sealed message, thus has become historically present in Isaiah, his children, and his disciples.

The message itself, "the testimony bound up, and the instruction sealed," is contained in the prophecy of the Prince of Peace (9:1–6), beginning with the lines:

> The people that walk in darkness
> have seen a great light.

This light, shining brightly over those who dwell in the shadow of death, is the newborn child, the future ruler (9:5):

> For a child is born to us,
> a son is given to us.

On his shoulders will rest the *misrah*—a term which occurs only in this context in the Old Testament and is perhaps best translated by the Latin *principatus;* and his name will be—among others, which the difficult text does not permit us to separate with certainty—Prince of Peace (9:5). The zeal of Yahweh will bring this about (9:6)

> For the increase of lordship [*misrah*], and for peace without end,
> upon the throne of David, and over his Kingdom,
> to establish it, and to uphold it,
> in justice, and in righteousness,
> henceforth, and forever.

This prophecy must be treated with caution, for its text is so terse that under pressure it will easily render any meaning desired. What can be asserted safely is the continuity with the Immanuel oracle: The child is still a ruler on the throne of David and over his Kingdom, wielding his *misrah* over the remnant of Israel, though we must note that the descent from the royal house is no longer stressed and even the royal style is carefully avoided. Beyond this point the interpretation becomes hazardous, which is all the more regrettable since the injunction of secrecy indicates that a matter of some importance is involved. What is so dangerously new about the Prince of Peace, that the prophecy must not be communicated to the public which is already in possession of the Immanuel oracle? Or is really nothing back of that secrecy but a human fear of unpleasantness at the hands of an irate populace or the authorities? Following the suggestions of Martin Buber we suspect that the answer to such questions is to be found in the closing line (9:6) that "the zeal of Yahweh of the hosts will perform this." If this phrase is taken at its full weight, it means that the transfiguration of history will no longer remain in the suspense which characterizes the meeting with Ahaz. The time for appeals will come to an end; God will not wait forever for a response that is not forthcoming, but will himself provide the man who responds, so that his *kabhod* will fill the earth in its realized order. That would indeed be a fundamental change in the position of Isaiah, and it would also explain why this knowledge should be "bound up and sealed." For such knowledge would be of no use to the men who do not respond to the appeal, least of all to the recalcitrant Kings of Judah; it is of importance only for the remnant, that is, for Isaiah and his disciples, who will have to wait until the present crisis has run its course and Yahweh provides them with the child that will rule over them as the new Israel.

This interpretation is confirmed by the last of the great metastatic prophecies, in Isaiah 11:1–9. The text is neither related to a concrete situation nor is the continuity discernible that would link it with the Prince of Peace prophecy, as the latter one is linked with the Immanuel oracle. Its place as the last one in the series of great prophecies related by their contents indicates probably a late date; perhaps it is something like a "last word" of Isaiah on these questions. It opens with a passage that restores the connection with the Davidic dynasty (11:1):

> A shoot shall come forth from the stem of Jesse,
> and a sprout shall spring out of his roots.

A stem, or stump, of the dynasty, thus, will survive the disaster; and from this Davidic remnant, as from the people's remnant the new Israel, its new ruler will spring forth. And he is the ruler not because he has refused evil and chosen good like Immanuel but because the spirit, the *ruach,* of God has descended upon him (11:2):

> There will come to rest upon him the *ruach* of Yahweh,—
> The *ruach* of wisdom and understanding,
> The *ruach* of counsel and might,
> The *ruach* of knowledge [*da'ath*] and fear of Yahweh.

With this endowment he will be the King after the model of David, in fear of Yahweh and in righteousness, but yet something more than a David, for he will judge not by what he sees and hears, but by true justice and fairness (11:3–5). The *kabhod* has penetrated the structure of the world indeed, and the metastasis is complete:

> And the wolf shall dwell with the lamb,
> and the leopard shall lie down with the kid.

There will be no harm nor destruction on all the God's Holy Mountain, for the earth shall be full of the *da'ath* of Yahweh, as the waters cover the sea (11:9).

The symbols of Isaiah 11:1–9, finally, are resumed in Isaiah 2:2–4 in order to enlarge the vision of the transfigured Israel into a vision of metastatic world peace. For in "the end of days" it shall come to pass that the mountain of Yahweh's house will be lifted above all hills, and the nations will stream to it, saying (2:3):

> Come! let us go up to the mountain of Yahweh,
> to the house of the God of Jacob;
> and he will teach of his ways,
> that we may walk in his paths;
> for from Zion goes forth Instruction [*torah*],
> Word-of-Yahweh from Jerusalem.

Yahweh himself will be the judge between the nations; "they will beat their swords into plowshares" and learn no more the art of war (2:4). Governmental institutions and their human incumbents are no longer mentioned.

The prophecies of Isaiah thus move from the appeal to the historically real King Ahaz to the "sign" of a more responsive, future Immanuel; from Immanuel to the Prince of Peace who will rule on the throne of David, not over the contemporary, empirical Israel, but over the remnant that is gaining historical concreteness in Isaiah and his disciples;

from the Prince of Peace to a "remnant" of the Davidic dynasty on whom the *ruach* has descended; and, finally to a vision of world peace in which the institutions have lost their distinctness. With the articulation of the metastatic experience, with the unfolding of its consequences, the institutional problems arising from human recalcitrance to the realization of the *kabhod* must indeed become irrelevant. For the *ruach* of Yahweh has transfigured human nature, so that the order of society and history has become substantively the order of the *kabhod*.

When the metastatic experience had been explored to its limits by Isaiah, prophetism had arrived at an existential impasse. While Amos and Hosea could still envisage a restoration of the Kingdom after the Davidic model, Isaiah had thoroughly eliminated the cultic tension of institutional order from the sequence of darkness and light; within two generations, the pressure of historical form had driven the cultic symbolism against the blank wall of the metastatic vision. The prophet's situation was no longer that of an Egyptian sage in the breakdown of empire between the Old and Middle Kingdoms. Since in the Egyptian crisis the cosmological form was not broken, the expectation of a Savior-Pharaoh— "Ameni, the triumphant, his name," "the son of a woman from the land of Nubia"—could be fulfilled through the re-establishment of imperial order. The metastatic faith of the prophet, on the contrary, precluded fulfillment through any pragmatic establishment.[12] Once the faith in the metastasis of social and cosmic order through an act of God had achieved the rigidity of full articulation, there was nothing one could do but sit down and wait for the miracle to happen. If it did not happen—and it has not happened to this day—the prophet would die while waiting; and if he had formed a group of disciples, who would transmit his faith to future disciples, generations might pass before the experience of their passing would become a motive of sufficient strength to re-examine the validity of what had become an article of faith.[13] Hence,

---

[12] That is the reason that comparisons between prophetic "Messianism" and Egyptian precursors, conducted on the level of literary history, are misleading.

[13] The question how long a metastatic expectation can last before it is affected by the lapse of time poses itself anew whenever a similar situation recurs in history. The most important case is the expectation of the Parousia and its transformation through the Pentecostal outpouring of the Spirit. Special problems are created when the metastasis is expected for a definite date, as for instance in the Joachitic movement of the thirteenth, or the American Millerite movement of the nineteenth, century. The time needed for the experiential breakdown can become very long in the modern movements, when the metastasis is operated not by an act of God but by human ac-

it was perhaps not merely a question of suppression by the new regime under Manasseh that no prophets appeared in the generation following Isaiah and Micah. Moreover, an abeyance of prophetism as a consequence of the metastatic impasse is suggested by the peculiar structure of the Book of Isaiah. In the collection that goes in the Bible under the name of "Isaiah" one can distinguish between the Isaianic prophecies proper (Isa. 1–35) with its appendixes (Isa. 36–39); the prophecies of the anonymous Deutero-Isaiah (Isa. 40–55), to be dated in the middle of the sixth century B.C.; and a collection of later oracles, of various unknown authorship, usually called the Trito-Isaiah (Isa. 56–66). If it is assumed that the three parts of the collection were not assembled by accident but that they represent the body of traditions preserved by a prophetic circle which in continuity derived from Isaiah and his disciples, there would be a gap of about a century and a half in the tradition between Isaiah himself and the Anonymous of the sixth century. If it be further assumed that the gap is not due to the accidental loss of the sayings of one or more great prophets but that indeed no prophet of note arose within the Isaianic circle during this time, the long silence would indicate the sterility of waiting for the metastasis. And finally, it is even doubtful whether the mere waiting and the lapse of time would have furnished a sufficient motive for the re-examination of symbols. For when prophecy is at last resumed in Deutero-Isaiah, the symbols of the anonymous prophet bear the imprint not only of the Isaianic tradition but distinctly of the work of Jeremiah.

In Jeremiah we have to look for the experiences which advanced the understanding of order beyond the metastatic visions of Isaiah. As the first motive must be noted the lapse of time, though its effect is difficult to gauge. Between the calls of Isaiah and Jeremiah more than a hundred years had passed. That was time enough for a prophetic personality which did not belong to the inner circle of Isaiah's disciples, but rather formed itself through the study of Hosea, to relax the tension of gazing into a future which never became present. For the order of being is the order in which man participates through his existence while it lasts; and the consciousness of passing, the presence of death in life, is the great cor-

---

tion in the economic and political sphere. When the metastasis is "in progress" through human action, the expectation can apparently feed on "installments" for centuries, as the progressivist metastatic faith did feed on the stages of the industrial revolution and the improvements of the material standard of living. And a similar duration seems to be in prospect for the communist metastasis and its feeding on realization in "installments."

rective for futuristic dreams—though it may require a strong personality to break such dreams, once they have become a social power in the form of accepted creeds. The fundamental concern of man is with the attunement of his existence, in the present tense, to the order of being. And Jeremiah indeed returned from the metastatic vision of the future to the experience of the untransfigured present. In this return, however, he did not have to break altogether with Isaiah. For his great predecessor, in spite of the extreme articulation of his experience in the symbols of the metastatic ruler, had achieved a solid advance, never to be abandoned, in the understanding of order: that the order of society in history is reconstituted in fact through the men who challenge the disorder of the surrounding society with the order they experience as living in themselves. The word of the prophet is not spoken to the wind, it is not futile or impotent, if it does not reform the society which he loves because it has given him birth. The Word that speaks through him is itself historical reality and forms the order of a new community wherever it is heard. In Isaiah, his sons and disciples, the "remnant" of Israel, which had been the contents of prophecies of salvation, had become the reality of salvation. The prophetic word about the future became historical present in the men who spoke and preserved it in community. And while the Israel that was pragmatically organized as the Kingdom of Judah went the way of all organizations, their governments, and kings in history, the Word spoken by the prophets and preserved by the communities which heard it, still forms the "remnant" of Israel in the present. This insight into the meaning of prophetic existence as the continuation of order in history, when its realization in the pragmatic order of a people is in crisis, was the heritage from Isaiah to be increased by Jeremiah.

Isaiah had received the "Messianic problem" from Amos and Hosea in its institutional form of an Israel under a king after the model of David. In his own experience of order the institutional form was preserved, even though it was now burdened with the metastatic act of trust he demanded of King Ahaz. When the King had the good sense not to make experiments in transfiguration, Isaiah neither abandoned the institutional form nor the metastatic will, but the metastasis had to be drawn out into the formation of a remnant by the prophet himself and its completion through the future appearance of a ruler. Moreover, in so far as being the carrier of the secret concerning the future ruler was the essence of the remnant, its formation had the characteristics of a first step toward the complete metastasis—in this respect the procedure of Isaiah foreshadows the later types of metastasis by "installment." If the problem of order was to be restored to its concreteness, Jeremiah had to reverse the futuristic projection of Isaiah and to bring the King back into the present. This he did, as we have seen, when in the oracles of his call he transferred the royal symbolism to himself. The order of Israel was complete in the present again, though contracted into the existence of the Jeremiah who enacted the fate of the people while carrying the burden of the Anointed. This is the third, the existential, phase in the prophetic occupation with the "Messianic problem."

The effort that went into this achievement must have been enormous. In order to see it in its true proportions, it should be recalled that this *tour de force* of recapturing the present was conducted within the limits which the compactness of the prophetic experience set to Jeremiah as much as to Amos, Hosea, or Isaiah. The prophetic symbolism, we remember, derived from the rites of defeat and victory in the New Year's festivals; under the pressure of the historical form, the cultic tension of order had dissolved into the successive periods of disaster and salvation. The prophetic experience, thus, was essentially metastatic. And we have traced the expression of this character in the prophets' criticism of conduct under decalogic categories, in their struggle for the existential order of man through virtues, and in their creation of the symbol of a new Covenant that will transfigure world and society. In all of these respects the prophecies of Jeremiah not only conformed to the type but even brought it to perfection. And no more than in the general structure of his prophecy did Jeremiah deviate from the type in his articulation of the "Messianic problem," especially in Jeremiah 23:1–8. That the problem had undergone a change of complexion for him became noticeable only in the fact that his prophecies did not continue or elaborate the Isaianic symbols but reverted to the prediction of a remnant under a Davidic model-king, as we found them in Amos and Hosea.[14] This firmness of the prophetic form was the burden that had to be carried by Jeremiah; it must be taken into account if one wants to estimate the strength that was necessary, not to break it—even a Jeremiah could not

---

[14] Not only the oracle concerning a remnant under a Davidic king, but the prophecies of salvation in general betray in numerous details the change of complexion. For the indexes of this change in Jeremiah cf. Buber, *Prophetic Faith*, 172 ff.

do that—but to become aware that the problems of order did not re-
volve around the empirical Israel and its institutions but around the man
who suffered concretely under the disorder. Hence, the greatness of
Jeremiah's achievement does not become manifest in the general body
of his oracles which run true to a standardized form, but in the oracles
of his call, in the enactment of Israel's fate, in the Temple Address and
the trial. Above all, however, it must be sought in his creation of a new
form of prophetic expression: What is new in his extant work are the
pieces of spiritual autobiography, in which the problems of prophetic
existence, the concentration of order in the man who speaks the word
of God, become articulate. The great motive that had animated the
prophetic criticism of conduct and commendation of the virtues had
at last been traced to its source in the concern with the order of personal
existence under God. In Jeremiah the human personality had broken the
compactness of collective existence and recognized itself as the authoritative source of order in society.

The type of experiences which forced Jeremiah back on himself and
into the recognition of his personality as the battlefield of order and
disorder in history, can be gathered from the notice about a conspiracy
against his life (18:18):

> Then they said:
>> Come, and let us devise devices against Jeremiah.
>> For the law shall not pass from the priest,
>> nor counsel from the wise, nor the word from the prophet.
>> Come, and let us smite him with the tongue,
>> and let us not listen to any of his words.

The motive of the plot was Jeremiah's assumption of personal authority
under God, which invalidated the people's traditional sources of authority
in the priests, the wise, and the prophets (the "false prophets" of Jeremiah); and its purpose was to silence the word emanating from the new
authority. In this danger Jeremiah turned to Yahweh with the question:
"Shall evil be repaid for good, that they have dug a pit for my life?"
(18:20). And assuming that this could not be God's intention he im-
plored him to visit the conspirators, their wives, and their children with
famine, pestilence, and violent death (18:21–23). In another notice of
a plot to murder him, Jeremiah formulated the motive in the demand
of his enemies: "You shall not prophesy in the name of Yahweh, lest you
die by our hands" (11:21); and the notice is accompanied by the same

heartfelt plea to see his enemies come to grief (11:20, 22–23). This vengefulness of Jeremiah must not be covered with charitable silence, or treated with genteel discreetness, as if it were a weakness unbecoming a distinguished public figure. For it is precious evidence of the spiritual passion that burned in him. The man who predicted the destruction of Israel, Jerusalem, and the Temple; who wished on the King of Judah (22:19):

> With the burial of an ass shall he be buried,
> dragged about and flung out beyond the gates of Jerusalem;

was not the man to make exceptions for personal enemies. On the contrary, since he was the representative of divine order, forgiveness for an attack on his life would have been a presumptuous attribution of importance to his private sentiments and a betrayal of his status. The prophet of Israel could not condone an attack on the life that served Yahweh.

Moreover, the justice of God was at stake. In the vengeful wishes of Jeremiah was involved, as the text has shown, the torturing question of repayment for good and evil. To be sure, Israel deserved punishment for its sins, but how should order ever be restored if the punishment of the wicked was visited on Israel collectively and engulfed the good? Josiah, the Reformer-King, had fallen in the battle of Megiddo against Egypt; and Jeremiah was the target of plots against his life. There always would be some wicked around, and if the divine punishment did not become more discriminate, there would be no end of suffering. Jeremiah put his questions before God in the complaints of 15:10, 15:

> Woe is me, my mother, that you bore me,
> a man of strife and a man of contention to the whole earth!
> I have not lent, nor have men lent to me,
> yet all of them curse me.
> You well know it,
> Yahweh, think of me, remember me,
> and avenge me of my persecutors.

God knows that the prophet suffers for his sake: Jeremiah cannot join the company of the sportive and make merry with them, because the hand of God is on him and forces him to sit alone (15:16–17). Why then is his pain unceasing, and his wound incurable? Will God be to him like a treacherous brook, like waters that are not sure? (15:18). To such questioning Yahweh answers (15:19):

> If you turn back, I shall take you back,
> and before my face shall you stand;
> and if you bring forth the precious from the vile,
> as my mouth shall you be.

There is no answer to the questions: The questioning itself is the defection, from which Jeremiah must return to the presence of God; only
when, through the return from questioning, he has brought forth the
precious from the vile will he be the speaker of God's word. The prophet
has to live with the mystery of iniquity. But that is not easy: "My grief
is incurable, my heart is sick within me" (8:18).

Jeremiah found no peace from these questions. He elaborated them
most profoundly in the great dialogue of Jeremiah 12, where he presented them as a legal case for judgment to the God with whom he had
the quarrel (12:1):

> In the right you are, Yahweh,
> if I contend with you—
> and yet of this case I must speak with you:
> Why is the way of the wicked happy?
> Why do those prosper who deal most treacherously?

Why does God not punish them individually but inflict misery collectively on the faithful together with the wicked (12:4):

> How long shall the land mourn,
> and the herb of the whole field wither?
> Because of the wickedness of those who dwell in it,
> the beasts are consumed, and the birds.
> For they said: "He will not see our way."

To the question again comes no answer that would solve the mystery
of iniquity, but the counterquestion (12:5):

> If you have run with the footmen,
> and they have wearied you,
> how then will you compete with horses?
> And if in the land of peace you fall down,
> how will you do in the jungle of Jordan?

Much more terrible things will happen than Jeremiah has experienced as
yet—and he will have to live through them, the questions unanswered.
But then the tension is relieved by the words of God, which must be
understood as a soliloquy to which Jeremiah is permitted to listen
(12:7 ff.):

> I have forsaken my house,
>> have abandoned my heritage;
> I have given the beloved of my soul
>> into the hands of her enemies. . . .
> My heritage has become to me
>> as a lion in the forest. . . .
> Many shepherds have destroyed my vineyard,
>> they have trodden my portion under foot. . . .
> The whole land is desolate,
>> yet no man lays it to heart.

What is the suffering of Jeremiah, compared with the suffering of God?

Prophetic existence is participation in the suffering of God. Beyond this insight gained by Jeremiah for his own person lies its application to everyman's existence. The prophet's secretary Baruch apparently was inclined sympathetically to experience the same sorrows as his master. When he had finished writing the words of Jeremiah, at his dictation, in a book, he must have complained often enough (45:3):

> Woe is me now!
> For Yahweh has added sorrow to my pain;
> I am weary with my groaning,
> and I find no rest.

For Jeremiah was authorized to transmit to him the succinct information, coming from Yahweh himself (45:4–5):

> Behold! What I have built, I will pull down;
> and what I have planted, I will tear up—
> and you seek great things for yourself?
> Seek them not!
> For behold! I will bring evil upon all flesh—
> says Yahweh—
> But your life will I give you, as a prize of war,
> in every place where you go.

§ 3. THE SUFFERING SERVANT

The problem of Israelite order was seen by the prophets, from the middle of the eighth century B.C. to the fall of Jerusalem in 586, in the discrepancy between the actual order of the Kingdoms and the order intended by the Message from Sinai. The discrepancy was intensely experienced as a defection from true order; only an immediate return could prevent the imminent divine punishment. And the expectation of disaster near at hand translated itself into the urgency of the call to return. The early prophets—Amos, Hosea, Isaiah, Micah—who had this intense experience, however, found no symptoms of a serious return in their environment; and at the same time they had to watch the disaster advancing in the form of the Assyrian invasion and the fall of the Kingdom of Israel. Hence, within the two generations of the early prophets, their call to return changed its complexion in as much as the expectation to see the institutions and mores of the concrete society reformed gave way to the faith in a metastasis of order after the present concrete society had been swallowed up by the darkness of a catastrophe. When the problem of order had gained this metastatic complexion, the prophets responded to it by developing the two distinct positions represented by Isaiah and Jeremiah:

(1) Isaiah engaged in the supreme effort of a political intervention which, if successful, was supposed to be the beginning of the metastatic order. When the King of Judah did not respond to the appeal, the prophet formed his group of disciples as the remnant of Israel beyond the present concrete society; and he entrusted the secret of the true order to his *limmudim* to be revealed only in the indeterminate future in which Yahweh would let his transfiguring *ruach* descend on the remnant's ruler. That secret had been indeed kept so well through the generations of disciples that nothing was heard of it during the remaining years of the Kingdom, nor in the early years of the Exile.

(2) A century later, Jeremiah was called to be the prophet to the nations. By the Message from Sinai Israel had been constituted as the holy center of all mankind, but the order of the Covenant and the Decalogue pertained only to the Israelite society; no order had been provided for the nations as a society of mankind. The blows of history had brought it home to Israel that there existed a mankind outside the Sinaitic order. The Philistine danger had made it necessary to supplement the theopolity by the organization of a kingdom; and the further events had shown that even the institution of kingship was no sufficient protection against Egypt, Assyria, and Babylon. The "nations," which during the recession of imperial power could remain on the margin of attention, had entered into the concrete relationship of war and conquest with Israel. If the Kingdom of Israel had fallen, and the Kingdom of Judah was on the point of extinction, the existence of man in society

under God apparently did not assume the concrete form of a small Israelite theopolity, even if supplemented by kingship, surrounded by mighty empires which respected it as the holy omphalos of their own order. If the Message from Sinai had revealed the order of history, obviously the wording of its intention could not be the last word in the history of order. This problem, recognized even by Amos, became fully articulate in Jeremiah's expansion of his prophetic concern from Israel to the Near Eastern oekumene. While "Israel" remained the holy center, the society under the new Message embraced the "nations"; and since both Israel and the nations were at the moment in a state of disorder, the center of order had contracted into the person of Jeremiah.

What the two responses have in common will come into view if their difference is characterized by the relative position of the time and space factors in their symbolization of order. Isaiah, after his experience with Ahaz, moved away from the concrete order of Israel into a future in which the true order of the "remnant" would become the center of a world society living in metastatic peace. Jeremiah moved spatially beyond the order of Israel into the contemporary disorder of Israel and the nations at war and expected it to give way in the future to the order of Yahweh which at the moment was concentrated in himself. Both prophets, thus, had in common the tendency to move away from the order of the concrete Israelite society toward an indeterminate goal.

The meaning of the movement can be approached through the questions suggested by its vague *terminus ad quem*. The concern of the prophets goes beyond the Chosen People, organized as a kingdom for survival in the pragmatic power field, toward a society which, though in some manner derived from the present people through survival and expansion, is certainly not identical with it. There is no answer to the question: Of which society are the prophets speaking when they envisage the carrier of true order? It certainly is not the society in which they live; and whether any concrete society that has formed in history since their time would be recognized by them as their object may be doubted. The same argument applies to the enlarged society that will embrace the "nations." Nor is there an answer to the second question: What kind of order will the society have? For it will be the transfigured order of a society after the metastasis. And a transfigured order was no object of knowledge to the prophets, nor has it become an object of knowledge to anybody since their time. Since neither the identity of the society nor the nature of its order can be determined, the suspicion will raise its head: Does the movement of the prophets make sense at all? If the analysis is driven against the wall of this suspicion, it will become clear that the sense of the movement can be found only if the apparent nonsense be taken as the starting point in the search for its motives.

The fact must be accepted that the questions can find no answer. The *terminus ad quem* of the movement is not a concrete society with a recognizable order. If the concern of the prophets with this apparently negative goal makes sense nevertheless, it must have been motivated by the insight, though unclear and insufficiently articulate, that there are problems of order beyond the existence of a concrete society and its institutions. The metastatic experience of Isaiah, which hitherto has been considered under the aspect of a sterile withdrawal from the realities of Israel's order, will appear in a new light if it is considered as an experience of the gulf between true order and the order realized concretely by any society, even Israel. And Jeremiah's experience of the tension between the two orders, his suffering participation in the divine suffering, is even articulate enough to make it certain that the prophet had at least a glimpse of the terrible truth: that the existence of a concrete society in a definite form will not resolve the problem of order in history, that no Chosen People in any form will be the ultimate omphalos of the true order of mankind. When Abram emigrated from Ur of the Chaldaeans, the Exodus from imperial civilization had begun. When Israel was brought forth from Egypt, by Yahweh and Moses his servant, and constituted as the people under God, the Exodus had reached the form of a people's theopolitical existence in rivalry with the cosmological form. With Isaiah's and Jeremiah's movement away from the concrete Israel begins the anguish of the third procreative act of divine order in history: The Exodus of Israel from itself.

The anguish of this last Exodus was lived through by the unknown prophet who by a modern convention is designated as Deutero-Isaiah, because he is the author of Isaiah 40–55. Since nothing is known about him except what can be inferred from his work, biographical preliminaries are not only unnecessary but hazardous, because they would prejudge the interpretation of the text. Even to speak of these Isaiah chapters as a "work" with an "author" involves commitments with regard to a series of much debated questions. This debate itself must remain outside the range of our study; but the commitments have to be set forth:

(1) The original material of Isaiah 40–55 is assumed to consist of a large number of brief oracles and songs which still can be well distinguished. The next level of organization consists of chains of the briefer pieces, forming self-contained units of meaning. Such chains, finally, are organized in a meaningful sequence, forming the "book."

(2) The chains of Isaiah 40–48, which are pervaded by the belief in Cyrus as the divinely ordained liberator and restorer of Israel, may well have been formed as "pamphlets" to be circulated among the exiles in Babylon. If the assumption is correct, both the component oracles and the chains will have to be dated in the years between Cyrus' conquest of Lydia in 546 B.C. and his conquest of Babylon in 538 B.C.

(3) The chapters Isaiah 49–55 still have the structure of chains of briefer oracles and songs, but the tone has changed. Cyrus has disappeared, together with the hopes set in him; and other sources of disappointment make themselves felt. The oracles of this later part probably were spoken and written during an indeterminate number of years after the fall of Babylon.

(4) In Deutero-Isaiah are embedded the four Servant Songs distinguished by Duhm: Isaiah 42:1–4; 49:1–6; 50:4–9; and 52:13—53:12. We assume that the songs have the same author as their context but that they represent the last phase of the prophet's work.

(5) Three of the Servant Songs are fitted into the later part of the work, whereas the first one, together with the pieces chained to it, is embedded in the earlier, the Cyrus part. Hence, we assume that the whole body of oracles was organized by the prophet as a literary unit after he had written the songs. The first song appears to be deliberately placed at the beginning of the Cyrus part, in order to stress the continuum of experience as it evolves from the expectation of a concrete order of Israel restored by Cyrus to the mystery of the Exodus from concrete order symbolized by the Suffering Servant. The movement toward the mystery is recognized by the prophet, in retrospect, to have been the undercurrent even at the time of the Cyrus diversion.

(6) We assume the prophet to have been a member of a circle which derived through the generations from the immediate disciples of Isaiah. In his self-understanding the prophet was one of Isaiah's *limmudim* entrusted with the secret of salvation.

These commitments must not be understood as assertions with a claim to certainty. They formulate probabilities as they are emerging from the exploration of details and the improvement of methods in the course of the last half century.[15]

[15] The debate about Deutero-Isaiah in general, and the Servant Songs in particular, is now easily accessible through the masterly study by Christopher R. North, *The Suffering Servant in Deutero-Isaiah. An Historical and Critical Study* (Oxford, 1948). Further information on the voluminous literature is to be found in H. H. Rowley, *The Servant of the Lord and Other Essays on the Old Testament* (London, 1952), especially in the studies on "The Servant of the Lord in the Light of Three Decades of Criticism" (pp. 3–57) and on "The Suffering Servant and the Davidic Messiah" (pp. 61–88). Important because of the succinct formulation of issues is Otto Eissfeldt, "The Prophetic Literature," in *The Old Testament and Modern Study* (1951), 115–61. In the following analysis the Isaiah commentaries by Duhm, Volz, and Bentzen were used.

Of the literature before 1940 the following studies proved of considerable importance: Sigmund Mowinckel, *Der Knecht Jahwaes* (Kristiania, 1921). Lorenz Duerr, *Ursprung und Ausbau der israelitisch-juedischen Heilserwartung. Ein Beitrag zur Theologie des Alten Testamentes* (Berlin, 1925). Hugo Gressmann, *Der Messias* (Goettingen, 1929). Otto Eissfeldt, *Der Gottesknecht bei Deuterojesaiah (Jes. 40–55) im Lichte der israelitischen Anschauung von Gemeinschaft und Individuum* (Beitraege zur Religionsgeschichte des Altertums, 2, Halle, 1933). J. S. van der Ploeg, *Les Chants du Serviteur de Jahvé* (Paris, 1936). Josef Begrich, *Studien zu Deuterojesaja* (Beitraege zur Wissenschaft vom Alten und Neuen Testament, 4:25, Stuttgart, 1938).

Since 1940 the study of Deutero-Isaiah has received several new impulses. One of them has come through Sidney Smith, *Isaiah Chapters XL–LV: Literary Criticism and History* (London, 1944). The book has met with considerable criticism, because the author wanted to make the prophet the leader of an underground movement (pro-Cyrus, anti-Babylon) who was killed by the exiles for his treasonable activities. Setting aside the imaginative extravagancies, the book has its merits, nevertheless, because it places the prophecies firmly in their historical context. The study by H. S. Nyberg, "Smaertornas man. En studie till Jes. 52, 13–53, 12," *Svensk Exegetisk Arsbok* (1942), 5–82, explores the background of mythical form in the fourth Servant Song and the emergence of the supra-individual Messianic symbol from the mythical form. C. R. North, *The Suffering Servant* (1948) finds his own interpretation in substantial agreement with Nyberg's. The symbolism of divine kingship in all four of the Songs is treated meticulously in Ivan Engnell, "Till fragan om Ebed-Jahweh-sangerna och den lidande Messias hos 'Deuterojesaja,'" *Svensk Exegetisk Arsbok* (1945), 31–65. Of this study the author himself has given an English version under the title "The Ebed-Yahweh Songs and the Suffering Messiah in 'Deutero-Isaiah,'" *Bulletin of the John Rylands Library*, XXXI (Manchester, 1948), 54–93. Engnell's study puts it beyond doubt that the cult form determines the language of the Songs. The search for a "historical" model of the Servant figure, be it the prophet himself or some other suffering personage of the time, must remain fruitless because the "clues" are cult symbols. This does not mean, of course, that the history of the age does not furnish cases of sufferers whose personal fate may have entered the prophet's experience. Such inspirations from royal sufferers of the time have been explored recently by J. Coppens, *Nieuw Licht over de Ebed-Jahweh-Liederen* (*Analecta Lovanensia Biblica et Orientalia*, II/15, Leuven, 1950). The problems of Messianic symbolism, with special attention to Deutero-Isaiah, are surveyed in Aage Bentzen, *Messias. Moses Redivivus. Menschensohn* (1948)—the best introduction to the Scandinavian literature on the subject. The understanding of Deutero-Isaiah is, furthermore, affected by the Scandinavian debate on the "tradition-historical" method in connection with prophetism. Cf. Sigmund Mowinckel, *Jesajadisiplene. Profetien fra Jesaia til Jeremia* (Oslo, 1925), the same author's *Prophecy and Tradition. The Prophetic Books in the Light of the Study of the Growth and History of Tradition* (Avhandlingen. Norske Videnskap Akademie, II, Oslo, 1946, No. 3), and Ivan Engnell, "Profetia och tradition," *Svensk Exegetisk Arsbok* (1947), 110–39. The whole complex of Messianic problems has recently been restated in Sigmund Mowinckel, *Han Som Kommer. Messiasforventningen i det Gamle Testament og pa Jesu Tid* (1951); cf. in particular Chapter VII on "Herrens tjener," pp. 129–73; and the extensive bibliography pp. 390–403. Because of the place

The text of Isaiah 40–55 is an accomplished literary composition *sui generis* which expresses certain experiences by means of the symbolic language developed in classical prophetism from Amos to Jeremiah. In the experiences expressed, clusters of motives can be distinguished. A first one is furnished by the historical events: the exile, the liberation through Cyrus, the fall of Babylon, and the vicissitudes of empire in general. A second cluster stems from the heritage of the great predecessors: the contraction of Israel into the solitary suffering of the prophet, the message to a mankind that embraces both Israel and the nations, and above all the Isaianic secret of the *kabhod* that will fill the earth. A third cluster, finally, is formed by the motives to which the author himself refers as the "new things": the message of salvation; the self-revelation of God in three stages as the Creator of the world, as the Lord and Judge of history, and as the Redeemer (*goel*); the consciousness that the present is the epoch between the second and third stages; the suffering of the second stage as the way to redemption; redemption as the existential response to the third revelation of God as the Savior and Redeemer; the role of Israel as the representative sufferer for mankind on the way to the response; and the climax in Isaiah 52:13—53:12, in the recognition of the Servant as the representative sufferer. While the distinction and classification of the motivating experiences is so amply supported by pieces of a meditative nature that the results are reasonably certain, the book as a whole is not a treatise in *oratio directa* on definite "doctrines." It is a symbolic drama which does not permit the separation of a contents from the manner of its presentation. Moreover, while the single motives can be distinguished, they have merged in the comprehensive experience of the movement that we have briefly characterized as the Exodus of Israel from itself. The text does not consist of a series of symbols expressing successive states of experience, so that it would be left to the reader to reconstruct from them a spiritual biography of the author. The construction is done by the author himself, to whom the movement is given as completed in the retrospect of his work. Beyond the component symbols, the drama as a whole is a unit of meaning. The

which the figure of the Suffering Servant has in the self-understanding of Jesus, the occupation with Deutero-Isaianic problems is almost exclusively Christian, predominantly Protestant. All the more important is the recent book by Martin Buber, *The Prophetic Faith* (1949), with its interpretation of Deutero-Isaiah, pp. 202–35. Buber's interpretation is especially valuable because it stresses the prophet's place in the Isaianic tradition as one of the *limmudim* of the master.

Exodus has happened in the soul of the author, and his work is the symbol of a historical event.

If this is the nature of the work, the methods most frequently used in its interpretation must be considered inadequate:

(1) The drama, to be sure, is autobiographical in substance, but the evolution of experience is mediated by the author's interpretation in retrospect. Hence, we know nothing about that experience except what the author chooses to reveal. It is reasonable to assume that the experience of the exile and the victories of Cyrus sparked the movement that reached its climax in the Fourth Song, and also that the beginning and the end were not joined in a flash of insight but were separated by a considerable number of years—but it is reasonable only because the text itself suggests this evolution over the years. Any attempt to go beyond the drama and to reconstruct the author as a "historical" person is therefore not only hazardous but contributes nothing to the understanding of the work.

(2) The meaning of the drama cannot be found by tearing an important symbol out of its context and treating it as if it were a piece of somewhat enigmatic information. There exists a library of studies on the question "Who is the Suffering Servant?" Is he the author himself, or some other suffering personage, or does the symbol prophetically envisage Christ—or is he no individual at all but Israel, and if that should be the case is he the empirical or the ideal Israel, and is he the whole of Israel or a remnant? Such attempts to understand the Deutero-Isaianic work through solving the puzzle of the Servant is, on principle, not different from an attempt to understand an Aeschylean tragedy by means of a study on the question "Who is Prometheus" or "Who is Zeus?" And even when Glaucon in the *Republic* (361e) draws the figure of the just man "who will have to endure the lash, the rack, chains, the branding-iron in his eyes, and at last, after suffering every kind of torture, will be impaled," nobody will search for the historical model of the sufferer, though the allusion to the suffering of the "historical" Socrates is considerably more probable than any lines that can be drawn from the Suffering Servant to a historical figure. If such studies can be undertaken in the case of Deutero-Isaiah nevertheless with at least a measure of sense, the reason must be sought in the difference between the Israelite historical and the Hellenic mythical form of order. The Aeschylean tragedy moves, in search of order, from its compact expression in the

polytheistic myth toward the Logos of the psyche; the Deutero-Isaianic drama moves from the compact revelation from Sinai toward the Logos of God. From Aeschylus the movement goes toward the Platonic Vision of the Agathon; from Deutero-Isaiah it goes toward the Incarnation of the Logos. When man is in search of God, as in Hellas, the wisdom gained remains generically human; when God is in search of man, as in Israel, the responsive recipient of revelation becomes historically unique. Since the human experience of revelation is an event in the history constituted by revelation, historicity attaches to the recipient of revelation, to the very historicity of Christ. As a consequence, the question "Who is the Servant?" is not as outlandish in an Israelite context as a comparable question with regard to an Hellenic literary text would be. Nevertheless, while these reflections will cast some light on the difference between the Logoi of philosophy and revelation, and while they will make intelligible the tendency to search for the historical figure behind the symbol of the Suffering Servant, they do not justify the procedure. Isaiah 40–55 remains a literary composition; and the symbols must be read as expressions of the author's evolving experience, even though what he tries to communicate is an insight concerning the revelation of God in history.

The various errors of interpretation, of which we have just adumbrated the two most important types, can be avoided only if one penetrates to their root in the multiplicity of time levels running through the work:

(1) The experience of the author evolves and matures over a period of perhaps ten or more years. Hence, there runs through the work the time of the experience from its inception to its completion. The temptation is great, therefore, to isolate this level and to use the clues of the text for a reconstruction of the "historical" course of the experience. This attempt, however, is bound to fail, as we have indicated, because the time of the experience has been absorbed into the structure of the work. The author's own reconstruction bars this possibility.

(2) The experience is inseparable from its expression in symbolic form. In so far as the component oracles and songs originate at various points of time in the course of the experience, the same argument applies to them as to the time of the experience itself. The text as a whole, however, is not a series of oracles in chronological order. It is a composition in which the single pieces, regardless of the time of their origin, are placed in such a manner that they express the meaning of the experience

as it has accumulated during its course. The compositorial work is itself part of the process in which the meaning of the experience is clarified; the revelation is received by the author completely only in the act of composition. Hence, the work is not the account of an experience that lies in the past, but the revelation itself at the moment of its supreme aliveness. From the human side, the time of the composition is the time which accumulates, the time in which one grows old and matures, the *durée* in the Bergsonian sense; from the divine side, it is the present under God in eternity. This is the time level to which in the literature on the subject practically no attention is given.

(3) The human response is an event in the history constituted by revelation. With the response begins the divine work of salvation, spreading through communication in space and time from the responsive human center. Since the symbols of the work picture the process of salvation, there is running through the work the time of salvation. And this time of salvation is not the inner time of a work of fiction, but the real time of the order of revelation in history. Hence, the symbols of the work, first, touch on the past history of revelation; they furthermore are concerned with the present revelation as received by the author, with the "new things" in the light of which the "former things" become a past of revelation; and they finally envisage the process of salvation as completed in the future through earthwide acceptance of the message that is received by the author, and communicated by his work, in the present. The time of salvation thus absorbs both the time of the experience and the time of the composition in so far as the historical process of the "new things" has its beginning in the experience of the author and continues in the composition of the work which communicates the revelation. This nature of the work as an event in the history of salvation, as the beginning of a process which in its symbols is imaged as extending into the future, is the inexhaustible source of difficulties for the interpreter. For there can hardly be a doubt that the Servant who dies in the Fourth Song is the same man who speaks of his call and his fate, in the first person, as the prophet in the Second and Third Songs. And is it not against common sense that a man gives an account of his death, as well as of its effects in the process of salvation? Such common-sense arguments have indeed become the basis for the assumption that the Fourth Song was written by a member of the circle after the death of the prophet who wrote the other three songs, and *a fortiori* that the work

as a whole (if it is a literary unit at all) could not have been written by
the prophet to whom certain parts of it may be conceded.

The structure of the work is so intricate that only an extended
commentary could do justice to it. For the purpose of this study it is
sufficient to indicate the main parts of the organization and then to
analyze the substantive problem which determines the detail of the
composition.

The main organization of the work is easily to be discerned, because
the incisions are marked by the position of the Servant Songs. The major
subdivisions are: (1) A Prologue (Isa. 40–41); (2) a First Part (Isa.
42–48, barring the dubious Isa. 47); (3) a Second Part (Isa. 49–53);
and (4) an Epilogue (Isa. 54–55). The Prologue sets forth the message
of salvation and its implications. The First Part, beginning with the
First Song, deals with the salvation of Israel. It culminates in the exhortation to the exiles to leave Babylon and to let the news of the redemption
spread to the ends of the earth (Isa. 48:20–22). The spreading of the
news of Israel's redemption forms the transition to the Second Part,
beginning with the Second Song. The process of salvation now expands
to the nations and culminates, in the Fourth Song, in the recognition
of the Servant as the representative Sufferer by the kings of the gentiles.
The hymns of the Epilogue, finally, envisage the process of salvation as
completed for Israel (Isa. 54) and the nations (Isa. 55). A redeemed
mankind will surround Jerusalem, in response to the Holy One of Israel.

The composition itself emerges from the substance of the revelation;
and this substance is to be found in the opening oracle of the book
(Isa. 40:1–2):

> Comfort, O comfort my people—
>   says your God—
> Speak to the heart of Jerusalem,
>   and call to her:
> That her time of service is ended,
>   that her guilt is paid in full,
> That she has received from Yahweh,
>   double for all her sins.

The oracle marks an epoch in the history of prophetism inasmuch as it
breaks with the classic form of the great prophets from Amos to Jeremiah and creates a new symbolic form. In the first place, it is not a "word

of Yahweh" spoken to the prophet, and through him, but a divine command of which the recipient is informed by heavenly voices. And to the mediation of the command in heaven there corresponds, second, a new mediating function of the prophet. For the hearer of the heavenly voices is no longer the mouth through which Yahweh warns his people to return to order, but the mediator of a message which supersedes the alternatives of punishment and salvation hinging on the existential appeal.

The meaning of this new type of prophecy will best be clarified through the elimination of suggestive misunderstandings:

(1) Since the guilt of Israel is atoned and the prophet has to bring the news of salvation without regard to the people's conduct, it is tempting to understand the message of the oracle as a prophecy of salvation of the older type. The new form would then not be so very "new," but a plain promise of salvation, unconditioned by reform of conduct; and it would become difficult to distinguish between Deutero-Isaiah and the "false prophets" of the eighth and seventh centuries. The new form, however, is not a mere matter of dropping one of the alternatives from the dual symbolism. For the suffering of Israel, far from having disappeared from the new prophecy, is one of its two major problems, balancing the concern with salvation. Hence, suffering and salvation are both present, but they have changed their complexion, as we may say provisionally, in as much as they are no longer "alternatives" linked by the appeal.

(2) Is the new complexion of suffering and salvation, then, due to the disappearance of the appeal? This assumption would be the second misunderstanding. For the salvation announced by Deutero-Isaiah is not a divine act that transfigures the order of Israel and mankind, but a revelation of God as the Redeemer. And since the revelation requires human response, the prophet has to appeal very energetically to the people not to reject the message of salvation (Isa. 44:22):

> I have blotted out, as a vapor, your transgressions,
>   and, as a cloud, your sins;
> Return to me, for I have redeemed you.

And the appeal is resumed in the Epilogue (Isa. 55:6):

> Seek Yahweh while he may be found,
> call upon him while he is near!

Hence, the appeal has disappeared no more than the alternatives, though it also has changed its complexion. For the whole question of the people's conduct lies now in the past: Israel *has* suffered for its defection, and it *has* been forgiven. The appeal is therefore no longer concerned with conduct as measured by the Sinaitic legislation, but with the acceptance of God the Redeemer.

(3) The form elements of the classic prophetic symbolism thus are all present, though in a different mode. Moreover, through the elimination of the misunderstandings, the cause of the change has been traced to the shift of the prophet's interest from the order of the Chosen People under the Sinaitic Berith to an order under the Redeemer God. The character of this new order is flashlike illuminated by the prophet's use of the berith symbol. In Isa. 42:6 the Servant is appointed as "a *berith* to the people, as a light to the nations." And more elaborately, in Isaiah 55:3–5, the prophet lets God say:

> Incline your ear, and come to me;
> hear, and your soul shall live!
> For I shall make you a berith forever,
> the mercies of David [*dwd*] which are sure.
> Behold, I have given him as a witness to the peoples,
> a prince and commander to the peoples.
> Behold, a nation you know not shall you call,
> and a nation that knows you not shall run to you,
> for the sake of Yahweh, your God
> and the Holy One of Israel, for he has glorified you.

If the two texts be conjoined, the "*berith* forever" of 55:3 is the Servant, who was appointed, in 42:6, as the "light to the nations" and is now given as the "witness, prince, and commander" to the peoples. This princely Servant, who is glorified by Yahweh, will call to the nations, and his call will be heard for the sake of the Holy One of Israel.[16] In this manner there will be established the order of mankind envisaged at the beginning of the work (Isa. 40:5):

> Then shall be revealed the *kabhod* of Yahweh,
> and all flesh shall see it together,
> for the mouth of Yahweh has spoken it.

---

[16] The line "the mercies of David which are sure," must be read as apposition to the *berith*, i.e. to the Servant. It is more intelligible without the Masoretic pointing of *dwd* as *dawid*. For without the points the *dwd* also carries the meaning of *dod*, i.e. the beloved, as in Isaiah 5:1. It could refer either to God or to the Servant; in either case the *dwd* is a divine-royal attribute.

The type of the new prophecy has now been sufficiently clarified to be placed in the history of Israelite order. From the imperial order in cosmological form emerged, through the Mosaic leap in being, the Chosen People in historical form. The meaning of existence in the present under God was differentiated from the rhythmic attunement to divine-cosmic order through the cult of the empire. The theopolity, supplemented by kingship for survival in pragmatic history, however, still suffered under the compactness of its order. The order of the spirit had not yet differentiated from the order of the people's institutions and mores. First, in his attempt to clarify the mystery of the tension, Isaiah split the time of history into the compactly unregenerate present, and a quite as compactly transfigured future, of the concrete society. Through Jeremiah this unregenerate present then gained its existential meaning, in as much as the prophet's participation in divine suffering became the omphalos of Israelite order beyond the concrete society. And through Deutero-Isaiah, finally, there emerged from existential suffering the experience of redemption in the present, right here and now. The movement that we called the Exodus of Israel from itself, the movement from the order of the concrete society toward the order of redemption was thus completed. The term "completion" must be properly understood. It means that the order of being has revealed its mystery of redemption as the flower of suffering. It does not mean, however, that the vision of the mystery is the reality of redemption in history: The participation of man in divine suffering has yet to encounter the participation of God in human suffering.

The work lives in the new dispensation which it proclaims; and inversely, the process of salvation moves through the work. The action begins with the first oracle, when a heavenly voice announces that Israel's sins are forgiven (40:1–2). In ever-widening circles of revelation the theme then moves through the heavenly hierarchy. A remoter voice calls that the glory (*kabhod*) of Yahweh will be revealed to all flesh (40:3–5); and a still remoter one antiphonally calls that all flesh is grass, and will wither like grass, but the word of our God will stand forever (40:6–8). The higher ranks now enter. A commander's voice orders the heralds of good news to let it be known in Jerusalem and the cities of Judah that Yahweh the Lord is coming with might—"Behold your God!" (40:9–11). A teacher's voice follows and sets forth the nature and attributes of the God who is about to appear. "The God everlasting is Yahweh, the Creator of the ends of the earth." He sits high above the circle of the earth, and stretches out the heavens like a curtain, like a tent to dwell in. Men are before his height like grass-hoppers. The princes and judges of the earth are before him a thing of nought.

> Scarce are they planted, scarce are they sown,
> scarce has their stock taken root in the earth,
> when he blows upon them, and they wither,
> and the whirlwind takes them away like stubble.

But he also gives power to the faint, and to him that has no might he increases strength (40:12–31). When the picture of God as the Creator and the Lord of Mankind has been drawn thus far, God himself appears. First he addresses the nations and points to the fall of Babylon as an object lesson of his power over history (41:1–4). Then (41:5–20) he speaks to Israel the promise and presence of his help:

> I myself help you—says Yahweh—
> and your Redeemer [goel] is the Holy One of Israel.

And, finally, he summons the gods of the nations before his throne and challenges them to interpret the "former things" or to announce the "new things." The dumbfounded he pronounces nought. He himself, however, has revealed the things that were to come. Moreover, he has roused the "one from the north" who treads down rulers like mortar, as the potter tramples clay. And he first told it to Zion and sent the heralds with the good news to Jerusalem (41:21–29). The God who is Creator, Judge, and Redeemer is also the Revealer who through the voices of his hierarchy ordered the prophet: "Comfort, O comfort my people!" The cycle of this Prologue in Heaven is closed. The drama proper, then, begins with the presentation of the Servant.

The summary will have given an impression of the author's literary art. The Prologue, reminiscent of certain scenes in *Faust,* must now be considered as the exposition of the leitmotifs which move through the main body of the work:

(1) The dominant motif of the work is the revelation of God as the *goel* of Israel, as the Redeemer (Isa. 41:14; 43:14; 44:6, 24; 48:17; 49:7; 54:5). The revelation marks so decisive an epoch in history that the whole past moves into the category of the "former things" to which now the "new things" can be opposed (43:16–19):

> Thus says Yahweh, who made a way through the sea,
> a path through mighty waters,
> who led forth the chariot and horse,
> the army and the power—
> they lie down together, they shall not rise,
> they are extinguished and quenched as a wick—:
> "Remember not former things,
> nor consider the things of old.
> Behold! I am doing a new thing,
> now shall it spring forth—
> will you not know it?"

The "new thing" is the liberation from the Babylonian yoke (43:14–15); and the text (16–19) expresses the epochal character of the event most drastically by suggesting that the "old thing," the Exodus from Egypt, may be relegated to oblivion as unimportant in comparison with the present act of liberation. From this center of intense experience the motif expands, following the logic of the received symbols. The Exodus is the first of the "former things," counting back from the present. Isaiah 51:9–10 completes the chain into the past:

> Was it not you that hewed Rahab to pieces,
> that pierced the dragon?
> Was it not you that dried up the sea,
> the waters of the mighty deep?

The creation of the world through the victory of Yahweh, symbolized as a Babylonian Marduk, over the waters of primeval chaos and the creation of Israel are the "former things" now to be followed by the redemption of Israel. The motif of creation is then pursued back from the beginnings of the world, through Israel, to the new salvation (45:8):

> Pour down, O heavens, from above,
> and let the skies rain deliverance [zedek];
> let the earth open, and bring forth salvation,
> and deliverance [zedakah] let her sprout together—
> I, Yahweh, have created it.

With a recall of the *toldoth* of heaven and earth (Gen. 2:4 ff.), the creation of the world is continued into the creation of salvation. To the three phases of world-history in the pregnant sense, then, correspond the names of God as the *bore*, the Creator of the world (40:28), of Israel (43:15), and of salvation (45:8). In this last capacity God also is the Redeemer (*goel*), the Holy One, and the King of Israel (43:14–15).

One may justly speak of Deutero-Isaiah as the author of the first theology of history.

(2) But why should the liberation be experienced as an epoch in world-history? The exiles in Babylon cannot have been too badly off. As a matter of fact, a large number of them preferred not to return to Jerusalem, but to stay with the fleshpots of the "oppression." What was the factor in the situation that made it possible to experience the events of power politics as an epoch of redemption in world-history? The concern with this factor furnishes the second great motif, concentrated in 40:6–8:

> All flesh is grass,
> and all its beauty is like the flower of the field.
> The grass withers, the flower fades,
> as the breath of Yahweh blows upon it—
> surely the people is grass—
> the grass withers, the flower fades,
> but the word of our God shall stand forever.

The fall of Jerusalem and the exile must have brought on a crisis of Yahwism in the sense that the power of empire seemed overwhelming and ultimate. The flesh did apparently not wither at all; Yahweh and Israel withered, while the gods and the people of Babylon prospered. It needed energetic reminders such as 51:12–13 that the powers of this world were mortal flesh, even if for the time being they seemed established forever:

> I, I, am your comforter—
> Who are you, that you should be afraid
>   of man that shall die,
> and of the son of man
>   that shall wither like grass?
> That you should forget Yahweh your Maker
>   who stretched forth the heavens
>   and laid to the earth its foundations?
> That you are in fear continually, all the day,
>   of the fury of the oppressor
>   as he makes ready to destroy?

And admonitions were required, such as 46:12–13:

> Listen to me, you downhearted ones,
> who count yourselves far from deliverance [zedakah]:
> "I bring near my deliverance, it is not far off,

and my salvation will not be delayed.
I will put salvation in Zion,
     for Israel my glory."

Such admonitions would surely become more convincing when the op-
pressive flesh of Babylon showed symptoms of withering like the grass.
The appearance of Cyrus must have been a relief beyond our full com-
prehension, not because of the political liberation, but because it proved
the reality of God and his power over the flesh. One can still sense this
relief in 45:1:

> Thus says Yahweh to his Anointed [*mashiach*]
> to Cyrus, whose right hand I have grasped
> to subdue nations before him,
> and to loose the loins of kings,
> to open doors before him,
> and that gates may not be closed. . . .

This is the convincing proof that Yahweh is God, and that no gods are
beside him (45:6). The rise and fall of empire is recognized as the way
of the flesh under the order of God (48:14–15):

> Assemble, all of you, and listen!
> Who among you has told these things:
> He whom Yahweh loves will do his pleasure on Babylon,
> and show his arm on the Chaldaeans?
> I, I have spoken; I have called him;
> I have brought him; and made his way prosperous!

And God has brought the deliverance for his own sake, that his name
will not be profaned in history (48:11); the people has burdened God
with its iniquities, but for his sake he blots out the transgressions (43:
24–25); the people has been tested in the furnace of suffering (48:10),
and now it is ready to hear the "new things," the news of the salvation
forever (45:17; 51:6).

(3) The liberation marks an epoch in history, because it brings
redemption from bondage to the false gods of empire. This is the third
theme running from the Prologue through the work. Quantitatively the
polemic against the false gods occupies considerable space, but the issue
is concentrated in the brilliant satire on Babylon, in Isaiah 47. The
chapter is probably from another hand, but it perfectly fits into the
context. Here Babylon the fallen is covered with scorn: "Come down,
and sit in the dust, O virgin daughter of Babylon!" "Get into darkness,

and sit silent, O daughter of the Chaldaeans!" The cause of the fall is formulated in the verse 47:10:

> Your wisdom and your knowledge
> have led you astray,
> So that you said to yourself,
> "I am, and there is none but me."

This is the caricature of the First Commandment, as well as of Yahweh's (48:12):

> I, I am the first,
> I also am the last.

In his pride of empire man apes God. This part of the truth contained in the Sinaitic revelation had remained veiled as long as the Chosen People under God was surrounded by longeval, politically and militarily effective empires. The fall of Assyria, Lydia, and Babylon within less than a century had brought it home that all flesh indeed withered like grass. And from the succession of imperial disasters, from the empirical crumbling of cosmic-divine order, emerged the insight that above the vicissitudes of empire "the word of our God shall stand forever" (40:8). This insight, however, establishes indeed a new aeon of history. For the God who has revealed himself as the first and the last, by blowing his breath on the flesh, is now revealed as the God of all mankind. The flesh that has aped God and withered for its guilt is the same flesh that now will see the *kabhod* of Yahweh revealed (40:5). Moreover, Israel as a concrete society in pragmatic history has perished together with the empires. Hence, the Israel that rises from the storm that has blown over all of mankind is no longer the self-contained Chosen People but the people to whom the revelation has come first to be communicated to the nations. It has to emigrate from its own concrete order just as the empire peoples had to emigrate from theirs. The new Israel is the covenant and light to the nations (42:6), the Servant of Yahweh through whom God will make his salvation reach to the end of the earth (49:6).

The task of the Servant is clear: From the center of its reception in Israel, the news of Redemption must be spread over the whole earth. The execution of the task, however, will encounter difficulties. For Israel as a society had been smashed into the leaderless population around Jerusalem, the exiles in Babylon, and the refugees scattered in all directions.

Who will listen to these pitiable remnants of a people to which nobody listened even when it was a power of moderate size? A century later, when Herodotus traveled through the Syrian and Palestinian area, apparently he never even heard of such peoples as Israel or Judah, or of a city named Jerusalem. Moreover, while Babylon had fallen, her empire was replaced by the Persians, to be followed by Macedonians and Romans. The power of empire had not disappeared with a prophet's experience of its withering like grass under the breath of Yahweh. And, finally, even if some sort of Israel should be reorganized in its old homestead, how many members of this people had indeed experienced the liberation from Babylon as the redemption from empire for all mankind? Hence, the task will be a laborious one; it will bring ridicule, humiliation, persecution, and suffering to the men who undertake it under such unauspicious circumstances. The empirical Israel will hardly embark on the missionary enterprise, for the people itself has not yet accepted the message of salvation. The prophet, at best surrounded by a group of like-minded disciples, will therefore move into the position of a Jeremiah, who enacts the destiny of the Servant as Israel's representative. And such a task, finally, will not be executed by the prophet within his lifetime; it will require the labors of generations of successors. The Servant will thus be a new type in the history of order, a type created by the prophet in Israel and for Israel, to be figured by others until the task is accomplished. This situation of the prophet must be realized if one wishes to understand the movement of the Servant symbol in his work from Israel the Servant of Yahweh, to the prophet himself as Israel's representative, and further on to the indeterminate successor who will complete the task that has to be left unfinished by the prophet.[17]

When the Prologue announcing the work of Redemption has come to its end, the Servant is presented by God to the heavenly audience (42:1–4):

> Behold! My Servant whom I uphold,
> my chosen in whom my soul delights!
> I have put my spirit [*ruach*] upon him,
> he shall bring forth right [*mishpat*] to the nations.

---

[17] The following translations of the Servant Songs are based on those by North, *The Suffering Servant*, 117–27. Numerous changes have taken into account the extensive debate on details. Suggestions by Bentzen, Buber, Engnell, and Nyberg were most frequently used.

He shall not cry, nor make any clamor,
nor let his voice be heard in the street;
a reed that is bruised he shall not break,
and the wick that burns dimly he shall not quench.

Faithfully shall he bring forth right,
he shall not flicker nor bend,
till on the earth he establish right,
and for his instruction [*toroth*] wait the coast-lands.

The royal symbolism of the First Song encloses the figure so completely
in its armor that nobody can tell whether Israel is meant or the prophet
as its representative. The immediately following oracle (42:5–9) gives
the Servant his place in the theology of history. The God who has created
the world and mankind now sets the Servant as "a covenant to the
people, and a light to the nations," to open blind eyes and bring the
prisoners out of the dungeon. That a blindness and prison of the spirit
is meant is shown by 42:16–17, where the darkness will be made light,
and the rugged places plain, and only those will be turned back who
still trust in idols. Before this can be accomplished through the Servant's
gentle action, however, the Servant himself must cease to be deaf and
blind. For at the present (42:19),

Who is blind, but my Servant?
And deaf like my messenger whom I send?
Who is as blind as my perfected one [*meshullam*],
and as blind as the Servant of Yahweh?

In this context the Servant is clearly the Israel (42:22–25) that has yet
to emerge from its deafness and blindness to become the perfected one
who can be a light to the nations (43:1–9). Only when the act of
redemption has touched the people will Israel be "the Servant whom I
have chosen" and be able to convince the nations that Yahweh is God
(42:10); and this act will consist in the breaking of the Babylonian
prison by the conqueror as God's instrument (42:14–15). Isaiah 45:1–7,
then, introduces Cyrus as the liberator; and the feat of political liberation
is followed by the brief hymn 45:8, quoted previously, in which the
heavens pour down deliverance and the earth brings forth salvation.

With the victory of Cyrus and the impending return to Jerusalem
the redemption of Israel is accomplished (48:20): "Say: 'Redeemed has
Yahweh his Servant Jacob.'" This does not mean, however, as the sequel

shows, that the empirical Israel has accepted the message of salvation. It means that redemption has been experienced by the prophet *for* Israel, as its representative. Israel has become the perfected one, because in its midst the revelation has found response in at least one man. For the Servant who has been destined in heaven in God's time now enters historical time in the prophet's own person as the speaker of the Second Song (49:1–6):

> Hearken, you coast-lands, to me,
> and give attention, you peoples afar!
> Yahweh has called me from the womb,
> before my birth he gave me my name;
>
> and he made my mouth like a sharp sword,
> in the shadow of his hand did he hide me;
> and he made me a polished arrow,
> in his quiver did he conceal me;
>
> and he said: "My Servant are you,
> Israel by whom I will get myself glory."
>
> But I said: "In vain have I labored,
> for nought and vanity have I spent my strength;
> yet surely my cause is with Yahweh,
> and my recompense with my God."
>
> And now, thus says Yahweh
> who formed me from the womb to be his Servant,
> to bring Jacob back to him,
> and that Israel to him should be gathered—
>
> (So was I honored in the eyes of Yahweh,
> and my God became my strength)—
>
> "It is too slight a thing that you should be my Servant
> to raise up the tribes of Jacob,
> and bring back the survivors of Israel—
> I will make you a light to the nations
>   that my salvation may reach
>   to the end of the earth."

The model of Jeremiah as the lord of history in royal form makes itself strongly felt in this Second Song. Israel has contracted into the Servant, who tries to move the empirical Israel—apparently in vain. But in spite of his temporary failure in the cause of Yahweh, God has assigned to him the even greater task of becoming the light to the nations. The cause of the failure to convince the people is set forth in the following text. Yahweh has indeed extended to the downtrodden Israel—"despised by men, abhorred by nations, the slave of rulers" (49:7)—his promise of salvation (49:7b):

> Kings shall see, and rise up,
> princes, and they shall bow down,
> because of Yahweh who is faithful,
> the Holy One of Israel who has chosen you.

Israel is meant to be the Servant, the "covenant to the people" (49:8)—but the circumstances disturbingly do not fit a world center of salvation for the nations (49:8–13). The empirical Israel still suffers; and its ample grounds of complaint require an answer in the extended comforts of 49:14—50:3.

In this rather confused situation the prophet, who may have become the target of unpleasant remarks if not of more tangible missiles, speaks the Third Song, expressing his trust in God, as well as his obedience to the divine command (50:4–9):

> The Lord Yahweh has given me
>   the tongue of the taught [*limmudim*, disciples],
> that I should know how to answer
>   the weary with a word.
> Morning by morning he wakens my ear
>   to hear as those that are taught.
>
> .   .   .   .   .   .
> .   .   .   .   .   .
>
> And I have not been rebellious
>   nor have I turned backward.
>
> My back I gave to the smiters
>   and my cheeks to the pluckers [of the beard];
> my face I hid not
>   from shame and spitting.
>
> But the Lord Yahweh will help me,
> therefore I am not confounded;
> I have set my face like a flint,
> and I know that I shall not be ashamed.
>
> Near is my vindicator:
>   Who will contend with me?
>   Let us stand up together!
>   Who is my adversary?
>   Let him approach me!

> Behold The Lord Yahweh will help me!
> Who then will put me in the wrong?
> Behold! They all shall wear out as a garment,
>   the moth shall eat them up!

In the Third Song the prophet characterizes his status as that of a *limmud*, of "one who is taught," of a disciple. Martin Buber has strongly stressed the fact that only in the context of Isaiah does the word *limmudim* appear with the meaning of "disciples." In Isaiah 8:16 the prophet binds up the testimony, and seals the instruction, "in the heart of my disciples"; and in Isaiah 50:4 his successor speaks with the tongue of the *limmudim*. Has the instruction sealed in the heart of Isaiah's disciples broken forth at this late hour in a member of the circle? And does the second Isaiah indeed speak with the tongue of a disciple of his master? The observation is astute and the assumption tempting, for Deutero-Isaiah uses indeed the language of the master and prophesies the advent of the *kabhod* of Yahweh. Nevertheless, I think Buber's assumption must be qualified. The passage Isaiah 8:16 is not quite clear in its context. The phrase "my disciples" may refer to the disciples of Isaiah, but the "my" may also refer to God: The prophet is perhaps ordered to seal the message in the hearts of God's disciples, who, to be sure, are at the same time Isaiah's disciples. And that also seems to be the meaning of *limmudim* in Isaiah 50:4, where the prophet presents himself as the man who is endowed by God with the disciples' tongue, as the man who morning by morning hears God as disciples do. Moreover, this conception of the *limmud* as the man who is taught by Yahweh pervades the work of Deutero-Isaiah. In the Prologue it is one of the attributes of God that he is not "taught" by anybody with regard to *mishpat* and *da'ath* (40:14). God is the untaught teacher who says of himself (48:17):

> I, Yahweh, your God,
> who teaches you for your profit,
> and who leads you the way you should go.

And in the Epilogue Israel is promised: "All your sons shall be *limmudim* of Yahweh" (54:3). The task of the Servant is fulfilled when every man has become a *limmud* of God, as the prophet is now. That is not to deny that the conception originates with Isaiah. But a disciple of Isaiah is at the same time a disciple of God; and the essence of discipleship, the being taught by God, must be stressed in order to avoid even the shadow of a "sociological" transmission of a message within a circle.

The prophet as the *limmud* is the man who has a word for the weary, however adverse the circumstances may be. And the pathos of his own existence is obedience in adversity. He does not rebel or turn backward (probably aimed at the questioning and complaining of Jeremiah); he will not be confounded by ill-treatment of his person; but trusting in God will he continue to speak with a disciples' tongue what he has been taught by God.

The prophetic autolouange of the Third Song is followed by prophetic action. Isaiah 50:10 is an exhortation to the weary, and 50:11 a prophecy of dire fate to the wicked. Isaiah 51:1—52:12 is a chain of oracles and hymns which resume the leitmotifs and elaborate them. The authority of the Servant is subtly supported by the transfer of predicates from the Servant to God himself. In the Prologue the prophet was commanded to comfort the people; now God assures them "I, I, am your comforter" (51:12–16). Formerly the Servant was the light to the peoples; now instruction (*torah*) shall go forth from God, and his *mishpat* be a light to the peoples (51:4–5). Moreover, the Servant's situation in the Third Song is transferred to the people at large. They are now those "in whose hearts is my instruction [*toroth*]" (51:7) and who, therefore, need not fear the reproaches of mortal men; and even the satisfaction of seeing their enemies consumed by the moth like a woolen garment is now granted to everybody (51:8). Finally, even the heralds with the good news of salvation reappear, announcing to Zion: "Your God has become King" (52:7). The section concludes with the exhortation to go out from the midst of the redeemed Jerusalem, from the omphalos of mankind, to bring the news of salvation to the nations and to spread it to the ends of the earth (52:8–12):

> Depart you! depart you! go out from thence!
>> Touch nothing unclean!
> Go out of the midst of her; keep yourselves pure,
>> you who bear the vessels of Yahweh!
> For you shall not go out in haste,
>> nor depart in flight,
> for Yahweh will go before you,
>> and the God of Israel will be your rearguard.

With the imagery of the Exodus from Egypt Israel is urged on to its Exodus from itself.

In the Second and Third Songs the prophet is the speaker; in the First and Fourth Songs it is God. The Exodus that is now to be undertaken leads into the future, beyond the time of the prophet and his work. The time of salvation which entered the time of the prophet runs beyond it toward fulfillment. In the First Song, God presented the Servant to the heavenly audience and revealed his intention of salvation; in the Fourth Song, God presents the Servant as their representative sufferer to the kings and the nations, so that all can accept him and be saved. The God who is first and last has the first and last words in the drama of salvation that reaches from heaven to earth.

In the first part of the Song, God presents the Servant as the exalted ruler over mankind (Isa. 52:13–15; the second and third lines of 52:14 are placed after 53:2):

> Behold! My servant shall prosper,
> he shall be exalted and lifted up, and be very high,
> As many were appalled at him
>
> . . . . . .
>
> So shall he startle many nations,
> because of him kings shall shut their mouth,
> for what has not been told them shall they see,
> and what they have not heard shall they understand.

The presentation is answered by a chorus which consists of the kings and the nations, and perhaps also of the prophet's own people. We can speak of it as a chorus of mankind. They at last believe what they have been told about the Servant and his representative suffering (53:1–9):

> Who could have believed what we were told?
> And the arm of Yahweh—to whom was it revealed?
>
> For he grew up as a small shoot before us,
> and as a root out of dry land.
> No form had he nor comeliness, that we should look at him,
> no appearance that we should delight in him,
> so disfigured his appearance, unlike that of men,
> and his form unlike that of the sons of man.
>
> Despised and forsaken of men,
> a man afflicted by pains, and marked by sickness,
> and as one from whom men avert their faces,
> he was despised and we regarded him not.

Yet ours were the sicknesses he carried,
and ours the pains he bore,
while we regarded him stricken,
smitten of God, and afflicted.

He was wounded for our transgressions,
he was bruised for our iniquities,
the chastisement for our weal was upon him,
and through his stripes we were healed.

All we like sheep went astray,
everyone his own way we turned,
and Yahweh made fall on him
the iniquity of us all.

He was oppressed—and he humbled himself
	and opened not his mouth—
as a sheep that is led to the slaughter,
and as a ewe before her shearers,
		he was dumb,
		and opened not his mouth.

Through violence in judgment he was taken off,
and to his fate who gave thought?
He was cut off from the land of the living,
for our transgressions the stroke fell on him.

And they made his grave with the wicked,
and with the rich in his deaths,
although he had done no violence
and there was no deceit in his mouth.

The unbelievable tale that now is believed, the mystery of representative suffering, is handed over from marveling mankind to heavenly voices which reflect (53:10):

Yet Yahweh was pleased to crush him with sickness,
truly he gave himself as a guilt-offering.
He shall see seed that prolongs days,
and the purpose of Yahweh shall prosper in his hand.

And from the heavenly voices the theme is finally taken over by God himself (53:11–12):

Out of the travail of his soul he shall see light,
he shall be satisfied with his knowledge:
My Servant shall bring deliverance to many,
and their iniquities he shall bear.

> Therefore will I assign as his portion the many,
> and numberless shall be his spoil:
> Because he bared his soul unto death,
> and with the transgressors he was numbered,
> while he bore the sin of the many
> and for the transgressors he interposed.

The Exodus from the cosmic-divine order of empire is completed. The Servant who suffers many a death to live, who is humiliated to be exalted, who bears the guilt of the many to see them saved as his off-spring, is the King above the kings, the representative of divine above imperial order. And the history of Israel as the people under God is consummated in the vision of the unknown genius, for as the representative sufferer Israel has gone beyond itself and become the light of salvation to mankind.

About the effectiveness of the prophet's vision in the history of Judaism almost nothing is known for the next five centuries. A trace here and there in the apocalyptic literature reveals that there are "wise among the people who bring understanding to the many" (Dan. 11:33) in the tradition of Deutero-Isaiah. And such discoveries as the Zadokite fragment and the Dead Sea scrolls prove that movements related to this tradition must have been much stronger than the canonical and rabbinical literature would let us suspect. These movements break to the historical surface again in Christianity. A prayer of such intenseness as the *Nunc dimittis* of Luke 2:29–34 cannot be explained as a literary reminiscence; it belongs to a living tradition of Deutero-Isaiah. And the preoccupation with the problem of the Suffering Servant is attested by the story of Acts 8: The Ethiopian eunuch of the queen, sitting on his cart and reading Isaiah, ponders on the passage: "Like a sheep he was led away to the slaughter." He inquires of Philip: "Tell me, of whom is the prophet speaking? of himself, or of someone else?" Then Philip began, reports the historian of the Apostles, and starting from this passage he told him the good news about Jesus.

Biblical References

[*Note:* Biblical references are set in italics to differentiate them from page numbers. For example, *Genesis 1:1–27*, page 91; *1:26*, page 16, etc.]

Modern Authors

Subjects and Names